1996

This major contribution to the history of philosophy provides the most comprehensive guide to modern natural law theory available, sets out the full background to liberal ideas of rights and contractarianism, and offers an extensive study of the Scottish Enlightenment.

The time span covered is considerable: from the natural law theories of Grotius and Suárez in the early seventeenth century to the American Revolution and the beginnings of utilitarianism. After a detailed survey of modern natural law theory, the book focusses on the Scottish Enlightenment and its European and American connections. Knud Haakonssen explains the relationship between natural law and civic humanist republicanism, and he shows the relevance of these ideas for the understanding of David Hume and Adam Smith. The result is a completely revised background to modern ideas of liberalism and communitarianism.

*Natural law and
moral philosophy*

Natural law and moral philosophy

From Grotius to the Scottish Enlightenment

Knud Haakonssen
Boston University

CAMBRIDGE
UNIVERSITY PRESS

Published by the Press Syndicate of the University of Cambridge
The Pitt Building, Trumpington Street, Cambridge CB2 1RP
40 West 20th Street, New York, NY 10011-4211, USA
10 Stamford Road, Oakleigh, Melbourne 3166, Australia

First published 1996

Printed in the United States of America

Library of Congress Cataloging-in-Publication Data
Haakonssen, Knud, 1947–
Natural law and moral philosophy : from Grotius to the Scottish
Enlightenment / Knud Haakonssen.
p.   cm.
Includes bibliographical references and index.
ISBN 0-521-49686-1. – ISBN 0-521-49802-3 (pbk.)
1. Natural law – History.   2. Philosophy, Scottish – 18th
century.   3. Enlightenment – History – Sources.   I. Title.
K455.H33   1995
340'.112–dc20   95-9657
                                                            CIP

A catalog record for this book is available from the British Library.

ISBN 0-521-49686-1 hardback
ISBN 0-521-49802-3 paperback

Contents

Acknowledgements

I am grateful to editors and publishers for permission to use material previously published under their auspices:

Section 0.2 of the Introduction is adapted from part of the introduction to *Traditions of Liberalism: Essays on John Locke, Adam Smith and John Stuart Mill*, ed. K. Haakonssen (Sydney: Centre for Independent Studies, 1988), pp. xi–xxi.

Chapter 1 is a revised and extended version of ch. 7, sect. 4, 'Divine/natural law theories of ethics', in *The Cambridge History of Seventeenth-Century Philosophy*, ed. Michael Ayers and Daniel Garber (Cambridge, UK: Cambridge University Press, forthcoming).

Sections 2.1 to 2.7 of Chapter 2 are revised from 'Natural law and moral realism: The Scottish synthesis', in *Studies in the Philosophy of the Scottish Enlightenment*, ed. M.A. Stewart (Oxford: Clarendon Press, 1990), pp. 61–85.

Chapter 3 is revised and abbreviated from 'The structure of Hume's political theory', in *The Cambridge Companion to Hume*, ed. David Fate Norton (Cambridge, UK: Cambridge University Press, 1993), pp. 182–221.

Chapter 5 is revised and extended from 'John Millar and the science of a legislator', *Juridical Review* (Edinburgh: W. Grant & Son), June 1985, pp. 41–68.

Chapter 6 is abbreviated and revised from the introduction to Thomas Reid, *Practical Ethics: Being Lectures and Papers on Natural Religion, Self-Government, Natural Jurisprudence, and the Law of Nations*, ed. K. Haakonssen (Princeton: Princeton University Press, 1990), pp. 38–85.

Sections 7.1, 7.2, and 7.4 of Chapter 7 are revised from my essay 'From moral philosophy to political economy: The contribution of Dugald Stewart', in *Philosophers of the Scottish Enlightenment*, ed. V. Hope (Edinburgh: Edinburgh University Press, 1984), pp. 211–32.

Chapter 8 is revised from 'The science of a legislator in James Mackintosh's moral philosophy', *History of Political Thought* (Exeter: Imprint Academic), 5 (1984), 233–66.

Chapter 9 is revised from my essay 'James Mill and Scottish moral philosophy', *Political Studies* (Oxford: Blackwells) 33 (1985), 628–41.

Chapter 10 is revised from 'From natural law to the rights of man: A European perspective on American debates', in *A Culture of Right*, ed. M. Lacey and K. Haakonssen (Cambridge, UK: Cambridge University Press, 1991), pp. 19–61.

Finally, I thank Elizabeth Short and Norma Chin for their great assistance in preparing the manuscript and Elizabeth Short for compiling the index.

Introduction: The Scottish Enlightenment in the history of ideas

0.1 The Scottish Enlightenment

The essays that make up this volume were written as more or less self-contained pieces, yet each is closely related to the rest. The unifying theme is that important parts of eighteenth-century moral philosophy were heavily influenced by the natural law theories that developed within Protestantism after Hugo Grotius. The general thesis is that Protestant natural jurisprudence harboured a tension between a natural rights and a natural law tendency and that this was of particular importance for much subsequent moral and political thought. This was especially true of moral philosophy in the Scottish Enlightenment. After an extensive survey of the seventeenth-century European natural law background, the argument therefore concentrates mainly on Scottish moral thought in the eighteenth century.

It has long been a commonplace that the thinkers of the Scottish Enlightenment understood the moral life and moral institutions of humanity in social and historical terms; in fact, they have been seen as pioneers of holistic methods of explanation and of historical sociology. Yet at the same time, the Scots have commonly been included in the roll of honour for the founders of liberalism, and this individualistic perspective was perhaps reinforced by the tendency of traditional history of philosophy to concentrate on the epistemic and moral powers of an abstract subject. This scene has been changed dramatically in less than a generation.[1] Of the many perspectives that have enriched our understanding of the Scottish Enlightenment, three stand out: that of practical morals and moralizing politics; that of natural jurisprudence; and that of scientism.

1 The best general bibliography is in Richard B. Sher, *Church and University in the Scottish Enlightenment: The Moderate Literati of Edinburgh*, Princeton, 1985, pp. 329–76. For more recent literature, see *Eighteenth-Century Scotland: The Newsletter of the Eighteenth-Century Scottish Studies Society*, 1987– , edited by Sher. The references in this introduction are selective pointers only.

The pioneering work of Caroline Robbins and John Pocock drew the Scots within the walls of revived republicanism, and the moralizing humanism that went along with this has been explained in its Anglo-Scots adaptations by Nicholas Phillipson and others.[2] Subsequently, additional forms of practical, social moralizing have been explored by Richard Sher and John Dwyer, and, more recently, detailed studies of the moral and political relevance of history, especially national history, have been added.[3] Furthermore, the humanist republicanism found in the Scots has been embraced by some American scholars in their search for a republican tradition unencumbered by individualistic liberalism and edified by communitarianism.[4]

These interpretative endeavours have been complicated by the simultaneous appearance of new studies of the role of natural jurisprudence in the Scottish Enlightenment. The issue was raised by a number of scholars in the context of the Scots' external connections – especially with Locke and with the European continent – and in the

2 Caroline Robbins, *The Eighteenth-Century Commonwealthman*, Cambridge, MA, 1959, ch. 6; same, '"When it is that colonies may turn independent": An analysis of the environment and politics of Francis Hutcheson (1694–1746)', *William and Mary Quarterly*, 3rd ser., 11 (1954), 214–51; J.G.A. Pocock, *The Machiavellian Moment: Florentine Political Thought and the Atlantic Republican Tradition*, Princeton, 1975, chs. 13–14; same, *Virtue, Commerce, and History: Essays on Political Thought and History, Chiefly in the Eighteenth Century*, Cambridge, UK, 1985. A particularly valuable working out of this perspective is John Robertson, *The Scottish Enlightenment and the Militia Issue*, Edinburgh, 1985. In addition to the articles by Nicholas Phillipson cited in note 5 to Chapter 8 in the present volume, see his *Hume*, London, 1989, and his 'Propriety, property and prudence: David Hume and the defence of the Revolution', in *Political Discourse in Early Modern Britain*, ed. Nicholas Phillipson and Quentin Skinner, Cambridge, UK, 1993, pp. 302–20.

3 Sher, *Church and University*; John Dwyer, *Virtuous Discourse: Sensibility and Community in Late Eighteenth-Century Scotland*, Edinburgh, 1987; same, 'Clio and ethics: Practical morality in enlightened Scotland', *The Eighteenth Century*, 30 (1989), 45–72; David Allan, *Virtue, Learning and the Scottish Enlightenment: Ideas of Scholarship in Early Modern History*, Edinburgh, 1993; Colin Kidd, *Subverting Scotland's Past: Scottish Whig Historians and the Creation of an Anglo-British Identity, 1689–c. 1830*, Cambridge, UK, 1993.

4 In addition to the references in Chapter 10 in the present volume, see e.g. Stephen B. Presser, *The Original Misunderstanding: The English, the Americans and the Dialectic of Federalist Jurisprudence*, Durham, NC, 1991. For a good discussion of these issues, see James T. Kloppenberg, 'The virtues of liberalism: Christianity, republicanism, and ethics in early American political discourse', *Journal of American History*, 74 (1987), 9–33. The continuity of ancient and modern republicanism has recently come under critical scrutiny in Paul A. Rahe's massive *Republics Ancient and Modern: Classical Republicanism and the American Revolution*, Chapel Hill, NC, 1992.

context of how to interpret Hume and Smith. It has subsequently been pursued in interpretation of a number of other Scottish thinkers, including Francis Hutcheson and Thomas Reid, and its central place in the university curriculum has come to be appreciated. The jurisprudential perspective has, however, allowed the question of liberalism – anachronistic though it is – to live on. Again, it has been the American passion for a usable past that has provided much of the energy. The well-known Scottish treatises on moral philosophy were discovered to have whole books and chapters on natural law and rights, and contractarian accounts of life's moral institutions that seemed like perfect substitutes for Locke, whose impact on moral and political thought in the eighteenth century was called into question by the republican interpretation.[5]

Meanwhile, a revolution in the history of science was taking place, and thanks to Roger Emerson and others, it touched the Scottish Enlightenment more than lightly.[6] The new social and contextual history

5 The literature on natural jurisprudence and the Scots is extensively cited and discussed in the subsequent essays and needs no supplementation here. Concerning the American connection, see notes 42–3 to Chapter 10 of this volume.

6 See esp. Roger L. Emerson, 'Natural philosophy and the problem of the Scottish Enlightenment', *Studies on Voltaire and the Eighteenth Century*, 242 (1986), 243–91; same, 'Science and the origins and concerns of the Scottish Enlightenment', *History of Science*, 26 (1988), 333–66; same, 'Science and moral philosophy in the Scottish Enlightenment', in *Studies in the Philosophy of the Scottish Enlightenment*, ed. M.A. Stewart, Oxford 1990, pp. 11–36. Other notable contributions to a large literature include M. Barfoot, 'James Gregory (1753–1821) and Scottish Scientific Metaphysics, 1750–1800', Ph.D. thesis, University of Edinburgh, 1983; same, 'Hume and the culture of science in the early eighteenth century', in *Studies*, ed. Stewart, pp. 151–90; J.R.R. Christie, 'The origins and development of the Scottish scientific community', *History of Science*, 12 (1974), 122–41; Christopher Lawrence, 'Medicine as Culture: Edinburgh and the Scottish Enlightenment', Ph.D. thesis, University of Edinburgh, 1984; C.M. Shepherd, 'Newtonianism in Scottish universities in the seventeenth century', in *The Origins and Nature of the Scottish Enlightenment*, ed. R.H. Campbell and A.S. Skinner, Edinburgh, 1982, pp. 65–85; same, 'The arts curriculum at Aberdeen at the beginning of the eighteenth century', in *Aberdeen and the Enlightenment*, ed. J.J. Carter and J.H. Pittock, Aberdeen, 1987, pp. 146–54; Paul B. Wood, 'Thomas Reid, Natural Philosopher: A Study of Science and Philosophy in the Scottish Enlightenment', Ph.D. thesis, University of Leeds, 1984; same, 'Science and the pursuit of virtue in the Aberdeen Enlightenment', in *Studies*, ed. Stewart, pp. 127–49; John P. Wright, 'Metaphysics and physiology: Mind, body, and the animal economy in eighteenth-century Scotland', in *Studies*, ed. Stewart, pp. 251–301. See also Dennis R. Dean, *James Hutton and the History of Geology*, Ithaca, NY, 1992; A.L. Donovan, *Philosophical Chemistry in the Scottish Enlightenment: The Doctrines and Discoveries of William Cullen and Joseph Black*, Edinburgh, 1975; P. Jones, ed.,

saw the exploration of nature as an integral part of polite culture and of the culture of the mind. This work made clear the full extent of the teleological and providentialist twist put on Newtonianism, and this again gave a better appreciation of how Newton was extended to the moral sphere. Science served better than anything to show humanity its place and function in the general order instituted by the Divinity, and science was therefore itself part of practical moralizing. At the same time, the 'mental sciences' could work out the details of the moral psychology that made moralizing possible.

In another development closely connected with these three lines of interpretation, M. A. Stewart and others have presented a new appreciation of the Stoic legacy and its Christianisation.[7] Many other areas of scholarship have become intertwined with these ideas. To mention a few obvious ones, the connection between practical moralizing and the arts is being explored; the traditionally accepted sharp boundaries between evangelicalism and polite moral enlightenment are being questioned, and liberal Catholicism has been drawn into the Enlightenment; the institutions of enlightenment are becoming more perspicuous and, especially in the work of Roger Emerson, this has provided a much better understanding of the politics of enlightenment.[8] Feminist

Philosophy and Science in the Scottish Enlightenment, Edinburgh, 1988; and R. Olson, *Scottish Philosophy and British Physics, 1750–1880,* Princeton, 1975.

7   M.A. Stewart, 'The origins of the Scottish Greek chairs', in *'Owls to Athens': Essays on Classical Subjects Presented to Sir Kenneth Dover,* ed. E. M. Craik, Oxford, 1990, pp. 391–400; same, 'The Stoic legacy in the early Scottish Enlightenment', in *Atoms, Pneuma, and Tranquillity: Epicurean and Stoic Themes in European Thought,* ed. Margaret J. Osler, Cambridge, UK, 1991, pp. 273–96; Dwyer, *Virtuous Discourse,* ch. 2; D. D. Raphael and A.L. Macfie, introduction to Adam Smith, *The Theory of Moral Sentiments,* ed. D.D. Raphael and A.L. Macfie, Oxford, 1976, pp. 5–10; Sher, *Church and University,* ch. 5; N. Waszek, 'Two concepts of morality: A distinction of Adam Smith's ethics and its Stoic origin', *Journal of the History of Ideas,* 45 (1984), 591–606.

8   Out of hundreds of items I mention a few recent, representative samples of these lines of scholarship: The papers in section 3, 'Music and art in the Enlightenment', and section 5, 'Literature of the Enlightenment', in *Aberdeen and the Enlightenment,* ed. Carter and Pittock; John Dwyer, 'Enlightened spectators and classical moralists: Sympathetic relations in eighteenth-century Scotland', in *Sociability and Society in Eighteenth-Century Scotland,* ed. J. Dwyer and R.B. Sher, Edinburgh, 1993, pp. 96–118; Ned C. Landsman, 'Presbyterians and provincial society: The evangelical enlightenment in the west of Scotland, 1740–1775', in ibid., pp. 194–209; Mark Goldie, 'The Scottish Catholic Enlightenment', *Journal of British Studies,* 30 (1991), 20–62; same, 'Common Sense philosophy and Catholic theology in the Scottish Enlightenment', *Studies on Voltaire and the Eighteenth Century,* 302 (1992), 281–320. Roger L. Emerson, *Professors, Patronage and Politics: The Aberdeen Universities in the Eighteenth Century,* Aberdeen, 1992; same, 'Lord Bute and the Scottish universities, 1760–1792',

work on the ideas of the Scottish Enlightenment has been limited so far,[9] but contributions in the fields of general history of philosophy and political theory have been rich and will be amply represented in this volume.

My concern in the following studies is not with the full variety of the Scottish Enlightenment but with a cluster of ideas and a pattern of argument that cut across the three interpretations just mentioned. My point of departure is, admittedly, one of the three, natural jurisprudence, but I shall show that this tradition is not what it has commonly been taken to be and that the form that was dominant in Scotland in the eighteenth century lent itself to synthesis with both practical moralizing and scientism. I shall, in particular, analyse some significant Scottish attempts to combine jurisprudence, civic humanism, and practical ethics in a coherent moral and political outlook.

The most important point to appreciate is that natural law theory in general was not deeply individualistic and dominated by the idea of subjective rights. There was, of course, a wide variety of purely *political* rights discourses in early modern Europe, not least in England. But few thinkers embraced, or even understood, the idea that moral agency, or personhood, might consist in asserting claims against the rest of the surrounding world with no other guidance than one's own lights and that any common, social world had to arise from accommodation of some sort among competing claims. We find attempts at this argument in Grotius and Hobbes and in parts of covenant theology. For these thinkers the moral life was – eschatology apart – an open-ended series

---

in *Lord Bute: Essays in Reinterpretation*, ed. Karl W. Schweizer, Leicester, 1991; Nicholas Phillipson, *The Scottish Whigs and the Reform of the Court of Session, 1785–1830*, Edinburgh, 1990; Richard B. Sher and Alexander Murdoch, 'Patronage and party in the Church of Scotland, 1750–1800', in *Church, Politics and Society: Scotland, 1408–1929*, ed. Norman MacDougall, Edinburgh, 1983, pp. 197–220.

9   See, however, Henry C. Clark's fine discussion of the literature that feminism has inspired, 'Women and humanity in Scottish Enlightenment social thought: The case of Adam Smith', *Historical Reflections/Réflexions historiques*, 19 (1993), 335–61. For discussion of women in eighteenth-century Scottish thought, see especially Jane Rendall's interesting 'Virtue and commerce: Women in the making of Adam Smith's political economy', in *Women in Western Political Philosophy*, ed. E. Kennedy and S. Mendus, New York, 1987, pp. 44–77. Other relevant studies include David Bowles, 'John Millar, the four-stages theory and women's position in society', *History of Political Economy*, 16 (1984), 619–38; David C. Cooper, 'Scottish communitarianism, Lockean individualism, and women's moral development', in *Women's Rights and the Rights of Man*, ed. A.J. Arnaud and E. Kingdom, Aberdeen, 1992, pp. 36–51; Sylvana Tomasselli, 'Reflections on the history of the science of woman', in *History of Science*, 29 (1991), 185–205.

of contractual adaptations among individuals. In ways traced in a previous work and pursued in this volume, Hume and Adam Smith became part-heirs to this tradition by transforming contractarian negotiation into a complex socio-political development that had to be understood historically.[10]

In general, however, natural law theory gave a very different idea of the moral condition of humanity. According to most natural lawyers in the seventeenth and eighteenth centuries, moral agency consisted in being subject to natural law and carrying out the duties imposed by such law, whereas rights were derivative, being mere means to the fulfilment of duties. Each person had a right to the acts he or she was under a duty to do and a right to what others had a duty to render. Similarly, contracts were means for implementing the performance of the duties imposed by natural law. Within this conceptual framework an intense battle was fought during the last three decades of the seventeenth and the early years of the eighteenth century. At issue was the old problem of whether natural law had moral force for humanity solely because it was God's will or whether in addition it had independent moral authority with us. Few disputed that natural law *existed* because of God's will; the question was rather whether or not there were moral values shared by God and humanity which entailed the moral obligations of natural law independently of our regard for God's willing this to be so. This was closely associated with the question of what powers of moral discernment human beings possessed, and that was in effect a question of the impact of original sin. The mainstream of moral philosophy in the Scottish Enlightenment was formed by dealing with these issues.

The question of the adequacy of humanity's moral powers was answered empirically in the well-known theories of 'moral sense' and 'common sense'. Similarly, an objective moral order was supposedly demonstrated empirically to be the telos of moral life as we know it, and this was accepted as an answer to the obligation to natural law. Realization of this moral order would consist of the perfect discharge of the myriad of complementary roles or 'offices' – that is, duties with matching rights – that make up human life. The activity of being a public moralist inculcating the virtues of fulfilling one's office in the communal life of one's group was therefore securely anchored in the natural law theory of duties. At the same time, the prima facie contractarian account of all the central moral and political institutions was

10 In setting Hume and Smith aside from the mainstream of Scottish moral thought, I am, of course, in line with Alasdair MacIntyre, *Whose Justice? Which Rationality?*, Notre Dame, IN, 1988, chs. 12–16, but I do not share most of his premises or his polemics.

reinterpreted in strongly anti-individualistic terms. The contractual obligations apparently upholding familial and civic roles were understood as implied by these roles, irrespective of whether the roles originated in free choice by the individual or in the coincidences of life. That line of argument is of importance for an understanding of the place of history in this type of moral thought. If moral life consists of the discharge of overlapping offices, and if these offices in general are formed communally, then the history of this process will help us to understand the content of each office. Or, more generally, the discharge of our offices is dependent upon our acquaintance with tradition. On the other hand, history – survival through time – is not by itself prescriptive. Natural law obliges to duty; history, tradition, and one's own choices detail the content of one's duty. But if history is merely informative, the future is prescriptive, and the science of morals can inform us of it. Moral guidance is in the future, in the ideal moral order and harmony of roles that are providentially appointed as our goals and described by moral science. Therein lies the great moral and political ambiguity of this line of thought. On the one hand it relies on a conservative notion of the historically given offices of life; on the other hand, it needs a teleological and providentialist norm, and that invites utopian scheming. This was, as we shall see, Thomas Reid's dilemma, from which Dugald Stewart tried to escape in a haze of historicist inevitability.

As we play this theme through with variations, we shall see that the educational value of history was not enough to give history a role in moral theory. It is no accident that those Scottish thinkers who pursued this line of argument with clarity contributed little or nothing to the historical work of the Scottish Enlightenment. I am thinking here of Francis Hutcheson, George Turnbull, Thomas Reid, George Campbell, James Beattie, James Oswald, Dugald Stewart. This is not to say that all those who did contribute histories had a different moral outlook; Lord Kames and Adam Ferguson, at least, bear witness against such a proposition. But I think it fair to say that for these eclectic thinkers the moral role of history was as a repository of exemplars, for good or for evil. For David Hume, Adam Smith, and John Millar, on the other hand, history was essential to moral theory, because moral consciousness, moral judgement, and moral institutions were formed by the accommodations reached at a given stage of society and in a given type of government. The 'historicism' of Smith, in particular, became a watershed in moral and political thought in the late phase of the Scottish Enlightenment. Consequently, my major themes are, in the later chapters in this book, discussed as part of the question of what became of Smith's historico-theoretical 'science of a legislator', which I reconstructed in an earlier book of that title.

0.2 *The history of ideas*

Despite the extraordinary variety of fruitful approaches to the Scottish Enlightenment that has emerged in recent years, there seems still to be an unaccountable hankering for *the* total history of the Scottish Enlightenment. It may be necessary to stress that the present work is not meant to satisfy such cravings. Although the moral philosophy with which I am concerned is central to any understanding of the Scottish Enlightenment, there is obviously much more to this phenomenon. Nor do I present this work as a history of the moral thought of the Scottish Enlightenment. My concern is with specific ideas and patterns of argument that are also to be found, in more or less comparable forms, elsewhere in Europe. This inevitably raises the question of the genre in which I write, and, in a methodology-conscious age, it may be as well to set this out clearly and briefly.[11]

During the past generation, one of the central disputes in the historiography of intellectual history has concerned the relationship between historical and theoretical endeavours. The general tendency has been to see intellectual – and, indeed, all – history as a sui generis study of the past which should not be defined and directed by modern theoretical concerns. This argument has been put forward with particular force by historians of morals and politics, notably Quentin Skinner and John Pocock.[12] Their argument is premised on the general view that the chief subject-matter of intellectual history is the linguistic behaviour of agents in the past. This view has some family resemblance to hermeneutic theory, and it has facilitated appreciation of hermeneutics in the Anglo-American world. The notion that linguistic usage should be an object of behavioural study does, however, have a distinct

11   The rest of this introduction is adapted from part of my introduction to *Traditions of Liberalism: Essays on John Locke, Adam Smith and John Stuart Mill*, ed. K. Haakonssen, Sydney, 1988, pp. xi–xxi.

12   It is not necessary for the points to be made here that I go into the differences between Pocock and Skinner or that I discuss the development of their methodological views. My *précis* relies on the following selection: J.G.A. Pocock, 'The history of political thought: A methodological enquiry', in *Philosophy, Politics and Society*, 2nd ser., ed. P. Laslett and W. G. Runciman, Oxford, 1969, pp. 183–202; chs. 1, 7, and 8 in Pocock, *Politics, Language and Time: Essays on Political Thought and History*, London, 1972; 'Reconstructing the traditions: Quentin Skinner's historians' history of political thought', *Canadian Journal of Political and Social Theory / Revue canadienne de théorie politique et sociale*, 3 (1979), 95–113; 'The concept of language and the *métier d'historien*: Some considerations on practice', in *The Languages of Political Theory in Early-Modern Europe*, ed. A. Pagden, Cambridge, UK, 1987, pp. 19–38. Skinner's main contributions are now collected in *Meaning and Context: Quentin Skinner and His Critics*, ed. J. Tully, Cambridge, UK, 1988.

source in Wittgenstein's theory of language and, more immediately, in the theory of 'speech acts' developed by thinkers such as J. L. Austin and J. R. Searle.[13] According to this theory, our use of language cannot be understood merely as oral or written utterance with propositional meaning, that is, with sense and reference – the so-called 'locutionary function'. We must, in addition, understand the use of language as an act, as a form of behaviour that meshes with the rest of the speaker's behaviour. Like other deliberate behaviour, it has a point, a purpose, a 'force' : this is the so-called 'illocutionary function', or force, of language.[14] In order to understand the illocutionary function – that is, what the author was doing in saying or writing something – we need to know the situation or context in which he or she was doing it. Otherwise we will not see the point of his or her action but will be left with a free-floating statement. Hence the method recommended by the 'speech activists' among the historians is often referred to as the 'contextualist method'. Although ideally we should study linguistic behaviour in the full context of the author's general behaviour, we cannot, of course, observe the behaviour of the past. To a large extent we must rely on linguistic reports of it, that is, on other speech acts, though historians naturally draw on a wide variety of additional evidence of past behaviour. The available context for a given past speech act is, therefore, primarily, though not exclusively, linguistic in character, as Pocock stresses.[15]

The effect of the contextualist turn in contemporary historiography of moral and political thought and, increasingly, in other areas of intellectual history, has been dramatic and generally beneficial. It has provided an ever-richer texture in many areas of history, and this has led in turn to an unprecedented rapprochement between the history of moral and political thought and other forms of history. It has begun to dispose of the numerous anachronisms in traditional histories in these fields. In some cases it has led to important revaluations of major thinkers in the traditional canon, and it has created a rising standard of historical sensibility in other areas of history.

It is questionable, however, whether the intended divorce of history and theory has been achieved, and even more problematic whether any failure in this respect is owing to inattention to the methodological lessons offered or to some inadequacy in these lessons. It seems to me that the historical and theoretical pursuits of moral and political ideas are as interwoven as ever, and, although this is not the place either to

13 J.L. Austin, *How to Do Things with Words*, Oxford, 1971; J.R. Searle, *Speech Acts: An Essay in the Philosophy of Language*, Cambridge, UK, 1969.
14 Austin, *How to Do Things*, pp. 99–131.
15 Pocock, 'The concept of language', p. 20.

document or to defend this practice, it is a place for putting forward another perspective on the study of intellectual history than that provided by the speech activists in banning theory from history.

At the heart of the matter is the speech-act theory. Although its proponents are aware that this theory encompasses both the locutionary and the illocutionary functions of language, they nevertheless allow the former no role when they apply the theory in their historiographical programme. The background to this neglect is undoubtedly Austin's insistence that the two functions are intertwined in every utterance, so that referential function must be understood in performative context. Although they adhere to a correspondence theory of reference, they insist that the truth of a description, considered as an utterance, is a matter of its adequacy to the linguistic community in which it is being uttered. 'True' means 'very well said', as has been said very well.[16]

Despite Austin's own attempt to achieve a balanced view, the referential function of language, as ordinarily understood, has to a large extent gone begging for a place in the contextualist methodology. For the purposes of formulating a methodology for, or even an attitude to, the study of the history of ideas, we do not, however, have to commit ourselves to an elaborate alternative metaphysical and linguistic theory about the 'real' referents and *the* proper referential function of language. We can take it as a matter for exploration, rather than assertion, that given utterances have identifiable objects of reference. If we accept that many utterances are intended to say something about these objects – in addition to whatever else the speaker may be 'doing' in the uttering – then it would seem to be part of the intellectual historian's task to write the history of the utterance not only as a performance but also as a reference. The latter, however, cannot be done except through an investigation of the purported objects of reference, which, in intellectual history, will primarily be the *ideas* employed by an historical speaker in making an utterance.

Once we see this as our task, we can no longer entirely reduce intellectual history to the history of discourse, in the sense of linguistic performance. We must always bear in mind that the speaker's choice of words may be inadequate to the formulation of the ideas he or she is trying to express. Since linguistic expression is the only immediate source for the ideas in question, historians seek to check their interpretation in various indirect ways. Some draw on socio-psychological theories of culture, in order to produce histories of 'mentalities'.[17] Oth-

---

16   John Passmore, *A Hundred Years of Philosophy,* London, 1966, p. 467.

17   In the study of the Scottish Enlightenment, Sher's *Church and University* is a notable example.

ers invoke one or another psychological theory, creating psycho-histories.[18] Marxists read the historical text as ideology and thus link it to the unfolding class struggle.[19] The contextualist historians protest against all of this in the name of 'genuinely historical history', insisting that the text be reread in terms of the specific socio-linguistic premises of a particular situation.[20]

At their best, all these, and still other approaches have yielded outstanding contributions to historical understanding. They have served to correct the merely anachronistic writing of history as the record of 'progress', or 'Whig history'. Yet unless we want to reduce ideas to the expression of collective mentalities, or to psychological processes, or to epiphenomena of social and economic forces, or to linguistic behaviour, there is evidently something missing – namely the history of *ideas*. When one or all of these methods of writing the history of thought have been tried, there will often be not only room but need for an investigation of the ideas thought, simply as ideas. In order to do this, however, the historian has to understand the ideas in question, not just as mental, social, and linguistic events but as intellectual phenomena with their own logic. By this I mean that historians have to reconstruct the premises for, and implications of, theories. They have to consider possible alternative formulations of distinctions and problems, and they have to do this in order to gauge exactly where, in this intellectual problem situation, specific historical formulations of ideas are to be located. Through an understanding of the logical possibilities in a theory or in a complex of distinctions and problems, the historian can appreciate not only the particular route taken by a past author but also the routes *not* taken – the logical implications of a theory which were not drawn, the inconsistencies which were not seen, the looseness of distinctions that were taken to be exhaustive. This is not to say that the historian's task is to record what might have been, the historical counterfactuals. It is to claim that our appreciation of the logical possi-

18 In the Scottish field there is a notable, if only partial, example of this: Charles Camic's use of theories of childhood socialization in *Experience and Enlightenment: Socialization for Cultural Change in Eighteenth-Century Scotland*, Edinburgh, 1983.

19 As far as the Scots are concerned, this began with Marx himself. In modern scholarship it has particularly affected Smith and Millar. I discuss the latter in Chapter 5 in this volume and the former in *The Science of a Legislator: The Natural Jurisprudence of David Hume and Adam Smith*, Cambridge, UK, 1981, ch. 8.

20 Most of the upsurge of work on the intellectual history of the Scottish Enlightenment has been affected in one way or another by this outlook. This has contributed to breaking down the barriers between intellectual and other forms of history – institutional, political, social – which have also experienced many new developments.

bilities in a situation structures the questions we must ask in order to make the historical agent's response intelligible to *us*.

Here the interchange between the history of ideas proper and the other approaches to intellectual history becomes particularly valuable. Very often we shall be satisfied that some logically possible implication or distinction was not in fact drawn because the author concerned did not find it within the mental horizon of the society in question, or because the person concerned happened to have some particular psychological block against it; or because it was not part of the discourse available to him or her and thus not part of what could be done in the situation. Although such answers, especially the last, often satisfy us, they are, from the standpoint of argumentative logic, extraneous, and they may be too easy a way out. More particularly, they may be resorted to prematurely. It is important, therefore, that our explanation of 'errors' and 'missed opportunities', as they appear to us in analysing a complex of past thought, be sought first in purely argumentative terms. Only then can we be confident that we have comprehended our author's understanding of the ideas he or she was trying to handle and thus that we can apply the other methods of explanation in the right place.

The suggested approach is not, as sometimes alleged, based on the assumption that our past author was perfectly rational, whatever that may mean. It is exactly because we do not know that person's rationality, its extent and its nature, that we must appreciate the logic of the ideas that he or she was trying to deal with. In doing this we cannot a priori exclude any theoretical insights. It would be foolish to assume that either the author's or the linguistic community's formulation of a set of ideas was exhaustive of the argumentative potential of these ideas. Although we should start from such formulations as our explananda, we should, as preparation for our explanations, utilise the theoretical insights gained from all periods, including our own. The purpose is not, of course, to ascribe to past authors ideas they did not have. The point is that fruitful intellectual history is not simply the record of successfully expressed ideas but also an appreciation of mistakes, of missed opportunities, of the only half understood. If we neglect this, we shall not press our historical material hard enough, nor shall we understand the intellectual problem situation or context that one generation, more or less unintentionally, presents to the next. It is not only an author's actual *utterances* that have unintended consequences; the *ideas* the author tries to express often have unintended implications of consequence. At the same time it must be emphasised that to pursue the history of ideas in this way is not to judge the truth value of past theories and complexes of ideas and thus to assess the 'contribution' of past thinkers to the present state of knowledge. A clear distinction between the validity of a conclusion given certain premises and the truth of the argument as a whole is to be maintained here.[21] The argumentative possibilities open to Locke, given his theological premises, and thus the connection between these premises and, say, his theory of rights is the business of the historian of ideas; the truth of the whole proceeding is a matter for the philosopher. It is quite possible, however, that the former will learn from the latter new ways of probing the material.

If the history of ideas is pursued in this manner, the relationship between history and theory is no longer entirely one-sided. In addition to any enlightenment that contemporary theory may derive from the great thinkers of the past, our understanding of their ideas may benefit from the insights of subsequent generations, including our own. This suggestion is an endorsement neither of anachronism nor of teleological history. In utilising the theoretical tools of a later period to elucidate the ideas of an earlier one, we must, of course, resist any temptation to transpose the former on to the latter. One of the main benefits of the contextualist fashion in modern intellectual history has been to make historians of ideas more honest in this regard. Similarly, the speech activists have served us well in criticizing all tendencies to 'explain' the past as a process whose goal is the present. There remains, however, a distinction between, on the one hand, gauging the logical or argumentative potential of past ideas by means of present insights and, on the other, saying that the latter were already there in the past, or that we can understand past ideas *because* they led to the present. (Whether this has happened, and how, is a different historical problem.)

Apart from the charges of anachronism and teleology, the history of ideas as outlined here is open to other, related suspicions. It may appear that such an approach presupposes that there are 'universal', trans-historical ideas, theories, and problems – such as A. O. Lovejoy's great 'unit-ideas'.[22] This is obviously not my presupposition. My point is simply that we have no means of knowing whether there are such ideas except by piecemeal investigation. We cannot start from them; whether we can end up with them is at least questionable. Since it

21 This is the only point that separates me from the distinction between 'intellectual history' and 'the philosophy of history' made by Richard Rorty, J. B. Schneewind, and Quentin Skinner, eds., in *Philosophy in History: Essays on the Historiography of Philosophy*, Cambridge, UK, 1984, pp. 1–14, esp. p. 4. By committing 'the philosophy of history' to a necessary concern with truth, they create an unnecessarily wide gap between the two disciplines, conceived as ideal types, which makes it harder for them subsequently to establish connections between them in practice. What they need is the concept of a history of ideas, such as the one indicated here.

22 A. O. Lovejoy, *The Great Chain of Being: A Study of the History of an Idea*, Cambridge, MA, 1936, repr. 1974, pp. 1–23.

seems impossible to specify what 'universe' is being referred to in talking about 'universal' ideas, it is extremely difficult to give the notion a specific meaning. The 'universality' of ideas is a matter of degree, and the degree is determined by the historical perspectives from which we choose to compare historically given ideas. In practice, we must elucidate ideas from different periods and contexts in the light of each other, and I suggest that it is up to our theoretical ingenuity to make this more and more enlightening for each idea in its context.

My insistence upon the possibility of a history of ideas is not to be taken to mean that this approach should replace all others. Intellectual history, perhaps more than any other historical field, calls for methodological pluralism, and I have no doubt about the necessity for an intimate connection between the contextualists' study of past thought as discourse and the sort of history of ideas advocated here. When such integrated history has been attempted, it has mostly been done by teams of historians writing encyclopaedic works; for the solitary scholar and the individual monograph, it may be a tall order. There is, however, a division of labour in intellectual history, and this can be legitimated by the methodological pluralism advocated here.

1

Natural law in the seventeenth century

The attempt to understand morality in the legalistic terms of a natural law is ancient but is now mostly associated with the formulation given it by Thomas Aquinas in the late thirteenth century. Earlier natural law is commonly seen as leading up to Aquinas's paradigmatic version, whereas later natural law is understood as deriving from it. This approach has resulted in long-standing disputes about the status of Protestant natural law vis-à-vis Thomism, disputes generally centring on the question of the originality of Hugo Grotius, commonly considered 'the father of modern natural law'. It is easy to understand why there should be such disagreements. The sources reveal an extraordinary degree of continuity between scholastic natural law (not only Aquinas's) and the natural law doctrines that dominated Protestant Europe during the seventeenth and much of the eighteenth centuries. Yet it seemed to moral philosophers of these centuries, especially to the modern natural lawyers themselves, that something decisively new happened with Grotius. Protestant natural law was seen as a distinct school of moral philosophy, until the history of philosophy was redrawn by Kant and by others working in the light of his philosophy.[1]

The resolution of these disputes has in some measure been frustrated by the concentration on the role of Grotius. Although Grotius's underlying theory conveyed to Protestant Europe large parts of natural law material utilized by the great scholastic thinkers, especially those of sixteenth-century Spain, it contained elements that his successors considered dangerous. In their commentaries on Grotius's text and in histories of their discipline, later natural lawyers glossed over or repudiated these elements and ascribed Grotius's novelty to ideas that were in fact not at all new with him but which were important to them. We

---

1 See Richard Tuck, 'The "modern" theory of natural law', in *The Languages of Political Theory in Early-Modern Europe*, ed. Anthony Pagden, Cambridge, UK, 1987, pp. 99–119.

must therefore distinguish between Grotius's true originality and the novelty of subsequent Protestant natural law theory.

1.1 Francis Suárez

The backdrop to these questions is, of course, scholasticism. Neither as a method nor as a body of doctrine was scholasticism a spent force by 1600, and work of various scholastic genres, including commentaries on Aristotle, continued to appear throughout the seventeenth century. Perhaps the greatest synthesis of scholastic moral-legal theory is a seventeenth-century work, *De legibus, ac Deo legislatore* (1612) by the Jesuit Francis Suárez. It issued from the Spanish schools, which, somewhat removed from the centres of Renaissance humanism and the Reformation, continued not only to teach scholastic doctrine but to renew it in response to novel problems, not least of a colonial and, to use an anachronistic term, international political-legal nature.[2] First of all, Suárez's theory is a carefully argued synthesis of earlier doctrines, reflecting some of the most prominent scholastic disputes, especially that between the Dominicans and the Jesuits over the respective roles of divine grace and human free will, and that between the nominalist-voluntarist tradition stemming from William of Ockham and the realist-intellectualist tradition descending from Gregory of Rimini and, most would say, Thomas Aquinas. Of these points, we can deal only with the last.

Like Aquinas, Suárez divides law into four categories: eternal law, natural law, divine positive law, and human positive law (I.3.v–vi; pp. 39–40).[3] In his analysis of these laws he does, however, emphasize the role of the will of the legislator a good deal more than Aquinas. Law, in the strict sense, is characterized by being obligatory upon creatures of reason and free will, and this is supposed to require willing on the part of the legislator. Eternal law is only in a tenuous sense a

---

2   See L.C. Green and O.P. Dickason, *The Law of Nations and the New World*, Edmonton, 1988; J.L. Holzgrefe, 'The origins of modern international relations theory', *Review of International Studies*, 15 (1989), 11–26; Anthony Pagden, 'The "School of Salamanca" and the affair of the Indies', in *Histories of Universities*, (1981), 1:71–112; same, 'Dispossessing the barbarian: The language of Spanish Thomism and the debate over the property rights of the American Indians', in Pagden, *Languages of Political Theory*, pp 79–98; J. B. Scott, ed., *The Spanish Origins of International Law*, Oxford, 1934. For the context, see also B. Hamilton, *Political Thought in Sixteenth-Century Spain: A Study of the Political Ideas of Vitoria, De Soto, Suárez, and Molina*, Oxford, 1963.

3   References of this form in the present section are to *Tractatus de legibus ac Deo legislatore* in Francisco Suárez, *Selections from Three Works*, 2 vols. (Classics of International Law), Oxford, 1944. I have occasionally corrected the translation included in this edition.

'law'. On the one hand, it is God's most general will, or Providence, for the moral (rational and free-willed) Creation, and so it is in a sense a law for the latter. On the other hand, it is only indirectly 'for' God's creatures, in as much as they cannot know it in more than the most general sense as part of God's nature (II.1.xi; pp. 150–1). Only when it is promulgated to rational creatures can it be called 'law' proper. This cannot be done directly, knowledge and obligation being temporal effects, and happens only when the eternal law takes the form of one or another of the other three kinds of law (II.4.ix–x; pp. 176–7). At the same time Suárez stresses that the eternal law cannot be seen as a law that God imposes upon himself (II.2.viii; p. 156). Law implies obligation, and obligation implies a superior as legislator, which is a contradiction where God is concerned.

The other forms of law are divided according to the different ways in which they, or those subject to them, participate in the overarching eternal law (I.3.vii–viii; pp. 40–1). Natural law is simply the way in which the eternal law applies to human moral nature. In the case of positive law, a legislator intervenes. Divine positive law comes about when God acts as a ruler who promulgates his law, in revelation, and binds those subject to it by his will and his power. This is the law of Scripture. It is an addition to nature which can aid human beings in this life, especially through its institutional forms in the church (I.3.xiv–xvi; pp. 45–7). In view of God's nature, there can of course be no conflict between this law and eternal law or natural law.

Human positive law issues from human rulers, and, like other human acts, it has natural law as the moral measure which it may or may not follow in particular cases. (In addition, some human law, of course, is built upon divine law.) Human law is better discussed in conjunction with Suárez's political theory, the fundamental principle of which is this: Given the nature of the moral creation, human beings have to arrange their affairs in one or other of a number of possible ways; such arrangements are, in other words, enjoined by the law of nature. However, which arrangement is to be adopted is a matter for people to settle among themselves. It is thus a natural necessity arising from the needs of human beings that they live in hierarchies of social groups, minimally the family and *some* sort of wider group. In order to have a coherent social group, there must be an organized concern for the common good, and this requires *some* kind of sovereign authority which in one way or another can legislate and enforce its legislation. In order to make use of the necessary goods of the world, *some* system of property has to be adhered to. This much is according to natural law, but the specific forms that property arrangements take have to be agreed upon by people.[4]

---

4   For the further development of the theory of property in modern natural law,

Accordingly, as far as society, political authority, and, by implication, private property are concerned, Suárez can be seen as a kind of contractarian. However, it is important to stress that the existence of these social institutions is natural and only their specific forms 'artificial', to use the language which was soon to become current in this connection.

This view of society, political authority, and legislation as necessary responses to the needs of human nature is clearly directed against the Reformers' political ideas. Social life and political governance are not to be seen as the necessary means of compensating for fallen man's loss of moral self-government. They are in fact part of the fulfilment of human nature. Original sin just makes it harder to achieve fulfilment in these as in other aspects of the moral life.[5]

The tenuousness of this kind of contractarianism was to persist in much of the debate about the basis for both civil and church government during the following two centuries. It is revealed in Suárez's discussions of the moral position that arises when the contractually instituted forms break down. In situations of extreme hardship, the needy have the right to make use of the private property (*dominium*) of others. This right does not derive from any duty on the part of the owners of private property. Rather, private property ceases to exist under such circumstances, and things return to the original common. It is similarly so with sovereign authority (also *dominium*). In cases of extreme need – namely, when government turns tyrannical – the contract transferring sovereignty to it is annulled, and sovereignty returns to its original natural source, the community. In both cases, the goals set by natural law – broadly speaking, the common good – override what was instituted by contract.

Finally, it should be pointed out that, in his attempts to capture the sense in which the institution of private property is permitted, or licit (*licitum*), under natural law, Suárez helped set in motion the clarification by the modern schools of natural law of the central deontic trichotomy 'obligatory permitted forbidden'.[6]

The natural law is the hub of Suárez's system. Apart from the fourfold distinction already mentioned, natural law must be distinguished from *ius gentium* (II.17–20), which again must be kept separate from the *ius civile*, or human positive law proper. *Ius gentium* is in effect customary

---

see S. Buckle, *Natural Law and the Theory of Property: Grotius to Hume*, Oxford, 1991; and T.A. Horne, *Property Rights and Poverty: Political Argument in Britain, 1605–1834*, Chapel Hill, NC, 1990, ch. 1.

5   For Suárez's general programme of criticism of the 'heretics', see I.18.ix–x.

6   See J. Hruschka, *Das deontologische Sechseck bei Gottfried Achenwall im Jahre 1767. Zur Geschichte der deontischen Grundbegriffe in der Universaljurisprudenz zwischen Suárez und Kant* (Joachim Jungius-Gesellschaft der Wissenschaften/ Göttingen), Hamburg, 1986.

law as found across civil societies. It is thus positive law but not civil law, in as much as it does not issue from a sovereign. The category of *ius gentium* provides the framework for Suárez's significant discussions of the laws of war and peace, discussions which, when combined with his in many respects modern concept of sovereignty, must be considered fundamental to what would eventually become international law.

Natural law must also be distinguished from law in the metaphorical sense, in which all of nature is 'law-governed' or subject to causal regularity. In this connection Suárez puts forward the old chestnut, now mainly known from Hume, that the same form of behaviour in an animal and in a person (e.g. promiscuity) has no moral significance in the former case whereas in the latter it has. In other words, natural law proper applies only to moral agents.

Law exists in the mind of the legislator, in the mind of the subject, and in some medium (I.4.iv; pp. 52–3). As far as the last is concerned, Suárez takes the traditional view that the law of nature is promulgated both in human reason and in the Decalogue (II.Introd.; p. 143). In the human mind, natural law exists in the form of an act of judgement which precedes and guides the will (I.4.v; p. 53). In the mind of the legislator, God, law exists as a combination of will and reason, since these are inseparable in God (I.4.vi; pp.53–4; II.1.viii; p. 156). It was through this suggestion that Suárez explicitly attempted to reconcile the two sides in one of the greatest scholastic disputes and presented a synthesis that remained at the heart of most natural law thinking for the following two centuries. At one extreme, he saw what we now refer to as the 'intellectualist' and 'realist' tradition, for which his main reference is Gregory of Rimini. At the other extreme, he presented the 'voluntarism' of William of Ockham, Jean Gerson, and Pierre d'Ailly (II.6.iii–iv; pp. 189–91).

Suárez characterizes the intellectualist and realist position as follows:

> the natural law is not a preceptive law, properly so-called, since it is not the indication of the will of some superior; but . . . on the contrary, it is a law indicating what should be done, and what should be avoided, what of its own nature is intrinsically good and necessary, and what is intrinsically evil.
>
> The natural law is not derived from God as a Lawgiver, since it does not depend upon His will, and . . . in consequence, God does not, by virtue of that law, act as a superior who lays down commands or prohibitions. Indeed . . . Gregory . . . says that even if God did not exist, or if He did not make use of reason, or if He did not judge of things correctly, nevertheless, if the same dictates of right reason dwelt within man, constantly assuring, for example, that lying is evil, those dictates would still have the same legal character which they actually possess, because they would constitute a law pointing out the evil that exists intrinsically in the object. (II.6.iii; pp. 189–90).

In contrast to this, Suárez formulates the voluntarist thesis in these terms:

> that the natural law consists entirely in a divine command or prohibition proceeding from the will of God as the Author and Ruler of nature; that, consequently, this law as it exists in God is none other than the eternal law in its capacity of commanding or prohibiting with respect to a given matter; and that, on the other hand, this same natural law, as it dwells within ourselves, is the judgment of reason, in that it reveals to us God's will as to what must be done or avoided . . . [Further] that the whole basis of good and evil in matters pertaining to the law of nature is in God's will, and not in a judgment of reason, even on the part of God himself, nor in the very things which are prescribed or forbidden by that law. The foundation for this opinion would seem to be that actions are not good or evil, save as they are ordered or prohibited by God; since God himself does not will to command or forbid a given action to any created being, on the ground that such an action is good or evil, but rather on the ground that it is just or unjust because He has willed that it shall or shall not be done. (II.6.iv; pp. 190–1).

Suárez objects to the intellectualist thesis on several grounds. First, there is a difference between a proposition and a law. Furthermore, a judgement about moral values is a judgement of facts, moral facts, and not of itself a guide to action; in order to have any relevance to action, as a law has, something must be added to the judgement (II.6.vi; p. 192).[7] The intellectualist thesis also implies that God himself is subject to natural law, since it is argumentatively presupposed in his will. Or, to put it differently, if 'good' implies 'is under obligation to', then God is under an obligation to follow the law of nature (II.5.vii; p. 182). But, as previously mentioned, this is an impossibility, since obligation presupposes a superior, a point underlined by the (question-begging) suggestion that self-command is a meaningless concept (II.6.i; p. 188). It is thus not only the case that natural law, on this reading of it, could be independent of God; it actually is so (II.5.viii; p. 182). It should be pointed out here that Suárez's formulation of Gregory's view, quoted earlier, polemically distorts it in a significant way. Gregory did not say, in the passage referred to by Suárez, that without God the dictates of right reason would still have the same 'legal character' (*rationem legis*) nor that they would constitute a *lex ostensiva*. He said only that, even without God, there would be sin, or moral evil (*peccatum*).[8] By imputing to Gregory the former view, Suárez is suggesting that the earlier

7 The reader may want to consider the transposition of this point to Hume's *Treatise*, III.1.i.

8 Gregorius Ariminensis, *Lectura super primum et secundum sententiarum*, ed. A.D. Trapp, V. Marcolino et al., 7 vols., Berlin, 1978–87, vol. 6 (1980), d. 34, q. 1. art. 2.

thinker had the idea that there could be obligation without God, a point that Suárez obviously took to be self-evidently absurd.

In view of his own position, Suárez's criticism of the voluntarist thesis is surprisingly muted and poorly formulated. His first point is 'that certain evils are prohibited, because they are evil. For if they are prohibited on that very ground, they cannot derive the primary reason for their evil quality from the fact that they are prohibited, since an effect is not the reason for its cause' (II.6.xi; p. 197). The implication is that either the argument moves in a vicious circle of prohibition and evil quality, or it moves in a hierarchy of prohibitions. But since God is involved, both an infinite regress and an unjustified fiat are impossible. Consequently, there must ultimately be a reason other than prohibition for the prohibitions of natural law. Suárez finds 'a posteriori' confirmation of this point in an attempted *reductio ad absurdum*. If natural law were simply a matter of God's will without the need for reasons, then it would in principle be possible that God could allow humanity to hate him. Hence this 'could be permitted, and it could be righteous' (*posset licere, vel esse honestum*; II.6.xi; p. 198).[9] However, to think that God is rightly the object of hatred is a contradiction in terms. Voluntarism leads to the notorious paradox normally ascribed to Ockham.[10] In this argument much of course depends on the notion of the licit. It is surprising that Suárez does not invoke here the clear distinction he makes elsewhere between *permissio facti*, the de facto indifference to an action, and *permissio juris*, the 'active' withholding of disapproval of an action.[11] Only the latter leads to Ockham's paradox, but it is arguable

---

9   Cf. the further discussion at II.6.xiv–xix: pp. 200–4. Although unacknowledged in Suárez, the example was well known from Ockham.

10   'If God could command this [that He be not loved for a certain time] – and it seems that He can do it without contradiction – then I maintain that the will in this situation cannot perform such an act, because merely by performing such an act the will would love God above all and consequently would fulfil the divine precept. For to love God above all means to love whatever God wills to be loved. But by the mere fact of loving God in this way one would not (according to our assumption) fulfil the divine command. Consequently by loving God in this manner one would love God and not love God; one would fulfil the precept of God and not fulfil it.' *Quodlibeta*, III, Q. xiii, in William Ockham, *Philosophical Writings: A Selection*, ed. and trans. P. Boehner, London, 1957, repr. 1967, p. 147. Whether Ockham in fact subscribed to the extreme form of voluntarism suggested by Suárez is at least doubtful; see John Kilcullen, 'Natural law and will in Ockham', in *Reason, Will and Nature: Voluntarism in Metaphysics and Morals from Ockham to Kant*, ed. K. Haakonssen and U. Thiel (*History of Philosophy Yearbook*, 1), Canberra, 1994, pp. 1–34. The voluntarist interpretation of Ockham may be part of a polemical tradition ratified and effectively conveyed by Suárez.

11   Suárez, *De legibus* [*Tractatus de legibus ac Deo legislatore*]. Ed. crit. bilingüe por

that the imputation to God of this kind of *permissio* is question-begging
for a voluntarist in at least one very important situation of God's permission. If we consider the human condition logically prior to, or in
abstraction from, God's imposition of the natural law, God's attitude to
humanity can hardly be conceived as one of *permissio juris*, since this
already contains a moral element. If the human situation prior to the
law is amoral, then God's attitude must be understood as a mere *permissio facti*. The question then is whether this *permissio* is consistent
with a Christian notion of the God who loves humankind. Clearly
Suárez's answer would have been no.

Suárez's own notion of natural law combines elements from both of
the extremes that he presents and rejects (II.6.v and xi; pp. 191 and 197–
8). The heart of the matter is that natural law is both indicative of what
is in itself good and evil, and preceptive in the sense that it creates an
obligation in people to do the good and avoid the evil. The natural law
thus reflects the two inseparable sides of God's nature, namely his
rational judgement of good and evil and his will prescribing the appropriate behaviour (II.6.xiii; pp. 199–200).

This brings us once more to the question of the necessity of God's
willing what is good. We have already seen that there cannot possibly
be any obligation upon God, since obligation presupposes a superior.
The question then is whether God can be said to derive an 'ought' from
his conception of what is good. The answer is that it is uncertain
whether Suárez has the conceptual apparatus required to deal with this
question. In one sense God is totally free – free, for example, to create
or not to create the known world (II.6.xxiii; p. 206). If we could conceive of his choice between creating this or another world, or no world
at all, as a moral choice, a choice between alternative constellations of
goods and evils, then we could see him as imposing upon himself
certain duties as a consequence of realizing one or another set of values. This rather common-sensical view is probably what Suárez intends. The problem is that it amounts to suggesting that human beings
can understand the eternal law by which God himself operates, not just
its adaptation in the natural law promulgated to humans. If human
beings could have this kind of insight, it is not clear why God the
legislator should be necessary as the ground of all human morality. On
the other hand, having made his choice of creation, he has too little
freedom: 'God could not have refrained from willing to forbid that a
creature . . . endowed [with reason and knowledge of good and evil]
should commit acts intrinsically evil, nor could He have willed not to
prescribe the necessary righteous acts' (II.6.xxiii; p. 206). In other

L. Pereña et al., 8 vols. (Corpus Hispanorum de Pace, 11–17, 21, 22), Madrid, 1971–
81, I.15.vii and II.14.xiii–xix.

words, the 'ought' is not self-imposed as a result of rationally considering the 'goods' but is the inevitable outcome of the fact that God did
choose one set of goods.

In the human world the problem is very different. On the one hand
Suárez is committed to the voluntarist thesis that it is God's will which
binds people. In accordance with this, he maintains that we are obligated to the natural law under pain of God's punishment. However,
such punishment cannot be part of natural law. It depends upon the
supernatural, and he explicitly admits that it is a matter of faith. This
makes the moral position of unbelievers uncertain – a problem he
sidesteps (II.9.ii–iii; pp. 224–5). On the other hand, his adoption also of
the intellectualist thesis brings him very close to a clear formulation of
the principle that 'good' implies 'ought', that is, that the preceptive
force of natural law can be derived from its indicative or demonstrative
content, and he calls this 'natural obligation' (II.9.iv–vii; pp. 225–7.
II.15.xviii; p. 298). Nevertheless, it was impossible for him to pursue
this line, for its conclusion would have been that human beings could
impose an obligation upon themselves by drawing the said conclusion,
and that would in effect have dispensed with God's role in Suárez's
moral theory.

In his theory of natural law Suárez generally used the traditional
term *ius naturale*, which to modern ears can mean either 'natural law'
or 'natural right'. He had, however, a clear idea of the distinction
between law and right and of their relationship: '*ius* sometimes means
the moral power [*moralem facultatem*] to get something [*ad rem aliquam*]
or over something [*in re*] . . . which is the proper object of justice . . . At
other times *ius* means law [*legem*] which is the rule of righteous behaviour, and which establishes a certain equity [*aequitatem*] in things and is
the rule [*ratio*] of those rights [*iuris*] of the former category [*priori modo
sumpti*] . . . which rule [*ratio*] is the very law' (II.17.ii; p. 326; cf. I.2).
'Subjective rights', as they would now be called, are means to the
realization of the goals set by the natural law. They basically encompass our powers, *dominia*, over ourselves (liberty), over the goods of
the world (property), and over others, that is, those familial and wider
social powers indicated by natural law and generally instituted by
contractual or quasi-contractual means. Subjective *iura* are therefore
also seen as concessions by the natural law, for 'natural reason not only
dictates what is necessary, but also what is permitted [*liceat*]' (II.18.ii;
p. 335). That is to say, liberty is granted us, but we can give it up or it
can be taken from us for an overriding natural law reason, such as
punishment; the world is conceded to us in common, but we can carve
it up if private property better serves the common good, and for the
same reason lawful authority can take away private property; we have
the liberty to marry or not according to our understanding of how best

to serve the Lord (II.14, esp. xiii–xix; pp. 275–80. II.18.ii–iii). In all
cases, what is instituted by the use of our *iura* is protected by the
natural law – until such time as it may require the dissolution of our
institutions.

Finally it must be noted that Suárez distinguishes between 'negative' and 'affirmative' precepts of natural law. The former prohibit that
which is in itself evil, and the latter prescribe the inherently good. In
view of the later uses of similar distinctions, it should be stressed that
the two kinds of precepts carry equal obligation (II.9.ix; p. 223. II.10.i;
pp. 231–2. II.13.iv; p. 260).

1.2   *Natural law and Protestantism*

Scholastic natural law theory, as represented by Suárez, was problematic for a number of reasons. Perhaps most fundamental, it was an
obvious target for the sort of moral scepticism which had been revived
at the Renaissance and which continued to have great influence in the
formulations given it by thinkers such as Montaigne and Charron.
Scholastic natural law seemed to presuppose a degree of knowledge
about God, the world, and human nature which it was only too easy
for sceptical criticism to undermine. Not least, it operated with an idea
of God and of the relationship between God and man which could
hardly be considered 'natural' unless it could be shown to be pervasive
outside the Christian world, for example in the new colonies in the
Americas and elsewhere. One of the main points of modern scepticism
was that this was not the case. Religious and moral notions were so
relative to time and place that no theoretically coherent account could
be given of them. Not least, such notions were relative to each person's
interest or individual utility. This connection of an Epicurean theme
with Renaissance relativism was made with particular effect when
Grotius in the 'Prolegomena' to his *De iure belli ac pacis* (1625) singled
out Carneades as the classical representative of all scepticism.[12] A con-

---

12 'This Man [Carneades] having undertaken to dispute against Justice, that
kind of it, especially, which is the Subject of this Treatise, found no Argument
stronger than this. Laws (says he) were instituted by Men for the sake of Interest;
and hence it is that they are different, not only in different Countries according to
the Diversity of their Manners, but often in the same Country, according to the
Times. As to that which is called NATURAL RIGHT, it is a mere Chimera. Nature
prompts all Men, and in general all Animals, to seek their own particular Advantage: So that either there is no Justice at all, or, if there is any, it is extreme Folly,
because it engages us to procure the Good of others, to our own Prejudice.' Hugo
Grotius, *The Rights of War and Peace in three Books*, ed. J. Barbeyrac, trans. anon.,
London, 1738, Prol. 5 (pp. xiv–xv). Presumably such use of Epicureanism by a

tinuing ambition of modern natural law was therefore to overcome such scepticism. That was Grotius's stated objective in *De iure;* it was still a driving force behind the work of Jean Barbeyrac three-quarters of a century later, his target being Pierre Bayle.

Protestant natural law's answer to scepticism started from its most fundamental objection to scholastic natural law, that it seemed to presuppose a moral continuity and interdependence between God and humanity.[13] For Protestant thinkers the starting point was the complete discontinuity between God and man, a discontinuity which made it impossible to give a rational account of human morality by reference to God and his eternal law. Only faith could bridge the gulf between humanity and its Creator. This led to a continuing ambiguity in Protestantism towards natural law as a rational account of morals. On the one hand, such an undertaking seemed impossible and pointless, since nothing but faith could sustain morality. On the other hand, precisely the circumstance that no ultimate account seemed attainable put pressure on thinkers to attempt whatever was possible in purely human and temporal terms. Thus if no amount of calculating human rationality could establish the link between people's behaviour and God's reward or punishment, then they had either to live by faith alone or to find a purely human and temporal foundation for reward and, especially, punishment.

We may see this ambiguity from a different angle. On the one hand, Protestant moral theology, Luther's in particular, is an ethics of duty, par excellence. There is here no room for degrees of perfection and improvement through good works, as in Catholic thinkers like Suárez. Nothing that a person can be or make of himself will justify him before God; only faith justifies, and that only by God's grace. Our duty towards God is thus infinite, and we may view our temporal life as a network of unfulfillable duties, which natural law theory may put into systematic form and give such worldly justifications as our limited understanding permits. On the other hand, if our duty is really infinite and unfulfillable, then it is hard to see it as a possible guide to action; it provides no criterion for what behaviour to choose. We therefore can live only by faith. This strongly antinomian line was adopted by a great many sects at the Reformation and later and must undoubtedly be

---

sceptic man of straw helped dissolve the Christianized Epicureanism of the Renaissance and thus prepare the way for Gassendi and Hobbes; cf. Jill Kraye, 'Moral philosophy', in *The Cambridge History of Renaissance Philosophy*, ed. C.B. Schmitt, Q. Skinner, and E. Kessler, Cambridge, UK, 1988, pp. 303–86, at pp. 382–6.

13   For a comprehensive survey of Reformation principles, their context, and social and political implications, see Q. Skinner, *The Foundations of Modern Political Thought*, 2 vols., Cambridge, UK, 1978, esp. vol. 2, pp. 3–19, 65ff., and ch. 7.

regarded as a target no less important than moral scepticism for Protestant natural law theory.

It is in this general perspective that we must view the overwhelming emphasis on duty in modern natural law. Notions of virtue were to be interpreted in terms of duty; rights derived from duty; prima facie supererogatory acts were to be seen simply as special duties.

These general points indicate the logic of the essential ideas. Few thinkers followed this to its full extent, and a large part of the interpreter's task is to account for deviations from it. The first and in many respects most formidable stumbling-block is Hugo Grotius.

1.3   *Hugo Grotius*

We have seen that Suárez, following tradition, divided *ius naturale* into two meanings, a subjective *facultas moralis* and the 'proper' sense of an objective *lex*. Grotius tried – in vain – to ensure that his breach with tradition would not be lost by introducing at the beginning of the first book of *De iure belli ac pacis* a division of *ius* into three meanings:

> [First] Right signifies meerly that which is just, and that too rather in a negative than a positive Sense. So that the Right of War is properly that which may be done without Injustice with Regard to an Enemy. Now that is unjust which is repugnant to the Nature of a Society of reasonable Creatures . . .
>
> There is another Signification of the Word Right different from this, but yet arising from it, which relates directly to the Person: In which Sense Right is a moral Quality [*qualitas moralis*] annexed to the Person, enabling him to have, or do, something justly . . .
>
> There is also a third Sense of the Word Right, according to which it signifies the same Thing as Law [*lex*], when taken in its largest Extent, as being a Rule of Moral Actions, obliging us to that which is good and commendable [*regula actuum moralium obligans ad id quod rectum est*]. (I.1.iii–iv and ix)[14]

Ius is first a type of action, that is, any action which is not injurious to others in such a way that social relations break down. In order to

14   Subsequent references of this form in this section are to Grotius, *De iure belli ac pacis libri tres*, ed. J.F. Gronovius and J. Barbeyrac, Amsterdam, 1735, and translations are from *Rights of War and Peace*. For the earlier history of *ius*, see esp. B. Tierney, 'Villey, Ockham and the origin of individual rights', in *The Weightier Matters of the Law . . . A Tribute to Harold Berman*, Decatur, GA, 1987, pp. 1–31; same, 'Conciliarism, corporatism, and individualism: The doctrine of individual rights in Gerson', *Cristianesimo nella storia*, 9 (1988), 81–111; same, 'Marsilius on rights', *Journal of the History of Ideas*, 52 (1991), 3–17; M. Villey, *La Formation de la pensée juridique moderne*, Paris, 1975.

determine what is injurious in this way, we have to turn to *ius* as a feature of persons, the second point. This is in itself a complex notion derived from two basic features of human nature (I.2.i), first the *prima naturæ*, which are the natural drives or instincts for self-preservation, and, second, right reason or sound judgement of what is *honestum*, that is, what makes life with others possible – which is in itself a natural inclination. Considered as a feature of the person, *ius* is the exercise of these two sides of human nature together. When we do so exercise them together, each of us maintains our own (*suum*), which is

> a Right properly, and strictly taken. Under which are contained,
> 1. A Power either over our selves, which is term'd Liberty; or over others, such as that of a Father over his Children, or a Lord over his Slave.
> 2. Property. . . .
> 3. The Faculty of demanding what is due, and to this answers the Obligation of rendering what is owing. (I.1.v)

Ius naturale in the strict sense is, then, every action which does not injure any other person's *suum*, which in effect means that it is every *suum* which does not conflict with the *sua* of others.

Grotius's point against scepticism and against religiously inspired antinomianism is that if we claim this much as moral knowledge and act accordingly, we can have society and thereby the fundamental elements of moral life, whereas if we deny it and act on the basis of such denial, we can have neither society nor humanity. This is his 'a priori' argument. In addition we find this reasoning confirmed 'a posteriori' in the history of humankind (I.1.xii; Prol. XL–XLI). It is, therefore, on sound moral grounds that people go to war to protect their rights, which is to say that there are moral reasons independent of religion for the punishment of injustice (injury). This is one of Grotius's main concerns, and it makes the title of his main work intelligible.

The *iura* we have sketched are 'perfect rights', and respect for them is 'expletive Justice, Justice properly and strictly taken' (I.1.viii). This is the minimal morality which is the foundation for social life. It is not, however, the whole of morals as we normally know it. In addition to the *facultates* by means of which we claim our *sua*, we have vaguer and more dispositional *aptitudines*, which may be considered imperfect rights (I.1.iv). To these correspond the ability of right reason to judge of *honestum* beyond what is necessary to the very existence of social life, that is, of goods which, in contrast to rights proper, cannot be claimed and, if necessary, defended by force. These imperfect rights are the subject of attributive or distributive justice, and they form the theoretical basis for the rules of charity, or love, which are made into positive law by religions and civil governments.[15]

In the characterization of *ius*, possessive and attributive features are intertwined. That is to say, *ius* is what a person has or has a claim to, but it is also an ability of the person to judge what he or she has or has a claim to. Further, the latter is not simply the ability to apply a natural law to a specific case, as one might perceive it in scholastic thought, for law does not play any role in this part of the argument. The notion of *ius* thus has a certain connotation of a moral power or moral sense.

The conceptual apparatus sketched here forms the basis for most of what Grotius is trying to do in his social and political theory. Individuals with natural rights are the units of which all social organization is made. They are people who balance pure self-interest and social inclinations by entering in contractual relations with others about property and about modes of living together, especially about authority. They consider it a right to enforce the obligations arising from such arrangements, that is, to punish their transgression. Over and above this, and to varying degrees, they may or may not do good to others by honouring 'imperfect rights'.

The emphasis is on what can be used towards the individual's self-preservation compatibly with similar striving by others. This is the case with the goods of the world. Originally held in common by humankind, they were gradually divided up into private property, because of avarice, population pressure, and other factors. However, in situations of extreme need the basic rights of the needy defeat the rights of others to private property. Similarly, claims to property right are rendered spurious by non-use – as was the case with Spain's claim to vast tracts of land and goods in foreign parts, which Dutch trading companies could well have found use for, not to speak of claims to ownership of the high seas, the use of which was clearly not improved by being held exclusively by any one power.[16] Furthermore, people could make use of their rights in extreme ways to secure their self-preservation, for example, by selling themselves into slavery or submitting to tyrannical government. These and similar political concerns were among the primary motivations of Grotius's enterprise.

15   See esp. II.17.ix; II.25.iii 3; III.1.iv 2; III.13.iv; cf. I.2.viii 3; II.1.xiii; II.12.ix 2. For the rules of charity, see J.B. Schneewind, 'Pufendorf's place in the history of ethics', *Synthèse*, 72 (1987), 123–55, at pp. 140–1.

16   See Grotius, *De iure praedae commentarius* [written c. 1604], with trans. by G.L. Williams and W.H. Zeydel, 2 vols. (Classics of International Law), Oxford, 1950; and Richard Tuck, *Philosophy and Government, 1572–1651*, Cambridge, UK, 1993, pp. 169ff.

The honouring of rights, perfect and imperfect, is in itself good, and as a consequence we can consider such behaviour as being prescribed by the Author of our nature. Such prescription is *lex*, the third sense of *ius naturale*. Grotius hastens to add that the behaviour prescribed by God is obligatory in itself – that is, without God – and that this distinguishes it from divine positive law as well as from human law (I.1.ix–x).

In this light we can make proper sense of a famous and controversial passage in the 'Prolegomena' to Grotius's major work. Having given a brief sketch of *ius naturæ* as encompassing both negative or perfect rights and positive or imperfect rights, he declares that all this 'would apply though we should even grant, what without the greatest Wickedness cannot be granted, that there is no God, or that he has no Care of human Affairs'. However, since Christians, at least, believe in God and his care for human affairs, 'this now becomes another Original of Right [*juris*], besides that of Nature, being that which proceeds from the free Will of God' (Prol. XI–XII).

The controversial point is whether Grotius is maintaining anything other than the old notion going back to Gregory of Rimini, if not further, which we considered previously. He obviously is. The scholastic point was that human beings have the ability to understand what is good and bad even without invoking God but have no obligation proper to act accordingly without God's command. Grotius is suggesting that people unaided by religion can use their perfect – and even imperfect – rights to establish the contractual and quasi-contractual obligations upon which social life rests. God is simply an additional source perceived by Christians – though it should of course be remembered that Grotius held the basic tenets of Christianity to be open to rational understanding.[17] Grotius's separation of natural law from the Christian religion is underlined in several ways. For instance, he firmly denies that natural law can be identified with either the Old or the New Testament (Prol. XLIX, LI), in sharp contrast to Suárez, who saw the Decalogue as containing the natural law.

Much of Grotius's natural rights theory originated in his attempt to justify the claims of Dutch traders to operate in the colonies of Spain; in fact the nucleus of his theory was already formulated in the first four laws of nature in his unpublished work *De Indis* (begun in 1604),[18]

---

17 See Grotius, *De veritate religionis Christianae* [1623]; in his *Opera omnia theologica*, 3 vols., Amsterdam, 1679, III, pp. 3–96.

18 Chapter 12 of this work was published in 1609 as *Mare liberum*; see *Mare liberum / The Freedom of the Seas*, ed. and trans. J. Brown Scott, New York, 1916. The full work was only rediscovered in the nineteenth century and published as *De iure praedae* (1864; cf. note 16 to this chapter). See W.S.M. Knight, *The Life and Works of Hugo Grotius*, London, 1925, ch. 5. For the development of Grotius's

except that he there gave natural law an unusual voluntarist foundation which was rejected in his later work.[19] Much of the energy of his
argument was generated by the analogy between sovereign states and
individuals, leading to a view of the natural state of man as morally
similar to the situation of states with respect to each other. The subsequent development of the argument in his great treatise *The Law of War
and Peace* had several additional concerns: the proof of an undeniable
core of morality against sceptics and antinomian radicals; proof that a
legal, including an international, order was possible independently of
religion, *pace* Europe's warring confessions; proof that absolutist government could be legitimate; proof of the circumstances under which
war is justified, namely in defence of rights and of the means to their
maintenance; and much else.

Grotius's legacy was rich and varied, and both he himself and his
ideas became European phenomena in several fields, including philosophy.[20] His early impact in England was particularly important. His
ideas played a central role in the Great Tew circle and were taken up by
John Selden and Thomas Hobbes.[21] Selden took the idea of man's natural freedom from moral laws a great deal further than Grotius, so far
in fact that according to him the only way in which moral community
could be understood was as an effect of God's positive imposition and
enforcement of the moral law as promulgated in the precepts given to
the sons of Noah.[22]

---

ideas, see above all Richard Tuck, *Philosophy and Government: 1572–1651*, Cambridge, UK, 1993, ch. 5.

19 See *De iure praedae*, I, pp. 8–9; and Tuck, *Philosophy and Government*,
pp. 172–3.

20 As Swedish ambassador in Paris from 1635 to 1645, Grotius was at the
centre of European diplomacy, politics, and intellectual life; Knight, *Life*, ch. 11. For
a possible attempt by Sweden's rival, Denmark, to attract him, see O. Carlsen, *Hugo
Grotius og Sorö Akademi. En Kritisk Studie*, Taastrup, 1938.

21 For the connections with Great Tew and Selden, see H. Trevor-Roper, *Catholics, Anglicans and Puritans: Seventeenth-Century Essays*, London, 1987, ch. 4; R. Tuck,
Natural Rights Theories, Cambridge, UK, 1979, chs. 4–5; same, *Philosophy and Government*, pp. 205ff. and 272ff.

22 John Selden, *De iure naturali et gentium juxta disciplinam hebraeorum libri
septem*, London, 1640. Cf. Selden, *Mare clausum: The Right and Dominion of the Sea in
Two Books*, trans. J.H., London, 1663; M. Crowe, 'An eccentric seventeenth-century
witness to the natural law: John Selden (1584–1654)', *Natural Law Forum*, 12 (1977),
184–95; J.P. Sommerville, 'John Selden, the law of nature, and the origins of government', *Historical Journal*, 27 (1984), 437–47; Tuck, *Natural Rights Theories*, ch. 4; same,
'"The Ancient Law of Freedom": John Selden and the civil war', in *Reactions to the
English Civil War, 1642–1649*, ed. J. Morrill, London, 1982, pp. 137–61 and 238–41;
and same, *Philosophy and Government*, pp. 205–21.

1.4 *Thomas Hobbes*

The relationship between Grotius and Hobbes is a complex matter. However, as far as concerns the role of natural jurisprudential concepts in their respective ethics, it has proven a particularly fruitful suggestion to see the *Elements of Law, De cive,* and *Leviathan* as descendants of *Mare liberum, De iure belli ac pacis,* and *The Truth of the Christian Religion.*[23] Like Grotius, Hobbes labours under a prima facie ambiguity. On the one hand, they both write from a theistic standpoint, according to which life and morals are part of the divine dispensation. On the other hand, they intend to account for the moral aspect of this dispensation in such a way that it explains how people without theistic beliefs can have a moral life. According to Grotius, the dispensation consisted partly of the world provided for our use and partly of human nature equipped with an urge and an ability to limit such use to the socially sustainable. According to Hobbes, humanity is also given the world for use, but the extent and form of this use is not limited by either a tendency towards sociability or an ability to judge from the other person's point of view. From the hand of nature, we all have an unlimited 'Right to every thing; even to one anothers body'. This

> *Jus Naturale,* is the Liberty each man hath, to use his own power, as he will himselfe, for the preservation of his own Nature; that is to say, of his own Life; and consequently, of doing any thing, which in his own Judgement, and Reason, hee shall conceive to be the aptest means thereunto.[24]

This right is being exercised by individuals who, according to Hobbes's elaborate anthropology, inevitably are concerned with self-preservation above all else. Human life consists in the satisfaction of a wide variety of desires, and the precondition for the satisfaction of any desire is to be alive. In view of the physical and intellectual equality among individuals in pursuit of self-preservation, the exercise of one's right to everything would be self-defeating, creating a war of everyone

23   See R. Tuck, 'Grotius, Carneades and Hobbes', *Grotiana,* n.s., 4 (1983), 43–62; same, 'Hobbes and Descartes', in *Perspectives on Thomas Hobbes,* ed. G.A.J. Rogers and A. Ryan, Oxford, 1988, pp. 11–41; and same, *Hobbes,* Oxford, 1989. Tuck even suggests that Hobbes, like Grotius, primarily sought an answer to scepticism; see esp. 'Optics and sceptics: The philosophical foundations of Hobbes's political thought', in *Conscience and Casuistry in Early Modern Europe,* ed. Edmund Leites, Cambridge, UK, 1988, pp. 235–63. This has been subjected to criticism by Perez Zagorin, 'Hobbes's early philosophical development', *Journal of the History of Ideas,* 54 (1993), 505–18.

24   Hobbes, *Leviathan,* ed. R. Tuck, Cambridge, 1991, p. 91. Cf. *De cive. The Latin Version / The English Version,* ed. H. Warrender, Oxford, 1983, 1:10; and Hobbes, *The Elements of Law Natural and Politic,* ed. F. Tönnies, Cambridge, UK, 1928, XIV.10.

against everyone.[25] In the interest of self-preservation, people therefore tend to heed certain precepts that limit their natural liberty or rights. These precepts are the laws of nature:

> A Law of Nature (*Lex Naturalis,*) is a Precept, or generall Rule, found out by Reason, by which a man is forbidden to do, that, which is destructive of his life, or taketh away the means of preserving the same; and to omit, that, by which he thinketh it may be best preserved.

The content of the laws of nature is that everyone should seek peace, or live sociably, in as far as at all possible, by laying 'down this right to all things; and [being] contented with so much liberty against other men, as he would allow other men against himselfe'.[26]

The rights of nature are not dependent upon any moral principle or law. By recognizing the laws of nature as heuristically obligatory, people do, however, create a kind of opposition between 'right' and 'law', in the sense that the latter limits the former, that is, commits the person to definite forms of action by ruling out endless other actions. The obligation is only heuristic, and, if the law-regulated behaviour does not serve self-preservation, the right to self-defence in the interest of preservation remains to be asserted by the individual.

There are, in other words, nowhere any obligations corresponding to the rights of nature; the latter are the primary moral feature of persons. But by recognizing an obligation to the laws of nature, people will strive to establish a realm of matching rights and obligations, namely those of contractual relations, which are the basis for civil society. The rest of the laws of nature specify the virtues which are required for the maintenance of such a system. The most important is '*That men performe their Covenants made*', which is 'the Fountain and originall of Justice'.[27] The others specify some essentials of sociability.

With this line of argument Hobbes took the Grotian idea of subjective rights as the primary moral feature of human personality to the limit. To his contemporaries it seemed a scandalous attempt to make out morals to be nothing but a human invention for self-serving purposes. To modern scholars it has rather seemed odd that he chose to couch such a programme in the antiquated language of natural law – to some, so odd that they deny that this in fact was his programme and instead interpret him as a 'genuine' natural lawyer, while to others the traditional language is little more than a radical thinker's bow to conventional wisdom, probably with an eye to his own safety and quiet.[28]

---

25   *Elements of law*, XIV.10–12; *De cive*, I.11–13; *Leviathan*, ch. 13.
26   *Leviathan*, pp. 91–2; cf. *Elements of Law*, XIV.1–2 and *De cive*, II.1–3.
27   *Leviathan*, p. 100; cf. *Elements of Law*, XVI.1 and *De cive*, III.1.
28   The most important proponents of the former view are H. Warrender, *The*

Behind much of this debate may lie an anachronistic assumption that Hobbes had to find his way among the same concepts of obligation as we do, that is, roughly, that obligation is either an implication of some kind of undeniable good, or that it is a special, self-imposed necessity. There is no doubt that Hobbes took a decisive step in the direction of the latter with his theory of the contractual foundations for the common moral virtues and institutions. At the same time it is undeniable that his theory is situated within a doctrine of natural law and natural rights – and this is neither traditional nor modern.

As already mentioned, Hobbes saw the world in a general theistic perspective, and there seems to be no good reason to doubt his profession of a Christian interpretation of this perspective or to doubt that he meant his deterministic metaphysics to be a philosophical elaboration of Calvinist necessitarianism. If anything, that only increases the difficulty of understanding his willingness to describe the rational precepts, or laws of nature, as divine commands for the direction of human behaviour. When the issue is at the focus of discussion, however, his words are carefully chosen:

> These dictates of Reason, men use to call by the name of Lawes; but improperly: for they are but Conclusions, or Theoremes concerning what conduceth to the conservation and defence of themselves; whereas Law, properly is the word of him, that by right hath command over others. But yet if we consider the same Theoremes, as delivered in the word of God, that by right commandeth all things; then are they properly called Lawes.[29]

Political Philosophy of Hobbes: His Theory of Obligation, Oxford, 1957, and A.P. Martinich, *The Two Gods of Leviathan*, Cambridge, UK, 1992, but see also A.E. Taylor, 'The ethical doctrine of Hobbes', in *Hobbes Studies*, ed. K.C. Brown, Oxford, 1965, pp. 35–55, and F.C. Hood, *The Divine Politics of Thomas Hobbes*, Oxford, 1964. Particularly important discussions of Hobbes on obligation are T. Nagel, 'Hobbes's concept of obligation', *Philosophical Review* 68 (1959), 68–83, and M. Oakeshott, *Hobbes on Civil Association*, Oxford, 1974, ch. 1. The latter view has taken many forms, but see esp. D. Gauthier, *The Logic of Leviathan: The Moral and Political Theory of Thomas Hobbes*, Oxford, 1969; M.M. Goldsmith, *Hobbes's Science of Politics*, New York, 1966; J. Hampton, *Hobbes and the Social Contract Tradition*, Cambridge, UK, 1986; F.S. McNeilly, *The Anatomy of Leviathan*, London, 1968; J.W.N. Watkins, *Hobbes's System of Ideas*, London, 1965. For particularly useful general assessments, see D. Baumgold, *Hobbes's Political Theory*, Cambridge, UK, 1988; D.D. Raphael, *Hobbes: Morals and Politics*, London, 1977; T. Sorell, *Hobbes*, London, 1986; and Tuck, *Hobbes*.

29 *Leviathan*, p. 111. Cf. Hobbes's explanation to Bishop Bramhall: 'After I had ended the discourse he mentions of the laws of nature, I thought it fittest in the last place, once for all, to say they were the laws of God, then when they were delivered in the word of God; but before, being not known by men for any thing but their own natural reason, they were but theorems, tending to peace.' *An Answer to a Book published by Dr. Bramhall, late Bishop of Derry, called "The Catching of the Leviathan"* (c.

So the legal quality of the precepts depends upon our consideration, and in such consideration the crucial concept is the 'right' by which God commands. Generally such authority arises from one or another form of contractual authorization, but since humanity, apart from a few and exceptionally inspired individuals, can have no communication with God, this cannot be the basis for divine moral authority.[30] Rather, it arises from God's irresistible power. God is in the same situation as all other moral agents in having a right to everything, but in contrast to other agents, he has the irresistible power to maintain this right successfully:

> Seeing all men by Nature had the Right to All things, they had Right every one to reigne over all the rest. But because this Right could not be obtained by force, it concerned the safety of every one, laying by that Right, to set up men (with Soveraign Authority) by common consent, to rule and defend them: whereas if there had been any man of Power Irresistible; there had been no reason, why he should not by that Power have ruled, and defended both himselfe, and them, according to his discretion. To those therefore whose Power is irresistible, the dominion of all men adhæreth naturally by their excellence of Power; and consequently it is from that Power, that the Kingdome over men, and the Right of inflicting men at his pleasure, belongeth Naturally to God Almighty; not as Creator, and Gracious; but as Omnipotent.[31]

Those who understand this situation will see everything they do towards their self-preservation, and especially their adherence to the precepts of reason, as done with the connivance of the irresistible power that could have ordered entirely otherwise. Those who do not, or will not, see it this way are enemies of this natural kingdom of God – but they still have the precepts of natural reason.

For Grotius there were two reasons why men in the state of nature could agree not only *that* others have the right to self-preservation, and the rights that follow therefrom, but also, to a significant extent, *what* those rights are in particular circumstances. First, transgressions against such rights are inherently wrong – so inherently wrong that not even God could make them acceptable. Grotius is, in anachronistic terms, a realist. Second, men have the moral power to recognize such objective values, as we saw earlier. This means that they have the ability to see what is good for others, as well as for themselves, and it is common knowledge among them that this is so. By contrast, Hobbes gave a completely subjectivist account of what is good and bad and of

---

1688), in *The English Works*, ed. W. Molesworth, London, 11 vols., 1839–45, 4:284–5. Cf. also *Elements of Law*, XVIII.1 and *De cive*, IV.1.

30 *Elements of Law*, XV.11; *De cive*, II.12; *Leviathan*, p. 197.

31 *Leviathan*, p. 397; cf. *De cive*, XV.5.

moral judgement. Of course he introduced into this scheme his notion of natural law as right reason bidding individuals to close off some of their endless possibilities or rights by seeking peace with others. However, in itself this does not help, as long as we have no objective standard for recognizing when others are or are not doing this, and a consequent common or intersubjective knowledge that this is happening. Only when the natural law has become institutionalized, that is, has become the sovereign's law, do we have such a standard and such common knowledge. Hobbes had to seek a political solution, the creation of an absolute sovereign, to the impasse in his moral theory. For Grotius the political establishment secures and extends the particular social arrangements which are direct expressions of the minimal morality of the natural state.[32]

This has led to extensive discussions, using modern notions from the theory of games, such as the 'prisoner's dilemma', as to whether Hobbesian individuals could rationally engage in contractual relations at all.[33] Hobbes himself seems to have taken the line that individuals in nearly all circumstances had to work together in order to preserve themselves. Any breach of trust would so tarnish a person's trustworthiness that his chances of future cooperation would be greatly diminished, and this was a sufficiently dangerous prospect to keep people cooperative in all but the most extreme personal danger.[34] The real question is, rather, whether the state of nature could exist.

In contrast to Grotius, Hobbes had an elaborate metaphysics and moral psychology, and these theories forced him to try to do without even the minimal moral equipment of the Dutchman. Whatever the philosophical merit of his attempt, historically the price he paid was high. To contemporaries and most successors he seemed to have arrived at a scepticism (relativism) even worse than the Renaissance variety which Grotius had seen as his target; natural law seemed to have been largely emptied of meaning, and it had become exceedingly difficult to see how human nature, on Hobbes's account of it, would even allow the formation of social relations. At the same time, Grotius's 'realism', though not his 'cognitivism', was seen as a relic of scholasticism. These were among the problems that Samuel Pufendorf faced.

1.5 *The German debate*

Samuel Pufendorf must be seen partly in the wider European context, partly as a major participant in a more local debate. In both arenas the situation was extraordinarily complex and beyond easy summary.

32 See Tuck, *Hobbes*, pp. 63–4.
33 Most of this debate began with Gauthier, *The Logic of Leviathan*.
34 *Leviathan*, pp. 204–5.

In Germany, Pufendorf was part of the Lutheran reaction to Grotius, which had begun somewhat later than the reactions in England and Holland and gained momentum only after the mid-century.[35] The German debate principally concerned the relationship between natural law and moral theology, with most orthodox Lutherans insisting that the former was based on or part of the latter. The source for this view was a protestant Aristotelianism considerably resembling scholastic Aristotelianism.[36] The original reformers, not least Luther, had revolted against the scholastic *imago Dei* doctrine. That is to say, they had rejected the possibility that men could have any rational knowledge of God's nature on the basis of which they could draw moral lessons for themselves – technically expressed, for example, as a denial that we can know that the natural law 'participates' in God's eternal law. Only faith and grace could guide and save humankind. Apart from being less than helpful as a social philosophy for troubled times,[37] this tendency in Lutheran thinking flew in the face of a metaphysics and anthropology which, being of an essentially Aristotelian bent, had great difficulty in giving up a teleological view of human nature. This kept alive the *imago Dei* notion, which was in fact central to much Lutheran orthodoxy in the seventeenth century. With it went the idea that the natural law could be derived only from that original state of innocence in which man was closest to being in the Maker's image. Although the Lutherans, more than their scholastic predecessors, emphasised the debilitating effect of the Fall upon man's moral faculties, they held that with the help of God's revealed word man could gain sufficient insight into the law to secure social living in the here and now – the hereafter being an entirely different question. Allowing for a great many variations, it is this theme of the dependence of natural law upon revealed religion which is one of Pufendorf's main targets.[38]

35   See E. Reibstein, 'Deutsche Grotius-Kommentatoren bis zu Christian Wolff', *Zeitschrift für ausländisches öffentliches Recht und Völkerrecht* 15 (1953–4), 76–102. For Pufendorf's background, see esp. D. Döring, 'Samuel Pufendorf (1632–1694) und die leipziger Gelehrtengesellschaften in der Mitte des 17. Jahrhunderts', *Lias*, 15 (1988), 13–48.

36   See P. Petersen, *Geschichte der aristotelischen Philosophie im protestantischen Deutschland*, Leipzig, 1921; and Horst Dreitzel, *Protestantischer Aristotelismus und absoluter Staat. Die 'Politica' des Henning Arnisaeus (ca. 1575–1636)*, Wiesbaden, 1970.

37   Cf. Suárez's polemic against the Lutherans as simple and dangerous antinomians, *De legibus*, I.18.ii. For a different view of the place of natural law in the Reformers' thought, see J.T. McNeill, 'Natural law in the teaching of the reformers', *Journal of Religion*, 26 (1946), 168–83.

38   The orthodox position was significantly clarified in the intense polemic which followed Pufendorf's two definitive natural law works from 1672 and 1673 and his defence of them, esp. in *Eris Scandica*, [1686], Frankfurt a.M., 1706. The most

These disputes were by no means divorced from the wider philosophical themes. The orthodox well understood that their chief enemy was a theological voluntarism. Disregarding, or perhaps misunderstanding, Grotius's potentially radical rights-based theory, they therefore often invoked his notable realism in their support. This must always be borne in mind when we find Pufendorf and his followers claiming to be Grotius's true successors. This was a polemical ploy and a misleading half-truth.

1.6 Samuel Pufendorf

Pufendorf took his stand against the Lutherans of his day by insisting on Luther's own assertion of the rational and moral gulf between God and man. However, whereas the reformer was led from this to a suspicion and neglect of natural law, the natural lawyer saw the possibility of developing it as a complete 'science of morals', sharply separate from moral theology and analogous to the new deductive science. This insistence on the scientific character of natural law, inspired by Cartesianism and by Hobbes, was a renewal of Grotius's ambition to use mathematics as the guiding ideal for natural law, an ideal mostly submerged by his humanist learning.[39]

Pufendorf's scientific ambition is patent in his early work, the *Elementa* (1660), which is intended to lay the foundations for natural jurisprudence as a hypothetico-deductive system and is cast in the form of one book of twenty-one definitions and another of two axioms and five observations. By the time of his major work, *De iure*, such formalities have been laid aside, but the substantial point is largely retained.[40]

---

extreme and clear position was that of Valentin Alberti, *Compendium juris naturæ, orthodoxae theologiæ conformatum*, Leipzig, 1678, and *Eros Lipsicus*, Leipzig, 1687. Cf. E.-D. Osterhorn, *Die Naturrechtslehre Valentin Albertis*, Freiburg i.B.: diss., Albert-Ludwig-Universität, 1962.

39 Concerning the connections between natural law and the methodological discussions, see W. Röd, *Geometrischer Geist und Naturrecht: Methodengeschichtliche Untersuchungen zur Staatsphilosophie im 17. und 18. Jahrhundert* (Bayerische Akademie der Wissenschaften, Phil.-hist. Klasse. Abhandlungen, N. F. 70), Munich, 1970. For Pufendorf, see also H. Denzer, *Moralphilosophie und Naturrecht bei Samuel Pufendorf*, Munich, 1972, pp. 279–96, and for his teacher, Erhard Weigel, see W. Röd, 'Weigels Lehre von den entia moralia', *Archiv für Geschichte der Philosphie*, 51 (1969), 58–84.

40 See Samuel von Pufendorf, *Elementorum jurisprudentiæ universalis libri duo* [1660], facsim. repr., ed. H. Wehlberg with trans. by W.A. Oldfather, 2 vols. (Classics of International Law), Oxford and London, 1931; *De iure naturae et gentium libri octo* [1672], facsim. repr. of 1759 ed., ed. J.N. Hertius, J. Barbeyrac, and G. Mascovius, 2 vols., Frankfurt a.M., 1967; and the English trans. by Basil Kennet, *Of the Law of Nature and Nations*, ed. J. Barbeyrac, 5th ed., London, 1749.

Just as God chose to create the physical world in such a way that it follows certain laws discoverable by the physical sciences, so he created a moral world which has certain permanent features, namely those of basic human nature. Beyond presupposing human nature as empirically given, however, moral science is not empirical. What makes it properly scientific is that it is an a priori, demonstrative or deductive discipline which in principle can give us certain knowledge analogous to that of mathematics (I.2).[41] This is because human nature in fact *creates* morals.

The basic features of human nature are a constant concern for self-preservation, recognition of one's insufficient ability to provide such security alone, a certain sociability, and a mutual recognition of these features in each other (II.3, esp. x–xi and xv–xvi). Given such a nature, groups of people will invent a language in which to articulate the recognition of their situation and to deduce basic rules enabling them to live together and, from these, more particular rules and institutions. Although the root of morals is God's will in choosing human nature as he did, the rest of morals is thus a human creation of which we have 'maker's knowledge', that is, demonstrative knowledge. In this respect, as in many others, Pufendorf's theory is clearly a precursor of Locke's in the *Essay Concerning Human Understanding*.

The moral and the physical world are two self-contained spheres, which is to say that there is no moral quality or purpose inherent in the physical world. Values are not among the natural qualities. The *entia moralia* are simply 'modes' that are introduced into the natural world supervening upon the particular substances of human nature. In order for things or events in nature to acquire value, they have to be related to a norm, and this can be done only by beings who can understand norms as prescriptions for actions and who can act upon this understanding, that is, beings of intellect and free will, who may or may not follow the prescription and will thereby do either right or wrong. Value is thus imposed upon that which in itself is morally neutral, when a rule is prescribed to guide a will. The human will can give such guidance to itself when it enters into pacts and promises and thus undertakes obligations; and one human will can guide another by legislating for it. These human impositions are, however, no more than deductions from the fundamental law of nature, which is inherent in human nature and as such a manifestation of God's will. Without the guidance of natural law, human volition and human action would be natural, non-moral phenomena like those we find in the rest of the animal creation.[42]

---

41 References of this form in this section are to Pufendorf, *De iure*, whereas translations are from *Law of Nature*.

42 Pufendorf illustrates his point in the manner we have already encountered

It should be stressed that Pufendorf's voluntarism in the first instance is ontological. It was in his choice of creation that God exercised his free will. However, once he had included a human nature of the sort he did, a certain set of moral entities was naturally fit to provide guidance for this nature.[43] The standard charge against voluntarism, that it makes God's prescription of natural law appear an arbitrary imposition, was thus in some measure misconceived, and a parallel complaint about the arbitrary choice of human nature would be impossible, since we have no means of knowing God's motives for creation. This train of reasoning we have already met with in Suárez (and it is to be found again in Locke), but in Pufendorf it was further strengthened by his particular understanding of Lutheranism – which contrasted so sharply with that of his contemporaries – as well as by his concern to make natural law independent of theology.

The language I have chosen already implies that Pufendorf was also a moral voluntarist for whom the basis for morality was the will or law of a superior. This does not, however, follow from his ontological voluntarism and has to be argued separately. After all, God might, for instance, have chosen human nature in such a way that men would primarily recognize a more or less extensive complement of subjective rights in each other, while any moral guidance beyond that would be derivative from such rights.[44] This would have brought Pufendorf very close to the standpoint of Grotius. Pufendorf's texts do, however, make it clear that he subscribes to a voluntarism according to which law is logically and causally primary, whereas obligation, duty, and right are derivative.

First, Pufendorf suggests that 'good' and 'evil', 'justice' and 'injustice', are conceptually derived from 'law'.[45] Second, he maintains that

---

in Suárez by suggesting that actions which are physically identical in man and in beast have completely different moral import (I.2.vi).

43 *Elementa*, I.xiii.14.

44 A succession of Swedish commentators seem to subscribe to something like this view: A. Hägerström, *Recht, Pflicht und bindende Kraft des Vertrages nach römischer und naturrechtlicher Anschauung*, ed. K. Olivecrona (Acta Societatis Litterarum Humaniorum Regiae Upsaliensis, 44:3), Stockholm, 1965; K. Olivecrona, *Law as Fact*, London, 1971; same, 'Die zwei Schichten im naturrechtlichen Denken', *Archiv für Rechts- und Sozialphilosophie*, 63 (1977), 79–103; and T. Mautner, 'Pufendorf and the correlativity thesis of rights', in *In So Many Words: Philosophical Essays Dedicated to Sven Danielson on the Occasion of His Fiftieth Birthday*, ed. S. Lindström and W. Rabinowics (Philosophical Studies, Philosophical Society and the Department of Philosophy, University of Uppsala, no. 42), Uppsala, 1989, pp. 37–59.

45 Pufendorf, *De officio hominis et civis juxta legem naturalem libri duo*, [1673], facsim. repr. of 1682 ed., with trans. by F. G. Moore, 2 vols. (Classics of International Law), New York, 1927, I.2.xi and xiii. The best translation is *On the Duty of Man and*

without law there is no possibility of moral judgement. There is no separate moral faculty or conscience, and moral judgement consists in nothing more than the correlation of action, legal prescription, and reaction of the lawgiver (or reward/punishment) (I.3.iv). Concerning the relationship between law and rights, Pufendorf's definition of *ius* must be remembered: *ius* is a 'Power of acting granted or left free by the Laws' (I.6.iii).

Pufendorf uses *ius* in the sense of subjective rights to refer to four different categories of deontic powers: power over one's own actions, termed *libertas*; power over another person's actions, termed *imperium*; power over one's own things – property, termed *dominium*; and power over another person's property, termed *servitus*.[46] The three last are 'adventitious', that is, they are instituted by men through contractual and quasi-contractual arrangements, and they thus presuppose the first power. *Libertas* encompasses the absence of subjection in a human being's command of his physical and moral personality – his life, actions, body, honour, and reputation. This right, or cluster of rights, does not depend on the agreement of others; it exists in a person by nature or innately. In fact, it exists ante-natally, in as much as a foetus has rights as soon as it is a recognisably human organism. The natural or innate character of *libertas* does not, however, mean that it is sui generis and independent of natural law. A clue is given in a passage concerning the rights of the foetus. There Pufendorf makes it quite clear that such rights exist as a result of the fact that other people have duties, imposed by natural law, to respect such rights. In order to appreciate Pufendorf's way of thinking, we must distinguish between the 'obligator', who is the person to whom one is bound in obligation, the 'obligee', who is the person thus bound, and the beneficiary of the obligation. The obligator and the beneficiary can be one person, as when A promises B to do something for him or her. However, in the case of *libertas* the obligator is God, to whom we are obligated to obey the law of nature by, among other things, respecting the *libertas* of our neighbour, but it is the neighbour who is the beneficiary of this obligation, his benefit being his *libertas*. This also explains why it is that in the state of nature there is no right of punishment in man. Such a right is an authority over others, but prior to agreements no individual has any authority over another, and the only authority in the state of nature is God. Each person does have a right of self-defense, as part of the right

---

Citizen According to Natural Law, trans. M. Silverthorne, ed. J. Tully, Cambridge, UK, 1991.

   46   See the discussions in Olivecrona, 'Die zwei Schichten im naturrechtlichen Denken', and Mautner, 'Pufendorf and the correlativity thesis of rights.'

to self-preservation, but Pufendorf is careful to distinguish this from the right to punish – in opposition to Hobbes (VIII.3.i–ii).

In this account a right is that which there is a duty to yield, whether to oneself or to others. Rights are, however, also related to duties and law in a different way. That which we have a duty to do, we must have a right to do, and in this sense a 'right' is a moral power to act, granted by the basic law of nature in order to fulfil the duties imposed by this law. Rights thus have a positive as well as a negative side, both of which are derived from duties conceived as impositions of natural law.

The reason for Pufendorf's obvious fear of considering rights as primary over law was that he saw such a position as a version of scholastic essentialism – the view that moral values were inherent in nature prior to God's moral legislation. This was exactly the view that he vehemently criticized in Grotius (I.2.vi and I.6.iv).

Of course one can rescue the thesis of the primacy of rights by resorting to the circumstance that the natural law is dependent on God's right to legislate, that is, to obligate those subject to the law. That, however, trivializes the thesis, as far as human morals are concerned, and to assimilate God's and man's 'right' is, furthermore, most un-Pufendorfian.

The vexed question of whether Pufendorf subscribed to the thesis of the correlativity of rights and obligations must then be answered in the affirmative, though with two important cautions which make the thesis different from that normally held. First, the thesis is, in the present context, philosophically interesting only concerning natural rights, since adventitious institutions may be made to include rights un-secured by obligations. Second, and more importantly, in the case of *libertas* there are indeed correlated obligations, but they are not directly to the rights holder, they are to God.

The character of Pufendorf's theory is in fact evident from the very structure employed in the *De iure* and the *De officio*. The basic natural law is that, given human nature, we should live sociably. This means that we must fulfil certain offices, *officia*. In order to do so, people need certain powers. Disregarding the obvious physical powers, for instance, of speech or procreation, the fundamental moral powers are the four groups of rights mentioned earlier, *libertas* being the fundamental one. In order for these rights to be effective, there must be specific duties (also mostly called *officia*) to respect them. As far as *libertas* is concerned, these duties are imposed by the law of nature; as far as the other rights are concerned, the duties are directly or derivatively self-imposed by contractual or quasi-contractual means or imposed by authorities established in this way. *Officia* in the broader sense are thus not simply 'duties', as the term is normally rendered in English. They

are the offices of life which encompass clusters of specific duties and
rights, and we are bound to them by an *obligatio*, or moral necessity.

The basic offices of life fall into three categories, that of being a
human being *tout court*; that of being a member of a family (as spouse,
parent, child, sibling, master, servant); and that of being a member of a
political society (as citizen, sovereign, any type of magistrate, or sol-
dier). These three groups of offices provide the foundation for Pufendorf's tripartite division of his material into analyses of the specific
natural jurisprudential relations of individuals as individuals, of
'oeconomical' (household) relations in the traditional sense, and of
civic relations. Self-consciously inspired by stoicism, this theory fitted
directly into the Christian stoicism of the Enlightenment and lived on
in the popular practical ethics of the eighteenth century as Pufendorf's
most pervasive legacy – though often on very different philosophical
foundations.[47]

It remains to consider the *obligatio*, or moral necessity, of the law of
nature. Pufendorf provides a dual foundation for natural law, namely a
Hobbesian idea of man's need for self-preservation and a Grotian idea
of man's social nature. It is debatable whether and to what extent the
latter is an independent principle, or whether it really reduces to the
former.[48] On the latter view, man's sociability is not an independent
principle but a means towards self-preservation; human beings are
rather de facto social than *sociabilis*, inherently sociable. It has been
argued that this view is often obscured by Pufendorf's attempts to
distance himself from Hobbes, and it is, at any rate, certain that the
polemics of the time soon forced Pufendorf to seek such distance.
However, he did see very clearly that obligation for self-interested
persons easily becomes conceptually confused with the threat of the
use of superior power. Such threat is indeed of the essence of obligation, but the distinguishing characteristic of the latter is that there are
morally good reasons for the threat of sanctions. The moral necessity in
obligation consists in the obligee's rational insight into the justifiability
of the obligator's imbuing him with fear through threat of sanctions if
the obligation is breached (I.6.v). This side of Pufendorf's argument
points to an independent status for the principle of sociability.

There is thus a fundamental ambiguity in Pufendorf's theory of the
obligation to natural law. If the emphasis is on self-preservation, then
obligation reduces to self-interest, in the mode of Hobbes, which Pufendorf evidently wanted to avoid. If the emphasis is on inherent
sociability, then an interesting dilemma arises. Sociability can be un-

47 See the subsequent studies in this volume.
48 For the latter view, see F. Paladini, *Samuel Pufendorf discepolo di Hobbes*,
Bologna, 1990.

derstood as a given, ultimate feature of human nature. This would dispense with any role for the Deity, except as creator. Morals would thus be entirely self-contained as a human enterprise, and the discipline dealing with it, natural jurisprudence, would be completely segregated from all theology. This segregation was one of Pufendorf's main concerns, and there is therefore a strong case for interpreting sociability as a natural ability or inclination. However, in that case it would make no sense to talk of sociableness as a *law*, and there would be no meaning in talking of obligation to it, let alone in invoking God. Pufendorf says all of these things. If, on the other hand, sociability *is* God's will for humanity, then the question of our obligation to God arises in all its sharpness after all.

1.7 *Reactions to Pufendorf*

These ambiguities gave rise to a debate which lasted for a generation or more, and which was as fierce as any in the history of philosophy. It also helped to secure to Pufendorf an influence that was European in scope and lasted well into the eighteenth century.[49] The chief

49 For some overviews, see R. Derathé, *Jean-Jacques Rousseau et la science politique de son temps*, Paris, 1988, esp. pp. 78–84; A. Dufour, 'Pufendorfs Ausstrahlung im franzözischen und im anglo-amerikanischen Kulturraum', in *Samuel von Pufendorf, 1632–1982*, ed. K.Å. Modéer, Lund, 1986, pp. 96–119; K. Haakonssen, 'Natural law and the Scottish Enlightenment', in *Man and Nature*, ed. D.H. Jory and J.C. Stewart-Robertson (Proceedings of the Canadian Society for Eighteenth-Century Studies, IV, Edmonton, 1985), 47–80; same, 'Natural law and the German tradition', ch. 9 of *The Cambridge History of Eighteenth-Century Political Thought*, ed. M. Goldie and R. Wokler, Cambridge, forthcoming; N. Hammerstein, 'Zum Fortwirken von Pufendorf's Naturrechtslehre an den Universitäten des Heiligen Römischen Reiches Deutscher Nation während des 18. Jahrhunderts', in *Pufendorf*, ed. Modéer, pp. 31–51; I. Hont, 'The language of sociability and commerce: Samuel Pufendorf and the theoretical foundations of the "four stages theory"', in *The Languages of Political Theory*, ed. A. Pagden, pp. 253–76; K. Luig, 'Zur Verbreitung des Naturrechts in Europa', *Tijdschrift voor rechtsgeschedenis/Revue d'histoire du droit*, 40 (1972), 539–57; T. Mautner, 'Pufendorf and eighteenth-century Scottish philosophy', in *Pufendorf*, ed. Modéer, pp. 120–31; J. Moore, 'Natural law and the Pyrrhonian controversy', in *Philosophy and Science in the Scottish Enlightenment*, ed. P. Jones, Edinburgh, 1988, pp. 20–38; H. Thieme, ed., *Humanismus und Naturrecht in Berlin-Brandenburg-Preussen* (Veröffentlichungen der Historischen Kommission zu Berlin, Bd. 48), Berlin, 1979. For important aspects of the more immediate impact of Pufendorf, see M. Bazzoli, 'Giambattista Almici e la diffusione di Pufendorf nel settecento Italiano', *Critica storica*, 16 (1979), 3–100; Thomas Behme, 'Pufendorf – Schüler von Hobbes?', in *Denkhorizonte und Handlungsspielräume. Historische Studien für Rudolf Vierhaus zum 70. Geburtstag*, Göttingen, 1992, pp. 33–52; L. Krieger, *The Politics of Discretion: Pufendorf and the Acceptance of Natural Law*, Chicago, 1965; Bo Lindberg,

problems concerned the role of God in the moral world and, consequently, the relationship between moral theology and natural law (or,
in modern parlance, ethics). On the one hand, Pufendorf was accused
of excluding God from human morals by making the content of the
latter entirely dependent upon post-lapsarian human nature and its
exertions. In this regard the accusations ranged from Hobbesian (and
Spinozistic) self-interest to mistaken reliance on the principle of sociability. On the other hand, Pufendorf was charged with ascribing to
God, if not too large a role, at least a mistaken one, by making all
obligation dependent upon God's will.

A sharpening of the orthodox Lutheran standpoint on these issues
was the most immediate and widespread reaction to Pufendorf and
cost him the greatest polemical efforts.[50] A rapidly deteriorating pamphlet war saw a clear formulation of the orthodox line by Valentin
Alberti, the central point of which was that natural law could be de-

---

Naturrätten i Uppsala, 1655–1720 (Acta Universitatis Upsaliensis, C: 33), Uppsala,
1976; P. Meylan, *Jean Barbeyrac (1674–1744) et les débuts de l'enseignement du droit dans
l'ancienne académie de Lausanne*, Lausanne, 1937; J. Moore and M. Silverthorne, 'Gershom Carmichael and the natural jurisprudence tradition in eighteenth-century
Scotland', in *Wealth and Virtue: The Shaping of Political Economy in the Scottish Enlightenment*, ed. I. Hont and M. Ignatieff, Cambridge, UK, 1983, pp. 73–87; same, 'Natural sociability and natural rights in the moral philosophy of Gershom Carmichael',
in *Philosophers of the Scottish Enlightenment*, ed. V. Hope, Edinburgh, 1984, pp. 1–12;
Osterhorn, *Die Naturrechtslehre Valentin Albertis*; F. Paladini, *Discussioni seicentesche
su Samuel Pufendorf. Scritti latini: 1663–1700*, (Pubblicazioni del Centro di Studio per
la Storia della Storiografia Filosofica, 6), n.p., 1978; same, 'Le due lettere di Pufendorf al Barone di Boineburg: Quella nota e quella "perduta"', *Nouvelles de la répub-
lique des lettres* (Naples), 1 (1984), 119–44; same, *Samuel Pufendorf, discepolo di Hobbes*,
Bologna, 1990; H. Rüping, 'Gottlieb Gerhard Titius und die Naturrechtslehre in
Deutschland um die Wende vom 17. zum 18. Jahrhundert', *Zeitschrift der Savigny-
Stiftung fürRechtsgeschichte*. Ger. Abt., 87 (1970), 314–26; René Sève, *Leibniz et l'école
moderne du droit naturel*, Paris, 1989; D. Tamm, 'Pufendorf und Dänemark', in *Pufendorf*, ed. Modéer, pp. 81–9.

50 It could have cost him more. Only royal patronage saved him in his pro-
fessorship at Lund, and the *De iure* was banned in Saxony. Cf. Oscar Malmström,
Samuel Pufendorf och hans arbeten i Sveriges historia, Stockholm, 1899, pp. 10ff.; Lind-
berg, *Naturrätten i Uppsala, 1655–1720*, pp. 50–3; and S. Jägerskiöld, 'Samuel von
Pufendorf in Schweden, 1668–1688. Einige neue Beiträge', in *Satura Roberto Feenstra
Sexagesimum Quintum Annum Aetatis Complenti ab Alumnis Collegis Amicis Oblata*, ed.
J.A. Ankum, J.E. Spruit, and F.B.J. Wubbe, Fribourg, 1985, pp. 557–70. In addition to
Paladini, *Discussioni seicentesche su Samuel Pufendorf*, see also the old but still valu-
able general account of the literary battle about Pufendorf by Hermann Friedrich
Wilhelm Hinrichs, *Geschichte der Rechts- und Staatsprinzipien seit der Reformation bis
auf die Gegenwart in historisch-philosophischer Entwicklung*, 3 vols., Leipzig, 1848–52, 2,
here esp. pp. 246ff.

rived only from the knowledge of man's state of innocence (*status integretatis*) which God's revealed word presented.[51] To base any universal natural law on the de facto sociality of fallen human nature instead of on the original human nature which God created in the purity of his own image was plainly as impossible as it was impious.[52]

Pufendorf provoked scores of attacks reflecting such ideas and remained for long the focus of this debate about the relationship between natural law and revealed religion. The chief support for his sharp separation of the two was provided by his most outstanding disciple, Christian Thomasius.[53] In a host of works, but most significantly in the *Institutiones jurisprudentiæ divinæ* (1688), Thomasius maintained the independence of natural law by delimiting the voluntaristic element to the bare minimum, arguing in effect that we cannot rationally know more about God's authorship of the law than the mere fact and that we can learn the rest from human rationality considered as a social practice. After a prolonged pietistic crisis of doubt about the adequacy of his own or any other rational reply to the criticisms of voluntarism and the associated principle of human sociality, Thomasius radically restated his position in *Fundamenta juris naturæ et gentium* (1705). He here reduces the status of *ius naturæ* from one of law proper to that of divine advice or a matter of conscience and stresses the role of positive law and social morality. This is the basis for his well-known distinction between *honestum*, *justum*, and *decorum*, respectively.

51 Most of the polemical pieces are collected in Pufendorf, *Eris Scandica*, and Alberti, *Eros Lipsicus*, Leipzig, 1687 (Eris was the goddess of strife, whom the pious Alberti thus answers with his Leipziger love).

52 See Alberti's main work, *Compendium Juris Naturae, Orthodoxae Theologiae Conformatum* . . . , Leipzig, 1678; the preface ('Ad Benev. Lectorem') contains the most important principles.

53 Concerning Pufendorf and Thomasius, see *Briefe Samuel Pufendorfs an Christian Thomasius (1687–1693)*, ed. E. Gigas (Historische Bibliothek, Bd. II), Munich, 1897; W. Schneiders, *Naturrecht und Liebesethik*, Hildesheim, 1971. For an English translation of Thomasius's central principles, see 'Christian Thomasius', in *German Political Thought in the Age of Absolutism*, ed. H.-E. Bödeker and K. Haakonssen, Cambridge, UK, forthcoming. Cf. also F.M. Barnard, 'Christian Thomasius: Enlightenment and bureaucracy', *American Political Science Review*, 59 (1965), 430–8, and 'The "practical philosophy" of Christian Thomasius', *Journal of the History of Ideas*, 32 (1971), 221–46; F. Battaglia, *Cristiano Thomasio, Filosofo e Giurista*, Bologna, 1982; H. Rüping, *Die Naturrechtslehre des Christian Thomasius und ihre Fortbildung in der Thomasius-Schule*, Bonn, 1968; W. Schneiders, ed., *Christian Thomasius, 1655–1728. Interpretationen zu Werk und Wirkung*, Hamburg, 1989; and G. Schubart-Fikentscher, 'Christian Thomasius. Seine Bedeutung als Hochschullehrer am Beginn der deutschen Aufklärung' (Sitzungsberichte der Sächsischen Akademie der Wissenschaften zu Leipzig, Phil.-hist. Klasse, Bd. 119, Heft 4), Berlin, 1977.

Thomasius's direct influence was more or less confined to the German-speaking (especially the Lutheran) realm, where it was very significant.[54] If we want to understand the wider European impact of the natural law debate, we have to go beyond Thomasius's development of Pufendorf's ideas. The most pervasive factor was a realist tradition that was readily invoked in the discussion, both in Britain and on the Continent. Another important feature was the attempt to use natural law to combat scepticism. But we shall here be concerned mainly with the former.

1.8   *Gottfried Wilhelm von Leibniz*

Throughout the seventeenth century there were strong currents of what today is often called 'moral realism', of partly Platonic, partly scholastic–Aristotelian provenance. While opposing voluntarism of the Cartesian, Hobbesian, and other varieties, these nevertheless had to find room somewhere for the voluntarist element required of any acceptable form of Christianity or of any natural religion compatible with Christian thought. In Germany the greatest representative of this tendency was Leibniz. Of his copious writings on natural law, only a few were published in his lifetime, and of these the best-known piece was primarily critical in character. The criticisms of Pufendorf's voluntarism, which we shall consider shortly, were based on the idea of a universal jurisprudence.[55] The object of this was a justice that was universal for all rational beings, and thus common between God and human beings. Since God cannot be indebted to humans, let alone be thought to harm them, this justice cannot be conceived in terms of the two traditional stricter forms of justice, giving each one his due and refraining from harm to others. Universal justice is a form of love or benevolence, though understood not as an emotive state but as an active principle guided by rational judgement. This is what Leibniz calls *caritas sapientis,* the charity of the wise person. He thus transposes the issue of voluntarism to the spheres of rational theology and moral psychology: In God (and, in pale imitation, in humanity), wisdom and will come together as 'the measure of justice', while 'power' – Hobbes's master principle, as Leibniz read him – is nothing but the temporal efficient cause:

54 Thomasius seems never to have been translated into either English or French during the eighteenth century.

55 See in general H.-P. Schneider, *Justitia universalis. Quellenstudien zur Geschichte des 'Christlichen Naturrechts' bei Gottfried Wilhelm Leibniz*, Frankfurt a.M., 1967; W. Schneiders, 'Naturrecht und Gerechtigkeit bei Leibniz', *Zeitschrift für philosophische Forschung*, 20 (1966), 607–50; and Sève, *Leibniz et l'école moderne.*

Justice is nothing else than that which conforms to wisdom and goodness joined together: the end of goodness is the greatest good, but to recognize it wisdom is needed, which is nothing else than knowledge of the good. Goodness is simply the inclination to do good to everyone, and to arrest evil . . . Thus wisdom is in the understanding and goodness in the will. And justice, as a consequence, is in both. Power is a different matter, but if it is used it makes right become fact, and makes what ought to be also really exist, in so far as the nature of things permits. And this is what God does in the world.[56]

On the basis of this theory, Leibniz launched his important and influential attack on voluntarism. He concentrated the central points in two minor works, one against Pufendorf, the other against the theocratic voluntarism of Heinrich von Cocceji and the latter's son Samuel. We shall here follow the order of argument in the former work, a lengthy letter subsequently appended to Jean Barbeyrac's influential French edition of Pufendorf's De officio together with Barbeyrac's own answer.[57] Leibniz's first point is that Pufendorf confines natural law, or

56 Leibniz, 'Meditation on the common concept of justice', in The Political Writings of Leibniz, ed. P. Riley, Cambridge, UK, 1972, pp. 45–64, at p. 50. The original ms. is printed as 'Méditation sur la notion commune de la justice' in a useful collection, G. Mollat, Rechtsphilosophisches aus Leibnizens ungedruckten Schriften, Leipzig, 1885, pp. 41–70.

57 Leibniz, 'Jugement d'un anonyme sur l'original de cet abrégé [De officio]: Avec des réflexions du Traducteur [Barbeyrac] . . .' in Pufendorf, Les Devoirs de l'homme, et du citoien, ed. J. Barbeyrac, Amsterdam, 1718, pp. 429–95. Leibniz had written the letter at the request of the Abbot of Loccum, G.W. Molanus, and it had previously been published with the author's name – which Barbeyrac says (p. 429) he 'has learned' – in A.A. Pagenstecher's edition of the Latin De officio, Groeningen, 1712 (namely in app. 3). For the publication history and the participants in the dispute, see Hinrichs, Geschichte der Rechts- und Staatsprinzipien, 3:64, n. 1. The letter is now available as 'Opinion on the principles of Pufendorf', in The Political Writings of Leibniz, ed Riley, pp. 64–75, while the Latin text is available as 'Monita quædam ad Samuelis Puffendorfii principia, Gerh. Wolth. Molano directa', in G. W. Leibniz, Opera omnia, ed. L. Dutens, 6 vols., Geneva, 1768, IV.3, pp. 275–83. For discussion of Leibniz's criticism of Pufendorf, see esp. Sève, Leibniz, pp. 49–63. Concerning Barbeyrac's partial defence of Pufendorf, see Meylan, Barbeyrac, esp. pp. 190ff. Concerning the dispute with the two Coccejis, see Samuel von Cocceji, Disputatio inauguralis de Principio juris naturalis unico, vero et adaequato . . . , Frankfort a.d.O., 1699, which was criticized in an anonymous journal article by Leibniz in 1700, subsequently reprinted as 'Observationes de principio juris', in Opera omnia, IV, pp. 270–5; this was again answered by the younger Cocceji in Tractatus juris gentium de principio juri naturalis unico, vero et adæquato, Frankfort a.d.O., 1702, Part II, pp. 5–51. Cf. J.A.R. von Stintzing, Geschichte der deutschen Rechtswissenschaft, completed by Ernst Landsberg, 3 vols. in 4, Munich, 1880–1910, 3. Abt., 1. Halbbd., pp. 112–17, 215–21; 2. Halbbd., pp. 64–8, 138–41; Hinrichs, Geschichte, vol. 3, pp. 316–38; H.-P.

morals as we know it, to this life. Yet the very fact of moral striving in earthly life points to a completion in a future life. Pufendorf allows some role for God, but the notion itself of divinity implies transcendent vengeance and reward.[58] The second criticism is that Pufendorf limits the scope of natural law to overt action, while he treats 'that which remains hidden in the soul' as a matter for moral theology, 'whose principle . . . is revelation'. However, the moral agent is one being, and the moral status of external actions cannot be separated from 'the internal movements of the soul'.[59] If they were separated, natural law would be concerned with nothing but human justice, in isolation from that which, as we shall see, gives the notion of justice its moral content, namely the divine justice which encompasses goodness and which is the true object of the soul's moral striving.

Third, Leibniz, like many Lutheran scholastics, is severely critical of Pufendorf's voluntaristic account of the obligation to natural law. First, if justice is simply a matter of God's will, then there is no rational account of why we should praise God as just. It is because 'justice follows certain rules of equality and of proportion [which are] no less founded in the immutable nature of things, and in the divine ideas, than are the principles of arithmetic and of geometry' that universal or divine justice encompasses the idea of truth in terms of which we can praise God as truly just. Otherwise Pufendorf would have to follow the 'unheard-of paradox by which Descartes showed how great can be the errors of great men', namely that truth itself is a matter of divine will.[60] Pufendorf had, of course, appealed to the justice of God's reasons for imposing the natural law, thus invoking a norm which is prior to God's will. But, Leibniz says, 'if the source of law is the will of a superior and, inversely, a justifying cause of law is necessary in order to have a superior, a circle is created, than which none was ever more manifest'.[61] Pufendorf tried to forestall criticism of this apparent breach of his own principle and prima facie blurring of his sharp division between natural law and revealed religion in the following manner. When he talks of sanctions being imposed justly, he means that they must come from someone with authority over the obligee. One agent's authority over another stems either from agreement by the latter or from some extraordinary benefit rendered by the former. Agreement with God being out of the question, Pufendorf rests his case on God's

---

Schneider, 'Die wissenschaftliche Beziehungen zwischen Leibniz und den beiden Cocceji (Heinrich und Samuel)', in *Humanismus und Naturrecht in Berlin-Brandenburg-Preussen*, ed. H. Thieme, Berlin, 1979, pp. 90–102.

58   Leibniz, 'Opinion', p. 67 ('Jugement', p. 441; 'Monita', pp. 276–7).
59   'Opinion', p. 68 ('Jugement', pp. 447–8; 'Monita', p. 277).
60   'Opinion', p. 71 ('Jugement', p. 466; 'Monita', p. 280).
61   'Opinion', pp. 73–4 ('Jugement', p. 485, 'Monita', p. 281).

extraordinary goodness to humankind, in the free gift of creating them as moral and social beings with the capacity to enjoy creation as we find it in ourselves, in others, and in the rest of the world. The natural reaction to this is gratitude for the gift, which is shown by looking after it as specified in the law of nature. Without presuming knowledge of God's motives, we are thus under a rational obligation to him.[62]

This argument does not quite get to the bottom of Leibniz's objection, for it is presupposed that man has the ability to recognize the goodness of God's gift independent of the law of nature, since this is the foundation of the obligation to the law. However, 'good' and 'evil' are given meaning only by the law of nature, and it is solely through the latter that we have a capacity for moral knowledge. On this basis Leibniz rejects Pufendorf's idea that the force of divine sanctions and the reasons of God's justice, though severally necessary, are conjointly sufficient for obligation to natural law.[63]

If Pufendorf had kept to the idea that human sanctions against ingratitude for 'God's gift' would do as the foundation for natural law, he would indeed have minimalized the role of God, and he would have provided the possibility of a purely human or social account of how we come to learn about 'good' and 'evil' or develop our moral powers (whether innate or purely acquired). Locke toyed with such thoughts, as we will see, and they were at the centre of the moral philosophy of the Enlightenment. The way was cleared for it in a somewhat circuitous manner through a return by several late seventeenth-century natural lawyers to some scholastic points, especially the distinction between the goodness and the obligation of natural law, which we have already met with in Suárez.

1.9 *Nathaniel Culverwell*

In the Platonic–Aristotelian ethics of the so-called Cambridge Platonists, the concept of natural law had an even more tenuous position than it had in Leibniz's thought.[64] In one of their eclectic students, Nathaniel Culverwell, there is, however, a determined attempt at compromise.[65] On the one hand, Culverwell was a Calvinist who had to

---

62   Cf. Schneewind, 'Pufendorf's place in the history of ethics', *Synthèse*, 72 (1987), 123–55.

63   'Opinion', pp. 73–4 ('Jugement', pp. 487–8; 'Monita', p. 282).

64   See e.g. Henry More, *An Account of Virtue* [1667], trans. E. Southwell, London, 1690, Book III. Richard Hooker was a crucial link between scholasticism and English ideas of natural law; cf. Peter Munz, *The Place of Hooker in the History of Thought*, London, 1952; John Passmore, *Ralph Cudworth: An Interpretation*, Cambridge, UK, 1951.

65   Nathaniel Culverwell, *An Elegant and Learned Discourse of the Light of Nature* [1652], ed. R.A. Greene and H. MacCallum, Toronto, 1971. Cf. also Greene and

reject the Platonists' theory of innate ideas as a trace of God's hand in the human mind and the associated notions of the soul as living or participating in the divine mind and therefore having an inherent goodness. On the other hand, he had to agree with the Platonists that goodness and justice could not simply be understood as effects of God's will; there was such a thing as inherently good and just behaviour. For this to make sense, there must be an overarching eternal law, to be understood as a purely conceptual link between God and the natural law prescribed for humanity. Against this uneasy background Culverwell drew well-known distinctions with origins in Suárez – between moral precepts discovered by reason in the nature of things and laws of nature prescribed for humans; between the matter and the form of the law of nature; between natural good and moral good; and between the natural obligation of rational precepts and the moral obligation of law proper.[66] Sadly, he is even further than his intellectual master, Suárez, from clarifying 'natural obligation', which seems to signify no more than recognition of natural goodness.

1.10   *Richard Cumberland*

The attempt to find a way between realism and voluntarism is also pursued by Richard Cumberland in his attempt to refute Hobbes.[67] He argues that only by serving the common good of the universal moral community of God and humanity, past, present, and future, will we serve our own good. We have a natural inclination, benevolence, to do this, and we develop rational precepts to guide this inclination. We will eventually appreciate that benevolent behaviour is also God's will and thus see that the rational precepts are proper laws of nature, that the inclinations are virtues, and that the common good is not only a natural but a moral good. The obligation to observe the basic law of nature concerning the promotion of the common good arises from the individual unifying his particular will with the general will of God. When Cumberland uses the traditional formulation that man's obligation stems from God's will, he means that obligation arises from us seeing that our will is part of God's general will. However, since moral good-

MacCallum's introduction to their edition, pp. ix–lvii, and Haakonssen. 'Moral philosophy and natural law: From the Cambridge Platonists to the Scottish Enlightenment', *Political Science*, 40 (1988), 97–110.

    66   Culverwell, *Discourse*, pp. 49–53.

    67   See Richard Cumberland, *De legibus naturæ disquisitio philosophica*, London, 1672, translated as *A Treatise of the Law of Nature* by J. Maxwell, London, 1727. Cf. K. Haakonssen, 'The character and obligation of natural law according to Richard Cumberland', in *English Philosophy in the Age of Locke*, ed. M. A. Stewart, Oxford, forthcoming; and L. Kirk, *Richard Cumberland and Natural Law*, Cambridge, UK, 1987.

ness is defined in terms of law, and since God cannot be subject to law, Cumberland is in the traditional dilemma. He takes the line that God's supreme reasoning and willing takes place *as if* he were following a law, and in his complete goodness and wisdom he binds himself to will the common good of the moral universe he has created. God is thus a sort of moral intuitionist who can undertake self-obligation to moral goodness, and this is the ultimate ground of all moral obligation. Although this is at best a marginal advance on attempts like those of Suárez and Culverwell, the formulation is so thoroughly anthropomorphic that this notion of *God's* ability to derive 'ought' from 'good' begs to be transferred to man. If man's moral ability is made as closely in God's image as humans think, cannot man make the same sort of inference, albeit imperfectly? Several thinkers set about exploring this possibility, some of them obviously inspired in part by Cumberland – for example, Shaftesbury, Clarke, and Hutcheson.

Cumberland's theory of natural law and its obligation as based upon love, benevolence, and man's sharing in the will of God presupposes a moral community of man with God. Traditionally this idea was associated with innatism, and often with Catholicism. The 'empiricist' critique of innatism is thus often used as part of anti-popish polemics, for example in Locke. Cumberland is of some significance in this connection. His combination of a strong critique of innate ideas and assertion of the moral community with God was a contributing factor in the formation of the kind of empirically based natural providentialism, or natural religious teleology, which soon became the framework for natural law thinking and, indeed, for the mainstream of Enlightenment moral thought.

1.11   *John Locke*

For Cumberland the loss of innate ideas of morals was amply compensated for by the knowledge acquired by reason and experience of the moral community in this world and the next. Despite Locke's reputation as the great 'empiricist' philosopher, there was no such easy replacement of innate with empirical knowledge in his development of a theory of morals.[68] Locke originally thought of natural law in traditional voluntarist-cum-realist terms, as we see from his unpublished *Essays on the Law of Nature* (1663),[69] although even then he rejected innatism. During the subsequent quarter of a century, as his epistemol-

---

68   For a rather naïve attempt to combine Locke and Cumberland, see James Tyrrell, *A Brief Disquisition of the Law of Nature* [1692], London, 1701.

69   John Locke, *Essays on the Law of Nature* [1663], ed. W. von Leyden, Oxford, 1954, pp. 111–13 and Essay VI. For a recent, somewhat different translation of this work, see Locke, *Questions Concerning the Law of Nature*, ed. and trans. R. Horwitz, J.S. Clay, and D. Clay, Ithaca, NY, 1990.

ogy and theology developed, the status of morals had to be rethought. However, Locke never published a comprehensive statement of his moral theory, and the partial presentations in *An Essay Concerning Human Understanding* (1689), the *Two Treatises of Government* (1690), and the works on education and religion left his contemporaries dissatisfied and confused, a condition matched by the disagreements that persist among modern scholars, even when they have been able to make use of Locke's correspondence and unpublished manuscript materials.[70] The disputes concern the relationship between reason and revelation.

In much of his philosophy relating to morals Locke is working out a programme similar to Pufendorf's, and, in view of Locke's stated admiration for the German thinker, he is likely to have been doing so with some degree of self-consciousness.[71] Like Pufendorf, Locke argues, as part of his criticism of innate ideas, that moral phenomena are created by moral agents and imposed upon nature, which, in abstraction from such activity, is value-neutral. Moral ideas are 'mixed modes', that is complex ideas deliberately put together from simple ideas so as to order our understanding of particular events for practical and, in particular, social purposes and thus facilitate our behaviour in the world. Like Pufendorf, he stresses the social aspect of this activity. Unless we arrange the particular events of life into groups and categories, we will have difficulty in communicating with and thus relating to others. The clear definition and labelling of moral ideas is therefore important in order to achieve some communal or social stability in such ideas. In short, morals is a mental construct used in social communication through the medium of language. Different individuals and, especially, groups of individuals can make different constructions and thus have different moral languages. Since morals are human-made, the study of morals can, as in Pufendorf, be a demonstrative science, for deductive proof consists in bringing ideas, over which we have command, into relationship with each other in the same way as we do in mathematics. The science of morals is thus a hypothetico-deductive system concerned with formal coherence. Whether anything

70 The most comprehensive modern discussion of Locke's moral theory is J. Colman, *John Locke's Moral Philosophy*, Edinburgh, 1983. In the Locke manuscripts there is an important overview of the main points in his moral theory, 'Of ethics in general', in Peter King, Seventh Baron King, *The Life of John Locke with Extracts from his Correspondence, Journals, and Commonplace Books*, new ed., 2 vols., London, 1830, 2:122–39.

71 See Locke, *Some Thoughts Concerning Education*, ed. J.W. and J.S. Yolton, Oxford, 1989, para. 186 (p. 239), and p. 322 ('Mr. Locke's extemporè advice &c'); also letter to the Countess of Peterborough, in *The Correspondence of John Locke*, ed. E.S. de Beer, 8 vols., Oxford, 1975–89, VI, pp. 212–16 at p. 215.

corresponds to it in the empirical world of the senses is an entirely different question, which does not strictly pertain to the science as such:

> the Truth and Certainty of *moral* Discourses abstracts from the Lives of Men, and the Existence of those Vertues in the World, whereof they treat: Nor are Tully's Offices less true, because there is no Body in the World that exactly practices his Rules, and lives up to that pattern of a vertuous Man, which he has given us, and which existed no where, when he writ, but in *Idea*. (IV.4.viii)[72]

Proof, in morals, consists more particularly in relating moral ideas and types of ideas to laws. In order for a rule to be a law, it has to issue from a lawmaker, that is, an authority who can back up the rule with reward and punishment. Laws are divided, according to their type of enforcement, into three kinds: the divine or natural law, stemming from God; the civil law, imposed by governments; and the law of opinion or reputation, arising in a given social group (I.3.xii; II.28.v–x).

All these forms of law are complex moral ideas which the mind constructs. The thing which, so to speak, anchors moral ideas in the world of action and thus makes the laws into practical principles is human beings' native desire for happiness and aversion to pain. The core of personality or agency is self-consciousness, which implies a concern for maintenance of the self, and this expresses itself in such desire and aversion (II.27.xvii–xviii). However, what counts as happiness and pain depends upon people's understanding of life, that is, upon their moral ideas. 'Hence naturally flows the great variety of Opinions, concerning Moral Rules, which are to be found amongst Men, according to the different sorts of Happiness, they have a Prospect of, or propose to themselves' (I.3.vi). It is the happiness or pain that we understand a lawmaker to attach to his rules as reward or punishment which make these rules into laws guiding our conduct and defining or demonstrating what is morally good or evil:

> Morally good and Evil, then, is only the Conformity or Disagreement of our voluntary Actions to some Law, whereby Good or Evil is drawn on us, from the Will and Power of the Law-maker; which Good and Evil, Pleasure or Pain, attending our observance, or breach of the Law, by the Decree of the Law-maker, is that we call *Reward* and *Punishment*. (II.28.v)

So far the argument amounts to a straightforward relativistic theory of morals, and Locke is in fact proud that he can account so economically for the moral diversity which history and geography exhibit. The question is, however, whether he can anchor the divine or natural law in

---

72 References of this form in this section refer to *An Essay Concerning Human Understanding* [1690], ed. P.H. Nidditch, Oxford, 1975.

something sufficiently permanent and universal to give him an absolute moral standard or a natural/divine law proper. This is where the main controversies arise. The central question is whether Locke did, or could, deliver something which, by his own standards, would be considered a rational argument for the proposition that God is a lawmaker for humanity in the sense just outlined, or whether he relied, or had to rely, on revelation at this point. The problem is compounded by evidence that Locke himself was uncertain and that his views changed over time. The most coherent line of argument in his main philosophical works is as follows.

Of all our ideas, two particular ones have a special veridical status, our knowledge of the self and our knowledge of God. The self, considered not as some kind of substance but as self-consciousness, is undeniable, and any attempt at denial confirms it. From this idea of the self and its properties of perception and reason, Locke argues causally or demonstratively to the existence of *an eternal, most powerful, and most knowing Being*' (IV.10.vi). Whatever we, from a post-Humean and post-Kantian perspective, may think of such an argument, it was of course entirely traditional, and there is little to suggest that Locke saw his own epistemology as undermining it.

Having established that the relationship between God and man is one of dependence, the question is whether this can be shown to mean that God is lawmaker. Commonly this is assumed to imply that Locke would have to show that there is an afterlife for the self and that God holds out the promise of reward and the threat of punishment through eternity. It seems clear that Locke did not think these things could be shown by reason, and it is frequently pointed out that he in fact undermines the usual arguments for the immortality of the soul.[73] But are such arguments in fact necessary in his scheme of things? Let us consider, first, immortality.

The essential point in Locke's account of the self in terms of self-consciousness is that personal continuity should be independent of the continuity of substance, whether material or immaterial, so that agency can be understood as continuous across changes of substance. And he explicitly links this to the idea of reckoning

> at the Great Day, when every one shall *receive according to his doing, the secrets of all Hearts shall be laid open.* [Locke's note: 'cf. 1 Cor. 14: 25 *and* 2 Cor. 5: 10.'] The Sentence shall be justified by the consciousness all Persons shall have, that they *themselves* in what Bodies soever they appear, or what Substances soever that consciousness adheres to, are the *same,* that committed those Actions, and deserve the Punishment for them. (II.27.xxvi)

73 See, for example, D. Wootton, 'John Locke: Socinian or natural law theorist?' in *Religion, Secularization and Political Thought: Thomas Hobbes to J. S. Mill*, ed. J.E. Crimmins, London, 1989, pp. 39–67.

In other words, although we cannot know anything of the immortality of the self as a substance, we can know that there is no reason why the self considered as self-consciousness should not continue to live.

Further, since, in an un-Lockean metaphor, it is of the essence of the self, understood as self-consciousness, to be concerned with self-preservation, or the securing of pleasure and the avoidance of pain, it is rational to assume that an infinitely more powerful being, upon whom we demonstrably depend for our very existence, has rewards and punishments in store for us, if he has any views on how we should behave. In other words, if it is rationally ascertainable that the Creator has intentions for his rational creatures, then it is a rational conclusion on the part of these creatures that they should 'play safe' by assuming that sanctions are attached to these intentions (II.27.vi; IV.3.xviii; IV.13.iii).[74] It does not of course follow that human beings as a matter of fact generally are rational and play it safe (II.21, esp. xxxviii).

Can God's intentions towards humanity, or the content of the law of nature, be discovered by human reason? In the *Essay Concerning Human Understanding* Locke makes only a few general remarks, to the effect that the law of nature is intended to secure the public happiness, the preservation of society, the benefit of all, that it is a 'Rule whereby Men should govern themselves', and the like (I.3.vi; II.28.viii). However, in *The Second Treatise of Government* he makes it clear that the fundamental law of nature is to preserve humanity in others as well as in oneself.[75] It is for this purpose that we must understand the rest of our moral powers, namely our 'rights' in ourselves and in the world around us, as well as the further rights which we create by contractual means. For Locke, as for Pufendorf, natural rights are powers to fulfil the fundamental duty of natural law.[76]

There is, however, an immensely important difference between the two thinkers here. In contrast to Pufendorf, Locke consistently maintains that among the rights entailed by the law of nature is the right or *'Power to Execute* that Law'.[77] He is clearly aware that this may be controversial, admitting that it 'will seem a very strange Doctrine'.[78] The point is that he has achieved too much, rather than too little, by means of reason, both for his own taste and for that of his contempo-

---

74 See also Bodleian MS. Locke f.3, fols. 201–2, 'Lex naturae' (journal entry 15 July 1678), printed in W. von Leyden, 'John Locke and natural law', *Philosophy*, 31 (1956), 23–35 at p. 35.

75 *Two Treatises of Government* [1689], ed. P. Laslett, Cambridge, UK, 1960, II, ch. 2, paras. 6–7.

76 Cf. J. Tully, *A Discourse on Property: John Locke and His Adversaries*, Cambridge, UK, 1980.

77 *Two Treatises*, II.2.vii.

78 *Two Treatises*, II.2.ix; again II.2.xiii and II.16.clxxx.

56 1 Natural law in the seventeenth century

rary readers. He has come dangerously close to making natural law independent of the Divinity, considered as a lawmaker as opposed to a mere creator. If we, unaided by revelation, can understand that the Divinity has a *ius creatoris* over us consisting in our duty to obey the law of nature, and if this rationally understood law entails a right on those who are subject to it to sanction it, then the Divinity's additional sanction, which is simply rationally *possible,* would appear to be deprived of much of its immediate relevance to the conduct of ordinary human affairs. And Locke does of course try to show that we, through our institutional arrangements, have a tolerable ability to sanction the law ourselves.

The need for sanctions of natural law arises because we, despite our rational abilities, all too frequently follow our immediate desires rather than the rational necessity of the good pointed out by natural law. In view of the prima facie hedonism we earlier found in Locke, this divergence between what is desired and what is good is in need of explanation. The background to this is that Locke does not identify desire and will as Hobbes did (II.21.xxx) and that although he defines 'good' in terms of 'pleasure', as we have seen, he does not, like Hobbes, define 'good' in terms of 'being desired'. He thus leaves an opening for objects of will that are not presently desired and therefore for goods that, though pleasant, are not currently pleasing. In this view, we have a liberty to will some good other than what we desire at the moment (II.21.xxxviii). The law of nature points out what the highest good is, namely the pleasures of a possibly eternal life, but the law does not constrain the will to do the good and thus terminate the individual's liberty.[79] Liberty consists in having compliance with the law as a rational option. This leaves scope for error and thus raises the need not only for sanctions but also for education. The most common error is that we remain satisfied with the goods of this life (II.21.lx), which, it might appear, we can secure through our own execution of the law of nature. Only the prospect of the incomparably greater pleasures of eternity can tear us from such erroneous inferences.

Much has been made of Locke's failure to fulfil his promise of a fully worked out theory of natural law. It has been suggested that he was so dissatisfied with his arguments concerning immortality and divine sanctions that he despaired of providing a rational foundation for natural law. In keeping with his increasingly Socinian leanings in theology, he ended by relying entirely on revelation.[80] In contrast, I want to

79 Concerning this conception of liberty, see the fine analysis in J. Tully, *An Approach to Political Philosophy: Locke in Contexts,* Cambridge, UK, 1993, pp. 294–8.

80 See Wootton, 'John Locke'; cf. Tully, 'Governing conduct: Locke on the reform of thought and behaviour', in his *Approach to Political Philosophy.*

suggest that Locke's natural law doctrine, as interpreted here, fitted some aspects of Socinianism exceedingly well. Any further elaboration of the theory would inevitably have strengthened the already fierce criticism of him for Socinianism and, since the latter was a serious crime, he was well advised not to pursue the matter further than he did in his anonymous works, leaving the final indications of his standpoint to the posthumous *Paraphrase and Notes on the Epistles of St. Paul*.[81]

The net result of the deliberations in the *Essay* was that immortality was rationally possible and that, given our demonstrable dependence upon an almighty Creator and given the character of humanity, it was reasonable to fear that divine sanctions were attached to the law of nature.[82] But although it was often asserted that God in fact holds such sanctions in store for us, it was never suggested that this could be proven. In the theological works, especially the *Paraphrase*, Locke repeatedly and emphatically reaffirms that the law of nature can be understood by natural reason and that it therefore is given to all human beings, irrespective of religion.[83] However, the divine sanction of the natural law in an afterlife, which reason could only show to be a sensible expectation and a rational possibility, was affirmed to be a reality by revelation. More particularly, it was Christ's special mission to teach this to humanity. Christ in fact repromulgated the law of nature, which had previously been known only partially by natural reason or through God's word to Moses, and taught it and its attendant sanctions more perspicuously than these other sources could. In this connection Locke strongly emphasises that reason, represented by philosophy, had in fact not developed a full system of morals, but he does not deny the possibility of such a philosophical enterprise. It could, of course, never be very effective with the bulk of humankind, who are incapable of rational demonstration and instead need direct com-

81 Concerning the danger of being accused of Socinianism, see J. Moore, 'Theological politics: A study of the reception of Locke's *Two Treatises of Government* in England and Scotland in the early eighteenth century', in *John Locke and / und Immanuel Kant*, ed. M. P. Thompson, Tübingen, 1991, pp. 62–82, and the literature cited there. Cf. W. M. Spellman, *John Locke and the Problem of Depravity*, Oxford, 1988.

82 See the tellingly hypothetical formulations in 'Morality', a manuscript printed in T. Sargentich, 'Locke and ethical theory: Two ms. pieces', *Locke Newsletter*, 5 (1974), 24–31 at p. 27, and the refrain of reasonable expectations in the pungent, brief journal entry 'Lex naturae', printed in von Leyden, 'John Locke', p. 35.

83 This is denied in Wootton, 'John Locke', pp. 42–3, but see Locke, *The Reasonableness of Christianity, as delivered in the Scriptures*, in *The Works of John Locke*, 12th ed., 9 vols., London, 1824, VI, pp.6:11–15, and *A Paraphrase and Notes on the Epistles of St. Paul to the Galatians, 1 and 2 Corinthians, Romans, Ephesians*, ed. A. W. Wainwright, 2 vols., Oxford, 1987, e.g. 2:496–7, 501, 687–8, 767. Cf. also the introduction by Wainwright, 1:46–7.

mands backed by sanctions. The mission of Christ was therefore at once to make clear to humanity what it had been fumbling for and, especially, to make it an effective force in people's lives by declaring the sanctions attaching to the moral law. However, Locke equally emphasizes that the revelation of the law itself, like all revelation, is subject to control by reason.[84] In other words, Locke's philosophical arguments in the *Essay* neatly left theoretical room for Christ to play exactly the practical role in the world that Socinian theology had allotted Him: to be the teacher of, more than the lawmaker for, humanity. It was clearly implied that His lessons would provide valuable guidance in the exercise of our natural duty-cum-right to impose our own preliminary sanctions, asserted in the second *Treatise*.

On the interpretation suggested here, it is possible that Locke worried about his arguments in the *Essay* and, not least, about the 'very strange Doctrine' in the (anonymous) second *Treatise*, not because they were weak but because they were so strong that they drastically reduced the role of a divine legislator, let alone of Revelation.

1.12 *Transitions to eighteenth-century Scottish moral thought*

Pufendorf's natural law theory and the great debate about the basic principles of natural law to which it had given rise were a European spectacle largely conveyed in Latin, yet the growing need to use the vernacular became a significant factor in the development of the doctrines under debate.[85] In the French- and English-speaking worlds, the mediation by the Huguenot refugee Jean Barbeyrac was of particular importance. Barbeyrac provided grand editions and French translations not only of Pufendorf but also of Grotius and Cumberland, in which he presented most of the European debate and gave a strongly Lockean slant to the natural law he himself wanted to reinforce.[86] The

84 *Reasonableness of Christianity*, pp. 138–47.

85 For apposite case-studies of the problems involved in the translation of natural law into the vernacular, see M. J. Silverthorne, 'Civil society and state, law and rights: Some Latin terms and their translation in the natural jurisprudence tradition', in *Acta Conventus Neo-Latini Toronotonensis* (Medieval and Renaissance Texts and Studies), Binghamton, NY, 1991, pp. 677–87.

86 Pufendorf, *Les devoirs de l'homme et du citoyen, tels qu'ils lui sont prescrits par la loi naturelle*, trans. J. Barbeyrac, Amsterdam, 1706, and *Le droit de la nature et des gens, ou système général des principes les plus importants de la morale, de la jurisprudence, et de la politique*, trans. J. Barbeyrac, 2 vols., Amsterdam, 1707; Grotius, *Le droit de la guerre et de la paix*, trans. J. Barbeyrac, 2 vols., Amsterdam, 1724; Cumberland, *Traité philosophique des loix naturelles*, trans. J. Barbeyrac, Amsterdam, 1744. Cf. also Meylan, *Barbeyrac*; Moore, 'Natural law and the Pyrrhonian controversy'; and S. C. Othmer,

French editions of Grotius and Pufendorf subsequently became the basis for English ones that had significant influence in the English-speaking world, especially in Scotland.[87] It was Barbeyrac more than anyone who streamlined the natural jurisprudential debate from Grotius onwards and delivered it to the eighteenth century as a coherently developing tradition, which was the most important modern school of moral thought and which had as a primary objective to combat modern scepticism, especially that of Pierre Bayle.[88]

In addition to Barbeyrac's impact on the two Glasgow thinkers Gershom Carmichael and Francis Hutcheson, there were many other links between the natural law doctrines of the seventeenth and early eighteenth centuries and British, especially Scottish, moral thought during the Enlightenment.[89] Most of these have been but little explored, but we can here only mention two natural lawyers whose importance in Scottish thought is discussed in more detail in subsequent chapters. The first is Johann Gottlieb Heineccius (or Heinecke), who, on the basis of a modified voluntarism in the Pufendorfian–Thomasian tradition – though he also expressed much sympathy with Cocceji's theocratic version of voluntarism – most effectively systematized the tripartite du-

---

Berlin und die Verbreitung des Naturrechts in Europa. Kultur- und sozialgeschichtliche Studien zu Jean Barbeyracs Pufendorf-Übersetzungen und eine Analyse seiner Leserschaft (Veröffentlichungen der historischen Kommission zu Berlin beim Friedrich-Meinecke-Institut der Freien Universität Berlin, Bd. 30), Berlin, 1970.

87 Grotius, *The Rights of War and Peace*; Pufendorf, *The Whole Duty of Man According to the Law of Nature.* The fourth edition, with the notes of Mr. Barbeyrac . . . , London, 1716, and *The Law of Nature and Nations.* There had been earlier English editions of Grotius and of the shorter Pufendorf. Cf. also D. Forbes, *Hume's Philosophical Politics*, Cambridge, UK, 1975, ch. 1; same, 'Natural law and the Scottish Enlightenment', in *The Origins and Nature of the Scottish Enlightenment*, ed. R.H. Campbell and A.S. Skinner, Edinburgh, 1982; Haakonssen, 'Natural law and the Scottish Enlightenment'; H. Medick, *Naturzustand und Naturgeschichte der bürgerlichen Gesellschaft. Die Ursprünge der bürgerlichen Sozialtheorie als Geschichtsphilosophie und Sozialwissenschaft bei Samuel Pufendorf, John Locke und Adam Smith*, Göttingen, 1973; Moore and Silverthorne, 'Carmichael and the natural jurisprudence tradition in eighteenth-century Scotland'; same, 'Natural sociability and natural rights in the moral philosophy of Gershom Carmichael'. For France and the French-speaking world, see esp. Derathé, *Rousseau*; A. Dufour, *Le Mariage dans l'école romande du droit naturel au XVIIIe siècle*, Geneva, 1976; and Meylan, *Barbeyrac*.

88 Barbeyrac, 'Historical and critical account of the science of morality', in Pufendorf, *Law of Nature*, pp. 1–75; cf. Moore, 'Natural law and Pyrrhonian controversy', and Tim Hochstrasser, 'Conscience and reason: The natural law theory of Jean Barbeyrac', *Historical Journal*, 36 (1993), 289–308.

89 In addition to the studies already mentioned, see, for an imaginative study of natural law and utilitarianism, J. Hruschka, 'The greatest happiness principle and other early German anticipations of utilitarian theory', *Utilitas*, 3 (1991), 165–77.

ties (to God, oneself, and others). This system was widely taught and used in Scottish classrooms and by Scottish jurists, as we shall see. The other important point about Heineccius to be foreshadowed here is that George Turnbull's translation of the German author's chief natural law work was central to the attempt to synthesize the jurisprudential and the civic humanist branches of the classical tradition.

Although Heineccius's wide-ranging text-book system was as modern as conventional wisdom could allow one to be in 1740, when nobody was reading Hume's *Treatise on Human Nature*, Samuel von Cocceji must have appeared to many to be a blast from the past. As will be shown in a subsequent chapter, he nevertheless gave the future a cue. Cocceji started from the ideas of his father, Heinrich von Cocceji, and, indeed, in his early work it is impossible to be entirely sure what is his and what the father's.[90] They both taught a starkly theocratic natural law doctrine, according to which God's will is the only true and adequate principle of natural law because God has indisputable maker's right over his creation, because all precepts of natural law can be deduced from this source, and because the moral faculties by which we grasp this principle are part of what God willed in creation.[91] It was a doctrine directed both against orthodox Lutheranism's idea of the Adamite *homo integer* as the reality from which natural law could be deduced and against the secular, Pufendorfian idea that natural law could be deduced from the rational-social nature of humanity. The latter issue made quite a stir when Samuel von Cocceji presented his dissertation to his father, who was also his *Doktorvater*. The central voluntaristic thesis of Samuel von Cocceji's arguments was immediately attacked by Leibniz with arguments similar to those employed in his more famous onslaught on Pufendorf, which we considered earlier, and this again led to a reply from Samuel von Cocceji.[92] Subsequently the younger Cocceji expounded and developed the parental natural law theory into an immensely interesting rights theory which seems to have been of some significance to Adam Smith.[93]

90   For details of the two Cocceji, see ch. 4, sect. 2.

91   Samuel Cocceji, *Tractatus juris gentium de principio juris naturalis unico, vero et adaequato*, Part I, quaest, ii, paras, 6–7. Part I is a republication of his dissertation from 1699, while Part II contains the reply to Pufendorf and other critics; see note 57 to this chapter.

92   See note 57 to this chapter.

93   The all-important work is Samuel von Cocceji, *Novum systema jurisprudentiae naturalis et romanae*, Berlin, 1740, known in another edition as *Elementa justitiae naturalis et romanae*. This work was then absorbed into the five hundred folio pages of his *Introductio ad Henrici L. B. de Cocceji . . . Grotium Illustratum . . .* , Halle, 1748, where it is the last of his twelve essays introducing his father's four-volume *Grotius Illustratus*. The first three volumes of the latter contain not only the elder Cocceji's

1.13 Conclusion

The history of natural law theory is to a significant degree a story of the continuities in moral thought. By the same token it accounts for the framework within which innovation took place. By the early years of the eighteenth century, natural law was established as the most important form of academic moral philosophy in most of Protestant Europe – Germany, the Netherlands, Switzerland, Scandinavia – and it was fast gaining ground in Scotland, in the academies of the rational Dissenters in England, and, eventually, in the North American colleges.[94] As the 'core curriculum' in practical philosophy, natural law became the seed-bed for new academic disciplines, notably political economy, and for political reform, especially law reform in Germany. Seventeenth-century natural law had received much of its inspiration from the need to settle confessional and colonial conflicts, and its eighteenth-century successors produced recognizably modern systems of the law of nations in response to great European wars. Seen in this perspective, it is hardly surprising that the theoretical aspects of natural law should continue to be a prominent part of philosophical endeavour.

The great questions which late seventeenth-century natural law theory, especially that of Pufendorf and Locke, had stated so forcefully were, in effect, the questions of in what sense, and to what extent, morals could be accounted for as a human construct without lapsing into 'scepticism', that is, relativism. This sent moral philosophers in two directions, often at the same time. On the one hand, they sought out moral powers in individual human nature, which, whether in the shape of moral sense, conscience, or reason, were both veridical and motivating. On the other hand, they traced the evidence for the collective effects of such moral powers in the moral institutions of humankind, ranging from money or the family to civil society or the international community. When interpreted in terms of Providence, the collective evidence certified the veridicity of the moral powers. This teleological or providential naturalism formed the mainstream of Enlightenment moral philosophy and was the basis for its 'scientific' approach to morals and its institutions. But when the sense of purpose was lost to the criticism of a Hume and a Smith, providential naturalism turned into the natural history of civil society, and the veridicality

---

extensive commentary on Grotius but also a great deal of material from the son's hand. The fourth volume is a significant compilation, with commentary by the younger Cocceji on Grotius's *Mare liberum,* Selden's *Mare clausum,* and a dozen related works. Cf. Chapter 4 in this volume.

94 It was, at times at least, practised with some distinction at Cambridge, and it had a significant impact in parts of Catholic Europe.

of the moral faculty was reduced to the question of what was minimally required for the existence of social life. This question was answered by a theory of negative justice harking back to Grotius's idea of
perfect rights, which was revived without appreciation of its paternity
in the astonishing theory of the younger Cocceji. Such ideas were,
however, exceptions in a sea of Christian–Stoic or neo-Aristotelian
teleology, in which rights remained derivative powers in the service of
the duties imposed by natural law. Within this framework it was next
to impossible to reach a philosophically coherent idea of the rights of
man – let alone woman – as the primary feature of moral agency. In so
far as it eventually was reached, it was via a notion of autonomy or
self-legislation, which amounted to the philosophical, if not the historical, death of natural law thinking proper. The following essays explore
these themes.

2

Natural law and moral realism: The civic humanist synthesis in Francis Hutcheson and George Turnbull

2.1 *Interpreting Scottish moral philosophy*

The following essays attempt to draw a number of connecting lines between Scottish moral thought in the eighteenth century and the history of European natural law theory. The latter is, however, as we have seen in the first essay, a less than uniform tradition. Protestant natural law theory in the century after Hugo Grotius was sufficiently multifarious that any attempt to use it, without differentiation, as a key – let alone *the* key – to the moral thought of the Scottish Enlightenment must lead to ungainly trimming. Furthermore, it is only when we attend to the differences and the fundamental debates within modern natural jurisprudence that we shall be able to appreciate how different kinds of natural law could be combined with ideas apparently foreign to the jurisprudential tradition, such as the notions of virtue, character, or quality of personality, which were central to the humanism of neo-republicanism and the evolving culture of politeness.

In some earlier essays I have sketched the way in which the division between a theory of subjective natural rights which must be traced partially to Grotius, and a Pufendorfian theory of natural law and natural duties, finds a kind of extension in Scottish moral thought in the eighteenth century.[1] David Hume's and Adam Smith's theory of justice as a negative virtue, sharply different from and holding cognitive, moral, and political priority over the rest of morality, distances

---

1   K. Haakonssen, 'Hugo Grotius and the history of political thought', *Political Theory*, 13 (1985), 239–65; same, 'Natural law and the Scottish Enlightenment', in *Man and Nature,* ed. D.H. Jory and J.C. Stewart-Robertson (Proceedings of the Canadian Society for Eighteenth-Century Studies, IV, Edmonton, 1985) pp. 47–80; same, 'Moral philosophy and natural law: From the Cambridge Platonists to the Scottish Enlightenment', *Political Science*, 40 (1988), 97–110; same, 'Natural jurisprudence in the Scottish Enlightenment: Summary of an interpretation', in *Enlightenment, Rights and Revolution,* ed. D.N. MacCormick and Z. Bankowski, Aberdeen, 1989, pp. 36–49.

them from the mainstream of moral philosophy among their contemporaries.[2] This division is certainly not in all cases and all respects a simple and neat one, nor by any means the only one, but it is nevertheless a fundamental feature of the moral thought of the Scottish Enlightenment.

The mainstream of Scottish moral philosophy in the eighteenth century I take to be a basically cognitivist and realist tradition. It stretches from Francis Hutcheson and George Turnbull via Lord Kames, Adam Ferguson, Thomas Reid, and the Common Sense philosophers, to Dugald Stewart and his circle; and it forms the philosophical backbone of more popular moralizing by enlightened clergymen and others, such as the group of 'moderate literati' now so well explored.[3] Though exhibiting variations in moral psychology, epistemology, and ontology, as well as theology, these thinkers generally claimed that mankind's potential for moral knowledge has an extent and a certainty quite beyond that allowed by Hume and Smith, and they took this to have important political implications. These range from Hutcheson's and Turnbull's more or less Harringtonian republicanism, via Reid's eventual resignation in the face of the utopian implications of his moral thought, to Stewart's historicization of this utopianism. Just beyond, but with clear connections, lies James Mill's replacement of the march of history with social engineering. In other words, this tradition subscribed to a view of morals which did not set the sorts of limits to the scope of politics which we find at the heart of Hume's and Smith's thinking.

The subsequent essays in this volume pursue this line of interpretation and deal with two obvious prima facie difficulties.

The first difficulty consists of the following pair of problems. In seeing Hume's theory of justice in the light of a theory of rights with roots in Grotius, I am in effect aligning the former with a theory which, in the seventeenth and early eighteenth centuries, was often assailed as a form of scholastic realism or essentialism – not least by Samuel Pufendorf. At the same time I may be seen as reinforcing the puzzlement which has often been expressed over the fact that Hume so studiously avoids the language of rights, a puzzle which may appear almost paradoxical when Hume's theory of justice is seen as leading to Smith's explicit theory of rights. But, as will become clear in the sequel, the concept of moral realism is complex, and it would not be surprising if, having used it, we should decide eventually to discard it, ladder-

2 See K. Haakonssen, *The Science of a Legislator: The Natural Jurisprudence of David Hume and Adam Smith*, Cambridge, UK, 1981.

3 R.B. Sher, *Church and University in the Scottish Enlightenment: The Moderate Literati of Edinburgh*, Princeton, 1985.

like, from our historical interpretations.[4] This may lend some flexibility to our understanding of the ontological implications of moral theories such as those of Grotius and Hume. In any case, the connection claimed here is limited[5] – not least because there is a good deal more to Grotius's theory of justice than his theory of rights.[6]

The second major difficulty I have referred to occurs on the other side of the divide by means of which I try to sort out some main lines in the moral thought of the Scottish Enlightenment. In claiming both that the mainstream of Scottish moral thought was, in our modern terms, cognitivist and realist and that it was significantly dependent upon a Pufendorfian natural jurisprudence, I must inevitably appear to be combining the incompatible. The heart of Pufendorf's theory is the notion of a law which institutes the moral realm by imposing duties upon agents possessed of free will. By contrast, the central concern of the moral realists is to show that there are moral values independent of any law. The crucial figure in this situation is Francis Hutcheson, volubly supported by George Turnbull.

2.2   Hutcheson: Voluntarism, realism, and egoism

It is incontrovertible that Hutcheson in his published work both criticizes the theory that morality is dependent upon law and expounds a system of natural jurisprudence which is largely derived from that of Pufendorf. It has, however, been argued with considerable force that Hutcheson never manages to integrate these two strands of his work – that he in fact presents two incompatible systems.[7] The first is that of his early work, published in the 1720s, in which he developed a moral theory which is realist and cognitivist in character. It is realist in maintaining that moral judgements have truth value; that there are facts about which some moral judgements are true; and that these facts

4   For a general defence of such apparent anachronism in the history of ideas, see the Introduction to the present volume.

5   See similarly D. Forbes, *Hume's Philosophical Politics*, Cambridge, UK, 1975, ch. 1.

6   See ch. 1, sect. 1.3, this volume, and R. Tuck, *Natural Rights Theories*, Cambridge, UK, 1979, ch. 3; same, *Philosophy and Government, 1572–1651*, Cambridge, UK, 1993, ch. 5.

7   James Moore, 'The two systems of Francis Hutcheson: On the origins of the Scottish Enlightenment', in *Studies in the Philosophy of the Scottish Enlightenment*, ed. M.A. Stewart, Oxford, 1990, pp. 37–59; same, 'Theological politics: A study of the reception of Locke's *Two Treatises of Government* in England and Scotland in the early eighteenth century', in *John Locke and/und Immanuel Kant*, ed. M.P. Thompson, Berlin, 1991, pp. 62–82 at pp. 78–80.

are the presence of certain qualities in persons, which cannot be reduced to subjective states of the person who judges. Hutcheson's theory is thus primarily concerned with qualities in persons, that is to say, virtues, which he considers to be natural to man. This is combined with a moral-sense cognitivism; that is, the idea that man is naturally supplied with a special moral sense which simultaneously approves or disapproves of, and occasions, the apprehension of moral qualities. Without committing himself to a doctrine of innate ideas, Hutcheson thus puts forward a moral theory according to which morals, in the sense of both sentiments and ideas, come naturally to man.[8]

This simple nucleus of ideas, around which a fairly elaborate moral and political theory is built, is critically aimed at a number of contemporary doctrines, the most important of which are the following. First, Hutcheson denies that post-lapsarian man is inherently sinful and that all apparent morality can be reduced to a more or less complicated function of this sinfulness. More particularly, he denies that man's moral institutions can be understood to arise from the prescriptions of an avenging God, whom his creatures follow in terror and in hope. It was exactly this kind of authoritarian voluntarism, legalism, and egoism that Hutcheson saw as the foundation of the natural jurisprudence of Pufendorf (and Locke) and that he rejected in his early works. Yet in his later works on morals he put forward a complete system of natural jurisprudence, which owes a good deal to Pufendorf and something to Locke. Not only that, but in a series of Latin text-books for his students he backed this second system of morals with a logic and a metaphysics which were entirely conventional in their dependence upon the sort of Augustinianism developed within reformed scholasticism in the Netherlands and Switzerland and imported into the Glasgow curriculum by Hutcheson's predecessor, Gershom Carmichael, and others.[9]

According to the two-systems thesis, it is an error to interpret this 'second system' as an integral part of Hutcheson's philosophical writing. Whereas the first system is Hutcheson's serious contribution to

8   This summary of Hutcheson's 'first system' is not Moore's but mine.

9   A small selection of Carmichael's central passages on natural law is to be found in Gershom Carmichael, *Supplements and Appendix to Samuel Pufendorf's 'De officio hominis et civis juxta legem naturalem libri duo . . .'*, ed. J.N. Lenhart, trans. C.H. Reeves, Cleveland OH (privately published), 1985. Concerning Carmichael, see J. Moore and M. Silverthorne, 'Gershom Carmichael and the natural jurisprudence tradition in eighteenth-century Scotland', in *Wealth and Virtue: The Shaping of Political Economy in the Scottish Enlightenment*, ed. I. Hont and M. Ignatieff, Cambridge, UK, 1983, pp. 73–87; and same, 'Natural sociability and natural rights in the moral philosophy of Gershom Carmichael', in *Philosophers of the Scottish Enlightenment*, ed. V. Hope, Edinburgh, 1984, pp. 1–12.

philosophy, the second system is largely pedagogical in intent, a conventional philosophy suited to the moral breaking in of youth and one which was acceptable to the academic, civil, and ecclesiastical authorities in Glasgow and in Scotland at the time. The interpretation of Hutcheson presented in the following pages is in fact headed in this allegedly erroneous direction, and we shall thus see whether we need to be quite so rigidly dualistic in our reading of him.

My main concern is with Hutcheson's moral thought, and I argue that it does manage to achieve a basic coherence between moral realism and natural law. Elsewhere I have related his attempted synthesis to a clear precedent, that of Richard Cumberland.[10] Here I am setting him against the background of the thinker who is traditionally seen as the main representative of voluntarist natural law, Samuel Pufendorf. However, while acknowledging that Pufendorf in one sense was a voluntarist and that Hutcheson saw him as such, we have already seen in Chapter 1 that in another sense one can easily see the German thinker as a realist. The purpose of this apparently perverse reading is twofold. I want to indicate that the problem situation Hutcheson faced was volatile and less than clear-cut and that his synthesis was closer to hand than might otherwise appear; and I want to maintain an awareness that a sharp separation between voluntarist constructivism and realism may eventually prove to be a hindrance rather than a help in the interpretation of early modern moral thought.

Once we appreciate the complex sense in which morality, according to Pufendorf, is 'imposed' upon a natural world that in itself is amoral, it becomes obvious that we cannot consider moral phenomena in any sense less real than physical nature in Pufendorf's theory. This is underlined by his nomenclature, according to which the elements of morals are *entia moralia*, by analogy with the *entia naturalia* of the material world. The whole purpose of the first couple of chapters in Pufendorf's major work is exactly to establish that morals are such an objective feature of God's creation that they can form the object of a properly scientific treatment. The fact that morals are created for man and thus contemporaneous with humankind does not in itself mean that they are less real than anything else in the finite creation. Pufendorf's concern is the origin and nature of an objective moral realm, not whether there is one or not. In this sense, at least, his discussion with Grotius and others may thus be seen as a discussion *within*, not *about*, moral realism. Both parties without doubt would subscribe to the following points, which, as I have implied earlier, may be taken to constitute

10 Haakonssen, 'Moral philosophy and natural law: The character and obligation of natural law according to Richard Cumberland', in *English Philosophy in the Age of Locke*, ed. M.A. Stewart, Oxford, forthcoming.

moral realism in the sense relevant to the present discussion – which is not to deny other possible senses of the phrase. These are, first, that moral judgements have truth value; second, that some moral judgements are true – that is, that there are facts about which moral judgements are true; third, that such facts in no sense of the term are reducible to subjective states, whether cognitive or affective, of the person judging morally about them.[11]

Although clearly Pufendorf's intention was to show that the reality or objectivity of moral objects could be compatible with a theological voluntarism and thus avoid what he saw as Grotius's essentialism, his solution, in the eyes of his successors, was beset with fundamental difficulties. The most important, as explained in Chapter 1, was that, by appearing to rest morality upon a voluntaristic theory of law, he was seen to run into problems concerning the moral status of this law itself, and his solution to these problems was considered to undermine his assertion of the objective reality of morals because it landed him in egoism. This was the end result of Leibniz's criticism of Pufendorf, and it was a point that in Scotland was pursued by Hutcheson's predecessor in Glasgow, Gershom Carmichael.[12]

Pufendorf's conclusion was that God's will is morally obligatory upon men because of the extraordinary good – not least their very existence as free beings – which God has bestowed upon them. The trouble with this argument was that it seemed to expose itself to a legitimate open question as to whether each man's own good is a moral good, and what lends it a moral quality. It is precisely this question which was implicitly posed by Pufendorf's successors, especially, as we shall see, by Hutcheson.

The point becomes much clearer when, in the second book of the *Law of Nature*, Pufendorf draws a distinction between the foundation of natural law as such and the basic law of nature derived from it. The former is each man's self-love and concern for himself. The egoistic *foundation* of morals, or natural law does not, however, imply that the basic law of nature, let alone all morality, is egoistic in character. For from the individual's egoism and his general weakness and natural needs follows his dependence upon his fellow men and hence the requirement to be sociable – which is the basic law of nature.[13] In other words, the bridge between our own good and that of others, and thus the basis for morals, is our natural weakness. Only when we contem-

---

11 The formulation of the first two points is indebted to G. Sayre-McCord, 'The many moral realisms', *Southern Journal of Philosophy*, 24 (1986), suppl., pp. 6–10.

12 See the studies by Moore and Silverthorne cited in note 9 to this chapter.

13 S. Pufendorf, *Of the Law of Nature and Nations*, ed. J. Barbeyrac, trans. B. Kennet, 5th ed., London, 1749, II.3.xiii–xv.

plate the goodness of God in creating us weak and interdependent, as well as egoistic, can we see that this goodness has a moral potential, namely our potential for creating moral institutions to make up for some of these weaknesses.

To a generation which was still shocked by Hobbes, this attempt to confine the effects of the alleged egoistic foundation of morals was less than persuasive; to the following generation which experienced the outrage of Mandeville, the need to maintain the reality of virtue against egoism as the paramount form of moral scepticism had simply become *the* fundamental problem of moral philosophy. Thus Hutcheson is quite prepared to acknowledge that when men act in accordance with Pufendorf's basic law of nature, their behaviour appears moral. The good produced is, however, a natural and not a moral good as long as the obligation to this pattern of behaviour is prudential rather than moral.[14] We shall return to this point later.

Furthermore, the link between a voluntaristic or law-based ethics and egoism had – whether rightly or wrongly – been strengthened by Locke's account in the second book of the *Essay Concerning Human Understanding*, as we saw in Chapter 1, and it is hardly surprising that such an ethics is invariably seen as egoistic by Hutcheson.[15] From beginning to end of his moral philosophical oeuvre, an important feature of his argumentative strategy is to show 'that we have Ideas of *Virtue* and *Vice*, abstractly from any *Law*, *Human* or *Divine*' and that these ideas are presupposed or implied by all 'Writers upon opposite Schemes, who deduce all Ideas of *Good* and *Evil* from the *private Advantage* of the *Actor*, or from Relation to a *Law* and its *Sanctions*, either known from *Reason* or *Revelation*'.[16] Further, that all attempts to reverse this order and make law basic to morals must end with a purely prudential obligation to this law, that is, an egoistic or self-interested foundation for morals, as we see especially in 'the definitions of *Puffendorf*, and of *Barbeyrac*'.[17]

The passage in Locke brings us to another point which it is reason-

---

14   See e.g. F. Hutcheson, *An Inquiry into the Original of our Ideas of Beauty and Virtue*, Dublin, 1725, p. 251; (unless otherwise indicated, I refer to the first ed. of the *Inquiry*). Also Hutcheson, *De naturali hominum socialitate oratio inauguralis*, Glasgow, 1730, p. 11; as trans. in Hutcheson, *Two Texts on Human Nature*, ed. and trans. T. Mautner, Cambridge, UK, 1993, pp. 134–5.

15   See Locke, *An Essay Concerning Human Understanding*, ed. P.H. Nidditch, Oxford, 1975, II.xxviii.5.

16   Hutcheson, *Inquiry*, pp. 249 and 247.

17   Hutcheson, *A Short Introduction to Moral Philosophy*, Glasgow, 1747, pp. 121–2. Cf. *Inquiry*, pp. 251 and 254–5; *A System of Moral Philosophy*, 2 vols., Glasgow, 1755, I, pp. 264ff.; and *An Essay on the Nature and Conduct of the Passions and Affections with Illustrations on the Moral Sense*, London, 1728, pp. 229–30.

able to see as part of Hutcheson's problem situation. Locke is saying that morality falls into the category of complex ideas called 'relations'; morality is a 'relation' of actions to rules or laws.[18] This argument has its problems, and those are problems which may be seen also to beset Pufendorf's moral theory.

Although Pufendorf, as noted earlier, talks of the furniture of the moral realm as 'entities', he is quite explicit that the similarity to physical things is purely analogical. In stricter metaphysical terms, the moral entities are *modi* of the substance 'human beings'.[19] However, from his whole account it is quite obvious that the only way in which human beings are, as it were, 'modified' by moral 'entities' is that they are subjected to some law and, ultimately, to the law of nature. This is the only way these so-called *modi* can be described. This description should, though, make it apparent that the basic ontological category in Pufendorf's moral theory in fact is that of *relation*, namely that of the relations between persons and laws, especially the law of nature. Apart from being an obvious inference from the text itself, it would certainly lie near to hand for subsequent thinkers like Hutcheson, who read Pufendorf with an empiricist epistemology in mind.

However, if one subscribes to a Lockean theory of knowledge, as Hutcheson did, and if one takes morals to be a relation between persons and laws, as we have seen Locke do explicitly and Pufendorf by implication, then one runs into the following problem. Both 'person' and 'law' are, in Lockean terms, mixed modes, but since mixed modes are made 'arbitrarily', the conclusion must be that the relations themselves, and thus morals, are 'arbitrary'.[20] It is not part of my present design to discuss Locke's attempt to get around this conclusion.[21] It is possible that he took 'arbitrary' to mean simply 'voluntary', but even then the doctrine would have appeared as pure Mandevillian scepticism to Hutcheson's generation.

We have sufficiently established some of the central elements in a problem situation, against the background of which a moral realism like the one ascribed to Hutcheson by recent commentators makes a good deal of sense.[22] The relevant problems may be summarized in the

18   *Essay,* II.xxviii.6–16.   19   Pufendorf, *Law of Nature,* I.1.vi.

20   I am here indebted to W. Leidhold, *Ethik und Politik bei Francis Hutcheson,* Munich, 1985, pp. 57–8.

21   But see Leidhold, *Ethik und Politik,* pp. 58ff.

22   D.F. Norton, 'Hutcheson's moral sense theory reconsidered', *Dialogue,* 13 (1974), 3–23; same, 'Hutcheson on perception and moral perception', *Archiv für Geschichte der Philosophie,* 59 (1977), 181–97; same, *David Hume: Common-Sense Moralist, Sceptical Metaphysician,* Princeton, 1982, ch.2; same, 'Hutcheson's moral realism', *Journal of the History of Philosophy,* 23 (1985), 392–418. See also, though more indistinctly, Leidhold, *Ethik und Politik,* ch. 4, sect. 2. This reading of Hutcheson is

following manner. Modern philosophy's criticism of what was seen as scholastic essentialism had made it difficult to see how morality could be a matter of qualities in persons. As far as natural jurisprudence is concerned, this is clearly exemplified by Pufendorf's criticism of Grotius. Nevertheless, Pufendorf's attempted solution was clearly intended to maintain a kind of realist framework, indicated by his language of 'entities' and 'modes', and the difficulties he ran into must be seen within this framework. It is precisely because they appeared to endanger a realist view of morals that they were perceived as problems. The traditional dilemma facing a voluntarist, law-based ethics was considered fatal. One of its horns appeared to leave morality without any other foundation than, at best, an infinite regress of justification, which was no foundation at all (except within a mitigated scepticism which seeks no ultimate justifying ground), while the other horn would gore morality by reducing it to mere prudence or egoism.

Furthermore, Gershom Carmichael's attempt to solve this problem by reducing the basis of morals to a divine injunction of love had problems of a different dimension. For by making love a matter of divine prescription, it made natural theology fundamental to morals, as Carmichael himself strongly emphasises.[23] It is one of the most important points in Hutcheson that he attempts a reversion of this order of priority, in the sense that some sort of morality is possible without a theological starting-point and that a theological perspective on morality is, so to say, the *completion* of morality.[24] In order to do so, he had to show that morality is an empirically ascertainable part of the world, and, as we have seen, this excluded the possibility that morals could be relational in character. This threw him back on a renewed attempt to show that morality was a matter of qualities in persons, but empirically ascertainable qualities. This is, I submit, the philosophical core of the turn to a language of *virtues* in Scottish moral philosophy.

2.3   *Hutcheson's moral realism and cognitivism*

In the present context there is no reason for rehearsing Hutcheson's efforts to show that disinterested behaviour is an empirical fact or for giving a detailed account of his theory of the mental powers by which

---

controversial; for criticism, see K. Winkler, 'Hutcheson's alleged realism', *Journal of the History of Philosophy*, 23 (1985), 179–94.

23   See Moore and Silverthorne, 'Carmichael and the natural jurisprudence tradition', p. 78.

24   The two points are to be found in several places, but see esp. sect. VI of the *Illustrations* (*Essay of the Passions*, pp. 301ff.) and, for the latter point, *Short Introduction*, pp. 101–2.

we judge such behaviour to be moral. This has been done by a succession of scholars with great thoroughness and analytical sharpness, and I have nothing to add to it.[25] All I need to establish here is that for Hutcheson our putative moral judgements are in fact real judgements; that the putative objects of such judgements are in fact real objects; and that these objects are empirically ascertainable features of human nature. Even on these points I can be brief, for, although his perspective is different, another recent commentator has done the basic work.[26] The issues can in fact be settled by examining a few central passages from Hutcheson himself:

> That we may discern more distinctly the Difference between *moral Perceptions* and others, let us consider, when we taste a pleasant Fruit, we are conscious of Pleasure; when another tastes it, we only conclude or form an Opinion that he enjoys Pleasure; and, abstracting from some previous *Good-Will* or *Anger,* his enjoying this Pleasure is to us a Matter wholly indifferent, raising no new *Sentiment* or *Affection.* But when we are under the Influence of a virtuous Temper, and thereby engaged in virtuous Actions, we are not always conscious of any Pleasure, nor are we only pursuing private Pleasures as will appear hereafter: 'tis only by *reflex Acts* upon our Temper and Conduct that we enjoy the Delights of Virtue. When also we judge the Temper of another to be virtuous, we do not necessarily imagine him *then* to enjoy Pleasure, tho' we know *Reflection* will give it to him: And farther, our Apprehension of his virtuous Temper raises Sentiments of *Approbation, Esteem* or *Admiration,* and the Affection of *Good-will* toward him. The Quality approved by our moral Sense is conceived to reside in the Person approved, and to be a Perfection and Dignity in him: *Approbation* of another's Virtue is not conceived as making the Approver happy, or virtuous, or worthy, tho' 'tis attended with some small Pleasure. Virtue is then called *amiable* or *lovely,* from its raising *Good-will* or *Love* in Spectators toward the Agent; and not from the Agent's perceiving the virtuous Temper to be advantageous to him, or desiring to obtain it under that View. A virtuous Temper is called *good* or *beatifick,* not that it is always attended with Pleasure in the Agent; much less that some small Pleasure attends the Contemplation of it in the Approver: but from this, that every Spectator is persuaded that the *reflex Acts* of the virtuous Agent upon his own Temper will give him the highest Pleasures. The admired Quality is conceived as the Perfection of the Agent, and such a one as is distinct from the *Pleasure* either in the Agent or the Approver; tho' 'tis a sure Source of Pleasure to the Agent. The Perception of the Approver,

25　In addition to the works of Norton and Leidhold, see J.D. Bishop, 'The Moral Philosophy of Francis Hutcheson', Ph.D. thesis, University of Edinburgh, 1977; W.T. Blackstone, *Francis Hutcheson and Contemporary Ethical Theory,* Athens, GA, 1965; H. Jensen, *Motivation and the Moral Sense in Francis Hutcheson's Ethical Theory,* The Hague, 1971; B. Peach, introduction to Hutcheson, *Illustrations on the Moral Sense,* ed. Peach, Cambridge, MA, 1971; D.D. Raphael, *The Moral Sense,* London, 1947.

26　Leidhold, *Ethik und Politik,* pp. 146–64.

tho' attended with Pleasure, plainly represents something quite distinct from this Pleasure; even as the Perception of *external Forms* is attended with Pleasure, and yet represents something distinct from this Pleasure. This may prevent many Cavils upon this Subject.[27]

Hutcheson might well be hopeful that this passage would prevent further cavils, for he could hardly have been more explicit. Moral perception is *not* a subjective affective experience; and moral judgements are thus not simply the expressions of such experiences. Whether we make moral judgements of our own behaviour or that of others, our moral perception and thus our moral judgement are explicitly *representative*, and thus either true or false. Further, moral judgements are emphatically representative of something quite distinct from the pleasures which moral behaviour may and, upon reflection, will occasion in agent as well as spectator.

The question is now what this something is which our moral judgement represents or which makes it true or false. At one level Hutcheson is quite clear about this. It is love or benevolence which 'excites toward the Person in whom we observe it' an 'Esteem, or Perception of moral Excellence'.[28] Benevolence, which is one of the two basic forms of human motivation, self-love being the other, is the quality of human nature which forms the object of moral judgement.

For a Lockean theory of knowledge like Hutcheson's, however, this solution to the problem of moral ontology does give rise to an obvious epistemological problem, namely, that of how we can know the motivation of other people and thus distinguish genuinely moral behaviour from counterfeits which spring from self-interest.[29] It has rightly been suggested that Hutcheson's intention is that we find the proper object of moral judgement by the use of reason. First we identify moral-looking behaviour by calculating the consequences of the action in question in accordance with the well-known 'greatest happiness' principle. Second, we try to reconstruct the motivation for such behaviour by drawing on our own experience – a point that was to be of particular interest to Hume and Smith:

> We judge of other rational Agents by our selves. The human Nature is a lovely Form; we are all conscious of some morally good Qualitys and Inclinations in our selves, how partial and imperfect they may be; we presume the same of every thing in human Form, nay of every living Creature. (*Inquiry*, pp. 131–2)

27 This passage is quoted from the fourth edition of the *Inquiry* (1738), pp. 129–31; it was first added in the third edition (1729), pp. 128–30.

28 *Inquiry*, p. 108.

29 Here and in what follows I am indebted to Leidhold, *Ethik und Politik*, pp. 155–6.

Finally, and more particularly, we seek out any available evidence that the agent may have had to surmount his self-interest in order to behave morally, though, while this is a sufficient reason for judging the motivation to be benevolent, it is not a necessary condition.[30]

Once reason has performed these preparatory tasks, which would bear some comparison with those allotted it by Hume and Smith, the moral sense has as good a chance as we can hope for of forming an adequate perception of the moral quality of the agent concerned. Whereas reason prepares moral judgements by establishing the subject of such judgements, namely the (likely) motivation to moral behaviour in each particular case, the moral sense perceives the moral quality of this motivation, when it approves or disapproves of the motivation, and this perception occasions an idea of the moral quality.

Unfortunately Hutcheson's text does not allow us to say much more about the nature of moral qualities and their perception and understanding. There are two necessary conditions for an action to have a good moral quality; its motivation must call forth a perceptible emotive reaction of love in observers suitably prepared through observation and reasoning; and its motivation must be benevolent, that is, tending towards actions that contribute to the over-all happiness of the moral creation, the 'moral system'. The correlation between moral quality and moral judgement therefore is an objective one, for it is not the subjective feeling that 'makes it true' (respective, false). But similarly the moral quality is not necessarily and generally esteemed *because* it contributes to the over-all happiness; only few have the capacity to judge in this way. Or in other words, the *motivation* for moral judgement is in a sense subjective and emotive, but that does not prevent the resulting moral judgement from having independent truth value. The grand aim of Hutchesonian moral education was to make a clear-sighted regard for the general happiness the *motivation* for more and more moral assessment.[31]

The interpretation offered here seems the most obvious way of reconciling Hutcheson's frequent 'subjectivist' language with his obvious assumption of objective truth in matters of morals. And it seems to be the most obvious way of explaining the stability of our moral ideas in

---

30 See *Inquiry*, p. 171, and Leidhold, *Ethik und Politik*, pp. 162–3. Concerning the role of reason in Hutcheson's theory of moral judgement, see also Norton's summary in 'Hutcheson's moral realism', pp. 404–5.

31 David Norton has ascribed to Hutcheson a theory of concomitant ideas in moral perception in analogy with those in external perception, and this has caused some controversy. See Winkler, 'Hutcheson's alleged realism', and Leidhold, *Ethik und Politik*, pp. 156–7, note 79, and Norton's answer in 'Hutcheson's moral realism', pp. 405–11. I do not think Hutcheson's texts allow a decision in the dispute.

parallel with Hutcheson's Lockean assumption of the stability of our ideas of the secondary qualities in external sensation. What is more, it integrates the relentless teleological rhetoric and makes it do some central work in his moral theory. This again points to a solution to the puzzlingly quick transformation of the scientific status of morals. Within a generation or so, 'the science of morals' had been transformed from Pufendorf's and Locke's demonstrative science into the Scots' empirical one. It seems to be commonly assumed that the Scots simply meant the empirical investigation of human nature. This reading is, I think, far too dominated by Hume's subversive and perverse use of language in the *Treatise*. While the investigation of human nature is certainly part of the Hutchesonian project, we have to understand 'the science of morals' in him and his like to be the mapping of the 'great system' of humanity, that is, of the moral community of which human nature is capable and for which it is *meant*. This is one of the significant implications of the rejection of the voluntarists' idea of morals-by-imposition and the Hutchesonian idea of natural or inherent goodness. The former was taken over and completely transformed by Hume and Smith in their 'secular' – meaning here the denial of even natural religion – historico-conventionalist theories, while the latter forms the backbone of the rest of Scottish moral thought.

2.4   *The political ambiguity of Hutcheson's moral theory*

From what has been said in the preceding section, it should be clear that moral perception, and hence moral judgement, are inherently fallible.[32] This fallibility in moral judgement follows directly from the combination of a Lockean theory of knowledge – in this case a theory about our knowledge of other minds – with a moral-sense cognitivism and a moral realism according to which the objects of moral judgement are the motives behind moral behaviour.[33]

The fallibility of moral judgement is of crucial importance for our

32   'In most Cases it is impossible for Men to know how far their Fellows are influenc'd by the one or the other of these Principles', i.e., self-love or benevolence (*Inquiry*, p. 130; cf. p. 171).

33   It may be suggested in passing that this fallibilism concerning moral judgement might be a fruitful point of departure if we were to seek an understanding of Hume's and Smith's moral ontology. For, in order to show how it is that, despite such fallibility, we can have a *common* moral world – a world so common that Hume could maintain that the ordinary person's moral judgement on the whole is *in*fallible – they had to construct a theory of how the objects of fallible moral judgements, i.e. other people's motives, in themselves are shaped by the same kind of preparatory reasoning which enables the observer to judge morally. This was the theory of the search through sympathy for the impartial standpoint.

understanding of some basic features of Hutcheson's political theory. First of all, since there is no certain way of settling that any man (in contrast to God) genuinely intends the good of others, there is no natural right in one to rule over others. Such a right has to be constructed by means of the consent of all concerned. Furthermore, it is not only the basis but also the form of civil society which must be shaped by the fallibility of our moral judgement; since we cannot have certainty about other men's moral judgement, we must rely on our own. As Hutcheson explains, in reference to 'the existence, goodness, and providence of God, and all the social duties of life, and the motives to them':

> Every rational creature has a right to judge for it self in these matters: and as men must assent according to the evidence that appears to them, and cannot command their own assent in opposition to it, this right is plainly unalienable: it cannot be matter of contract; nor can there be any right of compulsion as to opinions, conveyed to or vested in any magistrate. He can have no right to extort mens sentiments, or to inflict penalties upon their not agreeing to the opinions he thinks just; as such penalties are no evidences to convince the judgement, and can only produce hypocrisy. (*System,* II, p. 311)

Moral fallibility and the consequent necessity of self-judgement constitute the principles of what we may call the 'restraining' aspect of Hutcheson's politics. It is because of them that political power should not be concentrated but, rather, distributed in a Harringtonian balanced system; that there should be a comparatively wide religious toleration, freedom of opinion and of the press.[34]

Hutcheson's moral philosophy is, however, politically Janus-faced. At the same time as his moral fallibilism, which followed from his moral realism, is restrictive upon the exercise of political power, his realism is politically expansive in the following way. Morality is ultimately a matter not of maximizing happiness but of doing so intentionally, that is, with such maximization as the leading motive. This I take to be one of the ways in which a utilitarian moral theory is distinguished from what, drawing on theological language and Hutcheson's own usage,[35] may be called a 'beatific' moral theory; the latter is con-

---

34 *System,* II, pp. 310ff. For this side of Hutcheson's politics, see D. Winch, *Adam Smith's Theory of Politics: An Essay in Historiographical Revision,* Cambridge, UK, 1978, ch. 3; C. Robbins, '"When it is that colonies may turn independent"', *William and Mary Quarterly,* 3rd ser., 11 (1954), 214–51; same, *The Eighteenth-Century Commonwealthman,* Cambridge, MA, 1959, pp. 185–96. Also Leidhold, *Ethik und Politik,* chs. 9–10.

35 See the long quotation at note 27 to this chapter. [*Note:* citations saying '*at* note 27' mean 'in the text, near note 27'; citations saying '*in* note 6' mean 'in the text of note 6'.]

cerned with the creation of happiness as a consequence of the beatitude of its agent's soul. Consequently, our individual as well as our collective efforts, especially our political and institutional arrangements, must be centrally concerned with the motivation to moral behaviour, or, in other words, with virtue. This is precisely what we find in Hutcheson's politics. Civil society is essentially an institution for the moral improvement of mankind, and it is only limited in this regard to the extent that our moral fallibility, as indicated earlier, puts such improvement outside our reach. Subject to this restriction, civil society exists not just to maximize happiness but to inculcate the benevolent or beatific motivation of the citizenry. Thus morality and its extension in religion must be taught, partly by instruction, not least instruction of public-minded teachers and writers like Hutcheson himself, partly by the practice of participation by the citizens at large in the civil, the military, and the productive life of the commonwealth. In other words, the qualities which form the objects of moral judgements in Hutcheson's realism, far from constituting a timeless, Platonic realm, are historically conditioned, in the sense that they can be expanded by suitable institutional arrangements.

2.5 *Natural jurisprudence in Hutcheson's system*

(a) *Natural law and the common good*

If Hutcheson's moral theory is basically a theory of virtue, how can he accommodate a system of natural jurisprudence and, especially, a theory of rights, as he clearly attempts to do? We may approach this issue by considering the difficulties which a recent commentator has found in Hutcheson, and in the following passage in particular:

> Precepts of the law of nature . . . are deemed immutable and eternal, because some rules, or rather the dispositions which gave origin to them, and in which they are founded, must always tend to the general good, and the contrary to the general detriment, in such a system of creatures as we are. (*System*, I, p. 273)[36]

Hutcheson's supposed difficulties in combining moral sense and natural law are, it has been suggested, particularly evident here, where

> the expressions 'rules' and 'dispositions' appear next to each other: Hutcheson cannot make up his mind whether natural law consists of rules or dispositions. He himself seems rather inclined to interpret them as dispositions. That would, however, make natural law identical with the divinely created natural order, which is subject to immutable and eternal laws of

36 (Mis)quoted in Leidhold, *Ethik und Politik*, p. 210.

nature. Does the teleological concept of nature in the end turn out to be mechanistic?[37]

Whether or not there is some tension in Hutcheson between a teleological and a mechanical conception of nature, it is hardly to be found here. Hutcheson is not saying that the laws of nature may be seen either as rules or as dispositions but, rather, that it consists of rules which have their origin and foundation in certain dispositions. These dispositions are our moral abilities, essentially our capacity for benevolent motivation, and the law of nature is 'founded' in these because they 'must always tend to the general good . . . in such a system of creatures as we are'. The reasoning behind this is briefly as follows. Our moral experience will show that individual moral phenomena, that is, particular moral dispositions as judged by our moral sense, tend towards the general good, namely, towards a moral system of humanity in which the human moral potential is fully realised, that is, in which happiness is maximized intentionally, or in which all agents are effectively beatific. Our experience of this potential moral system of all humanity will, through a reasoning process analogous to the one which prepares our moral judgement of men, lead us to the conclusion that there is a superior moral motivation behind this system, namely the divine benevolence, which our moral sense will judge in the same way as it judges the moral qualities of men. In this way piety towards God is the completion of our moral life rather than its starting-point, though natural religion of course underwrites our natural moral ability.[38]

We may see the point in a different perspective. Having gained the insight that the moral system of humanity is not simply the aggregate of men's individual moral endeavours but in itself a moral good, because it flows as a whole from God's moral motivation, we morally approve of, that is, feel an obligation to, the rules which our reason works out to be God's prescriptions for how to realize the system.[39] In this way the moral sense is the basis for natural law and thus Hutcheson's means of solving the previously mentioned dispute on this point between Pufendorf and Leibniz, as he himself points out.[40]

(b) *Natural law and natural rights*

The consequences of seeing natural religion as the connecting link between the moral sense and natural law, however, go much further

37 Translated from Leidhold, *Ethik und Politik*, p. 211.

38 *Inquiry*, pp. 272–6; *Illustrations*, sect. 6; *Short Introduction*, pp. 59–60, 72–7, 100–1, 112; *System*, I, pp. 69–70, 168ff., 239.

39 *Short Introduction*, p. 112; *System*, I, pp. 264–5; *Inquiry*, 4th ed., pp. 267–77 (based on the recasting in the second ed.).

40 *System*, I, p. 264; and see ch. 1, sect. 1.8, this volume.

than this. Just as the concept of the common good, which ultimately must be understood in natural religious terms, is the foundation for natural law, so it is from this that natural rights must be derived. We may approach this point in the following way.

Once we have realized that the general good of humanity and its constituent parts are a moral good, in the strict sense that it flows from a motive judged to be morally good by our moral sense, we must reckon with the possibility that goods which are not perceived as morally relevant by the moral sense nevertheless have a moral aspect by being part of God's intention, that is, part of the common good. The typical and most important example is the pleasure derived from the satisfaction of our various needs. The actions involved here may often be considered morally neutral by the moral sense. Yet the fact that such actions have enough potential satisfaction in them to make them the object of the agent's intention means that they have a prima facie claim to be contributors to the sum of good in God's creation. Further investigation may, of course, reveal this not to be the case, but, in the absence of such evidence, any action which carries with it some pleasure, however modest, must be given some sort of moral position. In this way even actions which to the moral sense appear morally neutral gain a moral status as rights,

> as in fact it is for the good of the system that every desire and sense natural to us, even those of the lowest kinds, should be gratified as far as their gratification is consistent with the nobler enjoyments, and in a just subordination to them; there seems a natural notion of *right* to attend them all. (*System*, I, pp. 254–5; cf. *Short Introduction*, pp. 118–20, and *Inquiry*, p. 256)

The inclusion of that which in itself is morally neutral in the moral realm of rights, without its being imposed through law, may also be seen from the following. Rights can, according to Hutcheson, be ascribed to creatures which are incapable of moral motives and which, therefore, cannot possibly be the objects of the moral sense and moral judgement. This applies to animals and to unborn children. Along with the contemporary Danish philosopher Frederik Christian Eilschow, Hutcheson was the most consistent animal rights theorist of his age and helped establish a pattern of argument which became commonplace later in the century, when he maintained that the capacity of animals for pleasure and pain clearly includes them in the moral community instituted by God, to the extent that men have an obligation to respect their right to the seeking of pleasure and the avoidance of pain, even though animals themselves are incapable of undertaking obligations. Similar reasoning applies to the foetus (*System*, I, pp. 309–16; *Short Introduction*, pp. 147–9).

The point in approaching Hutcheson's theory of rights in this manner is to illustrate how entirely the concept of rights is derivative from the concept of the common good, and hence how wide the former concept is. A person has a natural right to perform every action by which he can best maximize the common good. This test applies not only to actions which are perceived by the moral sense to be morally neutral but likewise to actions which are judged morally good when seen in isolation. This is the argument with which Hutcheson begins his exposition of rights in both the *System* and the *Short Introduction*. 'From the constitution of our *moral faculty* . . . we have our notions of *right* and *wrong*, as characters of affections and actions.'[41] However, 'This is the *rectum*, as distinct from the *jus* . . . : the *jus* ensues upon the *rectum*.'[42] Hutcheson then proceeds to show how the subjective rights, *iura*, 'ensue upon' that which is right, *rectum*, when the latter contributes to the common good.[43] Since the common good is enjoined by the law of nature, he can also express the matter by saying that '*rights* as moral qualities, or *faculties*', that is *iura*, are 'granted by the law of nature'.[44] This relationship between law and right, apart from being evident from the presentation as a whole, is expressed in a phrase in the original Latin version of the *Short Introduction* which is left out in the English translation, '*Ut juri omni respondet lex quaedam, jus illud constituens aut confirmans, ita etiam obligatio.*'[45]

In view of this, it seems impossible to see a 'Grotian' theory of subjective rights as the foundation for Hutcheson's natural jurisprudence. This is further underlined by the fact that Hutcheson himself does not see in Grotius a subjective rights theory but, rather, a precursor of his own line of argument:

[Grotius] deduces the notion of right from these two; first, the *initia naturae*, or the natural desires, which do not alone constitute right, till we examine also the other, which is the *convenientia cum natura rationali et sociali*. (*System*, I, p. 255, note)[46]

41   *System*, I, p. 252; cf. *Short Introduction*, pp. 109–10, 119.
42   *System*, I, p. 252, note.
43   *System*, I, pp. 253–6; *Short Introduction*, pp. 118–20.
44   *Short Introduction*, p. 119.
45   Hutcheson, *Philosophiae moralis institutio compendiaria* [1742], 2nd ed., Glasgow, 1745, p. 126. The phrase '*jus . . . confirmans*' is not rendered in the English version. The differences between the Latin and the English versions of this work are sufficiently numerous to cast doubt upon the claim that Hutcheson himself was responsible for the translation; see A. Bower, *The History of the University of Edinburgh*, 2 vols., Edinburgh, 1817, 2:340; T.E. Jessop, *A Bibliography of David Hume and of Scottish Philosophy from Francis Hutcheson to Lord Balfour*, London, 1938, p. 145. This claim is in any case highly unlikely in view of the formulation of the 'Advertisement by the Translator' in the *Short Introduction*.
46   My denial that Hutcheson is in any strong sense a rights theorist has recently been reinforced by T. Mautner, 'Pufendorf and eighteenth-century Scottish phi-

For Hutcheson subjective rights, *iura*, are derived from natural law when our spontaneous notions of right action, *rectum*, are trimmed by considerations of the common good, into which natural theology gives us insight:

> Thus we have the notion of *rights* as moral qualities, or *faculties*, granted by the law of nature to certain persons. We have already sufficiently explained how these notions of our *rights* arise from that *moral sense* of right and wrong, natural to us previous to any considerations of law or command. But when we have ascended to the notion of a divine natural law, requiring whatever tends to the general good, and containing all these practical dictates of right reason, our definitions of moral qualities may be abridged by referring them to a law; and yet they will be of the same import; if we still remember that the grand aim of the law of nature is the general good of all, and of every part as far as the general interest allows it. (*Short Introduction*, pp. 119–20)[47]

(c) *Rights perfect and imperfect*

Once we have focussed sharply on this order of justification and, especially, on the primacy of the common good, we can provide some further clarification of Hutcheson's politics. Since the concept of the common good is that of the beatitude of God's creation, it encompasses the whole of human morality, or all the virtues. Consequently all rights, the exercise of which contributes to the common good, are morally well founded. When some rights are considered to have priority over others, this can be based only upon considerations of what in concrete situations will contribute most to the common good. Mankind

---

losophy', in *Samuel von Pufendorf, 1632–1982*, ed. K. Å. Modéer, Lund, 1986, pp. 125–7. Mautner does, however, deny the Pufendorfian ancestry to this.

47 The dependence of all *iura* upon the law of nature and thus upon the common good extends, of course, to property rights. This must be borne in mind when considering the claim that Hutcheson (like Carmichael) is a precursor of Adam Smith in transforming the labour theory of property into 'a theory of the natural and moral sentiments' (J. Moore, 'Locke and the Scottish jurists', paper presented to the conference on 'Locke and the Political Thought of the 1680s' sponsored by the Conference for the Study of Political Thought, Folger Shakespeare Library, Washington, DC, 21–23 March, 1980). In a sense this is quite true, but the important point is that this proto-Smithian theory – which in Hutcheson is simply an extension of the general moral-sense concept – occurs within the framework of the theory of natural law and the common good. In Smith, property rights, like all other subjective rights, are exactly *not* dependent upon a morally comprehensive concept of the common good. For other discussions of this point in Hutcheson, see R.F. Teichgraeber III, *'Free Trade' and Moral Philosophy*, Durham, NC, 1986, p. 71, and T.A. Horne, 'Moral and economic improvement: Francis Hutcheson on property', *History of Political Thought*, 7 (1986), 115–30 at pp. 122–3.

being what it is, this will on the whole mean that the negatively defined rights – rights not to be injured – or perfect rights, have practical
priority over the positively defined rights – rights to receive some
good – or imperfect rights.

> Yet the boundaries between perfect and imperfect rights are not always
> easily seen. There is a sort of scale or gradual ascent, through several almost
> insensible steps, from the lowest and weakest claims of humanity to those of
> higher and more sacred obligation, till we arrive at some imperfect rights so
> strong that they can scarce be distinguished from the perfect. (*Short Intro-
> duction*, pp. 122–3; cf. *System*, I, pp. 262–3)[48]

This being so, we cannot use the distinction between perfect and imperfect rights as a boundary line for the legitimate exercise of political
power. Indeed, as already indicated, Hutcheson does in fact charge
government with the promotion of a wide field of positive goods, and
he does not see claims to perfect rights as a barrier to government
intervention.[49]

Just as the framework for the exercise of political power is the concept of the common good, so the latter is the basis for this power.
The rationale for the institution of civil society is the promotion of the
common good, and political government is the trustee for this. At the
same time, Hutcheson is, of course, a well-known contractarian: 'all
human *Power*, or Authority, must consist in *a Right transferr'd to any
Person or Council, to dispose of the alienable Rights of others'*.[50] As we have
already seen, this is based upon the fallibility of our judgement of the
moral motivation of others. Hutcheson's politics is characterized by a
balance between the politically expansive claim to knowledge about
the common good and the politically restraining fallibility of our individual moral judgement. The balance is in general achieved by the
consoling thought that we can be assured by natural theology that in
principle there is no conflict between common good and individual
good.

2.6   *The coherence of Hutcheson's thought*

On the basis of the readings offered in the preceding section, I
suggest that Hutcheson's moral thought exhibits a fundamental coherence. By incorporating natural jurisprudence in his moral theory he

---

48   I cannot here pursue Hutcheson's handling of the traditional third category,
external rights; but see S. Buckle, *Natural Law and the Theory of Property*, pp. 218–22.

49   Cf. T.D. Campbell, 'Francis Hutcheson: "Father" of the Scottish Enlightenment', in *The Origins and Nature of the Scottish Enlightenment*, ed. R.H. Campbell and
A. S. Skinner, Edinburgh, 1982, pp. 176–7.

50   *Inquiry*, 4th ed., p. 294.

made a serious attempt to solve the issues which had been brought to a head in the debate about moral scepticism and the clash between a long tradition of moral realism, especially in England, and a renewed voluntarism, especially within natural jurisprudence. Given his premises, the attempt makes sense, nor is there any direct evidence that he was dissatisfied with this particular aspect of his system. Apart from some unspecific dissatisfaction in the later part of his life at his inability to write up a systematic synthesis of his moral thought, his expressed dissatisfaction was with the *Synopsis metaphysicae*, particularly the first edition which had been published without his knowledge. Here again we have no evidence of where he saw the deficiencies; he did, however, find it worth-while to revise the book and reissue it in a properly authorized version.

In general terms it is not hard to imagine Hutcheson's unhappiness at having to keep his text-books within a systematics which was directly transferred from the reformed scholastic curriculum, and, at least to that extent, there is a division between these text-books and the rest of his oeuvre. However, once we go beyond this to the basic doctrines, the lines become blurred. Only a detailed comparison of Hutcheson's Latin texts with their Continental models can reveal the degree of their orthodoxy and thus of their distance from his earlier work. Here I can pick up only a couple of significant points.

A cornerstone in any version of the sort of Augustinian dualism from which the Latin text-books derive is a strong notion of man's sinfulness and moral incapacity. On this point, however, the most striking feature of the *Synopsis metaphysicae* is an, admittedly poorly formulated, version of the idea of man's natural moral sense, or capacity for moral judgement.[51]

The second point, which has been cited as particularly strong evidence for the orthodoxy of the *Synopsis metaphysicae*, is Hutcheson's adoption of the traditional division between God's communicable and incommunicable attributes:

> Some attributes of God, such as omniscience, omnipotence, infinity, were described as 'incommunicable', i.e. were possessed by God alone. Other attributes, such as knowledge, volition, majesty, were described as 'communicable', or common to God and men; provided these men were redeemed from their sinful condition through the mediation of Jesus Christ.[52]

---

51 Hutcheson, *Synopsis metaphysicae, ontologiam et pneumatologiam complectens,* 2nd ed., Glasgow, 1744, pp. 53–5.

52 This and the next quotation are Moore's concise résumé of reformed scholastic doctrine, 'Two systems of Hutcheson', pp. 44–5. Hutcheson introduces the distinction between communicable and incommunicable attributes in *Synopsis metaphysicae*, pp. 97–8.

The importance of this distinction thus lies in its connection with 'the dogma of the Incarnation: that God became man in Jesus Christ while remaining God.' This flew in the face of the Arminian theology which Hutcheson taught in his public Sunday lectures, based on Grotius's *Truth of the Christian Religion*.

There is thus no doubt that the introduction of the distinction between God's attributes is a significant concession on Hutcheson's part. Yet the edge of it is completely blunted by the absence in the *Synopsis metaphysicae* of a clear commitment to the dogma of the Incarnation; without that the distinction becomes trite. It becomes even more innocent when it is not combined with the usual idea of selection of those to whom the communicable attributes are communicated as a sign of their task as moral and civic leaders. Add the notion of man's natural moral ability, and the *Synopsis metaphysicae* begins to look like an Arminian sheep in orthodox wolf's clothing; at least, it seems worth pursuing the possibility that a text which, from one point of view, undoubtedly was a major concession to the orthodox moral theology which Hutcheson in general fought, from another point of view is an attempt to empty the latter of some of its most distinctive doctrines. Despite, or perhaps because of, the muddled result, it may have contributed to the theological compromises characteristic of that mainstream of Scottish moral thought which Hutcheson's moral theory proper established.

2.7 *Hutcheson and the development of Scottish moral thought*

The interpretation of Hutcheson offered here has consequences in a number of areas. By way of conclusion I return to the two topics with which I opened, the coherence of his thought and the over-all development of the moral thought of the Scottish Enlightenment.

Just as Hutcheson's moral theology helped set the tone for subsequent Moderatism, so the duality which we found in his politics can be seen as a pointer for the development of Scottish political thought. When the fallibility of moral judgement is weakened by Thomas Reid's replacement of the moral sense with Common Sense, we see a tendency to weaken the restraints on political power, resulting eventually in a strong temptation towards the total politics of Utopia. Here traditional social relations, especially market and property relations, would be replaced by a system of public moral accountancy establishing moral merit as the basis for social standing.[53] If, on the other hand, we raise

---

53 See Reid's remarkable paper delivered to the Glasgow Literary Society in November 1794, 'Some thoughts on the utopian system', in Reid, *Practical Ethics*, Sect. XVIII; also ch. 6, sect. 6.10, this volume.

sceptical questions about the deity of natural religion, as Hume did, then the first casualty is our purported knowledge of this deity's good moral intentions and, hence, the concept of the 'common good' in the morally wide sense adopted by Hutcheson. Once the guarantee of an – in principle – all-encompassing harmony among individual goods has disappeared, the concept of the common good becomes an empirical and historical one: that is to say, it becomes a question of what sort of common good we can create in human society. The only common good about which we can have some degree of certainty, according to Hume, amounts to a great deal less than it did in Hutcheson, namely the enforcement of the rules of the negative virtue of justice. Any further common goods are not a matter of the principles of law but of the expediency of politics or the benevolence of private relations and thus, for a philosopher, mostly fit for empirical investigation as they occur in the progress of society. This is the message of Smith's combination of jurisprudence and political economy.

In short, for Hutcheson the whole realm of law, rights, and duties described by natural jurisprudence is dependent upon a collective view of humanity and a concept of the common good. This separates it from the individualistic morality of the moral sense. However, the two are tied together by Hutcheson's theory of natural theology. Once Hume had destroyed the latter, individual moral claims were, unnervingly, without a guarantee of mutual – even if only eventual – harmony. This is an idea which Hume and Smith may well have seen as a possibility in Grotius's theory of subjective rights. At the same time it is very close to the scepticism in morals against which Pufendorf's natural law theory was deployed by men like Barbeyrac, Carmichael, and Hutcheson. This is worth remembering, when we talk of 'the' natural jurisprudence tradition in Scotland.

2.8 *Turnbull and Heineccius*

As already indicated, Hutcheson had a close philosophical relative in George Turnbull. Like Hutcheson, Turnbull found much inspiration in Shaftesbury's philosophy and in the political ideals of Commonwealthmen such as Lord Molesworth.[54] On the fundamental points of

54 See the pioneering work of Robbins, *Eighteenth-Century Commonwealthman*, chs. 4–6. For a brief sketch of Turnbull's life, see M.A. Stewart, 'George Turnbull and educational reform', in *Aberdeen and the Enlightenment*, ed. J.J. Carter and J.H. Pittock, Aberdeen, 1987, pp. 95–103. Concerning Turnbull's involvement in the Rankenian Club in Edinburgh and the networking between this group and Molesworth's acolytes in Glasgow and Ireland, see a series of detective stories by M.A. Stewart, 'Berkeley and the Rankenian Club', *Hermathena*, 139 (1985), 25–45; 'John Smith and the Molesworth circle', *Eighteenth-Century Ireland*, 2 (1987), 89–102; and 'George Turnbull'. Concerning Turnbull's teaching at Aberdeen, see P.B. Wood,

moral philosophy in the narrower sense, Turnbull is in fact so similar to
Hutcheson that in this regard we can be brief. That is not to say that
Turnbull was dependent upon Hutcheson's work or that he did not
add to what Hutcheson had to say. Most of Turnbull's basic ideas seem
to have been developed simultaneously with those of Hutcheson and
are already present in his graduation speeches at Marischal College,
Aberdeen, in 1723 and 1726, especially his slogans about the similar
teleological order in the physical and the moral world.[55] As a gradu-
and from Turnbull's class, Thomas Reid undoubtedly listened to the
latter oration, and, as David Norton has explained, Turnbull did in fact
contribute to the development from moral sense to Common Sense in
British philosophy.[56] Our main interest here is, however, that Turnbull
also attempted a synthesis of realist and natural law ideas in the service
of a Christian Stoicism and a civic humanist 'republicanism'.

In the case of Hutcheson, the idea of a split between two systems in
his thought may have been nourished by the temporal gap between his
early, innovative moralizing works and his late natural law text-books
– although of course he did not entirely ignore natural law ideas in the
former. In the case of Turnbull, it is difficult to find support in chronology for a similar two-systems interpretation. Not only did he include
natural law topoi in his academic theses,[57] but he published his major
work in moral philosophy and his significant natural law text within a
year of each other.[58] It is therefore informative to use Turnbull as a

---

The Aberdeen Enlightenment: The Arts Curriculum in the Eighteenth Century, Aberdeen,
1993, pp. 40–9.

55   G. Turnbull, *Theses philosophicae de scientiae naturalis cum philosophia morali
conjunctione*, Aberdeen, 1723; and *Theses philosophicae de pulcherrima mundi cum materialis tum rationalis constitutione*, Aberdeen, 1726. Cf. Wood, *Aberdeen Enlightenment*,
pp. 47–49, and his 'Science and the pursuit of virtue in the Aberdeen Enlightenment', in *Studies in the Philosophy of the Scottish Enlightenment*, ed. M.A. Stewart,
Oxford, 1990, pp. 127–49 at pp. 130–6. Wood suggests that historians of the Scottish
Enlightenment, such as Richard Sher, have to mend their ways and stop seeing
Hutcheson as its 'father'. Not only does Turnbull have equal claims to paternity, but
such individualistic explanations have to make way for structural considerations of
socio-intellectual networks. See Wood, 'Science and the pursuit of virtue',
pp. 135–6; and cf. Richard B. Sher, 'Professors of virtue: The social history of the
Edinburgh Moral Philosophy Chair in the eighteenth century', in ibid., pp. 87–126,
and his *Church and University*, p. 167.

56   See Norton, *David Hume*, pp. 163–73. The most concentrated discussion of
the moral sense is in Turnbull, *The Principles of Moral (and Christian) Philosophy*, 2
vols., London, 1740 ('and Christian' was only added in the second volume), I,
pp. 107–41.

57   See the 'Annexa' to the two theses mentioned in note 55 to this chapter.

58   *Principles of Moral Philosophy* in 1740; and *A Methodical System of Universal
Law: Or, the Laws of Nature and Nations Deduced from Certain Principles, and applied to
Proper Cases*, by Johann Gottlieb Heineccius, trans. George Turnbull, 2 vols., Lon-

parallel to Hutcheson in our attempt to sort out the connecting links in what, to modern eyes, seems like a philosophical patchwork.[59] At the same time Turnbull is useful in another respect. While Hutcheson's discussion of natural law invoked the major names that today identify the tradition, especially Grotius and Pufendorf, Turnbull presents his ideas on natural law in the form of commentaries on his translation of a text-book by an author, Heineccius, who is now all but unknown outside the circle of German legal historians. Turnbull therefore takes us to intellectual connections that are disappearing from view.

Johann Gottlieb Heineccius (1681–1741) was a professor of philosophy and of law at the universities of Frankfort an der Oder and Halle, interrupted by a brief appointment at the West-Frisian University of Franeker.[60] Heineccius was among the ablest Roman lawyers of his time and one of those who applied his civilian skills to systematize domestic German law. In both branches of law he employed his 'axiomatic method', which essentially consisted of establishing definitions and general principles in the various areas of the law and employing these in the analysis and presentation of the legal material. Despite its name, it has nothing to do with a deductive or demonstrative method.[61] Most of the legal principles he established were in fact well known from natural law, and his works on both Roman and German law therefore contain much that is immediately recognizable as natural law. This had some significance in Scottish moral and legal thought. John Millar lectured on Roman law from Heineccius's text-books for many years, and it is quite clear that these influential lectures were in fact courses in general legal theory as much as in civil law in particular.[62] It is also clear that Heineccius influenced the 'institutionist' work of John Erskine and George Wallace, the latter invoking the German's

don, 1741. The former work admittedly derived from Turnbull's lectures in Aberdeen fifteen years earlier, but he clearly revised and updated them, not least with a good deal of Hutchesonian material.

59 David Fordyce's *Elements of Moral Philosophy* (1748), London, 1754, provides another, philosophically still feebler parallel but one of some influence; see ch. 10, sect. 10.3, this volume.

60 The main source for Heineccius's life is his son's brief biography: Johann Christian Gottlieb Heineccius, *De vita, fatis et scriptis Io. Gottlieb Heineccii, IC. commentarius*, first prefaced to the eight-volume *Opera omnia*, Geneva, 1744–8, I, pp. iii–liv. At Franeker in 1724–5, he taught the Prince of Orange, and this is said to have attracted many young Englishmen of rank; *De vita*, pp. xxvii–xxviii.

61 Heineccius gives a convenient brief explanation of the axiomatic method in the 'Praefatio' to his *Elementa iuris civilis secundum ordinem Institutionem* (1727), Amsterdam, 1733. For a brief discussion of his axiomatic method, see Jan Schröder, *Wissenschaftstheorie und Lehre der 'praktischen Jurisprudenz' auf deutschen Universitäten an der Wende zum 19. Jahrhundert*, Frankfurt a.M., 1979, pp. 140–2.

62 See ch. 5 at note 11, this volume.

axiomatic method.[63] Despite his inclination towards a formalistic method of presentation, Heineccius's jurisprudence is striking for much greater historical sophistication than was common in similar work at the time, and this undoubtedly appealed to John Millar and to the later historical school in German jurisprudence. It certainly appealed to Heineccius's greatest student, Edward Gibbon, who, in writing his famous history of Roman law in the forty-fourth chapter of *The Decline and Fall of the Roman Empire*, was 'directed by the most temperate and skillful guides', adding, 'At the head of these guides I shall respectfully place the learned and perspicuous Heineccius.'[64] In Gibbon's Lausanne journal we see how he was taken with the literary and philosophical importance of Heineccius's jurisprudence.[65] Heineccius's works on Roman and German law went through an extraordinary number of editions for more than a century, and their author retained a high European reputation.[66] At the close of the century, Sir James Mackintosh still remembered to pay Heineccius the sort of left-handed compliment at which he was an expert: 'It is hardly necessary to take any notice of the textbook of Heineccius, the best writer of elementary books with whom I am acquainted on any subject.'[67] Mackintosh's

63   See John Erskine, *An Institute of the Law of Scotland*, Edinburgh, 1773; George Wallace, *A System of the Principles of the Law of Scotland*, vol. I (no more published), Edinburgh, 1760, pp. xx–xxi. For institutionist thought in Scotland generally, see John W. Cairns, 'Institutional writings in Scotland reconsidered', *Journal of Legal History*, 4 (1983), 76–117; and cf. Neil MacCormick, 'Law and enlightenment', in *The Origins and Nature of the Scottish Enlightenment*, ed. R.H. Campbell and A.S. Skinner, Edinburgh, 1982, pp. 150–66. It still remains to analyse Heineccius's Romanist approach to German law alongside Millar's courses in Scottish and English law.

64   Edward Gibbon, *The Decline and Fall of the Roman Empire*, 3 vols., London, n.d., II, p. 621 and note 4. Heineccius is in fact present throughout the chapter. He and van Bynkershoek are the 'best judicial critics' (p. 622, n. 4); the history of edicts is composed 'by the master hand of Heineccius' (p. 627, n. 2).

65   *Le Journal de Gibbon a Lausanne 17 Août 1763 – 19 Avril 1764*, ed. Georges Bonnard, Lausanne, 1945, pp. 9, 14, 26, and 99–100. From these entries we learn that Gibbon first read the extracts from Heineccius's works in the *Bibliothèque raisonné des ouvrages des savans de l'Europe*.

66   His work on Roman legal antiquities, *Antiquitatum Romanarum syntagma*, Halle, 1719, had reached its twentieth edition by 1841; the lectures on Justinian's *Institutes* achieved about thirty editions by the turn of the eighteenth century, depending on how one counts the many edited versions. There are a vast number of other works, many in several editions; there were no less than three editions of the collected works; in eighteen volumes, Venice, 1743 (2nd ed. 1761); in eight volumes, Geneva, 1744–8 (2nd ed., 1768–71); and in twelve volumes, Naples, 1759.

67   James Mackintosh, *A Discourse on the Law of Nature and Nations* (1799), in *The Miscellaneous Works of the Right Honourable Sir James Mackintosh*, 3 vols., London,

praise presumably extended to Heineccius's text-book in philosophy as well as the one on natural law that sparked off his remark. The former was used by John Stevenson at the University of Edinburgh when Alexander Carlyle studied there in 1736.[68] It is the latter, however, the natural law work, that is our concern here. It went through five editions in thirty years, as well as the English edition by Turnbull.[69] The work is a very clear and well-organized presentation of a full natural law system in the general Pufendorfian–Thomasian tradition. It is noteworthy, however, that Heineccius, in many specific areas of discussion and for many of his copious references, follows Samuel von Cocceji's dissertation, although in basic philosophical ideas he differed widely from Cocceji.[70] Heineccius was a natural-law-and-duty theorist,

---

1846, I, pp. 339–87, at p. 362. The particular text-book to which Mackintosh is referring is the work on natural law which we shall consider later in this chapter. Similarly Heineccius's work on the *Institutes* was, inevitably, included among the civilian dogs to be kicked by Bentham when he finished *Of Laws in General* in the early 1780s; *Of Laws in General*, ed. H.L.A. Hart, London, 1970, p. 242.

68 See Alexander Carlyle, *Anecdotes and Characters of the Times* [1860], ed. J. Kinsley, London, 1973, p. 22. The text-book was the *Elementa philosophiae rationalis et moralis*, Amsterdam, 1728 (and at least half a dozen later editions plus reprints in the various collected works). Stevenson may also have used Heineccius's brief *Historia philosophica*: 'I always us'd to spend a fortnight [of the lecture course] in giving an account of the lives of the Philosophers without making use of any text; but now, I think of taking a compend of Heineccius for that purpose.' Stevenson to Charles Mackie, 10 September 1735, Edinburgh University Library, Laing MS II.91. I am indebted to Roger Emerson for this reference.

69 *Elementa juris naturæ et gentium*, Halle, 1737. There were also several French, Italian, and Spanish translations (including a Peruvian edition in 1832) which I have not inspected; and his work on the *Institutes*, in the opinion of a recent scholar, 'was probably the influential work most used in Latin America [in the eighteenth century]': Alan Watson, *Slave Law in the Americas*, Athens, GA, 1989, p. 95. A helpful general discussion of Heineccius's natural law theory is Ernst Reibstein, 'J.G. Heineccius als Kritiker des grotianischen Systems', *Zeitschrift für ausländisches öffentliches Recht und Völkerrecht*, 24 (1964), 236–64.

70 See especially *Methodical System*, Book I, Chapter 3, where the voluntarist element is to the fore and Heineccius in some passages is paraphrasing Samuel von Cocceji's *Tractatus juris gentium de principio juris naturalis unico, vero, et adæquato*, part I, Frankfort a.d.O., 1702. Cf. ch. 1, sect. 1.12, and ch. 4, sect. 4.2, of this volume. We may note that there were personal connections between Cocceji and Heineccius; the latter's elder son (and biographer) was tutor to the former's sons, and Heineccius saw fit to dedicate his work on German law to Cocceji, one of the most forceful Romanists. See Ernst Landsberg, in J.A.R. von Stintzing, *Geschichte der deutschen Rechtswissenschaft*, completed by Ernst Landsberg, 3 vols. in 4, Munich, 1880–1920, 3. Abt., 1. Halbbd., 'Noten', p. 124; and the dedication in volume 1 of *Elementa juris Germanici tum veteris tum hodierni*, 2 vols., Halle, 1735–6.

whereas Cocceji, as we shall see in Chapter 4, was an unusual individual-rights man. As so often, the common genre and topoi of natural law obscure fundamental differences.

2.9 *Natural law and Harringtonianism*

Through his translation of Heineccius, Turnbull presented his countrymen with a comprehensive overview of the intense philosophical debates that had taken place across Europe within the framework of natural law during the preceding couple of generations. In addition to the well-known figures from the seventeenth and early eighteenth century, we find here extensive use of those recent and contemporary German thinkers who are otherwise little known and often assumed to have been unknown in Britain in the eighteenth century: Thomasius, Wolff, and lesser names such as Alberti, Boecler, Buddeus, the two Cocceji, Koehler, Ludovici, and Ziegler. Most importantly, however, Heineccius sets out the ideas of a modified, Thomasian voluntarist with great clarity. When this is joined to Turnbull's criticism, we have a modernized replay of Hutcheson's struggle with the Pufendorfian legacy. For Turnbull tries to base natural law upon a moral-sense realism similar to that of Hutcheson, though more explicitly based on Shaftesbury and with occasional reference to Butler; and he seeks, more directly than does Hutcheson, to fuse a Harringtonian analysis of property and power with the natural law ideas of authority. Also like Hutcheson, he keeps firmly within a framework of providential naturalism.

Turnbull's central discussion of Heineccius's voluntarism is conducted in terms of obligation. Heineccius distinguished between internal and external obligation, that is, obligations to goodness and to justice, to moral rules, and to law, respectively. But while internal obligation to moral rules prescribing goodness is admittedly the 'nobler' sort, it is a highly uncertain guide in life, human nature being what it is. Consequently, external obligation imposed by a legislating authority, namely God, is necessary:

> Obligation is a connection between motives and free actions, and motives must consist either in the intrinsic goodness and pravity of actions themselves, or arise from the will of some Being whose authority we acknowledge, commanding and forbidding certain actions under a penalty. And therefore the former species of *obligation* is called *internal*; the latter is called *external*. The first excites to *good actions*, the other to *just actions*. But right is the correlate (as it is called in the schools) to both. For if one person be under an *obligation*, some other person hath a right or title to exact something from him. Hence it is manifest, that a rule which carries only an *internal obligation* with it, is not sufficient with respect to mankind: for since this obligation solely arises from the goodness of the action, and therefore only excites a

person to act by this motive, *viz.* that his action may be good; but man is so framed by nature, that he often embraces a false appearance of good for what is really such: Such a rule must be uncertain, and for that reason it is not deserving of being called a rule. But if a *rule* only carrying an *internal obligation* with it, would be uncertain, there is need of one which may produce an *external obligation* arising from the will of some Being whose authority we acknowledge.[71]

Finally, God's authority is evident from his infinite wisdom, goodness, and power, and from the fact of humanity's dependence on him.[72] To this Turnbull objects as follows:

it is plain, that the command of God to do, or to forbear an action can only be inferred from the intrinsic goodness or pravity of that action, i.e. in our author's language, the external obligation of an action can only be inferred from its internal obligation . . . But this being true, it evidently follows, That we cannot be more certain about the external obligation of an action, than we are about its internal obligation . . . It appears to me very odd reasoning to say, That considering how obnoxious men are to mistakes about good and evil, there must be a more certain rule for human conduct than the intrinsic goodness of actions, even the divine will; when at the same time we are told, that we cannot come at the knowledge of the divine will with respect to our conduct, otherwise than by first knowing what an action is in itself; or that we can only infer the divine will concerning an action from its intrinsic nature, its intrinsic goodness or pravity.[73]

Turnbull goes on to summarize some of the fundamental points of his *Principles of Moral Philosophy.* Since natural necessity forces us to recognize *natural* goods and evils (what helps or hinders our life processes), we will inevitably recognize that some of those natural goods and evils, namely those that are controlled by an agent, whether human or divine, are also *moral* goods or evils. We shall feel an internal obligation to do the one and avoid the other, and if there is a God – as the teleology of nature proves there is – it must be his will that we should feel such internal obligation.

Wherefore wherever there is internal obligation to act in such or such a manner, there is likewise an external obligation to act in the same manner . . . arising from the will of God. . . . Whatever therefore in respect of its internal obligation may be called a proper rule of conduct, is at the same time a *law,* in the proper and strict sense of the word, i.e. it is the will, the command of a superior who hath right to command, and power to enforce the obedience of his command.

71 Heineccius, *Methodical System,* I.7–9. This attempt to maintain both internal and external obligation was taken up in Scottish law by John Erskine, *An Institute of the Law of Scotland,* I.1.5–6.
72 *Methodical System,* I.10.
73 Turnbull, 'Remarks', in *Methodical System,* I.16.

A system of such rules of morals is the system of 'the natural laws of God concerning our conduct'.[74]

Turnbull's leading idea was that the moral world and the natural world were closely analogous and should be investigated in analogous sciences, the pivotal point in the analogy being the teleology of both worlds.[75] Just as the triumphs of Newtonian science proved to his satisfaction that the Author of nature had equipped humankind with the ability to ascertain physical facts and their regular connections, so the new 'experimental', or empirical, moral science would explain the reality of moral knowledge as a function of our moral sense and would delineate the orderly system that we as moral beings are capable of. Needless to say, both Turnbull's arguments for the existence of a veridical moral sense and for the providential order of the moral universe are developed, at considerable length, in order to combat moral scepticism.

As in Hutcheson, so in Turnbull moral knowledge is motivational as well as cognitive, and in its motivational aspect it is to be understood as benevolence or love. It is this issue of love that allows us to shed further light on the relationship between Heineccius and Turnbull. Having established that the *existence* of natural law is a matter of the divine will towards humanity, Heineccius proceeds to consider the principle by which we may *know* what this law is. He briskly presents and rejects as impossible all of the traditional principles: the 'sanctity' of God, as invoked by some orthodox Lutherans; the inherent justice of actions, without reference to any law; the consent of all nations, as sometimes suggested by Cicero and Grotius; the seven precepts of Noah, as suggested by John Selden (though not mentioned by Heineccius); the right of all to all things, as in Hobbes; the state of integrity, or original innocence, as in Alberti; the principle of sociability, as in Grotius, Pufendorf, and several ancients. Nor will he admit 'Other principles of natural law . . . highly boasted of by others; such as the order of nature, which the Creator intends in his works; the interest of mankind; a moral Theocracy, and other such like principles.'[76] Although Heineccius had in mind earlier thinkers, his rejection of 'the order of nature' and 'the interest of mankind' might as well have been directed against Hutcheson and Turnbull. This adds the question of method to that of love, in the following way.

74   Ibid., 'Remarks', I.17.

75   This is the primary purpose of the *Principles of Moral Philosophy*. A short and sharp analysis is provided by Norton, *David Hume*, pp. 153–63.

76   Heineccius, *Methodical System*, III.76. For the preceding, see III.69–75. Heineccius is following Samuel von Cocceji closely in these paragraphs; cf. note 70 to the present chapter. But by rejecting the idea of a moral theocracy as the principle of natural law, he is also distancing himself from Cocceji.

Heineccius rejects all the above-mentioned principles because they are not 'evident and adequate' – echoing language and arguments from Cocceji which we cannot go into here – and proceeds to replace them by invoking his axiomatic method. From the concept, or definition, of God as infinitely wise and good, it follows that he 'cannot will any thing else with regard to mankind but their happiness'. The pursuit of happiness is therefore our duty, and to pursue happiness is to love, 'hence we infer that God obliges us to love, and that love is the principle of natural law'.[77]

This was too much for Turnbull. He agrees that love is the principle of natural law, but it cannot be an 'external obligation' which we derive from the characteristics of God, as if we were dealing personally with the Deity and accepting a brief from him. Love of humanity and of the universe it inhabits must be felt and experienced as good, and we learn this through empirical observation of the orderly system of happiness to which such love contributes. Obligation is therefore in the first instance internal, the felt need to contribute the mite of love that Providence has made us capable of and which empirical observation can teach us:

> duty, obligation, or what is reasonable with regard to human conduct, must be inferred from human nature, and the constitution of things relative to him. But according to the frame of man and the constitution of things, the chief happiness and perfection of every man arises from the love and the pursuit of order within and without him; or from the observation of the prevalency of wisdom and good order, and consequently of greater happiness in the administration of the universe; and from such an orderly discipline of his affections as tend to produce universal happiness, order, and perfection, as far as his affections, and the actions they lead to, have any influence.[78]

Once we have learned God's mind through such experience of his works, namely that all this beautiful orderliness in the moral – as in the physical – world is his intention and will, an external obligation is added.

Returning to Heineccius, we see that, having established to his satisfaction that the duty to love is the basic principle of natural law, he distinguishes among various forms of love in order to organize the field of natural law. The proper object of love is perfection; love of beings more perfect than ourselves is the love expressed in devotion; love of our equal is the love expressed in friendship; and love of those less perfect than ourselves is the love expressed in benevolence. The love related to friendship is due among all human beings *qua* humans, but, in addition, the love related to devotion or benevolence may be

77 *Methodical System*, III.77–9.   78 Turnbull, 'Remarks', III.64–5.

due because of special circumstances such as high office or inferior abilities, respectively. Another distinction is among the objects of love, of which there are three: God, to whom we can owe only the love of devotion; ourselves; and others. Because love is our essential duty, this division is the foundation for the three general categories of duty that make up man's life on earth. This is the tripartite division that Pufendorf had made prominent and which Heineccius uses very effectively to arrange his material.[79] A third distinction is between degrees of love. Since the worst breach of the duty to love is to inflict hurt, the first and fundamental degree of love is not to hurt any one 'but to render to every one what is due to him, or to leave him in the undisturbed possession and employment of what he hath; which degree of love we call the *love of justice*'.[80] Because the object of love is excellence or perfection, a higher degree of love is to render a person more happy than he would be simply by being left alone, 'and this is a more sublime degree of love, which we call *love of humanity, or beneficence*'.[81] Both of these degrees of love are our duty, but they differ greatly in the obligation we have to perform them:

> whereas he who does not observe the love of justice . . . is a profligate person; he . . . who hath not the love of humanity and beneficence, can only be said not to perform the nobler and greater virtues. Now none may be forced to do virtuous actions, but all acts of wickedness may be restrained by punishments. Whence it is plain, that men may be compelled to acts of justice, but not to acts of humanity and beneficence. But when obligation is joined with coaction, it is *perfect*; when it is not, it is *imperfect*. We are therefore *perfectly* obliged to the love of justice, and *but imperfectly* to the love of humanity and beneficence.[82]

This well-known distinction identifies Turnbull's next important engagement with Heineccius. The sharp distinction between perfect and imperfect duties arises, in Turnbull's eyes, from the idea of God as a

79 *Methodical System*, I.91–3. This arrangement in natural law was by no means new in the Scottish setting. Not only was it well known from Pufendorf himself (cf. Carmichael's edition) and from Hutcheson, but it had also reached the Aberdonian classrooms at an early stage, as we see from David Verner's graduation dissertation at Marischal College in 1721, *Dissertatio philosophica de passionibus sive affectibus . . .*, Aberdeen, 1721, sects. xxii–xxiv.

80 *Methodical System*, I.82.

81 *Methodical System*, I.83. Heineccius explains that the difference between humanity and beneficence is that the latter, unlike the former, requires sacrifice in the doing of good. Heineccius makes the point that duties of humanity generally have been made enforceable at law (I.216), a point on which he was subsequently taken as an authority in Scottish law; see *Baron David Hume's Lectures, 1786–1822*, ed. G. Campbell and H. Paton (The Stair Society), 6 vols., Edinburgh, 1952, 3:182.

82 *Methodical System*, I.84.

superior magistrate who imposes external obligations that are either punishable or not in analogy with obligations that are either actionable or not in a court. Once we understand that obligation is internal and implied by moral goodness, we shall see that there is no sharp distinction but a scale of more or less important duties and, correspondingly, more or less serious 'crimes'.[83] This is underlined by the fact that the love of humanity and beneficence is obviously as much pointed out to us by our natural moral abilities as is the love of justice.[84] Turnbull maintains that since the teleology of human nature proves that benevolence is the basic duty of natural law, we need not be much concerned with all Heineccius's attempts to establish the duties of justice, for the latter is encompassed in the former as the lesser in the greater.[85]

Turnbull obviously sees Heineccius's error as the result of his 'axiomatic' idea of the person as an abstract individual under law, whereas Turnbull himself urges that we take as our starting-point what the empirical science of morals tells us about the teleology of human nature. This is not to say that Turnbull rejects the notion of moral equality, but it is worked out in a way that may be surprising to us. At the same time, it goes to the heart of his attempt to synthesize Heineccian natural law and Harringtonian civic humanism. First, let us document Turnbull's idea of equality under natural law; at the same time we shall also see one of his statements about the priority of duty over rights:

> All are equally bound by the law of nature; and for that reason, all are equally free from all obligations but those which the law of nature lays equally upon all. All are equally obliged to direct their conduct according to the law of nature; and therefore every one hath a right, an unalienable right, to make the law of nature his rule of conduct; and none hath a right so much as to advise, far less to force or compel any one to act contrary to the law of nature, or to hinder any one from making the law of nature his rule, and exercing [sic] his right to judge of it, and to act according to it: nay, none hath a right to dispose of, quit or resign this natural right and obligation. For that would be a right to throw off his natural obligations, and to choose or take another rule to himself.[86]

Being equally bound by the law of nature does not mean, however, that individuals are obliged to pursue the same virtues and actions. Turnbull found Heineccius and the natural lawyers quite confused on this point and urged a lesson from Harrington. If, instead of thinking only 'axiomatically' or abstractly about the human condition, we also

83 Turnbull, 'Remarks', I.164–5.   84 Ibid., 'Remarks', I.164–7.

85 Ibid., 'Remarks', I.152. It should be noted that Turnbull generally conflates Heineccius's beneficence and humanity into benevolence.

86 Turnbull, 'Remarks', II.18–19. Concerning the relationship between duty and right, see also ch. 10, sect. 10.2, this volume.

observe it empirically, we shall see that human beings are quite unequal from the hand of nature, by which he means 'abstractly from all
considerations of inequality occasioned by civil society'. This natural
inequality is divided into four categories. First, we are naturally dependent upon and subject to our parents. Second, some have more experience and prudence than others. Third,

> the Author of nature (as Mr. Harrington says in his Oceana) hath diffused a
> natural aristocracy over mankind, or a natural inequality with respect to the
> goods of the mind. And superiority in parts will always produce authority,
> and create dependence, or *hanging by the lips,* as the same author calls it . . .
> [Fourth,] Industry, to which, as the same excellent author says, *nature or God
> sells every thing,* acquires property; and every consequence of property made
> by industry is natural, or the intention of nature. But superiority in property
> purchased by industry, will make dependence, *hanging,* as that author calls
> it, *by the teeth* . . . All these inequalities, or superiorities and dependencies,
> are natural to mankind, in consequence of our frame and condition of life.[87]

The inequalities are, in other words, providentially prescribed, and as
such they are in themselves part of the law of nature. Being equal
under the law of nature thus means being bound by equal moral force
to perform to the best of our ability on the step of the ladder on which
we have landed. The performance itself consists of discharging our
duty to love God, ourself, and our neighbour with the means available
to us. Apart from the means provided by the inevitable family circumstances, such as parental authority, it is the goods of the mind and
material goods that shape the human world, and in both respects we
are unequal, because we have unequal purchasing power. As a consequence, relations of authority are created by the former means, relations of power by the latter.[88] Turnbull goes to great lengths to explain
both of these aspects of the 'law of purchase' by means of Harrington,
though making the ritualistic Scots bow to 'our Locke' on property but
without details, his 'book being in every one's hands'.[89] Both power
and authority are naturally appointed objects of man's ambition, and to
pursue them to the limit is our duty and, hence, our right under natural
law. The limit is that love of benevolence – comprehensively understood – which is the basic precept of natural law. Consequently, 'virtue
consists in benevolent desire of, and endeavour to have authority and
power in order to do good . . . It is in consequence of this principle that

87 Turnbull, 'Remarks', I.150–1.

88 Turnbull, 'Remarks', II.21: 'as superiority in respect of the goods of the mind
begets authority; so superiority in respect of external goods, begets power or
dominion.'

89 Turnbull, 'Remarks', I.196. By contrast, he thinks Harrington 'an excellent
author, unknown to foreign writers', 'Remarks', II.112.

it is lawful to have dependents and servants . . . or to exert ourselves to encrease our power and authority.'[90] The benevolent restraint on property and authority is of the 'utilitarian' kind we found in Hutcheson's Christian Stoicism. The use of property (or power) and authority is only justified if it creates happiness for all concerned, who consequently become mutually dependent upon each other, the rich upon the poor, superior upon subject, as well as vice versa.

Civil society, in order to retain stability, must institutionalize this interdependence, and Harrington's Oceanic scheme of a senate that has authority to propose legislation and a people that has power to choose is the ideal solution. There is nothing remarkable in Turnbull's recitation of the well-known principles of neo-republican government; the combination, however, with a resistance theory based on natural law but scornful of contractualism provides a suitable finale to this study.

Heineccius went out of his way to steer a middle course between the 'monarch-killers' – that is, Hotman, Sidney, Althusius, and Milton – and the 'machiavellians' – Machiavelli, Hobbes, and 'the asserters and defenders of passive-obedience [and non-resistance] in Great Britain', whom he thought equally 'pestilential'.[91] His basic proposition in this was that sovereign and people are equally subject to natural law. Nevertheless, he firmly maintained that there cannot be any judge in common between the sovereign and his people, other than God. Consequently sovereigns cannot be judged and punished, that is, resisted, under the law of nature – though subjects may, in extreme necessity, leave the country.[92] This sparks an eight-page polemical note from Turnbull. Although Turnbull invokes Sidney, Locke, and Hoadly for the defence of Machiavelli as 'explained' by Harrington, his own plea is phrased in the language of republican natural law which he is trying to establish:

> If the law of nature extends to all men, it extends to those vested with power, as well as to those under power; now, as far as the law of nature extends, the law of justice and benevolence, or in one word, the law of love extends; for that is the sum and substance of the law of nature. But so far as the law of love extends, justice is of perfect obligation, and benevolence of imperfect obligation: Princes therefore, being under the law of nature, are perfectly obliged to justice, and imperfectly obliged to benevolence. Now, since none (as our Author [Heineccius] often says) can be under an obligation, without giving some right to some other; it is plain a prince cannot be under the perfect obligation of justice, and the imperfect obligation of benevolence, without giving the people, to whom he is perfectly or imperfectly obliged, a perfect or imperfect right, correspondent to these his differ-

90 Turnbull, 'Remarks', I.200.
91 Heineccius, *Methodical System*, II.128–9.   92 Ibid., II.130–1.

ent obligations to them. The people therefore must have a perfect right to justice; that is, according to our Author's definition of perfect right, they must have a just title to exact, to demand, nay, to force it.[93]

The important point in this idea of a right to resistance is that it is a right that derives from the law of nature and therefore in effect is part of the duty to love and create happiness among humanity. This is underlined by Turnbull's forceful rejection of contractarianism.

Heineccius had argued that sovereignty could be established by means of pacts that stipulated restrictions on the normal natural law rights of either the sovereign or the people. If the pact limited authority, the sovereign could rightfully be resisted in case of transgression. Likewise, if the pact extended authority in tyrannical directions, the people could not complain. Turnbull characteristically takes up only the latter case, undoubtedly having Hobbes's and possibly Grotius's ideas of contractualist absolutism in mind:

> A pact by a people, giving a prince power to rule over them, otherwise than agreeably to the law of nature, that is, the law of justice and benevolence, or in one word, the law of love, and binding themselves to obey his commands, whatever they be, is a pact a people cannot make; it is an impossible pact, because an immoral one; and therefore it can never be obligatory, but to make it is a crime; and to stand to it, is to continue, nay, to increase the guilt. It is a mutual agreement between prince and people, to put the arbitrary will of a prince in the place of the law of nature, the law of God.[94]

2.10 Conclusion

In his elaborate manual for the education of the virtuous republican citizen and dutiful office-holder in the divine corporation, Turnbull includes the study of Roman law, followed by natural law, as essential. More particularly, he recommends Grotius, Pufendorf, and his own Heineccius – 'an excellent introduction to this most important study' – 'or any other of the celebrated doctors of the laws of nature and nations'.[95]

The preceding analysis of Turnbull's commentary on Heineccius shows that he had elaborate reasons for this opinion. In the midst of rambling, repetitive argumentation and unctuous rhetoric we find a concerted and often clear-headed effort to modify a typical natural law system to provide a suitable philosophical basis for Harringtonian political theory.

As in Hutcheson, the issue of what we have called 'moral realism' versus voluntarism was at the core of Turnbull's criticism of natural

93 Turnbull, 'Remarks', II.128–9.   94 Ibid., 'Remarks', II.132.
95 Turnbull, *Observations upon Liberal Education, in all its Branches*, London, 1742, p. 365.

law. Once he had rejected the residual voluntarism in Heineccius and reduced external to internal obligation, he could undermine the sharp distinction between perfect and imperfect duties and reduce the law of nature to the law of love. The second decisive move was to invoke the method of 'natural history' which pointed out the natural inequality of individuals and sought to explain the 'natural causes' as well as the teleological order of this inequality. When the evidence from natural history was viewed in a philosophical light, the teleology of inequality could be seen to be providential or part of natural law. Although all human beings are equally obliged by the law of nature, it is thus, on this view, inevitably an order of inequality that people are bound to uphold. This move, which creates the conceptual space for Turnbull's Harringtonian theory of property and politics, is much more distinct and tough-minded than anything in Hutcheson, and it provides the model for the combination of natural law and the history of moral institutions which is taken for granted in the mainstream of moral thought in the Scottish Enlightenment.

3

Between superstition and enthusiasm: David Hume's theory of justice, government, and politics

David Hume believed that most of the views about society and politics prevalent in his day had roots in one or another of 'two species of false religion': *superstition* and *enthusiasm*. Both were developments of conflicting theological doctrines that appealed to two different types of personalities. Both had come to be associated with opposing political interests. Both sprang from ignorance. And, although the two species had been universally present in society and in individuals in varying degrees throughout history, the peculiarity of modern post-Reformation Europe was the violent oscillation between them, as evidenced by the many wars of religion. Their more extreme adherents were also, not least, responsible for the plight of modern Britain, both North and South. One of the tasks of the philosophical historian, Hume believed, was to explain the preponderance at particular times of one or the other of these persuasions. The task he set for his political theory was to explain why both were philosophically misconceived, empirically untenable, and, in their extreme forms, politically dangerous.

3.1   The politics of religion

One part of humanity, Hume notes, has a tendency to 'weakness, fear, [and] melancholy, together with ignorance'. In this state, the imagination conjures up forces operating under the surface, and the mind is prone to grasp methods of influencing such forces by 'ceremonies, observances, mortifications, sacrifices, presents, or . . . any practice, however absurd or frivolous which either folly or knavery recommends to a blind and terrified credulity'. This condition and these practices Hume calls 'superstition'. In religion, priests, church establishments, and rituals are used to mediate between the individual and these forces. In society and in politics, the superstitious person is disposed to accept established forms and powers as inherent in the nature of things and to see society as a hierarchical structure with a monarch as the unitary source of authority and sovereignty as a divine right.[1]

In contrast, another part of humanity has a tendency to 'hope, pride, presumption, and a warm imagination, together with ignorance'. In this state, which Hume called 'enthusiasm', individuals take flights of fancy from the real world, presume direct rapport with higher powers, and incline towards ungovernable self-assertion. In religion, priests, church establishments, and ceremony are rejected. In society and politics, enthusiasts assert the rights of the individual. They often incline to forceful remodelling of authority and generally see self-government as the only proper government, at least in principle. Enthusiasts favour contractualist accounts of such authority as they will accept and insist on the protection of individual civil liberties.[2]

Hume's political theory is more than an outright rejection of such received ideas as those associated with superstition and enthusiasm. He meant his political writings to be also political *acts*, shaping the opinions or beliefs that in turn shaped politics and society. To achieve this, he sought to provide a theory of the nature of social and political phenomena different from those that served to reinforce superstition and enthusiasm. He proceeds, on the one hand, by analysing those beliefs which in recent history had tended to modify the ideal types of superstition and enthusiasm; on the other hand, he argues that such analysis in itself forms a set of opinions or beliefs with direct and beneficial political consequences. Speaking in the idiom of the time, he showed how his principles led him to take one or the other side in current debates. Often, of course, his topical conclusions obscured the theoretical premises, not only for his contemporaries but for subsequent generations of interpreters. The main problem in explaining Hume's political thought has always been figuring out how to provide a clear understanding of the close coherence between the general and the particular, and between the theoretical and the historical. His theory of the nature of social and political phenomena is mainly to be found

1 Hume, 'Of Superstition and Enthusiasm', in *Political Essays*, ed. K. Haakonssen, Cambridge, UK, 1994, pp. 46–50 at p. 74. (Unless otherwise indicated, all references to Hume's essays are to this edition.)

2 'Superstition and Enthusiasm', pp. 46–7. For examples of Hume's analysis of the origins of prominent modern forms of superstition, *viz.* Quakerism and Congregationalism, see Hume, *The History of England, From the Invasion of Julius Caesar to the Revolution in 1688*, foreword by W.B. Todd, 6 vols., Indianapolis, 1983, ch. 62 (VI:142–6) and ch. 57 (V:441–3). For a study of Hume's ideas of enthusiasm, see J.A. Passmore, 'Enthusiasm, fanaticism and David Hume', *The 'Science of Man' in the Scottish Enlightenment: Hume, Reid and their Contemporaries*, ed. P. Jones, Edinburgh, 1989, pp. 85–107.

in the third book of the *Treatise of Human Nature* and in the second *Enquiry*, whereas the particulars of the historically contingent situation of modern Britain and Europe are analysed in many of his *Essays* and in the *History of England*. In order to understand either, we have to grasp the sense in which basic social and political institutions are *artificial* according to Hume. This can best be achieved by looking at the *philosophical* ideas underpinning superstition and enthusiasm. Elsewhere this might have been called his 'metaphysics of politics'; Hume's aim was to unmask the politics of religious metaphysics.

3.2   Morals – found or constructed

Hume was keenly aware of the continuing influence of ideas derived from Aristotle and mediated by scholastic tradition. From this perspective, social forms, such as property and contract, and political roles, such as magistracy, have their foundation in essences, that is, inherent structures found in nature itself. On such a theory, specific actions are property-holding, contracting, or governing only in so far as they are an attempt to actualize the inherent meaning or the essence signified by these words. Moral, social, and political relations among people are not constructed by the individuals involved; such relations are established with reference to something over and above the persons concerned, namely, an objective structure of reality and meaning on which individuals try to draw. Hume saw these ideas as the philosophical equivalent, in religion, of the hocus-pocus of superstition (e.g., transubstantiation). Like most such ideas, this philosophy supported the need for authoritative interpreters of the meanings supposedly inherent in or essential to life in society. It was, in other words, the philosophy behind Catholicism, High Church Anglicanism, old-fashioned Toryism, absolutism, and divine-right monarchy.

The reactions in post-Reformation Europe to these directions in religion and politics were, as Hume realised more clearly than most, immensely complex and often contradictory. It is possible, however, to discern some of the philosophical ideas that were fundamental to much Reformation thought, and, as we saw in chapter 1, these ideas were eventually spelled out with great clarity by natural law philosophers such as Hugo Grotius, Thomas Hobbes, Samuel Pufendorf, and John Locke. With the partial exception of Grotius, these writers held that there were no moral or political meanings inherent in the structure of things. All meaning, or value, is willed or constructed, and imposed upon a natural world that *in itself* is amoral and apolitical. The essential act of will was that of God, who, in choosing the particular human nature he did, delegated to human beings the task of creating moral and political forms which would make possible the culture of humanity. According to most Protestant natural law thinkers, human reason could, unaided by revelation, derive from the character of human nature and the human position in the world a certain guidance in morals and politics, and this is what these thinkers called the law of nature. Generally speaking, the law of nature held that, since people are sociable and, indeed, had to be sociable in order to exist at all, various measures had to be taken. These measures were contained in derivative laws of nature, which specified the creation of moral and political institutions, ranging from marriage and property to civil government and the law of nations. A few thinkers, notably Grotius and Hobbes, tried to formulate a theory which dispensed with natural law as a guide for the human will. On this view, social and political forms are settlements negotiated among individuals with often conflicting claims and intentions, or *rights.* Natural law, in this scheme, is simply the lessons learned from such settlements, not the prescription for how to make them in the first place.[3]

The division between a natural law and a natural rights direction in Protestant natural law theory was of fundamental importance for the further development of political thought, as we shall see. For the moment, however, the significant point is that both forms of natural law theory apparently subscribed to the view that the institutions of moral and political life were contractually constructed by individuals.

The ideas of personal autonomy, of individual rights, of the absence of mediating factors between God and man and the consequent construction of morals and politics according to our own lights – ideas identified since with 'constructivists' – these parts of the philosophical argument could be taken to the extremes of enthusiasm, in religion, and of fanatical factionalism in politics. This had happened repeatedly in many parts of Europe, in Hume's opinion, but never with more devastating effect than in seventeenth-century Britain, marked by religious strife and civil war. Even in his own time, the political effect of the 'enthusiastic' cast of mind remained a danger to be guarded against; as Hume grew older, he sometimes feared that the battle against it might yet be lost.[4]

3 In addition, the law of nature was, of course, considered a positive law of God as revealed in his Word, but in this guise it could be considered a law only for those who had received the Word, Christian believers. For the relationship between natural law and natural rights in Grotius and Hobbes, see ch. 1, sects. 1.3–1.4, this volume.

4 In a number of letters in the late 1760s and early 1770s, Hume expressed his fear of and loathing for the London mobs rioting in support of the re-election to Parliament of the outlawed John Wilkes. Hume saw it as a degeneration of the demand for liberty to a senseless fanaticism which English freedom allowed to feed on itself, thus creating factionalism and 'barbarism' of a sort that could endanger

3.3 *Justice*

The theory of social artifice presented in the third book of the *Treatise* is an attempt to formulate a position mediating the two philosophical traditions that I have briefly outlined. Hume, of course, has no time for scholastic essences, and his naturalism precludes any role for the divine voluntarism of most Protestant natural law. Hume's individuals can expect neither inherent structures nor transcendent guidance. Only Hobbes had isolated humanity metaphysically and religiously as completely as Hume, yet the two thinkers reach very different conclusions about the human condition. It is not only that Hume gives a good deal more credit to the generous side of human nature. He also gives an account of the social relations among individuals which, while sharing the individualistic naturalism of Hobbes, is profoundly un-Hobbesian.

The actions that spring from the natural virtues and vices (beneficence, clemency, moderation, and their opposites, for example) are, according to Hume, 'entirely natural, and have no dependence on the artifice and contrivance of men'. Each of these actions is a simple or self-contained act that establishes relations between particular agents and particular patients.[5] An act of benevolence, or its opposite, is completed as one act or one occasion when that virtue, or vice, is being expressed, – for example, by the giving of a gift or the denial of a service. Such an activity may stretch over time, but it is nevertheless in a significant sense one act. Acts of benevolence may of course prompt reactions, such as gratitude, but these reactions are clearly *other* acts. Acts that result from natural virtue and vice are coherent and self-contained because they have a point or a meaning when taken *in isolation* – even when seen as nothing more than relations between specific individuals, a point Hume emphasizes by noting that we value each individual performance of a natural virtue (*T* III.3.i:579).

The natural virtues, 'commonly denominated the *social* virtues, to mark their tendency to the good of society', provide the basis for family life and intimate circles of friendship, but social life at large requires something else entirely, namely, a set of 'artificial' virtues (*T* III.2.ii:486–7). When I as agent abstain from taking the fruit of my neighbour's pear tree, pay my landlord his rent, or answer the govern-

---

this very freedom. See *The Letters of David Hume*, ed. J.Y.T. Greig, 2 vols., Oxford, 1969, 2:180–1, 191–2, 209–11, 212–13, 216, 261; *New Letters of David Hume*, ed. R. Klibansky and E. C. Mossner, Oxford, 1969, pp. 196, 199.

5 Hume, *A Treatise of Human Nature: Being an Attempt to Introduce the Experimental Method of Reasoning into Moral Subjects*, ed. L. A. Selby-Bigge; 2nd ed., rev. by P. H. Nidditch, Oxford, 1978 (hereafter referred to as *T*), Bk. III, Pt. 3, Sect. i: pp. 578, 574.

ment's military call-up, my actions cannot be understood *in isolation* as mere expressions of inherent features of my nature. These actions have reference to something else, to something beyond the other person or persons, the patient(s) affected by them. This patient may be unknown to the agent or may have been undeserving of the agent's behaviour: the neighbour may never harvest his fruit, the landlord may be excessively rich and grasping, the government may be conducting an unjust war. In such cases an agent's behaviour can only have meaning and only be evaluated through its relation to some additional factor beyond both the agent(s) and patient(s) involved. It has meaning only within a framework that is in an important sense objective and distinct from individuals and their qualities. The relations between people who hold property to the exclusion of others, who contract for exchange of goods or services, and who owe allegiance or support of some sort – these relations can only be established because the people involved have something other than each other's intentions to refer to, something which can shape their intentions. My giving money to another person does not constitute 'paying rent' merely because we have, respectively, intentions of giving and receiving. The transaction is given its particular meaning because it involves a social practice or institution, in this case a special form of contract. In other words, individual actions of this sort are not self-contained and complete. We cannot see their point and evaluate them without invoking the social practice to which they relate or on which they rely. Individual actions can be approved of as instances of such institutionalized practices as holding private property, keeping promises and contracts, paying allegiance, and the like, *because* such practices already exist and are approved of. This peculiar circumstance is, as Hume explains, well illustrated by actions which seem absurd when taken in isolation but which acquire meaning and can be evaluated once we assume their reference to a social practice of the sort mentioned. Consequently, when we see a poor person paying money to a rich one, we assume that a loan is being settled or goods paid for (*T* III.2.i:480–1).

Hume's analysis of the nature of social actions is a thorough rejection of will theories, such as contract theories. That is, he rejects theories according to which such social actions as respecting property claims acquire meaning because they derive from acts of will of the participating individuals. Like thinkers in the Aristotelian and Thomistic tradition, Hume holds that acts of will can establish social relations *outside intimate groups* only if these acts are given meaning by something over and above themselves.[6] In contrast to that tradition, how-

6 The scholastic theory of contract derives from Aquinas's theory of promises in *Summa Theologica*, II–II, q. 88. The late scholastics, especially in the Spanish

ever, Hume rejected the view that there are fixed and essential meanings for such social institutions as property and contract. Such institutions are no more than practices, a fact he signals by calling them and
their associated virtues and vices – justice and injustice, for example –
'artificial' (T III.2.i:483–4). They are artificial because they are human
creations. At the same time, Hume has deprived himself of the simple
contractualist account of these institutions as expressions of will. On
his account, property and contract must exist as social practices prior to
any acts of will relating to them. Hume has thus saddled himself with a
genetic problem, namely, how to account for the origins of the social
practices that constitute social institutions.

The solution Hume suggests involves luck, moderate foresight,
and imitative behaviour (T III.2.ii:484–501). We inevitably live in
family units, and although this is largely a response to natural passions and natural virtues as well as to 'the numberless wants and
necessities' with which nature has lumbered humans, it provides
some experience with relative divisions into *mine* and *thine* and with
trust. It requires only modest luck and prudence to attempt to imi-
tate this in relations with people outside the family group. The lack
of goods and abilities relative to needs and desires puts a premium
on making a success of such attempts. It is therefore easy to see how
it may become common practice to respect people possessing, transferring, and exchanging things that in one way or another are associated with them and then coming to trust each other's word about
future actions. The general pattern of such practices may be ex-

---

schools, made a sophisticated combination of this doctrine and the Roman law on
contracts. This combination had an enormous influence through the seventeenth
and eighteenth centuries – even on the natural lawyers who helped undermine the
philosophical basis for the doctrine – and we find it in civilian lawyers like Jean
Domat and Robert-Joseph Pothier, who influenced the French *Code civil* (1804). See
Domat, *Les Loix civiles dans leur ordre naturel,* Paris, 1689, Book I; Pothier, *Traité des
obligations,* Paris and Orléans, 1761–4. The modern alternative to the Aristotelian–
Thomistic idea of contracts as the actualization of the inherent essence of contracting was commonly seen to be the combination of nominalistic definitions and will
theories in thinkers such as Hobbes and Locke. See Hobbes, *Leviathan,* ed. R. Tuck,
Cambridge, UK, 1991, pp. 94–5; Locke, *An Essay Concerning Human Understanding,*
ed. P.H. Nidditch, Oxford, 1975, I.3, II.28, and IV.4; cf. Locke, *Two Treatises of Government,* ed. P. Laslett, Cambridge, UK, 1960, II.81. It must be stressed, however, that
the scholastic form of teleology was widely replaced by the teleological scheme of
natural religion, and the latter was not much more suited to support pure will
theories of promising and contracting than its predecessor. Eighteenth-century theories of promise and contract – legal as well as political – are therefore mostly
complicated and confused, a circumstance that makes Hume's theoretical clarification the more remarkable.

plained by the way the imagination works along empirically established associative lines (*T* III.2.iii–v:501–25).

It is a question how such practices gain sufficient strength to withstand the pressure of conflict, for instance in situations of social expansion and scarcity. The two basic requirements are that each practice should come to be valued independently of its individual instantiations and should be seen as binding or obligatory upon the individual. Rather than being just the sum total of what people do, social practices have to become independent rules specifying what is good and to be done.

Hume here offers a radical solution to what had proved to be one of the most intractable problems in moral philosophy, the relationship between *goodness* and *obligation*. At one extreme were those who thought that human nature had been so impaired by original sin that humankind had no insight into moral goodness and could be directed and governed only by being obliged to certain forms of behaviour. The obliging wills might be those of a hierarchy of authorities, terminating in God, as in much Lutheran thought; or they might be those of each individual, reflecting directly the will of God, as in much Calvinist thought. Either way we have a will theory of morals and politics of the sort Hume thought impossible, and we do not have an account that makes any necessary link between moral goodness and being obliged. In contrast to this line of thought were a wide variety of theories which all allowed that even in its fallen state, humanity was left with some natural capacity for moral insight. In Hume's recent past they ranged from Cambridge Platonism and the rationalism of Samuel Clarke to the moral-sense theories of Shaftesbury and Hutcheson. The proponents of such theories all had the task of explaining whether and how insight into moral goodness had implications for moral obligation. They all thought it did, and they all had extreme difficulty in accounting for it.

The problem was a serious theological one. If each person had a natural moral faculty which could bring moral understanding, and if such understanding imposed a moral obligation, then God's moral role in human life was severely curtailed. The morally good person would not need God, whose moral function would be reduced to that of policing the morally wayward. This was clearly unacceptable, for it would make morals ideally independent of God. Accordingly, in all these theories we find some residual element of divine voluntarism. Generally speaking, a way out was sought in some variation on the following theme. Since the relationship in God's nature between moral insight and moral will is unbroken – whatever account of the relationship theologians may give – and since humans to some extent share in the moral insight, a pale reflection of this relationship may be established in human nature if men and women can partake in God's will and in some measure make it their own. The chief way of accounting for this without resort to revelation was teleological. The particular and confined moral good which each person and community is able to effect may be understood as a contribution to the over-all good of the moral universe of all moral agents past, present, and future. This universal good is understood to be the intention of the Divinity, as shown in the purposefulness of creation. Consequently, our particular will to do the particular good in our power is part of God's general will for the moral creation as a whole. If on occasion we lack that particular will, or if it is weak and undecided, the thought of the teleological arrangement, that is, of God's will, is able to supply the want. We are then acting out of a sense of obligation.

This type of teleology and the associated 'Christian utilitarianism', as it is now often called, was probably the most pervasive style of moral and political thought in the eighteenth century.[7] An early formulation by Richard Cumberland had some influence, but the most important version was undoubtedly Francis Hutcheson's.[8] This line of argument provided the basis for the empirical 'science of morals' which characterized a great deal of Enlightenment social thought. Since so much depended upon the teleological arrangement of the universe, an important task of the science of morals was to provide a map of the moral world showing how its various components ideally fitted together. The popular science of morals was thus a description of the proper working of the moral institutions currently making up society – 'proper' being defined in terms of making social life possible as a contribution to the general happiness of humankind.

Hume matched this agenda point for point. Once such forms of behaviour as respect for the possessions of others and keeping of promises have become fairly common, it will be evident to all that they are socially useful by allowing things to be done collaboratively which otherwise could not be done. This social utility, or public good, is merely the outcome of individual actions, but it appears as though it were the result of a shared design. Consequently, individuals are inclined to approve of the behaviour that brings about the public good, for it appears as though this behaviour were aimed at this outcome, and contrariwise, to disapprove of behaviour having contrary effects. In this way the basic rules of justice pertaining to property and contract

7   Cf. J.E. Crimmins, 'John Brown and the theological tradition of utilitarian ethics', *History of Political Thought*, 4 (1983), 523–50.

8   For documentation of these points, see K. Haakonssen, 'The character and obligation of natural law according to Richard Cumberland', in *English Philosophy in the Age of Locke*, ed. M.A. Stewart, Oxford, forthcoming; and chapter 2 in the present volume.

come to be accepted as moral rules. In short, although the purposeful-ness of certain general patterns of behaviour is only apparent, the perception of this apparent purposefulness, or teleology, in itself be-comes an independent cause of such behaviour in the future. The prob-lem is that not every *application* of the rules of justice produces good results for all the individuals concerned or, in extreme cases, for any individuals. Nonetheless, because of their general public utility, we still think that the rules should be kept, or that they are obligatory. Whereas the popular moral philosophy sketched earlier invoked what we may call the 'internalization' of God's will, in order to account for obliga-tion, Hume suggests that we internalize a social 'will'. In a social group where just behaviour is generally approved as good because it pro-duces social utility, people who in a particular case lack any motive for justice – perhaps because neither they nor any other assignable person stands to gain anything from the action in question – will tend to have a motive supplied. Because everyone generally approves of just behav-iour, *as if* it sprang from a separate laudable motive, people lacking such a motive will feel morally deficient as compared with their sur-roundings and will come to disapprove of or hate themselves on that account. In this they will be reinforced by the disapproval of their fellows. This self-loathing becomes the motive or the will by which people act justly as a matter of obligation. We may also say that just behaviour has become an artificial accretion on the natural person. We disapprove of deficiencies – a lack of a certain degree of benevolence, for example – in the natural moral qualities and see it as an obligation to reinstate benevolence to its 'natural' place amongst our motives. In the same manner, we have learned to see the failure to have a motive to be just as constituting a deficiency. Since there is no motive to be reinstated in this case, we have to 'invent' one, namely the will to be complete moral characters like other people in our society. A crucial concept in Hume's analysis of obligation is thus that of character. Part of our moral character is natural, part of it derives from social living; deficiencies in the former evoke a natural, in the latter a socially in-duced, desire to repair our character. These desires are, respectively, our obligation to the natural and to the artificial virtues.[9] This causal

9 T III.2.ii:498–501; III.2.v:517–19, 522–3; III.2.viii:545; III.3.i:574–91; III.3.iii: 602–3; and, not least, III.2.i:478–9, where Hume on p. 479 explains:

> it may be establish'd as an undoubted maxim, that no action can be virtuous, or morally good, unless there be in human nature some motive to produce it, distinct from the sense of its morality. But may not the sense of morality or duty produce an action, without any other motive? I answer, It may: But this is no objection to the present doctrine. When any virtuous motive or principle is common in human na-ture, a person, who feels his heart devoid of that principle, may hate himself on that account, and may perform the action without the motive, from a certain sense of duty,

account of the moral obligation to pursue the artificial virtues, typified
by justice, is the crowning effort in Hume's subversion of the reigning
paradigms of moral and political philosophy. It had a number of no
less subversive repercussions.

3.4 *The basis for authority*

The rules of justice form the basis of any significant scale of organized social living. Yet the obligation to obey the rules of justice depends on nothing more than each person's perception of the general
social *opinion* of these rules. Although the formation of such opinion is

---

in order to acquire by practice, that virtuous principle, or at least, to disguise to
himself, as much as possible, his want of it. A man that really feels no gratitude in his
temper, is still pleas'd to perform grateful actions, and thinks he has, by that means,
fulfill'd his duty. Actions are at first only consider'd as signs of motives: But 'tis
usual, in this case, as in all others, to fix our attention on the signs, and neglect, in
some measure, the thing signify'd. But tho', on some occasions, a person may perform an action merely out of regard to its moral obligation, yet still this supposes in
human nature some distinct principles,which are capable of producing the action,
and whose moral beauty renders the action meritorious.

It has been objected to me by Robert Shaver that Hume is saying that the socially
created sense of duty is only one of several grounds for doing our duty; in Shaver's
view, this is why he gives additional accounts of obligation in terms of self-interest,
sympathy, etc. It is true, of course, that on Hume's view we often act out of self-
interest, sympathy, and other motives which it is 'in human nature ... to produce', in
doing actions that are our duty. But the relevant question is, Why can we say that an
act of justice which I happen to do out of self-interest or benevolence is *also* a duty?
Or, if we disregard the self-interest or benevolence (or if such motivation disappears), Why would it be meaningful for myself or others to appeal to my sense of
duty as a *further* motive? On my reading, it would be because the sense of duty is an
artificially or socially created addition to our character, existing alongside the natural features that helped foster it. As for these natural traits of character, or virtues,
the case is exactly parallel. We generally just have them – though now through
natural disposition – but in addition we also have them as *duties*, and to have
natural duties means to have a sense of natural character deficiencies, derived from
a sense of our common natural character: 'Tho' there was no obligation to relieve
the miserable, our humanity wou'd lead us to it; and when we omit that duty, the
immorality of the omission arises from its being a proof, that we want the natural
sentiments of humanity. A father knows it to be his duty to take care of his children:
But he has also a natural inclination to it. And if no human creature had that
inclination, no one cou'd lie under any such obligation' (*T* III.2.v:519). I am indebted
to Robert Shaver for private discussion of these issues; but see also his, 'Hume on
the duties of humanity', *Journal of the History of Philosophy*, 30 (1992), 545–56.

For further details of Hume's theory of obligation, see K. Haakonssen, *The Science of a Legislator: The Natural Jurisprudence of David Hume and Adam Smith*, Cambridge, UK, 1981, pp. 30–3, and the critical discussion by David Gauthier in 'Artificial virtues and the sensible knave', *Hume Studies*, 18 (1992), 401–27.

a strong and universal tendency in human life, it is clearly subject to severe disruption and fluctuation. People accordingly seek to protect the rules of justice by the institution of government (T III.2.viii:543). But then, one must ask, What is the basis for the authority of government to administer justice or to do anything else? Or, in Hume's language, What is the source of allegiance to government? In answering this question he follows a pattern similar to that employed in his analysis of the rules of justice.

The traditional Tory notion that authority is inherent in the social world in the form of a divine right has to be rejected because it invokes forces about which humans can know nothing. The traditional Whig notion that authority derives from contractual arrangements is, Hume argues, empirically false and conceptually confused.[10] It seems impossible to identify any contract by virtue of which any group living under a particular government owes allegiance to that government. The generality of humankind knows nothing of such a contract, and even if there had been some contract in the past, it would not carry authority beyond the original contractors. Hume finds incoherent the common suggestion that there is a 'tacit' contract, a contract about which a people does not know or think. The essential feature of a contractual arrangement is that it involves choosing whether or not to enter into the arrangement: but a choice that is unknown to a chooser is not a choice. Furthermore, individuals on the whole have no choice. We are generally born into societies that are already subject to government and find ourselves obliged to obey the laws of that government. People of a particularly enthusiastic cast may, of course, say that they always have the choice of dying rather than living with what they consider a tyran-

---

10 In the *History* Hume explains the labels 'Whig' and 'Tory' in ch. 68 (VI, p. 381) and accounts for the emergence of the Whig and Tory parties at the Revolution of 1688–9 in ch. 71 (VI, pp. 523–34). The basic party principles and their connection with the later division between Court and Country interests are laid out in 'Of the Parties of Great Britain', pp. 69–72, and 'Of the Coalition of Parties', passim. Pre-Revolutionary Tory ideas of divine right to rule owed a great deal to Robert Filmer's *Patriarcha* of 1680, in *Patriarcha and Other Writings*, ed. J.P. Sommerville, Cambridge, UK, 1991; among many post-Revolutionary restatements, Charles Leslie's voluminous output is representative, e.g. *The Constitution, Laws, and Government of England Vindicated*, London, 1709, and *The Finishing Stroke*, London, 1711. The role of John Locke's *Second Treatise of Government* (1689) – in *Two Treatises of Government*, ed. P. Laslett, Cambridge, UK, 1960 – for the formation of Whig principles continues to be a matter of dispute, as does the significance of radical contractarianism in general. Representative examples of the sort of Whiggism Hume has in mind are the anonymous *Vox Populi, Vox Dei: Being True Maxims of Government*, London, 1709; Daniel Defoe, *The Original Power of the Collective Body of the People of England, Examined and Asserted*, London, 1702; and Benjamin Hoadly, *The Original and Institution of Civil Government Discuss'd*, London, 1710, esp. Part II.

nical government. These are exactly the people Hume fears most of all, because in their fanaticism they could destroy existing government, and their wildness of temper could never sustain a lasting government (*T* III.2.vii–ix:534–50).

The contract theory of allegiance to government is, in any case, muddled in exactly the same way as the contractual account of property. It tries to reduce allegiance to acts of will by individuals, but in doing so it *presupposes* that there is a government, that is, an authority with some claim to allegiance to which individuals pledge that allegiance. Individual acts of obedience, in the form of promises, for instance, can be recognized as expressions of allegiance only if the object of such behaviour is the sort of person or group of persons to whom allegiance is due. Governmental authority must therefore rest on something existing prior to any such promise of allegiance. In the terms used in the account of property, we can see that the subjects of government must have an interest in government distinct from their interest in keeping their pledge of allegiance. The interest in question is, in general terms, an interest in external and internal protection and, especially, in the administration of justice. To the extent that such interest establishes obedience as a general pattern of behaviour, allegiance becomes, like justice, another artificial accretion on the natural personality of those involved. Once this has happened, the absence of sentiments of allegiance is perceived as a personal deficiency. In this way allegiance, like justice, becomes a matter not only of 'the natural obligations of interest . . . but also the moral obligations of honour and conscience' (*T* III.2.viii:545).

Hume's idea of the obligation of allegiance has a certain similarity to a form of contract theory that had some currency in his time but which he never mentions at all, namely 'implied contract'. In fact, in his rejection of 'tacit contract', he seems to suggest that he did not see any difference between these two theories. Those who did distinguish between tacit and implied contract saw the former as a voluntary commitment signalled in a non-verbal way but still as an identifiable behavioural event. On the other hand, an implied contract does not arise from any particular event; there is no act of will. The commitment of an implied contract follows from, is implied by, what a person *is* or what position or office (spouse, child, doctor, neighbour, citizen, magistrate) he or she holds. This was a way of thinking about social relations that had partly Aristotelian, partly Stoic origins, and that had been translated into the common teleologically-based systems of morals which were outlined earlier.[11] Hume, too, thought that duties arise from what a person is, but this could not be accounted for teleologically in terms

11   For the notion of implied contract, see ch. 10, sect. 10.3, this volume.

of the over-all aim of the system of moral beings, nor, because there is no act of will involved, was there any reason to invoke 'contract' to account for these duties.

Hume's theory of allegiance also saddles him with a genetic problem: how to account for the first origins of government. In his earlier works he is content to give a brief and bland explanation to the effect that, since government is superimposed upon social groups which already recognize the rules of justice, including the obligation to keep promises, it is possible to see the first institution of government as a matter of mutual promises. It is clear, however, that his concern is to discredit the idea that this has any implications for a continuing allegiance to government (*T* III.2.viii:541–2; 'Original Contract':470–1). After a lifetime of reflecting on the problem and, doubtless, after discussing it with his friend Adam Smith, Hume altered his argument in the last essay he wrote, 'Of the Origin of Government.' In this essay he suggests that government has its origins in people's habit of submission to military leaders in time of war. Such leadership would naturally attract non-martial functions, for example the administration of justice and the collection of revenue, and gradually become commonplace between bouts of warfare.[12]

3.5 *Opinion and the science of politics*

Irrespective of the historical account of the origins of government, Hume always maintained his position that contract and consent are not and cannot be the basis for continued allegiance to governmental authority. The basis for government is a combination of the two factors discussed in the *Treatise* and noted earlier: a people's perception of the public interest in protection, especially through enforcement of the rules of justice, and their perception of their obligation to allegiance. In the *Essays* he provocatively formulates this view by saying that it is 'on opinion only that government is founded'. This 'opinion is of two kinds, to wit, opinion of INTEREST, and opinion of RIGHT' ('First Principles of Government':32–3). People are generally born into and continue to live in societies that are under some form of government. The opinion of these subjects that their government can care for the public interest and has the right to exercise authority is the foundation of this government. Consequently, the central task of the science of politics is

---

12 'Origin of Government', pp. 39–40. Cf. Adam Smith, *Lectures on Jurisprudence*, ed. R.L. Meek, D.D. Raphael, P.G. Stein, Oxford, 1978, (A): v, 114–19, 127–8, 134–8; (B): 15–18, 93–6. For Hume, see D. Forbes, *Hume's Philosophical Politics*, Cambridge, UK, 1975, p. 76; for Smith, see Haakonssen, *Science of a Legislator*, pp. 129–31.

to account for the formation and transformation of these fundamental opinions.

Some of the causes of opinion are so universal that they can be explained in completely general terms; they are operative in practically all circumstances of human life. This applies to beliefs concerning the interest and obligation upon which pre-governmental institutions rest – the rules of justice pertaining to property and contract – and to the beliefs underlying government itself. A few additional features of politics may be explained in similarly general terms, but it very soon becomes necessary to draw on more particular factors, factors that are more historically specific. Although it is possible to discuss in general terms the relationship between 'liberty' and 'slavery' in government, one cannot introduce concepts like 'parties' into one's account without drawing on the experience of particular forms of government. To do so requires knowledge of specific events in individual countries. Consequently, Hume's science of politics ranges from a consideration of what some of his contemporaries would have called the 'natural history' of the human species, that is, from his examination of human understanding and the principles of morals, through historically based general maxims, to the civic history of particular cultures and states. This entire range of material is necessarily part of his *science* of politics, because, even in the explanation of the most specific event, there will be references to the universal principles of human nature underlying all moral thought and to the institutions to which those principles have led. Only rarely will our explanations depend on the idiosyncratic whims of individuals. And even in those rare cases, as for example the extremes of enthusiastic madness, deviations from principle can be understood as such only because we know the regularity that is being broken. At the same time the full range of explanations, from the most general to the most specific, is part of a science of *politics*, because all explanations are concerned with the formation of those opinions that support the institutions of society. The more general part of politics explains that such institutions are the kind of things that must have a history, while the more specific parts reveal the history they have actually had. The general principles of politics teach us that political action must start from an understanding of the particular political conditions to which history has brought us.

Hume's political theory is, in other words, an explanation of why political theorizing in abstraction from historical conditions is futile and often dangerous. Hume was acutely conscious of the fact that this was in itself a political opinion calculated to inform political conduct at a particular time and place. Indeed, this was undoubtedly part of the reason why he went to such lengths to popularize his theory in the *Essays* and the *History*. The formation of sound political opinions is the most basic political activity, and Hume's political theorizing was such an activity. There is often a sense of urgency in Hume's political writings, for he was always keenly aware that people's opinions are fickle. Under the influence of passions – of avarice, of factional or dynastic or confessional allegiances, of utopian dreams of perfection – our understanding of our situation and that of our society too often becomes clouded, particularly in situations of uncertainty and instability. When there is uncertainty about who has authority or about what those in authority may do, our habitual ways of thinking and behaving are broken. Under such circumstances, opinions and actions are much more likely to be influenced by imagined situations than by actual conditions, and passionate flights of fancy tend to take over. Since opinions are formed by experience, we can only have empirically well-founded opinions about who is doing what in society if there is a certain regularity of behaviour. The message of Hume's theory concerning the basic features of society is that such regularity cannot come from individual minds and wills alone; it depends upon something outside the individual, namely regular or rule-bound institutions that can guide our behaviour and consequently our expectations of each other. If such institutions, once acquired, are lightly given up, we lose habit and regularity, that is, the most important means of orienting ourselves to others. Consequently we cannot know what we ourselves may do with success, and we will have lost our most elementary freedom. This is the rationale for the enormous emphasis Hume placed on institutional stability.

3.6   *The distribution of justice*

Stability can be seen from two perspectives: the stability of what those in authority *do,* and the stability of who they *are.* These two topics are fundamental to Hume's political thought.

The conduct of government is stable and predictable only if it follows publicly known general rules – only if it is government in accordance with law. Government must therefore be concerned with issues that are suitable subjects of law. These are primarily forms of behaviour that are in the public interest, but not necessarily in the interest of each individual concerned in the particular instance.

> We are, therefore, to look upon all the vast apparatus of our government, as having ultimately no other object or purpose but the *distribution of justice,* or, in other words, the support of the twelve judges. Kings and parliaments, fleets and armies, officers of the court and revenue, ambassadors, ministers, and privy-counsellors, are all subordinate in their end to this part of administration. Even the clergy, as their duty leads them to inculcate morality,

may justly be thought, so far as regards this world, to have no other useful object of their institution. ('Origin of Government': 37–8; italics added)

While at first sight an example of the hyperbole to which Hume occasionally resorts in the *Essays*, this passage makes clear what carries most weight. Although Hume has no doubt about the necessity of a governmental agenda in defence and foreign affairs as well as in economics and culture, priority is given to maintaining those two basic institutions of justice – property and contract – which make social life possible beyond the confines of the family. In so far as the populace has a clear opinion that this balance of priorities constitutes the public interest and that 'the particular government, which is established, is equally advantageous with any other that could easily be settled', to that extent the government has a secure source of allegiance ('First Principles of Government':33).

It follows from this that Hume must reject policies that significantly break the rules of justice. He rejects, for example, the suggestion that governments should treat individual citizens according to their natural merit. Such a policy would create the greatest uncertainty. Merit is so dependent on each particular situation that it is impossible to formulate general rules for it; consequently no orderly allocation of goods could be based on it. The same criticism applies to all other schemes for the distribution of goods or status on the basis of alleged personal merits or virtues. Hume mentions in particular the claims of those religious fanatics who say *'that dominion is founded on grace, and that saints alone inherit the earth'* and points out that England had experienced such enthusiasm from the Puritans and from one of their political sub-sects, the Levellers, who claimed that there ought to be 'an equal distribution of property'.[13]

13 Hume, *Enquiries Concerning Human Understanding and Concerning the Principles of Morals*, ed. L.A. Selby-Bigge, 3rd ed. by P.H. Nidditch, Oxford, 1975; second *Enquiry*, Section III, Part 2: p. 193. In his fine discussion of 'Hume on the duties of humanity', *Journal of the History of Philosophy*, 30 (1992), 545–56, Robert Shaver takes me to task for suggesting that duties of justice, according to Hume, stand apart from duties of humanity by being of more urgent obligation and greater necessity to society. On Shaver's reading, humanity is a duty on a par with justice, as necessary to society; indeed, 'Justice presupposes humanity in that humanity is causally necessary as a motive and a restraint for producing people capable of justice' (p. 553). I have, of course, never denied that humanity, on Hume's view, is a moral duty – albeit a natural one – or that individuals need to be socialized in conditions regulated by duties, or virtues, of humanity in order to be morally equipped to risk regulation by justice. My point has always been the different one, that you cannot have a large society, a society beyond the extended family, unless you can trust that the total stranger has virtues, or adheres to duties, that fall quite outside the 'natural' repertoire and that the duties of justice fit this bill because of their simple

Regarding the distribution of property, Hume adds some further considerations of importance. Even if we assume that equality of property could somehow be achieved, its maintenance would be 'extremely *pernicious* to human society. Render possessions ever so equal, men's different degrees of art, care, and industry will immediately break that equality.' In order to keep people equal in their possessions, these 'virtues' would have to be controlled. To do so, would require a 'most rigorous inquisition', would impoverish society, and would break down social subordination and order (second *Enquiry* III.2:194). These remarks make it clear that Hume's notion of justice is not purely formal and procedural. The rule that everyone should have the same quantity of external possessions is as universal in form as Hume's rules concerning the allocation of property. But he rejects such a rule, because it would require tyrannical interference with individuals' natural qualities – with their virtues and with their personal freedom. The object of just laws is thus individual liberty, and, since the most obvious and most endangered expression of such liberty is the acquisition and use of property, justice is centrally concerned with property and, it follows, with contracts.

This order of justification is noteworthy, for in the *Treatise* Hume has sometimes seemed to limit the object of the rules of justice to securing property per se. He there says that we have three 'species of goods': the 'internal satisfaction of our mind, the external advantages of our body, and the enjoyment of such possessions as we have acquir'd by our industry and good fortune'. Of these the first cannot be taken from us, and the second, while transferable, can be of no use to others. 'The last only are both expos'd to the violence of others, and may be transferr'd without suffering any loss or alteration; while at the same time, there is not a sufficient quantity of them to supply every one's desires and necessities' (*T* III.2.ii:487–8). External goods are, accordingly, the *direct* objects of justice. What the passages from the second *Enquiry* (III.2:193–4) make clear is that through the protection of property the two other species of goods are indirectly being protected as well.

3.7 *The role of rights*

Hume hardly used the traditional notions of *rights* in his moral and political philosophy. Writers on these subjects commonly used a

---

negative and enforceable character. The fact that the duties of humanity are difficult and dangerous to enforce legally and yet 'causally necessary' just underlines the Humean theme of the precariousness of civilized political life and the need to foster a culture that accepts the enforcement of that which can be enforced, the duties of justice.

scheme based on materials from Roman law and developed by natural lawyers from Hugo Grotius onwards, as we have seen in chapter 1. On this scheme, certain features were inherent in each person *qua* human being, whereas others were acquired and added to the person through his or her activity in life. The former were natural or innate rights and correspond roughly to Hume's natural virtues; the latter were adventitious or acquired rights and correspond roughly to Hume's artificial virtues. Some of the natural rights were 'imperfect', others were 'perfect', as were all acquired rights. Kindness, benevolence, gratitude, and the like could be claimed as rights only imperfectly, because the qualities of the claimant that would justify the claim were too uncertain and variable to be the subject of law and the moral urgency of the claims was too limited to warrant the use of legal force to secure them. But the perfect natural rights – life, liberty, personal judgement – or bodily, behavioural, and mental integrity – and their adventitious or artificial extension of the person to property and contractual relations were sufficiently ascertainable to be regulated by law, and their protection by the force of law was deemed so important that it provided the main justification for the institution of government. The distinction between perfect and imperfect rights in respect of their certainty and enforceability sounds very much like Hume's distinction between artificial virtues such as justice and natural virtues such as beneficence. Yet, as we saw at the end of the preceding section, he recognized that in addition to property, certain natural qualities – the goods of mind and body – require the protection of law and that they receive such protection when property is legally safeguarded. These natural qualities or goods are the areas of life that, in theories of natural law, are protected as perfect 'natural rights'. In other words, in substance, Hume was in agreement with the popular natural law systems of morals, but he could not use the concept of rights to formulate his argument. When he does talk of rights, it is casually and in connection with property and contract, or it is in the context of authority – the right to govern.

Hume could not use the concept of rights because both of the rights traditions were unpalatable to him. On one view, rights were qualities of the person as a moral agent; they were the primary feature of moral personality. All moral institutions, such as rules of property or structures of authority, arose when individuals adapted their respective rights to each other. This view had received daring philosophical formulations by Grotius and Hobbes, for whom the qualities, or rights, in question were nothing more mysterious than the various claims of individuals on their surrounding world and on each other. In many respects this was close to Hume's way of thinking, but there were two good reasons why he could not accept it. First, this form of rights argument led directly to the contractarian will theories of social institutions that we have seen him reject. Only if he had found a way of seeing the ascription of rights to individuals as part of the process of socialization could he have reconciled rights with his moral theory.[14] A second reason for rejecting this form of rights argument was probably that it was too readily associated with politico-religious enthusiasm and politically dangerous. Religiously based claims to a freedom of the spirit to govern oneself were only too easily couched in terms of rights, or liberties.

On a second view, rights, far from being the primary moral feature of the person, were derivative from a natural law which ascribed duties and rights to individuals. This was by far the most pervasive view of the philosophical status of rights, based on traditional expositions of Christian notions of natural law as well as on the ideas of Samuel Pufendorf, Richard Cumberland, and other modern natural lawyers.[15] One leading characteristic of this theory was that rights, especially perfect rights, were dependent on duties; when one person has a right to something, others have a duty to abstain from it. This is similar to Hume's reasoning about the moral quality of the rules of justice. But if in these circumstances Hume had invoked a concept of rights, he would have been in great danger of being misunderstood. He had to avoid the traditional argument entirely, because, as we have seen, the natural law involved was part of a teleological and providentialist scheme of justification.

In sum, there are very good reasons embedded in Hume's theory of morals and politics for rejecting both of the common theories of rights. But this did not lead him to reject the entire jurisprudential approach to politics. His ideal of stable governmental action is couched in the juridical terms of rules of justice, and these rules cover the central areas of private jurisprudence in the systems of natural law, that is, the protection of natural and adventitious rights, especially real and personal rights such as property, succession, contract, and delict.

This ideal of government, or 'the rule of law', was, in the British political debate, associated with 'free' governments, whether purely republican like those of the Italian city-states and the United Provinces

14 This was one of the most significant philosophical achievements of Adam Smith, who explained justice in terms of rights, rights in terms of injury, and injury in terms of the reactions of spectators (ideal or actual). See Smith, *Lectures on Jurisprudence* (A): i.1 and 9–25; (B): 5–11. For detailed exposition, see Haakonssen, *Science of a Legislator*, pp. 99–104.

15 See Samuel von Pufendorf, *The Law of Nature and Nations*, ed. J. Barbeyrac, trans, B. Kennet, 5th ed., London, 1749, Bk. I, ch. 6, esp. sects. 3, 4, and 15, with the notes by Barbeyrac; Richard Cumberland, *A Treatise of the Laws of Nature*, trans. J. Maxwell, London, 1727, ch. 1, sects. xxii and xxvii–xxxv.

(The Netherlands), or 'mixed' like the British government. One of Hume's most provocative contributions to this debate was his partial divorce of the question of the nature and stability of government from that of the nature and stability of governmental action. He showed, first, that absolute monarchies like France under certain circumstances were perfectly able to adopt the rule of law and serve the public interest; and, second, that 'free' governments like that of Britain harboured forces that tended towards anarchy, and thereby tyranny and the undermining of the public interest. Having examined what Hume meant by stability of governmental action, we now turn to the second part of the issue of stability: the question of who governs.

3.8   *The right to govern*

All governments, Hume says, are founded on two opinions: opinion of interest, and opinion of right. The latter, he explains, 'is of two kinds, right to POWER and right to PROPERTY' ('First Principles of Government':33). We have discussed the first, what Hume describes as the 'sense of the general advantage which is reaped from government', in terms of the regular administration of justice as the ideal of what good government should do and what citizens should seek from their government. Opinion of right is concerned with who the people think should rule, and it is divided into two parts: opinion concerning the right to power, and opinion concerning the right to property. A government generally held by the people to have a right to power and to serve the public interest will be stable, unless its constitution allows for some popular influence, as in a republican or mixed constitution. In these cases people's opinion of the right to property normally includes the idea that there should be *some* proportionality between property and political influence. Hume remarks that a 'noted author' (that is, James Harrington) 'has made property the foundation of all government; and most of our political writers seem inclined to follow him in that particular'.[16] But Hume rejects Harrington's claim that the balance of political power is directly dependent upon the balance of property. There is a certain tendency for power to gravitate towards the propertied, but this process is normally influenced by several other factors,

16   'First Principles of Government', pp. 33–4. Hume is referring to one of the central theses of James Harrington in such works as *Oceana* and *The Prerogative of Popular Government*. See Harrington, *The Political Works*, ed. J.G.A. Pocock, Cambridge, UK, 1977, e.g. pp. 163–5, 181–2, 231ff., 404ff., 458ff. Hume discusses Harrington in 'Whether the British Government Inclines More to Absolute Monarchy, or to a Republic', pp. 47–8, and 'Idea of a Perfect Commonwealth', pp. 514–6 and 522-3.

such as reverence for settled constitutional forms – that is, opinion of right to power. Otherwise the British government would have become republican, given the weight of the propertied gentry represented in the House of Commons. In constitutions where property can have influence, there is always a danger that this may conflict with beliefs about the right to power, and consequently there is a danger of instability. This is the framework for Hume's analysis of factionalism in 'free' government in general and in that of Britain in particular. The danger is not great in governments, such as absolute monarchies, that rest primarily on the opinion of right to power, but monarchies may be fraught with other dangers.

Hume's analysis of the opinion of a government's right to power is in accordance with his general views regarding the connections between habitual behaviour, the creation of expectations, and the making of moral judgements.[17] He suggests that the factors which form such opinion may be divided into five categories: long possession, present possession, conquest, succession, and positive laws (T III.2.x:556–63). Long possession of power is the strongest and most common source of authority, as was dramatically demonstrated in Britain by the continuing influence of the Stuarts long after they had exhausted most other sources of authority, including that of present possession. Present exertion of power will always influence people's opinion about whom they owe allegiance to, as is shown by the repeated changes of sovereignty in Britain during the seventeenth and early eighteenth centuries. Conquest is a particularly forceful demonstration of present possession and has been used efficiently throughout recorded history. In the eyes of some, the accession of William of Orange to the British throne was an example of conquest. By 'succession', Hume means a situation in which the son succeeds to the father's authority as if it were property, even though such succession had not been long established. Finally, positive laws that regulate who should hold power will always have some impact upon a people's opinion of rightful authority, and this would undoubtedly be the case in Britain following the Act of Settlement (1701), which secured the Hanoverian succession to the thrones of England (after 1707, Great Britain) and Ireland. All these principles influence people's opinion of rightful authority, and if they all concur, the government has 'the strongest title to sovereignty, and is justly regarded as sacred and inviolable' (T III.2.x:562). Often, of course, the principles do not point in the same direction, and there is no general principle that will effectively sort them out. In the end, all politics is 'entirely subordinate to the interests of peace and liberty' (T III.2.x:562).

17 This process is outlined in connection with the obligation to justice in sect. 3.3 of this chapter.

Whatever the principles on which a government may try to rest its authority, if it too grossly invades these interests, the rationale for government has been removed. In that sense the people always have a right to resistance.

Whatever the principle or principles upon which a government bases its claim to sovereignty, the invocation of history will soon play a role. In monarchies the importance of history is reflected in the weight laid on the hereditary principle. Elective monarchies tend to be unstable but often make up for it through the principle of succession. In republics and mixed governments, historical justification is sought in the ancient origins of the constitutional forms followed. These invocations of the past for the purposes of legitimation are, of course, often mere myths, and Hume certainly rejected the various Whig ideas of an ancient English constitution as pure fiction. He clearly took it as one of the hallmarks of modern civilization that such myths could be subject to criticism without endangering the stability of government. Much of his historical and political writing was meant to educate modern Britons in this regard. By giving a candid view of the past, Hume hoped to provide a realistic understanding of how the passage of time influences the present. 'Time and custom give authority to all forms of government, and all successions of princes; and that power, which at first was founded only on injustice and violence, becomes in time legal and obligatory' (T III.2.xi:566). This was crucially important in Britain. Even if the accession of William of Orange could be seen as usurpation in 1688, the course of history had lent legitimacy to the whole of the succession set in train then. It was the latter that was important for the allegiance of British subjects in the middle of the eighteenth century. The task of non-partisan, philosophical history in the service of the science of politics was to disregard factions and factional myths and explain the process by which the nation had arrived at its particular present: by this process the 'interests of peace and liberty' had been shaped. It was necessary for the politically relevant part of the population to hold enlightened opinions about the government's rights on the basis of its present performance with regard to these interests. One of the most remarkable features of modern Europe was, Hume suggested, that this enlightenment was taking place not only within the mixed constitution of Britain but also in the Continental monarchies, or at least in France, the most modern of these.

Traditionally monarchies had, whenever necessary, created suitable opinions of governmental authority through the tyrannical and arbitrary exercise of force. Among Britons this was still the entrenched caricature of French 'slavery', a caricature which Hume thought it was important to dislodge. France was in the vanguard of an entirely new species of monarchy, the civilized monarchy.[18] This admittedly did not have the dynamism to generate the central elements of civilization in the first place; it imitated free societies like Britain. Once adopted, civilized modes of life were fairly secure in a monarchy, in some respects perhaps even more secure than under a mixed constitution.

Hume's analysis of the process of civilization is subtle and rich and beyond easy summary. The three main foci are the expression of the human spirit in arts and sciences, the protection of the person by means of law, and the acquisition and exchange of the goods of the external world (see *T* III.2.ii:487). In dealing with these three factors, Hume is showing the relationship between merely living and living well, to use the Aristotelian distinction. For a society to live at all, it needs, in addition to a government strong enough to protect it externally, a minimal system of justice and the wherewithal to feed itself. In a society where the government, for whatever reason, is restrained from doing much more than securing these things, a spirit of enterprise and individualism tends to predominate. There will be a growth of knowledge arising from experiments in living and producing, and it is on this basis that a commercial society like the British emerges. By living at all, a free society comes to live well. Intriguingly, monarchies can also become civilized by wanting to live equally well: in realizing this wish they may adopt some of the basic features of a free society. Monarchies are characterized by a crust of nobility, whose status is dependent upon the goodwill of the monarch rather than their own enterprise and whose life is guided by codes of honour and ritualized show. Such a class will feed off the arts and crafts developed in a free society and then will often outstrip that society in the fine arts, as exemplified by the superiority of French literature. Cocooned as he is within such a class of culture, the monarch is little inclined to take much interest in the life of society at large, and no social group is sufficiently propertied to make it necessary for him to do so. As long as the civil order is maintained by the enforcement of law, society can be left alone, and this, combined with the need for foreign goods, eventually leads to the growth of commerce. This was the model of the modern civilized monarchy emerging in France, which Hume admired and about which he tried to enlighten his countrymen.

18 Hume's analysis of modern monarchy in general and of that of France in particular is scattered through the *Essays*. The most important passages upon which this discussion is based are 'Of the Liberty of the Press', pp. 10–11; 'That Politics May Be Reduced to a Science', pp. 22–4; 'Of Civil Liberty', passim; 'Of the Rise and Progress of the Arts and Sciences', pp. 113–9, 124–33; 'Of the Original Contract', pp. 485–6. The issue is discussed in D. Forbes, *Hume's Philosophical Politics*, pp. 152–60, and N. Phillipson, *Hume*, London, 1989, pp. 61–70.

Despite his admiration for France, Hume never forgot that such a society enjoyed a regular administration of justice by default. There were no constitutional guarantees, because there was no constitutional counterweight to the Crown. For all its freedom and civilization, modern monarchy offered no political liberty. Hume thought social life with political liberty highly precarious, and, in his more pessimistic periods, when faced with libertarian excesses such as the Wilkes riots in London in the 1760s, he thought a civilized monarchy the safest long-term solution. What he feared in a free constitution was its tendency to breed factions and the tendency of factionalism to degenerate into fanaticism, disorder, and anarchy, out of which would grow tyranny. In other words, the very engine of civilized living, namely freedom under law, found its most refined protection in a system of political liberty which inevitably harboured forces that could become destructive of the engine. This was the situation in which contemporary Britain found itself, and the anatomy of factionalism was consequently a central concern in Hume's literary intervention in public life, his *Essays*, and much of the *History*.

The new and difficult point Hume had to impress on his readers was that in a free constitution political differences could not be *about* the constitution; they had to be *within* the constitution. Factionalism as he knew it was inconsistent with this: 'the influence of faction is directly contrary to that of laws' ('Of Parties in General':55). The general danger in factionalism was that it would lead to fragmentation by pitting group interests against each other at the expense of the public interest. Even worse, it tended to transform the recurring question of who should discharge the offices of government into a question of the balance among the powers of the constitution itself. This was particularly dangerous in a mixed constitution such as the British, where the main factions naturally would form around two different principles of government, the monarchical and the republican. The extraordinary thing was that Britain, as Hume saw it, was in the process of breaking away from this division. But his contemporaries did not appreciate this, and, by continuing the old factional rant, they endangered the precarious constitutional and political balance that was emerging. A readable analysis of factionalism was needed.

3.9 *Above parties*

'Factions' or 'parties' – Hume often uses the two words interchangeably – fall into two broad categories, 'personal' and 'real'. Personal factions are held together by personal relations, normally extensive family ties. Although such relations can play a role in any party, they most easily dominate politics as a whole in small republics, such as those of Italy. Real factions are the ones that can help us understand larger states, especially Britain. '*Real* factions may be divided into those from *interest*, from *principle*, and from *affection*.' Factions based upon interest typically arise when two different social groups, such as the nobility and the common people, have, or think they have, opposing interests. Since interest is inevitably a driving force in all human endeavour, such factions 'are the most reasonable, and the most excusable'. In England it had often been thought that there was a fundamental opposition between the interests of 'the landed and trading part of the nation', and this belief was an important aspect of the division of the political nation into 'Court' and 'Country' factions. But the theory was simply not true. If people are to avoid such false oppositions, they must be enlightened, so that the pursuit of interest, which is constitutive of human behaviour, is guided by the belief that the public interest is also the most important private one ('Parties in General':59–60).

In contrast, political factions inspired by principle, 'especially abstract speculative principle, are known only to modern times, and are, perhaps, the most extraordinary and unaccountable *phaenomenon*, that has yet appeared in human affairs' ('Parties in General':60). The key word here is 'speculative'. If division between factions is concerned only with differences of a speculative or theoretical sort, then there is no objective necessity for any division in political behaviour: that is to say, there is nothing outside the minds of those involved over which to divide. If the factional principles concerned things such as power or goods, which only one or other party could have, then there would be a prima facie case for division. In matters speculative, however, each mind could hold its own, were it not for a natural tendency to get other minds to conform to one's own and thus to one group. The factor that gave this natural tendency such sway in the modern world was, in Hume's opinion, the Christian religion. In its origins Christianity, in contrast to most other religions, was not an establishment faith. It was able to survive only by developing a strong priesthood to protect the sect against secular power. The priesthood therefore had a vested interest in continuing to govern its flock in separation from the state and from other sects. In order to do so, it had to invent speculative principles around which to rally its followers, and in this the priests sought reinforcement from speculative philosophy. When the universal Church broke up, the opposing forces burst upon modern Europe in the disastrous religious wars. 'Such divisions, therefore, on the part of the people, may justly be esteemed factions of *principle*; but, on the part of the priests, who are the prime movers, they are really factions of *interest*' ('Parties in General':62). The danger from the people is factions based on enthusiasm; from the priests, factions primed by superstition.

Hume feared factionalism based upon the opposing principles of superstition and enthusiasm most of all, because of its rabble-rousing potential. Couching their rhetoric in whatever was the political jargon of the day, leaders could take to the streets and the meeting-houses and appeal to the large segment of the population that was outside the reach of proper education. The only way to deal with such factionalism was to enlighten the potential leaders of the factions. To this purpose Hume supported every move that could secure the inclusion of the clergy in the world of letters. Clergymen of taste and learning would tend to see issues of doctrinal theology as matters for discussion amongst the educated, rather than as reasons for social divisions, and they would see their role vis-à-vis their congregations as a moralizing and civilizing one rather than as a sectarian one.

The British political system, however, also bred leaders of secular faction who based their causes on 'principle'. In the wake of the constitutional settlement after the Revolution of 1688, members of the old Tory and Whig factions had been weaving a complicated (and shifting) patchwork, the main components of which were a government, or Court, faction, consisting largely of modern Whigs, *and* a Country opposition, consisting of groups of Tories and old-fashioned Whigs who were only rarely able to act coherently as a group. Hume thought that this factionalism should be dealt with in two ways. At one level, the principles invoked by the factions should be criticized. At another level, this criticism should not take the usual form of political polemics but rather the detached form of polite literary debate. Politics had to be made polite and subject to civilized manners, just like art and literature; it had to be written about according to literary standards – as in Hume's *Essays* and *History* – not in the form of polemic or diatribe. The substantial criticism of factional principles Hume approached in a variety of ways. In the *Treatise,* the second *Enquiry,* and some of the *Essays,* he tried to show the untenability of the basic philosophical principles behind the factions which we considered at the beginning of this chapter: that is, the ideas of natural hierarchy and authority, on one side, and will theories of contract on the other. In the *History* and some of the *Essays* he rejected as spurious the historical authority invoked for party principles, and in several of the *Essays* he argued that the factions were politically blind to the realities of the contemporary situation and therefore potentially disastrous. This was not least the case with factions arising from 'affection', as distinct from those from interest and from principle.

Factions from affection 'are founded on the different attachments of men towards particular families and persons, whom they desire to rule over them' ('Parties in General':63). Such factions were powerful forces in history, and Hume analysed at some length the attachment of Englishmen and Scots to the Stuarts, and of the new breed of Britons to the Hanoverians, an issue that remained at the forefront of British politics until the defeat of the last Jacobite rising in 1745.[19] Political opposition based on such principles was irrational, since it could seldom serve the real interests of those involved. The voice of reason could only try to persuade people of this and, more generally, try to show that it mattered less *who* governed than *how* they governed. The best constitution was one of such stable procedures that even poor rulers might govern in the public interest. In at least his more optimistic moments, before the pessimism of the 1760s and 1770s set in, Hume thought that the British constitution was approaching, or could approach, such a stable and positive form. The problem was that factional cant was blinding Britons to this possibility.

3.10   *The stability of Great Britain*

The loudest charge against the post-Revolutionary political system, and especially against the long regime of Sir Robert Walpole, was that of 'corruption', by which was meant the manipulation of the House of Commons by the Crown and its ministers. Rejecting the use of such charged language, Hume pointed out that it was in fact a system of mutual dependence and the very thing that, however precariously, enabled political liberty to be combined with stability in a mixed constitution. In economic terms the Crown was infinitely weaker than the property represented in the Commons taken as a whole, a state of affairs constitutionally ratified in the Crown's dependence upon Parliament for supply. As a balance, the Crown had acquired a measure of control over parts of the lower house taken individually and in that way secured the stability of the policy pursued at any given time. This was possible because of the respect given to traditional constitutional forms and because the Crown was a great deal richer than any individual subject. Through distribution of offices in government and church, pensions and honours, procurement of secure parliamentary seats, and the like, the King and his ministers enrolled MPs in support of Court positions on decisive issues. The motives and indeed the characters of those involved might not stand the closest moral scrutiny, but that was not to be expected of people in power in any system. The point was that this system converted private – and not so private – vices into public interest.

The same could not, in Hume's eyes, be said about the other part of the charge of corruption, the undermining of the economy through

19 'Of the Protestant Succession', passim; 'Of the Parties of Great Britain', pp. 71–2; *History*, ch. 71: VI, pp. 530–4.

public debt. The government increasingly financed its business, including successive large-scale wars, by means of public loans from the community, guaranteed by the public treasury. Trading in these bonds became a major part of the finance market. The stability of this whole system was assumed to depend upon the ability of the government to honour the loans, and, as the public debt grew and grew, it seemed that the only barrier to national bankruptcy was trust in the future, which meant trust in the stability of the government to secure a future. Like many more traditional thinkers, Hume believed that landed property was a stabilizing influence on government. Since real estate could not be removed from the country, the landed interest was the interest of the country. But, in a commercial society, where land itself was increasingly a commodity and subject to the fluctuations of financial exchange, even land did not provide a terra firma for a government engaged in loan financing on a large scale. The whole financial system appeared increasingly to be a mental construct of the players involved, a kind of economic superstition, with decreasing reference to anything objective and extra-mental.

It was left to Hume's only peer in the metaphysics of markets, Adam Smith, to show that in this regard financial systems operated on rules not much different from the rules of justice, as Hume had expounded them. That such systems were useful and the result of choice distinguished them from those based on superstition. And it was left to Hume's only peer in the metaphysics of politics, Edmund Burke, to analyse the extraordinary revolutionary effect when superstition about paper credit was made to shore up French political enthusiasm. It is pleasant to speculate how both of these analyses would have informed a latter-day Humean interpretation of the longevity of the Anglican church-state's *ancien régime*.[20]

20 For a brief overview of the reception of and literature on Hume's political thought, see K. Haakonssen, 'The structure of Hume's political theory: Justice, government and politics', in *The Cambridge Companion to Hume*, ed. D.F. Norton, Cambridge, UK, 1993, pp. 182–221, at pp. 210–14.

4

Adam Smith out of context: His theory of rights in Prussian perspective

When, in the winter of 1763, he began his last series of lectures on jurisprudence as Professor of Moral Philosophy at Glasgow University, Adam Smith suggested that there were two alternative ways in which he could arrange his material: 'The civilians begin with considering government and then treat of property and other rights. Others who have written on this subject begin with the latter and then consider family and civil government. There are several advantages peculiar to each of these methods, tho' that of the civil law seems upon the whole preferable.'[1] Accordingly Smith adopted what he saw as the method of civil law, that is, first government, then the family, and finally the rights of the individual. The detailed notes from his lectures of the preceding year, 1762–3, and the very brief notes from one of the early years of his professorship, however, disclose that in these two years he followed the method of the 'others', leading us to presume that he in fact did so in all of his lectures until 1763.[2] The obvious question then is, Why did Smith change his system? It is also relatively easy to answer. Once we have outlined an answer, we shall see that it is no less obvious to ask, Why did Smith, even as he changed his method, see 'several advantages peculiar to *each* of these methods'? Indeed, we shall want to ask, why did he ever choose the way of the 'others' in the first instance? Esoteric though these questions may seem, they go to the heart of Smith's originality as a thinker about morals and, especially, about rights.

---

1 Adam Smith, *Lectures on Jurisprudence,* ed. R.L. Meek, D.D. Raphael, and P.G. Stein, Oxford, 1978, LJ(B), 11. The two sets of student notes in this edition are referred to, as usual, as *LJ(A)* and *LJ(B)*, designating lectures delivered in, respectively, 1762–3 and (almost certainly) 1763–4.

2 See LJ(A) and the 'Anderson Notes' in R.L. Meek, 'New light on Adam Smith's Glasgow lectures on jurisprudence', *History of Political Economy,* 8 (1976), 439–77, at 467–77.

4.1   Smith's theory of rights

The 'others' to whom Smith referred were the generality of natural
law thinkers in the seventeenth and eighteenth centuries, to whose
method he was introduced when a student of Francis Hutcheson's at
Glasgow University. These writers divided natural law into three principal parts. The first dealt with the individual in abstraction from social
groups; the second dealt with the individual as a member of the family
group (often called 'oeconomical jurisprudence' – that is, 'household
jurisprudence'); and the third dealt with the individual as a member of
civil society (sometimes called 'political jurisprudence'). To these topics
was normally added the jurisprudence of the international community,
the 'law of nations'.

At first it is puzzling that Smith should suggest that the 'civilians'
put political jurisprudence, or 'government', first. Plainly, no writer on
the civil law, by which Smith meant *corpus iuris civilis,* began with a
discussion of the principles of political governance (with a partial exception, to be considered later on). What Smith must have meant –
and, one may hope, explained to his students – was that the civil law
always *presupposed* the existence of political society, *civitas,* as a precondition for the law of the *civitas.* Smith himself, of course, did not simply
assume the existence of government; he set out to explain it, in original
historico-theoretical terms. But one of his basic messages was that there
was no pre-governmental condition of humankind, no state of nature.
The individual would always be living in some kind of social grouping
with systems of governance, even if only the most rudimentary ones,
as among bands of hunters and gatherers. The moral life, including
people's rights, would therefore be formed in governed societies, and
in this light it might well seem 'upon the whole preferable' to discuss
the basis for government before explaining the rights of the individual
and of members of private or household societies. In order to appreciate this preference, we have to look more closely at some basic features
of Smith's moral theory, not least his theory of rights.[3]

3   The following sketch of Smith's moral theory is closely linked to the detailed
discussions in K. Haakonssen, *The Science of a Legislator: The Natural Jurisprudence of
David Hume and Adam Smith,* Cambridge, UK, 1981, ch. 3. Since I wrote that book, a
number of comprehensive studies of Smith have appeared, including D. Brühlmeier, *Die Rechts- und Staatslehre von Adam Smith und die Interessentheorie der Verfassung,* Berlin, 1988; A. Hueber, *Die philosophische und ethische Begründung des homo
economicus bei Adam Smith,* Frankfurt a.M., 1990; *Adam Smith Reviewed,* ed. P. Jones
and A.S. Skinner, Edinburgh, 1992; P. Minowitz, *Profits, Priests and Princes: Adam
Smith's Emancipation of Economics from Politics and Religion,* Stanford, 1993; *Adam
Smith: International Perspectives,* ed. H. Mizuta and C. Sugiyama, London, 1993; J.Z.
Muller, *Adam Smith in His Time and Ours: Designing the Decent Society,* New York,

At the heart of Smith's moral philosophy is a social theory of the self. Consciousness of one's identity as a continuous self, separate from but standing in various relationships to other persons, is a function of neither a divinely implanted soul nor a specific natural power such as reason or a moral sense. The self is formed in our interaction with other people, according to Smith. We turn to other people not only out of need but out of curiosity or a spontaneous tendency to identify with the other, a tendency which Smith calls 'sympathy'. Consequently, when others turn to us, we are predisposed to see ourselves as objects of their observation. Awareness of being the object of other people's observation and assessment leads us to pre-empt their assessment by self-observation and self-assessment. We internalize the spectator and try to view ourselves as others might. The internal spectator therefore often prompts such adjustment of behaviour as would otherwise be demanded by external spectators in order to satisfy the inclination to or the need for agreement or conformity. This process of mutual adjustment through sympathetic search for a common standpoint of course often fails and leads to the quest for an ideal judgement transcending the various limitations of knowledge and bias of those actually involved. Once we begin a dialogue with such an imagined ideal of an impartial spectator, we have a moral conscience. To put it briefly, self-consciousness in our dealings with others is the basis for judgement of the behaviour of others, and the explicit or implicit conflicts this leads to prompt the ideal of objective moral judgement – the judgement of an *impartial spectator*. The moral life consists in our attempts sympathetically to identify the impartial spectator's stand-point.

The object of the impartial spectator's judgement is thus a socially formed self, but this does not mean that there are no universally constant features of humanity. Apart from the basic human needs and the tendency to take a sympathetic interest in others that lead to self-consciousness and moral judgement in the first place, the moral philosopher can trace certain patterns of moral reaction across different societies and cultures. These patterns are identified as the fundamental moral virtues, which have enough in common to allow comparison between ancient and modern, primitive and commercial, despotic and republican societies.

1993; S.J. Pack, *Capitalism as a Moral System*: *Adam Smith's Critique of the Free Market Economy*, Aldershot, UK, 1991; D.D. Raphael, *Adam Smith*, Oxford, 1985; G. Streminger, *Adam Smith*, Reinbek bei Hamburg, 1989; R.F. Teichgraeber III, '*Free Trade' and Moral Philosophy*: *Rethinking the Sources of Adam Smith's "Wealth of Nations"*, Durham, NC, 1986; Manfred Trapp, *Adam Smith – politische Philosophie und politische Ökonomie*, Göttingen, 1987; P.H. Werhane, *Adam Smith and His Legacy for Modern Capitalism*, New York, 1991.

When the spectator, whether the actual or the imagined impartial one, sympathetically enters into the situation of an agent, the result is approval or disapproval of the agent's judgement and action. When the agent is trying to promote the good or the welfare of someone, whether self or other, the spectatorial approval or disapproval tends to vary from one person to the next. For, although we tend to agree on what is good in broad outline, we have great difficulty agreeing what is good for particular persons in specific situations. By contrast, it is a constant element in moral life that humanity in any given society or period agrees on what counts as injury and, largely, on how deeply to resent it and how severely to punish it. As Gibbon put it, 'Virtue is praised without being known; known without being felt; and felt without being practised; but the case is different with vice.'[4] It is therefore in general easy to reach the impartial standpoint in questions of injury and, consequently, to avoid doing injury in the first instance. Avoidance of injury is, according to Smith, what defines the virtue of justice. For him, as for Hume, justice has a special status, apart from morality proper: it is a purely negative virtue, sharply distinct from the generally imprecise, and hence disputed, positive virtues.[5]

In strong contrast to Hume – a remarkable feature, which we shall consider later – Smith also explains his theory of justice in terms of *rights*.[6] Fundamentally, whenever, in the eyes of the impartial spectator, a person is injured, that person's right has been infringed, unless the injury is undertaken for a morally justified reason, such as punishment or self-defence – that is, in order to protect other rights. The virtue of justice therefore consists in respect for individual rights, and the rules of justice are safeguards for such rights. The concepts of a right and of justice thus rely crucially on the concept of injury, which again depends on the concept of a person:

> Justice is violated whenever one is deprived of what he had a right to and could justly demand from others, or rather, when we do him any injury or hurt without a cause. Let us consider then in how many ways justice may be violated, that is, in how many respects a man may be injured. – 1st, he may be injured as a man; 2dly, as a member of a family; and 3dly, as a citizen or member of a state.[7]

Individually, 'as a man', one may be injured as a physical being through bodily harm and by being deprived of the command of one's

---

4   Edward Gibbon, *An Essay on the Study of Literature*, London, 1764, p. 103.
5   Concerning positive and negative virtues and the theory of justice, see Haakonssen, *Science of a Legislator*, pp. 83–7.
6   See Haakonssen, *Science of a Legislator*, pp. 99ff.   7   LJ(A), i.9–10.

body (i.e. deprived of liberty). The individual may further be injured as a moral person through attack on his or her socially established identity; Smith refers to this as one's 'reputation'. Finally, the individual may be injured in certain extensions of his or her person into the surrounding physical and social world. For when the impartial spectator approves of a person's command over certain things in the world, a moral link is established between person and thing which it is consequently injurious to interfere with.[8] Similarly, when the spectator approves of one person's command over some aspect of another person's life – generally as a consequence of the latter's promise or delict – a morally protected connection is established. In the former case the result is property rights, in the latter contractual rights.[9]

As a member of familial and civil societies, one can be injured in one's standing as a husband / wife, parent / child, master / servant and citizen / magistrate. The important thing to note here is that such injury does not consist in breach of contract, for Smith does not see these societies as resting on contractual relations. Both familial and political roles depend on social or spectator recognition and are therefore primarily open to criticism from the point of view of the impartial spectator. One of the most important forms of such criticism is cast in terms of injury or infringement of rights.[10]

Smith recognizes the traditional distinction between 'natural' and 'adventitious' rights, saying that the rights to physical and moral integrity are natural, whereas the rest of the field of rights is adventitious, or acquired.[11] The sense of the distinction seems to be twofold: the two natural rights are more universal and are generally recognized as of greater moral importance than the adventitious right to property, since the former are found even in societies prior to the formation of property. As I have explained elsewhere, this is a distinction of dubious use in Smith, since all rights are acquired through spectator sympathy with

---

8 As I explain in *Science of a Legislator*, pp. 106–7, this spectator theory of property side-steps Locke's 'labour' theory. Investment of labour is simply one of the factors considered by the impartial spectator in establishing the link between person and thing.

9 For Smith's basic division of the field of rights, see LJ(A), i.9–26 and LJ(B), 5–11; *Science of a Legislator*, p. 105, fig. 1.

10 The law of familial society is dealt with in LJ(A), iii and LJ(B), 101–48; *Science of a Legislator*, pp. 123–7. Public law is in LJ(A), v. 54–86; 102–49; and LJ(B), 78–86; 91–9. For the special complications in the case of political rights, see my *Science of a Legislator*, pp. 127–33 and 145–6.

11 LJ(A), i.12 and 24, ii.93; LJ(B), 8, 9–10, 11, 149, 182; cf. *Science of a Legislator*, p. 205, n. 10.

resentment at injury done.[12] Furthermore, although the earliest society, that of hunters and gatherers, may not have had property, it did, by Smith's account, have possession, and one might have expected this to be included as a natural right.

However that may have been treated in Smith's own manuscript, it is clear from his students' notes that he saw the greatest extension of the personal sphere as occurring in the second stage of society, that of the shepherds. Here possession in things under each person's control, that is, a more or less physical relation, was extended into property in things beyond the person's immediate control, that is, into a moral relation. This step was so momentous that it could at first only be taken collectively; that is to say, property – especially in herds of animals – was at first recognized as invested in the social group as a whole. Only the ability of the chieftain to dominate the group, mainly through leadership in war, gave rise to the idea that their goods were his property. This idea of exclusive property right was immensely strengthened when it became possible for individual chieftains to exclude outsiders permanently from certain areas, that is, with the holding of land in property and the emergence of agricultural society. The most abstract, and fragile, extension of the personal sphere is through contract whereby one individual controls some part of another's personal sphere, whether goods, services, or other contractual means (e.g. credit or stock). Although elementary contracts may have been with humanity from the earliest times, contractual relations come to dominate as commercial society emerges from that of agriculture.[13] Each of these developments requires strengthening of government to protect the new rights, and when this is effective, people's pursuit of their needs will form the system of exchange that is the subject of political economy.

This brief sketch should suffice to make it clear that by basing rights upon the spontaneous spectatorial interaction among people, Smith makes rights integral to the structure of social life and its evolution. Rights are not pre-social moral equipment but part of living socially, and they have to be accounted for in the context of each form of society. To the extent that the four stages of society are seen as stages in the development of authority, or government, it is therefore hardly surprising that Smith should find it advantageous to account for this development first, so as to be able to relate the development of individ-

12   Haakonssen, *Science of a Legislator*, pp. 100–3.

13   For the four stages, see esp. R.L. Meek, 'Smith, Turgot and the "four stages" theory', *History of Political Economy*, 3 (1971), 9–27; Haakonssen, *Science of a Legislator*, ch. 7; and the critical discussion in J. Salter, 'Adam Smith on feudalism, commerce and slavery', *History of Political Thought*, 13 (1992), 219–41.

ual and familial rights to it. Furthermore, when history deviated from the 'natural' progress of the four stages, it was generally owing to revolutions in government, which again had a great effect on the development of humanity's moral, not least juridical, life. Thus when the energetic northerners toppled the Roman government, they set in motion the process leading to feudal government and law. And it was only the political alliance of monarchy and emerging cities that broke the back of this system and led to commercial developments long before the agricultural stage had reached maturity. In other words, both in the abstract natural, or conjectural, 'history' of the four stages of civil society and in the historical account of the past, an explanation of government seemed a necessary presupposition for Smith's theory of natural justice or natural law, meaning his theory of rights. Viewed in this light, it seems obvious that Smith should find the method of presentation of 'the civil law' – in his special understanding of this – 'upon the whole preferable'. How, then, could Smith have adopted the method of the natural lawyers for most of the formative years of his over-all system; how could he still find it attractive when he changed method at last?

4.2 *The jurisprudence of Samuel von Cocceji*

Smith's decision to change his method is not the only puzzle in the opening pages of his jurisprudence lectures of 1763. He began them with a brief survey of what he considered the main contributions to the modern literature on natural law.[14] According to this, the discipline was given its modern form and its most 'complete' treatment in Grotius's *De iure*, 'a sort of casuistical book' which, by drawing a parallel between the relations among states and among individuals in the state of nature, saw defence against and redress of injury as the heart of jurisprudence.[15] 'The next writer of note after Grotius was Mr. Hobbes', who, in 'utter abhorrence of the ecclesiastics', suggested that morals was a matter for positive determination by the sovereign power, not for individual consciences. Left in their natural state, the latter would produce a state of war which only a 'contract to obey one common sovereign' could obviate. Unspecified 'divines' sought to counter this by showing that humanity was capable of society without government:

> They endeavoured to shew that man in this state has certain rights belonging to him, such as a right to his body, to the fruits of his labour, and the

14   LJ(B), 1–4.

15   This is in accordance with Smith's brief remarks about Grotius in *The Theory of Moral Sentiments*, ed. D.D. Raphael and A.L. Macfie, Oxford, 1976, VII.iv.37.

fullfilling of contracts. With this design Puffendorf wrote his large treatise. The sole intention of the first part of it is to confute Hobbes.[16]

In other words, as Smith saw it, the modern natural law tradition was centrally concerned with humanity's pre-civil condition. He saw the tradition as fundamentally divided over the issue of whether the state of nature was an amoral state of war, as in Hobbes, or whether humankind had some moral capacity to form social relations independently of any political authority, as in the unnamed theologians and in Pufendorf. One senses Smith's frustration with this debate: 'it in reality serves no purpose to treat of the laws which would take place in a state of nature, or by what means succession to property was carried on, as there is no such state existing.'[17] Every state of society has some kind of political regimen; the formation of juridical categories, such as rights, and the growth of civic authority, such as the ability to judge and punish and to lead in war and peace, are equally part of moral 'progress' (in the eighteenth century, value-neutral sense). It may be that Smith was able to read some of this into Grotius and that this accounts for his obvious liking for the latter's great treatise. But what are we to make of his concluding remarks on the history of natural jurisprudence:

> The next who wrote on this subject was the Baron de Cocceii, a Prussian. There are five volumes in folio of his works published, many of which are very ingenious and distinct, especially those which treat of laws. In the last volume he gives an account of some German systems. Besides these there are no systems of note upon this subject.[18]

Since Smith never tells us any more about the reasons for including Cocceji with Grotius, Hobbes, and Pufendorf as those 'of note', we have to speculate against the background of the nature of this Prussian's theory of jurisprudence. It is a speculation which is more than a little curious.

The student's notes on Smith's lecture run together two barons von Cocceji, Heinrich von Cocceji (1644–1719), and his son, Samuel von Cocceji (1679–1755). This is hardly strange, for the younger Cocceji edited a four-volume work of his father's and issued it with heavy annotations, as well as with a companion volume of his own works. The five large folios tended to go together as one work,[19] nor was this

16   LJ(B), 3. Cf. TMS, VII.iii.1.1; VII.iii.2.1–5; and for Smith's general view of the character of natural jurisprudence, TMS, VII.iv.6–37.

17   LJ(B), 3.   18   LJ(B), 3–4.

19   Heinrich von Cocceji, *Grotius illustratus, seu commentarii ad Hugonis Grotii de Jure belli et pacis libros tres*, 4 vols., Bratislava, 1744–52; Samuel von Cocceji, *Introductio ad Henrici L.B. de Cocceji . . . Grotium illustratum, continens dissertationes proemiales XII in quibus principia Grotiana circa ius naturae . . . ad iustam methodum revocan-*

unjustified, since the son's natural jurisprudence was an explicit development of that of his father. The first three volumes of Heinrich von Cocceji's *Grotius illustratus* contain a detailed commentary on Grotius's *De iure*, while the fourth volume prints an important collection of works on the law of the sea, issued with the younger Cocceji's commentaries.[20] Samuel's own volume was meant as an introduction to his father's work, and it contains twelve 'preliminary dissertations', of which the twelfth, taking up half the volume, is a new edition of his *Novum systema* from 1740.[21]

The two Cocceji were no ordinary Prussian text-book writers. Heinrich von Cocceji was Professor of Natural Law and the Law of Nations at Heidelberg, in succession to Pufendorf. After a period at Utrecht, he taught from 1690 to his death at Frankfort an der Oder and served Frederick I and Frederick William I of Prussia as diplomat and legal adviser. Samuel was a student of his father's and became his colleague as *professor juris ordinarius* in Frankfort in 1702. He then entered government service and rose quickly under Frederick William, but it was only as first minister – Prussia's first *Grosskanzler* – under Frederick II, the Great, that he achieved his ambition of being an outstanding legal reformer and a powerful administrator second only to the king himself.[22] Although most of the younger Cocceji's reforms of the law and

---

tur . . . , Halle, 1748. The catalogues of Smith's library record the first three volumes of *Grotius illustratus* and Samuel's *Introductio* (as well as the latter's *Jus civile controversum*, Frankfort a.d.O., Leipzig, 1753). *A Catalogue of the Library of Adam Smith*, ed. James Bonar, London, 1894, pp. 24 and 45; Hiroshi Mizuta, *Adam Smith's Library*, Cambridge, UK, 1967, pp. 82 and 99. Heinrich von Cocceji's extensive oeuvre also includes *Prodromus iustitiæ gentium, sive exercitationes duas ad illustrationem tractatus Grotiani de Jure belli ac pacis* . . . , Frankfort a.d.O., 1719, an incomplete precursor of *Grotius illustratus*, also published posthumously by the son; and a widely used textbook, *Juris publici prudentia compendio exhibita*, Frankfort a.d.O., 1695. See also Christian Gottlieb Jöcher, *Allgemeines Gelehrten-Lexikon*, 4 vols., Leipzig, 1750–1, vol. I, cols. 1980–2; and Adam Friedrich Glafey, *Vollständige Geschichte des Rechts der Vernunfft*, Leipzig, 1739, esp. pp. 229–33.

20 In addition to Grotius's *Mare liberum* and Selden's *Mare clausum*, there are eleven other works, including ones by Conring and van Bynkershoek. The volume also prints Grotius's *Libellus de aequitate, indulgentia et facilitate, singularis*.

21 Samuel von Cocceji, *Novum systema jurisprudentiae naturalis et Romanae*, Berlin, 1740 (also published as *Elementa jurisprudentiae naturalis et Romanae*). The main work between the early dissertation (see ch. 1, at note 91, this volume. [*Note*: citations saying '*at note 91*' mean 'in the text, near note 91'; citations saying '*in note 6*' mean 'in the text of note 6'.]) and *Novum systema* was the widely used *Jus civile controversum*, 2 vols., Frankfort a.d.O., 1713, 1718, which Smith also owned. All Cocceji's important works went through several editions.

22 The standard accounts of Samuel von Cocceji's career are Adolf Stölzel, *Brandenburg-Preussens Rechtsverwaltung und Rechtsverfassung*, 2 vols., Berlin, 1888,

the judicial system remained unenforced and incomplete, they were a milestone not only in German but in European efforts at law reform in the Enlightenment.[23] In fact, Frederick the Great's plans, based on Cocceji's ideas, played a significant role in the British debate on legal reform in the 1750s and early 1760s.[24] The plan was translated in 1750, immediately after its inception, while the full code itself was first translated into French and then from French into English, published in two large volumes in Edinburgh in 1761.[25] We may note that the appearance in Scotland of this reformed legal code theoretically based on natural law coincided with the push by the Faculty of Advocates to have entrants to the group examined in the law of nature and nations, 'the fountain of Justice and equity', 'in so far as it is connected with the Civil Law or the Law of this Country'.[26] It was also at this time that

2:50–235, and Adolf Trendelenburg, *Friederich der Grosse und sein Grosskanzler Samuel von Cocceji. Beitrag zur Geschichte der ersten Justizreform und des Naturrechts*, Berlin, 1863. In one of his brief sketches of the Coccejian reforms of the legal system, the King introduced his Great Chancellor as 'a man of integrity, whose virtue and probity were worthy of the noble age of the Roman republic [– said the monarch!]. Learned and enlightened, he seemed like Tribonianus, born for legislation, and the good of mankind. This sage of the laws . . .' etc. *The History of the Seven Years War*, Part I, in *Posthumous Works of Frederick II, King of Prussia*, trans. Thomas Holcroft, 13 vols., London, 1789, II, p. 2.

23   There is a good brief account of the Coccejian reforms in H.C. Johnson, *Frederick the Great and His Officials*, New Haven, 1975, pp. 106–33. Cf. also Herman Weill, *Frederick the Great and Samuel von Cocceji: A Study in the Reform of the Prussian Judicial Administration, 1740–1755*, Madison, WI, 1961.

24   For a brief survey of the extensive periodical and pamphlet literature, see Manfred Schlenke, *England und das friderizianische Preussen, 1740–1763. Ein Beitrag zum Verhältnis von Politik und öffentlicher Meinung im England des 18. Jahrhunderts*, Munich, 1963, pp. 315–22. Concerning ideas of legal reform, see now first of all David Lieberman, *The Province of Legislation Determined: Legal Theory in Eighteenth-Century Britain*, Cambridge, UK, 1989; and, for an overview of attempts at reform, see Wilfrid Prest, 'Law reform in eighteenth-century England', in *The Life of the Law*, ed. P.W. Birks, London, 1993, pp. 113–23. Bentham still had Cocceji's code 'in his sights' in 1789; see *An Introduction to the Principles of Morals and Legislation*, ed. J.H. Burns and H.L.A. Hart, London, 1970, pp. 23 and 306.

25   *The King of Prussia's Plan for Reforming the Administration of Justice*, London, 1750; *The Frederician Code, or, A Body of Law for the Dominions of the King of Prussia. Founded on Reason and the Constitutions of the Country*, 2 vols., London, 1761 (of which Voltaire said, 'comme si le digeste [of Justinian] était selon la folie', Letter no. 12042, to J.B. de Beaumont, 26 September 1765, in *Voltaire's Correspondence*, ed. T. Besterman, 107 vols., Geneva, 1953–65, vol. 59). The great administrative work by Cocceji's friend and colleague Jacob von Bielfeld appeared in French simultaneously as *Institutions politiques*, 2 vols., Leyden, 1760.

26   Minutes of the Faculty of Advocates for 8 January 1760 and 24 November 1762, as quoted in John W. Cairns, 'Adam Smith's lectures on jurisprudence: Their

John Millar developed his course in Roman law at Glasgow University in such a way that it catered to the Faculty's call for competency in natural law.[27] Even Thomas Reid, who had previously paid little attention to natural law, felt obliged to make it an important part of his course in moral philosophy when he took over from Adam Smith at Glasgow in 1764.[28]

In sum, Smith was drawing his students' attention to one of Europe's foremost legal reformers – 'one of the greatest citizens of the century'[29] – and doing so in the middle of a domestic debate about law reform and the role of natural law (and also during the Seven Years' War, when everything Prussian was fashionable).

Samuel von Cocceji has come to be seen as the leading representative of the reform work of the conservative Prussian Enlightenment fostered by Frederick the Great, but his roots were in fact not Prussian. His father was born in Bremen, an independent city republic that was part of the lively network of Reformed (Calvinist) centres in Germany, the Netherlands, and Switzerland and with close connections to England and Scotland. Heinrich von Cocceji's mother's brother, Henry Oldenburg, was agent for Bremen in London and later became well known as the first secretary of the Royal Society in London.[30] The elder Cocceji himself received a doctorate of laws from Oxford in 1670. The family's connection with Britain was maintained by Samuel von Cocceji. During his European tour, from 1699 to 1701, Samuel stayed in England, where, as he tells us, he got to know John Shute. Shute (1679–1734) was a barrister who had received his education at Utrecht from 1694 to 1698 and, during that time, developed a theory of the world as a theocracy which interested Cocceji.[31] It seems also to have interested John Locke, with whom Shute was friendly in Locke's last years, but so far no evidence has come to light that Cocceji was in touch with Locke.[32]

---

influence on legal education', in *Adam Smith: International Perspectives*, ed. H. Mizuta and C. Sugiyama, London, 1993, pp. 63–83 at pp. 63–4.

27 See Ch. 2 at note 62 and Ch. 5 at note 11, this volume.

28 See Ch. 6, sect. 6.5, this volume.

29 *Westminster Journal*, 16 January 1749, as quoted in Schlenke, *England und das friderizianische Preussen*, p. 317.

30 See Thomas Birch, *The History of the Royal Society of London* . . . , 4 vols., London, 1756–7, vol. III, pp. 353–6.

31 Samuel von Cocceji's brief account of Shute in *Tractatus juris gentium de principio juris naturalis*, I, quæst. III, para. 8 (pp. 45–6). Cocceji's reference is Shute, *Dissertatio philosophica de theocratia morali*, Utrecht, 1697; cf. also *Dissertatio philosophica inauguralis de theocratia civili*, Utrecht, 1697.

32 See *The Correspondence of John Locke*, ed. E.S. de Beer, 8 vols., Oxford, 1975–89, VII (1982), Letters 2945 and 3074; VIII (1989), Letters 3374, 3394, and 3553. Shute was an occasionally conforming Presbyterian and wrote extensively in defence of

Although little is known of the details of the Cocceji family's dealings with their British connections, we can be reasonably sure of their
specific theological background. Partly influenced by the Frisian university at nearby Franeker, Bremen had become an important bastion
of covenant, or federal theology (*Föderaltheologie*), during the latter part
of the seventeenth century. One of the most influential covenant theologians, Johannes Coccejus (1603–69), was from Bremen and may have
been related to the Coccejis with whom we are concerned, though this
remains uncertain.[33] Be that as it may, it is clear that there are some
striking similarities between covenant theology and the jurisprudence
of the two Cocceji.

The most important point to appreciate is that the connection between God and man is a personal relationship. The individual has to
understand his or her life as if it were a personal gift from God which
establishes a personal bond of rights and duties. The life of the individual cannot be understood properly as part of some over-all whole –
creation – and its relationship to the Creator. The federal theologians
formulated this outlook in terms of an intricate system of covenants
between God and man, but the important point for us is the way in
which this individualistic or particularistic view informs the ideas of
natural law and human nature in the Coccejian theory.[34]

---

the Dissenters. One of these efforts, *The Rights of Protestant Dissenters*, London, 1704,
was targeted in Jonas Proast's late assault on the Lockean idea of toleration and
consequently was lumped in with Locke's defence: Locke, *A Fourth Letter for Toleration*, in *The Works of John Locke*, 9 vols., London, 1824, V, pp. 549–74. Shute later
added Barrington to his commoner name upon accepting an inheritance and was
eventually made first Viscount Barrington in the Irish peerage. The Whig government used him as a negotiator with the Scottish Presbyterians in the debate about
the Union. See 'Life of the first Lord Barrington', in *The Theological Works of the First
Viscount Barrington*, ed. George Townsend, 3 vols., London, 1828, I.

33 See *Neue deutsche Biographie*, vol. 1–, Berlin, 1953–, vol. 3 (1957), pp. 300–3;
s.v. 'Cocceji' and 'Coccejus'. For Johannes Coccejus's role in covenant theology, see
Charles S. McCoy, *History, Humanity, and Federalism in the Theology and Ethics of
Johannes Cocceius*, Philadelphia, 1980, and same, 'Johannes Cocceius: Federal theologian', *Scottish Journal of Theology*, 16 (1963), 352–70.

34 The following is based largely upon Samuel von Cocceji's *Introductio*. It
should, however, be noted that, as he himself emphasises, he is, in several respects,
presenting views already present in his father's work. As we have seen in chapter 1
at notes 91–2, Samuel's career began with a development and defence of his father's
theocratic theory of the basis for natural law. How much he himself added is
indicated by his commentaries to the summary of his father's principles in the tenth
dissertation of *Introductio*. In subsequent references I use Roman numerals for the
dissertatio in question and Arabic numerals for the paragraphs which run consecu-
tively through each dissertation across other divisions.

In line with the streamlining of the history of 'modern' natural law which both its friends and its foes undertook in the late seventeenth century, Cocceji saw a coherent tradition of natural law based on *socialitas* (in some sense or other) extending from Grotius through Pufendorf to many of his own contemporaries.[35] In one of his most original contributions to moral philosophy, Cocceji set about demolishing the theory of natural law as the law of 'sociality'.[36] Since the fact of human existence and the character of human nature are matters of divine choice, the existence of natural law is, in his eyes, plainly a matter of God's will.[37] God's will is the ground of existence (*principium essendi*) of natural law. It was futile of Grotius to maintain that there would still be a natural law even if God did not exist, for law requires obligation, and, as Cocceji's father (and he himself, in his earlier work) had tried to show, sociality could not be the source of obligation. A de facto (instinctual) feature of human nature, such as sociality, could not impose obligation,[38] for a self-imposed obligation arising from such a drive towards social living could be dissolved as easily as it could be assumed and was therefore no obligation at all.

Grotian radicalism concerning the existence of natural law had little following, but the hallmark of modernity in natural jurisprudence was the idea that natural law could be *known* as obligatory without reference to God, even if, as a matter of fact, it could not *exist* without the Divinity. As Cocceji saw it, the most widely supported *principium cognoscendi*, the idea that natural law could be *learned* from the social nature of humanity, was also derived from Grotius's theory of *socialitas*. According to Cocceji, the only way in which we can know the law of nature is by knowing it as God's will, but he agreed with the Grotian

35 Cocceji explains the Grotian basis for the tradition of using *socialitas* as the principle of natural law in chapter 1 of the first of the *Dissertationes Prooemiales*; he outlines the natural law tradition in the eleventh dissertation; and his refutation of *socialitas* theories, while present in many places, is concentrated in chapter 2 of the first dissertation. The elder Cocceji had already begun to demolish the concept of *socialitas* and to develop a theory of rights, *Prodromus jurisprudentiae gentium*, 'Exercitatio I', and 'Positiones parsulae et generalissimae loco quasi postulatorum explicationi juris gentium et praelectionibus Grotianis praemissae'. Cf. the convenient summary of his principles in the tenth of the son's dissertations in *Introductio*.

36 *Introductio*, I, cap. 2. This aspect of Cocceji's work has been analysed in an excellent master's thesis, which in fact provides the only previous discussion in English of Cocceji's philosophical ideas: Rebecca Lynn Reynolds, 'Samuel Cocceji and the Tradition of Natural Jurisprudence', M.A. thesis, Cambridge University, 1993. I am greatly indebted to Ms. Reynolds for permission to read and cite her thesis.

37 *Introductio*, XII.57, 65–6, 77, et passim.

38 Cocceji, *Introductio*, I.57 and XII.57. Concerning Grotius, see Ch. 1, sect. 1.3, this volume.

tradition in maintaining that we do not need revelation to acquire such knowledge, which is just as well, since natural law could otherwise not be binding upon non-Christians.[39] Instead he gives six grounds on which we can know natural law by reason alone.[40] The central mode of argument is that the Creator's will or intention can be read from the teleology of the creatures: that is to say, our various abilities imply the divine intention that we may use these abilities and whatever means they require to be effective. The world is thus open for us to use as we have ability, subject only to the restriction that we may not forcibly prevent others from exercising their equally God-given abilities. In short, God's will is rationally disclosed as a dispensation of individual or subjective rights.[41]

One of the distinctive features of Cocceji's theory is what we may call its 'distributive teleology'. God's purpose is manifested in each individual, as if each life were a pact with the Lessor of life. More specifically, there is no argument from any collective purpose for humanity, no use of the idea of the moral community of all moral agents, of the great 'system of humanity', and all the similar notions that informed most of moral theory and natural law theory in the Enlightenment. This is reflected in one of Cocceji's chief criticisms of the sociality theory, namely, that our natural abilities do not and cannot found a universal human society.[42] Our positive sociability, as well as our need to socialize in order to protect ourselves and satisfy our needs, are taken care of by the extended family grouping. A wider, political society is by no means always necessary for the exercise of our abilities, and a universal society is beyond anyone's social needs or means.

Cocceji's theory is also remarkable for the primary role of rights. In sharp contrast to the general natural law tradition, especially after Pufendorf, he does not arrange the field of natural law according to the standard set of duties (to God, oneself, and others).[43] This is in keeping with the absence of any common good – as in Hutcheson and others – from which such duties could be derived. True, the basis for natural law is an overriding obligation to obey the will of God, but even this is explained in terms of rights: God has certain rights in us, and they overrule any other rights.[44] The 'object' of natural law is to leave each person his or her own rights, and the 'effect' is that we each have a

39 *Introductio*, XII.59 (and cf. XI. pos. iv and commentary e).
40 *Introductio*, XII.42–8. He stresses his dependence upon his father in this connection (para. 43).
41 *Introductio*, XII.49.   42 *Introductio*, I.24–40.
43 The term *officium* occurs rarely in the *Introductio* and Cocceji's earlier works.
44 *Introductio*, XII.72–102.

right to exercise and defend our own abilities and means.[45] These are rights to use ourselves and the world around us according to our abilities; life, liberty, and property are rights, because they are means to such ends as the divine will has enabled us to set ourselves. We can engage others by means of mutual agreements – that is, in contractual relations – but from the hand of nature – or the will of God – individuals do not have rights in each other. Our relation with others is to leave them alone to exercise their license on life as they see fit. The core of natural law, or of justice, is to give each his or her own; all other rights derive from this 'single and sufficient' rule.[46]

Accordingly Cocceji makes a sharp distinction between the realm of rights and the realm of virtues among humanity. The 'precepts of the virtues' make up what Grotius called *jus naturæ laxius* and are the subject of the discipline of ethics.[47] But the virtues themselves have to be understood in terms of rights. God has a right in us and requires that we follow the precepts of virtue, for this is part of his right to our reverence (*cultus*) of him, namely our duty to live in his image.[48] The virtues thus consist in rendering other people active assistance in life, and they are exemplified by such qualities as 'liberalitas, caritas, misericordia, clementia, fortitudo, &c.'[49] Instead of accounting for the positive virtues in terms of imperfect duties and rights between individuals, as was usual in the natural law tradition,[50] Cocceji makes them out to be duties and rights on a par with those of justice – but, as such, the rights of virtue hold only between God and man. This is connected with the point that God is omniscient and can judge us by our mind, or intention. He can judge our efforts to do good and those to avoid harm equally well. People, on the other hand, can only judge with some certainty of overt behaviour that does no injury; and that is justice.[51]

Cocceji is unusual not only in making rights primary in his natural jurisprudence but also in his arrangement of the material. He divides all the rights that obtain among humanity into the classical three: the rights of the individual person (to life, liberty, etc.); real rights (to property, etc.); and personal rights (i.e. rights, such as contractual rights, vis-à-vis another person, as opposed to things). But he then explains that the first of these, the right of the person (*ius personarum*), means the

---

45   *Introductio*, XII.65–6.

46   *Introductio*, XII.51: 'Regula iuris naturae unica vera & adæquata, adeoque præceptum generale juris naturæ est: JUS SUUM CUIQUE TRIBUERE: Ad hanc enim regulam omnia & singula naturæ jura ultimo referri, ac per necessariam consequentiam inde deduci possunt'.

47   *Introductio*, II.15. The whole of the second dissertation is relevant.

48   *Introductio*, XII.97.   49   *Introductio*, II.36.

50   See Ch. 2, at note 48, this volume.   51   *Introductio*, II.37 and XII.39.

right arising from the 'state of man' (*ex statu hominum*); and Roman law supports this reading, he says, for the titles *de iure personarum* in the *Institutes* are in the *Pandects* called *de statu hominum*.[52] The state of man is the condition in which a person is fit (*capax*) for those rights that make up that state. There are three such states: that of a human being in general; that of a member of a family; and that of a member of a civil society. From the hand of nature, or under natural law, each person is fit for these three states.[53] Consequently Cocceji deals with the right of the person as the right of the three states of man. Only then does he proceed to real rights and personal (contractual) rights.

His approach contrasts markedly with the general natural law systems, which went from the right of the individual person to real and contractual rights and only then dealt with family and civil society as contractual formations. It is again Cocceji's focus on rights, and hence on injury, that is determining here. The individual can be harmed in his or her status as a member of a family or of a civil society without a breach of contract being involved; consequently we have to deal with such rights in these states as rights of the person. He reaches this conclusion by inspiration from Roman law, in which there was a class of actions for injury to such status rights, which, in Cocceji's opinion, did not fit properly into either of the main categories of actions, *actiones in rem* and *actiones in personam*; these were the *actiones praeiudicales* by which, for example, it was decided whether a person was free or a slave.

This, of course, amounts to a significant downplaying of the traditional concern with the contractual *origins* of the familial and civil states. Although Cocceji stipulates that the core of family society is a valid marriage and that this requires voluntary participation by both spouses, he is not concerned with marital consent as the beginning of a social formation; it is, rather, a commonly accepted factor in the conduct of life.[54] As for civil society, Cocceji makes it clear that it is based upon a pact among consenting families.[55] But the crucial point for him is clearly not the question of the origin but of the *effect* of being a member of a civil society. And the effect is that if one is being treated as a non-member, this is an injury for which one legitimately can seek redress, that is, membership entails rights.[56]

Having established that the right of the person embraces humanity's capacity for the three states of being an individual person under natural law, a member of a family, and a member of a civil society, Cocceji goes through real rights and personal rights and then returns to familial and civil society. The point of this return is to consider the centre of

---

52 *Introductio*, XII.104.   53 *Introductio*, XII.106–8.
54 *Introductio*, XII.108 and 151.   55 *Introductio*, XII.199–201.
56 *Introductio*, XII.202–3.

authority in these societies – the *pater familias* and the sovereign power – as forms of defence of the rights previously explained, partly against transgressions from other members of one's society, partly against other societies, that is, the law of war.[57] This is self-consciously analogous to Justinian's *Institutes*, of which the fourth and last book deals with wrongs, security, and actions.

4.3   *Smith and Cocceji compared*

I cannot show that Smith read Cocceji in the way outlined here and that this was why he included the Great Chancellor in his select group of notable modern natural lawyers. But it is not difficult to see why the Coccejian doctrine would have had strong attractions for Smith. Here was a conceptual model for interpreting Hume's theory of justice as a negative virtue in terms of rights. This could be done without incurring the burden of an elaborate system of duties imposed by a natural law that pointed the way to a fantastic scheme of the universal common good. True, the Coccejian scheme was deeply, conservatively theocratic, but God's role was very much a personal, individualized presence. Smith set about giving an empirical, socio-psychological explanation of this presence as conscience, the impartial spectator, the great inmate of the breast. The covenant of God was replaced by the inner dialogue of the moral character, divine jurisprudence by the theory of moral sentiments. Although speculative religion might lead one to project 'the man within' on to a cosmic sphere, he or she was the outcome of social interaction among people who had the sort of abilities and possibilities which, in Cocceji's traditional view, were the evidence of God's will. The individuated teleology outlined earlier, behind which we may perceive a covenanting legacy, must thus have been most suggestive to Smith. For when purposiveness in practice has to be understood in terms of individual purposefulness, apparently teleological explanations have been reduced to explanations in terms of motives and causes.

As I have explained elsewhere, it was a holistic, teleological view of humanity in thinkers such as Cumberland and Hutcheson that transformed the Lockean and Pufendorfian idea of morals as a demonstrative science into the idea of an 'empirical' science of the moral system that humanity was providentially appointed to and capable of.[58] Cocceji's criticism of these teleological theories of sociality is likely to have

57   *Introductio*, XII, Book VI: 'De defensione iurium naturali contra concives, ubi de origine summæ potestatis, eiusque iuribus, agitur', and Book VII: De defensione iurium naturali contra extraneos'.

58   See Chapter 2 in the present volume and Haakonssen, 'The character and obligation of natural law according to Richard Cumberland', in *English Philosophy in the Age of Locke,* ed. M.A. Stewart, Oxford, forthcoming.

helped Smith in his rejection of this approach to the problem and his formulation of the idea of an empirical study of the connection between individual action and spontaneously formed order.

Above all, Smith would have been attracted to the Coccejian view of natural jurisprudence as a system of rights. If he could use 'right', understood as a claim, as the primary jurisprudential concept, then he could turn the account of the jurisprudential system, and of the social life that this system made possible, into a theory of the changing adjustments of people's claims on each other. Smith did this in two ways. He adopted the 'statics' of the traditional jurisprudential systems, dividing rights into private, oeconomical, and political, and he developed the 'dynamics' of the four-stages theory of human society. In other words, I am suggesting that for most of his lecturing career, Smith was able to use the method of the 'others', of the natural lawyers, because he replaced their primary emphasis on law and duty with the primacy of individual rights (or claims). And I am further suggesting that he is likely to have found significant inspiration for this view in Cocceji. It is at least possible that this enabled Smith to brush aside the nearly universal myth of Grotius as a conventional natural lawyer and see in him the elements of a rights theory, and that this accounts for Smith's high regard for Grotius.

When Cocceji's somewhat formidable God was internalized as the ideal impartial spectator, the rights demanded by God of man were turned into the moral requirements of conscience. Just as the ultimate basis for the moral life, according to Cocceji, was the personal relationship between God and man, so the core of all morality, according to Smith, is the relationship between our empirical self of action and the ideal impartial spectator towards whom our conscience is striving. Our moral relations with other people all go before this higher, but private, tribunal – except for relations of harm, which in addition go before a more direct authority. For when we harm others, there is sufficient unanimity among people to make the moral tribunal public and charge it with the punitive and corrective powers of the magistrate. This is the basis for Smith's sharp distinction between legal justice and the rest of morals. He maintains that justice is a necessary and, in extreme (presumably temporary) circumstances, a sufficient condition for civil society.

Apart from the negative virtue of justice, the moral virtues are subject 'only' to the jurisdiction of private conscience. It is this that makes them 'moral', a point that is easily misunderstood. The privacy of conscience does not mean that it does not have public effects that are essential to social life. The positive virtues are obviously necessary for social life in general and are presumably always present in some measure in the familial societies that make up civil society. But if humanity

exhibited only those characteristics required by each social situation –
by the social spectator – then, by Smith's account, we would not say
that this constituted *moral* life. Such social accommodation would in
fact be unsustainable without the ideal of the impartial spectator; if we
did not believe that there is a right judgement to strive for, we should
have no reason – as we, according to Smith, obviously do – to see
social life as anything but a power play. So the public, social virtues
serve effectively towards social accommodation only if they are
checked by the proper moral virtues of private conscience.

Once the concept of rights had been liberated from the religious
commitments that seem to have restrained Hume from using it,[59] Smith
could apply a refined Humean method to the analysis of people's
mutual claims on each other. This became a socio-psychological theory
of human need fulfilment which, in its institutional aspect, became the
theory of the four stages and, within the framework of the latter, led to
the theory of the market mechanism.

For Hume, as for most other thinkers, natural law theory meant
contractarianism, and this applied equally to the scattered subjective
rights tradition of Hobbes (and Grotius) and to the mainstream of duty
theory, which we have examined in preceding essays. In a highly original move, Smith developed a subjective rights theory that allowed him
to reject contractarianism, and he may well have been helped towards
this standpoint by his reading of Cocceji. The latter's fascination with
Roman law led to his relative neglect of the contractual origins of social
forms and to accounts of rights that simply presupposed social living.
In Smith's hands, this became a theory of how rights changed as part
and parcel of social development and change.

As we saw, Cocceji was led by his theory of rights – especially
personal rights – to adopt the order of Roman law for his system of
natural jurisprudence. When we consider that Smith's praise of Cocceji
and his explanation of his own adoption of the method of the civilians
both occurred at the beginning of the same course – perhaps in consec-
utive lectures – it is hard not to infer that the Great Chancellor was
uppermost in his mind among the civilians. In that case we reach the
conclusion that Cocceji is likely to have served Smith on both sides of
his dilemma about how to arrange his course. On the one hand, the
primacy of subjective rights would have invited him to proceed from
individual via familial to civil society, thus following the 'others' – the
generality of natural lawyers – in form but not at all in content. On the
other hand, the new need for a socio-psychological and historical account of the intertwining of rights and the rest of social living would
have tempted him to follow Cocceji's Romanizing and put the account

59 See Ch. 3, sect. 3.7, this volume.

of social authority first. By 1763 Smith had found a way of doing so for his students. Sadly, he never found it good enough for the rest of the world.

4.4   *Kantian themes in Smith*

In 1798 Christian Garve, the greatest translator and conveyor of British moral and political thought to Germany in the eighteenth century, published a history of moral philosophy in which he ended the chapter on Adam Smith with a brief comparison of him with Immanuel Kant. He concluded,

> Smith assumes that a person has the rational ability to judge his own actions correctly when he does so at a certain distance. The greater the height from which reason surveys, and the more it includes not only the person's individual actions, but all other similar actions of other people; with so much the greater certainty can its decision be relied upon. But this is the height from which the legislator watches human behaviour. So Smith's sympathizing spectator is in fact Kant's legislator.[60]

Having read Smith through Samuel von Cocceji, we may be better able to appreciate how contemporaries could find the impartial spectator a somewhat Kantian figure.

It is well known that Kant himself found at least some inspiration in Smith's moral theory. We learn from correspondence that Kant by 1771

60   Christian Garve, *Uebersicht der vornehmsten Principien der Sittenlehre, von dem Zeitalter des Aristoteles an bis auf unsre Zeiten*, Breslau, 1798, p. 166. Meanwhile in Edinburgh in the same year, the Professor of Logic, James Finlayson, saw the matter in the opposite perspective: 'It is inconceivable to me how a people of such good natural sense as the Germans can be befooled by such shabby dress for old stuff. They could easily see that it is a mixture of the old stoic philosophy and the new of Shaftesbury etc.' Finlayson was reacting to Kantianism as presented in A.F.M. Willich's compilation, *Elements of the Critical Philosophy*, London, 1798, and it is a fair assumption that Smith was included in the 'etc.' For Finlayson's remarks, see the anonymous letter from Edinburgh, 8 June 1798, in *Neuer teutscher Merkur*, 1798 II, 398–9. (Part of the awkward English is included in the German text.) For an overview of the early reception of Kant in Britain, see Giuseppe Micheli, introduction to *Essays and Treatises on Moral, Political, and Various Philosophical Subjects*, by Emanuel [sic] Kant, facsim. repr. of London, 1798 ed., 2 vols., Bristol, UK, 1993, vol. I, pp. v–liii. For Garve's activity in translating and presenting English and Scottish literature, see Robert van Dusen, *Christian Garve and English Belles-Lettres*, Berne, 1970. For an overview of Garve's philosophy, see Michael Stolleis, *Die Moral in der Politik bei Christian Garve*, Diss. Ludwig-Maximilians-Universität, Munich, 1967; and Doris Bachmann-Medick, *Die ästhetische Ordnung des Handelns. Moralphilosophie and Ästhetik in der Popularphilosophie des 18. Jahrhunderts*, Stuttgart, 1989, pts. 1 and 3.

considered Smith his *Liebling*,[61] and subsequently the few direct references to Smith[62] and the use of Smithian notions suffice to make it clear that Kant took Smith for granted as part of the immediate moral philosophical background to his own work.[63] It seems that Kant focussed on two concepts: sympathy, and the spectator. On the former he probably saw Smith as a continuer of Hutcheson and Hume, but it is the latter that is associated with some central Kantian ideas.

The famous opening paragraph of the *Groundwork of the Metaphysics of Morals*, in which Kant begins his argument that there is nothing in the world or out of it which is good without qualification except a good will, ends thus:

> . . . not to mention that a rational impartial spectator never can have any pleasure at the sight of uninterrupted well-being in a creature that is not graced by a clean and good will. And so the good will appears the indispensable condition even to deserve happiness.[64]

61   In a letter to Kant of 9 July 1771, Marcus Herz says: 'Uber den Engländer Smith der, wie Herr Friedlander mir sagt, Ihr Liebling ist, habe ich verschiedene Remarken zu machen. Auch mich hat dieser Mann ungemein belustigt, aber gleichwol setze ich ihn dem ersten Theile von Home Kritik bey weiten nach': Kant, *Gesammelte Schriften*, hrsg. v. d. Königlich Preussischen Akademie der Wissenschaften, Bd. X, 2. Abt.: Briefwechsel, Bd. 1, Berlin, 1922, p. 126. Herz is referring to the recent translation of Kames's *Elements of Criticism*, namely *Grundsätze der Kritik*, trans. Johann Nikolaus Meinhard and Christian Garve, 3 vols., Leipzig, 1763–6; and, presumably, to the even more recent translation of Smith's *Theory of Moral Sentiments* (*Theorie der moralischen Empfindungen*, trans. Christoph Rautenberg, Braunschweig, 1770).

62   Other than to the *Wealth of Nations*. Concerning the early reception of Smith's economics in Germany, see for example H. Winkel, 'Adam Smith und die deutsche Nationalökonomie, 1776–1820. Zur Rezeption der englischen Klassik', in *Studien zur Entwicklung der ökonomischen Theorie*, ed. H. Scherf, Berlin, 1986, 5:81–109; and the brief, helpful overview by N. Waszek, 'Adam Smith in Germany, 1776–1832', in *Adam Smith: International Perspectives*, pp. 163–80.

63   In one of his reflections on anthropology, Kant says: 'Man rühmt sich, dass in Deutschland der Geschmack in schönen Künsten zugenommen hat. Aber wo ist der Schriftsteller, der die Geschichte und die trokensten philosophische Gegenstande mit Verstand und tiefer einsicht doch so schön abhandelt als hume oder die moralische Kentnis des Menschen wie Smith. Hievon muss man den Anfang machen, indem wir die muster des spielenden Geistes schon vor uns haben.' *Gesammelte Schriften*, Bd. XV, 3. Abt., Handschriftlicher Nachlass, Bd. 2ii, Berlin, 1928, p. 592 (Refl. 1355).

64   Kant, *Grundlegung zur Metaphysik der Sitten*, in *Gesammelte Schriften*, Bd. IV, Berlin, 1911, p. 393: 'ohne zu erwähnen, dass ein vernünftiger unparteiischer Zuschauer sogar am Anblicke eines ununterbrochenen Wohlergehens eines Wesens, das kein Zug eines reinen und guten Willens ziert, nimmermehr ein Wohlgefallen haben kann, und so der gute Wille die unerlassliche Bedingung selbst der Würdigkeit glücklich zu sein auszumachen scheint.'

Smith of course thought that moral praise and blame were directed towards people's motives, if one achieved the impartial standpoint, and that 'the influence of fortune' was the most pervasive distortion of humanity's actual moral judgement.[65]

In some of the *Reflexionen* in the manuscript Nachlass, Kant clearly associates impartial spectating with universality.[66] In a most intriguing, if obscure, reflection, he uses Smith to characterize moral feeling (what Smith would call 'approval') as arising from the impartial standpoint where the object of moral assessment can be considered in its 'form' (as falling under a rule?) rather than in its particularity:

> The ground of the moral feeling . . . is the necessity of the satisfaction with the form of actions, whereby we are consistent in our application of our [free] choice.*** The absence of the moral feeling arises . . . when one does not sympathize as much with the form as with the matter and does not view an object from the general perspective . . . This is no special feeling but really a manner of considering something from the general point of view . . .
> *** . . . In Smith's system: why does the impartial judge (who is not one of the participants) espouse that which is the general good? and why does he have some pleasure from it?[67]

The extent to which these snippets from the transcendental workshop provide evidence of a more general Smithian influence on Kant's ethics must be left for specialized investigation. The point here is the modest one that Kant's sporadic attention to Smith helps to highlight some peculiarly important aspects of the latter's thinking, not least those Smith seems to have been led to by reading Samuel von Cocceji.

65   TMS, II.iii.intro.
66   See the reflections on anthropology, *Gesammelte Schriften*, Bd. XV, 3. Abt., Handschriftlicher Nachlass, Bd. 2i, Berlin, 1923, p. 334 (Refl. 767); also Bd. XIX, 3 Abt., Handschriftlicher Nachlass, Bd. 6, Berlin, 1934, p. 117 (Refl. 6628), and p. 163 (Refl. 6796).
67   *Gesammelte Schriften*, Bd. XIX, 3 Abt., Handschriftlicher Nachlass, Bd. 6, Berlin, 1934, pp. 184–5 (Refl. 6864):

> Der Grund des moralischen Gefühls, [worauf das wohlgefallen an dieser Einstimmung nach principien beruht,] ist die nothwendigkeit des wohlgefallens an der form der Handlungen, wodurch wir mit uns selbst im Gebrauche unsrer Willkühr zusammen stimmen***. Der Mangel des moralischen Gefühls (Wir haben nothwendig wohlgefallen an Regeln.) beruht darauf, dass man an der form nicht so viel Antheil nimmt als an der Materie und einen Gegenstand nicht aus dem Gesichtspunkte der allgemeinheit betrachtet [oder auf sein Gefühl applicirt]. Dieses ist kein besonderes Gefühl, sondern eine Art überhaupt, etwas aus dem allgemeinen Gesichtspunkte zu betrachten . . .
> ***. . . In Smiths system: warum nimmt der Unpartheyische richter (der nicht einer von den participanten ist) sich dessen, was allgemein gut ist, an? und warum hat er daran irgend ein wohlgefallen?

A striking feature of Cocceji's theory is the focus on the individual will. The whole of moral life is due to the exertion of individual wills which are, in a way, delegated by God's will. In a significant sense, the Coccejian theory is a theory of the individual's self-legislation. In Smith this is developed into the idea of acting only in accordance with the ideal impartial spectator as present in our conscience. For Smith, the truly moral person is independent of partial and interested concerns in a given situation, including his or her own concerns. Conscience, when fully in control, can abstract from purely personal interests and hand down the verdict of an impartial judge. Consequently we find in Smith an ideal of duty and a rhetoric of overcoming deflections from it that has much in common with Kant. As in Kant, one of the means towards duty is the adherence to general moral rules – though rules admittedly are very much a secondary formation for Smith. Indeed conscience, in both Smith and Kant, is not only a judge, an internal court, a legislator; it appears as the voice of God, the vice-regent of the universe internalized. In accordance with this, religious belief is the *completion* of morals, the imagined eternal consummation of our moral ideals that cannot be achieved in this world.

In agreement with this common ideal of autonomy, that is, independence of circumstances and of authority, and the associated ideal of self-legislation, we find that for both Smith and Kant the proper object of moral judgement is the will or intention. Although duty consists in following self-imposed rules, mere overt rule-following behaviour has no moral merit. At the same time we find both thinkers insisting that there are wide areas of human exertion where we have no choice but to judge according to overt behaviour and without regard to the will or intention behind it. This applies to the mere abstention from injury or giving each person his or her own, which constitutes justice proper. And whereas in the domain of justice or law (*Recht*) we can justifiably be forced to comply with the rules, in the realm of the positive virtues or *Sittlichkeit*, moral merit arises from the free intention with which we act.[68] We should here remember Cocceji's idea of justice as giving to each his or her own; giving other people their own constituted human justice and the basis for law; giving God his own included doing good, exercising positive virtues, towards God's creatures. In Smith and Kant, the latter has become a matter of honouring the demands of one's individual conscience.

Smith had no idea of a 'noumenal' self which, as member of a transcendent realm of freedom, is the subject of a moral life that has to be lived in the phenomenal world of causal necessity. Nevertheless, he

---

68 See esp. Kant, *Die Metaphysik der Sitten*, 1. Theil: *Metaphysische Anfangsgründe der Rechtslehre, Gesammelte Schriften*, Bd. VI, Berlin, 1907, pp. 218–21.

makes his own division of the person, into the empirical self of immediate desires and actions and the ideal impartial spectator harboured in
our conscience beyond the sway of desires and the necessity of action.
Smith of course accounts for the formation of the impartial spectator in
empirical terms as a matter of social and psychological processes. Even
so, one has to allow that he is also making a conceptual point that has
some similarity to Kant's transcendental argument. Given the fact of
morals, how do we account for its possibility? Or, what is required for
moral life to exist? Smith's answer, in a nutshell, is the impartial spectator. If humanity had no capacity for forming the idea of an impartial
spectator – even allowing for wide departures from this ideal standard
– then there could be no moral life. The moral life consists in seeking to
acquire the standpoint of the impartial spectator, who is the ideal judge
of our behaviour. When we through sympathy attempt to make his
judgement our own, we are in effect trying to legislate to ourselves.
The crucial demand for us in this is to be impartial, which means doing
the right thing for its own sake, not for the sake of a particular person.
Impartiality is thus similar to universality in requiring that individuals
in relevantly similar circumstances must be judged similarly, if the
judgement and the will are to be considered moral. Although it may be
contingent that there is a human race and that it has developed a moral
life, there is a certain necessity, once we have such a moral life, in the
presence of the ideal impartial spectator. If we did not have this ideal,
we should have no means of characterizing what we are doing when
we are being partial. Since on Smith's account criticism of each other's
partiality is one of the most significant forces in humanity's moral
development, we must accept the implication that the impartial spectator is not a contingent factor in morals. In this perspective we can see
Smith's impartial spectator as a significant step towards Kant's notion
of the autonomous will that creates the moral life by willing in accordance with specifiable and necessary criteria.

It has quite rightly been suggested that a couple of thinkers before
Kant made some important approaches to his idea of a moral necessity
that is independent of contingent ends and desires and his idea of
autonomous self-legislation, notably C.A. Crusius and Jean-Jacques
Rousseau.[69] The foregoing reflections show that Adam Smith has a
claim to be included in this category. By looking at Smith in this manner, we take him, to some extent, out of his context, or at least float the
notion of the relevant context. This seems entirely justified if our objec-

69   See for example J.B. Schneewind, 'Autonomy, obligation, and virtue: An
overview of Kant's moral philosophy', in *The Cambridge Companion to Kant*, ed. P.
Guyer, Cambridge, UK, 1992, pp. 309–41, at pp. 313–14.

tive is to understand his *ideas,* as opposed to what he did with them, for it is clear that the logic of Smith's argument drove him to develop *some* ideas that cannot simply be understood as responses to his own context. But for the rest, we are happy to release him from the Prussian perspective.

5

John Millar and the science of a legislator

5.1 Introduction

Forty years ago Duncan Forbes developed his concept of 'scientific Whiggism' in a classic essay on Adam Smith and John Millar.[1] With subtle changes towards 'sceptical Whiggism' this line of interpretation was subsequently pursued in depth as far as Hume and Smith are concerned.[2] In Millar's case the field of interpretation has been dominated by scholars who, instead of seeing him as sceptical and 'scientific' in his approach to the great questions of political legitimacy and social and political change, see him rather as an extremely engagé bourgeois ideologist concerned with the preservation, in modern society, of humanist ideals of virtue and liberty and with the social and political changes required by this.[3] Some of these contributions have been as

1 D. Forbes, '"Scientific" whiggism: Adam Smith and John Millar', *Cambridge Journal*, 7 (1953–4), pp. 643–70.
2 See especially Forbes, *Hume's Philosophical Politics*, Cambridge, UK, 1975; 'Hume's science of politics', in *David Hume: Bicentenary Papers*, ed. G.P. Morice, Edinburgh, 1977, pp. 39–50; and 'Sceptical Whiggism, commerce and liberty', in *Essays on Adam Smith*, ed. A.S. Skinner and T. Wilson, Oxford, 1975, pp. 179–201.
3 One or more of these elements are to be found in Caroline Robbins, *The Eighteenth-Century Commonwealthman*, Cambridge, MA, 1959, pp. 214–17; J.G.A. Pocock, *The Machiavellian Moment*, Princeton, 1975, pp. 502–3; R.L. Meek, *Social Science and the Ignoble Savage*, Cambridge, UK, 1976, pp. 160–76; A.O. Hirschman, *The Passions and the Interests: Political Arguments for Capitalism before Its Triumph*, Princeton, 1977, pp. 87–113; Jürgen Kuczynski, *Zur Geschichte der Wirtschaftsge-schichtsschreibung*, Berlin, 1978, pp. 92–103; H. Medick and A. Leppert-Fögen, 'Frühe Sozialwissenschaft als Ideologie des kleinen Bürgertums: John Millar of Glasgow, 1735–1801', in *Sozialgeschichte Heute. Festschrift für Hans Rosenberg*, ed. H.-U. Wehler, Göttingen, 1974, pp. 22–48. Cf. also H. Medick, *Naturzustand und Naturgeschichte der bürgerlichen Gesellschaft. Die Ursprünge der bürgerlichen Sozialtheorie als Geschichts-philosophie und Sozialwissenschaft bei Samuel Pufendorf, John Locke, und Adam Smith*, Göttingen, 1973. W.C. Lehmann's monograph, *John Millar of Glasgow, 1735–1801: His Life*

much occupied with Millar's political and legal activities as with his writings, and much light has in fact been thrown on the former.[4] The result is, however, that one is often left in doubt about the relationship between his science and his politics. In its own way this serves to indicate that Millar's main works do not contain much in the way of explicit normative socio-political doctrine[5] and that their whole mode in this respect is the kind of sceptical indirectness which Forbes captured.

This picture is further complicated when we extend our field of inquiry to include the publication of some anonymous pamphlets. There are two such pamphlets which – either directly or indirectly – derive from Millar: the *Letters of Crito*[6] and the *Letters of Sidney*.[7] They

---

and *Thought and His Contributions to Sociological Analysis*, Cambridge, UK, 1960, while presenting much useful material, is interpretatively too vague to classify.

4   See esp. Medick and Leppert-Fögen, 'Frühe Sozialwissenschaft'.

5   Millar published two treatises: *The Origin of the Distinction of Ranks, or An Inquiry into the Circumstances which give rise to Influence and Authority, in the Different Members of Society*, first published in 1771 (under the title *Observations Concerning the Distinction of Ranks in Society*); all references are to the fourth edition, Edinburgh, 1806 – abbreviated *Ranks*. Millar's second major work is *An Historical View of the English Government from the Settlement of the Saxons in Britain to the Revolution in 1688. To which are subjoined some Dissertations Connected with the History of the Government from the Revolution to the Present Time.* The first and second editions (1787 and 1790) only took the history 'to the Accession of the House of Stewart', but in the post-humous third edition, 4 vols., Edinburgh, 1803, the editors and Millar's literary executors, John Craig and James Mylne (nephew and son-in-law, respectively), incorporated a volume covering the period to 1688, which was ready for the press, as well as a volume of dissertations, as indicated by the title. I refer to this third edition as *Hist. View*.

6   First as letters to the editor in *Scots Chronicle*, Edinburgh, from May to September, 1796. Republished as a pamphlet under the title *Letters of Crito, on the Causes, Objects, and Consequences of the Present War*, Edinburgh, 1796. Concerning the ascription to Millar, see Lehmann, *John Millar of Glasgow*, pp. 56, 404, 418; cf. Medick and Leppert-Fögen, 'Frühe Sozialwissenschaft', pp. 23–4.

7   First published in part as letters to the editor in *Scots Chronicle*, August to November, 1796. Published in full as *Letters of Sidney, on Inequality of Property, To which is added, A Treatise of the Effects of War on Commercial Prosperity*. Edinburgh, 1796. This work cannot with certainty be ascribed to Millar. Lehmann thought Millar's authorship 'a strong probability' (*John Millar*, p. 56) because of the close similarity between the *Sidney* and Millar's known views and because there 'is . . . nothing that speaks clearly against it' (p. 405). Medick has gone further and claimed that he could now prove Millar's authorship (Medick, *Naturzustand und Naturgeschichte*, p. 187, n. 42), but in fact his argument throws additional doubt on Millar's candidature. Medick argues that central parts of *Sidney* reappear verbatim in John Craig's *Elements of Political Science*, 3 vols., Edinburgh, 1814; but since this work is, in his opinion, largely a paraphrase of Millar's unpublished lectures on the science of

were occasioned by the debates on the French Revolution and the subsequent Anglo-French war, and they both contain very direct political messages, of which those of *Sidney* have the greater theoretical interest. In so far as scholars have paid serious attention to these messages, they have taken them as strong confirmation of a narrowly

government, which Craig had attended, he concludes that *Sidney* also must be Millar's (Medick, cf. Medick and Leppert-Fögen, 'Frühe Sozialwissenschaft', pp. 24 and 43, n. 29). There would seem to be at least one other obvious possibility, that Craig himself wrote *Sidney* as a paraphrase of Millar and later incorporated it into his major work – which is in any case much more than a mere paraphrase of Millar (see K. Haakonssen, 'Natural Justice: The Development of a Critical Philosophy of Law from David Hume and Adam Smith to John Millar and John Craig', Ph.D. thesis, University of Edinburgh, 1978, ch. 4). To Lehmann's rhetorical question, 'Who but a man like Millar would be quoting Harrington in 1796; and who else in Scotland would be likely to know of a law on testaments just passed in France, of which he had not yet seen "the specific regulations!" (*John Millar,* p. 404), we may fairly confidently answer that a student, a relative and friend, and an intellectual ally, in short a man like Craig, would be quite likely to do so. Harrington was not exactly forgotten among liberal and radical Whigs, especially in Scotland. Indeed, as is clear from his lectures on politics, Thomas Reid had for years preached Harrington and Harringtonian themes to his Glasgow students (see esp. Aberdeen University Library, Birkwood Collection, Ms 2131/4/III/6–7). On one copy of *Sidney* the title page is inscribed 'By John Craig, Esq.'. For an untrained eye it is not possible to tell certainly whether this handwriting is the same as Craig's own, which we find in a large number of marginal notes in his personal copy of the *Elements,* in the Australian National Library, nor do the couple of surviving letters in Craig's hand decide the matter. In sum, we cannot prove that *Sidney* is Millar's own writing, but there is no doubt that its intellectual content stems from him. Both *Crito* and *Sidney* have been issued in a modern edition, *Letters of Crito e Letters of Sidney,* ed. Vincenzo Merolle, Rome, 1984. Craig's *Elements* combines Godwin and Adam Smith, making the impartial spectator as anarchist the theoretical foundation for a comprehensive text-book in the political sciences. It may have been intended for the new professional course which the Professor of Logic, George Jardine, wanted introduced at the Scottish universities, to provide for 'the education of a numerous class of students who, from their birth, rank, and condition, may become statesmen, legislators, and magistrates'. George Jardine, *Outlines of Philosophical Education* (1818), Glasgow, 1825, p. 492. Craig's work was immediately translated into German (Leipzig, 1816) in support of the old-liberal, anti-revolutionary cause. He also published *Remarks on some Fundamental Doctrines in Political Economy illustrated by a Brief Inquiry into the Economic State of Britain since the Year 1815,* Edinburgh, 1821, which contributes to the formulation of the idea of marginal utility. It is also critical of Ricardo and became caught up in McCulloch's criticism of Smithian economics. McCulloch to Ricardo, 23 April 1821, in *The Works and Correspondence of David Ricardo,* ed. P. Sraffa, 10 vols., Cambridge, UK, 1962–6, VIII, p. 378. Along with Craig, James Reddie was the student who followed most closely in Millar's scholarly footsteps, and Francis Horner expressed the wish to see him in Millar's chair.

ideological picture of Millar.[8] In this way we have reached a point where our understanding of Millar is decisively based upon his anonymous works and his political involvement, whereas his two main works play a subsidiary and supplementary role. This of course gives rise to the question of how coherent Millar's position is, and it is not least to this that the present essay is devoted.

The *Historical View of the English Government* and the *Origin of the Distinction of Ranks* are both clear cases of the 'scientific Whig' approach to the development of society and its institutions, but they do not expound a political philosophy explicit enough to serve as the foundation for the politics of the pamphlets. On the other hand, the latter do not present a view of politics which makes it evident why Millar should be so concerned with the historical view of society. In order to answer our question it is necessary to go yet further afield for the sources of our interpretation.

It is well known that Millar's two treatises were developed from the lectures he gave as Professor of Law at Glasgow University from 1761 until his death in 1801, which have attracted some attention as a result.[9] Until recently this attention concentrated entirely on the 'Lectures on Government', but valuable new work by John Cairns has given a much fuller picture of Millar's contribution to legal and social thought.[10] Of particular importance for an understanding of Millar's philosophical

---

The Horner Papers: Selections from the Letters and Miscellaneous Writings of Francis Horner, M.P., 1795–1817, ed. K. Bourne and W. Banks Taylor, Edinburgh, 1994, p. 709; cf. James Reddie, *Inquiries Elementary and Historical in the Science of Law,* London, 1840.

8 See Medick and Leppert-Fögen, 'Frühe Sozialwissenschaft'. Michael Ignatieff uses them to draw a more complicated and interesting picture of Millar, which we shall consider later in this chapter. See 'John Millar and individualism', in *Wealth and Virtue: The Shaping of Political Economy in the Scottish Enlightenment,* ed. I. Hont and M. Ignatieff, Cambridge, UK, 1983, pp. 317–43.

9 See esp. the works by Medick; Medick and Leppert-Fögen; Meek; and Ignatieff. Cf. also notes 10 and 11 to this chapter.

10   John W. Cairns, 'John Millar's lectures on Scots criminal law', *Oxford Journal of Legal Studies,* 8 (1988), 364–400; same, 'Rhetoric, language, and Roman law: Legal education and improvement in eighteenth-century Scotland', *Law and History Review,* 9 (1991), 31–58; same, '"Famous as a school for Law, as Edinburgh . . . for medicine": Legal education in Glasgow, 1761–1801', in *The Glasgow Enlightenment,* ed. A. Hook and R.B. Sher, Edinburgh, 1994, pp. 133–59. Cairns has also been able to provide a great deal of clarification of the institutional background against which Millar is to be seen; in addition to the afore-mentioned essays, see his 'Origins of the Glasgow Law School: The professors of civil law, 1714–61', in *The Life of the Law,* ed. P. Birks (Proceeding of the Tenth British Legal History Conference, Oxford, 1990), London, 1993, pp. 151–94, and other works referred to there.

outlook are his 'Lectures on Civil Law', that is, on Justinian's *Institutes* and their significance for modern law, the second half of which was in effect a course in general jurisprudence.[11] A large number of students' notes from Millar's lectures are still in existence, and some of them evidently stem fairly directly from Millar's own notes. There is a great degree of correspondence between the sets of notes; several of them are of high quality and give a detailed account of the lectures.[12] In addition we also have the outlines of Millar's courses which his biographer, John Craig, presented in his *Life of Millar*.[13] By drawing on this much fuller oeuvre[14] it becomes possible to recognize an over-all structure in Millar's

11   For the first half of the course Millar's text-book was J.G. Heineccius, *Elementa juris civilis secundum ordinem Institutionum*, Amsterdam, 1725, just as, for another course on the *Digest*, he used Heineccius's *Elementa juris civilis secundum ordinem Pandectarum*, Amsterdam, 1727; see Cairns, 'Rhetoric, language and Roman law', p. 46, n. 90. These were standard works in civil law, but they also contain a good deal of general jurisprudence. For Heineccius in general, see Ch. 2, sect. 2.8, this volume.

12   Cairns, 'Millar's lectures on Scots criminal law', pp. 370–1, n. 33, has established that if Glasgow University Library MS Gen 289–91, 'Lectures on Government 1787–88' is not in fact a set of Millar's own lecture notes, it is directly derived from them. For general descriptions of these lectures, see, in addition to Cairns, Lehmann, *John Millar*, pp. 57–8 and 407–9, as well as his 'John Millar, Professor of Civil Law at Glasgow (1761–1801)', *Juridical Review*, 1961, 218–33 at p. 218, and 'Some observations of the law lectures of Professor Millar at the University of Glasgow (1761–1801)', *Juridical Review*, 1970, 56–73; further Medick, *Naturzustand und Naturgeschichte*, pp. 185–9. After study of a number of the sets of notes on the lectures on government (MS Hamilton 116, 1798; MS Gen 180 (1–3) 1789; MS Murray 88–90, 1790, all in Glasgow University Library; MS 99, 1771, Mitchell Library Glasgow; MS 133, 1782, Aberdeen University Library), I decided to refer only to the above-mentioned set, MS Gen 289–91, Glasgow University Library. Despite the clear date on this set, 1787–8, it contains a special lecture on the French Revolution. We have no explanation for this, but the tone and content of the Revolution lecture strongly suggest that this event had only just begun. I abbreviate these lectures as 'Govt.'. For Millar's lectures on civil law, I have used two sets, one of which covers only the general jurisprudential part of the course, *viz*. MS Hamilton 117, 1798, Glasgow University Library, abbreviated 'Juris.'. The other set is in Edinburgh University Library and is inscribed, 'Lectures on the Institutions of the Civil Law, by Professor Millar, Glasgow, 1794'. I abbreviate it here as 'Civil Law'. There are other notes from this course in Glasgow University Library and the National Library of Scotland.

13   This was prefaced to his 1806 edition of *Ranks* and is here referred to as 'Life'.

14   This does not quite exhaust the Millar sources. Not only are there notes from his courses on Scottish and English law, but Craig also tells us that Millar wrote 'a few articles in the Analytical Review' ('Life', p. lxxxvi). It has so far not been established which articles are to be ascribed to Millar.

standpoint, which both strengthens the scientific Whig thesis and provides a proper theoretical foundation for Millar's activism. In addition – and not least – this reading serves to demonstrate the very significant continuity between Millar, David Hume, and, especially, Adam Smith.

5.2 *A theory of justice and rights*

Fundamental to Millar's thought is a theory of justice which is based upon a general theory of moral evaluation.[15] Just as in Hume and Smith, it is to a large extent a theory of the relation between morality and law. Law is a branch of ethics, but a peculiarly distinct branch, which must not be confused with the rest. The former is dealt with in jurisprudence, the latter in the flimsy discipline 'casuistry'.[16] In order to understand this it is necessary to see what the general principles of moral evaluation are. Accordingly, we find that in Millar's civil law lectures there is a substantial treatment of those principles, and they even find a prominent place in a polemical *pièce d'occasion* like the *Letters of Sidney*.[17] It cannot be said, however, that this part of Millar's theory is nearly as important as Hume's and Smith's theory of morals. It is in fact little more than a summary and conscious restatement of their ideas.[18]

The central concept is that of the impartial spectator, whose standpoint is reached by the mechanism of sympathy and whose moral judgements are based on considerations of the propriety or impropriety, as well as the utility or lack of utility, of an action. The former we judge through sympathetic understanding of the situation of the acting person, the latter through sympathetic understanding of the situation of those who are the objects of the actions being evaluated. Both judgements in terms of propriety and those in terms of utility are considerably influenced by whether the action in question is customary and expected or novel and surprising. A similar influence arises from the unintended consequences which the spectator expects from the action, or from the motive, when he sees what type of action it is, and particularly which general rule pertains to it. Finally, it should be noted that the concept of utility employed by Millar has nothing to do with hedonistic utilitarianism. The term is always used in the broad sense of

---

15   I discuss Millar's moral thought in detail in 'Natural Justice', ch. 4.

16   'Life', pp. xxiv–xxv.

17   See 'Life', pp. xxvi–xxviii; *Sidney,* Letter 9; Civil Law, I, pp. 6–19; Juris., pp. 1–25; *Hist. View,* IV, pp. 267–75.

18   See 'Life', p. xxvi: 'Mr Hume and Dr Smith had written treatises [on the principles of moral approbation], equally eloquent and ingenious; and, to Mr Millar, little appeared to be wanting, but to combine their systems.'

that which somehow benefits another, and 'benefit' seems to mean no more than that which we as spectators can sympathize with. In this respect too Millar is following in the footsteps of Hume and Smith.[19]

The principles of moral approval naturally lead on to that which we approve of, namely the moral virtues. Millar divides these into two groups, the self-regarding, or personal virtues and the other-regarding, or social virtues. The former are again divided, on the classical pattern, into the three classes of prudence, temperance, and fortitude, the latter into the two groups typified by benevolence and justice.[20] It is the social virtues, and especially their division into the 'positive' virtue of benevolence and the 'negative' one of justice which are of significance in the present context. Justice has a number of qualities, as shown by the reactions of the impartial spectator, which mark it off from the rest of the virtues, and it is these which make it the foundation of law and which accordingly enable the separation of law from morals. The basic quality of the negative as opposed to the positive virtues is explained in terms of spectator reactions as follows:

> The rules of justice[21] . . . are satisfied, when a man abstains from injuring others, although he should make no addition whatever to general or partic-ular happiness. He who fails in prudence, in temperance, in courage, or beneficence, may become an object of dislike; he may destroy his own happiness, and disregard many opportunities of promoting that of others; but, having done no direct injury, he can scarcely become the object of general indignation. The infringement of the rules of Justice, on the other hand, never fails to excite resentment in the breast of the person injured, and indignation in that of the spectators.[22]

Judgement in matters of justice is further characterized by a clarity and precision not to be found in the other virtues, and it is, as already indicated, tied up with a judgement of punishability (enforceability):

19 'Life', pp. xxvi–xxvii. For Hume's and Smith's concept of utility, see Haak-onssen, *Science of a Legislator*, pp. 39ff. and 67–74.

20 This well-known division of the subject is found in *Hist. View*, IV, essay 6, where Millar deals with it from a sociological and historical point of view, asking about 'The Effects of Commerce and Civilization, upon the Morals of a People'. Both in his lectures (Civil Law, I, pp. 7–8, and Juris., pp. 3–5) and in the following essay 7 on 'The Progress of Science relative to Law and Government' he turns to the philosophical points involved.

21 The text says 'virtue', but this is corrected in the errata list.

22 This and the following two quotations are from 'Life', pp. xxxii–xxxiv, which summarize Civil Law, I, pp. 19–21, and Juris., pp. 25–8. The same points are in *Hist. View*, IV, pp. 266–8. As we shall see, this theory of justice is used in the central passages of the decisive ninth of the *Letters of Sidney* (pp. 44–5), where the author shows that the ultimate justification of property is that it is a basic rule of justice.

The rules of conduct prescribed by Justice, unlike the dictates of the other virtues, are always clear and precise. Frequently it may be a matter of some difficulty to determine what . . . may be most prudent or most beneficent; but never can any person be at a loss to know, when he deliberately diminishes the comforts or enjoyments of others, or be unconscious, that by so doing, he renders himself the object of merited punishment.

It is justice in this sense which must be the basis for all law:

For these reasons it is on the virtue of Justice, and on that virtue alone, that Laws, the object of which is to maintain rights and repress injuries, must be altogether founded.

In order to see how Millar intends to base law on this view of justice, we have to appreciate the point hinted at here, namely that evaluations in terms of justice lead to the recognition of natural rights, and natural rights are the objects of protection by the rules of justice. 'There are', says Millar, 'natural rights, which belong to mankind antecedent to the formation of civil society.'[23] These rights concern our personal safety, the 'exercise of our natural liberty, so far as it does not encroach upon the rights of others', and they concern our property, gained by occupancy or by labour. These rights continue on the whole to exist in society, though some are modified (the right to self-defence) and some are resigned to the civil power (the right to punish, and the right to part of our property – for taxes); in general 'we must yield obedience to the legislative power.' In all cases, however, we only give up rights in order to achieve the general purposes of social life, namely, the effective pursuit of our remaining individual rights while we live in community with others. It is this ability to combine a social life with maximum personal liberty that is the testing ground for 'the various political systems which take place in the world'.

5.3   *A theory of law*

Millar's theory of law follows from his theory of natural rights; just laws tell people to respect and protect natural rights. The justification of laws is obviously to be found in spectator reactions, the clarity, certainty, and strength of which distinguish law from mere moral duty. Law is the institutionalization of the clear, negative virtue of justice. The idea is that law grows spontaneously out of the conflicts of rights which are bound to arise when men are living together in social

---

23   For this and the following, see *Hist. View*, IV, pp. 300–1; *Govt.* I, pp. 21–3; and *Juris.*, p. 232. This theory of rights and the consequent theory of government is developed in much greater detail and clarity by John Craig in his *Elements of Political Science*, I, pp. 84ff.

groups.[24] Although in primitive society there will be a tendency to decide such disputes by force, self-interest and social pressure will more often lead to some kind of arbitration. Normally men of some social standing are chosen as arbiters; as time goes by they will increasingly be recognized as professional judges in disputes, and in the end society will also provide them with the power to enforce their decisions. As the extent of the job grows, it tends to become a separate profession, which leads to problems about the dependence of judges upon rulers or the people.

The professionalization of judges also has other consequences. It is a 'propensity natural to all mankind' to see similarities among different events and thus to form general rules. This naturally also happens in the case of decisions on disputes, but the tendency is greatly strengthened as it becomes a separate occupation for a certain group of citizens to decide disputes. They will tend more and more to look to previous cases to find precedents, and they will become more skilled in this than anyone else in the society. In this way the earliest known kind of law, common law, grows out of spectator reactions which have been institutionalized as the reactions of a particular group of people, namely judges. As the law grows in complexity and people increasingly become aware of its utility, they begin to amend the laws handed down by tradition, and the rules arising from this deliberate legislative activity constitute the beginning of statute law. The end result of this long development is that the law of a society, although arising from particular decisions, has become a large edifice, a theoretical entity, which is independent of individual cases and even determines how we are to see new individual cases.[25]

Law becomes the object of a new and independent science, but it is not created by that science. The legal speculators can begin work only when the object is already in existence:

> General systems of Law have rarely, if ever, been formed by the prospective wisdom of legislators, but have arisen gradually, and almost insensibly, from the slow progress of human experience.[26]

Legislators cannot create law a priori, for they must themselves to a very large extent be creatures of the society they legislate for. Otherwise they would have neither the knowledge nor the authority to do so:

> Before an individual can be invested with so much authority, and possessed of such reflection and foresight as would induce him to act in the capacity of a legislator, he must, probably, have been educated and brought up in the

24 The following is based on Hist. View, IV, pp. 275–81; Civil Law, I, pp. 19–21; Juris., pp. 25–7; Govt., I, pp. 133–43; and 'Life', pp. xxxiv–xl.
25 Hist. View, IV, pp. 281–2; Civil Law, I, p. 22; Juris., p. 29.
26 'Life', p. xxxiv.

knowledge of those natural manners and customs, which, for ages perhaps, have prevailed among the countrymen.[27]

All that so-called legislators can produce is some adaptation of already existing law:

> It is even extremely probable, that those patriotic statesmen . . . whose laws have been justly celebrated, were at great pains to accommodate their regulations to the situation of the people for whom they were intended; and that, instead of being actuated by a projecting spirit, or attempting, from visionary speculations of remote utility, to produce any violent reformation, they confined themselves to such moderate improvements as, by deviating little from the former usage, were in some measure supported by experience, and coincided with the prevailing opinions of the country.[28]

The legislator who tries to do more than that,

> he who frames a political constitution upon a model of ideal perfection, and attempts to introduce it into any country, without consulting the inclinations of the inhabitants . . . is a most pernicious projector, who, instead of being applauded as a Lycurgus, ought to be chained and confined as a madman.[29]

In sum, law is not an intended construction but the undesigned by-product of settlements of particular disputes, and only at a comparatively late stage do rational constructions play a role in systematizing, supplementing and, to some extent, changing the common law from views of 'utility'.[30]

All the decisive ideas in this line of argument Millar had heard in Adam Smith's lectures, and much of it he would also have read in Lord Kames. In fact one can consider these arguments of Millar's as variations on Smith's argument against a positivist theory of law, an argument to the effect that all positive legislation presupposes that people already have and apply basic ideas of justice and injustice. In this connection it is interesting to speculate that it is the idea of the limitation of our reasoning faculty, more particularly the point that we cannot construct ideas, and hence evaluate, independently of the elements in the situations surrounding us, which is the background to Millar's enthusiasm for Hume's 'metaphysics'.[31] Irrespective of this, there is another element in the theory, pointing beyond Hume. Some ideas, at

27 *Ranks*, p. 6.   28 *Ranks*, p. 7.   29 *Hist. View*, III, p. 229.

30 *Hist. View*, IV, pp. 58, 235ff., 278, and 281. For the general idea of unintended consequences among the Scottish theoreticians, see Ronald Hamowy, *The Scottish Enlightenment and the Theory of Spontaneous Order* (Journal of the History of Philosophy Monographs), Carbondale, IL, 1987.

31 Craig, 'Life', p. lxi, says that Millar was a 'zealous admirer of Mr. Hume's philosophical opinions' – specified in a note as 'metaphysical opinions' – 'which he had early adopted'.

least, are not just formed as reflections of reality but as part of an
ongoing activity. Aside from being interesting in itself, this is also of
importance as a possible indication of the theoretical background to the
(Smithian) idea that a society which increases the activity of the people,
as a commercial society does, is also productive of new knowledge.
This is particularly clear in Millar's essays in the *Historical View*,[32] and
John Craig pursues the same idea in the course of his argument for the
political involvement of the people.[33] By means of historical examples,
he reasons that all of the various aspects of culture have reached their
high points in the wake of political upheavals and exertions involving
the people. This involvement and its effects may become permanent
and yet avoid all the disastrous aspects of political unrest, if a form of
government is introduced which draws in the people, a line of argument much better known from Adam Ferguson's *Essay on the History of
Civil Society*.

5.4   *A theory of government*

A theory of natural rights such as Millar's implies equality of rights
and is therefore obliged to account for the major inequality which
seems to be generally acknowledged, namely the right in some to
govern. Millar 'dismissed, as scarcely worthy of refutation, the doctrine
of Divine Right',[34] and also rejected contract theories, though not without argument. His criticism is largely a restatement of Hume, for Millar
was, in his lectures on government, says Craig, 'at some pains to enforce Mr Hume's objections to the fiction of an Original Contract, long
the favourite opinion of the English Whigs'.[35] Millar maintained that
the idea of a contract was empirically false, that the concept of tacit
consent was contradictory, and in general terms that contract theories
imply a rationalization of social life of which mankind on the whole is
incapable. Not least, it is superfluous to suppose a contract, for it can
neither add to nor negate the obligation we have to protect the natural
rights of individuals. So, if a government provides such protection, we
have an obligation to support the government, irrespective of any contract, whereas, if it does the opposite no contract to support it can be
binding. All of which means that contract theories at best provide 'a
peculiar explanation' of the 'principle of utility', which says that support of government is justified when it is a useful tool for protecting
natural rights.

32 *Hist. View*, IV, essays 4–6.
33 Craig, *Elements of Political Science*, I, pp. 178–82.
34 'Life', p. xlix; this is borne out by Govt., I, p. 29.
35 'Life', pp. xlix–l. For the following, see *Hist. View*, IV, pp. 300ff.; Govt. I,
pp. 21–3; and Juris., p. 232.

As implied in this reference to the principle of utility, the right of government is, like all other rights, founded upon the basic principles of moral judgement. Of these the principle of propriety is only a necessary, not a sufficient, condition for moral approval, and we must therefore look in addition to the consequences of submitting to government, to its utility, in order to find the justification of governmental rights.[36] Government is justified in so far as it protects natural rights. Millar's point can also be expressed another way. Since we have a natural duty not to infringe the natural rights of others, we have a derivative duty to find means of implementing the former duty, and this must be a government: 'men, when they come into society, are bound to preserve the natural rights of one another; and, consequently, to establish a government conducive to that end.'[37] From this it would seem to follow that we have a duty towards some government, and that some government has the right to exercise authority. Beyond this we cannot go with general theorizing; the rest has to be added by a consideration of time and place. Here the other principle of government, the 'principle of authority', will generally play a major role, since it is the principle according to which we judge of legitimacy in terms of proper respect for established authority.

Finally, it should be pointed out that Millar's contrast between rights as fundamental and government – of whatever form – as derivative and a mere means is reflected in a very interesting distinction.[38] On the one hand, he sees rights as uniform and unchanging, whereas systems of government vary extremely from one society to another; this difference is reflected in Millar's organization of his lectures on civil law and on government, respectively.[39] Further, in so far as Millar by 'systems of government' means not only their constitution but also their political activity, it seems highly likely that he is drawing upon Adam Smith's important distinction between the general 'laws of justice' and the particular 'laws of police'.[40]

Millar's resemblance to Smith in approaching politics via the institutional framework of rights and law must be emphasised, for it puts into proper perspective the role played by the concept of 'interest' in Millar's political analysis. It is probably true, as Albert Hirschmann has argued, that Millar is more optimistic than Smith when he suggests that, with the development of commercial society, interest groups will be formed with greater ease than ever before and that these 'interests'

36 Cf. Govt., I, p. 5.   37 *Hist. View,* IV, p. 301.
38 Cf. 'Life', p. cxi: 'however highly Mr Millar valued Civil Liberty, he considered Personal Freedom as infinitely more important.'
39 See 'Life', pp. xliii–xliv; cf. ibid., pp. c–ci, and Govt., I, pp. 1–3.
40 See the discussion in Haakonssen, *Science of a Legislator,* pp. 93–8.

will naturally provide a check on the 'passions' of rulers. Another way of putting this is to say that Millar was on the whole more optimistic than Smith in welcoming the growth of the 'principle of utility' and the decline of the 'principle of authority' as the foundation for government.[41] The difference – and there are undoubtedly politically important differences[42] – would, however, seem to be more about matters of fact than of theory, for Millar's standpoint has more to do with institutional machinery than meets the eye at first. The premise on which he bases his welcome of the growth of the 'principle of utility', or the influence of 'interests', is that this may serve to make government function properly for its purpose, which is not simply to protect any set of powerful interests but – as we have seen – to protect fundamental rights defined by the principles of law. In other words, Millar's whole theoretical enterprise makes sense only when we understand that his welcoming of the influence of interests is conditional upon the coincidence of these interests with rights. Although he may have differed somewhat from Smith as to the degree to which this coincidence was in fact about to occur, there is hardly any theoretical difference between them. Conformably with this we find in Millar, as in Smith, no theory of the dwindling importance of strong government; their theories are concerned with the possibilities of limiting government, with the extent of government, while at the same time keeping it strong.[43]

Though so much of Millar's work was quasi-sociological in its approach, it was this concern with the institutional structure of society which determined his political views. In his well-known analysis in the *Historical View* and, more cautiously, in the lectures on government of the 1780s and 1790s, he argues that in Britain the influence of the Crown has grown since the Revolution of 1688, with the implication that only some sort of parliamentary reform to give the House of

41   See Hirschman, *The Passions and the Interests*, pp. 87–113, esp. pp. 87–93. Cf. *Hist. View*, IV, pp. 287–310; 'Life', p. i; Govt., I, pp. 13–29. For Smith's distinction between the two principles of government, see esp. *Lectures on Jurisprudence*, ed. R.L. Meek, D.D. Raphael, and P.G. Stein, Oxford, 1978, (A), v, pp. 119–22, (B), pp. 12–14; and cf. Haakonssen, *Science of a Legislator*, pp. 128–9.

42   This is explained by Donald Winch, *Adam Smith's Theory of Politics: An Essay in Historiographical Revision*, Cambridge, UK, 1978, pp. 100–2, in an interesting discussion with A.S. Skinner, *A System of Social Science: Papers Relating to Adam Smith*, Oxford, 1979, p. 178, and J. Cropsey, *Polity and Economy: An Interpretation of the Principles of Adam Smith*, The Hague, 1957, pp. 68–9.

43   Cf. Haakonssen, *Science of a Legislator*, pp. 127–33; and, concerning Smith's history of law and government, ibid., ch. 7. Hirschman's search for the fate of the optimism with which, in his view, Montesquieu and Sir James Steuart regarded economic expansion, would have been more generously rewarded by a look at Dugald Stewart; see chapter 7 in the present volume.

Commons more weight will redress the balance of the constitution.[44] The same institutional perspective dominates the extended analysis which John Craig derived from Millar.[45] Furthermore, the special lecture which Millar devoted to the French Revolution soon after it had broken out was wholly concerned with the new constitutional measures which had been taken.[46] And when Millar in the privacy of personal correspondence felt free to display his true colours as a liberal, Foxite Whig, he was occupied with the new French order at the beginning of 1790 as a model for British legal and constitutional reform – that is to say, as a slowly reforming influence on opposing opinions of interest.[47] Finally, when Millar (or Craig) in the *Letters of Sidney* did

44 Cf. Govt. III, pp. 15–8; and the discussion of the French Revolution, ibid., II, pp. 34–44.

45 *Elements of Political Science*, I, pp. 156–270.

46 This lecture is within the set of government lectures principally used here. It seems that this lecture was a special, probably additional one, which may have been given outside the actual course. In another set of notes, MS 180 (1–3), Glasgow University Library, dated 1789, the report of the lecture has clearly been inserted to be bound with the course notes (between pp. 256 and 257 in vol. II).

47 See Millar's letter to Samuel Rose, 16 February 1790: 'We have been a good deal alarmed by this late altercation which has fallen out between our two opposition friends [Burke and Fox]. By some accounts from London, I see people are disposed there to decide in favour of the invective against the French assembly. But this does not seem to be the opinion of any person I have conversed with here. The truth is, it grieves me to differ from so excellent a man as Burke, but I do not see in this instance how he can be vindicated. He is an enemy to the reform of parliamentary representation and to the repeal of the test-act – and seeing that the revolution in France is likely to forward both of those measures, he chooses to take the first word in declaiming against that revolution. It is all in vain however. The system established in France will have the effect of reflecting upon this country some of those rays which have been received from her through the medium of America. Our scruples concerning the repeal of the test-act will have a singular appearance, after the liberal sentiments on that subject, displayed by a Roman Catholic nation, the great leader of fashions and opinions upon the Continent. Is *our High*-church more strait-laced than that of Rome's? Is the *English* in greater danger, from latitude of opinions, than the *Gallican* establishment? Entre nous, I do believe it is in greater danger, from the greater stupidity, ignorance, and narrow prejudices, of the people by whom it is principally supported. As to the reform of parliament, I am not surprised that the measure should for a while longer continue to be unsuccessful. There is a great pecuniary interest that must lead many powerful individuals to oppose it, and it must require some length of time before the voice of the community at large is able to silence the opposition arising from private views. But I should think it impossible that the people of England will be contented with a national assembly so ill constituted, while they have the example of one so much superior in France.' (The Scottish archival source reference has been lost for this quotation.)

concern himself with proposals for social change, his arguments were
legal in character, as we shall see.

This institutional foundation of Millar's politics remained un-
changed throughout his career, despite the fact that his view of contemporary politics underwent significant changes. As Michael Ignatieff
has shown in a fine analysis of Millar, the 'ministerial crisis of 1784
dislodged his faith in [the] old Country Party nostrum', according to
which 'a union of talents and ranks' was necessary 'to limit the growing influence of the Court'.[48] Indeed, before the American war 'Millar's
account of royal prerogative and executive power was benign and
Humean in tone'; he even 'rejected the traditional Commonwealthman
and Country Party call for triennial Parliaments' and accepted the existing property qualifications for electors.[49] After the American war,
and especially after the dismissal of the North–Fox government, Millar's position on British politics was radicalized, and he began to adopt
'the language coined a century earlier by Whig Commonwealthmen
and Country Party opponents of King William's war'.[50] First of all,

> It was the electorate's apparent vulnerability to corruption in 1784 which
> convinced Millar, as Craig put it, 'of the necessity of henceforward founding
> national liberty on a much more general diffusion of political power.' In his
> government lectures of 1787, Millar gave his first explicit support to trien-
> nial Parliaments and to the enfranchisement of every male 'with as much
> property as a good labourer can earn by his daily labour, suppose £20 or £25
> a year'.[51]

Although these changes in Millar are politically important, they do not
signal any change in his theoretical politics. What changed was his
view of the political means to be used, whereas the justifying objective
remained the same: a legal order which maximized individual liberty.

Here I part ways with Ignatieff, who suggests that Millar's adoption
of the Commonwealthmen's ideas went so far as to include a 'preference for "virtue" over "justice", for "free government" over "regular
government"'.[52] It is impossible to accept this general conclusion, in
view of the primacy which Millar continued to give to 'justice' in his
post-1784 writings and lectures, as we have seen. Ignatieff, however,
rests his case on an argument which is interesting both in itself and
because it refutes his own conclusion. In a sparkling analysis with
which I wholly agree, he shows how Millar confined his 'preference for
"virtue"' in modern society to the private sphere of family life. It was

48 'Life', p. cii; Ignatieff, 'John Millar and individualism', p. 328.
49 Ignatieff, p. 327.
50 Ignatieff, p. 329, referring to *Crito*, pp. 84–101.
51 Ignatieff, p. 329, quoting Craig, 'Life', p. ciii, and Govt., III, p. 18.
52 Ignatieff, p. 332.

the marriage bond and the parental care of children which were under severe threat from the atomization and commercialization of life, whereas Millar 'agreed with Smith and Hume that commercial society had civilized manners in the "economic sphere". A free market encouraged relations of justice. And in the "political sphere", the independence of the rising ranks could be relied on to counterbalance the increasing proliferation of "police" and bureaucracy.'[53] This does not, however, constitute the 'intellectual disarray' in which Ignatieff would have us believe. According to him, Millar here espoused contradictions which were 'those of a theorist caught between two languages which bifurcate in his own lifetime – civic humanist moralism and political economy'.[54] But Millar's argumentative triumph is precisely to have helped to divide the two. The whole point in basing politics on the theory of justice was to remove most 'moralizing' from the political sphere and to subordinate the rest to the 'preference for "justice"'. This was the essence of 'scientific' or 'sceptical Whiggism', and Millar's firm commitment to it is clearly shown by its ability to keep his moralizing tendency in check. It is true both that this tendency is strong and that it often assumes the language of 'civic humanist moralism'; it is not true that Millar's separation of the private sphere of 'virtue' from the public sphere of 'justice' overturns his theoretical structure. This is, on the contrary, the direct implication of a 'scepticism' which bases politics upon a preference for negative justice.

5.5   A theory of property

Against the background of the argument in the preceding sections we may conclude that the theory of natural jurisprudence which Adam Smith presented in his lectures – attended by Millar – is taken over in all its essentials by the latter. We have the same idea of the relationship between justice and the other virtues and hence of the relationship between law and morality. For Millar, as for Hume and Smith, law is a phenomenon which must necessarily have a history and which can be understood only by reference to the formal elements of natural justice. This means that all questions of justice and right can be raised and settled only by reference to the social context or situation. Finally, Millar, like Smith, thinks that individual questions of justice are decided through the reactions of the impartial spectator by being referred to their context.

In spite of the evidence for such a line of argument, Millar's theory has most impressed scholars and critics as an historical and, not least, sociological theory of law. There are good reasons for this, as we shall

53   Ignatieff, p. 342.   54   Ignatieff, p. 341.

see, but for a comprehensive and consistent interpretation, which will also show the line of development from Hume and Smith, the jurisprudential aspect must be brought in.

To illustrate this in a more concrete way I will analyse what Millar had to say about property relations in contemporary Britain. These views are put forward in the anonymous *Letters of Sidney* and repeated in John Craig's *Elements of Political Science*.[55] As mentioned, it is impossible to decide whether Millar or Craig wrote the *Letters of Sidney*, but since they are based upon a theory of justice which is common to both and which Craig learnt from Millar, it hardly matters, for present purposes.[56] Much of the material in the *Letters of Sidney* is in any case derived from Millar's lectures on civil law, especially the sections on property and inheritance,[57] which do not, however, add anything of consequence to the published versions. Furthermore, in both the *Letters of Sidney* and Craig's *Elements*, general and generous acknowledgement is made to Millar's lectures.

The *Letters of Sidney*, so the subtitle tells us, are 'on Inequality of Property', and the first six maintain that in Britain, at the time, such inequality is so excessive as to have the most appalling effect on social life in a number of respects. It undermines both the private and social morality of the very rich as well as the very poor, and this evil spirit easily spreads to the whole community. It creates a corrupt atmosphere, ruinous to all public spirit and patriotism. Furthermore, it is economically disastrous, for economic growth is a matter of capital, and capital accumulation is much impaired under conditions of extreme inequality of fortune. In sum:

> I trust I have shown, that excessive inequality of property occasions misery both to the rich and to the poor; that it is subversive of morality, is the bane of patriotism, the prolific mother of the most flagitious crimes, that it is extremely hurtful to agriculture, commerce, and population. It seems altogether impossible for the mind of man to conceive more numerous and more destructive evils proceeding from one source.[58]

55 Craig, *Elements of Political Science*, Book II, ch. 5.

56 I do not agree with Ignatieff, 'John Millar and individualism', p. 323, that *Sidney* is 'more Jacobin than any text which can definitely be attributed to Millar'.

57 See Civil Law, I, pp. 79–123, and II, pp. 1–53; Juris., pp. 119–218.

58 *Sidney*, p. 27. Cf. G.E. Davie, *The Scottish Enlightenment*, London, 1981, p. 27: 'True to the spirit of David Hume and his secularised Calvinism, the principle which lay behind the moderate degree of planned redistribution of wealth [in Millar] was deemed an intellectual and not a moral one – that of keeping alive in the community the spirit of enterprise, and of preventing the stultification which too rigid class-divisions were supposed to bring'. (As will become clear, I would not use the expression 'planned redistribution' in connection with Millar.) Davie's discussion sets Millar's ideas clearly within the problematic of the relationship between Scotland and England in connection with the question of reform.

After this harsh criticism, the next two letters make it clear that it does not imply a scheme for the levelling of property. Indeed the author goes to some lengths to show that the frightening examples from history to which establishment 'alarmists' refer are misconceived, for they are all, in the view of the author, concerned with inequality of political and civil rights and not with property rights, which are natural rights. Whether this is true or not is, of course, questionable, but it is interesting to see the distinction between civil and natural rights being put to this kind of critical use.

Having cleared up this matter, the following letter, no. 9, states the central philosophical arguments. Justice and property are not rationally and deliberately constructed out of considerations of utility; more particularly, they are not the creatures of civil society. Social organization and government, on the contrary, are simply a means of protecting property, which is a natural right founded in the natural feelings of spectators. Natural rights, including property rights, arise spontaneously among men irrespective of their particular political organization; these rights are temporally and logically prior to civil society; indeed, the main function of civil society is to guard them. On this central issue Millar again finds it appropriate to invoke the authority of Hume: 'the ingenious writer, who has said that the whole apparatus of our Government is merely intended to support the twelve judges, has only erred by going a little too far.'[59]

After showing that rules of justice emerge spontaneously and only later gain strength through considerations of their utility,[60] the author goes on to apply them to the problem on hand, the excessive inequality of property. He first argues forcefully that levelling is ruled out as unjust[61] and goes on to suggest that it is useless as well. It does not pay economically, and it cannot function, because inequality springs up again immediately.[62]

This leads to the conclusion that while extreme inequality is bad, levelling is worse; though the former may have disastrous consequences, the latter not only has as bad or worse effects but is also fundamentally unjust. If we want to do something about the existing

59 *Sidney*, p. 46. A footnote refers to 'Hume's Essays, Part I, Essay V'. This is 'Of the Origin of Government', in *Political Essays*, ed. K. Haakonssen, Cambridge, UK, 1994, p. 20–3 at p. 20.

60 In this connection it is interesting to notice that Millar is concerned about the possible social dangers if considerations of utility become too prevalent. In *Hist. View*, IV, pp. 26off., he argues that when justice in 'opulent and luxurious nations' is judged more and more by 'considerations of interest', there is a danger that some people may find that their interest lies somewhere else. This can have catastrophic consequences. His examples are the Roman provincial governors and modern mercantile companies with a monopoly on trade 'in very distant countries'.

61 *Sidney*, pp. 47–8.   62 *Sidney*, Letter 10.

great inequalities, it must be done within the framework of just law, and that excludes the levelling of property. The author thinks the aim might be achieved by the following three measures, which would discourage extreme accumulation of wealth without infringing property rights: First, a change in the inheritance laws such that primogeniture is dissolved and all children inherit equally; second, a change in the inheritance laws such that only testaments for a limited part of a man's property are enforced; third, the distribution of the tax burden according to a somewhat progressive scale. For all three proposals the author argues that justice is not transgressed and that, since the measures are desirable for other reasons, namely considerations of utility, they ought to be carried out.

As to inheritance, the impartial spectator will approve that all those closest to a deceased person succeed to his property, and it is, therefore, naturally just that it should be so. This again means that it cannot rightfully be changed by statute, for there is a general presumption against changing by statute that which has not been introduced by statute.[63] Since deviations from this principle of justice in inheritance were in fact deliberately introduced, they ought accordingly to be abolished. Primogeniture was introduced in rude and violent times when it was important to have an agreed leader, especially in war, but as this consideration of expediency does not apply in the same way in modern times, there is so much more reason for returning to a just system of law, that is, to equal inheritance for all the children.

As to testaments, the author argues that they have no foundation whatever in human nature, that is, in the judgement of an impartial spectator. They are purely a matter of statutes, of expediency, and since the aim is to discourage large concentrations of wealth, only a certain part of a man's property should be allowed to be disposed of through testament.[64]

Finally, as to taxation, the author's point is that a tax burden divided equally among all members of the society deprives the poor of basic necessities, the better-off of conveniences, but the rich of luxuries.[65] Accordingly, taxation ought to be progressive.

An over-all view of the *Letters of Sidney* reveals a clear argumentative structure. For many reasons men are apprehensive about a particular feature of social life, namely extreme inequality of property. They are morally obliged to base their criticism of this situation, as well as

63 *Sidney,* p. 54.

64 *Sidney,* Letters 13–14. Entail obviously succumbs to the same argument (Letter 14). All of these arguments concerning inheritance derive from Smith; see Haakonssen, *Science of a Legislator,* pp. 109–11 and 142–3.

65 *Sidney,* Letter 15. The distinction between necessities and luxuries is well known from Smith's *Wealth of Nations,* V, ii, k.

their remedy for it, on the principles of justice. Both in order to find out what justice is in the case and in order to realize such justice, they must inquire into the history of the situation. Like Hume and Smith, Millar is insistent that justice is a negative virtue: it tells us what not to do. What the *Letters of Sidney* make particularly clear is that as long as we keep within this framework, our political actions can have all sorts of motives, but the limit of politics is set by the principles of justice.[66]

5.6 A question of ideology

Millar's approach to politics is fundamentally 'scientific', and his science of law and government is to be viewed in the jurisprudential tradition. At the same time he can to some extent accommodate the neo-humanist concern with morals and manners and its political significance by assuming a potential harmony between interests and rights, which can be realized through social and political enlightenment.[67] Like Adam Smith, he doubted the availability of such enlightenment for the lower orders, and, like him, he pinned his hopes mostly on a combination of basic education and the greater social mobility which commercial society provided by breaking down rigid class structures.[68] Again like Smith, he consequently thought that arguments from justice, arguments from economic expediency, and arguments arising from a concern with the moral stature of the people all pointed to legal reforms of the kind we have just rehearsed.

This delicate balance has led to the suggestion that Millar is fundamentally to be seen as the ideologist *des kleinen Bürgertums,* of the lower 'middling ranks', and that this ideological function is revealed in a number of significant inconsistencies, which are simply reflections of the contradictory situation of the lower bourgeoisie.[69] The most fundamental inconsistency, it is suggested, is to be found in Millar's theory of labour. For, when he analyses the process by which feudal society developed into modern commercial society, he uses labour (*viz.,* the

---

66 It is difficult to see *Sidney* in the way suggested by Ignatieff, 'John Millar and individualism', p. 323, as an 'Harringtonian appeal for an *equalization* of property through the abolition of primogeniture and entail' (my italics).

67 Cf. J.G.A. Pocock, *Virtue, Commerce, and History: Essays on Political Thought and History, Chiefly in the Eighteenth Century,* Cambridge, UK, 1985, pp. 298–300, and at note 41 to this chapter. [Note: citations saying '*at* note 41 mean 'in the text, near note 41'; citations saying '*in* note 6 mean 'in the text of note 6'.]

68 Cf. text at note 74 to this chapter.

69 Medick and Leppert-Fögen, 'Frühe Sozialwissenschaft', pp. 27–8. Medick has criticised Smith in similar terms in his important book *Naturzustand und Naturgeschichte der bürgerlichen Gesellschaft,* pp. 278ff.

labour of the middling ranks) as the foundation of property[70] and as
the precondition for the evolution of the political autonomy and liberty
of the individual. This theory becomes contradictory when Millar analyses the fully developed commercial society, for here the basic factor,
labour, itself becomes a commodity. This paradox is linked to a difficulty in the theory of capital. When Millar is dealing with pre-
commercial society, he says that 'capital is composed of what is saved
from the produce which [has] . . . not been consumed by individuals',
but when he comes to modern society the idea is completely transformed, and capital becomes an independent factor of production
along with the two natural ones of land and labour. As such, it is an
independent source of new property, namely profit, which is thus not
based on the owner's own labour.[71]

It is further argued that this leads to a split in Millar's class theory.
He sees clearly that in pre-commercial society there must be two broad
classes, those with, and those without property; and he sees that these
two classes must be opposed to each other as rulers and ruled. In
modern society, however, there must be three classes, corresponding to
the three means of production. Since Millar here suddenly asserts that
capital helps the labouring classes to support themselves, he is also led
to maintain that this class structure does not lead to any clear and
stable power structure nor to any antagonism. Here Millar is simply
blind to the fact that the new capital is based on exploitation. Historically, the middle class of small producers is the link between a feudal
and a fully developed capitalist society, but it differs from and is antag-
onistic to both. Millar wants to make the condition of this class the
permanent condition of society in general. His blindness to the true
character of capitalism, however, leads him to attack only one facet, so
to speak, namely, the feudal and feudal-seeming impediments to his
Utopia. This leads him, in the *Letters of Sidney*, to adopt the contradictory positions of first arguing clearly against inequality of property and
then defending private property even more strongly against all levelling schemes. The latter, indeed, is done with such excessive zeal that
he would maintain private property in the interests of a minority
against the will of the majority of the people.

Medick and Leppert-Fögen conclude that this contradiction between criticism of inequality and condemnation of levelling is impossible to resolve but that it can be explained. It is an expression of the

70 Medick and Leppert-Fögen, in 'Frühe Sozialwissenschaft', refer to Locke
(p. 44, n. 50): 'Millar schliesst sich in den "Letters of Sidney" explizit der Lockeschen
Arbeitslegitimation des Eigentums an; s. den Hinweis auf das klassische Kap. V des
II. "Treatise of Government" in Sidney, IX, 45'.

71 Ibid., pp. 30–1, quoting *Sidney*, p. 23.

small producers' ideology of 'reasonable economy', which on the one
hand requires the existence of private property but on the other excludes excessive possessions as leading to a bad economy. This is the
'petty-bourgeois view', the spoken and unspoken assumptions of 'the
petty-bourgeois economist' and, in the end, 'of the petty-bourgeois
moralist Millar'.[72]

Medick and Leppert-Fögen's view is obviously an interesting attempt to come to grips with Millar's argument, and, since it suggests
contradictions where I argue for consistency, it must be examined with
some care. At the heart of the matter is what I consider a clear mistake.
Millar does not adopt Locke's labour theory of property. Like Adam
Smith, he makes it clear that property has its origins in the approval of
the spectator, and he repeats this frequently.[73] He handles Locke's
labour theory of property exactly as Smith did, by transforming it into
a supporting argument for his own spectator theory. The idea is simply
that nothing heightens a person's expectations of having de facto possessions at his disposal more than having to work for them; because
any impartial spectator would entirely sympathize with this, his right
to the possessions is to that extent confirmed. Nor does Millar think
that labour as such is a precondition for political autonomy and the
liberty of the individual members of the emergent middle class; it is,
rather, labour performed in new circumstances, namely in a market
situation. It is the market which makes people free individuals, irrespective of what they have to offer in that market. This applies to
labour services as well as to goods, but of course the latter are the most
obvious commodity in the early stages of an evolving commercial
society. Accordingly, Millar says, 'the labouring parts of the inhabitants
. . . often find it more profitable to work at their own charges.'[74]

The thrust of a theory like this is that with the development of the
market, its liberating or independence-forming effects spread down-
wards to the lowest orders of the people. It is therefore creating a
situation in which even the poorest need no longer sell themselves but
only their services. This of course produces new social problems, but
that is, after all, not a contradiction but a practical problem. Millar sees
the development of Britain 'since the Reign of William III' as tending in
just this direction. In the important third essay in Volume IV of the
Historical View, he shows how capitalism in commerce and farming at
this period had increased freedom and independence in general and

72 Ibid., pp. 31–8.
73 See esp. the very important passage in *Sidney*, pp. 44–5; and cf. *Ranks*, p. 158.
Concerning Smith's identical idea, see Haakonssen, *Science of a Legislator*, pp. 106–7.
74 *Ranks*, p. 231. Cf. also Bruce A. Thor, 'The economic theories of John Craig:
A forgotten English economist', *Quarterly Journal of Economics*, 52 (1938), 697–707.

opened the opportunity for obtaining them to all. The consequence of such liberty is inevitably inequality, though not a final and monopolized inequality. For it is suggested that in the course of a few generations membership of the various ranks of society will change and that in order to achieve this laws of inheritance, testaments, and entail should be reformed.[75]

Similarly there is no contradiction in Millar's theory of capital. The mere savings of a pre-modern society can become capital, in the modern sense of independent means of production, only when a market has developed. The criticism that profit cannot really be property because it is not based on the owner's labour is refuted when we remember that Millar does not embrace the labour theory of property but substitutes for it a theory of spectator-perceived utility (which later led John Craig to develop the theory that value consists in utility).

Millar follows Smith closely in maintaining that the two broad classes of pre-commercial society oppose each other as rulers and ruled because there is no market system through which the property of the rulers can be circulated and thus benefit others besides themselves. The only ways in which property can be used or circulated are either as gifts, which create dependants, or through violence, which leads the propertied classes to use power and thus also creates dependants. This situation changes in commercial society, if it is not prevented by artificial maintenance of pre-commercial institutions and feudal laws. Savings turned into capital by the market can be spent and change hands. The three classes of modern society are accordingly not classes in the same absolute sense as the two classes of earlier periods, for their membership is continually changing. Although property will always greatly influence power, its influence will, in such a situation, be very much less.

Medick and Leppert-Fögen seem to lack an appreciation of the starting-point for Millar's various criticisms, namely his theory of justice and rights. It is because feudal institutions conflict with this that Millar criticizes them. And he does not criticize commercial society as such, because he perceives the society of small and medium producers as the most liberal, enforcing no monopoly or monopoly-creating laws and leaving room to remedy any social defects which arise. There is therefore no contradiction in his criticizing inequality of property while at the same time rejecting levelling. Both the excessive inequality then existing and any future levelling of property transgress the principles of justice and liberty in the same manner, and both are illegitimate interferences. It is not true to say that, according to Millar, it is Parlia-

---

75 *Hist. View,* IV, pp. 130–1; cf. Ignatieff as quoted in note 66 to the present chapter.

ment which should distribute property.[76] He only wants Parliament to abolish the old inheritance laws and then let the distribution of property run its own course, for he is more or less optimistic that this would lead to a much more finely graded scale of inequality. It is, accordingly, as a matter of justice, and only in that sense a matter of 'interest', that property has to be defended.

As regards Millar's 'petty-bourgeois outlook' and his zeal for 'reasonable economy', these are not aspects of an absolute and unchecked ideology but a set of moral, social, and economic ideals which are tried out against an overriding ideal of justice. In short, if Millar was indeed in a contradictory class situation, that fact is not reflected in the kind of intellectual difficulties which have been suggested.[77]

5.7   A role for history

The ideas of Millar with which we have been concerned have been within the general framework of Adam Smith's concept of a science of legislation, and it has been part of my purpose here to demonstrate this. Smith's 'science of a legislator' revolves around a theory of jurisprudence characterized by the interconnection between the descriptive and the normative theories of law, and, as we have seen, this relationship is neither severed nor confused in Millar's work. Millar's historical and sociological approach has, however, led a number of modern scholars to take his real achievement to be a materialist, or economic, interpretation of history similar to the one so often ascribed to Smith.[78]

---

76   Medick and Leppert-Fögen, 'Frühe Sozialwissenschaft', p. 23.

77   Louis Schneider has also found 'Tension in the thought of John Millar', *Studies in Burke and His Time* (Winter 1971–72), pp. 2083–98, some of it coinciding with what I have just discussed. I attempted to deal with this in 'Natural Justice', pp. 309ff.

78   For a discussion of this problem with special reference to Smith, see Haakonssen, *Science of a Legislator*, pp. 181–8. To the literature discussed there should be added Meek, *Social Science and the Ignoble Savage*, esp. pp. 160–76, and Kuczynski, *Zur Geschichte der Wirtschaftsgeschichtsschreibung*, pp. 92–103. The latter restates the idea of Millar as a proto-historical materialist, without qualification. A brief, balanced appreciation of Millar's historical method is T.P. Peardon, *The Transition in English Historical Writing, 1760–1830*, New York, 1933, pp. 82–4. The most sophisticated approaches to the problem of the role and character of history are Duncan Forbes, 'Sceptical Whiggism, commerce, and liberty', esp. pp. 198–200; same, 'Natural law and the Scottish Enlightenment', in *The Origins and Nature of the Scottish Enlightenment*, ed. R.H. Campbell and A.S. Skinner, Edinburgh, 1982, pp. 186–204, esp. pp. 201–2; and, on a much broader front, David Allan, *Virtue, Learning and the Scottish Enlightenment: Ideas of Scholarship in Early Modern History*, Edinburgh, 1993, esp. pp. 160–9. Cf. also Skinner, *A System of Social Science*, pp. 68–103, for a good

With Millar as with Smith it is often very difficult to ascertain precisely what this interpretation means and hence to see whether it is incompatible with the theory of law and government which has been ascribed to him here. Since Millar's theory of history is in all essentials the same as Smith's, the arguments which have already been put forward in the literature on Smith can here be extended briefly to Millar.[79] Like Smith, Millar uses as his explanatory unit the typified reactions of individuals to their situation, and, like Smith, he thinks that mankind's situation can be divided into four broad types, the four stages of social development. Likewise in agreement with Smith, Millar sees in each of these stages a multiplicity of elements which would influence the individuals living through that stage:

> the fertility or barrenness of the soil, the nature of its productions, the species of labour requisite for procuring subsistence, the number of individuals collected together in one community, their proficiency in arts, the advantages which they enjoy for entering into mutual transactions, and for maintaining an intimate correspondence.[80]

As in Smith, the economic elements dominate and are necessary for any social change, but they are hardly ever alone or sufficient. It seems a strange historical materialist who – in line with most of his contemporaries – would have as one of his recurrent themes, that

> the *ultimate* cause of this great phenomenon [the French Revolution] appears to be no other, than the general diffusion of knowledge, and the progress of science and philosophy.[81]

The main obstacle to the materialist interpretation of Millar is, however, the presence of a clear idea of natural law and rights. This theory would be unintelligible unless history, for Millar as for Smith, were an open-ended process with a plurality of factors at play, amongst which men's application of institutionalized rules of justice might be one. Millar's own intention and ability to apply such rules in a given situation have been demonstrated earlier in this chapter.

Finally, it should not be forgotten that, irrespective of his actual performance in the published works, Millar's intentions regarding the discipline of jurisprudence were the same as Smith's, and he declared them clearly at the beginning of his lectures on civil law. Like Smith, he saw comparative, including historical, studies of law such as his own

---

discussion of Smith's historical theory, and David Spadafora, *The Idea of Progress in Eighteenth-Century Britain*, New Haven, 1990, ch. 7, for a general presentation of the Scots view of progress.

79 See Haakonssen, *Science of a Legislator.*   80 *Ranks*, p. 2.
81 *Letters of Crito*, p. 3 (my italics); cf. *Govt.*, II, p. 34.

as a direct continuation of the work of Grotius and later natural law theoreticians.[82] In his view these philosophers did not achieve their goal, a universal system of ideal law, because they were too dependent upon Roman law and because they failed to distinguish exactly between law and morality. In Millar's view it was Montesquieu, Kames, and Smith who improved this situation by their comparative studies of law. The interesting thing is, however, that sociological and historical knowledge is not the only thing we get out of such studies. We 'obtain, at the same time, satisfactory evidence of the *uniformity of those internal principles* which are productive of such various and apparently inconsistent operations'.[83] It is only when we understand 'the uniformity of those internal principles' that we can see 'that there is any thing stable or precise in the moral sentiments of mankind'. This is 'that standard of perfection which nature holds up to the speculative mind', which lets us 'find no difficulty in conceiving' improvements in the practical system of law in any country.[84] In other words, the new study of law, which Millar sees himself as continuing, has the same ideal as the natural law tradition – as he saw this – namely that of 'delivering a system of law, free from the defects which occur in every practical establishment, and which might correspond in some measure, with our views of absolute perfection'.[85]

5.8 *Conclusion*

Michael Ignatieff has suggested that Millar contributed to the dissolution of Smith's project for a science of legislation, a dissolution which took place in the early decades of the nineteenth century with the separation of economics from the rest of moral philosophy:

> If Millar's theory of civil society went to show that the moral problem [in commercial society] was confined to the private and familiar sphere, it could be hived off as essentially irrelevant to the economic. The Smithian synthesis of economics, politics and history of civil society then began to seem, as Horner put it, like system-building, much better broken down into separate "treatises".[86]

82 See *Hist. View*, IV, pp. 282–5; Civil Law, I, p. 22; Juris., pp. 29–35; and 'Life', pp. xxiii–xxvi, for the following.

83 *Hist. View*, IV, p. 285 (my italics); cf. Civil Law, I, pp. 5–6; Juris. p. 35.

84 'Life', p. xxvi, and *Hist. View*, IV, pp. 281 and 284.

85 *Hist. View*, IV, p. 282. This is not to deny that both the element of historical 'materialism', such as it is, and the study of jurisprudence in Millar can be seen in an even wider perspective as parts of a general Scottish concern with the history of manners. See Allan, *Virtue, Learning and the Scottish Enlightenment*, pp. 164 and 168.

86 Ignatieff, 'John Millar and individualism', p. 343; cf. the discussion of Ignatieff at notes 52–4 to this chapter.

This does not, however, do justice to Millar. Not only does he maintain the separation of moral and legal criticism, which is at the very heart of the Smithian project and gives depth to its 'scientific' character, but he consistently follows Smith, as we have seen, in maintaining that history is integral to *both*. Furthermore, Ignatieff puts Millar into a scene where he hardly belongs. When the disciples of Dugald Stewart 'paired [*sic*] away' economics from the 'history of manners' and the demonstration of 'the moral problem', it was not because *Millar* had taught them to see the latter as 'marginal'.[87] They had, rather, come to see 'the moral problem' as marginal because they thought it could be *solved*, and this insight they derived from the realist moral philosophy of Dugald Stewart himself, who developed it from Reid.[88] It was precisely because Smith, and after him Millar, denied such moral realism and its implication for the solvability of 'the moral problem' that they insisted on the necessity of understanding this problem historically and of separating it from the problem of legal criticism and the consequent problem of the political means for legal reform.

The scholarly conjunction of Millar and Stewart may owe a good deal to the fact that they had common enemies. The reaction against the French Revolution after 1792 made public debate into a darkness in which all oppositional cats were grey, and, like Reid and Stewart, Millar was thrown into the ranks of the suspicious and had to show some caution in public life.[89] But despite all the attractions of streamlined traditions, it must be kept clear that intellectually Millar hails from a very different place than that of Common Sense philosophy. He had opposed Reid's appointment as Smith's successor in the Chair of Moral Philosophy at Glasgow and sought Smith's support in this, and it is likely that he developed the second half of his lectures on Justinian's *Institutes* into a course on pure Smithian jurisprudence and began his path-breaking lectures on government at least in part as a

---

87 Ignatieff, ibid.   88 See chapter 7, on Stewart, in this volume.

89 Francis Jeffrey's Tory father thought that his son had been politically corrupted by 'the mere vicinity of Millar' when Francis studied in Glasgow. As if prescient of which tradition was to adapt more easily to a morally conservative society, Francis had been sent to study moral philosophy with Reid's former assistant and then successor, Archibald Arthur. Henry Cockburn, *Life of Lord Jeffrey. With a Selection from His Correspondence*, 2 vols., Edinburgh, 1852, I, pp. 8–12. Cf. Philip Flynn, *Francis Jeffrey*, Newark, DE, 1978, ch. 1. Millar delayed continuing his *Historical View* beyond volumes 1 and 2 out of political caution, and they eventually had to be published posthumously. See James Reddie's report to Francis Horner that 'from what Mr. Millar had told him, he could gather that another volume was written out containing the last period ["from James I to the present time"] which was delayed and only by the present political temper.' *The Horner Papers*, p. 96. Concerning Reid and Stewart, see Ch. 7, sect. 7.1 and Ch. 8, sect. 8.1, this volume.

counter to Reid's arrival.[90] As we have seen, he had good philosophical reasons for this opposition. But even though Millar, basing himself upon the 'good old Humean philosophy', intended to be heir to Smith's whole science of a legislator, in practice he shifted the focus from jurisprudence in a philosophical sense to the history and sociology of law. This is obviously true of the published treatises, and it is largely true of his lectures as well. Although the latter contain a good deal of philosophical and critical material, their general approach to law is descriptive and explanatory. In so far as Millar contributed to the dissolution of the Smithian synthesis of the various branches of moral philosophy, the reason has to be sought in this change of emphasis and in the consequent obscuration of the relationship between explanatory history and critical theory.

90   See *The Correspondence of Adam Smith*, ed. E.C. Mossner and I.S. Ross, 2nd ed., Oxford, 1987, pp. 99–100), and Cairns, '"Famous as a school for Law . . .": Legal education in Glasgow', pp. 5–6. Alexander Carlyle, admiring student of Hutcheson and leading member of the Moderate establishment, recognized the combination of principles that made Millar dangerous: '[Millar had] begun to Distinguish himself by his Democratical Principles, and that Sceptical Philosophy, which young Noblemen and Gentlemen of Legislative Rank carried into the world with them, From his Law class, and many years afterwards, particularly at the Period of the French Revolution, Displayed with Popular Zeal, to the no Small Danger of Perversion to all those under their Influence.' Alexander Carlyle, *Anecdotes and Characters of the Times* [1860], ed. James Kinsley, London, 1973, p. 252.

6

Thomas Reid's moral and political philosophy

Thomas Reid is well known as an epistemologist, and to the extent that his moral philosophy has attracted attention, it has, until recently, concentrated on his idea of moral agency and moral judgement. The publication of his manuscript material on 'practical ethics', of which natural jurisprudence was the most prominent part, has enabled us to add significantly to this agenda.[1] The concern here is not, however, simply to add but to integrate. I want to show that Reid's practical ethics actually forms an integral part of his philosophy.

6.1 *Human knowledge*

Given Reid's presuppositions, the argumentative coherence of his moral thought is tight and systematic. The cardinal themes are the possibility of knowledge and, deriving from this, the possibilities in knowledge. The philosophy of mind shows what knowledge, including moral knowledge, is possible for man, and practical ethics shows what possibilities this gives man as moral agent. The basic presuppositions are theological and may be characterized as 'providential naturalism', a term that is appropriate also for George Turnbull and Lord Kames, Reid's principal mentors along with Butler in this regard.[2] For

1 See Thomas Reid, *Practical Ethics: Being Lectures and Papers on Natural Religion, Self-Government, Natural Jurisprudence, and the Law of Nations*, ed. K. Haakonssen, Princeton, 1990. I outline Reid's development and context in the introduction to that work, pp. 3–37; to the literature discussed there should be added Stephen A. Conrad, *Citizenship and Common Sense: The Problem of Authority in the Social Background and Social Philosophy of the Wise Club of Aberdeen*, New York, 1987.

2 See David Fate Norton, *David Hume: Common-Sense Moralist, Sceptical Metaphysician*, Princeton, 1982, ch. 4. For Reid's natural theology, see George Baird, *Notes from the Lectures of Dr. Thomas Reid, 1779–1780*, 8 vols., Mitchell Library, Glasgow, MS A104929, V. Reid's defence of the argument from design is in *Essays on the Intellectual Powers of Man*, in *Philosophical Works*, ed. Sir William Hamilton, facsim.

Reid – as for Turnbull, Kames, Butler, and most of their contemporaries – the world in both its material and immaterial aspects was a well-organized whole whose parts by their coherence indicated an intelligent, purposeful mastermind. The existence within creation of the human mind, with its apparent cognitive powers, thus gave rise to the presumption that the purpose of the mind is to explore the created world as it is presented to these powers. However, the world appears to us not as a coherent whole but as piecemeal, as discontinuous events and things, and we must therefore study it piecemeal, noticing similarities and regularities as they appear. If we go beyond this and form 'hypotheses' about connecting links outside our field of experience, we are in effect exceeding our cognitive brief and prying into God's affairs. In other words, there is strong theological sanction for the inductive method suggested by Francis Bacon and, in Reid's view, definitively developed and explained by Newton.

This method had been applied to the physical world with extraordinary results, but moral philosophers still employed it with what Reid considered insufficient stringency, thereby often being involved in unnecessary and dangerous problems. Modern philosophy – from Descartes via Nicolas Malebranche, John Locke, and George Berkeley – had made the possibility of knowledge more and more incomprehensible, until Hume finally drew the full sceptical conclusions.[3] Reid's interpretation of the course of modern philosophy soon became the textbook version and, as still surviving today, it must be conceded to be his most lasting influence on Western thought. Fortunately, modern scholarship has begun to reject his simplification of the history of philosophy, but we should not forget that such simplification was an important argumentative or polemical move. We may say briefly that Reid concentrated the battle against scepticism on one front by viewing epistemological scepticism as fundamental to all forms of scepticism and as pervading the whole of modern philosophy.

At the heart of the sorry confusion that was modern philosophy lay a general tendency to adopt a totally misleading analogy between body and mind in an attempt to replicate in moral philosophy the success of natural philosophy.[4] Treatment of the mind as analogous to

---

repr. of 8th ed., 1895, introd. Harry M. Bracken, 2 vols. in 1, Hildesheim, 1983 (henceforth abbreviated *IP*), pp. 457b–461b.

3 In general, see *An Inquiry into the Human Mind, on the Principles of Common Sense*, in *Philosophical Works* (henceforth abbreviated *HM*), ch. 1. See also Norton, *David Hume*, pp. 171–3 and 189–203.

4 The following sketch of Reid's epistemology and its critical implications is based mainly on the *Philosophical Orations of Thomas Reid*, ed. W.R. Humphries,

material mechanisms was naturally suggested and supported by the physical expressions ordinarily used to refer to its workings. Consequently the mental world was seen as composed of certain basic entities, namely simple ideas that were imparted to the mind by its surroundings in the form of sense impressions and from which complex ideas of things, events, and so on, were composed. The materialist and mechanistic analogy for the mind thus led directly to that other fundamental error of modern philosophy, 'the theory of ideas', as Reid called it – that is, the theory that ideas, not the objects of ideas, are the immediate objects of the mind's apprehension.

All this, for Reid, was fundamentally wrong. In fact, it rested on a total disregard of sound empirical method in the interest of formulating a purely speculative 'empiricist' (as it was to be known) philosophy. There was no empirical evidence to support the analogy between mind and body, and uncontaminated common sense clearly showed that the mind was in its nature quite different from and not comparable to the physical world. It is true that sensation suggests the presence of an object and occasions many of our ideas, but for many very important ideas – such as those of space, time, and power – this is not so. Furthermore, the process of perception, from sensation to idea, cannot be understood as a causal chain, like a physical process, for not only are mental 'images' of a totally different nature from their objects in the material world but the mind, far from being a passive recipient, is in fact active in so far as even simple perception is judgemental in character, judging that something is the case. Finally, it is empirically false that complex mental content is composed of simple ideas; on the contrary, even casual reflection shows that the mind spontaneously apprehends complex objects, which may subsequently be subjected to analysis. Reid even suggests that there is no empirical evidence whatever for the existence of ideas, in the sense of mental objects immediately present to the mind. Instead of acknowledging things and events of vary-

Aberdeen, 1937; the orations of 1759 and 1762; and on HM, ch. 1, with occasional reference also to IP. There is an English translation of the *Orations*, ed. D.D. Todd, trans. S.D. Sullivan, Carbondale, IL., 1989. Among several recent studies, I have benefitted from R.D. Gallie, *Thomas Reid and 'the Way of Ideas'*, Dordrecht, 1989; K. Lehrer, *Thomas Reid*, London, 1989; E. Lobkowicz, *Common Sense und Skeptizismus*, Weinheim, 1986; D. Schulthess, *Philosophie et sense commun chez Thomas Reid (1710–1796)*, Berne, 1983; J.C. Weinsheimer, *Eighteenth-Century Hermeneutics: Philosophy of Interpretation in England from Locke to Burke*, New Haven, 1993, ch. 5. See also S.A. Grave, *The Scottish Philosophy of Common Sense*, Oxford, 1960; C.J. McCracken, *Malebranche and British Philosophy*, Oxford, 1983; and J.W. Yolton, *Perceptual Acquaintance: From Descartes to Reid*, Minneapolis, 1984.

ing complexity that common experience shows to be present to the mind, philosophers have speculatively created an intervening phantom world of ideas.

Reid believed this was not only false but also dangerous, leading to scepticism. In order to solve their self-created problem of the epistemic adequacy of the ideas through which the mind is supposed to apprehend the world, philosophers have had to embark on a wild-goose chase in search of proof of such adequacy. However, because all suggested guarantors of our ideas – such as Berkeley's God – can be apprehended only through ideas or are in some other way subjective in character, the inevitable conclusion is that each person lives in his own world of ideas with no means of knowing that there is either a physical world or other minds or a God around him. This progressive impoverishment of the world reaches the height of absurdity with Hume's argument, as Reid understood it, that we do not even know that there is a self, because we can form no idea of it.

Reid's various arguments against the theory of ideas are further buttressed by the well-known 'reflexivity argument', as we may call it, the argument that sceptics like Hume are entirely inconsistent, because in the practive of living they presuppose the reality of all those things of whose existence their theory of ideas denies them knowledge. Even in writing down their sceptical ideas and addressing them to others they are affirming what their words deny – a line of argument well know to Hume himself.[5]

If we abandon the materialist and mechanistic view of the mind as a passive recipient of ideas causally implanted by sense perception, we have, according to Reid, cleared the way for a proper empirical investigation of the mind. This reveals that the mind is by its very nature constituted as a highly active cognitive agency. Apart from the operations that it acquires or learns (habits), the mind is provided with various innate powers, among them instincts and such faculties as the ability instantly to form judgements or shape beliefs about objects of perception – that is, without a learned process of reasoning. Finally, the mind is issued with a large number of 'first principles of common sense, common notions, self-evident truths' or, in other words, 'intuitive judgments . . . which are no sooner understood than they are believed'.[6] These naturally absorbed First Principles are not subject to

5 For further discussion of this, see L. Marcil-Lacoste, 'The seriousness of Reid's sceptical admissions', *Monist*, 62 (1978), 311–25, and Lobkowicz, *Common Sense und Skeptizismus*.

6 IP, p. 434b.

proof but themselves unquestionably supply the starting-point for all further cognitive activity:

> In every branch of knowledge where disputes have been raised, it is useful to distinguish the first principles from the superstructure. They are the foundation on which the whole fabric of the science leans; and whatever is not supported by this foundation can have no stability. In all rational belief, the thing believed is either itself a first principle, or it is by just reasoning deduced from first principles.[7]

The First Principles of human knowledge are of two kinds: 'They are either necessary and immutable truths, whose contrary is impossible; or they are contingent and mutable, depending on some effect of will and power, which had a beginning, and may have an end.'[8] The former are divided into six categories: principles of grammar, logical axioms, mathematical axioms, axioms of taste, first principles of morals, and first principles of metaphysics.[9] The contingent truths are not organized, but they are illustrated by twelve examples, demonstrating that they basically guarantee our knowledge of our own mental world, our personal identity, the content of our memory, ourselves as free agents, the external world, other minds as intelligences and free agents, the uniformity of nature, and reliable signs and evidence. These principles, together with the intellectual powers that harbour them, are what Reid calls Common Sense.[10]

As we have seen, the defence of Common Sense is that its principles are inescapable or incontestable, a view often expressed in the familiar reflexivity argument ad hominem. This is repeatedly reinforced by the theologico-teleological argument that because Common Sense is part of our natural constitution it is, like nature in general, instituted to fulfil its ostensible function in creation by helping us to survive and lead human lives by supplying us with knowledge. Its truthfulness is therefore part of the providential arrangement of nature.[11]

---

7   Reid, *Essays on the Active Powers of Man*, in *Philosophical Works* (hereafter *AP*), p. 637a. For the role of First Principles in general, see IP, VI.IV.

8   IP, p. 441b.   9   IP, VI.VI.

10   IP, VI.V. See also Reid, 'Cura prima. Of Common Sense,' ed. David Fate Norton, in L. Marcil-Lacoste, *Claude Buffier and Thomas Reid: Two Common-Sense Philosophers*, app., Kingston, 1982.

11   See David Fate Norton, 'From Moral Sense to Common Sense: An Essay on the Development of Scottish Common Sense Philosophy, 1700–1765', Ph.D. thesis, University of California at San Diego, 1966, pp. 53–4.

6.2 *Human agency*

The foundations of Reid's providential naturalism and its meth-odological implications were laid early, in Turnbull's classroom.[12] They were probably reinforced by later reading of Turnbull's *Principles of Moral Philosophy*; Hutcheson's *Inquiry* and probably his other works; and not least Butler's *Analogy* and subsequently Kames's *Essays on the Principles of Morality and Natural Religion*. By the time of his graduation orations at King's College in the 1750s and early 1760s, it is clearly the framework for Reid's developing theory of Common Sense as the an-swer to scepticism. That theory itself was long in the making, and it is quite likely that the characteristic reflexivity argument – that all claims to knowledge, including sceptical claims that appearances of knowl-edge are deceptive, necessarily presuppose the principles of Common Sense – had been developed before the theory of ideas was identified as the source of the sceptical malaise. There are already clear traces of this argument in the 1730s, which, together with Reid's interest at the time in the notion of human agency, make it possible that he was then using the reflexivity argument to show the reality of human agency. If so, then he may have begun to see epistemological scepticism as funda-mental to moral scepticism and consequently Common Sense as the answer to both, before the publication of Kames's arguments in his *Essays* of 1751. Certainly he was prepared for Kames's theory and thoroughly absorbed it, including many of the key elements in the Common Sense solution to the problems of scepticism, particularly the First Principles.[13]

In any case, whatever the chronology or origin of the view, by the time of his *Inquiry into the Human Mind on the Principles of Common Sense* (1764), Reid had clearly come to see the struggle against moral scepticism in the tradition of Shaftesbury, Hutcheson, Butler, and Turn-bull as a mere side-skirmish in the general battle against epistemologi-cal scepticism, with Hume as the principal antagonist on both fronts. This polemical narrowing of the idea of scepticism in general and of Hume's scepticism in particular may well be Reid's second most signif-icant legacy, and again one making more argumentative sense in his problem situation than its historical accuracy would lead us to believe.

The central problem was the concept of human agency. If the mind did not have direct access to the objects of cognition except as a se-

12 Concerning Turnbull, see also Chapter 2 in this volume. For Reid's develop-ment, see Haakonssen, introduction to Reid, *Practical Ethics*, pp. 6–37.

13 For an incisive comparison of Reid and Kames, see Norton, 'From Moral Sense to Common Sense,' esp. pp. 271ff., and same, *David Hume*, pp. 189–91.

quence of discrete ideas, as Reid's reading of the theory of ideas would have it, then not only were causal connections between events unintelligible but it would also be impossible to ascribe actions to agents, or indeed to have an idea of continuous and coherent agency whether in oneself or in others. Consequently it would be impossible to ascribe moral qualities, such as virtue and vice, to agents on the evidence of their behaviour, and it would make no sense to hold a person responsible for his actions. Hence, reward and, especially, punishment would be impossible, and there would in general be no foundation for the enforcement of law or the upholding of society. As Reid says, in explanation of the wider perspective of the *Inquiry*'s otherwise narrow refutation of epistemological scepticism,

> upon this hypothesis [the theory of ideas], the whole universe about me, bodies and spirits, sun, moon, stars, and earth, friends and relations, all things without exception, which I imagined to have a permanent existence, whether I thought of them or not, vanish at once . . . I thought it unreasonable . . . upon the authority of philosophers, to admit a hypothesis which, in my opinion, overturns all philosophy, all religion and virtue, and all common sense.[14]

More specifically directed against Hume, on the lines indicated earlier, we find this remarkable, ironic aside:

> We were always apt to imagine, that thought supposed a thinker, and love a lover, and treason a traitor: but this, it seems, was all a mistake; and it is found out, that there may be treason without a traitor, and love without a lover, laws without a legislator, and punishment without a sufferer . . . or if, in these cases, ideas are the lover, the sufferer, the traitor, it were to be wished that the author of the discovery had farther condescended to acquaint us whether ideas can converse together, and be under obligations of duty or gratitude to each other; whether they can make promises and enter into leagues and covenants, and fulfil or break them, and be punished for the breach. If one set of ideas makes a covenant, another breaks it, and a third is punished for it, there is reason to think that justice is no natural virtue in this system.[15]

For Reid, as for so many of similar moral and theological outlook, such as the 'Moderate Literati' and the moderate clergy in general, it was of the utmost importance to establish the reality of free human agency.[16] Although Joseph Butler, in *The Analogy of Religion, Natural and Revealed, to the Constitution and Course of Nature*, had asserted free will and agency, he had neither explained nor defended them. After Hume, such a defence of moral freedom was badly needed, because it was

14 HM, p. 96.   15 HM, p. 109b.
16 For a detailed discussion of this issue, see W.L. Rowe, *Thomas Reid on Freedom and Morality*, Ithaca, NY, 1989.

seen as the necessary precondition for the possibility of morals. Without it, moral education seemed a mere illusion, and social improvement through education, in the widest sense, was impossible. Moral freedom was the necessary presupposition of moral personality seen as the basis of civil society, the unit of which social structure and political institutions were composed. Ultimately, moral freedom was at the heart of a vision of humanity as God's moral viceregents on earth, set there to realize a moral potential both in each individual life and in the collective life of society and the species as a whole.

In its context, the doctrine of moral freedom was a two-edged sword.[17] On the one hand, it was, as I have shown, directed against modern philosophy's materialist analogy of the mind, seen as necessitarian, whose logical conclusions were perceived to be moral scepticism and a Godless universe; of this Hobbes and Hume were seen as the chief representatives. On the other hand, the notion of moral freedom and its attendant ideas flew in the face of traditional Calvinist necessitarianism, with its emphasis on election and justification by faith alone.

Reid's solution to the problem of moral freedom should be viewed partly against the background of classical determinism as represented by Hobbes and its continuation, for Reid, in Hume's notion of 'freedom', partly as a response to a controversy of the 1750s. Stated briefly, the problem is as follows. Hobbes, like many simpler minds, had held that moral freedom simply meant freedom to act as one willed. However, if one adopted a determinist theory of the will, as Hobbes did, this definition of freedom seemed quite inadequate to most moralists, because determinism was held to make ideas of moral worth and moral responsibility, and thereby morality as such, meaningless. On the other hand, it was difficult to make sense of moral freedom as freedom of the will, because this was thought to lead to an infinite regress of acts of will: one is free to will, because one can will to will, ad infinitum – a point made by Locke.[18] In his *Essays on the Principles of Morality and Natural Religion* (1751), Kames tried to solve this problem within a determinist framework by arguing that although our acts of

17 The following outline of Reid's theory of free moral agency is based upon AP, essay IV; the letters to James Gregory (Reid, *Works*, pp. 62–89) and to Kames (ibid., pp. 50–2); and I.A. Ross, 'Unpublished letters of Thomas Reid to Lord Kames, 1762–1782', *Texas Studies in Literature and Language*, 7 (1965), 17–65 at pp. 48–51. In the critical literature, I am especially indebted to Barfoot, 'James Gregory (1753–1821) and Scottish Scientific Metaphysics, 1750–1800', Ph.D. thesis, University of Edinburgh, 1983, pp. 135–58; and J.A. Weinstock, 'Reid's definition of freedom', in *Thomas Reid: Critical Interpretations*, ed. S.F. Barker and T.L. Beauchamp, Philadelphia, 1976, pp. 95–102.

18 See Weinstock, 'Reid's definition of freedom', p. 98.

will, like all other natural events, are determined, we do in fact have an illusory sense of power over our will. Furthermore, because we have this natural though false belief in the freedom of will, we naturally ascribe moral worth and moral responsibility to ourselves and others, and these moral notions thus become part of the causal determinants of our will.

Despite his misguided attempt, using Jonathan Edwards as representative, to present this view as compatible with Calvinist doctrine, it caused Kames considerable trouble with great numbers of the clergy and led to charges that he was, like Hume, a sceptic and an infidel, although one of his principal aims in the *Essays* had been to refute Hume's views. After protests from Jonathan Edwards too, Kames dropped his theory from the second edition of the *Essays* (1758),[19] but Reid took up the issue by offering an alternative analysis of the concept of power over one's will. Put simply, Reid broke the infinite regress of acts of will by his insight that power over one's will is not itself an act of will but rather the ability to judge rationally of what it is that one wills. Thus animals, small children, and people whose minds are permanently or temporarily defective may certainly be said to act according to their will, but they cannot therefore be said to act with moral freedom and responsibility, because their willing is deficient, inasmuch as their judgement of what it is that they will is either lacking or very imperfect or distorted. Moral freedom is therefore a matter of being able or competent to judge of what it is that one is willing, especially to judge in terms of the First Principles of Common Sense and thus to control the will. Because the exercise of judgement does not presuppose an act of will, the infinite regress does not arise. Furthermore, once willing is seen to be linked with the power of judgement, the issue of determinism or necessitarianism is simply sidestepped, since judgement as a mental activity cannot be understood in mechanistic causal terms but must be seen as sui generis.[20] Put another way, Reid is not in fact maintaining the freedom of the will as such, because the will is determinable by judgement. However, this determining power of judgement cannot meaningfully be talked about in causal terms, as for

19   Concerning the whole episode, see Weinstock, p. 101, n. 27; I.S. Ross, *Lord Kames and the Scotland of His Day*, Oxford, 1972, ch. 8; and R.B. Sher, *Church and University in the Scottish Enlightenment: The Moderate Literati of Edinburgh*, Princeton, 1985, pp. 65–74. Reid's interest is underlined by his four-page abstract of Jonathan Edwards's *Freedom of the Will* (1754); see MS 2131/3/11/6, Birkwood Collection, Aberdeen University Library.

20   The latter seems to be overlooked by Weinstock, but I do not deny his charge ('Reid's definition of freedom', pp. 97 and 99) that there is some confusion in Reid between the issue of moral freedom and the issue of determinism.

instance being 'determined' by this or that motive. When we are talking about agency, 'causality' is simply a category mistake.

6.3   Principles of moral judgement

Reid's doctrine of moral freedom and free moral agency (or active power) as a power of judgement over the will is vastly more complicated, both in what Reid says about it and in what it presupposes or implies. The brief outline given here should, however, suffice to indicate how knowledge in the form of judgement is determining for moral action. The general possibility of knowledge, or of epistemically adequate judgement, has already been outlined in the discussion of Common Sense, particularly its First Principles. It remains to apply this specifically to moral knowledge, to show how moral judgements are available to determine the will of moral agents. It is this combination that makes moral *action* possible, and it is the possible world of moral action that is charted in Reid's *Practical Ethics*.

As so often in Reid, his own theory of moral knowledge is reached through criticism of the theories of others. Reid's main targets are Hutcheson and Hume, and the starting-point is Reid's general criticism of the empiricist theory that all simple ideas stem from sense or feeling whereas all complex ideas are constructed by the mind from simple ideas. This, according to Reid, is as false of moral knowledge as of all other knowledge, first, because the moral faculty in fact begins with complex ideas and only by analysis reaches simple ones, and second because such analysis reveals the presence of ideas – for example, the moral First Principles of Common Sense – which are not derived from any form of sensation but rather from the native operations of the mind. Furthermore, attention to the actual workings of the moral faculty shows that these are not simply a matter of feeling but a matter of judgement. When one makes 'a moral judgement', as the familiar term significantly has it, of one's own or other's behaviour, one is directly conscious that one not only has a feeling but is also asserting a proposition that, in contrast to a feeling, may be true or false, and that this proposition is about the behaviour, not about the feeling.

> That other men judge, as well as feel, in such cases, I am convinced, because they understand me when I express my moral judgment, and express theirs by the same terms and phrases. Suppose that . . . my friend says 'Such a man did well and worthily, his conduct is highly approvable'. This speech . . . expresses my friend's judgment of the man's conduct . . . Suppose, again, that in relation to the same case, my friend says – 'That man's conduct gave me a very agreeable feeling'. This speech, if approbation be nothing but an agreeable feeling, must have the very same meaning with the first . . . But this cannot be, for two reasons.

First, Because there is no rule in grammar or rhetoric, nor any usage in language, by which these two speeches can be construed so as to have the same meaning. The *first* expresses plainly an opinion or judgment of the conduct of the man, but says nothing of the speaker. The *second* only testifies a fact concerning the speaker – to wit, that he had such a feeling.

Another reason why these two speeches cannot mean the same thing is, that the first may be contradicted without any ground of offence, such contradiction being only a difference of opinion, which, to a reasonable man, gives no offence. But the second speech cannot be contradicted without an affront: for, as every man must know his own feelings, to deny that a man had a feeling which he affirms he had, is to charge him with falsehood.[21]

So far from being constitutive of the operation of the moral faculty, feeling is in fact causally dependent upon our judgement: it is the judgement that some act or person is good or bad that causes certain feelings about it.

Reid's principal antagonist, Hume, would not of course have denied that judgement is relevant to the formation of our moral sentiments, commonly termed 'judgements', nor that the relationship is often a causal one. Thus the judgement that A is a means to B leads to an evaluation of A, if B is already considered to have some value or other. Such relational judgement may again lead to the evaluation of B in relation to C. But this process will have to stop somewhere, with something considered of value in itself and not simply a means, and Reid believed that this consideration was for Hume a matter of feeling and not of judgement. This was how Reid understood Hume's maxim that reason is and ought to be the slave of the passions, a maxim that Reid rejected:

among the various ends of human actions, there are some of which, without reason, we could not even form a conception; and . . . as soon as they are conceived, a regard to them is, by our constitution, not only a principle of action, but a leading and governing principle . . . These I shall call rational principles; because they can exist only in beings endowed with reason, and because, to act from these principles, is what has always been meant by acting according to reason.[22]

Foreshadowing a later point, we may say that for Reid relative value judgements imply not facts (such as feelings) but judgements of facts – that is, of *moral* facts. Such judgements are arrived at by application of his 'rational principles', or ends, of which there are two – 'to wit, *What is good for us upon the whole,* and, *What appears to be our duty'*.[23] The former, also called 'prudence', is a principle of cool, rational self-interest. It presupposes that we are creatures with a complex of animal

21 AP, p. 673.   22 AP, p. 580.   23 Ibid.

principles, desires, and aims in life, whose immediate or long-term
satisfaction or disappointment suggests to us a plurality of goods and
evils. Prudence, or 'practical reason', as it is also called,[24] is a judgement on the best attainable balance of these, based on past experience
and a reasonable assessment of the future. This can plainly not be
calculated on some simple, unitary scale, but, though sometimes approaching value pluralism, it cannot be denied that Reid's concept of
'our good upon the whole' depends on a teleological concept of the
true nature (purpose) of human personality.

This is particularly clear in the lectures on practical ethics, where
Reid treats 'prudence' as our duty to ourselves, or the duty of self-
government.[25] The proper exercise of prudence, he thinks, will show,
as most ancient moralists, particularly the Stoics, had pointed out, that
our good upon the whole consists in the exercise of three of the four
classical virtues – prudence, temperance, and fortitude – and indirectly leads to the fourth, justice:

> according to the best judgment which wise men have been able to form, this
> principle leads to the practice of every virtue. It leads directly to the virtues
> of Prudence, Temperance, and Fortitude. And, when we consider ourselves
> as social creatures, whose happiness or misery is very much connected with
> that of our fellowmen . . . from these considerations, this principle leads us
> also, though more indirectly, to the practice of justice, humanity, and all the
> social virtues.[26]

It is of the utmost importance to realize that, as was usual in late
seventeenth- and eighteenth-century moral thought, when Reid talks
of duty he adopts the Stoic (Ciceronian) concept of *officium* and adapts
it to Christian beliefs by adding the notion of being 'called' or 'appointed' to the offices of one's life, as indicated by a natural power to fulfil
these. By the same token, we are called upon to know and worship the
Creator and to promote the 'good upon the whole' of the rest of creation. Consequently Reid's lectures on our duties to ourselves are preceded by a discussion of our duties to God and followed by an elaborate treatment of our duties to others. In short, the language of virtue,
as the exercise of natural powers of moral judgement, and the language of duty, as the fulfilment of appointed offices, are one and the
same and are seen to be so.

The ancient tripartite division of man's duties had become a common device for the organization of lecture courses and text-books,
especially after Pufendorf adopted it in his *Duty of Man*.[27] However,

24 AP, p. 582a.   25 *Practical Ethics*, pp. 127–37 and 184–7.
26 AP, p. 584. See ibid., pp. 581–4 and 638.
27 See the discussion in this volume of Pufendorf in Ch. 1, sect. 1.6; of Turnbull
and Heineccius in Ch. 2, sects. 2.8 and 2.9; and cf. Ch. 10, sect. 10.3. A popular

because the English word 'duty', unlike *officium,* had lost the sense of a prudential duty to realize one's 'good on the whole', the *utile,* and retained only the sense of *honestum* – that is, the performance of one's duties to others – Reid in his published work dropped the organization he had employed in the lectures and restricted 'duty' to the latter use.[28]

This led Reid on to the further point that although prudential regard for our good on the whole is a basic end or principle of practical reason, it is not a genuinely moral one; only duty is that. Reid acknowledges that the two are so similar in their effect on human life that they lend plausibility to the attempts by 'many of the ancient philosophers, and some among the moderns, to resolve conscience, or a sense of duty, entirely into a regard to what is good for us upon the whole'.[29] In fact, as he points out, if the regard to our good on the whole is fully developed it will produce the same behaviour as a regard to duty. The problem is that few, if any, can 'attain such extensive views of human life, and so correct a judgment of good and ill, as the right application of this principle [of prudence] requires'.[30] Consequently the principle of duty is necessary as the foundation of morals. Furthermore, even when truly virtuous behaviour arises from a prudent pursuit of our good on the whole, it is not considered as meritorious as when it arises from a sense of duty.[31] Finally, the direct pursuit of our own good as the ultimate end, which Reid polemically tends to identify with happiness, is generally counter-productive, leading instead to 'fear, and care, and anxiety'.[32] The performance of duty for its own sake alone gives real and lasting happiness. Duty as a contribution to the common good is what man is charged with as a moral being, while his ultimate happiness is God's reward.[33]

All this seems to Reid to indicate that regard to our good on the whole and regard to duty are two very different ends or principles of practical reason, that the latter cannot be reduced to the former, and that duty is the only properly moral principle:

---

account of the three general duties was that of Samuel Clarke, *A Discourse concerning the Unchangeable Obligations of the Natural Religion, and the Truth and Certainty of the Christian Revelation,* London, 1716, pp. 65–6 and 81–104. The three duties of natural religion corresponded to the three theological virtues of revealed religion: faith, hope, and charity.

28 AP, p. 588a.   29 AP, p. 582b.   30 AP, p. 584b.

31 AP, p. 585. For Joseph Butler's somewhat different emphasis, see 'Of the Nature of Virtue', in *Works,* 2 vols., Oxford, 1874, I, pp. 333–5.

32 AP, p. 585b.

33 AP, p. 586a. The idea that the piety derived from the insights of natural religion is the necessary premise for and completion of morals is forcefully stated at pp. 598b–599a.

This principle of honour, which is acknowledged by all men who pretend to character, is only another name for what we call a regard to duty, to rectitude, to propriety of conduct. It is a moral obligation which obliges a man to do certain things because they are right, and not to do other things because they are wrong . . . Men of rank call it *honour* . . . The vulgar call it *honesty, probity, virtue, conscience*. Philosophers have given it the names of *the moral sense, the moral faculty, rectitude*.

What we call *right* and *honourable* in human conduct, was, by the ancients, called *honestum* . . . [and they] distinguished the *honestum* from the *utile*, as we distinguish what is a man's duty from what is his interest.[34]

He goes on to make the point noted earlier, that 'duty' – the English rendering of the Latin *officium* (which in Latin includes the sense of *utile*) is commonly restricted to *honestum*. The basis of all morality is thus the doing of duty in the sense of fulfilling one's office for its own sake, and the moral faculty, by whatever name it is commonly known, is the sense of duty or conscience.

Reid, as we have seen, has no objection to calling the moral faculty a 'sense', provided this is understood, as in ordinary usage, to include judgement.[35] But two kinds of judgement are required of the moral faculty.[36] First, it must assent to the First Principles of morals previously referred to.[37]

Second, the moral faculty judges the moral worth of particular actions by relating such actions to the moral end – duty – through subsuming them under the relevant First Principle or Principles.[38] Following ordinary usage, Reid commonly calls this form of judgement 'moral judgment'. Whereas the First Principles of morals constitute certain knowledge to any competent moral judge, the particular moral judgements are inherently fallible because we can never have perfect knowledge of the 'real essence' of contingent beings such as those related in moral judgements – namely, particular agents and their particular behavioural circumstances.[39] He often muddles this point badly, when, by a confused and rhetorical use of the term 'axiom' to mean First Principles as well as particular moral judgements, he transfers the certainty of the former to the latter.[40] The necessity and importance of the point is, however, quite clear when he insists that the self-evidence of First Principles does not dispense with the need for moral education or vitiate the role of moral experience in such education. This assertion would not be intelligible if particular moral judgements

34 AP, pp. 587a–588a.
35 AP, pp. 589b–590. See also Butler, "Of the nature of virtue," p. 329.
36 Reid is not able to distinguish the two clearly, as D.D. Raphael has pointed out in a searching discussion, *The Moral Sense*, Oxford, 1947, pp. 172–89.
37 IP, p. 453b, and AP, p. 637.   38 AP, pp. 589b–591a.
39 IP, p. 479b.   40 See Raphael, *Moral Sense*, pp. 175–6.

had the same epistemic standing as moral First Principles, for it is the ease of error in the former that often obscures the latter. Despite lapses, Reid manages to avoid the common error in responses to scepticism of trying to prove too much.[41]

6.4 Duty and virtue

Turning now from moral judgement to the objects of moral judgement, we must make explicit what has already been hinted at. Reid acknowledges that in ordinary language moral judgements concern the moral quality of either actions or agents or duty. However, Reid believes that philosophical scrutiny makes it clear that an action considered in abstraction from an agent and his motives can have a moral 'quality' only in the sense that it is a duty either to do it or to avoid it. As we shall see, this is the crux of his criticism of Hume. If we judge a particular action as resulting from the agent's motive, we are judging the merit or demerit of the agent.[42] However, since the exercise of virtue is a duty, all judgements of moral merit ultimately depend on judgements of duty. Even when a moral quality such as benevolence is the ostensible object of a moral judgement, we must understand that it derives its moral status from the fact that it is a duty.

Thus, because all moral judgements are ultimately about duty, their objects must be relational in character:

> If we examine the abstract notion of Duty, or Moral Obligation, it appears to be neither any real quality of the action considered by itself, nor of the agent considered without respect to the action, but a certain relation between the one and the other.
>
> When we say a man ought to do such a thing, the *ought*, which expresses the moral obligation, has a respect, on the one hand, to the person who ought; and, on the other, to the action which he ought to do. Those two correlates are essential to every moral obligation; take away either, and it has no existence. So that, if we seek the place of moral obligation among the categories, it belongs to the category of *relation*.[43]

41 AP, pp. 640b–643a. Although Reid, in accordance with his rational religious outlook, maintains that revelation must be consistent with reason, he also subscribes to the not uncommon view that the moral teaching of revelation may lead corrupted mankind to *see* the moral First Principles, which are used by reason. This is clearly how he viewed the work of Christ. See AP, p. 641b. For a similar view of revelation, see Butler, *The Analogy of Religion, Natural and Revealed, to the Constitution and Course of Nature,* in *Works,* I, Part II, ch. 1.

42 AP, p. 649a. There are lively discussions of this in the manuscripts; see esp. 2131/7/V/17. For Butler's similar standpoint, see 'Of the Nature of Virtue', p. 330.

43 AP, pp. 588b–589a.

Judgements are moral in character when they express a duty relationship; a person is virtuous because he does his duty, and actions are good because they are duties to be done by people in particular circumstances.

We have already seen that Reid's theory of the moral sense as a faculty of judgement constitutes a break with moral-sense theory, especially as formulated by Hutcheson, though it may be more limited than Reid thought and rather less dramatic than most scholars would have it. Hutcheson has generally been presented as an affective subjectivist, for whom moral judgements were expressions of certain affections of the moral sense. In line with some recent studies, I incline to believe that he was a 'moral-sense cognitivist' and a 'moral realist', who saw the moral sense as a cognitive faculty perceiving moral qualities.[44] As we have seen, he had been forced, by a complicated set of problems arising out of the debate on Pufendorf's voluntaristic natural law theory, into trying to show that morality concerned personal qualities that were empirically ascertainable by the moral sense, a view that helped ensure that much eighteenth-century Scottish moral thought was couched in the language of *virtues*.

This makes the real nature of Reid's break with Hutcheson clear. It was a division not between subjectivism and realism but between two kinds of realism, two kinds of cognitivism, and two kinds of moral judgement. For Hutcheson, the moral world consists of qualities that are perceived by the moral sense and ascribed to people in moral judgements. For Reid, the moral world consists of relations that are judged to be the proper ones between particular people and actions in the light of the First Principles of morals. For the former, the language of virtue is the primary one; for the latter, the language of duty is primary.

It appears that Reid was precluded from an adequate appreciation of the relationship between his own common-sense theory and the classical formulation of the moral-sense theory by his reading of Hume. Like most of his contemporaries, Reid understood Hume as being a self-confessed sceptic for whom morality was entirely a matter of subjective states, and not a body of objective knowledge. Once scepticism was seen as the result of moral-sense theory, the possibility that the moral sense was a cognitive faculty giving access to an objective moral world was lost from sight, and only its affective side was remembered.[45]

Leaving aside the adequacy of Reid's interpretation of Hume, we may elucidate the central point of his criticism.[46] He starts from the

44 See Ch. 2, Sect. 2.3, this volume, and the literature referred to there.
45 See IP, p. 421b.
46 This is part of the critical reflection contained in the last four chapters of

question 'Whether an action deserving moral approbation, must be done with the belief of its being morally good',[47] and his affirmative answer to this question introduces his criticism of Hume's theory of the artificial virtues. As Reid and most other readers have understood him, Hume maintains that it makes sense in ordinary language to say that the motive for an action is good because the action itself is good. This assumes that of certain categories of action, typically acts of justice, we can say why in the final analysis they are good. However, moral goodness cannot rest in the external action as such but must depend upon a morally good motivation, so we are in effect arguing in a circle: the motive is good because the action is good, and the action is good because the motive is good.[48] Hume breaks the circle with his well-known argument that when actions of the justice type in general are performed within a group this contributes to the common good of the group, whether or not this was the intention. Because of our sympathy with the public good, we approve of such actions, and this becomes their 'artificially' engendered *moral* motive, turning them into proper acts of justice.[49]

Reid has several criticisms of this theory, but behind them all is one arising from the ideas just discussed. Hume's alleged circularity of motive and action, Reid declares, is false; it never existed, and his elaborate scheme for breaking it is therefore futile. We are perfectly entitled to say that a person's motive is good or virtuous if the person intends a good action, for the goodness of the action itself does not depend on the motive. We must distinguish between the goodness of the doer of a specific good action and the goodness of the act considered in abstraction from its being done at a particular time by a particular person. Goodness in the latter case simply derives from the fact that the action in the abstract is a type or category of action that is a prima facie duty for *any* moral agent:

> what do we mean by goodness in an action considered abstractly? To me it appears to lie in this, and in this only, that it is an action which ought to be done by those who have the power and opportunity, and the capacity of perceiving their obligation to do it . . . And this goodness is inherent in its nature and inseparable from it. No opinion or judgment of an agent can in the least alter its nature.[50]

Active Powers, which have the character of appendices rather than integrated parts of the systematic exposition; see Reid's remarks about their origins, AP, p. 645b.

47   AP, p. 646a.

48   Hume, *Treatise of Human Nature*, III.ii:1, esp. pp. 479–80. Reid quotes the central passages, AP, p. 648a.

49   *Treatise*, III.ii:1–2.   50   AP, p. 649a.

As I understand it, this is just another way of saying that the judgement that an act considered in the abstract is good is a moral First Principle and, further, that when a particular act of this kind is related to an agent by his application of this First Principle, that is, by his judging that the particular act is his duty – then his motive is morally good. If the same action is related to the agent by sheer coincidence or by some non-moral principle of practical reason, such as self-interest, then there is no 'transfer' of moral goodness from the action to the agent.

This interpretation hinges upon the identification of actions in the abstract as the subjects of moral First Principles. It seems to be borne out by Reid's example of an action considered abstractly, 'that of relieving an innocent person out of great distress',[51] that this is a duty is clearly a principle that could take its place among Reid's explicit First Principles of morals. His criticism of Hume thus rests upon the idea that there are such undeniable First Principles that make actions good and obligatory independently of the motive of the agent.[52]

I have stressed Reid's switch from a theory of virtue to a theory of duty, in the sense of offices, partly because this is an often neglected structural feature of his moral philosophy, as published in the *Essays on the Active Powers of Man*, and partly because it is a precondition for an adequate understanding of the wider system of practical ethics which he developed in his lecture course. As we have seen, there are rules of translation between the two languages, of virtue and of duty, so that either can be used for normative and didactic purposes – that is, in practical ethics. Even so, Reid considered 'duty' more proper and natural than 'virtue' in this regard also, and he arranged his lectures accordingly:

> Morals [practical ethics] have been methodized in different ways. The ancients commonly arranged them under the four cardinal virtues of Prudence, Temperance, Fortitude, and Justice; Christian writers, I think more properly, under the three heads of the Duty we owe to God – to Ourselves – and to our Neighbour. One division may be more comprehensive, or more natural, than another; but the truths arranged are the same, and their evidence the same in all.[53]

This brings us to the final point to be made here concerning the primacy of duty in Reid's theory. We saw earlier that, considered as virtues in the

51   Ibid.
52   Reid engaged in intensive discussion of all significant contemporary philosophers over these matters, as we see from his manuscripts. For the most important, see Haakonssen, introduction to *Practical Ethics*, pp. 55–6, n. 52, and the references given there.
53   AP, p. 642b.

traditional sense of qualities of persons, even the cardinal virtues were not properly *moral*, but only *prudential* ends or principles of practical reason. However, if the same behaviour is considered as *duty*, then not only the other-regarding justice but also the prima facie self-regarding prudence, temperance, and fortitude are properly moral principles. Accordingly, the last three are included in Reid's lectures as 'duties to ourself', alongside 'duties to God' and 'duties to others' (justice).

The apparently paradoxical notion of duties to ourselves is explained by the fact that these duties are only prima facie self-regarding. We have a duty to cultivate the cardinal virtues of prudence, temperance, and fortitude because we are created with a moral nature and have been given a divine brief to develop it to the best of our ability. The duties to ourselves are thus really owed to God, and their value to ourselves can be seen as a moral good only insofar as it is a contribution to the good of the world as a whole, the striving for which is a duty imposed by God upon mankind individually and collectively.

This religious perspective is very important. Not only does practical ethics presuppose the pneumatological explanation of the divine as well as of the human mind, but practical ethics itself has as its fundamental first part 'duties to God'. As Reid explains it in his published work; 'That conscience which is in every man's breast, is the law of God written in his heart, which he cannot disobey without acting unnaturally, and being self-condemned', and again, 'Right sentiments of the Deity and of his works, not only make the duty we owe to him obvious to every intelligent being, but likewise add the authority of a Divine law to every rule of right conduct'.[54] The ultimate foundation of morality is divine law, and we can thus appreciate why Reid generally respected the traditional distinction between duty and obligation.[55] Morality is a matter of duties imposed, not of obligations undertaken; obligations, like virtues and all other moral categories, presuppose duty and law. Remembering the inspiration Reid derived from the Stoics, we may also say that morality is an elaborate network of 'offices' of greatly varying extent to which God has appointed us.

Pneumatology explains the appointed place of mind within the creation, and the cognitive powers and epistemic principles that make knowledge possible to the mind. The theory of morals is the part of pneumatology that explains that the mind is an active power: it has moral (and metaphysical) freedom to act and the power of judgement

54 AP, pp. 638b and 639b.
55 The distinction had become obscured, and Reid occasionally confuses the subjective and objective concepts, though mostly using 'obligation' either for the subjective state of the person who has a duty or for an obligation undertaken, e.g. by contract.

to guide its action, and it can acquire the moral knowledge to guide its judgement. Practical ethics, or morals, is not in the same way explanatory; it is, rather, a taxonomic discipline that systematically arranges the principles of our duty and thus provides a map of the network of typical offices that constitute the moral world.[56] We must take it that the world that is thus depicted is not the actually existing moral condition of mankind but rather that which, given the moral powers of man, is possible in principle and a guiding ideal in practice. In this sense, 'systems of morals' are supportive of our haphazard moral judgements of our duty. This is what Reid understood by practical ethics.

6.5 *Natural jurisprudence*

We have already seen that in the lectures on practical ethics Reid adopts both of the traditional divisions of morality to structure his course: the three duties (to God, to ourselves, and to others) and the four virtues (prudence, temperance, fortitude, and justice). The three duties provide the basic structure of the lectures, and of these the last is by far the most extensive; duties to ourselves consist in the exercise of the three virtues of prudence, temperance, and fortitude, while the fourth, justice, applies to our duties to others. Reid often reserves the label 'natural jurisprudence' for the justice section of his course. The opening discussion of duties to God is brief, drawing on his pneumatology lectures on natural religion, and is generally organized around the traditional distinction between internal and external worship. Together with the lectures on the duties to ourselves, it presents an integration of Christian and Stoic ideals, now sometimes called Christian Stoicism, which was a common theme in the moral thought

---

56 As he once defines it, 'Ethics the knowledge of these Rules or Laws by which men ought to regulate their Actions' (MS 2131/6/1V/2, 1R). See also AP, p. 642b: 'A system of morals is not like a system of geometry, where the subsequent parts derive their evidence from the preceding, and one chain of reasoning is carried on from the beginning; so that, if the arrangement is changed, the chain is broken, and the evidence is lost. It resembles more a system of botany, or mineralogy, where the subsequent parts depend not for their evidence upon the preceding, and the arrangement is made to facilitate apprehension and memory, and not to give evidence.' This point is central to his claim that morals, or practical ethics, in contrast to the (pneumatological) 'theory of morals', is not a matter of reasoning in the sense of deductive inference but is open to any ordinary intelligence (see Raphael, *Moral Sense*, pp. 165–172). 'Morals' is thus not an *inference* from 'the theory of morals'. The latter explains how morals is possible for man, but that is a point never doubted by anyone in the practical conduct of life, and the only practical implication in demonstrating it is to rebut sceptical metaphysicians, whose sophistries might otherwise derange the moral Common Sense of some people.

of the period. The important point here is the analysis of the classical theory of virtue in terms of a Christian theory of duty and law within a teleological framework.

The section on natural jurisprudence, or duties to others, is by far the most extensive in Reid's course on practical ethics. The basic division of the topic is between the rights and duties of individuals and those of societies. Although he draws the traditional parallels between the two groups, Reid is careful to point out the significant differences, which fully justify a separate treatment of international law. The tripartite division of the law of nature pertaining to individuals is, again, entirely traditional. In 'private jurisprudence' we consider the individual in isolation from any organized society and in that sense in a state of nature, whereas the other two sections deal with the individual's rights and duties within the household and within civil society. Though Reid adopts the old use of 'oeconomical' as the adjectival form of *oikos* and operates with the traditional extended concept of the household, he was well aware that historically the juridical roles of the household were steadily being transferred to the state. Finally, political jurisprudence deals with rights and duties between rulers and the ruled in civil society and between citizens *qua* citizens.

Basic to Reid's idea of natural jurisprudence is the concept of natural law. In common with all modern natural lawyers, he sees this as God's command to man, apprehended by human reason (as opposed to revelation), and he identifies it simply as the precept of our moral power or conscience. It is worth noting that Reid does not take this opportunity to revive the old dispute about a voluntarist versus a realist foundation for the obligation to natural law, which had played a significant role in modern natural law and which we have followed in some detail in earlier chapters. The law of nature so orders the moral world of human actions into rights and duties that for every right there is a corresponding duty, whereas there are some duties that cannot be claimed as rights.[57] This applies most obviously to our duties to ourselves but also to some other cases, which we shall look at shortly. Ignoring duties to God and to ourselves, Reid in the *Active Powers* takes the systems of rights and of duties to be alternative ways of dealing with morals, but, more judiciously, in the lectures he sees them as complementary.[58] This is not solely or even primarily because of the odd status of duties to God and to ourselves but because the law of nature in some cases appoints the rights as primary and the matching duties as consequent upon them, whereas in others the reverse is true.

---

57 *Practical Ethics*, pp. 143ff.

58 AP, pp. 643–5. See *Practical Ethics*, p. 202, where Reid explicitly excepts duties to ourselves.

Thus our rights of liberty (to be and to do, put simply) and our 'real' rights (our rights in things, i.e. property) are primary, and it is as a consequence of granting us those that the law of nature appoints duties to respect them. Our 'personal' rights (i.e. our rights to some performance by other persons, usually contractually established), on the other hand, are derived from the duties imposed by natural law on those others.[59] The important thing is that, irrespective of what in this sense is primary and what is secondary, the law of nature maintains the correspondence between natural rights and duties. Reid believes that the moral world is in principle well ordered by a natural law whose relationship to natural rights and duties is analogous to the relationship between positive law and legal rights and duties.

My emphasis here on the role of natural law may meet with some scepticism as being far too voluntaristic for a moral realist like Reid. And so it would be if we stopped there, but when we look at the concept of the common good I hope that such scepticism will be reassuringly mitigated.

Apart from the divisions of rights according to their 'nature' (liberty rights, real rights, and personal rights), and according to their 'relations' (private, oeconomical, and political), Reid divides rights according to their 'source' or 'foundation' into innate, or natural, rights and adventitious rights.[60] It is interesting to note that in the *Active Powers* Reid introduces the concept of rights as deriving from that of injury, a traditional notion that Adam Smith had developed into a highly original theory by means of the idea of the impartial spectator.[61] On this basis, though without using Smith's theory, Reid lists six rights:

> A man may be injured, *first*, in his person, by wounding, maiming, or killing him; *secondly*, in his family, by robbing him of his children, or any way injuring those he is bound to protect; *thirdly*, in his liberty, by confinement; *fourthly*, in his reputation; *fifthly*, in his goods, or property; and *lastly*, in the violation of contracts or engagements made with him. This enumeration, whether complete or not, is sufficient for the present purpose.[62]

Reid's purpose then was to criticize Hume for his neglect of the first four rights, the 'natural rights', in his theory of justice – just as Smith's spectator theory of justice is obviously meant to correct Hume on exactly this point.[63]

59 *Practical Ethics*, p. 199.
60 Sometimes he adds 'acquired' rights as a third category; sometimes instead he subdivides adventitious rights into 'original' and 'derived'. *Practical Ethics*, pp. 147, 199–200, 201, 206, 208.
61 See Haakonssen, *Science of a Legislator*, pp. 99ff. 62 AP, p. 656.
63 See Haakonssen, *Science of a Legislator*, pp. 102–3.

The basis for the distinction between innate or natural rights and adventitious or acquired rights is that the former do not presuppose any human action, whereas adventitious rights do. Innate rights are thus typically life, liberty, and free personal judgement. Original adventitious rights are principally the right to property, which arises from mere occupation and derives in a way from innate rights, insofar as its justification is that it helps us to preserve the latter (sustaining life, etc.). Here it should be mentioned that, according to Reid, the whold world is given to mankind from the hand of nature (or the Creator) in 'negative community' – that is, everything is equally open to occupation by everyone.[64] Derived rights presuppose the prior existence of original adventitious rights, which can be transferred or otherwise transformed through succession, contracts, testaments, and the like. Finally, he also divides rights according to their 'mutability', into alienable and inalienable rights – real rights, personal rights, and 'some parts of our Liberty' being alienable.[65]

The most important division is, in some ways, that between perfect rights and imperfect rights.[66] Reid rejects the most common grounds for this distinction: that perfect rights can be legally enforced, whereas imperfect rights cannot, and that perfect rights alone are absolutely necessary to the very existence of society. Instead, he relies on a more general reason: he takes perfect rights to be rights matched by negatively defined duties – for example, duties not to injure – whereas imperfect rights are matched by positive duties to render some good.[67] Though adopting this traditional distinction for conceptual clarification, Reid does not think that it has the moral and political significance often ascribed to it. First, he never gives the two kinds of rights and their matching duties different epistemological status. The moral qualities that people show in exercising them are equally objective and equally open to appreciation by our moral powers. Second, he does not

64   *Practical Ethics*, pp. 204–5 and 210; AP, p. 658.   65   *Practical Ethics*, p. 201.

66   Although Reid occasionally talks of the distinction between perfect and imperfect rights as a general division of the field, his more considered view was that the distinction was really only relevant to personal rights. (*Practical Ethics*, p. 198). I take his point to be that liberty rights and real rights are all obviously perfect. It should also be noticed that Reid, in accordance with the jurisprudential tradition, distinguishes a third category, external rights (*Practical Rights*, pp. 202, 209; AP, p. 644). These are in fact a mere *fictio juris* created to match duties arising from ignorance, as in the case where one person innocently borrows something from another, who has in fact stolen it. The law of nature here imposes an obligation on the former, in his ignorance, to restore the thing borrowed, and although the latter actually has no matching right, he has a semblance of right, which is called 'external'.

67   See *Practical Ethics*, p. 197; AP, p. 645b; and pp. 193–4; AP, pp. 643b–644a.

think that they are so very different in moral urgency; in this regard the line between them will often be uncertain.[68] Third, because of this he does not think that a society can exist merely on the basis of the protection of perfect rights. Fourth, he consequently sees it as the task of government to protect both perfect and imperfect rights by legally enforcing their corresponding duties.[69]

Reid does not name his adversaries in this argument, but it should be noted that these four points collide head-on with the views of both David Hume and Adam Smith. As we have seen in preceding chapters, Hume, and especially Smith, had argued that some fundamental features of justice, conceived negatively as a matter of the protection of perfect rights (terms that Hume did not employ), are much more universally recognizable than other parts of morality. The uncertainty of the latter, the 'positive' virtues, in itself makes them less morally urgent and makes it both difficult and dangerous to enforce them as legal duties. This does not, however, mean that the positive virtues on their view are irrelevant to the well-being of society; indeed, in some form or other they are indispensable to its stability, and in many historical situations it may be necessary for governments to support them by educational and cultural policies, if for any reason they are endangered. For Hume and Smith the pursuit of some of the positive virtues is thus a matter of policy; for Reid it is a matter of legal enforcement. It is important to be aware of this contrast, for it makes clear the far-reaching political implications of the form of the doctrine of rights.

6.6   *Property*

The world then, is given to mankind in negative community from the hand of the Creator: that is, everything is equally open to occupation by everyone. The justification for this is that it is a means to secure our innate or natural rights, such as life and liberty, but this conventionally individualist argument is combined with views of a different tendency. In occupying the world, man not only must discharge his obligation to look after his own natural rights but also is under a constant obligation to look after the rights of others. Reid illustrates this by a splendid allegory, taken from Epictetus and Simplicius, in which human life is depicted as a party, and the natural world as the refreshments provided by the host (the Lord).[70] While looking after himself, every guest must still be constantly concerned for the satisfaction of his neighbour, the general happiness of the party, and the

68   *Practical Ethics*, pp. 202–3; AP, p. 645b.

69   I return to this later in connection with political jurisprudence; in the meantime, see AP, p. 645b.

70   *Practical Ethics*, pp. 204–5.

honouring of his host. In short, individual claims are legitimate rights only when they do not conflict with the common good but as far as possible contribute to it.

When Reid says that the law of nature gives us all an equal right to occupy and use the non-human creation, he is not implying that this had been so arranged in order that we may realize our natural rights. The point is that we should do so in order to realize the common good, for only those requirements – of liberty, of goods, and of services – whose satisfaction contributes to the common good are in fact rights at all. This is the true significance of maintaining that all rights are matched by duties. Because all duty is pointed out by natural law, whose ultimate objective is the realization of the common good, the assurance that there are no free-floating rights unengaged by duties shows that all genuine rights claims are in harmony with the common good.

I am aware that this use of the concept of the common good (or public good) may lead to a charge of inconsistency, in view of Reid's well-known criticism of Hume for using 'public utility' as the justifying ground for the artificial virtues, especially justice. This issue is connected with his problematic use of natural law, and the two problems can in fact be resolved together when we know more about Reid's concept of the common good. Meanwhile, we may take the 'common good' to mean the fullest possible honouring of duties and hence protection of rights.

All this is simply to say that the right to property is heavily circumscribed.[71] We may occupy only such parts of nature as are necessary for the satisfaction of the needs and wants of ourselves and those dependent upon us, and we may do so provided only that we do not injure others in their similar rights. (The basic sufficiency of nature is an unstated premise here; it was a common one.) Further, such things as air, water, and the ocean, which can benefit us without becoming private property, may not be occupied by individuals (or societies). This leads Reid to the interesting Lockean suggestion that perhaps only what is actually consumed may become private property, whereas things of a 'permanent Nature' may 'be left in the Community of Nature or at least remain in a State of positive Communion'.[72] Although Reid does not use it as an example of such durable things, he undoubtedly meant to include all real estate, especially land, and this view is very close to that sometimes ascribed to Locke.[73] Reid's own

71   See *Practical Ethics*, pp. 206–8; AP, pp. 658b–659a.

72   *Practical Ethics*, p. 210; AP, p. 658a.

73   J. Tully, *A Discourse on Property: John Locke and His Adversaries*, Cambridge, UK, 1980.

references are to Plato, 'Utopia' (undoubtedly More's), and 'Paraguay', by which he means the Jesuit social experiments. In his lectures, as in *Active Powers*, Reid rejects this idea, and it would indeed have been extraordinary if the professor had lectured his young charges on the illegitimacy of private property in land. In his final political statement, however, he did toy with the idea in its most radical, utopian form, as we shall see.

The reasons Reid gives in the lectures for the legitimacy of private property, in durable as well as consumable things, are such that it is not a long step to arguing for the abolition of private property. Prominent among the reasons is the idea that the acquisition of such property is a means to make us realize our moral potential, partly by making us more diligent and thus socially useful, partly by enabling us to show generosity. In fact, the overriding justification for all private property is that it is a means to create a common good; once civil society has been instituted as the guardian of the common good, it has a complete prerogative over private property:

> In General as Property is introduced among Men for the Common Good it ought to be secure where it does not interfere with that end but when that is the Case private Property ought to yield to the Publick Good when there is a repugnancy between them. Individuals may be compelled in such cases to part with their Property if they are unwilling, but ought to be indemnified as far as possible.[74]

In fact, 'A Man or a Nation may be hindred from acquiring such an extent of Property as endangers the Safety and Liberty of others', which Reid takes to imply the abolition of private monopolies and the legitimacy of restricting 'the disposal of Property by will or by Entails'. Further, 'A Proprietor has no Right to destroy his Property when the common Good requires that it should be preserved, nor to keep up Mercatable Commodities when the common Good requires that they should be brought to Market.' Finally, the state may secure its own political stability by setting 'Bounds to the Acquisition of Property by Agrarian Laws or other Means of that kind' and may secure itself militarily by confiscating required property.[75] In line with this, Reid

---

74 *Practical Ethics*, p. 208.

75 *Practical Ethics*, p. 207. Reid was always suspicious of the emerging market society and its alleged acquisitiveness. The most extreme expression of this occurs in his utopian scheme, discussed later, but note his reaction to Bentham's *Defence of Usury*. Writing to James Gregory on 5 September 1788, Reid says: 'I am much pleased with the tract you sent me on usury. I think the reasoning unanswerable, and have long been of the author's opinion, though I suspect that the general principle, that bargains ought to be left to the judgement of the parties, may admit

condemns entail, on natural law grounds, as contrary to the moral good of both the individual and society and thus adds his voice to the chorus of Scots philosophers who campaigned against this institution during the eighteenth century. Reid's juristic justification of the classical republican idea of an agrarian law and his whole treatment of property emphasise the very direct political implications of his jurisprudential system.

6.7   Contract

Following the systematics of the natural lawyers, Reid's lectures on practical ethics turned from 'real' rights – in things – to 'personal' rights: rights to some prestation from particular people, and this was the framework for some of his most original ideas in his published works. As was common, Reid considered not only the paradigm of contract but also the wider question whether the use of language as such gives rise to rights and obligations. This leads to a fruitful combination of his theory of language with moral and political themes.[76]

Behind Reid's idea of language lies his important distinction between 'solitary' and 'social' acts of mind.[77] The essential point here is that the second, unlike the first, presupposes the existence and (in some sense) presence of another mind or other minds. Social acts are necessarily communicative, and thus a matter of signs, while solitary acts may or may not be expressed. Examples of the latter are seeing, hearing, remembering, judging, reasoning, deliberating, deciding, while the former include questioning, testifying, commanding, promising, contracting, and the like. For mental acts to be social, there must therefore be a community of signs, so that mutual understanding is possible, and nature has in fact provided such a community of signs. It

---

of some exceptions, when the buyers are the many, the poor, and the simple – the sellers few, rich, and cunning; the former may need the aid of the magistrate to prevent their being oppressed by the latter. It seems to be upon this principle that portage, freight, the hire of chairs and coaches, and the price of bread, are regulated in most great towns. But with regard to the loan of money in a commercial state, the exception can have no place – the borrowers and lenders are upon an equal footing, and each may be left to take care of his own interest' (Reid, *Philosophical Works*, p. 73a).

76   See the chapter on contract in the *Active Powers* (AP, pp. 663ff.) and a paper on implied contract given to the Glasgow Literary Society, *Practical Ethics*, pp. 237–44.

77   IP, pp. 244a–245b; AP, pp. 663b–666b.

is, however, not only language in the conventional sense that functions as a set of signs. Any behaviour directed by a will and judgement and perceived to be so is a sign, or part of language. Consequently, verbal promises and contracts are only special cases of the wider question concerning the moral implications of communicative behaviour. Because this is a large part of voluntary behaviour, it is subject to ordinary moral judgement in terms of the principles of duty. Veracity in our use of signs must thus be a First Principle of morals, and as such Reid maintains it. Veracity is an *undeniable* principle in the use of signs, for were it not assumed as the prima facie duty of all sign users, no communication would be possible, and to attempt it would involve a contradiction. The reflexivity argument encountered earlier is obviously not far off: How can Hume hope to argue that fidelity to promises is an artificial virtue without presupposing that the general virtue of veracity is being naturally imputed to him by the readers of this argument?

The voluntary undertaking of obligations and consequent creation of rights in others is, in traditional subjective rights theories, the fundamental operation upon which morality rests. The fact that Reid reduces such obligations and rights to the operation of the principles of duty and thus to natural law merely strengthens the thesis with which we began. This is reinforced when we see how he extends the argument to contractual obligations. Because any voluntary behaviour may function as a sign and thus 'engage' the agent to some obligation, well-known patterns of behaviour or common roles must invariably do so, and they are then, in the proper Ciceronian sense, the offices of human life. These offices will be known in their general character to any competent moral agent and, although all the moral facts making up the role may not be foreseen by the agent, the office is prima facie binding once the latter has signalled its beginning by his behaviour. Once the agent has initiated a role, the reliance of others upon his fulfilment of it shows that his behaviour has been taken as a sign and puts him under an obligation to complete the role, as if he had promised or contracted to do so. Failure in this would be to deny that the preceding behavior was what it pretended to be.

In other words, by broadening the concept of signs (or language) Reid relativizes the distinction between explicit and implicit promises and contracts and reduces the moral status of both to that of voluntary behaviour in general. He almost certainly arrived at this idea by generalization from natural law ideas of quasicontract, probably by following up a brief hint in Hutcheson, as we shall see. And it was undoubtedly with the aim of reinterpreting the idea of a contractual basis for government that Reid developed the theory.

6.8   *Political jurisprudence: The contract of government*

The theory of contract, including quasicontract, belongs to the jurisprudence of the individual person but is at the same time the foundation for the jurisprudence of collectives, since these are made up of
contracting individuals. In line with jurisprudential tradition, Reid divides the relevant collectives into the family and the state, which are
the subject of, respectively, oeconomical and political jurisprudence.[78]
It is the latter that is our concern here.

Reid distinguishes sharply between the actual historical origins of
political society and the question of 'The Reasons that ought to induce
men Sufficiently enlightened to prefer the Political State to that of
Natural Liberty'.[79] As was common at the time, he sought the origins
of government in the need for leadership in tribal warfare and collective expeditions and ventures, subsequently reinforced by the need for
arbitrators in internal disputes. The rational person's motivation for
living in civil society is partly prudential, partly moral: he will gain
protection and better living conditions, and he will be enabled to develop morally as an active member of the moral community that the
Creator obviously intended for mankind.[80]

This rational foundation for political society must be understood in
what appear to be contractual terms, but instead of operating with the
conventional ideas of explicit and tacit contract and consent, Reid constructs an ingenious argument around the difficulties of contract theory by which he largely deprives 'contract' of its usual meaning and
role. In an important paper on contract his use of the idea of implicit
contract was probably inspired by Carmichael's and Hutcheson's speculations on the concept of obligations *quasi ex contractu*, which Grotius
and Pufendorf, among others, had originally constructed from Roman
law materials.[81] More particularly, Reid appears to be seeking to sup

78   *Practical Ethics*, pp. 170–2 and 217–36. Oeconomical jurisprudence is ex-
plained in the introduction, pp. 68–9. For a general discussion, see also J.C. Stewart-
Robertson, '"Horse-Bogey Bites Little Boys"; or, Reid's Oeconomicks of the Family',
Studies in Eighteenth-Century Culture, 16 (1986). 69–89.

79   *Practical Ethics*, p. 248.   80   *Practical Ethics*, pp. 174ff. and 247ff.

81   Reid, *Practical Ethics*, pp. 237–44; Carmichael, suppl. IV, 'De Quasi Contract-
ibus', in Pufendorf, *De officio*; Hutcheson, *Short Introduction*, pp. 223–7; and same,
System, 11.77–86. Implied contract and quasi-contract are complex topics in modern
natural law. Some details are supplied in *Practical Ethics*, pp. 355–8, nn. 122–7; pp.
402–3, n. 4; and 405–7, n. 9; but see principally Peter Birks and Grant McLeod, 'The
implied contract theory of quasi-contract: Civilian opinion current in the century
before Blackstone', *Oxford Journal of Legal History*, 6 (1986), 46–85, for the wider
context. On pp. 50–1, Birks and McLeod draw attention to the connection that
Blackstone saw between the original contract and quasi-contractual obligation, but

port the idea of a contractual basis for political authority by developing Hutcheson's suggestion, already noted, that continuing obligation to government 'is an obligation *quasi ex contractu*'.[82]

Reid's strategy here is to argue that there is no moral difference between an explicitly stated contractual obligation, a tacitly implied contractual obligation, and an obligation implied *as if* (*quasi*) there were a contract when in fact there is none. That the obligation is not altered by these different situations is underlined by the fact that we are not always able to draw clear distinctions between them. The point is that contractual obligation does not really depend upon contract at all but upon the assumption of an 'office' as a position carrying specificable obligations. In short, Reid's idea is that, whatever our walk in life or whatever social action we engage in, we assume an office or a set of duties pointed out to us by the common good and the law of nature, which are matched by corresponding rights and which our moral powers enable us to perceive immediately. This applies as much to the offices of magistrate and citizen as to any other offices. To hold the position of a magistrate carries with it certain obligations, and these point out the rights that the citizens hold against him. The same is true in reverse for the duties implied in being a citizen and the rights in being a ruler. These rights and duties are held together as if they had arisen from a contract, but they are in fact 'in the nature of things', to use the natural lawyers' idiom.

This interpretation of the relationship between rulers and the ruled means, for Reid, that the origins of goverment have nothing to do with its justification. Just as a marriage originating in rape is legitimate, according to Reid, if the offices of husband and wife are subsequently discharged properly, so a government begun in violence, conquest, or the like is legitimate if the governors proceed to carry out the duties of their office. Its origins are entirely irrelevant. 'A Government unjustly imposed may afterwards acquire Right by tacit consent',[83] if we understand 'tacit consent' in the wide sense of implied contract as characterized by the mutual offices and rights of rulers and ruled, which are matched by the law of nature so as to promote the common good. Accordingly we find Reid repeatedly emphasising the classical principles that 'The Sole End of Government is the Good of the Society', that is, 'The Publick Safety [is] the Supreme Law to Prince & People'.[84]

This argument is explicitly directed against Hume's criticism of con tract theory, and I believe it is also implicitly directed against his rejec-

---

there is no evidence that this weighed with Reid; they do not discuss Carmichael or Hutcheson.

82 Hutcheson, *Short Introduction*, p. 287.
83 *Practical Ethics*, pp. 242–3 and 177.   84 *Practical Ethics*, p. 252.

tion of the providential justification of government.[85] Put very simply, we may say that Hume conflated the various theories justifying the post-Revolutionary settlement of British government into two main categories that often functioned as one, namely contract and consent, and what may be called 'providential de factoism'.[86] In the former I include the many attempts to rest the new settlement upon one or more contractual arrangements, such as the Convention Parliament's call to William and Mary, the Oath of Allegiance and the Coronation Oath, and/or the supposed consent of the people, as shown, for example, in their acceptance of the benefits – the provision of protection and law and order – offered by the government. Hume's rejection of these ideas is too well known to need repetition here.[87] 'Providential de factoism' is the general idea that providence has appointed government to secure the common good of society and that any government that does so is ipso facto legitimate.

Hume rejects the notion of providentially appointed aims of government but retains the idea that a government that serves the common good, understood as the interests of the governed, is legitimate as long as it is seen to serve the common good. This brings Hume close to one aspect of de facto theory in the stricter sense: the argument that the Stuarts remained kings de jure but that the line that was settled by the Revolution, that is, by an historical accident, was the only government that could function, and it was therefore owed allegiance de facto. Although denying that the de jure question could be settled by history, he accepted the second part of this argument, virtually reducing the de jure question to a de facto one.

Reid agreed that the legitimacy of government did not depend on its origins, and to that extent he was predisposed towards some form of 'de factoism', but he could not accept in Hume the idea that opinion of interest was the basis for de facto government, since this would make it an amoral institution. For Reid, government was a moral institution resting upon moral judgement, but because such moral judgement could not properly be held to be expressed in an original contract, and because tacit consent, as commonly understood, seemed to be empirically meaningless, he had to reinterpret it as a matter of Common Sense perception of the implications of the respective offices of ruler and ruled. Finally, because the offices of life were divinely instituted in natural law, Reid's theory may be seen as a refinement of 'providential de factoism'. Civil society was ultimately legitimated by its end, which

85 For further discussion, see also *Practical Ethics,* pp. 402–8.
86 I am indebted to Conal Condren for a discussion of these matters.
87 But see Ch. 3, sect. 3.4, this volume.

was the common good elevated by natural law, and the offices of rulers and ruled were instituted accordingly.

6.9   *Rulers and ruled*

As indicated earlier, the relationship between rulers and the ruled may be considered either from the point of view of the rights of the individual and the duties of the government or from that of the rights of the government and the duties of the governed. When Reid takes the former line, he sounds at first almost libertarian: the task of the government is to protect the rights of its citizens, who may legitimately hold it to its task, because government rests on consent and is limited in its authority by the law of nature. Although this is the impression eager eyes may get from some of the manuscript papers, there are a number of difficulties. First, it is disquieting that Reid indicates neither which rights are to be protected nor to what extent. This problem will be solved when we look at it from the point of view of the government's rights; we shall then find that all rights, even those one might have thought inalienable, may on occasion be overruled by concern for the common good. Let us deal first, however, with the question of resistance.

Reid is quite clear that the authority of government is bounded by what is in accordance with the law of nature and that rulers 'are not to [be] obeyed in things unlawful'. This is further explained in brief notes: 'Active Obedience due onely in things lawfull . . . Passive Obedience . . . Due in many cases where our Rights are violated. Due wherever the publick good requires it. The Example of Socrates.' The legitimacy of a government's action is one thing, the right of resistance to such action quite another, for the right of the governed that the governors fulfil their duty to act according to natural law is obviously not identical with a right of resistance. The latter is a separate natural law question – whether the exercise of such a right of resistance contributes to the common good – and this will normally be doubtful: 'Changes in a form of Government that hath been established & acquiesced in ought not to be made without very weighty Reasons.' Indeed, 'The great mischief arising from violent changes of Government shew that they ought not to be attempted without urgent Necessity'.[88] The right of

88 *Practical Ethics*, pp. 251, 252, 253, and 177. See also the first pages of Reid's paper on the utopian system there, pp. 277–99, esp. p. 279: 'violent & sudden Changes of the Form of Government . . . are so dangerous in the Attempt, so uncertain in the Issue, and so dismal and destructive in the means by which they are brought about, that it must be a very bad form of Government indeed, with circum-

resistance is certainly there, in cases of dire necessity, but so it was for everyone who employed natural law modes of thinking, including Hobbes and the various German natural lawyers who were concerned with legitimating absolutist forms of government. The fact is that for the mainstream of natural law until late in the eighteenth century the right of resistance was heavily circumscribed, and Reid plainly agreed with them. The true character of Reid's politics is revealed in the relationship between rulers and ruled, seen as a matter of the former's right over the latter. He here elaborates a point implicit in natural law architectonics, that the rights of the political society over its members derive from its duties under natural law. First he argues that the state consists of moral individuals who

> unite in one incorporate Body . . . so as to have in a manner one Understanding one will one Active power, & thereby resemble one person, and consequently this political Person must be a moral Person and partake of the Nature of the individuals of which it is made up. . . . Political Bodies therefore or States are under the Same Obligation to regard . . . each others Rights as individuals. And hence it follows that the Law of Nations is in reality a very exact Copy of the Law of Nature. As therefore we Divided the Duty of Individuals into that which they Owe to God to themselves and to others we might divide in the same Manner the duty of Nations or States.[89]

Usually the analogy between individuals and states led only to the third category mentioned here, that of the rights and duties contained in the law of nations, but Reid develops it more fully.

Nations are as dependent as individuals upon the deity, and like them cannot well live without the four cardinal virtues, for which 'the most powerfull motive' is religion. 'It necessarly follows that a State neglects one of its most essential Interests if it neglects Religion and leaves that altogether out of its Consideration.'[90] The state must by law provide for the religious education of the citizens by establishing an official religion, which, if it is to serve its moral function, cannot be a mere form of worship but must have a doctrinal content. Because not even 'good and pious men' can agree on such matters, 'it is necessary in every State, that there be a Tolleration for those whose sentiments do not allow them to joyn in the National Religion, while at the same time they may have no notions of Religion that are inconsistent with their being good Subjects and good members of the Society'.[91] Reid does not make it clear how wide a religious toleration he would accept. This

---

stances very favourable to a Change concurring that will justify a Wise and good Man in putting a hand to them.'
89 *Practical Ethics*, pp. 254–5. Cf. p. 181.
90 *Practical Ethics*, p. 256. For the following, see pp. 257–9.
91 *Practical Ethics*, p. 258.

comes under the general principles of the state's duty to itself, which are that 'A State may lay restraints upon Actions of Men that are hurtfull though not criminal' and that it may not only restrain but also punish as a crime actions that spring from a 'malus animus', such as immorality, even when not injurious to other individuals.

> Whatever impairs the Morals, enervates the mindes, or bodies of the Members of a State is hurtfull to the State and as every individual so every political Body has right and is obliged to use its endeavours to preserve all its Members in that Sound State which fits them for being most usefull to the Society.[92]

In this way the four cardinal virtues very appropriately find a place in the jurisprudential system at the collective, political level, becoming in effect civic virtues. Indeed, when we remember Cicero's broadly practical interpretation of them, the following sample of the state's duties appears much less heterogeneous than it otherwise might:

> The duty of a State to promote Industry Agriculture Arts and Science. To provide for the Necessities of the Poor. to Punish idleness Riot and Dissipation. To manage the Publick Revenue to provide Ships & Harbours and all the Implements of forreign Trade to drain Marches make highways Bridges Canals Fortresses. To polish the Manners as well as preserve the Morals of its Subjects. To maintain the Respect due to Magistrates Parents Seniors persons of Superior Rank . . . To attend carefully to the Glory of the Nation. The Dominium Eminens of the State over the Lives & Property of the Subjects.

Reid's elaboration of this last right of the state over its citizens (or duty under natural law) not only spells out the full extent of the authority of civil society but also shows the structure of the general argument:

> The State not onely ought to defend the property of its Subjects against all who invade it, but has also a Right to Use it in as far as the publick Good Requires. When a Mans personal Service and even his life itself is . . . due to his country when its Safety demands it, it would be very odd to imagine that his Country should not have right to demand a farthing of his Money without his Consent. In a State the good and Safety of the whole is the very End of the Political Union . . . and therefore must be the supreme Law to which both the Life and the property of Individuals must submit as far as the Publick good Requires.

One part of this *dominium eminens* is the right of taxation. This is, naturally, restricted to what is necessary for the public good, and taxes must be 'frugally managed' and 'made as equal as possible':

> But there does not appear to me a Shadow of Reason why the Consent of a Subject should be necessary to his bearing an equal Share of the publick

92 Ibid.

burdthen which the service of the State demands. An Error of Mr. Locke on this Subject Second Treatise concerning Government §138.[93]

The pivot of his argument is clearly the natural law idea of the common (or public) good. It is this that allows such rights as individuals have and that imposes the duty on civil society to exercise a range of rights over its members, a duty limited only by the requirements of the common good. The rights of individuals are by no means open-ended claims to satisfaction, subject to the vicissitudes of fortune, the bargaining of life. Consequently it is quite erroneous to think with Locke that the state's *dominium eminens* over the property of individuals is a matter of negotiation, to be settled by consent. The common good settles this and all similar questions. The rights of individuals are not claims against others, including the state, beyond what the law of nature and the common good allow, and the same applies to the rights of the state against citizens. Although the principle is symmetrical, the outcome is far from being so.

6.10   *Utopia*

In view of this, it is hardly surprising that Reid in his final political statement[94] argues that maybe private property ought not to be recognized as a right at all but should be abolished in favour of communal ownership. The first premise for Reid's argument is that, apart from the desire for self-preservation,

the Desire of Distinction and Preeminence among his fellowmen is one of the strongest Desires of Man; And when his whole Activitiy is not necessarily employed in providing the means of Subsistence, is the strongest, the most general, & lasting spring of Activity and Exertion. Now Riches, in all

93   *Practical Ethics*, pp. 258–60. On *dominium eminens*, see AP, p. 659. Reid's view of taxation and consent is exactly the opposite of that put forward by Americans and their British supporters in the Stamp Act crisis and the debates leading up to the American Revolution. See *Practical Ethics*, p. 260 and pp. 425–6, n. 24. There is scant evidence from Reid's own hand about his attitude towards the American conflict, though his interest is clear from a letter written during the Stamp Act crisis (*Philosophical Works*, p. 43b), and a student's notes from his lectures in 1776 confirm his hostility to the American cause and its Lockean principle (Robert Jack, 'Dr. Reid's Lectures, 1774–1776', Glasgow University Library MSS 116–8, Lecture xx, pp. 667ff). For a brief discussion, see J.C. Stewart-Robertson, 'Sancte Socrates: Scottish reflections on obedience and resistance', in *Man and Nature* (Proceedings of the Canadian Society for Eighteenth-Century Studies, I) ed. R.L. Emerson, G. Girard, and R. Runte, London, Ontario, 1982, pp. 65–79.

94   Aberdeen University Library MS 3061/6, an address to the Glasgow Literary Society in 1794 entitled 'Some Thoughts on the Utopian System', in *Practical Ethics*, pp. 277–99.

civilized Societies, seem to have advantages above all other Qualifications for gratifying this Desire.[95]

The second premise is that acquisitiveness totally corrupts the morals of both poor and rich, mainly because it divides people into poor and rich. Third, Reid suggests that when all but the most basic exertions of men are concerned with the acquisition of private property, a sharp division will occur, both between the interests of individuals and between those and the public or common interest of society. The result will be a strife-ridden society in which public spirit and all concern for the public good is lost.[96]

The remedy is 'the Utopian system', largely inspired by Thomas More, which has as its fundamental principle that moral exertion should replace economic exertion. Property arises out of labour, so if we abolish private property in favour of communal ownership we shall all be working for the state, and that is a much more direct and effective manifestation of the benevolent side of our moral character than anything made possible by private property.[97] As for the acquisition of property as a spur to activity, this can readily be replaced by a system of public honours for moral exertion and merit that will also provide a much better social stratification than one based directly or indirectly on riches. Further, moral merit may be reinforced and its influence enhanced by state allowances of 'Servants, Horses, Chariots, Houses and Furniture', though it must be stressed that servants remain in the employment of the state, whomever they serve, and presumably the rest remains the property of the state, whoever benefits from it from time to time.[98]

For such a system to work, the people must be properly educated. This does not mean simply literacy, numeracy, high scholastic education, and vocational training:

> to form the Character to good Habits and good Dispositions, & to check those that are vicious; this is the Soul and Spirit of right Education. To accomplish this as far as can be done by human Means, requires great Knowledge of human Nature, constant Attention, great Temper, Patience and Assiduity. The diseases of the Mind while it is pliable and docile as well as those of the Body may, by prudent Means, be cured or alleviated.[99]

Such moral training must be given to all the people, because 'Nature has not made the Talents of Body or Mind that are usefull in Society, hereditary, or peculiar to any Rank'. But equality of opportunity does not mean equality in the result, and 'in such a State there will be a much greater variety of Ranks than in any other'. In order to establish

95 *Practical Ethics*, p. 285.   96 *Practical Ethics*, pp. 286–7.
97 *Practical Ethics*, pp. 283–5.   98 *Practical Ethics*, pp. 291–2.
99 *Practical Ethics*, p. 289.

the membership of these ranks, it is necessary that a constant supervision and record is kept of each individual's contribution to the common good in all its aspects:

> As the Labour in every Employment is for the Publick, it must be overseen by Officers appointed by the Publick, who shall at stated times make a Report to superior Officers of the Industry, Skill and moral behaviour of every Individual under their Charge.[100]

According to how people fare in this assessment, they will be given 'Distinctive ba[d]ges or habits, by which every Mans Rank & the Respect due to him may be known'; similarly 'a Man may be made to carry about him the Marks' of 'Dishonour & Disgrace'. If this system of incentives and disincentives is not sufficient for some 'to make them act their part in Society', Utopia has recourse to punishment. Indeed, 'Such Persons have the Temper of Slaves and ought to be degraded into that state, being altogether unworthy and incapable of being Citizens of Utopia.' The task with which the utopian state is burdened is thus extensive:

> The Education of all the Youth of both Sexes. The Oversight of all the labouring hands. The collecting, storing and dispersing the Produce of their Labour. The publick Registers that must be kept of the Merits and Demerits of every Individual, & of every Step of his advancement in Honour and Rank. The Regulations for confering Degrees with Justice and Impartiality, and the Management of the trading Stock of the Nation.[101]

Reid argues at some length that the legislative and judiciary branches of government in Utopia will be relieved of so much work as will easily compensate for the increased executive load.

It is now abundantly clear that the overriding element in Reid's notion of the common good is moral perfection. The striving for all-round moral perfection is the basic precept of natural law that justifies the imposition of all necessary duties. Against this, individual rights have no force; there are simply no other rights than those whose enforcement is in keeping with this common good.

This enables us to consider the two central problems, noted briefly earlier, concerning the role of natural law and the common good. We may unite them and describe Reid's suspected dilemma as follows. As we have seen, he was a moral realist in the sense that he held that the essential moral category is an 'objective relation', namely, duty between a person and an action; the relation is 'objective' in the sense that it is established by moral First Principles, which cannot in any sense be reduced to subjective states, whether cognitive or emotive, of the agent

---

100 *Practical Ethics*, pp. 289, 291, and 290.
101 *Practical Ethics*, pp. 290, 292, and 293.

or the spectator. At the same time, he held that human actions are sorted into rights and duties by the law of nature, which God prescribes for man in order to create the common good. Are these views not mutually exclusive?

Reid does not, of course, suggest that natural law makes actions good or bad; it points out which actions *are* in fact good or bad, for it is internalized as each person's conscience or moral faculty. Further, the actions that are good and that natural law therefore prescribes do indeed contribute to the common good. This is moral in character, which means that it is realized when the doing of one's duty – that is, the carrying out of morally right actions – is optimal. We can therefore take it as a sign that an action is not morally right if it conflicts with the common good, and if an individual claims a right to perform such an action we can be certain that he has no right in the matter, for there cannot be any duty to respect his claim.

We may also understand Reid's position by contrasting it with the theory of the artificial virtues, particularly justice, which he found in Hume.[102] As Reid saw it, Hume maintained that acts of justice have no inherent or natural moral quality but are lent a certain moral colouring by their connection with public utility; they are morally justified because in general they contribute to the public good. By contrast, Reid maintains that the common good is made up of actions that are in themselves or inherently morally good. Moreover, although not the ground justifying the moral goodness of actions, the common good may obviously be the criterion by which we can discern morally right actions in situations where their direct contemplation is not sufficient, such as situations with competing rights claims or situations where people's moral sense is warped by selfishness or criminal inclinations. This is why the concept of the common good plays a key role in Reid's system of *practical* ethics and hence in his utopian polity. The idea of the common good as a sign or criterion of recognition, rather than a ground of justification, should also make it clear that Reid is not a consequentialist in his political theory, save in the trivial sense that political institutions serve an end; but that end is moral rightness.

When Reid's version of Pufendorf's system of natural law is combined with the idea that all morality can be certainly taught, his utopian vision follows readily:

> if ever civil government shall be brought to perfection, it must be the principal care of the state to make good citizens by proper education, and proper instruction and discipline . . . The end of government is to make the society happy, which can only be done by making it good and virtuous. That men

102 AP, V.v, and pp. 667–70. On Hume's and Smith's concept of public utility, see Haakonssen, *Science of a Legislator*, pp. 40–1, 87–8, 120–3.

in general will be good or bad members of society, according to the education and discipline by which they have been trained, experience may con-
vince us. The present age has made great advances in the art of training men
to military duty . . . and I know not why it should be thought impossible to
train men to equal perfection in the other duties of good citizens. What an
immense difference is there, for the purposes of war, between an army
properly trained, and a militia hastily drawn out of the multitude? What
should hinder us from thinking that, for every purpose of civil government,
there may be a like difference between a civil society properly trained to
virtue, good habits, and right sentiments, and those civil societies which we
now behold?[103]

6.11   *Revolution or reform*

Reid's political theory is at one level an unusually explicit synthesis
of one brand of natural jurisprudence with humanist utopianism. The
former undoubtedly developed during his tenure of the Glasgow chair,
with its jurisprudential tradition from Carmichael, Hutcheson, and
Smith; the latter probably dated from his early introduction to the
republicanism of the Commonwealth tradition and its sources and
certainly remained of primary concern throughout his life. Not only do
republican and utopian authors figure prominently in his Aberdeen
Orations and in the Glasgow lectures on political jurisprudence, but the
lectures on politics, following on pneumatology and practical ethics in
his Glasgow course, were strongly influenced by James Harrington.
When William Ogilvie, his successor at King's College and subsequently Professor of Humanity, published his utopian scheme for
agrarian reform, Reid approved of it.[104]

103   AP, pp. 577b–578a. There is in Reid a never-resolved tension between this
kind of moral perfectibilism, which points towards a 'perfect moral commonwealth', and an acceptance of man's inherent moral imperfectibility, which points to
institutional arrangements that will make up for this, i.e. a Utopia proper. For this
general distinction, see J.C. Davis, *Utopia and the Ideal Society: A Study of English
Utopian Writing, 1516–1700*, Cambridge, UK, 1981, ch. 1. While this cannot be adequately discussed here, it should be kept in mind in the following section. The
former line leads readily to Dugald Stewart's historicism (see the following two
chapters in the present volume), whereas the latter is more amenable to the possibility of institutional reform, to which Reid is attracted for reasons set out in the next
section.
104   See Reid's letter to Ogilvie of 7 April 1789 in William Ogilvie, *Birthright in
Land*, with biographical notes by D.C. MacDonald, London, 1891, pp. 151–2.
Ogilvie's *Essay on the Right of Property in Land* was published anonymously in 1781
or 1782 (see *Birthright*, p. 186). On Ogilvie's usefulness in the nineteenth century, see
J. Morrison Davidson's quaint Georgist tract *Concerning Four Precursors of Henry
George and the Single Tax*, London, n.d. (c. 1890).

Yet Reid was far from being a Harringtonian republican. Although an agrarian law might improve existing social conditions, it still founded civic virtue and political authority on property, and 'It may be doubted whether there is in this Model sufficient provision for preserving that degree of Morals and publick Virtue which is necessary in a Commonwealth.'[105] Nor would agrarian redistribution affect any of the other forms of property that had emerged in modern society and that seemed much more difficult to control.[106] Political reform could thus not be guaranteed by a change in property relations but had to rely on moral reform.

This brought Reid into conflict not only with the Harringtonians but also with the theory, favoured by Hume, Smith, and Millar, of a necessary though not exclusive link between forms of property and forms of government. It is not implausible to see Reid's utopian moral commonwealth as yet another criticism of Hume, in this instance of his adaptation of Harrington to a more advanced 'Idea of a perfect commonwealth'.[107] It is a sobering study of the complexities of the reaction to the French Revolution and of the concept of Whiggism to contrast Reid's scheme with the reform program of his colleague John Millar in the latter's *Letters of Sidney* two years later.[108]

Further light on Reid's views on the French Revolution may be gained indirectly. William Ogilvie thought that Reid's agrarian scheme might be useful in India, and, in a letter written in 1805 to Sir James Mackintosh, his former student and then recorder at Bombay, he tried to engage the latter's interest:

> I do not suppose that you, any more than myself, have embraced the philosophy of common sense, as it has been called, in all its latitude; but surely Dr. Reid's eminence in various sciences, and his successful endeavours to throw light on that which he cultivated, cannot have escaped your notice, any more than the merits of the 'Vindiciae Gallicae' escaped him. Mrs. Carmichael, his surviving daughter, at whose request I take the liberty of giving you this trouble, informs me that he was struck with admiration on reading that Essay, and used frequently to speak of it as one of the most ingenious works of the kind he had ever met with.[109]

105   Aberdeen University Library, Birkwood Collection, MS 2131/4/111/6,4v. This is part of his lectures on politics.

106   Ibid., Fol. 4r.

107   See Hume, *Political Essays*, ed. K. Haakonssen, Combridge, UK, 1994, pp. 221–33. On Smith, see Haakonssen, *Science of a Legislator*, pp. 181–8. In this regard, Reid was preceded by Robert Wallace's *Various Prospects of Mankind, Nature, and Providence*, London, 1761, which may well have inspired him.

108   [John Millar], *Letters of Sidney, on Inequality of Property*, Edinburgh, 1796; and see Ch. 5, sect. 5.5, this volume.

109   Ogilvie to Mackintosh (received in June 1805), in *Memoirs of the Life of . . .*

This leads one to wonder whether Mrs. Carmichael's 'request' perhaps echoes a wish of her father's. It certainly indicates that Reid's esteem for Mackintosh's youthful radicalism survived the reaction against the French Revolution after 1791, lasting until Reid's death in 1796. Why else would the daughter who cared for him in his last years be so concerned with it nearly ten years later?

Seen against this background, it is hardly surprising that Reid supported the early, hopeful phase of the French Revolution, when it was still possible for British sympathizers to see it as a delayed 'English' revolution. It is thus of more than symbolic significance that when the Glasgow Friends of Liberty in 1791 called a Bastille Day celebration, at which Reid officiated as a steward, the public announcement echoed the language that Britons had been using for a century about their own Revolution of 1688: 'The 14 of July being the anniversary of the late glorious revolution in France, by which so many millions have been restored to their rights as men and citizens, the Friends of Liberty in Glasgow and neighbourhood are invited to celebrate the second anniversary of that revolution.'[110]

This liberal Whig constitutionalist perspective, combined with Reid's moral progressivism, non-necessitarian Calvinism, and republican leanings, explains his enthusiasm for the French Revolution as a renewed attempt to implement moral freedom and in that sense the 'rights of man', but to see Reid as the protagonist of some modern ideology of subjective rights of man is a misunderstanding of both his morals and his politics.[111] Reid himself brought together a number of these traditionalist elements in his account, to an anonymous correspondent, of the Glasgow celebration and its aftermath:

Sir James Mackintosh, ed. R.J. Mackintosh, 2 vols., London, 1836, 1:380. For Mackintosh's answer and his appreciation of Ogilvie, see ibid., pp. 17 and 381–6. Cf. also Chapter 8 in the present volume.

110 *Glasgow Mercury*, 5 July 1791. See also P.B. Wood, 'Thomas Reid, Natural Philosopher: A Study of Science and Philosophy in the Scottish Enlightenment', Ph.D. thesis, University of Leeds, 1984, pp. 181ff.

111 Seen in this light, neither Reid's recommendation of Mary Wollstonecraft's *Vindication of the Rights of Woman*, London, 1792, nor his qualification of it, is surprising: 'Have you [Dugald Stewart] read a *Vindication of the Rights of Woman*? I think a Professor of Morals may find some things worthy of his attention, mixed, perhaps, with other things which he may not approve' (letter to Stewart, 21 January 1793, in John Veitch, 'A Memoir of Dugald Stewart', in Dugald Stewart, *Biographical Memoirs of Adam Smith . . . William Robertson . . . Thomas Reid . . .* , in Dugald Stewart, *Collected Works*, ed. Sir William Hamilton, facsim. repr. of 1854–60 ed., introd. Knud Haakonssen, 11 vols., Bristol, UK, 1994, 10:cxlviii).

Dear Sir,

I have been in your Debt as a Correspondent since Christmas. You then rejoiced in the Return of that Anniversary, & in the great Events which had happened in our Neighbouring Kingdom both Civil & Ecclesiastical. In all this I think you did what might become a good Praefectorian, & I give you the right hand of Fellowship. Among the other Wonders of our Day, let the pure Wine of Rome & Geneva mix, leaving the Dregs behind! . . .

I have been very long persuaded, that a Nation, to be free, needs onely to know the Rights of Man. I have lived to see this Knowledge spread far beyond my most sanguine hopes, and produce glorious Effects. God grant it may spread more & more & that those who taste the Sweets of Liberty may not turn giddy but make a wise and sober Use of it.

Some few here think or affect to think, that to be a Friend to the Revolution of France is to be an Enemy to the Constitution of . . . Britain, or at least to its present Administration. I know the contrary to be true in my self, & verily believe that most of my Acquaintance who rejoice in that Revolution agree with me in this.

In this belief, upon the sollicitation of some friends in the College & others, I permitted my Name to be used, for a meeting of Friends to the French Revolution on the 14 of July, upon the Condition & promise of my fellow Stewarts that no unfavourable Reflection direct or oblique either on the Constitution or present Administration of Great Britain was to be heard. I meant nothing more than to own myself not ashamed to be thought a friend to the French Revolution, & thought no Mortal needed to take offence at this. But I have within this four and twenty hours received an Anonymous letter in a feigned hand professing friendship, and great Surprize *that my Name should appear at the bottom of an Advertisement calling together a set of political Madmen and Blackguards; and acquainting me that the time is fast approaching when I and some of my brethren will repent the steps we have taken.*

Whether you do think it more odd that an old deaf Dotard should be announced a Stewart of such a Meeting, or that it should give any Man such offence.[112]

When mixed, the 'pure wine of Rome and Geneva' was obviously heady enough to stir the octogenarian Reid to action, and he caused further offence when, in the following year, with many others, he gave money to the French National Assembly.[113] After that he could no longer approve of the course of the Revolution, and by 1794 he was prepared to indicate this publicly, in his Utopia paper. It is, however, a misunderstanding to see this as a political volte-face.[114] It was the political situation that had changed, not Reid's position. His defence of

112   MS 2131/3/III/8. The draft letter is neither addressed nor dated; it was presumably written soon after 14 July 1791, clearly to someone close to Reid.

113   See M. Forbes, *Beattie and His Friends*, London, 1904, p. 273.

114   See H.W. Meikle, *Scotland and the French Revolution*, London, 1969, pp. 155–6.

the British constitution in that paper is entirely in line with his 'rights-of-man' letter quoted earlier and with everything he had previously said on the topic.

By emphasising his esteem for Mackintosh and the sort of token support for the beginnings of the French Revolution that many liberal and radical Whigs gave, we have let Reid slide away from utopianism toward the third element in his political thought, which tempers this and brings us back to natural law. Reid was apprehensive of the uto-pian implications of his moral thought. In the course of unravelling these implications,[115] he breaks off in alarm: 'But I fear I shall be thought to digress from my subject into Utopian speculation.' Six years later he again indulged in utopian speculation in a lengthy paper he presented to the Glasgow Literary Society, but he prefaced that passage with a caution against the dangers of sudden, wholesale political inno-vation and praised the British constitution as a vehicle for gradual, peaceful change. The paper as a whole is entitled 'Some Thoughts on the Utopian System', but only the prefatory remarks were published in a local newspaper, under the title 'Observations on the Dangers of Political Innovation'.[116]

By the 'British constitution' Reid undoubtedly meant the 1688-9 principles of government, interpreted on liberal Whig lines, though it is difficult to determine exactly which lines. What is important is that this respect for constitutional principles in Reid demonstrates a more general constitutionalist bent – that is, a tendency to see politics as a rule-governed system. It is significant that, along with Harrington, Montesquieu is the dominant influence on Reid's lectures on politics. In the lectures on Harrington, Reid is obsessively concerned with the labyrinthine regulations of the Commonwealth of Oceana, and it is easy to imagine his fascination with the mechanical politics of other utopias. To such a mind, the idea of organizing all morality into neat jurisprudential categories of duties and rights governed by natural law must have had strong appeal, especially as an extension of a moral

115 See at note 103 to this chapter. [*Note*: citations saying '*at* note 103' mean 'in the text, near note 103'; citations saying '*in* note 6' mean 'in the text of note 6'.]

116 *Glasgow Courier*, 18 December 1794. We do not know whether Reid himself initiated its publication or chose the title. The newspaper article is, oddly enough, reprinted in the *Discourses on Theological and Literary Subjects*, Glasgow, 1803, of Reid's successor, Archibald Arthur, and the editor, William Richardson, says that it was 'published with his [Reid's] consent in the Glasgow Courier' ('An account of some particulars in the life and character of the Rev. Mr. Archibald Arthur, late Professor of Moral Philosophy in the University of Glasgow', in Arthur, *Discourses*, p. 514 n.; see also ibid. p. 518). Richardson, however, is so determined to lump Reid and Arthur together as upright, consistent opponents of the French Revolution that both his judgement and his intentions are suspect.

philosophy that showed there were objective, universally valid principles of moral knowledge. Consequently the moral uncertainty, historical chance, and mere political probability inherent in radical political change appalled him. Indeed his dislike, even fear, of these often seems to amount to a mistrust of politics as such, and it is not surprising that in his Utopia, politics are replaced by moral accountancy. The constitutionalist element in his thought is thus the natural result of his dread of a life governed by political chance, which Hume and Smith had accepted as the inevitable lot of humankind but which Reid felt it his moral and philosophical duty to oppose.

Reid's desire for a different society and his fear of change as a means of achieving it constitute the traditional utopian dilemma, and he had not yet succumbed to the temptation of seeking refuge in the future. It was left to his self-appointed disciple Dugald Stewart to find a way out of the dilemma in the historicist idea of the inevitable and unpolitical march of the mind towards the moral commonwealth of the future.[117] If this was a fitting response to the political ambiguity of post-revolutionary Europe, the reader may be left to consider whether Reid was too simple or too honest to adopt it, or whether he was spared by living too soon.

117 See the following chapter on Stewart. In his last years, Reid was close not only to Stewart but also to the intellectually minded artists around him, one of whom, Raeburn, made Reid the subject of an outstanding portrait painted in the year of the Utopia paper, dramatically echoing Ramsay's portrait of Rousseau. Another painter, Alexander Nasmyth, also probably influenced by Reid's and Stewart's theory of perception, apparently found in Reid support for his own utopian leanings. See Duncan Macmillan, *Painting in Scotland: The Golden Age,* Oxford, 1986, pp. 145–6.

7

Dugald Stewart and the science of a legislator

7.1 Smith or Reid

The Smithian concept of a science of legislation is carried on in the work of Dugald Stewart, and yet the content of the discipline, as well as its philosophical presuppositions, undergoes changes which from hindsight we can see amount to its dissolution. Viewed in narrowly disciplinary terms, Stewart identifies the science of a legislator with political economy, but he then reconstitutes the content of political economy by making jurisprudence part of it.[1] At the same time he virtually excludes what he calls 'politics proper', that is, the theory of government, from the discipline and, more or less, from scientific treatment at all.[2] Finally, he makes it plain that he considers political economy in this sense to be a direct extension of moral philosophy and that he sees himself in this respect as continuing a tradition which had so far reached its height in the Scottish academic tradition.[3] But despite his awareness of his intellectual ancestry, he finds no theoretical function for history in his political economy. At the level of disciplinary history, it is this explicit rejection of history and the less explicit reduc-

1 *Lectures on Political Economy*, 2 vols. (c. 1809–10; hereafter *Pol. Econ.*), in Dugald Stewart, *Collected Works* (hereafter *Works*), ed. Sir William Hamilton, facsim. repr. of 1854–60 ed., introd. K. Haakonssen, 11 vols., Bristol, UK, 1994, vols. VIII–IX; here VIII, pp. 9–29. *Dissertation Exhibiting the Progress of Metaphysical, Ethical and Political Philosophy since the Revival of Letters in Europe* (1815–21; hereafter *Diss.*) in *Works*, vol. I; here at p. 22. Cf. Donald Winch, 'The system of the north; Dugald Stewart and his pupils', in *That Noble Science of Politics: A Study in Nineteenth-Century Intellectual History*, by S. Collini, D. Winch, and J. Burrow, Cambridge, UK, 1983, pp. 23–61; and B. Fontana, *Rethinking the Politics of Commercial Society: The "Edinburgh Review", 1802–1832*, Cambridge, UK, 1985, pp. 7–8. For a more general view of Stewart's context, see ch. 8, sect. 8.1, this volume.

2 *Pol. Econ.*, VIII, pp. 20–9; IX, pp. 413 and 419–21; *Diss.*, pp. 93–4.

3 *The Philosophy of the Active and Moral Powers of Man*, 2 vols. (1828; hereafter *Powers*), in *Works*, vols. VI–VII; here VII, pp. 364–6; *Diss.*, I, pp. 171, 178–9, 192–3.

tion of jurisprudence to a subsidiary role within a more comprehensive discipline which are characteristic of Stewart as compared with Smith.

Behind these changes in the idea of how to study human beings in their social aspect lies a metaphysics of social phenomena and a theory of the historical process which are significantly different from those of Smith. The key to this is, however, to be found at an even more fundamental level, namely in the profoundly different theory of moral knowledge to which Stewart – following Thomas Reid – subscribed. The broad perspective suggested by the following argument is, therefore, that the moral theory of Common Sense philosophy contributed in an important way to the dissolution of Smith's science of a legislator.[4]

The chief objective of Stewart's moral philosophy was to counter the subjectivism and relativism which he saw as the dangerous legacies of much of the moral philosophical tradition; at the same time he wanted to avoid the kind of rationalism which he found in Clarke, Cudworth, Wollaston, and others. The subjectivism with which Stewart was principally concerned was that inherent, as he saw it, in the various eighteenth-century theories of the foundation of moral judgement in some form of sensing or feeling – the theories of such philosophers as Shaftesbury, Hutcheson, Hume, and Smith. The objects of his attacks on relativism were philosophers, such as Mandeville, who taught that moral judgement is formed by education and political indoctrination.[5] Normally the two lines of argument were combined and the second, moreover, developed from a conspiracy theory of moral and social phenomena into increasingly sophisticated developmental theories, a process which in most respects reached its climax in Smith, who, in addition, attempted to transcend relativism by his ingenious theory of the abstract normative principles inherent in the ideal impartial spectator. The interesting thing is that although Stewart recognized these new developmental theories as of the greatest importance in modern

---

4 Richard Sher has suggested that Stewart, at least in his early years, was greatly indebted to Adam Ferguson; Richard B. Sher, 'Professors of virtue: The social history of the Edinburgh Moral Philosophy Chair in the eighteenth century', in *Studies in the Philosophy of the Scottish Enlightenment*, ed. M.A. Stewart, Oxford, 1990, pp. 87–126, at pp. 123–4. This may well be true, but it leaves us guessing what it was – course outlines apart – that Stewart got from his predecessor as Professor of Moral Philosophy at Edinburgh. One guess is that Ferguson provided long-lived proof of the need to think through the relationship between the Hume–Smith and the Reidian traditions.

5 *Powers*, VI, pp. 264–74. For a useful overview of the polemical agenda of Stewart's philosophy as a whole, see Fontana, *Politics of Commercial Society*, pp. 86–93.

philosophy, he was unable to accommodate them in his own moral and social philosophy.

7.2 *Elements of a theory of morals*

The central argument in Stewart's moral philosophy proceeds along two complementary lines, one concerning the understanding of moral qualities, the other concerning the reality of moral values as objects of understanding.[6] The latter argument is simply to show that moral qualities are irreducible attributes of actions, attributes which are analogous to the primary qualities of matter. On this point Stewart is explicit, whereas Reid never made the analogy clear.[7] But then Stewart is quite happy to talk about moral attributes as qualities, whereas Reid explicitly denies this and maintains that they are relational. It would seem that this creates more difficulty for Reid's analogy between aesthetic and moral attributes than those that D.D. Raphael points out, and it makes it hard to see how the distinction between primary and secondary qualities can be of much help in understanding Reid, as opposed to Stewart. In this matter Stewart may well be taking up a point from his other teacher, Adam Ferguson, who criticized Lord Kames for having 'started a question, whether moral excellence be not a secondary quality'.[8] However, what Kames had in mind was an analogy between primary and secondary qualities, on the one hand, and the determinism of human behaviour versus the appearance of free will, on the other.[9]

Moral qualities are, on Stewart's view, immutable and have real existence independent of their perception by any human mind. Corresponding to this, the human mind has a certain ability to perceive such moral qualities, and these 'moral powers' of the mind are original and

6   *Outlines of Moral Philosophy* (1793; hereafter *Outlines*), introduction and Part I in *Works*, vol. II; Part II in *Works*, vol VI; here VI, paras. 181–210; *Powers*, VI, pp. 219–32; 280–301.

7   Cf. D.D. Raphael, *The Moral Sense*, Oxford, 1947, pp. 177–8.

8   Adam Ferguson, *Principles of Moral and Political Science*, 2 vols., Edinburgh, 1792, II, p. 133. Ferguson's work is peppered with the conventional ideas that we have met repeatedly and will meet again later in this volume, about a general moral order which may be progressively realized if the universal moral faculty is freed of corruption of various kinds. But he does on occasion talk in very different terms, and the discussion of Kames seems to have been a catalyst for this. Instead of the langauge of qualities and the perception of qualities, of virtues and moral faculties natural to man, he switches to the language of moral *ideals* which may be striven for, realized, deviated from, used as standards, etc. *Principles*, II, pp. 133–4, and cf. pp. 2 and 123–6.

9   [Henry Home, Lord Kames], *Essays on the Principles of Morality and Natural Religion*, Edinburgh, 1751, pp. 190–2, 212, 215.

irreducible in the sense that they are as much part of human nature as
the rest of our mental faculties. The traditional attempts to analyse the
moral powers in terms of such principles as 'a regard to character',
'sympathy', 'the sense of the ridiculous', 'taste', or – most importantly
– 'self-love', are thus futile and of course dangerous, in as much as they
tend to obscure the permanency and reality of human morality.[10] Stewart does not want to identify the moral powers with a separate moral
sense, nor does he want them understood as an aspect of reason, if by
reason is meant the ability to draw logical inferences. The moral faculty
is a complex of reason and feeling, in as much as it partly consists in
the ability to recognize and form judgements about the special attributes of actions which are called 'moral', and partly in experiencing
certain feelings which accompany such judgements. Although the ability to judge is, in a sense, of primary importance, the moral faculty or
the moral power is a single original feature of our intellectual nature
which it does not make sense to try to analyse any further.[11]

The most obvious objection to a doctrine of this nature is that human
morality, at different times and in different places, has taken on so
many diverse and often incompatible forms that it is exceedingly difficult to see what is permanent and immutable in them. Stewart deals
with this kind of objection at some length, pointing out that

> it is necessary to attend to a variety of considerations which have been too
> frequently overlooked by philosophers; and, in particular, to make proper
> allowances for the three following: – I. For the different situations in which
> mankind are placed, partly by the diversity of their physical circumstances,
> and partly by the unequal degrees of civilization which they have attained.
> II. For the diversity of their speculative opinions, arising from their unequal
> measures of knowledge or of capacity; and, III. For the different moral
> import of the same action under different systems of external behaviour.[12]

In order to illustrate the first point, Stewart points out – very much in
the style of Hume – that whereas the specific content of the concept of
property right, and consequently of what constitutes theft, varies according to what people for physical or social reasons hold as property,
this does nevertheless not prove that there is any variation in the
fundamental moral principle of not 'depriving an individual of an

10 For the criticism of systems of self-love, or prudence, see *Outlines*, VI, paras.
159–70; *Powers*, VI, pp. 205–18. For the criticism of the other attempts at analysis, see
Outlines, VI, paras. 222–38; *Powers*, VI, pp. 327–41.

11 *Powers*, VI, pp. 279–80. In keeping with his general eclectic tendency, Stewart allows the four principles of 'a regard to character', 'sympathy', 'the sense of the
ridiculous', and 'taste' to be supportive of the moral powers but insists that it is this
very circumstance which has misled philosophers to think that one or another of
them constituted the moral powers.

12 *Powers*, VII, p. 237.

enjoyment which he had provided for himself by a long course of persevering industry'. Similarly, the fact that in pre-commercial society money-lending on interest is considered sinful and, often, criminal, whereas in commercial society it generally is accepted as much as any other form of business, does not prove any disagreement about the moral regard for the interests and happiness of other people. The point is that in the former kind of society loans cannot have the objective, market-determined value which is a reflection of mutual interests between lender and borrower, and consequently the taking of interest tends to be the direct exploitation of a particular individual's weakness.[13]

In explanation of the second point Stewart gives the following example:

> there is a wide diversity between the moral systems of ancient and modern times on the subject of suicide. Both, however, agree in this, that it is the duty of man to obey the will of his Creator, and to consult every intimation of it that his reason can discover, as the supreme law of his conduct. They differed only in their speculative opinions concerning the interpretation of the will of God, as manifested by the dispensations of his providence in the events of human life.[14]

The final point is that the same mode of behaviour can receive completely different moral appreciations in different moral systems. Thus, if pain and violence are considered criteria of an honourable and happy death, then it may be benevolent to torture. And similarly, when actions are symbolic or expressive of moral ideas, or ideas of politeness, they are often completely conventional, and the same idea may be expressed in widely different ways.

Although one cannot accuse Stewart of avoiding the issue, it is hard to be satisfied with this attempt to cope with the historical and geographical diversity of morality within his moral theory. For if we accept the arguments and illustrations, the most they show is that human morality has been constant in this, that men have always and everywhere made moral distinctions and recognized moral qualities, but they have varied extremely in the content of these distinctions and recognized qualities – and that is hardly saying much more than that mankind has always and everywhere had some sort of morality. The problem is that for an objectivism of Stewart's strong brand it is not enough to show that actions which are prima facie different are yet preceived to be of the same moral value. He has to show that the actions have a real, intrinsic quality in common which exists indepen-

---

13 *Powers*, VII, pp. 237 and 239–43. Cf. Hume, *A Treatise of Human Nature*, ed. L.A. Selby-Bigge, 2nd ed. rev. by P.H. Nidditch, Oxford, 1978, II.II.3.
14 *Powers*, VI, p. 246.

dently of perception. Presumably such an argument would take the form of showing that whatever the perceptual qualities of an action, apart from being perceived to be right, nothing follows about whether the action is right. None of Stewart's arguments goes anywhere towards showing this, and in general he simply assumes – falsely – that because the rightness of an action is independent of the judgement that the action is right, its rightness has no relation to perception or feeling. But the subjectivists distinguished the judgement that an action causes a certain perception or feeling from the perception or feeling itself, which, on their view, makes an action right, and they would properly reject Stewart's assumption.

Stewart's inability to accommodate the facts of history within his moral theory does not, of course, provide an argument against the possibility of moral objectivism, but it highlights the fact that in such a doctrine the history of moral phenomena plays no other role than that of providing possible obstacles in the form of counter-examples. Right moral judgement is a matter of understanding certain natural attributes of human action, and there is nothing to show that such attributes could have an historical aspect and need an historical understanding. It is, therefore, not surprising that Stewart never sees it as part of his moral philosophical task to put forward a theory of the development of moral phenomena. In this he is very far from Hume and Smith. Hume had begun and Smith continued the speculation that the only basis in human nature for moral judgements is provided by a set of simple emotional responses to the behaviour of other people and an ability to perceive such responses in others through sympathy. This parsimony with respect to 'natural' principles in each individual then forces Hume and Smith to account for all other aspects of moral judgement by reference to the circumstances in which the individuals concerned find themselves. Rejecting what they take to be Montesquieu's idea that the physical circumstances will suffice, they come to the general conclusion that moral judgements can be fully understood only if we understand the society in which people live. A group of individuals is made into a society by the collective effect of their moral judgements – judgements concerning human behaviour – some of these judgements being institutionalized, pre-eminently in the form of law; some of them being pseudo-institutionalized, such as the received code of general behaviour; and some of them standing as the more or less influential verdicts of individuals. Moral judgements are therefore to be understood as formed under the influence of a vast complexity of previous moral judgements, either directly or as they are internalized by the individual, and normally both. And at the same time the present judgement may of course well contribute to, and possibly change, this social store of moral knowledge. In this way the theory of the development of moral phenomena becomes a necessary element in the theory of morality, and this theory of development is turned into history, once we add the particular circumstances of the society in question – its relationship to other societies, its physical circumstances, its exposure to accidental factors of all sorts.

For Smith the search for the moral standpoint is the search for impartiality, and the conditions of impartiality are in each case set by the historically given social situation. Whether the history is one of wisdom or of ignorance (e.g. of just or unjust law), it is equally necessary for an understanding of the moral judgement and the behaviour to which it may lead. For Stewart, on the contrary, the moral standpoint is a matter of the recognition of natural moral qualities in actions and, although such recognition may be obscured by historically given prejudices or enlightened by illustrious examples from the past, this is by no means inherent in the judgement as such but a mere circumstantial factor which can be disregarded when the minds of moral agents can be enlightened by direct education.

These reflections should make it intelligible why Stewart not only does not, but cannot, take over Smith's complicated idea of the role of history in moral theory. The situation has the appearance of a pleasant paradox, for while Smith has stacked the cards so thoroughly in favour of subjectivism that he has to produce a sophisticated socio-historical theory in order to cope with the facts of social morality – and in the end also with the ideal morality of the impartial spectator – Stewart's optimistic objectivism in morals leads him to put the full explanatory burden on the moral powers of the subject.

7.3   Knowledge and social progress

Adam Smith saw the modern commercial world as fundamentally different from the ancient and medieval worlds, and indeed from all other civilizations, in a number of respects. At the core of this novelty was the fact that modern society was based on free labour and thus on a much more thorough-going market economy than any previous society. This again was made possible by the creation of a strict legal system, protecting individual rights and presupposing for its administration the existence of strong government. But in Smith's preoccupation with the characteristics of modernity there is never any suggestion of a particular 'break' or leap in history – past, present, or possible – brought about by a change in the forces which shape the historical process. Smith's picture is that of an ongoing, ever more complicated social environment which we have to understand historically.

Stewart's idea of the novelty of the modern world goes much further. Although he admits the importance of all the factors stressed by

Smith and others,[15] he considers it his special contribution to point out and explain the one element that was rapidly transforming the very stuff of which history was made, namely the growth and spread of knowledge, which was altering all moral relationships, and thus changed the basis for the most central political and social institutions. The explanation for this new development is the invention of the printing press: 'Among all the circumstances . . . which distinguish the present stage of mankind from that of ancient nations, the invention of printing is by far the most important; and, indeed, this single event, independently of every other, is sufficient to change the whole course of human affairs.'[16] So radical is this break in the historical development that it effectively makes it impossible for us to learn anything from history that is of any use for our understanding of the forces which are shaping the future. These forces, preeminently the dissemination and growth of knowledge due to printing, 'render the condition of the human race essentially different from what it ever was among the nations of antiquity, and . . . of consequence, render all our reasonings concerning their future fortunes, in so far as they are founded merely on their past experience, unphilosophical and inconclusive.'[17] And, to anticipate a theme for later discussion, it should be pointed out that this of course means that statesmen cannot find principles to guide them in the past but have to 'search for the rules of their conduct chiefly in the peculiar circumstances of their own times, and in an enlightened anticipation of the future history of mankind'.[18] This explicit rejection of history, which we had already been led to expect from our analysis of Stewart's theory of moral judgement, will later be seen to be further supported by a number of methodological considerations. But for the moment we must pursue the view we have attained of two of the most powerful elements in his social thought, a cognitivist theory of morality, according to which moral behaviour is a matter of knowledge; and a kind of sociology of knowledge, according to which knowledge is becoming increasingly available to mankind.

As already mentioned, the printing press functions in two directions, 'in securing and accelerating the progress of knowledge' and 'in facilitating the diffusion and dissemination of knowledge among the lower orders'. As far as the former is concerned, printing simply gives knowledge a much more durable form, and in doing so, it also aids

15 See *Elements of the Philosophy of the Human Mind*, 3 vols. (1792; hereafter *Elements*), in *Works*, vols. II–IV, vol. II, p. 242; *Pol. Econ.*, VIII, pp. 31–3. In the *Lectures on Political Economy* Stewart repeatedly contrasts the modern with the ancient world in connection with such topics as slavery, wealth, and education.

16 *Elements*, II, p. 242; cf. *Diss.*, I, pp. 500ff., and *Pol. Econ.*, IX, pp. 397–9.

17 *Elements*, II, p. 242.   18 *Elements*, II, p. 223.

the division of intellectual labour, making it more and more international and world-wide. These considerations give Stewart occasion to
put forward a theory of the objectivity, or non-psychological and non-
subjective character of knowledge. This objectivity again leads to
steady progress towards truth by the elimination of error – an optimism which Stewart rather pointedly illustrates by Europe's, and especially Scotland's, rapid transformation of superstition into what are
supposed to be just views of the divine arrangements.[19] That this has
more to do with Stewart's change of Smith's science of legislation into
'political economy' than immediately occurs to the modern reader remains to be seen.

The spread of knowledge to the people at large presupposes that the
people have at least their most basic material needs provided for. It can
therefore take place only in a modern society where the growing market economy increasingly diffuses wealth; and the spread of knowledge again sustains the market society by helping to render individuals effective agents in the market. Furthermore, the institutional
arrangement of leaving the press free of censorship is a necessary
prerequisite, as Britain's proud example showed. The most important
means of conveying knowledge to the people were, in Stewart's opinion, the periodical press and the pamphlet literature, but before everything else and presupposed by everything else, an elementary school
system such as the Scottish parochial schools constituted. The provision of such a system was among the most important duties for a
government, though Stewart is deliberately non-committal about the
extent to which the content of education should be regulated by the
government.[20]

There are three important aspects of this education of the people: its
background in moral psychology, its cognitive content, and its momentous political and social consequences. The psychology of moral education[21] is, according to Stewart, a matter of the development of certain
cognitive abilities and is thus completely parallel with our education to
reason about theoretical matters. There is an innate capacity, or natural
faculty, which is brought out partly by direct instruction and partly by
the practice of a common social life. But although this faculty is common to humankind, it cannot be expected that it will have the same
degree of excellence in all individuals, and even those who have the

19   *Diss.*, I, pp. 503–10; *Pol. Econ.*, IX, pp. 338–41.
20   *Diss.*, I, pp. 510–15; *Pol. Econ.*, VIII, p. 54.
21   The following remarks are primarily based upon *Elements*, II, pp. 57–76;
Diss., I, pp. 515–23; *Powers*, VII, pp. 361–66; *Pol. Econ.*, VIII, pp. 48–56, and IX,
pp. 327–49.

most superior abilities to reason about moral matters will often be deficient in moments of action. It is therefore important that moral education, like other education, takes advantage of the laws of association in the human mind by simply inculcating moral truth while the mind is still tender and in the process of forming its associative patterns, leaving it to later intellectual development to support by reason that which has been instilled by authority. Stewart's perspective is that thanks to the growth of moral knowledge we now have much more of the truth to dispense, and thanks to the printing press we have the means, not only of impressing it on young minds in the making but also of following it up by further education for ever-broader segments of the population.

Stewart is always emphatic that the moral educability of the human mind, far from supporting what he takes to be Mandeville's denial of the reality and permanency of moral abilities, in fact provides some proof of this, and he takes this to be in itself an important moral lesson against scepticism.[22] But although this undoubtedly is too philosophical for the common mind, the most important object of moral education is clearly to inculcate an understanding of the relationship between private happiness, morally right conduct, and public happiness. Stewart argues first, much in the style J.S. Mill later adopted, that the generally educated mind is susceptible to a higher kind of happiness than the uneducated mind, and second, that the highest kind of individual happiness arises, not from behaviour which has happiness as its immediate aim but as an inherent by-product of behaviour which aims at moral correctness. Third, and crucially, he argues that there is a complete coincidence between private happiness understood in this way and public happiness; that we can *know* that this is the case, thanks to the modern science of political economy; and that the most important goal of education is to convey this knowledge. Often Stewart puts his point negatively by saying that the task of education and enlightenment is to dispel all prejudices which exaggerate the role which the pursuit of self-interest plays in human happiness.[23]

According to Stewart, one of the noblest tendencies of learning is to give the mind a liking for generalizations and abstractions in preference to particular things and events. This is nowhere more important than in our understanding of human society, for society is pre-eminently an abstract order, and to the extent that we understand it as

22 *Elements,* II, pp. 67–71.

23 *Diss.,* I, pp. 515–18; *Outlines,* VI, paras. 172 and 443–4; *Powers,* VII, pp. 223–6 (esp. p. 224) and VI, pp. 362–6; *Pol. Econ.,* IX, pp. 347–9.

such, to that extent we shall see ourselves and our particular circumstances through that order as parts of it.

> It is from this tendency of philosophical studies to cultivate habits of *general-
> ization*, that their chief utility arises; accustoming those who pursue them to
> regard events, less in relation to their own immediate and partial concerns,
> than to the general interests of the human race; and thus rendering them at
> once happier in themselves, and more likely to be extensively useful in the
> discharge of their social duties.[24]

To see that society is such an abstract order involves an understanding
that it is not the particular creation of some assignable individual or set
of individuals but that it is the unintended result of the interaction
between the individual members of the society in question.[25] With
regard to this relationship between individual element and over-all
order, there is a complete analogy between the moral and the physical
world. And Stewart takes this analogy one step further, for just as the
marvellous order in the material universe is proof of divine institution,
so is the no less wonderful order in the moral or social universe.

> A firm conviction . . . that the general laws of the moral, as well as of the
> material world, are wisely and beneficently ordered for the welfare of our
> species, inspires the pleasing and animating persuasion, that by studying
> these laws, and accommodating them to our political institutions, we may
> not only be led to conclusions which no reach of human sagacity could have
> attained, unassisted by the steady guidance of this polar light, but may
> reasonably enjoy the satisfaction of considering ourselves . . . as *fellow-
> workers with God* in forwarding the gracious purposes of his government. It
> represents to us the order of society as much more the result of Divine than
> of human wisdom; the imperfections of this order as the effects of our own
> ignorance and blindness; and the dissemination of truth and knowledge
> among all ranks of men as the only solid foundation for the certain though
> slow amelioration of the race.[26]

This teleological theme is very important to Stewart, not only because
he obviously believes that it is true but also because it provides a
religious aid in moral education which can supplement and, for weaker minds, even replace the more philosophical arguments.[27]

Apart from natural theology, the two important disciplines are,
however, 'moral philosophy' in the narrower sense, which explains the
character of true human happiness as consisting in right moral behaviour, and 'political economy', which Stewart sees as a special branch of
moral philosophy because its task is to explain the nature of public

---

24 *Diss.*, I, p. 520.   25   *Elements*, II, pp. 232 and 248.
26 *Diss.*, I, pp. 491–2; cf. *Elements*, II, p. 247; *Powers*, VII, pp. 120–60.
27 As we shall see later in this chapter, it has an even more fundamental role.

happiness and the connection between public and private happiness.[28] Stewart never offers an analysis of what he means by either private or public happiness, but whereas the former seems to be taken in very broad, common-sense terms about which little can be said, the latter clearly must mean something like the maximum compatibility which can be established among individuals in their pursuit of happiness.[29] This means that public happiness is a matter of order among individuals, and hence we have Stewart's vague idea of the moral importance of that intellectual discipline which explains the nature and possibility of such order, namely political economy. If we add to this the theological perspective mentioned earlier, that this possible social order is of divine ordination, we can see why Stewart talks of a natural social system as a directive ideal for humankind in general and for statesmen in particular.

> To delineate that state of political society to which governments may be expected to approach nearer and nearer as the triumphs of philosophy extend, was, I apprehend, the leading object of the earliest and most enlightened patrons of the economical system [i.e. the physiocrats and Adam Smith]. It is a state of society which they by no means intended to recommend to particular communities, as the most eligible they could adopt at present; but as an ideal order of things, to which they have a tendency of themselves to approach, and to which it ought to be the aim of the legislator to facilitate their progress. In the language of mathematicians, it forms a *limit* to the progressive improvement of the political order; and, in the meantime, it exhibits a standard of comparison by which the excellence of particular institutions may be estimated.[30]

When we return to this last point we should remember that, by teaching that society is a sui generis order spontaneously emerging from the activity of individuals, the political scientist is at the same time showing that this order or system is not a political creation and that political

28 *Powers*, VII, pp. 364–6.

29 See *Elements*, III, pp. 354–7; *Powers*, VI, pp. 224–5, and VII, pp. 235–6.

30 *Elements*, II, p. 236; cf. *Powers*, VI, p. 225, and *Account of the Life and Writings of Adam Smith, LL.D.*, (1793; henceforth *Life of Smith*) in *Works*, vol. X, pp. 5–98 at pp. 64–5. Stewart is using the term 'government' in a loose sense in *Elements*, II. It was only later, and possibly as a result of misunderstandings of this early work, that he made the sharp distinction between the theory of government and political economy one of his primary concerns – although it is clearly enough implied already in *Elements*, II. For Stewart's reaction to the political turmoil in the midst of which his first book appeared (in 1792), see the footnotes to the second edition of this work (1802), pp. 237 and 240–41 (in the edition used here); also *Life of Smith*, note G (to p. 53), p. 87; *Pol. Econ.*, VIII, pp. 306–8. Cf. John Veitch, *Memoir of Dugald Stewart*, in Stewart, *Works*, vol. X, pp. vii–clxxvii at p. l; and the letters printed in ibid., pp. cxix–cxxxvi.

activity is therefore the road neither to private nor to public happiness. This was not the least important part of moral teaching for Stewart, for it was exactly error in this regard that had led both the French Revolutionists and some of their British friends astray by making participation in the political process a condition for both private and public happiness. That separation of the political from the social which Stewart saw as an inherent part of progress should therefore be reinforced through education by simply creating as little interest in it as possible and by showing that the interest it might have is entirely secondary to that of political economy.[31] This latter point was further supported by some methodological differences between the two disciplines, as we shall see later.

Hitherto we have talked of education in quite general terms, without making any distinction between elementary literacy and more advanced intellectual work culminating in academic studies. Similarly, we have not pursued the difference between formal schooling and a general pursuit of knowledge and enlightenment. Although these distinctions are not of great significance for our understanding of those discussions of principles in Stewart with which we are dealing, it should be pointed out that Stewart was well aware of them, and particularly that he was realistic enough to see that for the foreseeable future only a minority of the population could be educated above fairly minimal standards, beyond which the authority of their betters and of religion would have to take over from reason. But he also thought that this trust in authority would be more forthcoming and firm when the mind had been broken in by *some* education. This being said, there is, however, no doubt at all that Stewart was immensely optimistic as to how far education could be pushed in both extent and depth, and part of his point seems clearly to be that what has been started by formal schooling will be continued by the general diffusion of knowledge by means of the printed word.[32]

Stewart was keenly aware that in preaching the power of knowledge he was attempting a self-fulfilling prediction, and he seemed to see this as an important rationale for his activity as an intellectual and, probably, as a public teacher. In the end this work was directly in the service of God, for although God's impression of order on the material universe was a natural fact, his plan for a social order based upon moral insight was a natural possibility which required the interposition of moral education. So, although the history of humankind hitherto

31 See esp. *Pol. Econ.*, VIII, pp. 20–9; and cf. Donald Winch's discussion of Stewart's reversal of the order of political economy and 'politics proper', i.e. the theory of government; 'The system of the north', pp. 37–8.

32 *Elements*, II, pp. 57–76; *Pol. Econ.*, VIII, 49–56, and IX, pp. 327–49.

had been the natural history of how social order has been maintained on the strength of prejudice – much as instinct has maintained order in the animal world – this would soon be changed into a no less natural, but now properly moral, history.[33] For it would become the history of how we, instead of being spectators of the passage of our past and present into the future, would be the makers of our own present and future.

> In enlightened ages . . . there cannot be a doubt that political wisdom comes in for its share in the administration of human affairs; and there is reasonable ground for hoping, that its influences will continue to increase, in proportion as the principles of legislation are more generally studied and understood. To suppose the contrary, would reduce us to be mere *spectators* of the progress and decline of society, and put an end to every species of patriotic exertion.[34]

As already indicated, this is not to be taken in the rationalistic sense that we should be able to construct our society according to some preconceived plan. Stewart is as critical as Hume and Smith of utopianism, simply because he, like them, believed that the matter of social life is far too intractable to be manipulated and too complicated to be known in sufficient detail.[35] His point is rather that we should be grafting onto the present social order, which is being maintained by a mixture of knowledge and prejudice, more and more knowledge of the future social order that would be maintained by moral insight. For it is such appreciation of the future that makes the future possible, by providing the very moral insight that will edge us spontaneously towards

33 *Elements*, II, 247; and 248–9: 'A great variety of prejudices might be mentioned, which are found to prevail universally among our species in certain periods of society, and which seem to be essentially necessary for maintaining its order, in ages when men are unable to comprehend the purposes for which governments are instituted. As society advances, these prejudices gradually loose their influence on the higher classes, and would probably soon disappear altogether, if it were not found expedient to prolong their existence, as a source of authority over the multitude. In an age, however, of universal and unrestrained discussion, it is impossible that they can long maintain their empire; nor ought we regret their decline, if the important ends to which they have been subservient in the past experience of mankind, are found to be accomplished by the growing light of philosophy. On this supposition, a history of human prejudices, as far as they have supplied the place of more enlarged political views, may at some future period, furnish to the philosopher a subject of speculation, no less pleasing and instructive than that beneficent wisdom of nature which guides the operations of the lower animals, and which even in our own species, takes upon itself the care of the individual in the infancy of human reason.' Also most of the final, fragmentary chapter of *Diss.*, I (pp. 487–523) is relevant here.

34 *Diss.*, I, pp. 191–2.   35 *Elements*, II, pp. 232–3; cf. *Life of Smith*, pp. 62–5.

it. Of course Stewart is not blind to the fact that legal and other institutional obstacles to progress have to be removed by political intervention, but he is always quick to warn against forcing matters and to stress the necessity of spontaneous or natural growth, and that is for him essentially a matter of knowledge.

What then more precisely is it that Stewart expects to happen as a result of the spread of moral enlightenment? At the most fundamental level, mere literacy will make it possible for man to expend excess energy in a more profitable manner than he otherwise can. Instead of shortening 'his hours in inaction with the agitations of gaming and the *delirium* of intoxication', elementary education will give the common man 'those early habits, which render some degree of intellectual exertion a sort of want or necessary of life'. And apart from directly preventing disorderly tendencies, such 'cultivation of mind . . . which books communicate, naturally inspires that desire and hope of advancement which, in all the classes of society, is the most steady and powerful motive for economy and industry'.[36]

Stewart, who viewed the ill effects of the division of labour with as much seriousness as did Smith, Ferguson, and Millar, thus sees education as the most immediate and obvious remedy for this problem. At the same time he also optimistically suggests that the problem leads to its own dissolution, since the division of labour promotes the invention of machinery, and this will in the end lead to a substitution of 'mechanical contrivances for manufacturing work'.[37]

It is not just the activity of learning but also, and more importantly, the content of learning which has its influence on the common mind:

> It is not merely as a resource against 'the pains and penalties of idleness' that habits of reading and of thinking are favourable to the morals of the lower orders. The great source of the miseries and vices which afflict mankind is in their prejudices and speculative errors; and every addition which is made to the stock of their knowledge has a tendency to augment their virtue and their happiness.[38]

And, as we already know, such knowledge will ideally consist in a growing insight into the coincidence of private and public happiness, mediated by morally right behaviour. The over-all effect of these developments will therefore be a radical change in the sources of social order. Instead of being created by more or less considered manipula-

36 *Diss.*, I, pp. 518–9.

37 *Pol. Econ.*, VII, pp. 329–31. Stewart's rhetoric about the workshop that eventually will become a completely automated engine has escaped the ridicule heaped upon Godwin's picturesque self-moving plough.

38 *Diss.*, I. p. 519.

tion of common prejudices, social order will spring immediately from the internal fount of our rational moral powers:

> Under all governments, even the most despotic, the superiority in point of physical force must belong to the multitude; but, like the physical force of the brutes, it is easily held in subjection by the reason and art of higher and more cultivated minds . . . In proportion as public opinion becomes enlightened, the voice of the people becomes the voice of reason; or, to use the old proverbial phrase, it becomes like the voice of God, unchangeable, irresistible, and omnipotent.[39]

It is partly as a result of this reasoning that Stewart reaches three important conclusions that are closely connected. First, and obviously – granted the premises – less and less legislation will be required as society progresses. Secondly, legislation will be on a safer intellectual footing than previously. And third, the power of governments will be more secure than ever before.[40]

That it requires less legislation to govern people whose individual self-government spontaneously forms a harmonious whole seems clear enough. But in order for it to become reality, it is necessary both that the legislators and statesmen understand this and that they have the courage to act on this understanding by entrusting more and more to the forces of the natural social system and to attempt less and less regulation by legislative means. As to the understanding of the connection between the individual's behaviour and the system, Stewart has few apprehensions, for – as he goes to paradoxically great lengths to explain – political economy has during the latter half of the eighteenth century developed so magnificently that it is now very close to a both complete and very simple explanation of this, the most important social phenomenon. In fact, Stewart thinks that it will be relatively easy to map out the natural system of society which, with its divine imprint, should form the ultimate, directive ideal for all changes to the present society. As to the courage and will of statesmen to change their ways, Stewart makes the point that this will simply become a necessity as they are dealing with an enlightened populace, purged of prejudice. Further, in so far as statesmen understand the new developments, they will also see that in a morally enlightened society the power of a government which is confined within the limits suggested by the morality of the people will be as secure as any government can be. The people will have an understanding of the necessity of such governance, based on insight into the connection between private and public happiness. As a result of the diffusion of knowledge through education and the printing press, and of the progress of knowledge in that most important branch of moral philosophy which Stewart calls 'political

39 *Diss.*, I, p. 524.   40 *Elements*, II, pp. 232–3.

economy' (and occasionally the 'science of legislation'), modern society will see less political activity than before and have government that will be more steady and secure against revolutionary upheavals than at any earlier period. Or, in Stewart's own words, the effect of this development will be to

> enlarge the basis of equitable governments, by increasing the number of those who understand their value, and are interested to defend them. The science of legislation . . . with all the other branches of knowledge which are connected with human improvement, may be expected to advance with rapidity; and, in proportion as the opinions and institutions of men approach to truth and to justice, they will be secured against those revolutions to which human affairs have always been hitherto subject.[41]

This development will have to be a natural one, in the sense that it cannot be deliberately constructed and centrally directed. On the other hand, it is by no means an historical inevitability, for it presupposes a moral enlightenment which culminates in a rational insight into itself as a possibility.[42] It is perfectly understandable that the first dawn of social enlightenment should lead many to err in the former respect and thus tempt them to become revolutionaries who prejudice the possibility of progress by upsetting the stability of society:

> When the economical system [i.e. the natural system of modern political economy] . . . is first presented to the mind, and when we compare the perfection which it exhibits with the actual state of human affairs, it is by no means unnatural that it should suggest plans of reformation too violent and sudden to be practicable.[43]

But although this is indeed extremely dangerous, as the excesses of the French Revolution so tragically illustrated, the answer is not to prevent enlightenment, for that might well provoke social upheavals by not supplying what progress demands. The only solution is more knowledge and a full understanding of the relationship between the particular circumstances of our present society and the natural system of a possible future. Stewart's theory of the watershed in modern history is supported by a number of methodological reflections on the study of politics which have been touched upon in the preceding and which must now be brought out more fully. At the same time this will also throw more light on his criticism of both conservative and revolutionary tendencies. Part of this criticism is that both these tendencies un-

---

41 *Elements*, II, pp. 243–4.

42 Cf. the fine discussion in H. Medick, *Naturzustand und Naturgeschichte der bürgerlichen Gesellschaft. Die Ursprünge der bürgerlichen Sozialtheorie als Geschichtsphilosophie und Sozialwissenschaft bei Samuel Pufendorf, John Locke und Adam Smith*, Göttingen, 1973, pp. 145–70.

43 *Elements*, II, p. 238; cf. *Diss.*, I, pp. 520–3.

derrate the power of spontaneous social forces and overrate the efficacy of political action – either to undertake change or to halt it. They
are, therefore, revealing ignorance not only of the modern science of
political economy but also of the traditional theory of government, and
this ignorance is owing to methodological naïveté. Stewart wants to
distinguish between two approaches to the study of political and social
matters:

> there are plainly two sets of political reasoners; one of which consider the
> actual institutions of mankind as the only safe foundation for our conclu-
> sions, and think every plan of legislation chimerical, which is not copied
> from one which has already been realized; while the other apprehend that,
> in many cases, we may reason safely *a priori* from the known principles of
> human nature combined with the particular circumstances of the times.[44]

His primary concern is to show that the study of politics should be of the
latter kind, that is, that it is properly a 'theoretical' study based simply
on observation of actual political forms of the past and the present. This
is brought out clearly in an interesting criticism of Machiavelli:

> the bent of Machiavel's mind seems to have disposed him much more
> strongly to combine and to generalize his historical reading, than to re-
> mount to the first principles of political science, in the constitution of human
> nature, and in the immutable truths of morality. His conclusions, according-
> ly, ingenious and refined as they commonly are, amount to little more (with
> a few very splendid exceptions) than empirical results from the events of
> past ages.[45]

The science of politics is, in other words, properly aiming at general
laws rather than accounts of particular phenomena, and the point behind this is, of course, that the former may provide us with some sort
of knowledge of the future, which the latter cannot do. This is so
because general explanations have no inherent reference to time; they
are equally concerned with past facts and with future 'facts':

> as the chemist, from his previous familiarity with the changes operated
> upon bodies by heat or by mixture, can predict the result of innumerable
> experiments, which to others furnish only matter of amusement and won-
> der; – so a studious observer of human affairs acquires a prophetic foresight
> . . . with respect to the future fortunes of mankind; a foresight which, if it
> does not reach, like our anticipations in physical science, to particular and
> definite events, amply compensates for what it wants in precision, by the
> extent and variety of the prospects which it opens. It is from this appre-
> hended analogy between the future and the past, that historical knowledge

44 *Elements*, II, p. 220; cf. III, pp. 330–5.
45 *Diss.*, I, p. 46. Cf. *Pol. Econ.*, VIII, p. 13: '[The Political Economist's] conclusions rest, not on the details of any particular art, but on the principles of human
nature, and on the physical conditions of the human race.'

derives the whole of its value; and were the analogy completely to fail, the records of former ages would, in point of utility, rank with the fictions of poetry.[46]

The negative part of Stewart's argument in effect takes the form of showing that an historical approach to the study of politics is fruitless; we cannot in a simple sense 'learn' from history, because the history of political society is largely our own theoretical construction and by no means the pure perception of facts of a political nature. What we may think of as facts are themselves theoretical constructions or interpretations: 'By far the greater part of what is called matter of fact in politics, is nothing else than theory; and very frequently, in this science, when we think we are opposing experience to speculation, we are only opposing one theory to another.'[47] This is so partly because of the sheer complexity of social phenomena, and partly because of the connected difficulty of capturing the full extent of social reality in language and conveying it to posterity or to people of another society. It is these rather modern ideas, which Stewart put forward in his earliest work, that explain why the history of social phenomena, according to him, had to be 'Theoretical or Conjectural', though in the now much better-known account in the *Life of Smith*, all he seems to be saying is that 'theories' or conjectures have to stand in when facts are missing in the historical record:

In [the] want of direct evidence, we are under a necessity of supplying the place of fact by conjecture; and when we are unable to ascertain how men have actually conducted themselves upon particular occasions, of considering in what manner they are likely to have proceeded, from the principles of their nature, and the circumstances of their external situation.[48]

The point is, however, that 'gaps' in history are not simply given but are relative to a theory of history, and 'facts', however many, do not by themselves add up to a coherent history. The history of man in society is thus not a magnificent natural fact which is given to us for our instruction but an intellectual puzzle for our construction. When we add these considerations to Stewart's idea of the decisive break between the past and the future in modern society and his theory of the structure of moral judgement, we can see why for him history lacks the kind of theoretical importance it had for Smith.

In his more positive ideas concerning the study of politics, Stewart explicitly follows the lead of Hume, arguing that general explanations of social phenomena, as of other phenomena, have to be based on 'determinate and known causes'. These causes are the permanent or

46 *Elements*, III, p. 163; cf. *Pol. Econ.*, VIII, pp. 30–1.   47 *Elements*, II, p. 224.
48 *Life of Smith*, X, pp. 33–4; cf. *Diss.*, I, pp. 69–70.

fixed features of the human mind that are known, which, to Stewart and his contemporaries, meant the basic needs, wants, and interests of man. Consequently, behaviour which arose from less permanent causes in the human mind and which might be the result of chance, and of the '"whim, folly, and caprice" of single persons',[49] could not – at least as yet – be given general explanations. Social explanations would therefore inevitably be concerned with certain general features of social situations, not with all details; they would be what has been called 'explanations of principle'.[50]

It is exactly these methodological ideas which are behind Stewart's argument that the theory of government, as opposed to political economy, is not yet a 'scientific' study but at best a collection of historical knowledge, aided by the classical taxonomic system of three pure types of government.[51] It is here important to know that by 'theory of government' Stewart means the theory of the *form* of government, for the *function* of government is of course an important part of what political economy explains. The form governments assume is, in Stewart's opinion, so completely dependent upon the particular circumstances of the country in question and upon the 'whim, folly and caprice of single persons' that it is not possible to find any 'determinate and known causes' which will explain any general future of them all. Here again Stewart finds support in Hume's authority, just as he follows him in the hope that the growth of knowledge may in the future extend to the theory of government. Or, in his own words in the *Dissertation*;

> Through the whole of this Discourse, I have avoided touching on the discussions which, on various occasions, have arisen with regard to the theory of government, and the comparative advantages and disadvantages of different political forms. Of the scope and spirit of these discussions it would be seldom possible to convey a just idea, without entering into details of a local or temporary nature, inconsistent with my general design. In the present circumstances of the world, besides, the theory of government (although, in one point of view, the most important of all studies) seems to possess a very subordinate interest to inquiries connected with political economy, and with the fundamental principles of legislation.[52]

There are thus in Stewart's opinion good methodological reasons for treating the theory of government as separate from and of secondary

49 *Elements*, II, p. 250, quoting Hume, 'Of the rise and progress of the arts and sciences', *Political Essays*, p. 59.

50 *Elements*, II, p. 222, and III, p. 165; cf. F.A. von Hayek, *Studies in Philosophy, Politics, and Economics*, London, 1967, ch. 1.

51 *Pol. Econ.*, IX, pp. 353–4, 413, and 420–1; *Elements*, II, pp. 397–8.

52 *Diss.*, I, 93, the note; cf. *Elements*, I, pp. 250–1.

importance to political economy. The latter point is connected with the idea mentioned earlier, that to give the theory of government its traditional prominence is tantamount to suggesting a dangerously exaggerated role for government. This idea of the sharp division between the broadly social and the narrowly political and the priority of the former over the latter is an often repeated and forcefully formulated theme in Stewart which we have already touched upon a number of times. The possibility of separating political from social life is, in Stewart's opinion, one of the main fruits of the progress of humankind. In so far as people fully understand this progress, they will see that the form of government is of little importance compared with what system of law and policy it follows, and they will appreciate the wisdom of Hume when he pointed out that the real aim is a 'government of laws, not of men', and that 'the vast apparatus of our Government' has 'ultimately no other object or purpose but the distribution of *justice,* or the *support of the twelve judges'*.[53] In his adoption of this Humean theme Stewart even goes so far as to quote Hume's panegyric on the achievements of the absolute monarchies of modern Europe with regard to the rule of law.[54] One of the most important results of the new scientific treatment of modern society, as opposed to the constitution-mongering of the philosophical tradition, is thus the understanding that 'the happiness of mankind' does not depend upon political participation in the 'enactment of laws' but on 'the equity and expediency of the laws that are enacted'. Stewart takes this as a healthy reversal of the priority of 'political liberty' over 'civil liberty' which had 'been so widely disseminated in Europe by the writings of Mr. Locke'.[55]

The endorsement of Hume's old thesis about the role of the political is supplemented by a couple of themes which are more peculiar to Stewart. He suggests that political freedom to take part in the legislative process ought to be valued only as a means to better legislation. This does not mean what it might at first suggest to the modern reader, for he goes on to maintain that political freedom can be exercised only by an intelligent and virtuous population – and that such qualities arise only under good laws.[56] Political freedom is, in other words, not in itself a vehicle for progress but one of the fruits of progress. It is therefore a mistake to aim at it for its own sake, for it is not constitutive

53   Hume, 'Of civil liberty', *Political Essays*, p. 56, quoted in *Pol. Econ.*, IX, p. 400; and Hume, 'Of the origin of government', *Political Essays*, p. 20, quoted in *Pol. Econ.*, IX, p. 22.

54   *Diss.*, I, pp. 46–7.

55   *Life of Smith*, X, pp. 54–6; *Pol. Econ.*, VIII, pp. 21–5, and IX, pp. 376 and 399–401.

56   *Life of Smith*, X, p. 55. By 'good laws' Stewart here means a 'natural order' of society.

of happiness and may lead to the opposite, if it is premature. But as intelligence and virtue are achieved, political activity will be just another of the exercises of our moral powers. When Stewart thus says that political freedom ought to be valued as a means to better legislation, his point is that in the fullness of time enlightened minds will be able to contribute to the search for the morally right legislation. So, although Stewart does not provide any anticipation of the Millian idea of the educational effect of politicial activity, he does suggest some political effect of education.

The form of government which might come about as a result of the steady progress of society is somewhat lost in the haze of Stewart's rhetoric. He does, however, suggest that a natural aristocracy is a fact among humankind and that the best constitution is the one in which the principles of monarchy and democracy are strong enough to temper the influence of the aristocracy.[57] The implication would seem to be that with the general spread of enlightenment, the democratic principle will grow in strength. This is supported by his general Humean principle, which we have noted, that political authority rests on opinion and has to adapt to opinion, even – or, perhaps, especially – when it changes into knowledge.[58] But the thing he always stresses most strongly is that political reformation must be slow, gradual, and a mere consequence of general progress, and that it is anyway of secondary importance.[59] Stewart obviously also thought that in the life of the individual the role of the political would dwindle in importance. He draws one of the contrasts between the ancient world, by which he means the ancient republics, and the modern commercial society which is in the making, by suggesting that in the former, men – free-

---

57 *Pol. Econ.*, IX, pp. 418–19: 'Since . . . there is in every society a natural aristocracy, arising partly from original inequalities among men, and partly from the influence of birth and fortune, in what manner shall the legislator avail himself of the assistance of those who compose it, and, at the same time, guard against the dangers to be apprehended from their uncontrolled authority? The answer seems obvious. Form that order of men who, from their situation in life, are most likely to comprehend the greatest number of individuals of this description, into a *senate* possessing no share of the executive power, and control their legislative proceedings by the executive magistrate, *on the one hand,* and by an assembly of popular representatives *on the other.* "The people without the senate," says Harrington, "would want wisdom; the senate without the people would want honesty."' Cf. also *Pol. Econ.*, VIII, p. 328, and VIII, p. 417, where it is pointed out – again in words that might have been George Turnbull's three-quarters of a century earlier – that these political arrangements are implied by 'the appearances of design in the human constitution'.

58 *Elements*, II, p. 233.

59 *Pol. Econ.*, IX, pp. 419–20; *Life of Smith*, X, pp. 55–6.

men, the only men that counted – lived a significant part of their lives
in politics, whereas in the latter, men are leading predominantly domestic and private lives, adding that this means lives in which women
play important, if not quite equal, roles. Consequently, although he
wants to avoid feminist 'absurdities' – meaning probably those of Godwin and Mary Wollstonecraft – we have to put very significant efforts
into educating the female intellect for its company with the male.[60]

7.4   *Jurisprudence and political economy*

The preceding account of the leading ideas in Stewart's moral and
political thought at length brings us to what he had to say about
jurisprudence, and since the theory of natural jurisprudence constituted the heart of Adam Smith's science of a legislator, the following
discussion will at the same time provide the focus for a closer comparison of Smith and Stewart. Stewart never put forward a separate theory
of natural jurisprudence; in fact he suggested that it would be a mistake to do so,[61] and our primary concern here is to account for this
significant difference from Smith. But though the difference is significant, it is at the same time strangely elusive and hard to formulate
clearly, not only because there are a number of things in common
between the two but also because Stewart often uses language which
tends to suggest that the common ground is more extensive than is in
fact the case.

At a very basic level Stewart is, of course, able to speak the language
of any natural law theory, namely that there is a notion of justice
among humankind which has certain natural and permanent features
and thus provides the basis for critical assessment of all positive law.[62]
Together with the Continental natural lawyers, with Hume, and with
Smith, he takes this to be the foundation for criticism of the Hobbesian
idea that we can ascribe 'moral distinctions . . . to the positive institutions of the civil magistrate'. But, like (the older) Hume and Smith, he
rejects the natural lawyers' attempt to combine the idea of natural
justice with the unhistorical, 'unscientific' idea of a state of nature.[63]

From the doctrine of natural justice it does not follow, however, that
there is an independent discipline of natural jurisprudence; and the
philosophical justification for such a doctrine can, furthermore, vary
extremely, being in Stewart's case the Common Sense moral theory
outlined earlier. But in his discussion of justice, Stewart explicitly says
that what 'properly forms the subject of that part of ethics which is

---

60   *Pol. Econ.*, VIII, pp. 55–6.   61   *Powers*, VII, p. 259.

62   For example *Diss.*, I, pp. 181–2, 183–4, 187. See also the panegyric on Bacon,
ibid., pp. 71–3.

63   *Diss.*, I, pp. 173–4.

called Natural Jurisprudence' is justice in the sense explained by Hume and Smith, namely the negative virtue which is distinct from all the other virtues in two respects:

> in the first place its rules may be laid down with a degree of accuracy of which moral precepts do not in any other instance admit. Secondly, its rules may be enforced, inasmuch as every breach of them violates the rights of some other person, and entitles him to employ force for his defence or security.[64]

It was, he suggests, the accuracy of justice which led natural lawyers to attempt to formulate it in fixed rules.[65] Stewart also strikes up a number of other natural law themes. Thus he tries to show that the right to individual property has a natural foundation in our recognition of the value of labour expended on the acquisition of property.[66] Similarly he maintains that there is a foundation in natural justice for testamentary succession, and he indicates a natural justice aspect to his criticism of the laws of entail and primogeniture in the same context.[67] Finally, when Stewart is dealing directly with Smith, we find him adopting Smithian principles with much firmness:

> It is evident . . . that the most important branch of political science is that which has for its object to ascertain the philosophical principles of jurisprudence; or (as Mr Smith expresses it) to ascertain 'the general principles which ought to run through and be the foundation of the laws of all nations.'[68]

It is therefore by no means clear that Stewart rejects the idea of natural jurisprudence in every sense of the word, despite his suggestion that it should not be dealt with as an independent discipline. What is clear is that he rejects what he takes to be the Continental lawyers' idea of a natural or universal code of law. Montesquieu and the Scottish school of social thinkers – especially Smith – had sufficiently taught him that law in the strict sense is an historical phenomenon.[69]

---

64 *Powers*, VII, p. 255; cf. *Diss.*, I, p. 175, and *Outlines*, VI, paras. 363–4.
65 *Powers*, VII, pp. 256–7; *Outlines*, VI, para. 370.
66 *Powers*, VII, 260–73. Stewart's argument is not entirely clear but seems to be similar to Smith's radical transformation of Locke's labour argument into a spectator theory. See Adam Smith, *Lectures on Jurisprudence*, ed. R.L. Meek, D.D. Raphael, and P.G. Stein, Oxford, 1978, LJ(A), i.37; 'Anderson Notes', in R.L. Meek, 'New light on Adam Smith's Glasgow lectures on jurisprudence', *History of Political Economy*, 8 (1976), 439–77 at 467–7; and K. Haakonssen, *The Science of a Legislator: The Natural Jurisprudence of David Hume and Adam Smith*, Cambridge, UK, 1981, pp. 106–7.
67 *Pol. Econ.*, VIII, pp. 204–10 and 197–204.
68 *Life of Smith*, X, p. 55; cf. *Diss.*, I. p. 72.
69 *Diss.*, I, pp. 69–70 and 188–93. Stewart discusses the natural lawyers in ibid., pp. 170–87. He has a very clear idea of the importance of natural law thinking for

Stewart's standpoint is perhaps best approached through a significant encounter with Bentham – and we are thus also hearing the voice of the future, so to speak:

> [Mr Bentham's] expressions . . . are somewhat unguarded, when he calls the Law of Nature 'an obscure phantom, which, in the imaginations of those who go in chase of it, points sometimes to manners, sometimes to laws, sometimes to what law is, sometimes to what it ought to be.' Nothing, indeed, can be more exact and judicious than this description, when restricted to the Law of Nature, as commonly treated of by writers on Jurisprudence; but if extended to the Law of Nature, as originally understood among ethical writers, it is impossible to assent to it, without abandoning all the principles on which the science of morals ultimately rests. With these obvious, but, in my opinion, very essential limitations, I perfectly agree with Mr Bentham, in considering an abstract code of laws as a thing equally unphilosophical in the design, and useless in the execution.[70]

In other words, there are fundamental moral principles which are natural to humankind and which ought to run through all systems of law, but which are not in themselves law; and the sound point in talking of natural jurisprudence is to draw attention to this. Put in such broad and general terms, Smith would certainly agree with Stewart's standpoint, but Smith's background for this was a distinctive theory of justice based on his idea of the impartial spectator, and the question is whether Stewart had anything similar to fill his general principle.

For a start, it cannot escape our notice that although Stewart mentions Hume's and Smith's distinction between the negative virtue of justice and all the positive virtues and refers to precision and enforceability as the two distinguishing characteristics of justice, he never furnishes any theoretical explanation of this. Nor does he refer to Smith's explanation that injury and harm are universally recognized with greater certainty and reacted to with greater force than their opposites and that consequently the virtue which protects against the former is on a much more secure and permanent footing than those which endorse the latter. This mere omission on Stewart's part may not in itself seem significant – although omissions generally may be more significant in an author who repeats his central doctrines in work after work – but it does lead us to speculate how he could have accounted for the distinction within his own moral philosophy. And it is far from evident that he could, for in his theory, the virtues consist in doing actions which have certain natural qualities of one moral colour or another, and presumably justice and all the other moral qualities must

---

the development of the Scottish school of social thought; cf. H. Medick, *Naturzustand und Naturgeschichte*, pp. 145–70 and 305–13.

70 *Diss.*, I, p. 187, quoting Jeremy Bentham, *An Introduction to the Principles of Morals and Legislation*, ed. J.H. Burns and H.L.A. Hart, London, 1970, p. 298.

be equally natural to or inherent in their respective actions. They may of course not be equally easy to know; but if we assumed that to be Stewart's intention in distinguishing between the negative virtue of justice and the positive virtues, then we would be looking for some indication as to whether it is an epistemological point or simply a report on the actual state of our knowledge. If it were to be taken as the former, we would be looking for a theory to the effect that it is somehow inherent in our moral knowledge that we know more about, or know with more certainty about, the negative virtue – which is Smith's point. But not only does Stewart not give us any such theory; all indications are in the opposite direction. If on the other hand Stewart's point in adopting the distinction is to report that humankind at the moment in fact knows more – or with more certainty – about justice than about the other virtues and thus to imply that this may well be different in the future, as moral enlightenment spreads, then he has drastically altered Smith's distinction, and it is difficult to see that justice in particular should distinguish a special sub-division of moral philosophy called 'natural jurisprudence'.

Stewart is anything but lucid in these matters, and it is quite likely that he is simply confused about the different implications of Smith's spectator-based moral philosophy and his own common-sense theory. It is, however, clear that the latter of the proposed readings of his adopted distinction fits in with his often repeated message about the great progress which knowledge has begun and will continue to make in the world. At the same time it finds general confirmation in his tendency to speak as if all our moral duties are derived with equal immediacy from human nature. And it is also of interest to notice that Stewart's overture to accepting Hume's and Smith's distinction between justice and the positive virtues is to emphasise that this applies only to one special meaning of 'justice' and that the concept also has a positive side (which can be identified with 'candour').[71] Much more important, however, is his criticism of Hume's well-known thesis that justice is an artificial virtue, in the sense that it does not have direct reference to motives which form an inherent or natural part of the human frame, but depends for its reality on the interaction of individuals in social groups.[72] Smith's spectator theory had entirely by-passed this issue: for him, all the virtues were equally 'artificial' (or equally

71 *Outlines*, VI, paras. 358–62; *Powers*, VII, pp. 243–4, 248–54.

72 D. Hume, *A Treatise of Human Nature: Being an Attempt to Introduce the Experimental Method of Reasoning into Moral Subjects*, ed. L.A. Selby-Bigge, 2nd ed. rev. by P.H. Nidditch, Oxford, 1978, III.3.1; and *Enquiries Concerning Human Understanding and Concerning the Principles of Morals*, ed. L.A. Selby-Bigge, 3rd ed. rev. by P.H. Nidditch, Oxford, 1975, second *Enquiry*, III.2. Cf. Haakonssen, *Science of a Legislator*, pp. 21–6. Stewart's criticism is in *Outlines*, VI, paras. 365–7, and *Powers*, VII, p. 255.

'natural'), in the sense that they all arose from interpersonal, 'social'
(spectator-induced) modifications of natural motives and passions and
reached their perfection from the modification induced by the ideal
impartial spectator. For Smith, the special character of justice thus centred only on its negativity and all that that involved. But Smith's way of
arguing is lost on Stewart, who goes directly back to Hume's argument,
maintaining that justice and the virtue of benevolence – the archetypal
positive virtue – are equally natural to humankind because they both
depend on a direct understanding of two natural qualities. 'So far . . .
as benevolence is a virtue, it is precisely on the same footing with
justice; that is, we approve of it, not because it is agreeable to us, but
because we feel it to be a duty.'[73]

It seems difficult to find any raison d'être for Smith's distinction
between justice and all the other virtues – and thus for his original idea
of a new natural jurisprudence of sorts – in Stewart's moral philosophy. This is entirely borne out by a consideration of what Stewart had –
and did not have – to say about law. It is a significant fact that Stewart
never in any way indicates that he wants to distinguish between laws
of justice and laws with some other moral foundation. This is not to say
that he did not recognize the usual divisions of the law; only that he
did not present any philosophical rationale for this. Smith, on the other
hand, had an elaborate theory of the division of law into laws of justice,
on the one hand and, on the other, such laws as those of 'police,
revenue, and arms', which were based on considerations of public
utility. This is clearly illustrated by the case of the law relating to
marriage – the enforcement of monogamy and prohibition of polygamy. Although Smith and Stewart were in agreement that it was necessary to have such law, Smith was quite explicit that this was not a
matter of justice but purely of public utility.[74] Stewart, on the other
hand, not only does not make any such distinction but explicitly argues
that the moral values protected by the marriage laws are as much part
of the arrangement of nature as the justice which is protected by the
laws of several property:

> marriage . . . is the result (in the first instance) of that order of things which
> nature herself has established; and the proper business of the legislator is
> here, as in other cases, limited to the task of seconding and enforcing her
> recommendations, by checking the deviations from her plan which are occa-
> sioned by the vices and follies of individuals. The fact is precisely similar
> with respect to *Property*. The idea of property is not created by municipal

73 *Powers*, VII, p. 255.

74 For Smith's arrangement of the law, see LJ(A), i.1–26 and LJ(B), 1–11. Concerning marriage, see LJ(A), iii. 23–48 and LJ(B), 111–17; cf. Haakonssen, *Science of a
Legislator*, pp. 124–5.

laws. On the contrary, one of the principal circumstances which suggested the necessity of laws and magistrates, was to guard against those violations to which the property of the weak was found to be exposed amidst the turbulence of barbarous times. It is with great propriety, therefore, that Horace classes these two *objects* of law together, the preservation of property and the protection of the marriage bed; – objects, however, which so far from being the *creatures* of municipal institutions, may be justly considered as the chief *sources* from which municipal institutions have taken rise . . . They are indeed the two great pillars of the political fabric, and whatever tends to weaken them, threatens, we may be assured, the existence of every establishment essential to human happiness.[75]

Despite all that Stewart had learnt from Hume and Smith about social evolution, he is here operating with a rather simplistic dichotomy between the natural and the positively instituted which is reminiscent of – and perhaps echoes – the early Mandeville and which hardly does justice to his implied opponent and thereby to the argument.[76] Thus Smith would certainly agree with Stewart that marriage is not a deliberate institution but has a foundation in moral values which people come to subscribe to for natural reasons. But this does not mean that these reasons, unaided by positive law, will have the same degree of uniformity in any given society or historical period, as will the reasons for protecting individual rights; nor does it mean that people will react with the same natural certainty to deviations from the moral values embedded in marriage as they do to infringements of the individual rights protected by rules of justice. Part of Smith's point here is, of course, that the latter cases concern the rights of other people, whereas the former cases are about the agents' own moral values – assuming that all the parties to whatever deviation we are talking about (e.g. polygamy) are acting voluntarily.[77] Without implying that marriage as such is entirely factitious, Smith can therefore argue that the reasons for settling a particular form of marriage by law must derive from considerations of public utility (or 'expediency') and that they are therefore quite different from the reasons behind laws of justice, such as those protecting private property. This line of argument is closed to Stewart by his Common Sense moral philosophy, which saw all moral attributes as equally natural qualities in human actions.

Although Stewart thus, as we should expect, preserves the general idea that law is founded on a morality which is natural to humankind, he abolishes Smith's idea of a distinctive discipline of natural jurisprudence based on the peculiar features of the negative virtue of justice.

75   *Pol. Econ.*, VIII, pp. 79–80. The whole discussion of marriage, pp. 67–82, and of polygamy, pp. 82–92, is relevant.

76   Cf. Stewart's general discussion of Mandeville in *Powers*, VI, pp. 264–73.

77   See Smith, LJ(A), iii. 23–5, and LJ(B), 111–12.

This lack of distinction is behind his idea of one all-encompassing socio-political science, for which, as mentioned earlier, he wants to adopt the label 'political economy', despite its traditionally narrow reference to wealth and population:

> I think that the same title may be extended with much advantage to all those speculations which have for their object the happiness and improvement of Political Society, or, in other words, which have for their object the great and ultimate *ends* from which political regulations derive all their value; and to which *Wealth and Population* themselves are to be regarded as only subordinate and instrumental. Such are the speculations which aim at ascertaining those fundamental Principles of Policy, which Lord Bacon has so significantly and so happily described, as 'Leges Legum, ex quibus informatio peti possit, quid in singulis Legibus bene aut perperam positum aut constitutum sit.'[78]

The contrast between Smith's jurisprudence-based science of a legislator and Stewart's reconstituted 'political economy' can be taken even further if we consider Stewart's handling of the Smithian theme of justice and 'expediency' – or 'public utility', since 'expedient' measures seem to be those which promote public utility. Stewart is also here more inclined to be sanguine and often speaks of 'public happiness'. In Smith's work as a whole – not just *The Wealth of Nations* – 'public utility' is a complex notion which is never clearly analysed, but it can be said that the publicly useful is the aggregate of everything which will tend to safeguard the maximum pursuit of private interest by each individual citizen in the long run. It is therefore in a sense a *means* to private interest or utility, which is the *end* – but an end the content or character of which is never specified, as it was by later hedonistic utilitarianism: it is for Smith a strictly individual or private matter. This very nature of individual happiness does, however, mean that a utilitarian approach to politics is impossible; according to Smith, we simply cannot know enough to make a simple aggregation of happiness the general criterion for policy. Commonly all we can do is to try to secure the individual in the pursuit of his own happiness as he sees it, and that means protecting his individual rights – which is exactly what the moral primacy of justice points out as our duty anyway. In this loose sense, therefore, public utility and justice can well be said to coincide, but it should be quite obvious that this does not mean that measures of justice will always be of public use in all respects in all societies, or that

---

78   *Pol. Econ.*, VIII, p. 10, quoting Bacon *De fontibus juris*, Aphor. 6; it means, 'Laws of laws from which we can determine what is right or wrong in the appointments of each individual law.' See Stewart, *Works*, XI, p. 2. Cf. *Pol. Econ.*, VIII, pp. 57–8, and II, p. 22.

the publicly useful will be in all respects just or of direct relevance for questions of justice.

To take the former first, it is certainly just and – as it is Smith's particular pride to show – at the same time overwhelmingly useful to enforce the strict system of law which makes possible a market economy in commercial society. But, as it is also his concern to show, this does sometimes in some societies lead to disutility in certain areas, such as defence and the intellectual development of the poor.[79] Accordingly, special policies motivated by public utility may have to be adopted in these and other areas. As to the reverse situation, Smith maintains, for instance, that it is necessary for the social fabric of modern Europe that monogamous marriage be legally enforced but yet makes it clear, as we saw earlier, that this is not prescribed by natural justice. Further, public works, like harbours and bridges, may well be of great public utility by facilitating modes of behaviour which would otherwise not have been possible, but their relevance to issues of justice is rather indirect – as long as they are not paid for out of taxes.[80]

The relationship between justice and utility in Smith is thus inherently complex. In the narrowly economic field he is confident that he can show that they may closely coincide at that time and in that type of society. But the pursuit of just this kind of policy leads to problems in other areas. Although he is fairly optimistic that these problems might be solved without infringement of the fundamental rules of justice, he is certainly not issuing any guarantee on behalf of God, History, or Nature – whether severally or as a trinity. The history of human society is open-ended for Smith, not in the sense that we can do as we like with it – all his work was concerned to show the nature of the forces within which we have to act – but in the sense that it has openings for a diversity of developments, and human wisdom and folly will play their roles alongside other factors in determining which course is taken.

Turning to Stewart, we again find a good deal of the language and concerns to be those of Smith, so much so that the first impression may well be that of a Smithian turned overly optimistic. The point is, however, that there are philosophical reasons for Stewart's optimism and that these in effect amount to a significant break with Smith. For a start, it should be noticed that Stewart operates with the two notions of justice and expediency (or utility) as the possible foundations for policies and laws. Thus, 'It was preserved for modern times to investigate

79   A. Smith, *An Inquiry into the Nature and Causes of the Wealth of Nations*, ed. R.H. Campbell and A.S. Skinner, Oxford, 1976, V.i.f.

80   Ibid., V.i.c–e.

those universal principles of justice and of expediency, which ought under every form of government, to regulate the social order.'[81] But the ease with which Stewart mentions the two together in the same breath, and the surprising idea of 'universal principles' not only of justice but also of expediency arrest the attention and make one wonder about the significance of the distinction for him. Since measures of expediency, by their very nature, must be aimed at taking care of particular exigencies of particular societies at particular times, it is questionable how much sense it makes to talk of universal principles behind them, but it may well make more sense in a situation where we have a 'universal' social order. This, combined with the normative mode which Stewart applies, gives us our clue; he is talking of the great social order that can be in the future, the natural system which will gradually unfold with the growth and spread of knowledge.

Stewart is undoubtedly well aware that in society as it is, the relationship between justice and utility is complicated, but the belief that the two will increasingly coincide is at the heart of the social progress which he envisages. This natural system will become a more and more universal social order, for not only will it unite existing societies internally by breaking down – however slowly – such divisions as hereditary orders, but it will also unite different societies into one great international social order.[82] This optimism of Stewart's sets him apart from Smith simply by its supreme confidence, a confidence which is never obscured by all his warnings against precipitate actions to speed up the natural course of events, his encouragement to gradualism, merely to 'clearing the way'. The real difference from Smith is, however, Stewart's doctrine that we now know that society can develop into the natural system and, indeed, that it will so develop, since human folly can only delay it.

> What else is wanting, at this moment, to the repose and prosperity of Europe, but the extension to the oppressed and benighted nations around us, of the same intellectual and moral liberty which are enjoyed in this island? Is it possible, in the nature of things, that this extension should not, sooner or later, be effected? Nay, is it possible, (*now* when all the regions of the globe are united together by commercial relations,) that it should not gradually reach to the most remote and obscure hordes of barbarians? The prospect may be distant, but nothing *can* prevent it from being one day realized, but some physical convulsion which shall renovate or destroy the surface of our planet.[83]

81   *Life of Smith,* X, p. 54; cf. *Diss.,* I, pp. 71–3.
82   *Elements,* II, pp. 239, and 250–1.   83   *Diss.,* I, p. 490.

He arrives at this theory by superimposing the central element of his own Common Sense moral philosophy upon the methodological doctrines which he takes over from Hume:

> in proportion as these prospects, with respect to the progress of reason, the diffusion of knowledge, and the consequent improvement of mankind, shall be realized, the political history of the world will be regulated by steady and uniform causes, and the philosopher will be enabled to form probable conjectures with respect to the future course of human affairs. It is justly remarked by Mr Hume, that 'what depends on a few persons, is, in a great measure, to be ascribed to chance, or secret and unknown causes: what arises from a great number, may often be accounted for by determinate and known causes' . . . From these principles, it would seem to be a necessary consequence, that, in proportion as the circumstances shall operate which I have been endeavouring to illustrate, the whole system of human affairs, including both the domestic order of society in particular states, and the relations which exist among different communities, in consequence of war and negotiation, will be subjected to the influence of causes which are 'known and determinate'. Those domestic affairs, which, according to Mr Hume, are already proper subjects of reasoning and observation, in consequence of their dependence on general interests and passions, will become so more and more daily, as prejudices shall decline, and knowledge shall be diffused among the lower orders: while the relations among different states which have depended hitherto, in a great measure, on the 'whim, folly, and caprice' of single persons, will be gradually more and more regulated by the general interest of the individuals who compose them, and by the popular opinions of more enlightened times.[84]

For Hume and for Smith, the causes which were found to be 'determinate and known' from their recurrence in the generality of humankind were on the whole basic needs, wants, and interests; and this was the foundation for a scientific explanation of the economic and some of the more elementary political features of human society. But to these causes Stewart can foreshadow the addition of knowledge. Normally we tend to think that knowledge and ideas bring diversity rather than uniformity to human behaviour and thus make it more difficult to understand. But the kind of knowledge Stewart has in mind is naturally the moral knowledge we dealt with earlier, knowledge of the true moral qualities of actions, including their coincidence with private and public happiness. His point is, therefore, that moral knowledge makes human behaviour regular and thus subject to general explanation because it is knowledge of The Truth. For, as he says – ironically with a

84 *Elements,* II, pp. 249–50, quoting Hume, 'Of the rise and progress of the arts and sciences', in *Political Essays,* pp. 58–77 at p. 58.

quotation from Hume – 'Truth . . . is *one thing*, but errors are numberless, and every man has a different one.'[85]

Against this background it is hardly surprising to find Stewart declaring that it 'is easy for the statesman to form to himself a distinct and steady idea of the ultimate objects at which a wise legislator ought to aim, and to foresee that modification of the social order to which human affairs have, of themselves, a tendency to approach'.[86]

Although Smith certainly thought it most important for the statesman and legislator to seek a systematic understanding of the social order and its possible development, he had no foundation for such confident claims to knowledge, and his taciturnity on the subject of the future does indeed seem nearly demonstrative. For him, men's moral judgement, and hence their behaviour, had an inherently historical and thus contingent element. But that point inevitably escaped Stewart, partly because of the nature of his moral philosophy and partly because he tended to see any reference to history in moral matters as nothing but prescriptive traditionalism in the style of vulgar Whiggism and Edmund Burke. This is particularly evident in his repeated insistence that the 'natural' or permanent foundation for law is to be found directly in the principles of human nature, not in the historical record.[87] It is true that in these contexts he often talks of human nature and 'its circumstances', but he never clarifies what that means or how it influences the operation of moral judgement, and he certainly never takes Smith's point that among 'the circumstances' are inescapable historical elements.

Stewart has turned Smith's science of a legislator into a science of the possible – and more than just possible – future but in so doing has shifted the focus from the individual moral agent to the moral system of which the former is a part, and he has transformed the normative issue from the justice of individual human action to the goodness of the whole system. This may not be immediately evident, for from one point of view Stewart is, of course, the complete individualist. It is the morally well-informed behaviour of individual members of society which will make up the natural order of society, and it would therefore seem obvious that it is the moral rightness of such behaviour which justifies that system. But although this is quite true, the perspective changes rather drastically once we realize that the morally right action coincides with the publicly useful, the action which contributes to the system, and that it is part of the moral enlightenment of people to make them see this. This makes it intelligible why Stewart is never very clear about where the ultimate ground of justification lies, for it raises

85   *Powers*, VII, p. 212; cf. *Diss.*, I, p. 524.   86   *Elements*, II, pp. 230–1.
87   See e.g. *Pol. Econ.*, VIII, pp. 69–72, 86, 91–2; *Powers*, VII, pp. 260–73.

the possibility that it is not the moral rightness of individual actions which justifies the natural system but that the latter provides some sort of justification for the former, and consequently we are faced with the question of what could provide some independent justification of the natural system itself.

This is where Stewart's religious views play a significant role. He always makes it clear that he sees not only the physical but also the moral world in teleological terms. There is a benevolent design of divine origin which is slowly unfolding as humankind progresses, and this design provides the directive ideal which informs and justifies our individual actions.[88] The natural order of society which is described by political economy thus carries a divine imprint which makes it prescriptive for statesmen and legislators – but of course it is one of the most important aspects of the design, and thus of the prescription, that it will unfold itself spontaneously, not by the deliberate planning and construction of humanity.

Stewart held his teleological views strongly and gave lengthy teleological arguments for the existence of God.[89] He did distinguish, however, between final and efficient causation, and he quotes Smith's criticism of the confusion between the two to support this. But instead of drawing the conclusion which Smith drew, namely that explanation by means of final causes is vacuous, Stewart maintains that the two kinds of causes are equally valid explanatory principles, as long as they are not confused – although he himself tends to speak of efficient causes in teleological terms, as means or tools in the over-all design of the universe. He blames Smith for inconsistently using teleological language despite his criticism of teleological explanations, thus showing that he misses Smith's point, namely that although there is a natural tendency in the human mind to view things teleologically, this cannot be sustained by rational explanatory principles. It is therefore hardly surprising that when Smith speaks of 'the natural course of things' in society, Stewart takes this to mean that we have to understand it as a divinely instituted design of things and quotes it as identical with the view of Quesnay: 'Ces lois forment ensemble ce qu'on appelle la loi naturelle. Tous les hommes et toutes les puissances humaines doivent être soumis à ces lois souveraines, instituées par l'Etre Suprème: Elles sont immuables et irréfragables, et les meilleures lois possibles.'[90] But of course Smith's whole concern was to explain social

---

88 *Diss.*, I, pp. 489–92; *Elements*, II, p. 247; *Powers*, VII, pp. 120–60.

89 *Powers*, VII, pp. 12–160; *Outlines*, VI, paras. 252–315; cf. *Elements*, III, pp. 335–7.

90 *Powers*, VII, pp. 106–7; 'These laws make up what is called the law of nature. All men and all human powers must be subject to these sovereign laws instituted by

order without having recourse to design; and whether or not we should take order as evidence of design was a question the answer to which he left obscured by a haze of conventional and ambiguous language.

The idea that the natural order with its divine backing has some sort of moral primacy over the behaviour of individuals shows how close Stewart is to the mainstream of Scottish moral thought in the Enlightenment and how distant he is from Hume and Smith. This significant difference from Smith sheds light over the fate of his science of a legislator and, particularly, of the natural jurisprudence on which it centred. For Smith the fundamental moral problem of social significance was that of the justice of individual actions, and the discipline which dealt with this problem, namely natural jurisprudence, was therefore both the connecting link between fundamental moral philosophy and all social and political studies, and also the organizing principle for the latter. But once the crucial moral problem in society becomes that of the relationship between individual actions and an over-all order, the moral goodness of which is divinely assured, the organizing principle for all study naturally becomes this order, and Stewart saw his 'political economy' as the all-encompassing discipline which would study the natural order as a whole.

> Although the obligations of Justice are by no means resolvable into considerations of Utility, yet in every political association they are so blended together in the institutions of men, that it is impossible for us to separate them completely in our reasonings . . . It seems, therefore, to be proper, instead of treating of jurisprudence merely as a system of natural justice, to unite it with Politics, and to illustrate the general principles of justice and of expediency, as they are actually combined in the constitution of society. This view of the subject (which properly belongs to the consideration of man as the member of a political body) will show, at the same time, how happily these principles coincide in their application.[91]

The consequence is that the study of justice and of its institutionalization in the legal establishments becomes a subordinate part of this new total study of public and private happiness and their coincidence. The study of law will remain an especially significant, although dwindling part, for the immediate future,[92] but it will nevertheless be subordinate to the wider vistas of 'political economy'.

---

the Supreme Being. They are immutable and irrefutable and the best possible laws.' See pp. 102–4 for the preceding.

91 *Powers*, VII, p. 259.   92 See *Diss.*, I, pp. 191–2.

8

The science of a legislator in James Mackintosh's moral philosophy

8.1 *Adam Smith and Dugald Stewart*

Paying tribute to Dugald Stewart's work during his tenure of the Chair of Moral Philosophy at Edinburgh, Sir James Mackintosh remarked that 'Without derogation from his writings, it may be said that his disciples were among his best works.'[1] This parallel is no less accurate for being drawn by one who might well be considered a disciple himself. For just as Stewart produced a substantial philosophical oeuvre which in its main lines derives from that of Thomas Reid, so too he decisively influenced a large number of men who must all, in varying degrees, be characterized as intellectual epigoni. Although Stewart and his circle produced few new and original ideas, they nevertheless deserve some attention, not just because of their influence but also because of an intellectually interesting pattern to their eclecticism, an understanding of which is necessary for an appreciation of the precise nature of their influence.

It is with this pattern of thought – or at least an example of it – that I am concerned here, not with the question of their influence. The latter is fairly well known and documented – how they created the *Edinburgh Review*; influenced the Whig Party and, beyond that, liberal politics in the nineteenth century; were involved in the making of the Reform Act of 1832; contributed to the spread of educational institutions, ranging from Lancastrian schools to London University.[2] The peculiar interest

---

1 James Mackintosh, *Dissertation on the Progress of Ethical Philosophy*, 2nd ed., Edinburgh, 1837, p. 345 (hereafter, *Dissertation*).

2 Concerning the *Edinburgh Review*, see J. Clive, *Scotch Reviewers: The "Edinburgh Review", 1802–1815*, London, 1957; and esp. B. Fontana, *Rethinking the Politics of Commercial Society: The "Edinburgh Review", 1802–1832*, Cambridge, UK, 1985. The fullest and most interesting impression of Scottish involvement is gained through the standard volumes of life and letters on all the main figures. The best general discussion of the Stewart circle is Donald Winch's chapter 'The system of the north: Dugald Stewart and his pupils', in S. Collini, D. Winch, and J. Burrow, *That Noble*

of the Stewart circle for the historian of philosophy, however, is that its members believed themselves to possess a philosophical basis for their public lives, and yet their philosophical enterprise – in contrast to their public works – has, until lately, all but disappeared from the scholarly debate. Much of their philosophizing is admittedly little but posturing and planning, with disappointingly little substance, even in the case of so able a mind as that of Francis Horner,[3] or, alternatively, merely an attempt to get 'a clear view of the next step, and a wise intention to take it',[4] as in the case of Henry Brougham. But even allowing for a good deal of both, it remains a fact that Dugald Stewart inspired his eminent students with a grand view of the structure and historical importance of human knowledge, the fate of which is worth investigating.

This quest for Stewart's legacy can be, and recently has been, approached in a number of different and to some extent complementary ways. As Nicholas Phillipson has stressed, a primary concern for Stewart was to make Reid's Common Sense philosophy socially effective by making it teachable to the potential leaders of society.[5] As Stewart saw

---

Science of Politics: A Study in 19th Century Intellectual History, Cambridge, UK, 1983, pp. 23–61. See also J.H. Hollander, 'The Founder of a School', in J.M. Clark et al., *Adam Smith, 1776–1926,* New York, 1966, pp. 22–52, esp. pp. 22–42. The relevant parts of the extensive literature on the formation of 'classical political economy' in the early decades of the nineteenth century are discussed in Fontana and in Collini, Winch, and Burrow. A valuable addition is a better understanding of Stewart's influence on the formation of a modern High Anglican political economy: P. Corsi, 'The heritage of Dugald Stewart: Oxford philosophy and the method of political economy', *Nuncius,* Fasc. 2 (1987), 89–144; and cf. A.M.C. Waterman, *Revolution, Economics, and Religion: Christian Political Economy, 1798–1833,* Cambridge, UK, 1991, and same, 'The nexus between theology and political doctrine in Church and dissent', in *Enlightenment and Religion,* ed. K. Haakonssen. Stewart's methodological legacy is also discussed in Neil di Marchi, 'The case for James Mill', in *Methodological Controversy in Economics: Historical Essays in Honour of T.W. Hutchison,* ed. A.W. Coats, New York, 1983, pp. 155–84.

3   This is not to detract from his contribution to the discussion of economic problems (see *The Economic Writings of Francis Horner in the "Edinburgh Review," 1802–6,* ed. F.W. Fetter, New York, 1957) or from his role in Parliament. The papers, journals, and letters printed in *The Horner Papers: Selections from the Letters and Miscellaneous Writings of Francis Horner, M.P., 1795–1817,* ed. K. Bourne and W. Banks Taylor, Edinburgh, 1994, give a good impression of the development of the mind behind the action. Cf. also the older collection, *Memoirs and Correspondence of Francis Horner, M.P., 1795–1817,* ed. Leonard Horner, 2 vols., London, 1843.

4   Walter Bagehot, 'The First Edinburgh Reviewers', in *The Collected Works of Walter Bagehot,* ed. Norman St. John-Stevas, 8 vols., London, 1965, I, p. 318.

5   I am here referring especially to Nicholas Phillipson, 'The Scottish Enlightenment', in *The Enlightenment in National Context,* ed. R. Porter and M. Teich, Cam-

it – and I am not here concerned with the adequacy of this reading – Reid's importance lay in having furnished the means of refuting David Hume's and Adam Smith's 'theory of ideas', which endangered human knowledge of both the physical and the moral world, not to speak of the providential guidance thereof. Reid's method of refuting scepticism and moral conventionalism was a painstaking piecemeal investigation of the intellectual and active powers of the mind, showing that they were capable of veridical apprehension of both physical and moral objects. There was therefore no reason for believing the world to be a mere veil of ideas nor for reducing the rules of behaviour to socially inculcated, historically variable maxims of propriety. In Phillipson's opinion, Stewart's main complaint against this Reidian philosophy was that it did not sufficiently stress the organic unity of the mind's intellectual and active powers. Consequently it failed to make clear that the effect of philosophizing could and should be a general culture of the mind, a *Bildung*,[6] consisting on the one hand of the command over the intellect exercised by a morally trained free will, and on the other of the intellectual enlightenment of the active powers which is possible because morals can be taught (and not just socially assimilated).[7]

---

bridge, UK, 1981, pp. 19–40 (esp. pp. 37–40), and 'The pursuit of virtue in Scottish university education: Dugald Stewart and Scottish moral philosophy in the Enlightenment', in *Universities, Society, and the Future*, ed. Nicholas Phillipson, Edinburgh, 1983, pp. 82–101. Phillipson's general interpretation of the Scottish Enlightenment as developed in a series of papers is also relevant: 'Adam Smith as civic moralist', in *Wealth and Virtue: The Shaping of Political Economy in the Scottish Enlightenment*, ed. Istvan Hont and Michael Ignatieff, Cambridge, UK, 1983, pp. 179–202; 'Culture and society in the 18th-century province: The case of Edinburgh and the Scottish Enlightenment', in *The University in Society*, ed. L. Stone, 2 vols., Princeton, 1974, 2:407–48; 'Hume as moralist: A social historian's perspective', in *Philosophers of the Enlightenment*, ed. S.C. Brown, Brighton, UK, 1979, pp. 140–61; 'James Beattie and the defence of Common Sense', in *Festschrift für Werner Gruenther*, ed. B. Fabian, Heidelberg, 1978, pp. 145–54; 'Lawyers, landowners, and the civic leadership of post-Union Scotland', *Juridical Review* (1976), 97–120; 'The Scottish Enlightenment and the science of man', in *Theoretische Geschiedenis*, 8 (1981), 3–19; 'Towards a definition of the Scottish Enlightenment', in *City and Society*, ed. P. Fritz and D. Williams, Toronto, 1973, pp. 125–47.

6 Cf. Winch, 'The system of the north', p. 49.

7 As a matter of fact, this was also Reid's argument, but that is admittedly clearer in his unpublished lectures on the culture of the mind than in his published work. See also the discussion of 'duties to ourselves' in Reid, *Practical Ethics: Being Lectures and Papers on Natural Religion, Self-Government, Natural Jurisprudence, and the Law of Nations*, ed. K. Haakonssen, Princeton, 1990, pp. 127–37 and 184–7. Cf. J.C. Stewart-Robertson, 'The Well-principled Savage, or the child of the Scottish Enlightenment', in *Journal of the History of Ideas*, 42 (1981), 503–25; and 'Sancte Socrates:

It was this ideal of the philosophically cultured mind which Stewart
instilled into his students and which for some of them – notably
Brougham, Horner, and Mackintosh – led to grandiose plans for a new,
comprehensive map of knowledge, showing how all the sciences centred on moral philosophy.[8] As we saw in Chapter 7 and as Phillipson
also stresses, Stewart's moral teaching marks the end in Scotland of the
neo-humanist ideal of the active citizen.[9] For Stewart the relationship
between moral education and political action had been reversed: virtue
was a precondition for political participation, no longer a concomitant
thereof. Nor was there for Stewart an inherent link between ownership
of property and political exertion: on the contrary, the most successful
of his students clearly demonstrated the point that politics was now for
men of intellect as well as for men of property. But Stewart's philosophical cultivation of the mind did not primarily aim at civic virtue at
all but at the creation of a far-sighted leadership in public life. His ideal
was for an élite, not for all citizens.

Stewart did, however, also have a theory concerning the moral condition of humanity at large, as we saw in Chapter 7.[10] It is a view according to which a future society that is maintained through moral
excellence is emerging because of the spread of enlightenment about
this prospect. Stewart's historicist notion of the march of the mind is
combined with a realist and cognitivist moral theory, and he takes the
implication of this combination to be that politics and the law increasingly will become marginal as the morally well-ordered society
emerges spontaneously. As a consequence, the theory of government
and jurisprudence will give way to 'political economy', as Stewart calls
the comprehensive science of the great society of the future.

These ideas were, as we have seen, to a large extent a response to
Adam Smith. There is much more to Stewart than this, but for the
present my particular concern is with the fate of the complex of ideas
which he developed from Smith's philosophy. This is central to an
understanding of the wider question of what became of the Enlightenment in Scotland, and at the same time it provides an important ave-
nue into the thought of Stewart's pupil Sir James Mackintosh, with

Scottish reflections on obedience and resistance', in *Man and Nature*, ed. R.L. Emerson, G. Girard, and R. Runte, London, Ontario, (Proceedings of the Canadian Society for Eighteenth-Century Studies, I) (1982), 65–79.
  8   See Winch, 'The system of the north', pp. 44 ff.
  9   See Phillipson, 'The Scottish Enlightenment', p. 39.
  10   Cf. also Istvan Hont, 'The "rich country – poor country" debate in Scottish
classical political economy', in *Wealth and Virtue*, pp. 271–315, at pp. 310–18; and
Winch, 'The system of the north'.

whom we shall be concerned in this chapter. In saying this, I have already indicated that I am not undertaking an exhaustive discussion of Mackintosh; that would require a much wider net than the present study.[11] Although I shall touch upon additional themes in Mackintosh, the centre of interest is his use of the ideas just introduced. There are two reasons for concentrating on Mackintosh. Of all the men in the Stewart circle, it was he who addressed himself most fully to the range of ideas in which we are interested and who most extensively transformed his philosophical self-consciousness into theoretical work. In addition, his work presents a particular challenge, because he set out from an apparently much more radical standpoint than the rest of the Stewart coterie. In tracing the themes which are our major concern we therefore inevitably raise the additional issue of the continuities in Mackintosh's thought.

8.2   *The* Vindiciae Gallicae

The greatest difficulty in understanding Mackintosh is perhaps that of not overrating him, while taking him seriously enough to be worth investigating as more than a purely political creature. This difficulty is particularly brought out by the question of the continuity or discontinuity between his early *Vindiciae Gallicae* and his later work. We err in the former respect if we think him capable of developing two alternative political philosophies. We err in the latter respect either if we take him to be mindlessly shifting from one philosophical standpoint to another or if we take the fact that his changing attitude to the French Revolution was philosophically shallow as grounds for rejecting him from the history of ideas. The singular interest of the *Vindiciae* is that it allows us a rare insight into a mind in the making. It combines elements from at least three distinct, though often overlapping, traditions of political thought: some echoes of the republican, or 'Commonwealth', tradition;[12] Scottish moral philosophy and philosophical history; and a vague form of natural rights thinking which Mackintosh derived from Rousseau. The result is a standpoint which is philosophically ambiguous and undeveloped, because it is based on no clear moral theory. In his later work Mackintosh does develop a moral theo-

11   The more important discussions are referred to later in this chapter. See, in addition, the general biography by Patrick O'Leary, *Sir James Mackintosh, the Whig Cicero*, Aberdeen, 1989.

12   For this influence on Mackintosh, see L.A. McKenzie, 'The French Revolution and English parliamentary reform: James Mackintosh and the *Vindiciae Gallicae*', *Eighteenth-Century Studies*, 14 (1981), 264–82.

ry, but of a realist kind like that of Dugald Stewart, and we are consequently in a good position to see what havoc this causes among the
political ideas from which Mackintosh started.

The Commonwealth tradition, with its humanist ideal of the civic
virtues, its emphasis on the importance of an agrarian basis for civil
society, its hostility towards modern commercialized and urbanized
society, and its republicanism, was the earliest political-philosophical
influence on Mackintosh. Before going to Edinburgh he was a student
at King's College, Aberdeen, where he would have met a strong local
Commonwealth tradition, represented especially by William Ogilvie.
Ogilvie, who succeeded Thomas Reid when the latter transferred to
Adam Smith's chair in Glasgow in 1764 and who was subsequently
professor of 'humanity', was actively engaged in schemes for the enlightenment of the general public and for agrarian reform.[13] This Aberdonian tradition was, to some extent at least, shared by Thomas Reid
and adds a further dimension to his differences with Hume and Smith,
as we have seen in the chapter on Reid.[14] Although Mackintosh does
not refer to Ogilvie in the *Vindiciae Gallicae,* we know from the *Memoirs
of Mackintosh* that he was influenced by and retained a respect for
Ogilvie long after he had changed his own political ideas.[15] Already by
the time he came to write the *Vindiciae,* Mackintosh had broadened his
political-philosophical horizon, and Commonwealth ideas cannot be
said to provide the organizing principles of his thought; nevertheless,
the republican line of argument is clearly and explicitly present in the
Vindiciae. Thus he specifically links up with George Buchanan, James
Harrington, John Milton, Algernon Sidney, William Molyneux, and
Andrew Fletcher and sees the English Revolution of 1688 as an imperfect and unfinished attempt to realize some of the ruling principles of
the Commonwealthmen.[16] Furthermore, for Mackintosh, as for John

13 See William Ogilvie, *Proposals for a Public Library at Aberdeen,* Aberdeen,
1764; and the rambling 'Biographical Notes' by D.C. MacDonald in his edition of
Ogilvie's *Essay on the Right of Property in Land,* entitled *Birthright in Land: With
Biographical Notes,* London, 1891 (hereafter MacDonald). For the original, see [Wil-
liam Ogilvie], *An Essay on the Right of Property in Land, With Respect to Its Foundation
in the Law of Nature, Its Present Establishment by the Municipal Laws of Europe, and the
Regulations by Which it Might be Rendered more Beneficial to the Lower Ranks of Mankind,* London, n.d. The work was finished in 1781 but perhaps not published until
1782: see MacDonald, p. 186. Cf. T.A. Horne, *Property Rights and Poverty: Political
Argument in Britain, 1605–1834,* Chapel Hill, NC, 1990, pp. 216–19.

14 Cf. G.E. Davie, *The Scottish Enlightenment,* London, 1981, pp. 18–19.

15 *Memoirs of the Life of . . . Sir James Mackintosh,* ed. R.J. Mackintosh, 2 vols.,
London, 1836, I, pp. 17 and 380–6. Cf. MacDonald, pp. 243–4, 297–8, 300–6, 317–18.

16 James Mackintosh, *Vindiciae Gallicae: A Defence of the French Revolution and its
English Admirers, against the Accusations of the Right Hon. Edmund Burke* (hereafter

Millar, Thomas Reid, Dugald Stewart, and so many other Britons who welcomed it, the first stages of the French Revolution were a delayed English Revolution, just as the American Revolution had been. Like the Americans, the French might well have greater success in realizing Commonwealth principles and thus show the way to reform in Britain itself.[17] We even find Mackintosh playing with the old idea of 'that free constitution which France, in common with the other Gothic nations of Europe, once enjoyed'.[18] There is, too, a good deal of republican stock-in-trade about the connection between moral stature and political and military exertion,[19] but even here, and without looking at all the other elements which go into the *Vindiciae*, we find cause to think that this line of reasoning does not go very deep with Mackintosh, although the resulting political position was undoubtedly sincerely held. For while it is quite clear that Mackintosh linked virtue with political freedom, it is not at all clear which is productive of which, whether it is participation in the political process that forms the moral character, or whether the formation of a virtuous character is a requisite for the functioning of a free constitution, towards which the moral education of mankind must lead. This is a crucial issue for Mackintosh to be unclear about, for once the horrors of the later stages of the French Revolution had led him to the conclusion that mankind had not yet achieved a suitable level of moral enlightenment, it took only a clarification of it in the latter direction and he had the premises for Whig gradualism on the question of political reform. On the way to this conclusion he was aided not only by events in France but also by a number of ideas from the Scottish philosophical tradition which he had undoubtedly picked up while a student in Edinburgh.[20]

The structure of the *Vindiciae Gallicae* was largely determined by its role as a reply to Burke's *Reflections on the Revolution in France* and a contribution to the debate on the affairs of the day, but its underlying structure of thought may be displayed as follows. First there is a potted historical survey of modern Europe, with special attention to a comparison of England and France, which shows the possibilities for action; second, there is a discussion of the justifiable moral and political ideals to follow in action; and third, there is a discussion of what are the

---

VG), in *The Miscellaneous Works of the Right Honourable Sir James Mackintosh* (hereafter *Miscellaneous Works*), 3 vols., London, 1846, III, pp. 136–8.

17   *VG*, pp. 146–8, 153–7.   18   *VG*, p. 36; cf. pp. 10–11.

19   For example *VG*, pp. 28–9, 39–40, 126–9.

20   The general outline of Mackintosh's Scottish background has been drawn in Jane Rendall's fine study of Mackintosh, 'The Political Ideas and Activities of Sir James Mackintosh (1765–1832)', Ph.D. thesis, University of London, 1972, esp. chs. 1 and 2. Cf. *Memoirs of Mackintosh*, I, ch. 1.

justifiable means of realizing these ideals in the historically given circumstances. Looking at each of these steps in turn, we shall see that Mackintosh mixes elements from the other two traditions of thought on which he draws, namely Scottish moral philosophy and an unspecific theory of the rights of man, of a kind which was common amongst the more radical sympathizers with the French Revolution.

(i) The first thing to notice about Mackintosh's historical sketches in the *Vindiciae* is that he goes out of his way to align himself with one of the main principles of Scottish philosophical history, namely that explanations should as far as possible refer to 'general causes' rather than to the actions and conspiracies of individuals, and he eagerly quotes Hume in support of this.[21] This Humean lesson and the more general one implied – that history should be explanatory rather than a mere narrative of events – was one that remained with him for the rest of his life. This is undoubtedly one of the reasons behind his grand declaration, a quarter of a century later, that Hume's history of the Stuarts was 'the most remarkable work which ever issued from the Scottish press'.[22] It was one of his main criticisms of Fox's *History of James the Second* that it was purely narrative and neglected the historian's duty to give causal explanations.[23] And Francis Jeffrey must have known that he took up a cause as dear to Mackintosh's heart as to his own when, in his obituary on Mackintosh, he took the latter's historical works as the occasion for his own last and fierce defence of the old mode of explanatory history and for attack on the modern 'notion that history should consist of narrative only'.[24]

Mackintosh applies his idea of historical explanation to sketch a view of European history containing a number of elements which are

21   Hume is quoted in *VG*, p. 28. The general-causes theme is a recurrent one, but see esp. pp. 10, 28, 30, 61–2, 87. Cf. his advice to William Smyth on 'universal history', *Memoirs of Mackintosh*, I, pp. 412–13; H. Ben-Israel, *English Historians on the French Revolution*, Cambridge, UK, 1968, pp. 83–5. See also Jane Rendall's discussion of how Mackintosh and a group of other Scottish orientalists in the period between 1800 and 1830 applied the basic principles of conjectural history in the study of India and other Asian societies: 'Scottish orientalism: from Robertson to James Mill', *Historical Journal*, 25 (1982), 43–69.

22   'Preface to a Reprint of the *Edinburgh Review* of 1755', in *Miscellaneous Works*, II, p. 474.

23   *Edinburgh Review*, July, 1808, Art. I, pp. 283–5. It should, however, be pointed out that this did not prevent Mackintosh, eclectic as he was, from expressing a number of romantic ideas on how to write history; see his review of Sismondi's *History of France*, *Edinburgh Review*, July, 1821, pp. 488–509; and the discussion of this in Ben-Israel, *English Historians*, pp. 119–20.

24   *Edinburgh Review*, October 1835, Art. XI, p. 249.

immediately recognizable from philosophical historians such as Hume and Smith. Thus it was commerce that broke the back of feudalism, and it was the emergence of a large, enlightened middle class that was characteristic of modern Europe.[25] Similarly the large number of feudal remains, such as class and church privileges, especially in continental Europe, were to be understood as petrifactions of arrangements which were useful to society in an earlier stage but which had been artificially extended through unholy alliance with despotically minded monarchs. Thus what were once offices had turned into ranks; and a natural way of remunerating the clergy in a pre-commercial society, namely through the use of land, had turned into large-scale landownership with all its attendant privileges. In short, artificial interventions had prevented or distorted natural growth, especially in the distribution of property and the formation of a scale of ranks on merit.[26] The result was that governments lost their foundation, for – and this is the most important Humean influence on Mackintosh – a stable government power is grounded in opinion. This is the background to the most pervasive theme in the *Vindiciae,* namely that opinion constitutes the most general of all general explanatory causes in human history: ideas led to the English Revolution, but because the ideas were confused, it became a confused and unfinished revolution. The same ideas were behind the American Revolution. Above all, ideas and nothing else created the French Revolution.[27] In all these cases the previous spread of enlightenment through the commercialization of society had been artificially prevented from becoming a power base for government.

This is, however, not just a simple continuation of the old Hume–Smith line of thinking about power. There is a vagueness in Mackintosh's presentation of the view which may easily conceal that it could take a turn very different from that of its ancestry. For Hume and Smith (and for John Millar), the idea that power rests on opinion was in itself a rather empty formula, a formal schema, to be filled in by the socio-historical analysis of each society or epoch. Thus the opinions and ideas which could form the basis of power might be economic interests, religious ideas, heroic identification with the tribal leader, or aesthetic identification with the great. But in Mackintosh there is a very strong tendency to treat those ideas which support government as the morally right and justifiable ones, with little apparent awareness of the obvious problem of how to explain the existence of governments which do not rest on such fortunate grounds. The ideas in question are,

---

25 *VG*, pp. 62–6, 91–2.

26 *VG*, pp. 33–48 and 75, note. Cf. O. von Gierke, *Natural Law and the Theory of Society, 1500–1800,* Cambridge, UK, 1958, p. 370.

27 *VG*, sect. v, p. 147; and pp. 20, 30, 58–9, 61–2.

of course, about the natural rights of men; in other words, Mackintosh combines an evaluative element with his analysis, whereas the two are always separate in Hume and Smith and even in the much more en-gagé Millar. Once this tendency in Mackintosh is premised by a realist moral theory and put into a providentialist framework, another stone is added to a very different philosophical structure from the one he began with.

(ii) The conclusion of Mackintosh's sketchy analysis of modern Europe is that the forms of political power have not developed in tune with their natural support in ideas. Since the latter constitute the kind of 'general causes' in human history which cannot be changed at will, the avenues of action seem to be either continued repression or political reform. The former is becoming ever more difficult, according to Mack-intosh, and he believes that the reforms begun in France must sooner or later spread to the rest of Europe.[28] Since political reform is thus demanded by the spread of ideas, the next question concerns what line such reform should take, and this must naturally be determined by the content of the ideas in question. In dealing with this problem of justi-fication, Mackintosh is clearly influenced by Rousseau on one impor-tant point, the assertion of equal human rights. But he deliberately eschews all discussion of the philosophical basis for such a theory of rights and, indeed, any clarification of the concept of rights. That is because it is not required by his polemic against Burke, who agrees that there are natural rights, but one inevitably gets the impression that the real reason is that Mackintosh's position in moral philosophy is com-pletely unclear at this stage.[29] This is underlined by his apparent blind-ness to the need to explain how a Rousseauan idea of natural rights is compatible with other, more Scottish-sounding ideas which he uses in the same context – that there was no state of nature, that society is coeval with humanity, that property rights are coeval with society, and especially that the institutions of civil society have made possible the protection of natural rights.[30]

It was probably Hume who inspired this last idea. This can be seen from the polemical context in which it appears and from the conse-quent speculations about just laws, which are immediately recog-nizable as in the Hume–Smith tradition. As Mackintosh read him, Burke maintained that, although it was sensible to ascribe natural rights to men, this had no implications whatever for civil society, for on entry into society all such rights had to be understood as renounced; all the institutions and laws of civil government were purely matters of

28   *VG*, pp. 157–66.   29   *VG*, pp. 96–7.
30   *VG*, pp. 45–6, 96–7.

convenience, and any rights which the member of civil society could claim were privileges granted by society. But, says Mackintosh, if this were the case, then we must expect the civil and criminal laws to be what we should call *enabling* ordinances, just like the special laws creating the 'rights', that is, the powers and privileges, of public officers, whereas in fact criminal and civil law is restrictive in character. It so limits the exercise of already existing rights that social living becomes possible. The implication of this view is, of course, that the right to personal freedom which is protected by just law is negative and unspecific in character; it is everything that is not prohibited.[31]

In true eclectic style Mackintosh, however, immediately combines this with a Rousseauan idea. For, he reasons, since all men have equal natural rights and since they must be understood to have the same basic purpose in submitting to civil authority, namely to gain as much protection of their natural rights as is ncessary to make these effective, they must also be understood to have submitted to an equal degree of restriction and thus to have an equal amount of right or freedom left. But since men in civil society thus have an equal degree of self-government, it follows for Mackintosh – and this is his Rousseau-inspired non sequitur – that all men must have an equal right to a voice in the politically institutionalized government of themselves.[32]

This episode is a good example of Mackintosh's eclecticism in the *Vindiciae*, and it demonstrates how easy – in an intellectual sense – it must have been for him to weed out such extraneous elements as the last-mentioned and yet retain a large number of elements for a much less radical Whig philosophy. Although the work has to be seen as the meeting-place of a number of traditions, this can be overdone, as it was in the most famous interpretation of Mackintosh. Elie Halévy's suggestion that the *Vindiciae Gallicae*, in line with other transitional works between Adam Smith and the utilitarians, suffers from the strain between a natural rights doctrine and a proto-utilitarian line of argument, is wrong.[33] It is, however, a very interesting mistake, because it serves

31 *VG*, pp. 95–6; and pp. 99–100.   32 *VG*, pp. 97–8.

33 Elie Halévy, *The Growth of Philosophic Radicalism*, trans. M. Morris, Boston, 1966, pp. 184–6. McKenzie, 'French Revolution', pp. 276–7, follows Halévy in maintaining that there is some strain in Mackintosh, though the following observation indicates further possibilities in Mackintosh's position: '[Mackintosh argued] with some ingenuity that a declaration of rights, for example, would be useful in recording those maxims that tended to promote public happiness. Such maxims, as it happened, would coincide with man's natural rights. A declaration of rights, in short, was a useful expedient that would serve to keep alive "the public vigilance against the usurpation of partial interests" by "perpetually presenting the general interest to the public eye."'

to bring out some of the ideas which were to remain fundamental to Mackintosh's later thought.

Here as elsewhere we have to apply sharper concepts than those used by the subject of our analysis. We should distinguish much more clearly than Mackintosh himself ever does in the *Vindiciae* between two levels of utility considerations. On the one hand there is the question of the utility of the institutional means of protecting natural rights, on the other the question of the utility of these rights themselves.[34] The former question is unproblematic and readily seen to have nothing to do with utilitarianism, for it is simply the view that institutions must be judged according to whether they serve whatever purpose is thought to be morally justified – in Mackintosh's case, the protection of natural rights. This broad view conflicts only with those who maintain that institutions have some inherent value, whether derived from their supposed divine origin or from their long establishment. This is exactly the point Mackintosh makes: government 'may be made to be respected, not because it is ancient, or because it is sacred, – not because it has been established by barons, or applauded by priests, – but because it is useful'.[35] If this were to be called 'utilitarianism', then the 'right-to-life' movement in our own day, for example, would also have to be described as utilitarian: it sees great utility in laws prohibiting abortion. It is, of course, a 'utilitarianism' which Mackintosh retained in all his post-Revolutionary thought.

Much more important is the second level of utility considerations in the *Vindiciae*. These occur when Mackintosh confronts the view of government which we earlier saw him ascribe to Burke, namely that government is wholly a matter of convenience as determined by tradition. The answer to this has already been given – that government is a matter of convenience only up to a point, and that is because it has a point – the point of protecting natural rights as these are contained in the rules of justice. But in the present context Mackintosh launches into the following, much more difficult speculations:

> All morality is, no doubt, founded on a broad and general expedience . . . Justice is expediency, but it is expediency speaking by general maxims, into which reason has consecrated the experience of mankind. Every general principle of justice is demonstrably expedient; and it is this utility alone that confers on it a moral obligation. But it would be fatal to the existence of morality, if the utility of every particular act were to be the subject of deliberation in the mind of every moral agent. Political principles are only

34 Mackintosh touches upon the former in a number of places, but *VG*, p. 136, is particularly relevant. The latter question is discussed on pp. 100–1.

35 *VG*, p. 136.

moral ones adapted to the civil union of men. When I assert that a man has a right to life, liberty, etc. I only mean to enunciate a moral maxim founded on the general interest, which prohibits any attack on these possessions. In this primary and radical sense, all rights, natural as well as civil, arise from expediency. But the moment the moral edifice is reared, its basis is hid from the eye for ever. The moment these maxims, which are founded on an utility that is paramount and perpetual, are embodied and consecrated, they cease to yield to partial and subordinate expediency. It then becomes the perfection of virtue to consider, not whether an action be useful, but whether it be right.[36]

It is anachronistic to talk of utilitarianism in a work of 1791, but if we nevertheless accept it for the sake of discussion, we can see that the one thing which is clear in this central passage is that Mackintosh rejects what is now called 'act utilitarianism' because it would be fatal to human morality, and goes in for what looks like 'rule utilitarianism'. But what is 'this utility that alone confers on [rules of justice] a moral obligation'? From the first few sentences it might seem that it is a utility which is inductively demonstrated through the history of mankind. But if that were the intention, what then can be meant by 'the moment the moral edifice is reared'? And how can its basis be 'hid from the eye for ever'? If the utility in question were a matter of calculation, would we not be in the same danger as if we tried to base morality on act utilitarianism? How could we be sure that we had found the 'utility that is paramount and perpetual'?

To these crucial questions there is not the shadow of an answer in the *Vindiciae*, nor are we ever let into the secret of what 'the general interest' mentioned consists of. But if we add to this vague scheme of ideas a Christian providentialism, as we shall see Mackintosh do later, then the interest and utility in question will be that of mankind as a whole, stretching into a life beyond the present. Furthermore, it will be a utility and an interest which is not at all a matter of human calculation but one which is fixed and determined by the Deity, and the inductive demonstration from history will simply be a confirmation of this arrangement. Within such a framework of ideas, it would make perfect sense to talk of 'the moment the moral edifice is reared' and of its basis being hidden 'from the eye for ever'. Similarly the semi-religious talk of the rules of morals being 'embodied and consecrated' suddenly becomes very appropriate. If we further add a moral theory which distinguishes sharply between the 'objective' question of moral rightness and the 'subjective' question of the moral motivation of human behaviour, then we can see the criticism of 'act utilitarianism' in

36 *VG*, pp. 100–1.

the *Vindiciae* as a rejection of a possible answer to the subjective question, and the somewhat special kind of 'rule utilitarianism' as the right answer to the objective question.

With these two additions we have arrived at two of the essential elements in Mackintosh's later thought, and we shall seek a fuller explanation of them later in this chapter. But for the moment I have, at one and the same time, shown the unfinished character of his ideas in the *Vindiciae* and indicated the nature of the continuity between this and his later work. Above all, I have shown that there is no strain between utilitarianism and natural rights thinking in the early work, for the simple reason that Mackintosh has no real conception of the former.

(iii) On the basis of these two ideas, – that men have equal natural rights, and that general enlightenment has now spread sufficiently for men to understand this doctrine of rights and its political implications, – Mackintosh tackles the question of what should be done. This takes two forms, first a defence of nearly all that had been done in the French Revolution up to the publication of the *Vindiciae* in 1791, and second, an analysis of the English Revolution and its effects, showing that it had been very imperfect indeed and that further and drastic reform was necessary. In France, repression had continued for so long that revolutionary change was the only possibility. In Britain sufficient steam had been let off in 1688 for piecemeal reform to be adequate.[37] The French Revolution was a grossly delayed, but now much more perfect, realization of the right political principles, and the British would have to take action to catch up and thus enter fully into the era of modern civilization.

It was undoubtedly Mackintosh's later repudiation of the revolutionary mode of changing society which was the most conspicuous element in his conversion from the French Revolution. With him, as with so many others in Britain who supported the early stages of the Revolution, it is natural to explain this by reference to Revolutionary atrocities and the surfacing of the authoritarian elements of the Revolution after the publication of the *Vindiciae*. It is, however, of interest for our understanding of Mackintosh's later thought to try to intellectualize his reaction in this respect more precisely. Of his two premises, the moral doctrine of natural rights was never repudiated, but then it was so vague that it could easily be fitted into his later moral thought without having any significant function. So our attention is concentrated on the historical thesis about the spread of enlightenment, and here Mackintosh simply took the later events in the Revolution as

37   *VG*, pp. 153–7.

evidence that his historical analysis was wrong, that enlightenment was by no means as widespread as he had thought.[38] The conclusion was clear: change must be a matter of education, and that necessitated reform rather than revolution.

This line of thought also provides the clue to another important change between the *Vindiciae* and Mackintosh's later work, namely his changing attitude to perfectibilism. There is in the early work a clear leaning towards what we may call 'scientific perfectibilism', which incorporates what has been called a 'constructivist rationalism' in politics.[39] I have in mind the view that the institutions of civil society can be reconstructed according to preconceived ideas and can thus be brought ever closer to perfection, though it is important to notice Mackintosh's declaration that 'It is absurd to expect, but it is not absurd to pursue perfection.'[40] He expounds this view in a polemic against Burke's thesis that the French Revolution issued from wildly speculative ideas, whereas politics should be based on experience. The question must be, however, in what way should we be guided by experience? Surely we should not simply be led to conserve this or that form of civil institutions of which we have experience? In that case we would never have progressed beyond the stage of the most primitive savage. On the contrary, we should, like the scientist dealing with the material world, learn from experience the underlying principles of the moral world. This would then allow us to treat our institutions as the practical mechanic does his materials, forming them into ever-better machinery. This knowledge was readily available in the existing 'science of politics' which philosophers had developed during the preceding century, and all that the French legislators had done was to try to use it in practice. Furthermore, in its essentials this knowledge was rapidly filtering through to the population at large, thanks to the modern printing press; accordingly, both the pressure for and every possibility of its realization existed.

This broad concept of empirical science undoubtedly derived from Mackintosh's training in Edinburgh, and its development here against Burke sounds very much like a rehearsal, not only for the dispute many years later between the utilitarians and Macaulay but also for James Mill's onslaught on Mackintosh himself. The question of why Mackintosh changed his view does not allow an entirely satisfactory

38 This is well documented and discussed in W. Christian, 'James Mackintosh, Burke, and the cause of reform', *Eighteenth-Century Studies*, 7 (1973–4), 193–206 at 200–1.

39 See F.A. Hayek, 'Kinds of rationalism', in his *Studies in Philosophy, Politics, and Economics*, London, 1967, pp. 82–95.

40 *VG*, p. 55. The following discussion is based mainly on pp. 53–61.

answer, but it seems fairly obvious that, just as experience refuted his early optimism concerning the spread of knowledge, so his youthful naïveté about the completeness of moral science was soon dispelled by the further studies which, as we know from his letters, he pursued for the rest of his life. At any rate, throughout his later work, political economy is the only one of the moral sciences which is talked of as certain and testable, and late in life he declared, at the conclusion of his *Dissertation on the Progress of Ethical Philosophy*, that 'Ages may yet be necessary to give to ethical theory all the forms and language of a science, and to apply it to the multiplied and complicated facts and rules which are within its province.'[41] Just as mankind as a whole was sent back to the classroom and the periodical press, so the philosophers were again to be kept to the inductive grindstone. In conformity to this, the hero of scientific methodology in all Mackintosh's subsequent work becomes Bacon, who, for him as for the rest of the Stewart circle, became an all-purpose sage.[42]

The concrete institutional changes suggested or supported by Mackintosh do not warrant much attention in the present context, and they are probably the best-known part of the *Vindiciae*. He indulges in Rousseauan talk of the general will as the basis of legitimate government and in Lockean talk of trust between the people and the government. The theory of equal natural rights leads him to support manhood suffrage, but he severely criticizes direct democracy and advocates a representative form of government based upon a system of indirect voting. The doctrine of equality further leads him to vehement criticism of the political privileges pertaining to special orders – the nobility and the Church – and thence to a preference for an undivided Parliament, and to a plea for some parliamentary reform in Britain. He supports the separation of powers, though he wants ministers in Parliament; and he has doubts about the propriety of a veto power in the executive. In Mackintosh's presentation of these ideas there are a number of tensions, especially between democratic and traditional Commonwealth principles, but, although these are interesting in themselves, they do not significantly point beyond the *Vindiciae* and may therefore be ignored here.[43]

41 *Dissertation*, p. 400. Concerning political economy, see 'Discourse Read at the Opening of the Literary Society of Bombay', in *Miscellaneous Works*, II, pp. 572–8.

42 At the same time Stewart forcefully adapted Baconianism to his own purposes; see A. Pérez-Ramos, *Francis Bacon's Idea of Science and the Maker's Knowledge Tradition*, Oxford, 1988, pp. 24–5. Cf. S. Rashid, 'Dugald Stewart, "Baconian" methodology, and political economy', *Journal of the History of Ideas*, 46 (1985), 245–57; J.C. Robertson, 'A Bacon-facing generation: Scottish philosophy in the early nineteenth century', *Journal of the History of Philosophy*, 14 (1976) 35–45.

43 But see McKenzie's interesting discussion, 'French Revolution'.

It should be pointed out, however, that all these reforms are purely political and institutional in character; Mackintosh is emphatic that his political egalitarianism must not be mistaken for a 'Utopian and level-ling madness'. It has nothing to do with property nor with other forms of social inequality. On the contrary, the purpose of political reform is to create a system of government which is able to maintain a strict system of justice within which a natural distribution of property can take place.[44] This was a standpoint which would remain with Mackin-tosh. Finally, the list of specific ills which he saw as stemming from the unrepresentative character of the British Parliament was one to which he would subscribe for the rest of his life: the suppression of Catholics, especially of Catholic Ireland; the Test Acts; the feudal remains in Scottish law; restrictions on the press; limitations on trial by jury; and hindrances to free trade.[45]

8.3   *After* Vindiciae Gallicae: *Moral philosophy*

One of the vapours from William Hazlitt's *Spirit of the Age* is the idea that Mackintosh's shift away from the principles of the French Revolu-tion was 'sudden and violent' and that it occurred as a result of a visit to the old and sick Edmund Burke at Beaconsfield at the end of 1796.[46] But Hazlitt exaggerates and simplifies, for there is no reason to doubt Mackintosh's own account of how events in France themselves worked on his standpoint over the years.[47] Although his change may well be described as 'violent' in its political aspect, it was not quite so drastic in philosophical terms. In fact, by taking our lead from the latter, we can put the nature and extent of the former into perspective. We may, furthermore, find an intellectual rationale for the ambiguity which the later Mackintosh always felt towards his early work – an ambiguity which often puzzled him and which continues to intrigue commen-tators.[48]

44   *VG*, pp. 38 and 34–5. Mackintosh also slams all legally nourished 'corpora-tion spirit'.

45   *VG*, p. 152.

46   William Hazlitt, *The Spirit of the Age*, in *The Complete Works of William Hazlitt*, ed. P.P. Howe, 21 vols., London, 1930–4. XI, p. 100. Cf. *Memoirs of Mackintosh*, I, pp. 86–94.

47   See *Memoirs of Mackintosh*, I, pp. 128–36; his son's statement, ibid., pp. 122–3; Christian, 'James Mackintosh'; and S. Deane, *The French Revolution and Enlighten-ment in England, 1789–1832*, Cambridge, MA, 1988, pp. 50–3.

48   See Melvin Lasky's discussion of Mackintosh in *Utopia and Revolution: On the Origins of a Metaphor, or Some Illustrations of the Problem of Political Temperament and Intellectual Climate and How Ideas, Ideals, and Ideologies Have Been Historically Related*, Chicago, 1976, pp. 543–9.

Another 'personalities-and-events' approach to Mackintosh's development, which may be more of a hindrance than a help, if not used with care, is to consider his attitude to Godwin. It is true that they met and became friends as supporters of the French Revolution; it is not only true, but important, that when Mackintosh publicly announced his conversion from the Revolution in 1799 he used, as we shall see, an only slightly concealed – and vicious – attack on Godwin's radical utilitarianism as one of his basic organizing principles.[49] However, when Mackintosh wrote the *Vindiciae* he was not a utilitarian properly speaking, and, as noted earlier, he very clearly outlined a criticism which could be directly applied to the act utilitarianism which Godwin was to put forward in his *Political Justice* in 1793. It is precisely this criticism which was seminal for some of Mackintosh's most important later works.

These began with his 'Lectures on the Law of Nature and Nations', which he delivered at Lincoln's Inn Hall in the winter of 1799 and repeated the following year, and which were fundamental to the moral and political philosophy which he was to expound in a number of lengthy articles in the *Edinburgh Review,* in a few of his more significant speeches, and in his *Dissertation on the Progress of Ethical Philosophy* of 1830. Discussion of the 'Lectures' might well tempt us into the sphere of conjectural history of ideas, for not only have Mackintosh's brief notes for them apparently been lost but contemporary accounts of the lectures deal with them mainly on the personal or purely political levels. Mackintosh did, however, publish a preliminary *Discourse on the Law of Nature and Nations* as an advertisement for the lectures, and in the *Memoirs of the Life of Sir James Mackintosh* his son printed a couple of excerpts from the manuscript.[50] Together these sources give us a good idea of the philosophical basis of Mackintosh's course.

The most striking feature of the 'Lectures' is that Mackintosh has exchanged his utopian-perfectibilist talk of deliberate, large-scale political change for a very Burkean discourse on gradual, spontaneous growth and the need to learn from the wisdom of the past.[51] Mackintosh's rhetoric was so florid on this point that his contemporaries took

49   Concerning Mackintosh's mean and arrogant treatment of Godwin in the 'Lectures on the Law of Nature and Nations', see Hazlitt, *Spirit of the Age,* p. 98; and D. Locke, *A Fantasy of Reason: The Life and Thought of William Godwin,* London, 1980, pp. 161–2. See also Godwin's protest in *Thoughts Occasioned by . . . Dr. Parr's Spital Sermon . . .* , London, 1801, pp. 12–20. For Mackintosh's later attempts to make amends, see *Memoirs of Mackintosh,* I, pp. 134–5, and Locke, *Fantasy of Reason,* pp. 200, 263, 334–6, 350–1.

50   *Memoirs of Mackintosh,* I, pp. 111–15, 116–22.

51   See e.g. *A Discourse of the Law of Nature and Nations* (hereafter *Discourse*), in *Miscellaneous Works,* I, pp. 375–6.

him to be entirely against political reform.[52] In a wider – one is tempted to say more liberal – perspective, the 'Lectures' seem to herald a return to the kind of political thinking we find in Hume and Smith, according to which the institutions of justice form the framework for civil society and its development.

Mackintosh was prompted to develop the moral philosophical standpoint of the *Vindiciae* in the 'Lectures' by Godwin's uncompromising utilitarian analysis of human morality, according to which the criterion of right and wrong at both the individual and the institutional level was a rational calculation of the balance of consequent happiness. The nub of the question for Mackintosh, as for so many other contemporary critics of consequentialism, was that men in fact are not and cannot be rational calculating machines of this sort but need a moral framework to live by, which is provided for them externally, as it were, in the form of the traditional morality of their society.[53] This appeal to tradition does not, however, rely on the ancient form of conservatism that is founded on a sceptical argument to the effect that, since man can have no moral knowledge, he must live by whatever local tradition happens to provide. We cannot even see Mackintosh, at this point, as yet another representative of the kind of reformism which Francis Jeffrey presented so well and which springs from a more or less mitigated scepticism, according to which we are so fallible in moral as in all other knowledge that we have to be content with cautious, gradual reform, whenever the use of our knowledge touches other people, unless dire necessity commands the opposite – the attitude that tradition must have the benefit of all doubt. For when Mackintosh wants to rely on tradition, it is because history reveals a completely universal human morality, and although there are certainly local aberrations, it is on the whole certain that at any time and in any place the generally accepted morality contains these universal standards.

> History . . . is now a vast museum, in which specimens of every variety of human nature may be studied. From these great accessions to knowledge, lawgivers and statesmen, but, above all, moralists and political philosophers, may reap the most important instruction. They may plainly discover in all the useful and beautiful variety of governments and institutions, and under all the fantastic multitude of usages and rites which have prevailed among men, the same fundamental, comprehensive truths, the sacred master-principles which are the guardians of human society, recognised and revered (with few and slight exceptions) by a succession of wise men from the first dawn of speculation to the present moment. The exceptions, few as

52 See Jeffrey in the *Edinburgh Review*, October 1835, Art II, p. 217.
53 See esp. *Memoirs of Mackintosh*, I, pp. 111–15.

they are, will, on more reflection, be found rather apparent than real. If we could raise ourselves to that height from which we ought to survey so vast a subject, these exceptions would altogether vanish; the brutality of a handful of savages would disappear in the immense prospect of human nature, and the murmurs of a few licentious sophists would not ascend to break the general harmony. This consent of mankind in first principles, and this endless variety in their application, which is one among many valuable truths which we may collect from our present extensive acquaintance with the history of men, is itself of vast importance. Much of the majesty and authority of virtue is derived from their consent, and almost the whole of practical wisdom is founded on their variety.[54]

This idea of the universality of basic moral principles recurs again and again in Mackintosh's subsequent work until it finally forms part of the full statement of his moral thought in the *Dissertation on the Progress of Ethical Philosophy*. Thus he maintains that speculative opinions, even of the strongly held religious kind, cannot completely submerge universal morality. For example, in all countries and sects where Calvinist necessitarianism reigns supreme as the speculative religion, we yet find the most active devotion to moral rules and virtues. This shows that in such matters there is a 'sacred neutrality of morals'.[55] The same point is again brought home to us when we study the moral thought of the Catholic theologians of the Middle Ages:

> To find the exact agreement of such a work as that of Aquinas with the moral precepts of our own age, has some tendency to heighten our reverence for the Rule of Life which thus preserves its unchangeable simplicity, amidst the fluctuations of opinion, under the most unlike and repugnant modes of thinking, and in periods the most singular, or, if it so pleases the reader, of the most perverted speculation.[56]

In fact, this perspective was undoubtedly one of the main inspirations for Mackintosh's vigorous attempt, especially in the reviews of Stewart's *Dissertation* and in his own *Dissertation*, to re-evaluate the general culture of the Middle Ages and thus to contribute to the mediaevalism of the time.

We are encouraged, accordingly, to 'look at the code of Moses', to explore 'the Institutes of Menu', to open 'the books of false religion', and to 'examine the codes of nations', in order thoroughly to learn the lesson that 'morality admits no discoveries'.[57] But although we find the fundamental 'Rule of Life' in this way, we have not yet found the foundation of this morality itself. Both in the 'Lectures' and in the *Dissertation* Mackintosh pursues the argument which he began in the *Vin-*

54   *Discourse*, p. 359.   55   *Edinburgh Review*, October 1821, Art. 10, p. 257.
56   *Edinburgh Review*, September 1816, Art. 9, p. 203.
57   *Memoirs of Mackintosh*, I, pp. 119–20; cf. *Discourse*, p. 357.

diciae, that although the immediate test of the morality of human actions is their conformity to the universal rules of morality, the morally binding character of these rules themselves arises from utility. This is a utility computed not by man but by God, as part of Providence; it is the utility of mankind as a whole, and it is utility in the long term, into eternity.[58] It is thus part of God's utilitarian design for the world to have erected a framework of moral rules by which we can live, but it is a grave error for humankind to try to go beyond this framework and live directly by the light of utility. For, although we can see the utility of general categories of actions, we cannot calculate the effects of particular actions, rules, and institutions.

> A correct examination of facts will lead us to discover that quality which is common to all virtuous actions, and which distinguishes them from those which are vicious and criminal. But we shall see that it is necessary for man to be governed, not by his own transient and hasty opinion upon the tendency of every particular action, but by those fixed and unalterable rules, which are the joint result of the impartial judgment, the natural feelings, and the embodied experience of mankind. The authority of these rules is, indeed, founded only on their tendency to promote private and public welfare; but the morality of actions will *appear* solely to consist in their correspondence with the rule . . . Beneficial tendency is the foundation of rules, and the criterion by which habits and sentiments are to be tried: but it is neither the immediate standard, nor can it ever be the principal motive of action. An action to be completely virtuous, must accord with moral rules, and must flow from our natural feelings and affections, moderated, matured, and improved into steady habits of right conduct.[59]

58 Some of the best passages are *Discourse,* pp. 346–7 and pp. 364–5; *Dissertation,* pp. 355–61. Mackintosh held one of the conceptual gains of eighteenth-century moral philosophy to be the realization that 'utility' could mean 'the interest of all men', not just of the individual; *Edinburgh Review,* September 1816, Art. 9, p. 220.

59 *Discourse,* pp. 364–5, my italics. Cf. *Dissertation,* pp. 360–1: 'A perfectly good being, who foresees and commands all the consequences of action, cannot indeed be conceived by us to have any other end in view than general well-being. Why evil exists under that perfect government, is a question towards the solution of which the human understanding can scarcely advance a single step. But all who hold the evil to exist only for good, and own their inability to explain why or how, are perfectly exempt from any charge of inconsistency in their obedience to the dictates of their moral nature. The measure of the faculties of man renders it absolutely necessary for him to have many other practical ends; the pursuit of all of which is moral, when it actually tends to general happiness, though that last end never entered into the contemplation of the agent. It is impossible for us to calculate the effects of a single action, any more than the chances of a single life.' Compare this passage with the one from *Vindiciae Gallicae,* discussed at note 36 to the present chapter. [*Note:* citations saying '*at* note 36' mean 'in the text, near note 36'; citations saying '*in* note 6' mean 'in the text of note 6'.]

It is here that, according to Mackintosh, one moral philosopher after another had gone wrong. Among the moderns, the Benthamites in particular had rightly promoted the idea that utility is the criterion of morality, but they were wrong in thinking that man could use this criterion to assess individual actions, rules, and institutions.[60] Again, although the 'excellent' William Paley's *Moral and Political Philosophy* taught Mackintosh that the Creator is a utilitarian, his conclusion that so, too, are his creatures was mistaken.[61]

These merely philosophical errors became disastrous when proponents of social change spread them beyond the walls of the scholar's study, as the French Revolutionary thinkers and their British counterparts such as Godwin did, and as the Benthamites would have liked to do. These people in effect asked the general population to undertake utilitarian analyses of their traditional morality and its social institutionalization and, since this is impossible even for philosophers themselves, they contributed to the breakdown of those habitual rules and social institutions without which the moral life, and thus society, is impossible.[62]

We have two layers in the moral world, a providentialist utilitarianism and a structure of moral rules or virtues, which, although they may appear in changing guises, are universal and unalterable in substance. Whether Mackintosh wants us to distinguish a third class of moral elements, which are largely conventional, although ultimately deriving from universal morality, or whether he wants us to regard them simply as the changing appearances assumed by universal morality, is unclear. He does, for example, tend to talk of positive law and international conventions as something separate, at least for the purposes of jurisprudential discussion.[63]

This theory of the objective structure of the moral world is supplemented by a theory of the moral subject as an agent in this world. The development of this theory is the major concern of the *Dissertation on the Progress of Ethical Philosophy*, but there are clear signs in the 'Lectures' that it was already developing when they were written. Basic to Mackintosh's theory is a distinction between, on the one hand, the

60 See *Dissertation*, pp. 284–313.
61 *Discourse*, pp. 362–3; and *Dissertation*, pp. 276–9.
62 See *Memoirs of Mackintosh*, I, pp. 111–15; *Dissertation*, pp. 302–6; and esp. *Discourse*, p. 361. This was a standard criticism of utilitarian moral theories at the time. For another example, which is modelled directly on Adam Smith, see Thomas Green, *An Examination of the Leading Principle of the New System of Morals, as that Principle is Stated and Applied in Mr. Godwin's Inquiry Concerning Political Justice, in a Letter to a Friend*, London, 2nd ed., 1799, esp. pp. 22–4.
63 *Discourse*, pp. 343–4, 383–6.

question of how man's moral faculty, or conscience, is formed and, on the other, the question of how it functions and what status it has, once formed.[64] He makes large and quite false claims to this as his own original contribution to moral thought and uses it as the organizing principle and as the criterion of appreciation in his discussion of all other moral philosophers in the *Dissertation*. It is clear what Mackintosh hopes to achieve by this distinction. It allows him to exploit developments in psychology, and thus to honour the claims of 'science', but also makes possible, he believes, a theory of the moral faculty which will match his moral realism. By showing that a 'scientific' theory of the formation of the moral faculty does not derogate from its moral authority, he would overcome one of Reid's and Stewart's chief complaints about Hume and Smith.

We know that in the 'Lectures' Mackintosh had already applied the 'science of human nature' to suggest how the moral subject is formed, and, although we have no details, in the surviving fragments of the lectures, of how he did this, we know from Hazlitt's *Essay on the Principles of Human Action* (1805) that he made use of Hartley's associationist psychology.[65] In the *Dissertation* Mackintosh strongly maintained that Hartley had provided the key to this problem of moral psychology, although admitting that there was still a long way to go before a fully satisfactory theory would be developed.[66] The general point was, however, clear, namely that each individual is exposed to social reinforcement of associative links between, on the one hand, things like social acceptance and, on the other, behaviour in accordance with the basic moral rules in whatever form they are found in a given society and period. The result is that through habituation, a moral faculty or conscience is formed which thereafter can operate independently of social reinforcement. Mackintosh maintains that, however this moral faculty is formed, it is universally the same in all individuals; it is the unitary centre of human agency, which functions in accordance with the rules of universal morality. In this fashion he carries into his 'science of human nature' a substantive moral content; it is no longer just a matter of those flexible principles of human nature which Hume was con-

64 This distinction pervades the *Dissertation*, but some of the most extensive discussions are at pp. 58–67, 197–202, 324–34, 390–3.

65 *Discourse*, pp. 355–7; and William Hazlitt, *An Essay on the Principles of Human Action: to Which are Added Some Remarks on the Systems of Hartley and Helvetius*, in *Complete Works of Hazlitt*, I, pp. 63 ff.

66 *Dissertation*, pp. 254–61, 324–8. For Mackintosh's own sketch of a theory, pp. 366–81, 351–2. He thought Smith's theory of sympathy, pp. 238–40, a most valuable attempt to explain the formation of conscience.

cerned to show were as morally neutral as the law of gravitation, which made the Rhone flow one way in its particular circumstances and the Rhine the opposite way in its place.[67]

Mackintosh's attempt to reconcile a genetic theory of the moral faculty with a theory of this faculty's universal authority – which brought him close to another of Stewart's pupils, Thomas Brown – enabled him, he thought, to mark his independence of Stewart, whom he otherwise followed so closely. As Mackintosh understood him, Stewart's argument ran like this: Whenever a person observes a particular virtuous action, he will recognize it as such, because he has a moral faculty containing the ideas of the various virtues, which, when applied, are accompanied by the conception of moral beauty, and these moral emotions are the activating part of the moral faculty. Mackintosh's objection was that there is no evidence to suggest that any thought process intervenes between the perception of the action and the occurrence of the moral emotions and that this connection can instead be understood to be forged through associative mechanisms operating from the earliest age. Furthermore, Stewart was left without any explanation of the formation of the moral faculty, because he was afraid of applying associationist psychology, which he mixed up with consequentialism in moral theory – and for him that meant egoism. In other words, for Stewart the associationist explanation of the formation of moral notions simply consisted in pointing to an association between the idea of doing an action (or kind of action) and the idea of the good consequences flowing from this for the agent, and of taking the latter as moral goodness. But for Mackintosh there was no reason why this should be the associative pattern, and, even if it were, we must still distinguish between the moral quality of the formation of the moral faculty and the moral authority and independence of this faculty once formed. Finally, although 'reason' – namely reasoning about universal moral qualities – is thus excluded from the formation of moral judgement, this does not mean that moral qualities in action (i.e. the virtues) become dependent upon, or relative to the moral faculty of the judging subject. They are as objective as always; it just so happens – or, rather, is so arranged – that when they are related to our moral faculty, they produce a moral judgement.[68]

Summing up, we can say that Mackintosh's moral philosophy is structured by two distinctions. First, he distinguishes between the universal morality, which consists of God's utilitarian providence, and the conventional 'superstructure' of positive moralities, which give con-

67 Yet Mackintosh thinks he can find support in exactly this passage in Hume. See *Discourse*, p. 343.
68 See *Dissertation*, pp. 324–34, esp. pp. 331–4.

crete expression to the former. Secondly, he distinguishes between the objective question of the ground of morality and the subjective question of the motivation to moral behaviour; of these, the former is answered by referring to universal morality, while the latter is answered, partly by a doctrine of the absolute moral supremacy of the moral faculty, or conscience, and partly by a socio-psychological theory of how the moral faculty is formed under the influence of the conventional form of morality. In all this there is little originality, despite Mackintosh's grand claims concerning the failures of his predecessors in moral philosophy. As James Mill pointed out with glee in his *Fragment on Mackintosh*, the second distinction had been playing its role in Scottish moral thought from Hutcheson to Brown; and of course the whole question had become acute with Hume's theory of the 'artificiality' of justice and allied virtues; but first of all, Mackintosh's whole moral theory is very close to the theological utilitarianism which runs from George Berkeley and John Gay through John Brown and Abraham Tucker to William Paley and Edmund Law – and beyond.[69]

8.4 *After* Vindiciae Gallicae: *History and jurisprudence*

While Mackintosh has found an opportunity to satisfy his wish to demonstrate a certain independence of his philosophical master, there is never any doubt about their agreement on the fundamental point, that there is an objective moral order set down by providence and that this order in itself is independent of the vicissitudes of history and of the mental development of each individual. Mackintosh, however, formulates his position so vaguely as to make the best of several worlds. For although there is a universal moral order, this has, as we have seen, assumed a wide variety of external forms in the history of mankind – in the different religions, philosophies, moral habits, legal codes, political institutions, and literatures. Hence it is possible for Mackintosh to maintain that the historical study of humankind is necessary, not only to teach the edifying lesson about the universality of morality but also to enable men to adapt new moral conventions to existing conventional expressions of universal morality, when changes, for one reason or another, become necessary. This is the background to the other side of Mackintosh's argument, his strong insistence on the importance of 'time and place' in moral, political, and legal argument. This insistence is alternately couched in the Burkean language of slow growth and tradition or in Scottish terms of adaptation to the 'stage of society', and

69   James Mill, *A Fragment on Mackintosh*, London, 1835, pp. 4–9. Cf. J.E. Crimmins, 'John Brown and the theological tradition of utilitarian ethics', *History of Political Thought*, 4 (1983), 523–50.

it is of course particularly prominent in his discussions of legal and
political issues.[70] After he had used history in the 'Lectures' to demonstrate the universality of morals, and associationist psychology to show
the formation of the universal moral faculty in the individual, he
would toss a number of historical considerations into his discussion of
government, state, and the various areas of law – private, criminal,
constitutional, and international law. In this he was, like his Scottish
forebears, inspired by Montesquieu.[71] Although he considered these
topics from an historical as well as a systematic angle, Mackintosh
would have nothing to do with the unhistorical, 'unscientific' ideas of a
state of nature, a social contract, or the classical simple forms of constitution.[72] By undertaking a proper historical analysis, he thought himself able to show the uniqueness of modern Europe (especially in connection with the law of nations), for, under the influence of Christianity
and the theory of the law of nations, as propounded by Continental
natural lawyers, Europe had become a great 'Commonwealth' in
which, for the first time in the history of mankind, international relations were increasingly regulated by law.[73] At the same time the European nations were increasingly linked by commerce, which needed
this legal framework, and had, furthermore, developed a technology
which for the first time would make civilization secure both externally
and internally. For Europe now had the means to protect itself against
all outside force and, by inventing the printing press, had given knowledge a form so durable that it could never again be lost, as it had been
on the demise of classical civilization.[74] All that was necessary to secure the emergence of this new international commonwealth was,
therefore, to spread and inculcate knowledge about its underlying
principles. Here the most important means included the teaching of
international law and its foundation in the law of nature, which was
part of universal morality; general schooling, with emphasis on a clas-

70   In the *Discourse*, pp. 375–6, the two modes are particularly well blended.

71   Although he praises Montesquieu as the great pioneer of the historical
study of law and government, Mackintosh mentions all the points of criticism
which had become standard in Scottish moral philosophy: *Discourse*, pp. 359–60.
For an account of Mackintosh's constitutional thought in his historical works, see
M. Francis and J. Morrow, *A History of English Political Thought in the 19th Century*,
London, 1994, pp. 82–9.

72   *Discourse*, pp. 367, 370–1, 377.

73   *Discourse*, pp. 349–50; and *Edinburgh Review*, September 1816, Art. 9,
pp. 235–7. Mackintosh thought Grotius's *De iure*, Locke's *Essay*, Montesquieu's *Spirit of the Laws*, and Smith's *Wealth of Nations* the four most important influences on
European opinion during the preceding two centuries (he undoubtedly means after
Bacon), *Edinburgh Review*, October 1821, Art. 10, p. 244.

74   *Edinburgh Review*, October 1821, Art. 10, p. 223; *Discourse*, pp. 349–50; *Dissertation*, pp. 89–92.

sical education;[75] the security of a free press;[76] and the arrangement of political institutions – in particular, of course, Parliament – in such a way that political power was firmly based on public opinion.[77]

In all this Mackintosh is clearly very close to Stewart. It is true that he is much more explicit on the topic of political reform, but then he was a Member of Parliament and could not avoid the issue. Moreover, although Stewart thought it dangerous to pin too many hopes on political reform, especially during the period of the French Revolution and the subsequent wars with France (where Mackintosh clearly indicates his agreement),[78] there was never any doubt that he agreed with the movement for moderate reform. The only topic which Mackintosh adds to Stewart's agenda is that of international law, although the disagreement here is undoubtedly more about the past than the future. He severely criticizes Stewart for denying the importance in European history of the natural law movement, for although Stewart rightly saw it as philosophically shallow, the continued promotion of the idea of a legal order independent of the individual state contributed significantly to the practical realization of such an order in Europe.[79] Mackintosh sees himself and his contemporaries as being in a position where, by combining the legal and philosophical harvests of the eighteenth century, they can provide a proper intellectual foundation for the new legal order.[80] In this perspective the French Revolution was but a temporary aberration, disastrous in its tendency but easily checked by the

75 Mackintosh was involved in both the Lancastrian school movement and in the foundation of London University. See also his discussion of classical education in *Memoirs of Mackintosh*, I, pp. 116–22; and *Memoirs and Correspondence of Francis Horner*, I, pp. 295–6, concerning the great hopes which the Scots attached to Lancaster's schools, *viz.* that they might become for England what the parish school had been for Scotland.

76 This was always a concern of Mackintosh's; for an especially forceful expression of it see 'A Speech in Defence of Jean Peltier', in *Miscellaneous Works*, III, pp. 241–300.

77 See *Edinburgh Review*, December 1818, Art. 8, pp. 165 ff.; *Edinburgh Review*, November 1820, Art. 12, pp. 461 ff.; and 'Speech on the Second Reading of the Bill to Amend the Representation of the People of England and Wales', in *Miscellaneous Works*, III, pp. 535–65.

78 See 'Discourse Read at the Opening of the Literary Society of Bombay', in *Miscellaneous Works*, II, pp. 577–8. Cf. *Memoirs and Correspondence of Francis Horner*, I, pp. 130–1.

79 *Edinburgh Review*, September 1816, Art. 9, pp. 235–7.

80 *Discourse*, pp. 355–7; cf. *Memoirs and Correspondence of Francis Horner*, I, pp. 223–4, 238–9, where Horner is encouraging the Glasgow advocate James Reddie to pursue his scheme for a treatise on international law. Reddie eventually produced a work that has to be seen as a direct descendant of eighteenth-century Scottish jurisprudence: *Inquiries Elementary and Historical in the Science of Law*, London, 1840.

formidable weapons which universal morality had found in modern Europe.[81]

Mackintosh's concern with time and place is thus based on two closely connected ideas: the idea that universal morality always exists in some historically particularized form, and the old idea, adopted from Hume, that the authority of government and law, including international law, rests on public opinion. It was this philosophic mule which carried him into the criticism of Bentham that so enraged James Mill:

> Mr Bentham . . . is much more remarkable for laying down desirable rules for the determination of rights, and the punishment of wrongs, in general, than for weighing the various circumstances which require them to be modified in different countries and times in order to render them either more useful, more easily introduced, more generally respected, or more certainly executed. The art of legislation consists in thus applying the principles of jurisprudence to the situation, wants, interests, feelings, opinions, and habits of each distinct community at any given time. It bears the same relation to jurisprudence which the mechanical arts bear to pure mathematics. Many of these considerations serve to shew, that the sudden establishment of new codes can seldom be practicable or effectual for their purpose; and that reformations, though founded on the principles of jurisprudence, ought to be not only adapted to the peculiar interests of a people, but engrafted on their previous usages, and brought into harmony with those national dispositions on which the execution of laws depends.[82]

As this and other passages make clear, the historical consideration of morality and law was for Mackintosh in principle a matter of form rather than substance, of practicability rather than principles. This, however, was an attitude which a utilitarian also could adopt, and the debate was therefore bound to be confused. To the extent that Mackintosh emphasises the universal substance of morals, he is considerably closer to the utilitarian idea of a universal measure of value than he is to the formalism-cum-historicism of Smith's impartial spectator. But in so far as he stresses the idea of the historically particular form of morality, there is an issue of contention, for it then becomes hard to see how any universal standard can be said to be used in moral decisions – time and place become more than a matter of mere practicability. This difficulty, which Mackintosh never overcomes, can also be expressed in terms referring to my interpretation of Smith: Mackintosh cannot at one and the same time strengthen the universal aspect of moral judgement by turning the merely formal rules of moral reasoning embodied

---

81 *Edinburgh Review,* September 1816, Art. 9, pp. 216–19; and *Edinburgh Review,* July 1808, Art. 1, pp. 277–8.

82 *Dissertation,* pp. 289–90.

in the impartial spectator into a substantive moral code and also preserve the historically contingent as a necessary part of moral judgement. Although his position here is philosophically weak, it should be
acknowledged that his attempt to make room for the history of morals
and its institutions of course was the influential part of his argument
and that it was this which led to the debate with James Mill and the
utilitarians.

As will have become clear, Mackintosh stresses the institutional,
especially the legal, framework of society and its development. Like
Stewart, he takes the spread of knowledge about this framework, and
reflection on its underlying values, as the prime mover of development. Unlike Stewart and more like Smith, he never engages in optimistic speculation that the moral development of society will lead to a
steady decrease in the importance of law; he simply seems to adopt the
more common-sensical position that moral development will strength-
en authority for law and government – and this may well be why he is
prepared to criticize Stewart for his unwillingness to discuss the theory
of government.[83]

This emphasis on the importance of law leads us to look at the
relationship between law and morality, between jurisprudence and
the theory of morals, and thus to consider the general composition of
the science of morals according to Mackintosh. In the 'Lectures' he
complains that neither ancient philosophers nor modern natural lawyers have distinguished between law and morality, and in the *Dissertation* he similarly criticizes Bentham for mixing the treatment of the
two.[84] It is immediately clear that all he has in mind is the distinction
between *positive* law and the underlying universal morality. This is
confirmed when we enquire whether Mackintosh has any theory
which allows him to distinguish justice as the foundation of law from
the rest of morality. In the 'Lectures' he tells us that natural law consists
of that part of morality which is enforceable by law, but the only reason
he gives seems to be that the virtues which are enforced by law are
those which are absolutely essential to the preservation of society – in
other words, a consideration of utility, rather than justice.[85] In the
Dissertation he explains his position as we would expect, considering
his general moral theory, and does so, significantly, in the form of a
criticism of Hume, who

---

83   See *Edinburgh Review*, September 1816, Art. 9, pp. 220–1.

84   *Discourse*, p. 349; *Edinburgh Review*, September 1816, Art. 9, p. 236; *Dissertation*, p. 306.

85   See *Discourse*, p. 343, and the discussion of property and marriage law,
pp. 368 ff.

very unnecessarily distinguishes the comprehensive duty of justice, from other parts of morality, as an artificial virtue, for which our respect is solely derived from notions of utility. If all things were in such plenty that there could never be a want, or if men were so benevolent as to provide for the wants of others as much as for their own, there would, says he, in neither case be any justice, because there would be no need for it. But it is evident that the same reasoning is applicable to every good affection and right action. None of them could exist if there were no scope for their exercise.[86]

In other words, all parts of morality are equally binding and have the same foundation, namely that of utility – in the sense explained earlier. Despite all the trumpeting about the importance of jurisprudence within the moral sciences, despite the fact that Mackintosh more than anyone else in the Stewart circle wanted to reconstitute the theory of natural law, it is clear that he has in fact adopted a moral philosophy which does not allow him to distinguish justice as the basis for law from the other virtues.[87] For him as for Stewart, morality is a seamless web. This conclusion is further underlined by the fact that Mackintosh, like Stewart, takes the law relating to property and the law relating to marriage to be equally fundamental to the legal system.[88] The virtues contained in them are equally part of universal morality, and what singles these virtues out for legal enforcement is equally a consideration of what is necessary for the very existence of society. The difference from Smith is clear: for Smith the two sets of virtues were morally different and hence had to be included in the law for different reasons – for reasons of justice and utility, respectively.[89]

Mackintosh's difference from Smith and essential agreement with Stewart are shown also by the fact that the language of subjective rights has disappeared and been replaced by 'duties' and 'virtues'. As with Stewart, his brand of moral realism does not have room for the morally open spaces called 'subjective rights'; his moral world is entirely ordered by a natural law that imposes duties, not just structured by a natural law that allots rights.

We may gain some impression of what Mackintosh's theory might have been had he articulated it more fully, by looking briefly at the more systematic Thomas Brown. He presents a considerable discussion of duties – which, since the moral world is well ordered, have each

86 *Dissertation*, pp. 224–5.

87 The papers of Francis Horner make it clear that he was equally keen on a science of jurisprudence, but there is no indication that he had any clear theory at all of its basis and scope. See *Memoirs and Correspondence of Francis Horner*, I, pp. 51–2, 127–8, 130, 207–8, 223–4, 238.

88 *Discourse*, pp. 367–9.

89 See K. Haakonssen, *The Science of a Legislator: The Natural Jurisprudence of David Hume and Adam Smith*, Cambridge, UK, 1981, ch. 4.

their corresponding right – and organizes it according to the traditional division into negative duties, which are nearly synonymous with
justice, and positive duties, typically represented by benevolence.[90] He
concludes this extensive section of his lectures by pointing out that the
law only recognizes certain duties (and, hence, rights) as enforceable,
simply as a matter of political expedience, for all duties and rights have
the same moral status, and Brown therefore sees little significance
in the distinction between perfect and imperfect rights about which
jurisprudence-infected moralists trumpet so loudly. Morally speaking,
all rights are equally perfect. This does lead him to a theoretical perfectibilism in politics, which, however, he immediately qualifies by strong
warnings against revolutionary rashness – warnings which he com-
pletes with Smith's well-known cautions against princes imbued with
the 'spirit of system'.[91] Brown thus perfectly illustrates the confusion
and dilemma into which Smithian political thinking was thrown by a
realist moral philosophy, which made no theoretical distinction between the foundation of justice and of the rest of morality and thus
formed no theory concerning the limits of law.

As with Stewart, both Mackintosh's and Brown's moral philosophies lose the ability to organize the 'science of a legislator' into clearly
defined areas. Stewart compensated for this by presenting his idea of
'political economy' as an all-encompassing science of the universal
social order of the future. Brown put more emphasis on the role of
active politics, with his aggressive assertion of a moral duty to seek the
perfection of society but obviously saw 'the political department of our
science'[92] (including political economy and jurisprudence) as resting
upon a unified moral theory of the kind outlined earlier.[93] In Mackintosh there are, as mentioned, few indications of this sort of optimism. It
is true that he believed in progress, and his moral philosophy of course
entailed that the moral world could be ordered and harmonious –
between the individual and the collective, between each nation and the

90   Thomas Brown, *Lectures on the Philosophy of the Human Mind*, 4 vols., Edinburgh, 1820, IV, pp. 183–398. See pp. 394–5 for the correspondence of duties and
rights. For another example of the longevity of this arrangement of morals, see the
lectures John Young gave at the new college in Belfast, published in part as *Lectures
on Intellectual Philosophy*, edited with a memoir of the author by William Cairns,
Glasgow, 1835. Young had studied at Glasgow.
91   Brown, *Lectures*, IV, pp. 384–95. The quotation from A. Smith, *The Theory of
Moral Sentiments*, ed. D.D. Raphael and A.L. Macfie, Oxford, 1976, VI.ii.2.18, is at
pp. 391–2.
92   Brown, *Lectures*, I, p. 10.
93   Brown dealt with political economy in a separate course, apparently for
purely heuristic reasons, and this course has not been published. See *Lectures*, IV,
pp. 614–15.

international community, between past, present, and future.[94] It is also true that he followed Stewart in thinking that political economy is a universally valid science, which can be tested and applied anywhere in the world and hence is more fundamental and important than the theory of government,[95] for the form of government is only a question of the most convenient means of protecting the values of universal morality, and it is disastrous to confuse these two areas of moral thought. Thus, to take the politically most pressing case, 'property exists for the benefit of the proprietor; political power exists only for the service of the state', and again: 'Of all doctrines which threaten the principle of property, none more dangerous was ever promulgated, than that which confounds it with political privileges.'[96] Although all the elements are there, the fact remains that Mackintosh never drew them together as Stewart did. In particular he never clarified the relationship between his idea of natural jurisprudence (and the universal morality which sustained it) and political economy. Upon the only occasion on which he did confront this problem, he simply made a historical point. The natural jurists, he said,

> became, as Mr Stewart states, the forerunners of the beneficent science of political economy – spreading the same spirit which it breathes, and reaching, with a sort of practical coarseness, some of its results, – though their reasonings did not, we conceive, lead by any logical process to the establishment even of its first principles. The connection is rather historical than philosophical.[97]

But he does not tell us what the philosophical connection is. In Stewart we see jurisprudence dealing with the particular (and temporary)

94 'Discourse Read at the Opening of the Literary Society of Bombay', p. 578: 'It is not only absurd, but contradictory, to speak of sacrificing the present generation for the sake of posterity. The moral order of the world is not so disposed. It is impossible to promote the interest of future generations by any measures injurious to the present; and he who labours industriously to promote the honour, the safety, and the prosperity of his own country, by innocent and lawful means, may be assured that he is contributing, probably as much as the order of nature will permit a private individual, towards the welfare of mankind.'

95 Ibid., pp. 576, 577–8; *Edinburgh Review*, September 1816, Art. 9, pp. 196–7.

96 'Speech on the Second Reading of the Bill to Amend the Representation of the People of England and Wales', pp. 551–2. Cf. *Discourse*, p. 372: 'Liberty is . . . the object of all government. Men are more free under every government, even the most imperfect, than they would be if it were possible for them to exist without any government at all: they are more secure from wrong, more undisturbed in the exercise of their natural powers, and therefore more free, even in the most obvious and grossest sense of the word, than if they were altogether unprotected against injury from each other.'

97 *Edinburgh Review*, September 1816, Art. 9, p. 237.

means, 'political economy' with the general order or moral economy that is the justifying goal. In Mackintosh this relationship is never settled. Although he had obviously moved beyond a return to any classical republican idea of the inevitable demise of the polity, he was not yet able fully to subscribe to Stewart's optimistic 'historicism';[98] consequently the rearrangement of the science of a legislator which this entailed fell apart for Mackintosh, although his own moral philosophy pointed in the same direction. We might well employ Mackintosh's words, from a different context, and ask, 'What shall [now] be said of the very distinct sciences comprehended under the common name of Moral Philosophy in our Scottish Universities?'[99]

98 Cf. Winch, 'The system of the north', p. 44.
99 *Edinburgh Review*, September 1816, Art. 9, p. 236.

9

James Mill and Scottish moral philosophy

9.1 *Introduction*

James Mill is commonly known as the utilitarian theoretician of government, law, and education and as the leader of the circle of radical political activists who worked to apply Bentham's ideas to virtually all the social, political, and legal problems of the first half of the nineteenth century. This view is certainly true in so far as any over-all assessment of Mill's work must see Bentham's utilitarianism as by far the most important influence on it – even allowing for some truth in John Stuart Mill's contention that his father reached a measure of philo-sophical independence by combining elements from Hartley, Malthus, and Ricardo. The purpose of this chapter, however, is confined to elucidating the structure of Mill's thought by reference to the moral philosophy in which he was first educated and with which his later Benthamite utilitarianism had to come to terms – or which had to come to terms with his utilitarianism.

This moral philosophy was the extraordinarily complex and com-posite Scottish academic tradition, which, especially in the work of Dugald Stewart, tried to encompass ideas derived from David Hume, Adam Smith, the idiosyncratic eclectic Adam Ferguson, and the Com-mon Sense philosopher Thomas Reid. From a philosophical point of view, these conflicting lines of Scottish moral thought may seem to be transcended by the mature Mill's Benthamite utilitarianism, and yet, as is argued in the second half of this chapter, closer consideration will show that Mill's utilitarianism has some fundamental affinity with one strand of the Scottish legacy, namely the objectivist moral theory of the Common Sense school. This thesis immediately raises another prelimi-nary problem concerning Mill's attitude to the well-known Scottish 'conjectural history' of the moral institutions of society. For although it is clear that Mill saw himself as continuing the line of conjectural historians, the objectivist moral theory of Reid and Stewart had very little use for conjectural history. In order to appreciate the relationship between Mill and the Scottish legacy in moral and political thought, we have, therefore, to start with an assessment of Mill as a conjectural historian of civil society.

Mill's early training in Scottish moral philosophy, his continuing enthusiasm for Stewart's lectures, and his very wide reading in the Scottish thinkers and the literature on which they drew are all well-known facts.[1] It is evident that his interest was a lasting one; thus when, late in life, he made his fierce onslaught on Sir James Mackintosh's moral thought, he typically used all the main Scottish eighteenth-century thinkers from Hutcheson to Brown to set the scene for the discussion.[2] The question is, however, what did Mill take from this tradition, apart from his great interest in the philosophy of mind and in the whole range of moral sciences? As mentioned, it has been suggested that he at least adopted the main ideas of the Scottish conception of conjectural history and that he later tried to negotiate a modus vivendi between this and his utilitarian theory of politics.[3] The crucial question

1   See especially Alexander Bain, *James Mill: A Biography*, London, 1882, pp. 13–21. On p. 16 Bain quotes the following passage from one of Mill's letters to Macvey Napier many years later, in 1821: 'All the years I remained about Edinburgh, I used as often as I possibly could, to steal into Mr Stewart's class to hear a lecture, which was always a high treat. I have heard Pitt and Fox deliver some of their most admired speeches; but I never heard anything nearly so eloquent as some of the lectures of Professor Stewart. The taste for the studies which have formed my favourite pursuits, and which will be so to the end of my life, I owe to him.' When I first published the present essay in 1984, I was not aware of Robert A. Fenn's dissertation, 'James Mill's Political Thought', Ph.D. thesis, University of London, 1971, in which he argues for the importance of seeing Mill's thought as a continuous development from his Scottish beginnings. When Fenn published a revised version of this dissertation in 1987, he was apparently unaware of all the more recent literature linking Mill to his Scottish intellectual origins (cf. note 3 to this chapter). Fenn's published study does, however, contain the only detailed evidence for just how close Mill stayed to Reid, especially in mental philosophy, up until 1806; Robert A. Fenn, *James Mill's Political Thought*, New York, 1987. Unfortunately, Fenn has no eye for the difficulty of accounting for the fact that this affiliation occurred simultaneously with Mill's strong allegiance to Millar.

2   James Mill, *A Fragment on Mackintosh*, London, 1835, pp. 4–9.

3   The pioneering study here is Duncan Forbes, 'James Mill and India', *Cambridge Journal*, 5 (1951–2), 19–33; and the approach is developed by Donald Winch in his introduction and editorial material to James Mill, *Selected Economic Writings*, ed. D. Winch, Edinburgh, 1966; by John Burrow in *Evolution and Society: A Study in Victorian Social Theory*, Cambridge, UK, 1970; and by J.H. Burns in 'The light of reason: Philosophical history of the two Mills', in *James and John Stuart Mill: Papers of the Centenary Conference*, ed. J.M. Robson and M. Laine, Toronto, 1976, pp. 3–20. The most important treatment of Mill's position in the general Scottish methodological tradition is N. de Marchi, 'The case for James Mill', in *Methodological Controversy in Economics: Historical Essays in Honour of T.W. Hutchison*, ed. A.W. Coats, New York,

is, however, exactly which elements in the theory of conjectural history Mill adopted, for the answer to this will determine the precise sense in which the second half of the suggestion can be accepted.

9.2   *The use and abuse of conjectural history*

From some of his earliest reviews in the *Literary Journal*, through his extensive notes on the translation of Charles François Dominique de Villers's *Essays on the Spirit and Influence of the Reformation of Luther*, his contributions to the *Edinburgh Review*, the *Monthly Review*, and the *Eclectic Review*, to *The History of British India*, Mill draws very heavily on the Scottish philosophical historians. Of these, John Millar is the most important to Mill; Millar continued Hume's combination of philosophy and history; he was far 'more philosophical' than Montesquieu in his concentration on government rather than power; and in dealing with the consequences of commerce he covered much the same ground as Smith, but did so independently and showed himself to be 'of equal originality and depth of thought'.[4] Further, in *The History of British India* Mill makes it quite clear that he sees his work, in some respects, as a direct continuation of that of Millar, for Millar's historical theories 'though highly important, were but detached considerations applied to particular facts, and not a comprehensive induction, leading to general conclusions'.[5] This gives us our clue to what Mill thought he particularly learned from the Scots: to look for 'general conclusions' rather than history. This is a theme which Mill strikes up already in his first review of Millar's *Historical View of the British Government* (1803), where he maintains that, admirable as Hume's pioneering efforts were in combining history and philosophy, it must nevertheless be feared that the two will ultimately get in each other's way:

> For this reason we are of opinion, that the relation of public events, and transactions, the simple business of history, and disquisitions with respect to the causes and consequences of these transactions, and with respect to the tendency and operation of the political arrangements in any country, which successively take place, form two different subjects, which ought to be treated apart. The first is properly speaking history, the last might be called

----

1983, pp. 155–84. For perceptive comparisons between Mill and the other Scottish orientalists who were influenced by Dugald Stewart and the canon of conjectural history, see Jane Rendall, 'Scottish orientalism: From Robertson to James Mill', *Historical Journal*, 25 (1982), 43–69.

4   *Literary Journal*, 2 (October 1803), 325–33 and 385–400, at pp. 325–6, 327 and 390–1.

5   James Mill, *The History of British India*, 4th ed., with notes and continuation by H.H. Wilson, 9 vols., London, 1840–48, II, p. 157.

philosophical considerations on history; or more shortly the one might be denominated history, the other the philosophy of history.[6]

In order to produce such 'philosphy of history', we would have to apply the laws of human nature to provide causal explanations, physical causes being inadequate. By means of these and of comparative studies of cultures, we would be able to construct conjectural accounts of periods with missing or deficient historical evidence, and we would be able to study history as a progression, in which each stage should be considered as a coherent whole.[7] However, Mill does not commit himself clearly to any particular view of the stages in 'the progress of improvement', though he does see these as matters of 'statistical fact'.[8]

These are the themes in Mill's historical method and in his own practice as a philosophical historian. Although admittedly he did not quite follow his own suggestion to separate narrative history from 'the philosophy of history' when he came to write *The History of British India*, there is nevertheless a clear division between his highly 'philosophical' history of Hindu society and his narration of the facts pertaining to British connections with India. The former, which constitutes the backbone of the work, is in many ways as perfect an example of 'rationalist' history as any from the previous century. In fact, if one reads Mill's work in the fourth edition by Horace H. Wilson, Professor

6 *Literary Journal*, 2 (October 1803), 326.

7 There are many examples of these forms of explanation in *History of British India*, the more notable ones being I, pp. xxvi–xxvii, 171–9, 211–17 (the judicature), 243–4 (inheritance), 249–50 (testaments), 252–3 (very Smith-like account of the origin of criminal jurisdiction and government), 299–301 (property), 330–45 (natural history of religion), 445–7 (natural history of marriage – with the editor protesting in the name of historical fact), 466–7; II, pp. 2–3 (natural history of 'the arts'), 48–50 (natural history of literature: poetry is the language of the passions and a mnemonic aid – therefore the first literature, beyond which the Hindu has hardly reached), 74–9 (abstract speculation is natural and not a sign of high civilization – *vide* Arabs and Turks, as well as Hindus!), 205 ('The science of political economy' can make a 'demonstration' that a society at the Hindu stage could not have had money of gold and silver, to which the editor remarks, 'These assertions are all at variance with facts, but facts must give way to the "science of political economy"'). For emphasis on comparisons, see I, pp. 182–4 note, 211, 264–6, 303–20 and II, pp. 9–11, 74–9, 86, 210–32, 499–514. Concerning moral causes, see I, pp. 466–7, 480–1. There is also a glorious use of 'the known laws of human nature' to criticize any idea that the prospect of reward or punishment in a future life carries any moral weight for mankind in general, and this is then illustrated and confirmed by the case of the common Hindu: I, pp. 434–6.

8 See *History of British India*, II, p. 479; and compare with Mill's review of De Guignes, *Voyages à Peking*, in the *Edinburgh Review*, July 1809, p. 413, where he complains that philosophers have not yet fixed exactly the criteria for the progress of civilization.

of Sanskrit at Oxford, the confrontation between Mill's text and Wilson's extensive editorial notes often reads like a caricature or parody on the standard view of the transition from eighteenth- to nineteenth-century historiography.[9] This may serve to sharpen our enquiry: What is it that makes Mill's *History* such an aridly rationalist exercise when compared, for example, with the works of Smith and Millar? It would seem that there are two elements in particular which may account for this. First, in Mill there is no emphasis on the principle of unintended consequences, or on the heterogeneity of ends;[10] and second, closely connected with this, Mill constantly puts a quite extraordinary emphasis on the role of individual human agency in the development of society. He has in fact little or no theoretical conception of social and institutional change, and in virtually all important cases of development in Hindu society Mill allots the decisive role to deliberate intervention by some individual or institution.

It is true that Mill begins his philosophical history with the classical 'sociological' point that civilization requires a certain density of population.[11] But beyond that, he roundly declares: 'The form of the government is one, the nature of the laws for the administration of justice is the other, of the two circumstances by which the condition of the people in all countries is chiefly determined.'[12] This is later modified when Mill says that it is nearly impossible to decide whether it is religion or the combination of government and law which is the major social determinant in Hindustan, for the whole of Hindu life and all its institutions are understood in religious terms.[13] We might, of course, take all this as an indication that Mill is really subscribing to a pluralism of the sort which we find in Smith and Millar.[14] But apart from the fact that religion itself is understood simply in terms of a conspiracy theory, according to which religion is a weapon for power-seeking priests,[15] all hopes of pluralism are ruled out by Mill's explanatory

9   For a substantial survey, see T.P. Peardon, *The Transition in English Historical Writing, 1760–1830*, New York, 1933; Mill is discussed briefly on pp. 266–71.

10   In drawing up the lines of development from the Scottish social thinkers of the eighteenth century to the Mills, Duncan Forbes also makes this point: '"Scientific" Whiggism: Adam Smith and John Millar', *Cambridge Journal*, 7 (1953–4), 643–70, specifically p. 670. But in all fairness it should be mentioned that in his early first review of Millar, Mill did emphasise this point: *Literary Journal*, 2 (October, 1803), 333.

11   *History of British India*, I, pp. 172ff.   12   *History of British India*, I, p. 289.

13   *History of British India*, I, pp. 329–30.

14   On Smith's historical pluralism, see K. Haakonssen, *The Science of a Legislator: The Natural Jurisprudence of David Hume and Adam Smith*, Cambridge, UK, 1981, ch. 8; on Millar, see Chapter 5 in the present volume.

15   This is the general message of the long chapter on Hindu religion in *History of British India*, I, pp. 329–436.

practice. Thus, although growth of population made government necessary, history shows that government was generally created by some outstanding individual.[16] Furthermore, when society was ripe for it, the intervention of a great legislator created the division of labour, and in Hindustan this took the form of the four-caste system. In societies, such as those of the Arabs and the Tartars, which have lacked such a legislator – 'one of those superior men, who are capable of accelerating the improvement of society' – the division of labour, and hence the division of society into classes, has never taken place, 'natural and simple as it may appear'.[17] Just as it was the inactivity of one monarch which allowed the mixing of the four original castes to get out of hand, so 'it required the wisdom of [a] virtuous king to devise a remedy' for the resulting disorders; and by classifying the mixed race and assigning the classes to different occupations, he at the same time met the need for further division of labour. 'This, accordingly, was the commencement of arts and manufactures.'[18] Obviously this was a significant step forward in Hindu society, but 'having reached this stage, it does not appear that it has made, or that it is capable of making, much further progress'.[19] The implication of all this is clear: another great legislator is required, one who is not trammelled by the Hindu stage of civilization – maybe one from Great Britain.[20]

Finally, we should look at Mill's very important discussion of property in land. This is perhaps the most curious case of all for, sandwiched between two paragraphs which briefly but clearly indicate a general natural history type of explanation of the historicity of property, we find the following extraordinary declaration, which sounds as if it had strayed in from his *Essay on Jurisprudence*:

> the different combinations of benefits which are included under the idea of property, at different periods of society, are all equally arbitrary . . . they are

16 *History of British India*, I, p. 178: 'In every society there are superior spirits, capable of seizing the best ideas of their times, and, if they are not opposed to circumstances, of accelerating the progress of the community to which they belong. The records of ancient nations give us reason to believe that some individual of this description, exalted to authority by his wisdom and virtue, has generally accomplished the important task of first establishing among a rude people a system of government and laws.'

17 *History of British India*, I, pp. 180–3.

18 *History of British India*, I, pp. 199–200.   19 *History of British India*, I, p. 200.

20 Remember Bentham's dictum: 'Mill will be the living executive – I shall be the dead legislative of British India', in *The Works of Jeremy Bentham*, published under the superintendence of his executor, John Bowring, 11 vols., Edinburgh, 1838–43, X, p. 490. As Forbes points out, Mill's *History* was 'a standard work for officials of the East India Company, and eventually became a text-book for candidates for the Indian Civil Service' ('James Mill and India', p. 23), and he was, of course, a high official in the company.

not the offspring of nature, but the creatures of will; determined, and chosen by the society, as that arrangement with regard to useful objects, which is, or is pretended to be, the best of all.[21]

As if this were not bad enough from Millar's admirer, Mill goes on to maintain that since the creation of private property in land is such 'a great revolution', it can be done only by the sovereign sharing out the territory and that in order to do this he must come to be regarded as the owner of all land. Mill then embarks on a lengthy demonstration that this was generally the case in primitive societies and that the Hindus had reached this particular stage of sovereign ownership of the soil.[22] This is of great importance for his general argument, since he wants to show that neither the ryots nor the zemindars have anything approaching property right in the land they use – contrary to what many previous observers and administrators had thought.[23] It is, then, possible for him to argue that the British state should be considered as the sovereign power which could settle the peasants on the land (the 'ryotwar' system) and reap the rental of the land as revenue.[24]

Altogether, Mill's way of writing history emasculates the type of history he so much admired. The view he presents is of a few stages or periods, which are outlined very briefly in natural history terms as more or less static and are connected only through the dynamic forces of individual exertion. Since Mill believed that he could 'make the human mind as plain as the road from Charing Cross to St. Paul's'[25] by means of associationist psychology, we have the prospect that even these moving forces of history could be explained by the laws of science. We are thus very near to an identification of the view of the past with what the methods of conjectural history can produce. It is of course true that Mill's great legislators responded to their historical situation, but he displays little or no sense of the limitations this might have placed upon their actions and planning generally, 'All great changes in society, are easily effected when the time is come.'[26] Consequently, just as the past could be understood according to 'scientific'

21   *History of British India*, I, p. 501.   22   *History of British India*, I, pp. 302–20.

23   *History of British India*, I, pp. 320–8, and V, pp. 480 ff.

24   For a discussion of the contribution which Mill, and the utilitarians in general, made to the discussion of the whole spectrum of British policy towards India, see Eric Stokes, *The British Utilitarians and India*, Oxford, 1969. For the problems of land and land revenue, see especially pp. 60–1 and ch. 2. See also Donald Winch's introduction to the excerpts from *The History of British India* in Mill, *Selected Economic Writings*, pp. 383–95.

25   Quoted from a letter to Francis Place in William Thomas, *The Philosophic Radicals: Nine Studies in Theory and Practice, 1817–1841*, Oxford, 1979, p. 121.

26   Quoted from a letter to Ricardo in Mill, *Selected Economic Writings*, p. 390; see also Winch's surrounding discussion.

formulae, so the future could be constructed according to such 'scientific' principles. As Mill reassured Ricardo;

> I have no doubt about removing all your difficulties; and showing you that instead of being a science, the practical results of which must always be uncertain, rendering it always prudent to try to remain in the state we are in, rather than venture the unknown effects of a change, legislation is essentially a science the effects of which may be computed with an extraordinary degree of certainty; and the friends of human nature cannot proceed with too much energy in bearing down every obstacle which opposes the progress of human welfare.[27]

John Burrow has suggested that Mill was able to reconcile the two strands of his thought, namely his historical approach and his utilitarian activism in politics, by postulating a sort of break in history. This break separated, on the one hand, the more primitive stages of social development, which the West had put behind but which could still be found in places such as India, from, on the other hand, the developed society which Europe had achieved. The former could be explained by the canon of conjectural history, whereas the latter was open to the influence of utilitarian reform.[28] Furthermore, it has even been suggested that although Bentham himself never wrote anything about the past comparable to Mill's *History of British India*, the whole of Bentham's oeuvre should nevertheless be seen in pretty much this light.[29] Although we may disregard this speculation here, it should be clear that Mill follows in the footsteps of Dugald Stewart and his Whig disciples in so far as he maintains the idea of a sharp break between modern society and all previous history and thus impoverishes the relationship between normative political theory and historical considerations.[30]

This is a very complex issue, however, for it is by no means clear why Mill takes that position. According to Burrow's reading, Mill's position is, in brief, as follows. In the 'Essay on Government' Mill argues that the decisive premise for the advocacy of representative government is 'that men can recognize their own interest',[31] not that they just pursue their interest, namely pleasure – for the latter applies universally, irrespective of what form of government may be appropriate. But in *The History of British India* Mill argues that the Hindus have not reached a stage where they can recognize their own interests; con-

27 Quoted from a letter to Ricardo in Mill, *Selected Economic Writings*, p. 187. Cf. Winch's discussion of this in relation to Mill's influence on Ricardo, pp. 179–88.

28 See Burrow, *Evolution and Society*, pp. 59–64.

29 See E.J. Eisenach, 'The dimension of history in Bentham's theory of law', *Bentham Newsletter*, 5 (1981), 2–21.

30 See Chapter 7 in this volume.   31 Burrow, *Evolution and Society*, p. 61.

sequently, the argument of the *Essay* does not apply to India. In other words, 'Mill has a philosophy of history which teaches him to be a gradualist in India, just as he has a philosophy of mind which teaches him to be a democrat in England.'[32] Without necessarily disagreeing with this, we may think that the situation is more complicated and that Mill's attempt to reconcile his political theory with his philosophical history is much more difficult to rescue. First of all, it should be made clear that as far as all the social institutions are concerned, Mill is not 'a gradualist in India'. The general point of his discussion of Hindu civilization is to debunk the idea that it has reached any degree of sophistication or any high level of development. And the measure which is constantly applied to do this is that of utility: 'In looking at the pursuits of any nation, with a view to draw from them indications of the state of civilization, no mark is so important, as the nature of the End to which they are directed. Exactly in proportion as Utility is the object of every pursuit, may we regard a nation as civilized.'[33] On this basis, all parts of Hindu culture and all institutions, not least law, can be judged and are found to be utterly wanting. As Eric Stokes has thoroughly demonstrated, Mill's diagnosis was that the ills of India stemmed from exactly the same source as the ills of Europe: bad government.[34] The cure too was the same: good government. Consequently, as Stokes shows, Mill proposes to reconstitute the legal framework of India completely by introducing a Benthamite code and attendant institutions. In this there is no gradualism whatsoever, and we must conclude that for most of the institutions of fundamental importance to the philosophical historians in whose footsteps Mill professedly follows, he refuses their most basic lesson: that these institutions form part and parcel of the social life of a people and that they cannot for the purpose of reform be separated from the rest of the intractable, historically-conditioned matter of society.

Because Mill's belief in the power of education has become particularly well known, it should perhaps be pointed out here that he does not believe even in the piecemeal improvement of the Hindus through schooling.[35] His concept of education is, however, much wider than that; for him it includes 'every thing, which acts upon the being as it comes from the hand of nature, in such a manner as to modify the

32   Burrow, *Evolution and Society*, pp. 61–2.

33   *History of British India*, II, pp. 149–50.

34   Stokes, *The British Utilitarians and India*, pp. 66ff. Since this was written, Javed Majeed has argued at length that it was central to Mill's *History* to use 'British India to fashion a critique of British law in particular and British society in general': *Ungoverned Imaginings: James Mill's "The History of British India" and Orientalism*, Oxford, 1992, p. 133.

35   Stokes, *The British Utilitarians and India*, pp. 55–8.

mind, to render the train of feelings different from what it would otherwise have been'.[36] In this wide field, the influence of 'the political machine' is the most important of all:

> The Political Education is like the key-stone of the arch; the strength of the whole depends upon it. We have seen that the strength of the Domestic and the Technical Education depends almost entirely upon the Social. Now it is certain, that the nature of the Social depends almost entirely upon the Political; and the most important of the Physical (that which operates with greatest force upon the greatest number, the state of aliment and labour of the lower classes), is, in the long run, determined by the action of the political machine. The play, therefore, of the political machine acts immediately upon the mind, and with extraordinary power; but this is not all; it also acts upon almost every thing else by which the character of the mind is apt to be formed.[37]

As we have seen, only this, the most important part of education, is fit and necessary for the Hindus, and it is a lesson which could be given once and for all. But the results of this lesson will presumably come about piecemeal, and it is this which opens the possibility of Burrow's argument, from which we started.

The only respect in which there is room for gradualism in Mill's theory is the one pointed out by Burrow, specifically concerning the introduction of representative government. But even here there are difficulties. The argument Burrow must have in mind, on Mill's behalf, must be to the following effect. With the introduction of a rational utilitarian legal framework, man's natural individualism in his pursuit of his interest, namely pleasure, will gradually gain strength amongst the Hindus. The main obstacle is religious nonsense, but since this has force only through the power of priests, it will disappear as their power disappears, for 'the known laws of human nature' demonstrate that the prospect of reward or punishment in a future life in itself has no influence on people.[38] As the natural pursuit of interests becomes the common pattern, the Hindus will in time come to recognize that this is what they are doing – which, as we saw, is the qualification for representative government. The problem is just that, as far as is known, there is no evidence that this is what Mill expects or even hopes. On the contrary, he went out of his way to argue against the introduction of Indians into any part of the higher administration of their country,[39] and he 'obviously believed India was a case where autocracy needs not

36 James Mill, 'Education', in *James Mill on Education*, ed. W.H. Burston, Cambridge, UK (1969), p. 70.
37 Mill, 'Education', pp. 117–18.   38 *History of British India*, I, pp. 434–6.
39 See Stokes, *The British Utilitarians and India*, pp. 64–6.

lead to tyranny'.[40] So, even as far as government itself is concerned, there is little to be said for Mill's application of a social and historical perspective.

Our general conclusion must be that Mill's view of the past had been taken over completely by a conception of conjectural history, so simplified by the exclusion of the principle of unintended consequences,[41] and thus by its view of social causation, that it could not possibly modify his highly rationalist and constructivist theory of politics. Further, on the one point where his quasi-historical view of Hindu society should have influenced his ideas of the mode of political change, it clearly did not.

9.3 Politics in a morally well-ordered world

Mill's narrow view of history and dim view of its theoretical importance must be borne in mind when we try to understand his more theoretical work. Since much of this, especially after *The History of British India* (1817), was at least in part produced as his contribution to the radical group's attack on Whig thinking, an interpretation in terms of 'theory versus history', 'reason versus tradition', is both obvious and, consequently, common. The first major battle was sparked off by Mackintosh's (1818) review of Bentham's *Plan of Parliamentary Reform*.[42] This led to a number of utilitarian rejoinders during the 1820s, all resting on the theory of Mill's *Essay on Government*. This debate was in many ways a rehearsal for the much more famous one between Macaulay and the Benthamites, which we shall ignore here.[43] The general outlines of these discussions are well known, and they have been summarized aptly with special reference to Mackintosh and Mill:

> Mackintosh's approach was the very antithesis of Bentham's and Mill's. Where they saw society as a mechanism, he saw it as an organism. They appealed to reason; he appealed to history. The changes they demanded to maximize human happiness he rejected as likely to squander what happiness had been achieved. They saw the social changes around them in the

40 Stokes, *The British Utilitarians and India*, p.68.

41 As Forbes says, 'What Alexander Bain later described as a "grand sociological display" was in reality an example of the parochialism of Rationalist history so extreme as to be almost a caricature', 'James Mill and India', p. 28.

42 *Edinburgh Review*, December 1818, pp. 165–205. See Mackintosh in *Edinburgh Review*, November 1820, pp. 461–501, and George Grote, *A Statement of the Question of Parliamentary Reform*, London, 1821; cf. Thomas, *The Philosophic Radicals*, pp. 127–8 and 412–3.

43 The main contributions to this debate are now collected in *Utilitarian Logic and Politics: James Mill's 'Essay on Government', Macaulay's Critique and the Ensuing Debate*, ed. J. Lively and J.C. Rees, Oxford, 1978.

light of an increasing popular enlightenment; he saw them as symptoms of popular ignorance, threatening a repetition of the disorders of the English Civil War. They brushed aside the Whigs as a party blighted by aristocratic folly and greed; he saw in the Whig party the only hope for stability because only they combined desire for change with a respect for constitutional forms. He condemned Bentham's *Plan* as revolutionary in effect if not in intention, and proposed instead a much more gradual programme of piece-meal disfranchisement of rotten boroughs and slow extension of the franchise, a solution which almost seemed to them no solution at all. The difference in approach could hardly have been more marked, and it recalls the argument of Burke and Paine thirty years before.[44]

With the exception of the point about popular enlightenment, which is not valid for Mackintosh's work in general, this would seem to cover the agenda for the debate very well. And yet, if we keep in mind the Scottish tradition in moral philosophy, which forms part of the background to the debate, it must be apparent that there is more to be said. Could the 'difference in approach' not 'have been more marked'? If we look at it from a philosophical angle and draw in the later encounter between Mackintosh's *Dissertation on the Progress of Ethical Philosophy* and Mill's *Fragment on Mackintosh*, then it would seem that it could.

First of all we have to locate the exact point of disagreement beneath all the conventional rhetoric, and this is by no means as simple as it may appear. In his review of Bentham's *Plan* Mackintosh sets out from the following declaration, which one would hardly have expected from Thomas's description:

> In discussion with Bentham, we have the advantage of agreeing in a common principle. Like him, we consider utility as the test of every political institution . . . The dispute about Reform must finally be decided by the principle of Utility . . . Before we enter on the argument, we wish to waive all advantage, which may be supposed to be possessed by those who defend established principles against untried projects. We shall compare different plans of representation, as if they were for the first time presented to the judgment and choice of a nation, borrowing no aid from the established system, but the experience with which it has supplied us.[45]

In agreeing with the principle of utility, Mackintosh is, of course, being either facetious or superficial, as his concluding reference to the experience furnished by the established system indicates. When he wants to use a measure of utility, he refers to the preservation, not necessarily of a particular set of given institutions but of the form of moral life which is lived within these institutions. It is not a utility that is compounded of the interests of individuals but a utility that is compounded of the interests of the various national and local orders which traditional

44 Thomas, *The Philosophic Radicals*, p. 125.
45 *Edinburgh Review*, December 1818, p. 174.

morality has formed. Hence the appropriate form of political representation is not universal suffrage but one that adequately follows the movements of social morality. Such is the burden of both this and his subsequent contributions to the debate about Parliamentary reform.[46] Further, this view must be understood against the background of Mackintosh's theory of morality, according to which the traditional and conventional moral forms in any given society are the 'superstructural' expression of the underlying objective, universal, and unvarying morality.[47]

For Mill too there is a universal morality, and this in fact is a theme to which he recurs a number of times:

> nations differ less from one another in the knowledge of morality, and of its obligations (the rules of morality have been taught in all nations in a manner remarkably similar), than in the degrees of steadiness, with which they assign the preference to moral, above other acts.[48]

Similarly, that part of morality which is of particular importance for legislation, namely rights, is essentially the same everywhere:

> The particular powers or privileges which it is expedient to constitute rights, are, in the great points, so distinctly and strongly indicated by common experience, that there is a very general agreement about them among nations in all the stages of civilization. Nations differ chiefly in the mode of securing those rights.[49]

For both Mackintosh and Mill the ultimate criterion of morality is the maximization of happiness, and it is a criterion which in the world of affairs has always been more or less submerged by conventional morality and its institutions. But whereas for Mackintosh the universal criterion is wielded only by the Deity, for Mill it can be applied by the individual. Consequently, according to Mill, we do have a measure for the quality of the conventional superstructure of morality, so the latter cannot be taken for granted as an expression of universal morality. Mill's onslaught on the traditionalism of Mackintosh and the Whigs takes place, then, on the basis of a difference in attitude to the role of

46 In addition to the references in note 42, see also Mackintosh's 'Speech on the second reading of the Bill to amend the representation of the people of England and Wales', in *The Miscellaneous Works of the Right Honourable Sir James Mackintosh*, 3 vols., London, 1846, III, pp. 535–65.

47 See Chapter 8 in the present volume.

48 *History of British India*, I, p. 421; cf. II, p. 86.

49 *History of British India*, II, p. 500. This is repeated in *A Fragment on Mackintosh*, p. 145. Mill is here referring to more fundamental rights than legal rights, which he discusses, for example, in the 'Essay on Jurisprudence', in *Essays on Government, Jurisprudence, Liberty of the Press, and Law of Nations*, New York, 1967, pp. 4–6.

religion and the status of man's claim to moral knowledge. But important as this is, one cannot help feeling that there is a certain superficiality about the debate, which can perhaps be revealed by drawing up the opposing positions in yet another manner.

Mackintosh's idea of the relationship between the historically-given morality and the underlying universal morality is inherently vague, so it is always possible for him to rebut any charge of moral historicism and relativism – by asserting that of course there are universal moral standards; we just cannot apply them universally. Mill, on the other hand, is in a position to assert, as he does in the *Fragment on Mackintosh,* that he and Bentham do have regard for the historically-given morality and institutions – after all, that is the very object for utilitarian criticism in any given case.[50] But the real point is that for Mackintosh the historically-given is not an object for moral judgement, because it is not the deliberate creation of men, whereas for Mill this is precisely the case. Most of the positive morality we find is created by power-hungry priests; and positive law and institutions are the making of corrupt legislators and judges. Mill is led to this standpoint by his 'rationalist' conception of history and social change. Underlying these differences there is, nevertheless, a strange unanimity. For Mill, as for Stewart and Mackintosh, the moral world is ultimately without uncertainty. It is true that we can make mistakes, but we know that there is always a right answer to any moral problem, that one action in each alternative set will make the maximum contribution to happiness, and that in this sense the moral world is in principle completely well ordered. Both the philosophical Whig's argument against large-scale intervention in the moral and institutional fabric of society and the utilitarian's argument for such intervention therefore spring from similar claims to certain moral knowledge. In this they both differ from Adam Smith, for whom the moral world was a genuinely open and uncertain one, in which the only point of certainty was constituted by a few formal or procedural requirements of natural justice, which, when minted into law, would provide sufficient attention to natural justice to make social life on a wide scale possible – anything else being a more or less lucky bonus.

Against this background we may give a new twist to Elie Halévy's famous interpretation of the discussion between Whigs and utilitarians in terms of an opposition between the idea of 'natural' and 'artificial' harmony in society.[51] Whether the harmony is growing out of the steadily increasing adequacy of man's moral faculty to grasp the objectively well-ordered moral world, as in Stewart; whether it is assured

50   *A Fragment of Mackintosh,* pp. 145–6.
51   Elie Halévy, *The Growth of Philosophic Radicalism,* Boston, 1966, esp. pp. 455–78.

when the traditional morality of society is left to shape the universal moral faculty of the individual (even if the starting-point is a psychologically egoistic being), as in Mackintosh; whether harmony is created when psychologically egoistic individuals, by the erection of the right institutional forms (and hence the right 'education'), are made to live according to utilitarian calculations of the maximization of happiness, as in Mill: in every case, the striking point behind the differences to which Halévy directs our attention is the idea of assured harmony. At least, this is what is striking if we contrast these thinkers with Hume and Smith.

It is also this which makes Mill's idea of the political sciences so very different from Smith's science of a legislator. The character of Smith's science of legislation was determined by the relationship between the formal requirements of natural justice and the empirical results of the 'history' of law and society, and, as this relationship has been presented elsewhere, it may to some extent be understood by analogy with the reasoning of a common law judge upon a case presented to him.[52] But with Mill what springs to mind immediately is the relationship between pure and applied science. The pure science of human nature, while taking for granted the physical needs of man which are so decisive for political economy, consists mainly of the genetic explanations of our psychological make-up provided by associationist psychology. There is hardly any doubt that with his own rounding off of Hartley's work, in the *Analysis of the Phenomena of the Human Mind*, Mill thought that this science had been largely completed and that the human mind had become 'as plain as the road from Charing Cross to St Paul's'. The other 'pure science' must be conceived to be utilitarian value theory, which for Mill consists in a reduction of the traditional virtues and rules of morality to the utilitarian standard of the maximization of happiness. The part of this theory that deals with the values which, when adopted into the law, become known as 'rights' he sometimes refers to as the 'science of legislation'.[53] Again, he clearly thought that this discipline had been completed by Bentham, with occasional assistance from himself[54] and in fact he is generally content simply to take it for granted.[55]

52   See Haakonssen, *Science of a Legislator*, chapter 5.

53   See *A Fragment of Mackintosh*, p. 145.

54   See Halévy, *The Growth of Philosophic Radicalism*, pp. 473–4, concerning Mill's contribution, mainly in the form of a suggestion to reconstitute the four classical virtues on a utilitarian basis, a suggestion which influences Bentham's *Deontology* and is of some importance in Mill's essay on 'Education'.

55   The *Fragment on Mackintosh* is the only work in which Mill discusses moral philosophy at length (see esp. pp. 248–65). But chs. 16–25, esp. ch. 23, of the *Analysis of the Phenomena of the Human Mind*, New York, 1967, as well as the essay on 'Education' are also important.

In relation to these basic sciences, the rest – political economy, the theory of government, and jurisprudence – are simply derivative, technological disciplines. They deal with the social and institutional devices which, if they are applied according to the utilitarian prescription, will make it possible for men, who are psychologically egoistic, to live together according to the utilitarian rules of morality. Mill's aim is thus a scientifically demonstrated institutional solution to the problem which from an early date had bedevilled the discussion of utilitarianism, namely its relationship with egoism. Although this problem had already been effectively dealt with by the two founders of Scottish moral philosophy, Gershom Carmichael and Francis Hutcheson, some of the utilitarians of the late eighteenth century, such as Thomas Belsham, and indeed all critics of utilitarianism from the Common Sense philosophers onwards, automatically identified the two.[56] But the Benthamite utilitarians, from Bentham, in the *Introduction to the Principles of Morals and Legislation*,[57] through to Mill, especially in the *Fragment on Mackintosh* and beyond,[58] constantly emphasized that utilitarianism was not an egoistic moral theory, although Mill at the same time subscribed to a more or less clearly distinguished psychological egoism. This position was bound to be misunderstood, and Mill himself was never as systematic in the presentation of the whole as of the parts. Nevertheless, it is an important perspective on his work. Since his psychological theory seemed to make it difficult to understand how men actually could live in accordance with the moral doctrine to which he subscribed, the attendant disciplines of political economy, government, and jurisprudence became necessary to demonstrate which institutional framework would do the trick. Precisely because he took his science of human nature and his moral theory to be complete and certain, the derivative sciences could be conceived with deductive certainty. So why should a legislator worry more about time and place than any other engineer?

When all the traditional differences have been allowed for, it is clear that Stewart's course in moral philosophy and the derivative 'political economy' provided a better preparation for this standpoint than Smith's science of legislation.

56   Cf. J.B. Schneewind, *Sidgwick's Ethics and Victorian Moral Philosophy*, Oxford, 1977, ch. 4, especially pp. 127–8 and 131.

57   Jeremy Bentham, *An Introduction to the Principles of Morals and Legislation*, ed. J.H. Burns and H.L.A. Hart, London, 1970, chs. 1 and 2. The long note in ch. 2, to para. 14 (pp. 26–9) is particularly important, for its point is that all moral philosophers, of very different schools, are really just a bunch of disguised subjectivists who become despotic when their principles are turned to politics, whereas the principle of utility is an objective one between individuals. The concluding dialogue is particularly clear on this.

58   Mill, *Fragment on Mackintosh*, pp. 248–65, are again the most valuable pages.

From natural law to the rights of man:
A European perspective on American debates

10.1 *English and American jurisprudence*

As the first ten amendments were making their way through the provisions of the new Constitution they were to amend, American jurisprudence was being systematically formulated by the recently appointed Professor to the new Chair of Law at the College of Philadelphia. With much rhetorical force and eclectic learning, James Wilson presented a public course of lectures, one important aim of which was to give an American answer to the jurisprudence of Sir William Blackstone. In doing so, Wilson effectively provided one of the earliest sustained analyses of the contrast between the American cultivation of rights as the basis for social ethics and politico-legal institutions and the British reliance on a combination of common law and policy. Wilson would, in fact, have recognized all the leading themes in a recent analysis of this kind.[1]

Nowhere is the theoretical scope of Wilson's polemics brought out more dramatically than in his discussion 'of the natural rights of individuals'.[2] Here Blackstone is joined by Edmund Burke's recent *Reflections on the Revolution in France* as the epitome of British thinking. Wilson understands the two British thinkers to be maintaining that all, or – allowing for Blackstone's lack of clarity in the matter – at least all significant, natural rights are given up in civil society in return for such fundamental legal rights as those contained in Magna Charta, that is, 'civil privileges, provided by society, in lieu of the natural liberties given up by individuals'.[3] Thus in his eyes the British held rights to be

1   Alan Ryan, 'The British, the Americans, and rights', in *A Culture of Rights: The Bill of Rights in Philosophy, Politics and Law – 1791 and 1991*, ed. M.J. Lacey and K. Haakonssen, Cambridge, UK, 1991, pp. 366–439.

2   James Wilson, 'Lectures on Law', in *Works*, ed. J. Dewitt Andrews, 2 vols., Chicago, 1896, II, pp. 296–336.

3   Ibid., p. 302.

a kind of communal property to be granted to individuals, and they held individuals to be 'nothing but what the society frames'.[4] It is as a contrast to this view that he formulates the well-known 'American' ideas of human beings as the carriers – in society and out of it – of certain inalienable natural rights, and of civil society and its government as the means 'to secure and to enlarge the exercise of the natural rights of its members'.[5]

The striking thing about American jurisprudence, then as now, and the thing that has been seen as the main difference from British jurisprudence, is this emphasis on basic rights. For long periods this jurisprudence has been taken as the key to understanding both political thought and action in America in the last third of the eighteenth century. When major challenges to such interpretations have been launched, normally to establish the independent efficacy of politics and the political vis-à-vis jurisprudence and the law, a central problem has been to explain the prima facie prominence of rights talk. In these grand debates comparatively little attention has been paid to the concept of rights itself. The purpose of this chapter is to sketch some of the argumentative structure surrounding this concept in the eighteenth century. This will show that the status of rights was different from that commonly assumed and that at least some of the divisions in the scholarly disputes run along rather anachronistic lines.

10.2 *Law, duty, and rights*

In the mainstream of natural jurisprudence in the eighteenth century, natural rights derived from natural law and natural duty. Natural rights were understood as part of a morally well-ordered universe, a universe structured and lent certainty by the law of nature. Natural rights theory was much less individualistic and anti-authoritarian than it has later been taken to be. Furthermore, the natural law theory of which it was part was developed by a wide variety of British thinkers so as to accommodate a great deal of traditionalism, including that inherent in English constitutionalism and common law thought. This cluster of doctrines constituted a formidable hindrance to the development of a subjective rights theory proper, that is, a theory according to which rights are the primary and fundamental moral feature of humanity. However, a number of steps towards such a theory were taken, and it is in the resulting complex situation that we have to locate some important attempts by Americans to conceptualize their position. One such step was the strong emphasis upon the inalienability of certain rights, an idea that was already part of traditional natural law theory

4   Ibid., p. 303.   5   Ibid., p. 307.

and became crucial in a revolutionary situation. Another was the suggestion that the moral world might not be well ordered even in principle, or, in other words, that clashes between rights might not be the
result simply of human folly or blindness but might be ultimate and
unresolvable. A third move in the direction of a theory of subjective
rights was the emergence of the idea of autonomy, understood as the
ability to impose obligation upon oneself, not as an effect of the moral
law but as the foundation for all morals.

The moral philosophical paradigm based upon natural law was so
dominant that these steps were taken uncertainly and with difficulty –
the last two with such difficulty, in fact, that it remains uncertain when
they were clearly made. In order to understand why this should be so,
one must have an appreciation of the complexity of the natural law
tradition as it was developed into the conventional moral philosophy
in which educated Britons and Americans alike were reared. Natural
law became a prevalent academic form of moral philosophy in the
eighteenth century, as it was taught in the two major Scottish universities and in many English dissenting academies and American colleges, as well as in latitudinarian Cambridge. Natural law was, in fact,
school-book stuff, for it was generally taught to boys aged fourteen to
eighteen as part of the arts curriculum that prepared them for all
further education. It was thus crucial in forming a moral outlook and
provided a framework into which other moral ideas had to fit or within
which they must be tested. This applies not least to any innovations on
a central point like the idea of rights.

In the preceding chapters we concentrated on the way in which
leading Scottish thinkers worked out a natural law–based moral philosophy. In this chapter we will consider what American thinkers in the
Revolutionary period did with this philosophy. We will begin this
consideration by looking briefly at an English (and Anglican) statement
of the paradigm, that of Thomas Rutherforth, who, like Grotius, Pufendorf, Locke, Hutcheson, and Burlamaqui, was taken for granted by
James Wilson as a household name amongst his educated audience.[6]

As Regius Professor of Divinity at Cambridge from 1756 to 1771,
Rutherforth was at the heart of Cambridge latitudinarianism,[7] whose
philosophical basis is spelled out in his main works in the form of the

6   Concerning the importance of Jean-Jacques Burlamaqui in America, see
M. White's important analysis *The Philosophy of the American Revolution*, New York,
1978, and section 10.7 in this chapter.

7   See John Gascoigne, *Cambridge in the Age of the Enlightenment: Science, Religion, and Politics from the Restoration to the French Revolution*, Cambridge, UK, 1989,
ch. 5: same, 'Anglican latitudinarianism, rational dissent and political radicalism in
the late eighteenth century', in *Enlightenment and Religion: Rational Dissent in
Eighteenth-Century Britain*, ed. K. Haakonssen, Cambridge, UK, forthcoming.

traditional theory of natural law, 'or the Knowledge of Right and Wrong' (as Isaac Watts defined it):[8]

> The actions of men are, in their own nature, either good, or bad, or indifferent . . . The law of nature . . . enjoys all those actions, which are morally good, and forbids all those which are morally bad. By this means the former become duties, and the latter crimes . . . But when any actions, which are indifferent in themselves, are commanded or forbidden by any express revelation of Gods will; those actions likewise . . . become duties, and . . . crimes: however, as the actions in themselves, or in their own nature, affect the common good of mankind neither one way or other, as they have nothing in them either morally good or morally bad; this sort of duties are called positive duties.[9]

The forms of behaviour which are pointed out by natural law as good are those that bring happiness, on the whole, to ourselves and to our neighbour and that please God.[10] In other words, Rutherforth presents the usual combination of moral realism and Christian utilitarianism,[11] and on this basis he goes on to clarify the relationship among law, right, and obligation:

> Our actions or our possessions are just, where they are consistent with law; and consequently the right which any person has to do any action, or to possess any thing, is nothing more than his power of doing this action, or

8   I. Watts, *The Improvement of the Mind, or, A Supplement to the Art of Logick*, London, 1741, p. 341.

9   Thomas Rutherforth, *Institutes of Natural Law* [1754], 2nd ed., Cambridge, 1774, pp. 17–18.

10   Ibid., pp. 9–13. For Rutherforth's influence on Paley, see D.L. Le Mahieu, *The Mind of William Paley*, Lincoln, NB, 1976, p. 124.

11   Cf. Blackstone, to add but one other genre in which we find this combination (we might as well have taken, say, Philip Doddridge's text-book for the dissenting academies): '[God] has laid down only such laws as were founded in those relations of justice, that existed in the nature of things antecedent to any positive precept. These are the eternal, immutable laws of good and evil, to which the creator himself in all his dispensations conforms . . . He has so intimately connected, so inseparably interwoven the laws of eternal justice with the happiness of each individual, that the latter cannot be obtained but by observing the former; and, if the former be punctually obeyed, it cannot but induce the latter. [Accordingly] he has not perplexed the law of nature with a multitude of abstracted rules and precepts, referring merely to the fitness or unfitness of things, as some have vainly surmised; but has graciously reduced the rule of obedience to this one paternal precept, "that man should pursue his own happiness." This is the foundation of what we call ethics, or natural law.' Sir William Blackstone, *Commentaries on the Laws of England*, 4 vols. Oxford, 1765–9, I, pp. 40–1. How could Bentham not give credit for this! For Doddridge, see *A Course of Lectures on the Principal Subjects in Pneumatology, Ethics, and Divinity* [1763], 4th ed., 2 vols., London, 1799, I, pp. 188ff. Cf. also J.E. Crimmins, 'John Brown and the theological tradition of utilitarian ethics', *History of Political Thought*, 4 (1983), 523–50.

possessing this thing consistently with law. Right and moral power are expressions of like import. A mans natural power extends to every thing, which his strength enables him to perform, whether the law allows it or not. But his moral power extends to such things only, as his strength enables him to perform consistently with law. For in a moral sense, or in reference to such rules as a man is strictly obliged to observe in his behaviour, he is not supposed to have any more power than what the law allows him to exercise.[12]

In these circumstances it is not surprising to find that 'obligation and right are correlative terms: where any person has a right, some one or more persons are under an obligation, which corresponds to that right', and vice versa.[13] Rutherforth draws the traditional distinctions between perfect and imperfect rights and duties, natural and adventitious rights, and alienable and inalienable rights, both sides of the distinction in each case being entirely dependent upon natural law. The consequence of the logical primacy of law is that right and duty become not only correlative in this sense but, in the case of the basic rights, interchangeable with duties in the manner I have already explained.[14] We should therefore not be surprised to find, in a chapter devoted to a discussion 'Of the Right which a Man has in his own Person', a subheading, 'Duty towards ourselves', under which Rutherforth sets out rights and duties in a way that reveals the nature of his theory very clearly:

It seems to be self-evidently true, that no man can have a right to manage his own person, or to dispose of it in such a manner, as will render him incapable of doing his duty. For his duty is a restraint, which arises from the law of nature: he cannot therefore have any right to free himself from that, unless he has a right to free himself from all restraints, which the law of nature has laid him under. The consequence of this is, that a mans right to his life or his limbs is a limited right; they are his to use, but not his to dispose of. As they were given him to use, whoever deprives him of them does him an injury. But then, as they are not his to abuse or dispose of, it follows, that he breaks through the law of nature, whenever he renders himself incapable of complying in any instance with that law, which the author and giver of his life

12   Rutherforth, *Institutes of Natural Law*, p. 27. Cf. Jefferson: 'Of liberty then I would say that, in the whole plenitude of its extent, it is unobstructed action according to our will, but rightful liberty is unobstructed action according to our will within limits drawn around us by the equal rights of others.' Letter to Isaac H. Tiffany, 4 April 1819, in *The Political Writings of Thomas Jefferson*, ed. E. Dumbauld, Indianapolis, 1955, p. 55.

13   Rutherforth, *Institutes of Natural Law*, pp. 29–30.

14   See ch. 6, sect. 6.5, this volume. Cf. Jean-Jacques Burlamaqui, *The Principles of Natural and Politic Law* [1747–8], trans. T. Nugent, 2nd ed., London, 1763, 2 vols., I, p. 74: 'There are rights which of themselves have a natural connexion with our duties, and are given to man as means to perform them.'

and limbs, has required him to observe . . . A duty, which we can release ourselves from at pleasure, is unintelligible; it is in effect no duty. The law of nature could not in any respect be binding upon a man, if we suppose him to have such a right in his own person, that he may at any time, by his own voluntary act, lawfully release himself from the whole obligation of it, or in any respect render himself incapable of performing it.[15]

We can hardly find a clearer expression of the common dogma that a self-imposed obligation cannot be the foundation of morals,[16] from which it was inferred that rights must in some sense be derivative from some higher moral standard.

10.3 *Rights and contractarianism*

The prevalence of this line of argument in the eighteenth century leads to some reconsideration of the basics of much moral-political thought in the period. Rights are not simple powers granted, but powers granted for a purpose; they have a right use, namely, that of contributing to an over-all moral order. Consequently they are never granted as open-ended powers, but always in conjunction with matching duties – duties to use them properly, and duties on others then to respect them. As John Witherspoon put it in his lectures at Princeton, 'Right in general may be reduced, as to its source, to the supreme law of moral duty; for whatever men are in duty obliged to do, that they have a claim to, and other men are considered as under an obligation to permit them.'[17]

It is the package deal of rights and duties in a person that is so often referred to as that person's office, role, station, or even character, but since the Latin *officium* was also often translated as 'duty', we find a great deal of linguistic confusion.[18] Although the sense of 'the rights and duties of one's office' is immediately intelligible, 'the obligations of one's office', not to speak of 'the moral obligations of duty',[19] are somewhat desperate attempts to keep separate the particular actions

15 Rutherforth, *Institutes of Natural Law*, pp. 146–7.

16 Cf. sect. 10.7 in this chapter.

17 John Witherspoon, *An Annotated Edition of "Lectures on Moral Philosophy"*, ed. J. Scott, Newark, NJ, 1982, p. 110.

18 See also the quotation from Fordyce at note 29 to this chapter. [*Note:* citations saying '*at* note 29' mean 'in the text, near note 29'; citations saying '*in* note 6' mean 'in the text of note 6'.]

19 As, for example, in Hume, *A Treatise of Human Nature: Being an Attempt to Introduce the Experimental Method of Reasoning into Moral Subjects*, ed. L.A. Selby-Bigge; 2nd ed. rev. by P.H. Nidditch, Oxford, 1978, p. 568. Similarly, Witherspoon wanted to derive 'the nature or obligation of duty' from human nature; see *Lectures on Moral Philosophy*, p. 79.

which one's office, in the sense of 'station', requires – and not only desperate but unfortunate, for 'obligation' had a separate function to indicate the moral necessity one is under in fulfilling a duty.

Once we think about the impositions of natural law as offices, the individualistic contractarianism that is traditionally ascribed to natural law theory looks rather different. The relations constituting the family or the more extensive society cannot simply be understood as negotiated deals abridging the potentially open-ended claims of individuals. Rather they are specifications of the relationship among the offices imposed upon individuals by natural law. This idea is exactly what made it so easy to interpret all contracts as tacit contracts, implied contracts, or quasi contracts, and this interpretation, again, made it easier to evade criticism of the unhistorical character of contractarianism and promoted the assimilation of the prescriptive use of history into natural law contractarianism.

Once again, we have to contend with fluid and uncertain language. Tacit contract is not always clearly distinguished from 'implied contract', and in modern scholarship the latter has all but disappeared, except among legal historians who remember its civil law ancestor, 'quasi contract'.[20] However, using various Roman law materials, natural lawyers and moral philosophers through the seventeenth and eighteenth centuries slowly, and by apparently uncertain steps, which I have indicated elsewhere,[21] achieved an interesting distinction. The main point is that a tacit contract is simply an unspoken contract, that is, it is an event involving an act of will by the contracting parties, which gives rise to an obligation.

By contrast, an implied contract is not an event; it is rather a purely implied and fictional thing which is inferred from a relation between two or more parties, of such a nature that it is *as if* it were based on a contract, though, in fact, it is not. An implied contract therefore does not presuppose an act of will in the same way that both explicit and tacit contracts do. An implied contractual obligation may simply arise from a situation one happens to find oneself in. The nature of such obligations can therefore not be inferred from what the contracting parties did intend to will; it must rather be inferred from the nature of the situation in which they find themselves, that is, from the role or

20   See the splendid article by Peter Birks and Grant McLeod, 'The implied contract theory of quasi-contract: Civilian opinion current in the century before Blackstone', *Oxford Journal of Legal Studies*, 6 (1986), 46–85.

21   See ch. 6, sects. 6.7–6.8, this volume, and the 'Commentary', pp. 356–8 and 405–7, in Reid, *Practical Ethics, Being Lectures and Papers on Natural Religion, Self-Government, Natural Jurisprudence, and the Law of Nations*, ed. K. Haakonssen, Princeton, 1990; and, again, Birks and McLeod, 'The implied contract theory of quasi-contract'.

office they have in that situation. If you find yourself alone, faced with a disaster on your absent neighbour's property, you have an obligation of care as if you had promised him to look after the place. Or you find yourself to be a child of parents you did not choose, but you have the obligations of a child as if you had, because a child is what you are. You are a citizen / subject and have the obligations of this office, because that is what you are. Questions of voluntariness arise, of course, but the point of this approach is that voluntariness is not a matter of either / or, but of more or less. Within a range of voluntariness that cannot be specified a priori for all cases, once a person signals that he or she is playing a certain role, the performance is judged in terms of the obligations that generally pertain to that role.

This is where history comes in. Our notions of the many offices which make up human life are inevitable derived from experience, and so it is by using the ways institutionalized in the past that a king can signal his office and be understood, just as it is with the barber hanging out his sign, or the spouse who continues to behave in the ways expected of this role. It is not the passing of time which creates obligation; the obligation arises from the office discharged as if we had contracted to do it; but we can discharge the office only because the past tells us what it is. I submit that this is the general tenor of a great deal of so-called contractarianism in the eighteenth century. Once the natural law legacy from Pufendorf and others concerning the offices imposed by natural law is read in this way, it can assimilate most forms of traditionalism in morals and politics, including traditional English constitutionalism.

It is of course a moral philosophy which was tailor-made for a conservative Enlightenment.[22] With its emphasis upon the recognizable offices of life and society, it seemed to make traditional social arrangements both understandable and justifiable. At the same time, the suggestion of a possible balance between duties and rights lent credibility to the ideal of moral improvement through enlightenment and thus to the justifiability of social betterment. The philosophical foundations were mainly laid in the moral philosophy classes of the

22 See J.G.A. Pocock, 'Post-puritan England and the problem of the Enlightenment', in *Culture and Politics from Puritanism to the Enlightenment*, ed. P. Zagorin, Berkeley, 1980, pp. 91-111; same, 'Clergy and commerce: The conservative Enlightenment in England', in *L'Età dei Lumi: Studi storici sul settecento europeo in onore de Franco Venturi*, ed. R. Ajello et al., 2 vols., Naples, 1985, 2:23-68; same, 'Conservative Enlightenment and democratic revolutions: The American and French cases in British perspective', *Government and Opposition*, 24 (1989), 81-105; same, 'Josiah Tucker on Burke, Locke, and Price: A study in the varieties of eighteenth-century conservatism', in Pocock, *Virtue, Commerce, and History: Essays on Political Thought and History, Chiefly in the Eighteenth Century*, Cambridge, UK, 1985, pp. 157-91.

Scottish universities, especially in the work of Francis Hutcheson and Thomas Reid,[23] but the general train of ideas became the stable core of the popular moral philosophy that penetrated to an ever-growing reading public.

A good example is David Fordyce's *Elements of Moral Philosophy.* Fordyce taught moral philosophy at Marischal College in Aberdeen and was one of many direct links between the Scots enlighteners and the English dissenters.[24] His work on moral philosophy was first written for *The Preceptor,* a comprehensive popular course in all the arts and sciences aimed at 'trying the Genius, and advancing the Instruction of Youth', engineered by the author and publishing entrepreneur Robert Dodsley.[25] Subsequently another Scottish dealer in ideas with an eye for a wider market, William Smellie, used Fordyce's work – in the meantime also published as a successful book[26] – for the extensive article on 'Moral Philosophy' in his new *Encyclopaedia Britannica.*[27] The

23   In addition to the preceding essays, see R.B. Sher, 'Professors of virtue: The social history of the Edinburgh Moral Philosophy Chair in the eighteenth century', in *Studies in the Philosophy of the Scottish Enlightenment,* ed. M.A. Stewart, Oxford, 1990, pp. 87–126. For the general context, see Sher, *Church and University in the Scottish Enlightenment: The Moderate Literati of Edinburgh,* Princeton, 1985.

24   We get a taste of Fordyce's teaching in his manuscript 'A Brief Account of the Nature, Progress and Origin of Philosophy delivered by the late Mr. David Fordyce, P.P. Marish. Col: Abdn. to his Scholars, before they begun their Philosophical course. Anno 1743/4', Aberdeen University Library MS M 184. In the list of modern luminaries, ethics is represented by 'Cumberland who gave us a beautiful detail of the laws of nature in the moral world'. Fordyce adds Samuel Clarke but without detail, ibid., para. 35. For an overview of Fordyce's teaching, see Paul B. Wood, *The Aberdeen Enlightenment: The Arts Curriculum in the Eighteenth Century,* Aberdeen, 1993, pp. 50–5.

25   *The Preceptor: Containing a General Course of Education: Wherein the First Principles of Polite Learning Are Laid Down in a Way Most Suitable for Trying the Genius, and Advancing the Instruction of Youth,* 2 vols., London, 1748. Concerning Fordyce, see, in addition to Wood, *Aberdeen Enlightenment;* W.H.G. Armytage, 'David Fordyce: A neglected thinker', *Aberdeen University Review,* 36 (1956), 289–91; J.C. Stewart-Robertson, 'The well-principled savage, or The child of the Scottish Enlightenment', *Journal of the History of Ideas,* 42 (1981), 503–25; P. Jones, 'The polite academy and the Presbyterians, 1720–1770', in *New Perspectives on the Politics and Culture of Early Modern Scotland,* ed. J. Dwyer, R.A. Mason, and A. Murdoch, Edinburgh, 1982, pp. 156–78.

26   David Fordyce, *Elements of Moral Philosophy,* London, 1754. For the use of this work at Harvard, see D.W. Robson, *Educating Republicans: The College in the Era of the American Revolution, 1750–1800,* Westport, CT, 1985, pp. 16–17, 82, and 168.

27   *Encyclopaedia Britannica,* 3 vols., Edinburgh, 1771, III, pp. 270–309. See R.L. Emerson, 'Science and moral philosophy in the Scottish Enlightenment', in *Studies in the Philosophy of the Scottish Enlightenment,* ed. Stewart, pp. 11–36 at pp. 25–8;

Unitarian minister and educator John Prior Estlin gave Fordyce's conventional version of a very conventional moral philosophy further coverage by basing his 'familiar lectures' on it.[28]

Fordyce's philosophy was, in most respects, close to that of Turnbull. We find the same 'scientistic' idea of moral philosophy as a perfect parallel to natural philosophy, dealing with an orderly, law-bound world – albeit one *in potentia* only. The normative force of moral philosophy was thus entirely owing to the teleological view of the world that it unravelled:

> Moral Philosophy enquires, not how Man *might have been,* but how he is *constituted*; not into what *Principles,* or *Dispositions* his Actions *may be artfully* resolved, but from what Principles and Dispositions they *actually* flow; not what he *may,* by Education, Habit, or foreign Influence, come to *be,* or *do,* but what by his *Nature,* or *Original Constituent Principles* he is *formed* to *be* and *do.* We discover the *Office, Use* or *Destination* of any *Work,* whether *natural* or *artificial,* by observing its Structure, the Parts of which it consists, their Connection or joint Action. It is thus we understand the *Office* and *Use* of a Watch, a Plant, an Eye, or Hand. It is the same with a *Living Creature,* of the *Rational,* or *Brute Kind.* Therefore to determine the *Office, Duty,* or *Destination* of *Man,* or in other words what his *Business* is, or what *Conduct* he is *obliged* to pursue, we must inspect his *Constitution,* take every Part to pieces, examine their *mutual Relations* one to the other, and the common Effort or Tendency of the Whole.[29]

Even wider circulation of such ideas resulted from their adoption into one of the most popular genres of the time, the conduct books for women, many of which analysed women's domestic and social relations in terms of the proper discharge of offices, derived from the standard section on 'oeconomical jurisprudence' in any system of natural jurisprudence.[30] This part of natural jurisprudence was also the source of professional ethics, of which medical ethics, considered as systems of mutually related offices – or implied contracts - between doctor and patient, was only the most spectacular.[31]

A. Murdoch and R.B. Sher, 'Literary and learned culture', in *People and Society in Scotland,* ed. T.M. Devine and R. Mitchison (*A Social History of Modern Scotland, 1760–1830,* vol. 1), Edinburgh, 1988, pp. 127–42 at p. 137.

28 John Prior Estlin, *Familiar Lectures on Moral Philosophy,* 2 vols., London, 1818.

29 Fordyce, *Elements of Moral Philosophy,* p. 8. Book II of the work is devoted to 'man's duties to himself, to society, to God'.

30 A useful survey of the sheer extent of this genre is in W. St. Clair, *The Godwins and the Shelleys: The Biography of a Family,* London, 1988, pp. 504–10.

31 Lisbeth M. Haakonssen, *Medicine and Morals in the Enlightenment: John Gregory, Thomas Percival, and Benjamin Rush,* Amsterdam, forthcoming (Wellcome Series in the History of Medicine).

In an entirely different genre, even the most influential system of international law, that of Vattel, largely follows this pattern.[32] Finally, we may refer to an ambitious attempt by the latitudinarian divine Thomas Gisborne to map the whole of 'the Duties of Men in the Higher and Middle Classes of Society in Great Britain, resulting from their respective stations, professions, and employments', beginning with the duties of the sovereign and ending with those of 'persons engaged in trade and business' and of 'private gentlemen'.[33]

The authors of such works had generally been taught moral philosophy in a Scottish university or a dissenting academy. The most philosophically sound presentation was that of Thomas Reid in Glasgow.[34] As for the dissenting academies, we know that many of the most important of these regularly taught natural law in the way just outlined.[35] The moral philosophy section of the most popular of textbooks in the academies, Philip Doddridge's *Course of Lectures on the Principal Subjects in Pneumatology, Ethics, and Divinity*, followed the established pattern of duties to God, to others, and to ourselves, based on a straightforward Christian utilitarianism, and this seems to have been typical of the academy curricula in moral philosophy.[36]

32   Emerich de Vattel, *The Law of Nations, or Principles of the Law of Nature applied to the Conduct and Affairs of Nations and Sovereigns* [1758], 2 vols., London, 1759–60. See the introduction for a survey. Vattel organizes much of his material into the state's duties to itself and to others, with duties to God incorporated into the former (Bk. I, ch. 12). For a general study, see F.S. Ruddy, *International Law in the Enlightenment: The Background of Emmerich de Vattel's "Le Droit des Gens"*, New York, 1975.

33   Thomas Gisborne, *An Inquiry into the Duties of Men in the Higher and Middle Classes of Society in Great Britain, Resulting from their Respective Stations, Professions, and Employments*, [1794], 6th ed., 2 vols., London, 1811. The full list of duties includes those of the Sovereign, Englishmen as subjects and fellow citizens, peers, members of the House of Commons, executive officers of government, naval and military officers, the legal profession, justices of the peace and municipal magistrates, the clerical profession, physicians, persons engaged in trade and business, and private gentlemen. The philosophical foundations are given in exactly the manner to be expected in Gisborne's *Principles of Moral Philosophy Investigated, and Applied to the Constitution of Civil Society*, [1789], 4th ed., London, 1798. One is not surprised that he added, for good measure, the four hundred pages of *An Enquiry into the Duties of the Female Sex*, London, 1797, which reached eleven editions in nineteen years.

34   See chapter 6 in this volume.

35   For a brief survey, see Anthony Lincoln, *Some Political and Social Ideas of English Dissent, 1763–1800* [1938], New York, 1971, ch. 3. Cf. Haakonssen, 'Enlightened dissent: An introduction' and J. Seed, '"Advocates of an overstrained moderation": The social logic of Rational Dissent, 1770–1800', both in *Enlightenment and Religion*, ed. Haakonssen.

36   Philip Doddridge, *A Course of Lectures on the Principal Subjects in Pneumatol-*

Many more examples could be given of the pervasiveness of this conventional moral philosophy and its adaptation of the natural law framework. In the present context its political-constitutional use is, however, of the greatest importance, especially as we find it in the great Whig oracle Blackstone himself. After ridiculing the mere idea that civil society has its beginnings in historical contracts and briefly sketching instead a Scottish-type 'stages' theory of society, he writes:

> But though society had not it's formal beginning from any convention of individuals, actuated by their wants and fears; yet it is the *sense* of their weakness and imperfection that *keeps* mankind together; that demonstrates the necessity of this union; and that therefore is the solid and natural foundation, as well as the cement, of society. And this is what we mean by the original contract of society; which, though perhaps in no instance it has ever been formally expressed at the first institution of a state, yet in nature and reason must always be understood and implied, in the very act of associating together: namely, that the whole should protect all it's parts, and that every part should pay obedience to the will of the whole; or, in other words, that the community should guard the rights of each individual member, and that (in return for this protection) each individual should submit to the laws of the community; without which submission of all it was impossible that protection could be certainly extended to any.[37]

To us this notion of implied contractual obligations, inferred from a more or less tradition-bound notion of the office that implies the obligation, may well appear as the death of 'real' contractarianism – but then, we eighteenth-century scholars have probably been brought up on more Hobbes than is good for us. My point is just that a Hobbesian theory of subjective rights as the basis for contractual relations is foreign to what is conventionally known as the great 'age of contractarianism'. This is further underlined by Blackstone's discussion of rights in the first chapter of his great work. After explaining natural rights in the conventional natural law terms with which we are now familiar, he sketches the major steps by which these rights have been declared through English history. For Americans, at least, such declarations could mean only that the natural rights had been surrendered and then returned as a grant from civil government. This point was the target of James Wilson's critique, as we saw at the beginning of this chapter.

---

ogy, Ethics, and Divinity, 4th ed., 2 vols., London, 1799, I, pp. 169–312. Doddridge, typically, also meant his course to be a guide to the literature for the students' self-education. His copious reading lists to this part of the course most frequently cite Pufendorf's *De jure* and *De officio*, with Grotius's *De jure* a close second, followed by Fénelon, Locke's *Second Treatise*, Hutcheson, Hoadly, Barbeyrac, Grove, and others.

37 Blackstone, *Commentaries*, I, pp. 47–8. Cf. D. Lieberman, *The Province of Legislation Determined*, Cambridge, UK, 1989, chs. 1–2.

10.4 *Natural law theory and moral philosophy in America*

The derivative nature of rights and the watering down of contrac-tarianism were intimately connected, and, when used to assimilate the English constitution into the traditional natural law framework, this contractarianism constituted one, if not the major, stumbling-block for the American attempt to formulate a theory of natural rights as the foundation for American civil society and its constitution. The Ameri-cans broke the connection between traditionalism and the derivative character of rights, and they got rid of the former – or at least reduced it significantly. But apparently nobody achieved a radical theory of subjective rights of the sort whose beginnings we encounter in Grotius and Hobbes. Philosophically, rights remained derivative.

This is hardly surprising, for Americans drew upon the same natu-ral law tradition as their British contemporaries, and they shared its development into the broader, conventional moral philosophy outlined earlier. In saying this, I am not trying to enter into the rather common monocausal, or at least single-track, patterns of explaining American intellectual life, American independence, or American constitutional-ism. I have no method of intellectual calibration that allows me to measure the relative significance of the roles played in these wider contexts by natural law, common law, evangelicalism, liberalism, or republicanism, of whatever stripe. My explanandum is a good deal narrower than the intellectual origins of the American ideology of independence. On the assumption that natural law theory and the moral philosophy built on it had a presence of some significance in America in the later eighteenth century, my concern here is to explain the conceptual structure of such theories and so contribute to a charac-terization of the culture of rights in which events such as the adoption of the first ten amendments to the Constitution took place.[38] But I am happy to add that such a concern is a necessary preliminary to consid-

---

38 Even with this modest agenda I may be in conflict with J.P. Reid's interest-ing attempt to reduce everything to common law ideas; see his *Constitutional History of the American Revolution: The Authority of Rights*, Madison, WI, 1987, e.g. p. 95: 'There was little substantive difference between natural rights and positive rights. To dissect a natural right was to find a British right and it was natural because the British possessed it . . . Natural rights were the reflection, not the essence; they were the confirmation, not the source, of positive rights.' Even if this view were correct – and it is hard to square with the central texts – the historian must still ask whether the loose natural rights talk makes sense on the premises of those using it, why people indulged in it at such great length from an early age, and *how* at the time many people could see the theories of natural law and British constitutionalism to be compatible.

erations of how natural law theory related to other moral and political theories.

Whatever the exact role of natural law and the associated moral philosophy in the great events in North America in the last third of the eighteenth century, the assumption mentioned seems well founded and is widely documented in the literature.[39] Perhaps the most important point to remember is that this material was, in effect, school-learning. Several important American colleges, following the British pattern already discussed, taught a natural law–based moral philosophy as part of the arts curriculum.[40] Apart from general political talk of rights, the theory of rights outlined here was thus the first, and certainly the first systematic, exposition of the topic to which significant parts of the American intelligentsia were exposed while still boys in their teens.[41]

39   The literature bearing on this wide topic is extensive. Much of it is marred by a lack of distinctions between various strands of European natural law thought and by neglect of the connection between some of these and eighteenth-century moral thought. Philosophically the outstanding and most directly relevant discussion is White, *Philosophy of the American Revolution*, but see also N. Fiering, *Jonathan Edwards's Moral Thought and Its British Context*, Chapel Hill, NC, 1981; B. Kuklick, *Churchmen and Philosophers: From Jonathan Edwards to John Dewey*, New Haven, 1985, chs. 1–6; E. Flower and M.G. Murphey, *A History of Philosophy in America*, 2 vols., New York, 1977, vol. 1. Of the more broadly historical studies I have used in particular B. Bailyn, *The Ideological Origins of the American Revolution*, Cambridge, MA, 1967; H.F. May, *The Enlightenment in America*, New York, 1976; G. Wood, *The Creation of the American Republic, 1776–1787*, Chapel Hill, NC, 1969; and same, *The Radicalism of the American Revolution*, New York, 1992. Cf. also D. Walker Howe, 'European sources of political ideas in Jeffersonian America', *Reviews in American History*, 10 (1982), 28–44; and F. McDonald, *Novus ordo seclorum: The Intellectual Origins of the Constitution*, Lawrence, AR, 1985.

40   See in general H. Miller, *The Revolutionary College: American Presbyterian Higher Education, 1707–1837*, New York, 1976; and D.W. Robson, *Educating Republicans*, Westport, CT, 1985, esp. pp. 82–7, 123–6, 148–52, 162–71, 191–4 and 206–9. Cf. also D.C. Humphrey, *From King's College to Columbia, 1746–1800*, New York, 1976; M.A. Noll, *Princeton and the Republic, 1768–1822*, Princeton, 1989; D. Sloan, *The Scottish Enlightenment and the American College Ideal*, New York, 1971.

41   It is not surprising that the Revolutionary principles were often seen as less than revolutionary. As Jefferson repeatedly emphasised late in his life, his work on the Declaration of Independence was meant 'not to find out new principles, or new arguments, never before thought of, not merely to say things which had never been said before; but to place before mankind the common sense of the subject in terms so plain and firm as to command their assent, and to justify ourselves in the independent stand we are compelled to take'. Letter to Henry Lee, 8 May 1825, in *The Writings of Thomas Jefferson*, ed. A.E. Bergh, 20 vols., (Thomas Jefferson Memorial Association of the United States), Washington, DC, 1907, 16:118. Cf. also letter to James Madison, 30 August 1823, 15:462.

It is uncertain and controversial how much direct influence was exerted by the seventeenth-century natural lawyers, especially Pufendorf and Locke.[42] However, whether Americans read the original texts or learned their ideas from text-books like those of Hutcheson, Rutherforth, Fordyce, or Burlamaqui – to mention only the few already referred to in this chapter – the common theoretical framework for teaching and learning was certainly natural law theory. It was generally based on Christian utilitarian principles of one sort or another, and, if not, such principles were still expounded at length as the chief object of the lecturer's criticism – and followed by the usual system of duties.[43] An early example of the former is Francis Alison's lectures at the College of Philadelphia from the 1750s onward; an example of the latter is

42   Concerning Pufendorf, see H. Welzel, 'Ein Kapitel aus der Geschichte der amerikanischen Erklärung der Menschenrechte', in *Zur Geschichte der Erklärung der Menschenrechte*, ed. R. Schnur, Darmstadt, 1964, pp. 238–59; Clinton Rossiter, *Seedtime of the Republic*, New York, 1953, esp. pp. 212ff.; A. Haddow, *Political Science in American Colleges and Universities, 1636–1900*, New York, 1939; D. Klippel, *Politische Freiheit und Freiheitsrechte im deutschen Naturrecht des 18. Jahrhunderts*, Paderborn, 1976, ch. 3. Concerning Locke, see, for example, J. Dunn, 'The politics of Locke in England and America in the eighteenth century', in *John Locke: Problems and Perspectives*, ed. J.W. Yolton, Cambridge, UK, 1969, pp. 45–80; D. Grimm, 'Europäisches Naturrecht und Amerikanische Revolution: Die Verwandlung politischer Philosophie in politische Techne', *Ius Commune*, 3 (1970), 120–51; T.L. Pangle, *The Spirit of Modern Republicanism: The Moral Vision of the American Founders and the Philosophy of Locke*, Chicago, 1988; Pocock, *Virtue, Commerce, and History*. For more general surveys, see Charles F. Mullett, *Fundamental Law and the American Revolution, 1760–1776*, New York, 1933; B.F. Wright, Jr., *American Interpretations of Natural Law*, Cambridge, MA, 1931.

43   The American connections with the Scottish Enlightenment have been cultivated with particular intensity. There are several surveys of the literature, but see especially D. Walker Howe, 'Why the Scottish Enlightenment was useful to the framers of the American Constitution', *Comparative Studies in Society and History*, 31 (1989), 572–87, and R.B. Sher, 'Introduction: Scottish-American Studies, past and present', in *Scotland and America in the Age of the Enlightenment*, ed. Sher and J.R. Smitten, Princeton, 1990, pp. 1–27. Of particular interest for the following are Garry Wills, *Inventing America: Jefferson's Declaration of Independence*, New York, 1979, and the criticism by R. Hamowy, 'Jefferson and the Scottish Enlightenment', *William and Mary Quarterly*, 36 (1979), 503–23; P.J. Diamond, 'Witherspoon, William Smith and the Scottish Philosophy in Revolutionary America', in *Scotland and America*, ed. Sher and Smitten, pp. 115–32; D.F. Norton, 'Francis Hutcheson in America', *Studies on Voltaire and the Eighteenth Century*, 154 (1976), 1547–68; C. Robbins, '"When it is that colonies may turn independent": An analysis of the environment and the politics of Francis Hutcheson (1694–1746)', *William and Mary Quarterly*, 11 (1954), 214–51; and S.C. Stimson, '"A Jury of the Country": Common sense philosophy and the jurisprudence of James Wilson', in *Scotland and America*, ed. Sher and Smitten, pp. 193–208.

Thomas Clap's teaching at Yale, soon to be followed by Witherspoon's at Princeton, which we shall encounter later.[44] By the end of the century such adaptations of natural law theory had acquired the same quality of academic orthodoxy as they had somewhat earlier in Britain. The ethical and political sections of Samuel Stanhope Smith's undergraduate lectures at Princeton bear a very close resemblance to those of several of his older Scottish colleagues, especially Thomas Reid,[45] and James Wilson's systematization of American jurisprudence in 1790–1 represents, in its theoretical aspects, an excellent summing up, complete with a virtual guide to the literature, of the tradition with which we have been concerned here.[46]

Having grown up with natural law theory and the associated moral philosophy, it is hardly strange that Americans found use for such ideas in their own writings and, eventually, in the documents of independence and constitution-building. It is in these fields, especially the latter, that the great historiographical controversies are raging concern-

44   See Sloan, *Scottish Enlightenment and American College Ideal*, pp. 88–94; Norton, 'Hutcheson in America', and Thomas Clap, *An Essay on the Nature and Foundation of Moral Virtue: Being a Short Introduction to the Study of Ethics: for the Use of the Students of Yale-College*, New Haven, 1765. Another interesting perspective on this matter, which cannot be pursued here, is that these three intellectual leaders were of different theological orientations, Alison an Old Side Presbyterian, Clap a strongly anti-revivalist Congregationalist, and Witherspoon a Scottish evangelical who in America was expected to align himself with New Side Presbyterianism and yet managed to include elements of Butlerian and Hutchesonian moral philosophy.

45   Samuel Stanhope Smith, *The Lectures, Corrected and Improved, Which Have Been Delivered for a Series of Years, in the College of New Jersey: On the Subjects of Moral and Political Philosophy*, 2 vols., Trenton, NJ, 1812. Like Reid, Smith massively increased the treatment of the philosophy of mind. Reid's lectures were not published at the time; see Reid, *Practical Ethics*. The most important discussion of Smith is Noll, *Princeton and the Republic*.

46   There was more than this, of course, to Wilson's teaching. Cf. the important studies by S.A. Conrad, 'Polite foundation: Citizenship and Common Sense in James Wilson's republican theory,' *Supreme Court Review*, 1984 (1985), 359–88; and 'Metaphor and imagination in James Wilson's theory of federal union', *Law and Social Inquiry*, 13 (1988), 170; and by Stimson, 'A Jury of the Country'; and *The American Revolution in the Law: Anglo-American Jurisprudence before John Marshall*, London, 1990, pp. 127–36. Wilson draws on a wide variety of sources. By far his most frequent reference is Blackstone, followed by the ever-present Bacon. Then come John Millar for legal history, Pufendorf for legal theory, Reid for epistemology and moral psychology, and Cicero for everything. Behind these come Burlamaqui, Paley, Grotius, Vattel, Beccaria, Burke, Gibbon, Heineccius, Locke, Hooker, Wooddeson, Montesquieu, Pope, Rutherforth, Shaftesbury, Hume, Rousseau, Hutcheson, Kames, Barbeyrac, Bolingbroke, Hobbes, plus a number of legal sources.

ing the relative importance of different traditions. The unwary reader is tossed around between 'liberal', 'republican', and 'evangelical' interpretations of American action and mind.[47] Of these, the liberal line of argument traditionally promoted the importance of natural rights. After a decade or more out of the scholarly limelight, liberalism has returned, broadened beyond the earlier rights agenda and, according to many, consequently bettered. It has supposedly benefitted from the growing understanding of the Scottish Enlightenment and its influence in America and can accordingly now see that the liberal individual of Revolutionary and independent America exercised his rights with a moral sense. Since moral-sense theory, furthermore, can be seen as a theory of virtue, and since 'republicanism' is centrally concerned with virtue, some rapprochement between the two great 'isms' has appeared possible.[48]

This syncretic move has its problems. It still assumes that it makes sense to talk of liberalism in this context, and that, whatever else liberalism might have been about, it was also concerned with natural rights. But liberalism is a nineteenth-century construct that is best kept out of these discussions, and the Scottish philosophy that influenced Americans was concerned with rights only within the natural law and duty framework. Americans did not change this framework, and it was this inherited natural *law* that could provide a certain assimilation of republicanism. Throughout the eighteenth century the languages of duty and of virtue were practically interchangeable – for moral-sense theorists as well as ethical rationalists – and switching from the jurisprudential concept of duty to the republican concept of virtue never seemed to trouble those of a neoclassical republican tendency, such as Hutcheson and Turnbull.[49] Virtuous behaviour was duty, and the performance of duty was virtue. Rights had their place in this scheme, but it was a logically subordinate one, as we have seen. It is thus primarily the anachronistic use of a vaguely rights-based liberalism which has made it appear to scholars that there was a deep division between it

47 Excellent overviews are provided by J.T. Kloppenberg, 'The virtues of liberalism: Christianity, republicanism and ethics in early American political discourse', *Journal of American History*, 74 (1987), 9–33; and P.S. Onuf, 'Reflections on the founding: Constitutional historiography in bicentennial perspective', *William and Mary Quarterly*, 46 (1989), 341–75.

48 See Kloppenberg, 'The virtues of liberalism', esp. pp. 28ff. For the wider debate on the relationship between republicanism and liberalism, see also Onuf, 'Reflections on the founding', pp. 346–50.

49 See Haakonssen, 'Natural jurisprudence in the Scottish Enlightenment: Summary of an interpretation', in *Enlightenment, Rights, and Revolution: Essays in Legal and Social Philosophy*, ed. D.N. MacCormick and Z. Bankowski, Aberdeen, 1989, pp. 36–49.

and republicanism. This is not to deny that the traditions of natural law and republicanism have different classical and early modern ancestries or that there remained republicans with no use for natural law. The point is that by the eighteenth century the popular moral philosophy based on natural law, which was taught in the colleges, was not only no hindrance to republican politics; its notion of the duty to virtue provided more of a philosophical foundation for the latter than it had had before.[50]

This harmony was not to last. Just as the emerging emphasis on rights disrupted the assimilation of English common law traditionalism into a natural law framework, so it eventually led to a new phenomenon, liberalism, at loggerheads with much of the republican legacy. This was the outcome of the search for a rights theory, not the cause of it. In order to conceptualize the search itself, we must remain within the theoretical framework already outlined: In other words, we must explain how rights could be effective in argument even though they were justified in terms of law and duty. However, in order to underline how complex and difficult a matter it was to break with this tradition and approach a subjective rights theory proper, we shall also trace two imperfect steps in that direction. The final sections of this essay will therefore be devoted to three lines of argument. The first concerns the inalienability of rights; the second questions the Christian-utilitarian idea of rights as derivative from a common good prescribed by natural law; and the third deals with the ideas of individual autonomy and the ability of individuals to impose obligations upon themselves.

10.5 *Inalienable rights*

The problem concerning the inalienability of rights was fundamental to Americans' understanding and justification of their dispute with Britain, as James Wilson explained.[51] If certain basic rights were to be the moral touchstone by means of which the conduct of all instituted authority was to be checked, such rights must exist on a basis that made them transcend all institutions of authority. They must somehow be inherent to the human species and thus continue to be justifiably held by persons in society as well as out of it. Furthermore, the institutions of civil society must be seen primarily as safeguards for such rights. This argument was at the heart of the theoretical rationale of the American rebellion against British authority and the institution of a new civil society. The question then was, How could one justify

50 Cf. Chapter 2 in this volume.
51 Cf. White, *Philosophy of the American Revolution*, ch. 5; and same, *Philosophy, "The Federalist," and the Constitution*, New York, 1987, pp. 32–4.

the proposition that certain rights are fundamental in this sense, and which rights are these?

The answer is, in a way, simple to the point of triviality within the natural law tradition we have been tracing.[52] Indeed only the great need of the Founders, particularly Jefferson, to formulate in theoretical terms the crucial locus of British transgression brought the question to the fore. Even then, it was hardly explained. It was a matter of course in theory, which now needed to be asserted in practice. Yesterday's matter of course is commonly today's puzzle, and so it has often been in this case. If natural rights are derivative from the duties imposed by natural law, in the sense that rights are powers granted by the law in order to fulfil its duties and thus its purpose, then the rights are necessary to human life under the natural law, that is, to all moral life. There can therefore be no moral justification for alienating such rights. A right is a duty and a duty a right.

It should be pointed out here that there was considerable confusion concerning the term 'natural rights'. In the broadest sense, natural rights were those that people had possessed in the state of nature as distinct from the positive rights instituted by civil society. In this sense, natural rights encompassed rights to property and contractual rights – rights that were excluded by the other common and more restrictive sense of the term. For natural rights were also distinguished from adventitious or acquired rights, which are the result of human activity or arrangements – typically the acquisition of property or the establishment of contracts – whereas natural rights pertain to individuals without any such initiatives being taken. Some of the rights which are natural in this sense can, however, be alienated whereas others cannot, and it is to this group that I have occasionally referred, noncommittally, as 'basic'.[53]

---

52 In the following discussion I agree with Morton White, in the works cited earlier, concerning the most essential point, that the inalienability of rights derives from the dependence of rights upon duties. I work the thesis out somewhat differently from White, and I do not go into the details of these differences, because they would require considerable discussion.

53 Cf. Witherspoon's explanation: 'The distinction between rights as alienable and unalienable is very different from that of natural and acquired. Many of the rights which are strictly natural and universal may be alienated in a state of society for the good of the whole as well as of private persons; as for example, the right of self defense; this is in a great measure given up in a state of civil government into the hands of the public' (*Lectures on Moral Philosophy*, p. 111). Witherspoon is bound to have confused his students when he added, 'and the right of doing justice to ourselves or to others in matters of property is wholly given up'. Property is precisely an acquired right, but it is 'natural' in the wider sense of obtaining in the state of nature. Cf. Reid, *Practical Ethics*, pp. 188–203; and ch. 6, sect. 6.6, this volume.

Clearly only a limited number of natural, nonadventitious rights can be inalienable. In fact, of *specific* rights, only the rights to life and liberty could be considered inalienable within the natural law theory presupposed here. We have a duty, and consequently a right, to maintain God's creation as we find it in ourselves. Similarly we have a duty, and hence a right, to maintain ourselves as moral agents under natural law, and consequently we cannot justifiably give up all of our liberty: a vestige must always remain in the form of the right of judgement. This was the reason why there could not be natural slavery; a being without a minimum of moral judgement about himself or herself is simply not a person or moral agent. This minimum must be preserved even in lifelong servitude – the legitimacy of which was commonly allowed within natural law theory. In addition, it was not uncommon to think that if a person was already morally 'dead', having made himself a non-person through incurable moral depravity, then slavery was in order; it was, in effect, moral death in place of physical.

In addition to the two basic rights of life and liberty we also have a duty, and therefore a right, to seek out the means to maintain these two rights for ourselves. As far as our physical being is concerned, we must appropriate things around us. This right is commonly referred to as a 'right to property' though, strictly speaking, as an *inalienable* right it can never be more than a right to *seek* property (plus, according to some, a right to subsistence). As for our moral being, we must seek the means to independence of judgement, namely freedom of opinion and speech.

There is, however, a clear difference between the two basic duties/rights to life and liberty and the derivative duties/rights to the means of maintaining life and liberty. The derivative duties/rights form a kind of framework-rights, because they may be implemented through a variety of institutional arrangements. Consequently Jefferson, for the purposes of the Declaration of Independence, had to choose the broad and somewhat vague phrase concerning the right to 'the pursuit of happiness' (which could also encompass the pursuit of both physical and moral means). This broadening and the implied exclusion of a specific inalienable right to private property was controversial but entirely consonant with accepted natural law doctrine. Although the right to the pursuit of happiness, considered as a framework-right, is indeed necessary and inalienable, the specific forms it takes in any given place will be a matter of human action, and the specific rights to which they lead (for example, communal versus several property) are, therefore, both alienable and adventitious.[54] Similarly all other rights,

54 As Jefferson explains, well knowing the traditional rhetoric concerning property, 'It is a moot question whether the origin of any kind of property is derived from nature at all . . . Bar an universal law, indeed, whatever, whether fixed

although ultimately deriving their justification from the basic, inalienable rights and, hence, from the law of nature, are adventitious devices to implement the law.

This solution to the problem of rights is the most coherent interpretation that can be given of the central, mainly Jeffersonian, formulations of the American standpoint. It provided a foundation for the common rejection of English traditionalism and conventionalism, of the sort we have met with in Blackstone, as far as the ultimate natural rights are concerned. It thereby also gave meaning to contractarianism of a kind somewhat closer to the modern notion than the implied contractarianism outlined at the beginning of this chapter. The contract supporting civil government was between individuals who retained an identifiable core of rights, for the sake of whose protection other rights were alienated to create government. At the same time, by limiting the natural rights proper to the well-known three, it underlined the alienable and adventitious character of the rest and so allowed wide scope for the assimilation of the historically contingent.[55]

In a sense this solution simply follows the logic of traditional natural law theory: Certain basic rights are inalienable because they are duties under natural law, and all other duties / rights derive their ultimate justification more or less directly from these. None of the American theoreticians put forward a clear idea of rights as underived, primary features of the person, and one inevitably gets the impression that some of the apparent moral certainty stemmed from the fact that Americans stayed well within the comfortable moral world of traditional natural law theory, with its assurance of an in-principle harmony of individual rights and duties.

If this account is correct, the question remains why Americans (and a growing number of Britons) increasingly claimed life, liberty, and the pursuit of happiness (or some more or less clearly conceived equivalent) as *rights* when they might as well have asserted them as duties. One obvious answer is that it was rhetorically and polemically more forceful to point out that your just claims were being denied than that your duties were being taken out of your hands. Another, theoretically much more interesting, answer can be found by attending to an appar-

---

or movable, belongs to all men equally and in common, is the property for the moment of him who occupies it, but when he relinquishes the occupation, the property goes with it. Stable ownership is the gift of social law, and is given late in the progress of society'. Letter to Isaac McPherson, 13 August 1813, in *Writings of Jefferson*, 13:333. Cf. White, *Philosophy of the American Revolution*, pp. 213–28.

55   Cf. Jefferson's dictum that '[our government] is a composition of the freest principles of the English constitution, with others derived from natural right and natural reason'. 'Notes on Virginia', in *Writings of Jefferson*, 2:1–261, at p. 120 (Query VIII).

ently unconnected question, which also arises from the present interpretation, namely, What became of the duties to others?

As we have seen, it was a common point in natural law theory that
we have a basic duty to preserve God's moral creation wherever we
encounter it, in ourselves and in others, which means that we have to
be sociable and promote the common good. However, the basic inalienable rights in American theory are all derivative from our duties
to ourselves only. Here the equality of basic rights comes in. Since life,
liberty, and the pursuit of happiness are equally duties for all, they are
equally rights for all, and accordingly there is a duty on everyone not
to disturb this equality, that is, to leave all others to enjoy their basic
rights. The primary duty to others is simply to leave them alone.[56]

Behind this doctrine lies the assumption that God's moral creation is
best nurtured when each person looks after his or her own part of it,
namely him- or herself. This assumption is in fact twofold. The first is
that, if each person did not look after his or her own basic duties/
rights, then he would simply not have a complete moral personality;
and the more people are in that condition, the further away is the
optimal common good. This fundamental natural-law – and in the end
Protestant – idea of the necessity of personal judgement in morals
always favoured the rights side of the Janus-faced notion of duty/
right. It also provided an opening for further development, as we shall
see later. The other assumption is that in practical terms it is most
realistic and efficient that each person cultivates his or her own life,
liberty, and pursuit of happiness. It is most realistic because it is taken
for granted that self-love is one, if not the most, fundamental feature of
human nature. Consequently it is also most efficient, because people
on the whole are more motivated to pursue their own good than that of
others. When eventually combined with an economic theory of the
market, this aspect of rights theory became recognizably political in the
narrower sense. Possessive individualism did come about, though a
couple of centuries too late to fit the scholarly bill.[57]

---

56   Cf. Jefferson: 'No man has a natural right to commit aggression on the equal
rights of another: and this is all from which the laws ought to restrain him; every
man is under the natural duty of contributing to the necessities of the society; and
this is all the laws should enforce on him; and, no man having a natural right to be
the judge between himself and another, it is his natural duty to submit to the
umpirage of an impartial third. When the laws have declared and enforced all this,
they have fulfilled their functions; and the idea is quite unfounded, that on entering
into society we give up any natural right.' Letter to Francis W. Gilmer, 7 June 1816,
in *Writings of Jefferson*, 15:24.

57   I refer here to C.B. Macpherson's interpretation of seventeenth-century political thought, *The Political Theory of Possessive Individualism: Hobbes to Locke*, Oxford,
1962. In a more general explanation of American political thought, the ideas set out

A standard controversy concerned the moral situation when these assumptions did not hold, especially when individuals were not the best judges of their own good, whether because of ignorance or because their judgement was irrelevant, as in illness or famine.[58] The logic of traditional natural law theory was that such persons still had basic rights under natural law. The duty/right to life entailed at least a right to subsistence, and the duty/right to liberty entailed at least that one could not sell one's person but only one's services. To that extent, if no further, I am my brother's keeper. As we know, this logic was not always appreciated in practice.

However, it was obviously assumed that on the whole the strict or perfect duties to others, that is, duties essential to the very existence of society, were discharged by simply respecting the basic rights of others. In this light it is not strange that life, liberty, and the pursuit of happiness should be emphasized as rights rather than as duties, though duties they also were.

10.6   *Evangelicalism and Christian utilitarianism*

A cornerstone in the natural law theory discussed here is the proposition that the law of nature prescribes duties and grants matching rights that, when properly taken care of, contribute to the general common good or greatest happiness in God's creation. As part of the general providentialism of the age, this idea was found as much in America as in Britain. As long as rights were thought of within this scheme, there was no real chance of developing a subjective rights theory proper. In such a theory there would be no guarantee that the maze of individual rights, or claims, even in principle could exist harmoniously as part of the common good. On the contrary, in such a theory no such assumption could be made the justifying ground for rights, and in its absence individuals, starting from no other moral assumptions than their own and others' several claims, would seek temporal, historically contingent guarantees through contractual arrangements of moral (social and political) institutions.

---

in the text should be related to Revolutionary thinkers' understanding, and possible readjustment, of the balance between self-interest and the public good in republican theory, as discussed in R.C. Sinopoli, 'Liberalism, republicanism and the Constitution', *Polity*, 19 (1987), 331–52; and L. Banning, 'Some second thoughts on virtue and the course of Revolutionary thinking', in *Conceptual Change and the Constitution*, ed. T. Ball and J.G.A. Pocock, Lawrence, AR, 1988, pp. 194–212, esp. pp. 199–201.

58   I disregard conditions like childhood, insanity, and various forms of dependence, because they raise a question of a different sort, namely, When is a person a person? Natural lawyers developed a variety of intricate standpoints on these issues.

In so far as the eighteenth century had any clear idea of such a rights theory, it associated it with irreligion and Hobbesian chaos and the concomitant authoritarianism.[59] Alternatively, eighteenth-century moralists would have associated such ideas of the moral primacy of the individual spirit and its claims with religious 'enthusiasm' and generally antinomian evangelicalism.[60]

There is a long-standing tradition in American scholarship for seeking the springs of individualism, independence, and self-government in one or another form of evangelical religion.[61] The question here is, however, a different and much more modest one, whether there were any conceptual points of contact between evangelicalism and natural law. Although evangelicalism is often represented as a doctrine of the Christian virtues, it was by the same token also a doctrine of Christian duty. The emphasis on duty was a quite fundamental point in common with natural law, and this in practice provided evangelicals who became teachers with an opening for preserving elements of both lines of thought. At the same time they could use evangelical religion to undermine natural law, and it is from this quarter that we encounter a clear blow at the conventional Christian-utilitarian basis of natural law. It was delivered at one of the main centres for the education of the new American mind, in John Witherspoon's lectures on moral philosophy to the Princeton undergraduates.

Witherspoon's lectures are notoriously eclectic, and he was not a good enough moral thinker to make a coherent whole of what he picked up from his many sources.[62] He was, however, quite clear-

---

59   The reaction of Cumberland in 1672 remained typical until the end of the eighteenth century. See Haakonssen, 'The character and obligation of natural law according to Richard Cumberland', in *English Philosophy in the Age of Locke*, ed. M.A. Stewart, Oxford, forthcoming.

60   Cf. the discussion of Hume in ch. 3, sect. 3.7, this volume.

61   The pioneering study is P. Miller, *Errand into the Wilderness*, Cambridge, MA, 1956. As an outsider I have found P.U. Bonomi's *Under the Cope of Heaven: Religion, Society, and Politics in Colonial America*, New York, 1986, particularly useful, not least for its explanation of the fusion of Old Light rationalism and New Light emotionalism with Whig resistance ideology. Cf. also A. Heimert, *Religion and the American Mind: From the Great Awakening to the Revolution*, Cambridge, MA, 1966; N.O. Hatch, *The Sacred Cause of Liberty: Republican Thought and the Millennium in Revolutionary New England*, New Haven, 1977; W.G. McLoughlin, *Revivals, Awakenings, and Reform: An Essay on Religion and Social Change in America, 1607–1977*, Chicago, 1978, chs. 2–3; R.H. Bloch, *Visionary Republic: Millennial Themes in American Thought, 1756–1800*, Cambridge, UK, 1985; and H.S. Stout, *The New England Soul: Preaching and Religious Culture in Colonial New England*, New York, 1986.

62   Concerning Witherspoon generally, see Noll, *Princeton and the Republic*, chs. 3–4; Diamond, 'Witherspoon, William Smith'; R.K. Donovan, 'The popular party of

headed enough to see where the real dividing line lay between his own evangelical notions of man's duty and those of mainstream natural law moralists, of whom his former compatriot and opponent Francis Hutcheson was the archetype. On the whole, Witherspoon's course follows the natural law–derived organization that was standard in Scottish moral philosophy courses and in the many text-books and treatises, of which we encountered several examples earlier. He obviously thought that it was important to instruct his students in the usual system of duties and rights and that he could simply adjust the theoretical foundations. Although it cannot be said that he worked out the implications of his scattered objections to conventional theory, these objections are significant as disturbing elements in the theoretical situation surrounding American ideas of rights.[63]

Witherspoon begins his lectures traditionally enough by identifying the subject of moral philosophy as being 'the laws of Duty' that reason derives from human nature independently of, though in consonance with, revelation. However, he goes on to stress that moral philosophy has its limitations because of the complexity of human nature, which we know only in its fallen and corrupt state, and

> this depravity . . . must be one great cause of difficulty and confusion in giving an account of human nature as the work of God. This I take to be indeed the case with the greatest part of our moral and theological knowledge. Those who deny this depravity, will be apt to plead for every thing, or for many things as dictates of nature, which are in reality propensities of nature in its present state, but at the same time the fruit and evidence of its departure from its original purity. It is by the remaining power of natural conscience that we must endeavour to detect and oppose these errors.[64]

Witherspoon goes on to sketch a theory of conscience that owes much to Bishop Butler. In the process he rejects moral-sense theories, espe-

---

the Church of Scotland and the American Revolution', in *Scotland and America*, ed. Sher and Smitten, pp. 81–99; N.C. Landsman, 'Witherspoon and the problem of provincial identity in Scottish evangelical culture', in ibid., pp. 29–45; T.P. Miller, 'Witherspoon, Blair, and the rhetoric of civic humanism', in ibid., pp. 100–14; L.E. Schmidt, 'Sacramental occasions and the Scottish context of Presbyterian revivalism in America', in ibid., pp. 65–80; Sher, 'Witherspoon's dominion of Providence and the Scottish jeremiad tradition,' in ibid., pp. 46–64; and J. Scott, introduction to Witherspoon, *Lectures on Moral Philosophy*, pp. 1–61.

63 My emphasis here is on Witherspoon's contrasts with natural law theory and Hutchesonian moral philosophy. If instead he is contrasted with evangelical and New Side attitudes and with Jonathan Edwards, he naturally comes out a good deal closer to the former theories. See Noll's excellent discussion in *Princeton and the Republic*, 36–52.

64 Witherspoon, *Lectures on Moral Philosophy*, p. 66.

cially that of Hutcheson. His principal objection is that such theories tend to assume that that which appears (feels) good to the human mind in its present state is good in an absolute sense. He allows that human beings are provided with a moral sense which offers some moral guidance, but it is in need of correction by reason. Although this correction is fallible too, reason and sense combine to jolt into action whatever they have left of a conscience, or sense of duty, after Adam brought death into the world.

Accompanying this thought is the point we are after here. Because of people's sinfulness, the moral world is complex and confused, and our moral powers are weak and easily deceived. In such a world it is impossible for individuals to discern a common good which could guide their moral sense and judgement, although they may try when nothing else points to a decision. As Witherspoon says, in a passage where he typically tries to have it a little both ways:

> True virtue certainly promotes the general good, and this may be made use of as an argument in doubtful cases, to determine whether a particular principle is right or wrong, but to make the good of the whole our immediate principle of action, is putting ourselves in God's place, and actually superseding the necessity and use of the particular principles of duty which he hath impressed upon the conscience.[65]

Witherspoon does not deny that we should and can enlighten our conscience, or that we should hold fast to the belief that conscience is God's voice speaking through us. But we should not think that we can make God's purpose, the greatest common good, into our purpose in our actions. We simply have to do our duty as we see it by the limited light of our conscience. This is God's law. What it adds up to is God's business, not ours. Witherspoon made the point pithily in his Fast Day sermon at Princeton on 17 May 1776: 'There is the greater need to take notice of this that men are not generally sufficiently aware of the distinction between the law of God and his purpose.'[66] This statement is his indictment of those polite moral philosophers, such as Hutcheson, who thought they could build a system of natural law and its duties on the idea of the common good that God has in store for humankind. They entirely forgot that humankind is fallen and corrupt and that individuals have to grope their way without such rationally established moral certainty.

Witherspoon got no further than this with his rethinking of the basis for natural law. His ideas are not particularly remarkable in them-

65 Ibid., p. 87.
66 Witherspoon, 'The Dominion of Providence over the Passions of Men', in *The Selected Writings of John Witherspoon*, ed. T. Miller, Carbondale, IL, 1990, pp. 126–47 at p. 127.

selves, but they deserve notice because of the explicit attempt to introduce them into the conventional system of natural law, and because
this attempt was made as part of the teaching of moral philosophy at
such a prominent institution. The point is that at the time no other line
of thought had much chance of breaking the Christian-utilitarian foundation for natural law and of persuading people to consider seriously
the possibility that the moral world of humankind may be, if not chaotic, at least without guarantee of order, even in principle. It is beyond
the scope of this chapter to investigate how far evangelicalism was
successful in this regard, let alone what it did to create a climate later
for the development of a proper subjective rights theory.

10.7 Self-government and obligation

The last argument that tended to chip away at the conventional
natural law theory in favour of a subjective rights theory will be presented not through an American voice but through one much heard in
America in the late eighteenth century. I refer to the Swiss thinker Jean-
Jacques Burlamaqui.

A central feature of eighteenth-century moral thought is, as we have
seen, the apparently paradoxical proliferation of theories stressing the
moral autonomy of the individual while retaining the natural law foundation for morals. However, neither the supposed moral sense, nor
reason, nor conscience provided as much autonomy as might at first
appear; for most thinkers the moral power derived its strength from
guidance by natural law. This went hand in hand with another feature
of traditional natural law theory, the idea that obligation presupposes a
superior authority. The common assumption was that a necessary condition for the obligation of natural law was that it issued from God's
authority and that all other obligations, that is, those undertaken by
individuals, derived their force from the binding character of natural
law. Only very few early modern thinkers, Grotius among them, clearly articulated the idea that there could be obligation without reference
to divine authority. It is true that many, probably most, rejected outright voluntarism of the Pufendorfian kind, but they did so by the
redeployment of a scholastic distinction, between the content and the
form of natural law. The content of the law was the specification of
what was good and virtuous and could be grasped by people's native
moral power (however conceived). But in order for this specification to
be obligatory upon them as a guide to action, it had to have the form of
law, and obligatory law required a lawgiver of supreme authority,
namely, God.[67] The idea that human beings could have sufficient au-

---

67 See Chapter 1 in the present volume and cf. James Wilson, who, discussing
Pufendorf and political obligation, says: 'Consent is the sole principle, on which any

tonomy to impose obligations upon themselves without any ultimate reference to a higher law and authority was extremely difficult to accept, for it was assumed that if they had such autonomy, morals would be possible without reference to any deity – as Grotius had also pointed out. Since an account of morals in terms of subjective rights required the ability to enter into contractual obligations without reference to a higher law, this common line of thought was one of the main hindrances to the development of a subjective rights theory.[68]

One can point to a number of attempts in the later eighteenth century to formulate the idea of sui generis obligation, but, as with other elements in the subjective rights theory discussed here, it is not possible to point to one particular breakthrough that goes the whole way, at least in the Anglo-American world. The closest might be said to be Richard Price's theory of obligation and self-determination,[69] but he too has a moral safety net, though of a Platonist cut.[70] The attempt by Burlamaqui is, however, of significance, partly because it is clearly stated, partly because it occurs within the framework of a natural law theory, and finally because Burlamaqui was so significant for the American intellect.[71]

---

claim, in consequence of human authority, can be made upon one man by another. I say, in consequence of human authority: for, in consequence of the divine authority, numerous are the claims that we are reciprocally entitled to make, numerous are the duties, that we are reciprocally obliged to perform. But none of these can enter into the present question. We speak of authority merely human. Exclusively of the duties required by the law of nature, I can conceive of no claim, that one man can make upon another, but in consequence of his own consent' ('Lectures on Law', in *Works*, vol. 1, p. 190; cf. his tortuous but remarkable discussion of self-imposed obligation in ibid., pp. 102–3).

68   For a detailed discussion of obligation, see S. Darwall, 'Norm and normativity in eighteenth-century ethics', ch. 25 in *The Cambridge History of Eighteenth-Century Philosophy*, ed. K. Haakonssen, Cambridge, UK, forthcoming.

69   Richard Price, *A Review of the Principal Questions in Morals* [1758], ed. D.D. Raphael, Oxford, 1974, chs. 5 and 6; *Observations on the Nature of Civil Liberty, the Principles of Government, and the Justice and Policy of the War with America*, 3rd ed., London, 1776, pp. 2–6; *Additional Observations on the Nature and Value of Civil Liberty, and the War with America*, London, 1777, pp. 1–15.

70   See, e.g., *Additional Observations*, p. 11.

71   See Burlamaqui, *The Principles of Natural and Politic Law*. Burlamaqui was professor at the University in Geneva and contributed significantly to its reputation as, in Jefferson's words half a century later, one of 'the two eyes of Europe', the other eye being Edinburgh. After the French Revolution had spilled over into Geneva, Jefferson actively promoted the idea of importing the whole of the Geneva faculty, at George Washington's expense, and locating it 'so far from the federal city as moral considerations would recommend and yet near enough to it to be viewed as an appendix of that, and that the splendor of the two objects would reflect usefully on each other'. Letter to George Washington, 23 February 1795, in *Writings*

Burlamaqui's great two-volume work presents a full system of 'natural and politic law', which in its external form largely follows the systematics that had become traditional since Pufendorf. Behind the conventional facade is an often sharply argumentative mind, as can be seen in the case of particular interest here, the notion of obligation upon which all morality rests. His starting point is an account of what we might call 'practical reason'. Human action, as opposed to mere bodily locomotion, is goal directed, it has some sort of aim or purpose, however vague, and a rule of action is simply pointing out the connection between action and aim.

> This being premised, I affirm that every man who proposes to himself a particular end, and knows the means or rule which alone can conduct him to it, and put him in possession of what he desires, such a man finds himself under a necessity of following this rule, and of confirming his actions to it. Otherwise he would contradict himself; he would and he would not; he would desire the end, and neglect the only means which by his own confession are able to conduct him to it.

The acknowledgement of a rule of action under such circumstances is thus a 'reasonable necessity' or an obligation, 'because obligation, in its original idea, is nothing more than a restriction of liberty, produced by reason, inasmuch as the counsels which reason gives us, are motives that determine us to a particular manner of acting, preferable to any other'.[72] This is the natural condition of humankind. It is inevitable that reason in this sense regulates our behaviour, and 'consequently reason alone is sufficient to establish a system of morality, obligation, and duties; because when once we suppose it is reasonable to do or to abstain from certain things, this is really owning our obligation'.[73]

---

of *Jefferson*, 19:113; see also the letters to Wilson Nicholas, 22 November 1794, and M. D'Ivernois, 6 February 1795, 9:291ff. and 297ff. I should perhaps point out that within fifty years Burlamaqui's great work appeared in thirty-eight editions (the next fifty years adding another nineteen) in eight countries and was translated from the original French into seven other languages. There were seven American editions from 1792 onwards. There is one solid modern monograph on Burlamaqui: Bernard Gagnebin, *Burlamaqui et le droit naturel*, Geneva, 1944, and useful chapters in A. Dufour, *Le Mariage dans l'école romande du droit naturel au XVIIIe siècle*, Geneva, 1976, pp. 65–82; and S. Zurbuchen, *Naturrecht und natürliche Religion*, Würzburg, 1991, ch. 6. See also R.F. Harvey, *Jean Jacques Burlamaqui: A Liberal Tradition in American Constitutionalism*, Chapel Hill, NC, 1937, which gives the bibliographic information, pp. 188–92. The best discussion of Burlamaqui's influence on American thought is in White, *Philosophy of the American Revolution*, passim. See also U.M. von Eckardt, *The Pursuit of Happiness in the Democratic Creed*, New York, 1959, ch. 8.

72   Burlamaqui, *Principles of Natural and Politic Law*, I, pp. 207–8.
73   Ibid., p. 210.

Burlamaqui goes on to confront all the traditional objections to the notion of self-imposed obligation: that the very idea of obligation implies an agent who obliges and who is distinct from the obligee; that one cannot have a contract with oneself; that one cannot impose a necessity on oneself, because a removable necessity is not a necessity; that obligation implies a law, and law a superior. Acknowledging that these are indeed the received opinions,[74] Burlamaqui rightly points out that they beg the question and goes on to explain:

> It is true that man may, if he has a mind, withdraw himself from the obligations which reason imposes on him; but if he does, it is at his peril, and he is forced himself to acknowledge, that such a conduct is quite unreasonable. But to conclude from thence that reason cannot oblige us, is going too far; because this consequence would equally invalidate the obligation imposed by a superior.[75]

The consequence is that a voluntarist account of natural law is impossible, for even our obligation to God as moral legislator is a self-imposed obligation (and the same, of course, applies to human legislators). The covenant had been turned into a philosophical theory, and Hobbes would have been amused.[76]

Most of the elements in Burlamaqui's argument may have been anticipated in various earlier rationalist theories of ethics, such as those of Leibniz, the Cambridge Platonists, Samuel Clarke and his followers, and indeed, earlier still, by Suárez. But the Swiss thinker is unusually clear-headed in insisting that his line of argument means that all morals rest on rationally self-imposed obligation. As we saw earlier, he also appreciates that in that case there is no guarantee of the moral life

---

74   Cf. the quotation from Rutherforth at note 15 to the present chapter and the one from Wooddeson in note 79. [*Note*: citations saying '*at* note 15' mean 'in the text, near note 15'; citations saying '*in* note 6' mean 'in the text of note 6'.]

75   Burlamaqui, *Principles of Natural and Politic Law*, I, p. 213; cf. pp. 65–6.

76   For a typical example of the sort of public mind that would be receptive to a philosophical theory of self-government, we may take the notable abolitionist Granville Sharp. For him all law and authority, including God's, are based on covenant. Consequently he must reject Pufendorf's authoritarian voluntarism – of which the idea of Parliament's absolute sovereignty is a consequence – and warn his readers of 'the Errors of this celebrated Civilian, because the studying of his Works . . . is at this time considered as a material part of Education in our Universities; so that *the rising Generation* of the very best Families in this Kingdom are liable to imbibe (as it were with the Milk of Instruction) these poisonous Doctrines' (*A Declaration of the People's Natural Right to a Share in the Legislature*, London, 1774, pp. xx–xxi). Elsewhere he attacks the common combination of Christian utilitarianism and (residual) voluntarism, using as his starting-point the passage in Blackstone's *Commentaries* quote in note 11 to this chapter: Sharp, *A Tract on the Law of Nature, and Principles of Action in Man*, London, 1777, pp. 57ff.

beyond human rationality. This point is, however, considerably obscured by a good deal of the usual sunny providentialism concerning
the essential harmony between individual rational judgements, including the correlativity between rights and duties.[77]

This combination of a strong theory of human moral self-government
with a tradition-bound theory of how such self-government works out
is characteristic of the deep philosophical ambiguity of the so-called
rights-of-man theories of the later eighteenth century. Those, such as
Burlamaqui and cognate spirits among rational dissenters, who were
finding their way to the idea of moral autonomy and the possibility of
self-imposed obligation, found it hard to accept the implication that self-
government makes moral harmony an open-ended task and not a
justifying ideal. Those, like Witherspoon, who were able to toy with the
idea of a more or less chaotic moral world in which all semblance of
order was man-made and transitory, found the strength to do so in the
eschatology of evangelical religion. However, from whichever side they
came, their idea of the moral self easily adopted the old *political* rhetoric
of self-government and gave the latter an individualistic sense it had not
had. For a short season, people of many persuasions – although differ-
ing about the key terms such as 'right', 'self-government', and 'nature' –
could agree with Jefferson that 'every man, and every body of men on
earth, possesses the right of self-government. They receive it with their
being from the hand of nature. Individuals exercise it by their single will;
collections of men by that of their majority.'[78]

The man who saw most clearly what this could lead to – and dis-
liked what he saw – was Edmund Burke, who thought it had to do
with a new idea of the rights of man. He was both right and wrong.
Many people certainly talked of such rights, and a few even talked of
the rights of women. This chapter has been concerned with the history
of the ideas of rights, not with the discourse about them, but if my
argument is correct, few people understood exactly what they were
talking about. There were, if not good, at least intelligible reasons for
this situation, as I have tried to show. In the end the talk may have led
to a more coherent theory, but that end probably lies well beyond the
eighteenth century. On the whole, the conceptual structure of natural
law, duty, right, with its comfortable orderliness, persisted on both

77   Burlamaqui, *Principles of Natural and Politic Law,* I, p. 71. In Burlamaqui, as in
many earlier and later thinkers, there is always some ambiguity as to whether the
correlativity thesis is purely definitional or whether it is a statement about the
(ideal) moral world.

78   Jefferson, 'Opinion Upon the Question Whether the President Should Veto
the Bill, Declaring That the Seat of Government Shall Be Transferred to the Potomac,
in the Year 1790', 15 July 1790, in *Writings of Jefferson,* 3:60.

sides of the Atlantic, as shown in the lectures of Blackstone's successors, of Witherspoon's successor, and of James Wilson.[79] As Wilson said, 'The laws of nature are the measure and the rule; they ascertain the limits and the extent of natural liberty.'[80] Within this framework, however, American thinkers managed to rid themselves of the traditionalism that the British had grafted onto it and thus to create a culture in which rights talk could flourish, whatever it meant.

79 Opening his lectures as Vinerian Professor of Law at Oxford in 1777 with a lecture on 'The Laws of Man's Nature', Richard Wooddeson warned his students: 'Those, who think man's sociability . . . might suffice to preserve some order and justice in the world [in a note he cites Grotius, *De iure belli ac pacis*, Prol., VI, VIII, XI], and those, who speak of obligation arising from the mere approval of reason [note: Burlamaqui, *Natural Law*, Part 2, ch. 7, i.e., the chapter that I quote at notes 73 and 75], both sorts of speculatists, excluding natural theology from the argument, seem to deal in unprofitable refinements, not considering things as they are, but upon a subject so serious inventing and dwelling on arbitrary suppositions. Besides, if rules so founded could obtain, they could not properly be termed laws, which cannot be abstracted from the authority of a lawgiver. It may be added, that in unlettered minds the conceptions of moral right and wrong immediately raise impressions of the pleasure or displeasure of the Deity; which cannot be wholly ascribed to habitual association; for it does not rest there' (*Elements of Jurisprudence Treated of in the Preliminary Part of a Course of Lectures on the Laws of England*, London, 1783, pp. 6–7). Cf. Robert Chambers, *A Course of Lectures on the English Law Delivered at the University of Oxford, 1767–1773*, ed. T.M. Curley, 2 vols., Oxford, 1986, I, pp. 83ff. (Lecture 1); Stanhope Smith, *Lectures on Moral and Political Philosophy*, esp. II, pp. 94ff. (Lecture 18); and Wilson, 'Lectures on Law', *Works*, I, pp. 95ff., esp. pp. 104ff. (Lecture III). See also Noll's splendid discussion of Stanhope Smith's synthesis, a 'Republican Christian Enlightenment', *Princeton and the Republic*, esp. ch. 10.

80 Wilson, *Works*, I, p. 276.

Bibliography

Manuscript sources

Aberdeen University Library

Ms 133, 1782 (John Millar).
MS M 184: David Fordyce, 'A Brief Account of the Nature, Progress and Origin of Philosophy delivered by the late Mr. David Fordyce, P.P. Marish. Col: Abdn. to his Scholars, before they begun their Philosophical course. Anno 1743/4'.
Birkwood Collection, MSS 2131/3/II/6; 2131/4/III/6–7; 2131/3/III/8; 2131/6/IV/2 (Thomas Reid).

Bodleian Library

MS Locke f.3, fols. 201–2, 'Lex naturae' (Journal entry 15 July 1678). Printed in von Leyden, 'John Locke'.

Edinburgh University Library

MS Dc 2.45–6 (John Millar).
Laing MS II.91: John Stevenson to Charles Mackie, 10 September 1735.

Glasgow University Library

MS Gen 289–91; MS Hamilton 116, 1798; MS Gen 180 (1–3) 1789; MS Murray 88–90, 1790 (all concerning John Millar).
MSS 116–18: Robert Jack, 'Dr. Reid's Lectures, 1774–1776'.

Mitchell Library, Glasgow

MS 99, 1771 (John Millar).
MS A104929 (Thomas Reid).

Printed sources

Alberti, Valentin, *Compendium juris naturæ, orthodoxæ theologiæ conformatum*, Leipzig, 1678.
  Eros Lipsicus, Leipzig, 1687.

343

Anonymous, see entries under individual titles.

Ariminensis, Gregorius, *Lectura super primum et secundum sententiarum*, ed. A.D. Trapp, V. Marcolino et al., 7 vols., Berlin, 1978–87.

Arthur, Archibald, *Discourses on Theological and Literary Subjects*. With an account of some particulars in the life and character of the Rev. Mr. Archibald Arthur, late Professor of Moral Philosophy in the University of Glasgow, by William Richardson, Glasgow, 1803.

Bagehot, Walter, 'The first Edinburgh reviewers', in *The Collected Works of Walter Bagehot*, ed. Norman St. John-Stevas, 8 vols., London, 1965, vol. 1.

Barbeyrac, Jean, 'Historical and critical account of the science of morality', in Pufendorf, *Law of Nature*, pp. 1–75.

Barrington, *see* Shute, John.

Bentham, Jeremy, *An Introduction to the Principles of Morals and Legislation*, ed. J.H. Burns and H.L.A. Hart, London, 1970.

Of Laws in General, ed. H.L.A. Hart, London, 1970.

The Works of Jeremy Bentham (published under the superintendence of his executor, John Bowring), Edinburgh, 1838–43, vol. 10.

Bielfeld, Jacob von, *Institutions politiques*, 2 vols., Leyden, 1760.

Birch, Thomas, *The History of the Royal Society of London . . .*, 4 vols., London, 1756–7.

Blackstone, Sir William, *Commentaries on the Laws of England*, 4 vols., Oxford, 1765–9.

Bower, A., *The History of the University of Edinburgh*, 2 vols., Edinburgh, 1817.

Brown, Thomas, *Lectures on the Philosophy of the Human Mind*, 4 vols., Edinburgh, 1820.

Burlamaqui, Jean-Jacques, *The Principles of Natural and Politic Law* [1747–8], trans. T. Nugent, 2nd ed., 2 vols., London, 1763.

Butler, Joseph, *The Analogy of Religion, Natural and Revealed, to the Constitution and Course of Nature*, in *The Works of Joseph Butler*, 2 vols., Oxford, 1874, vol. 1, pp. 1–327.

'Of the nature of virtue', in *The Works of Joseph Butler*, vol. 1, pp. 328–9.

Carlyle, Alexander, *Anecdotes and Characters of the Times* [1860], ed. J. Kinsley, London, 1973.

Carmichael, Gershom, *Gershom Carmichael's Supplements and Appendix to Samuel Pufendorf's 'De officio hominis et civis juxta legem naturalem libri duo . . .'*, ed. J.N. Lenhart, trans. C.H. Reeves, Cleveland, OH, (privately published), 1985.

Chambers, Robert, *A Course of Lectures on the English Law Delivered at the University of Oxford, 1767–1773*, ed. T.M. Curley, 2 vols., Oxford, 1986.

Clap, Thomas, *An Essay on the Nature and Foundation of Moral Virtue: Being a Short Introduction to the Study of Ethics: for the Use of the Students of Yale-College*, New Haven, 1765.

Clarke, Samuel, *A Discourse concerning the Unchangeable Obligations of the Natural Religion, and the Truth and Certainty of the Christian Revelation*, London, 1716.

Cocceji, Heinrich von, *Grotius illustratus, seu commentarii ad Hugonis Grotii de Jure belli et pacis libros tres*, 4 vols., Bratislava, 1744–52.

Juris publici prudentia compendio exhibita, Frankford a.d.O., 1695.

Prodromus iustitiæ gentium, sive exercitationes duas ad illustrationem tractatus Grotiani de Jure belli ac pacis . . ., Frankfort a.d.O., 1719.

Cocceji, Samuel von, *Disputatio inauguralis de Principio juris naturalis unico, vero et adaequato, . . .,* Frankfort a.d.O., 1699.

Introductio ad Henrici L.B. de Cocceji . . . Grotium illustratum, continens dissertationes proemiales XII in quibus principia Grotiana circa ius naturae . . . ad iustam methodum revocantur . . ., Halle, 1748.

Jus civile controversum, 2 vols., Frankfort a.d.O., 1713, 1718 (also Frankfort a.d.O., Leipzig, 1753).

Novum systema jurisprudentiae naturalis et romanae, Berlin, 1740.

Tractatus juris gentium de principio juris naturalis unico, vero et adæquato, Frankfort a.d.O., 1702.

See also [Frederick the Great, King of Prussia].

Cockburn, Henry, *Life of Lord Jeffrey. With a Selection from His Correspondence,* 2 vols., Edinburgh, 1852.

Craig, John, 'Account of the Life and Writings of John Millar, Esq.', in John Millar, *Origin of the Distinction of Ranks,* pp. i–cxxiv.

Elements of Political Science, 3 vols., Edinburgh, 1814.

Remarks on some Fundamental Doctrines in Political Economy illustrated by a Brief Inquiry into the Economic State of Britain since the Year 1815, Edinburgh, 1821.

Culverwell, Nathaniel, *An Elegant and Learned Discourse of the Light of Nature,* [1652], ed. R.A. Greene and H. MacCallum, Toronto, 1971.

Cumberland, Richard, *De legibus naturæ disquisitio philosophica,* London, 1672.

Traité philosophique des loix naturelles, trans. J. Barbeyrac, Amsterdam, 1744.

A Treatise of the Laws of Nature, trans. J. Maxwell, London, 1727.

Defoe, Daniel, *The Original Power of the Collective Body of the People of England, Examined and Asserted,* London, 1702.

Doddridge, Philip, *A Course of Lectures on the Principal Subjects in Pneumatology, Ethics, and Divinity,* [1763], 4th ed., 2 vols., London, 1799.

Domat, Jean, *Les Loix civiles dans leur ordre naturel,* Paris, 1689.

Edwards, Jonathan, *An Inquiry into the Modern Prevailing Notions Respecting that Freedom of the Will,* 1754 [reprinted, Bristol, UK, 1993].

Encyclopaedia Britannica, 3 vols., Edinburgh, 1771.

Erskine, John, *An Institute of the Law of Scotland,* Edinburgh, 1773.

Estlin, John Prior, *Familiar Lectures on Moral Philosophy,* 2 vols., London, 1818.

Ferguson, Adam, *Principles of Moral and Political Science,* 2 vols., Edinburgh, 1792.

Filmer, Robert, *Patriarcha* [1680], in *Patriarcha and Other Writings,* ed. J.P. Sommerville, Cambridge, UK, 1991.

Fordyce, David, *Elements of Moral Philosophy* [1748], London, 1754.

[Frederick the Great, King of Prussia], *The Frederician Code, or, A Body of Law for the Dominions of the King of Prussia. Founded on Reason and the Constitutions of the Country,* 2 vols., London, 1761.

The History of the Seven Years War, part I, in *Posthumous Works of Frederick II, King of Prussia,* trans. Thomas Holcroft, 13 vols., London, 1789, vols. 2–3.

The King of Prussia's Plan for Reforming the Administration of Justice, London, 1750.

Garve, Christian, *Uebersicht der vornehmsten Principien der Sittenlehre, von dem Zeitalter des Aristoteles an bis auf unsre Zeiten,* Breslau, 1798.

Gibbon, Edward, *The Decline and Fall of the Roman Empire*, 3 vols., London, n.d.
 An Essay on the Study of Literature, London, 1764.
 Le Journal de Gibbon a Lausanne 17 Août 1763–19 Avril 1764, ed. Georges Bonnard, Lausanne, 1945.
Gisborne, Thomas, *An Enquiry into the Duties of the Female Sex*, London, 1797.
 An Inquiry into the Duties of Men in the Higher and Middle Classes of Society in Great Britain, Resulting from their Respective Stations, Professions, and Employments, [1794], 6th ed., 2 vols. corrected, London, 1811.
 The Principles of Moral Philosophy Investigated, and Applied to the Constitution of Civil Society [1789], 4th ed., London, 1798.
Glafey, Adam Friedrich, *Vollständige Geschichte des Rechts der Vernunfft*, Leipzig, 1739.
Glasgow Courier, 18 December 1794.
Glasgow Mercury, no. 5, July 1791.
Godwin, William, *Thoughts Occasioned by . . . Dr. Parr's Spital Sermon . . .*, London, 1801.
Green, Thomas, *An Examination of the Leading Principle of the New System of Morals, as that Principle is Stated and Applied in Mr. Godwin's Inquiry Concerning Political Justice, in a Letter to a Friend*, 2nd ed., London, 1799.
Grote, George, *A Statement of the Question of Parliamentary Reform*, London, 1821.
Grotius, Hugo, *Le Droit de la guerre et de la paix*, trans. J. Barbeyrac, 2 vols., Amsterdam, 1724.
 De iure belli ac pacis libri tres, ed. J.F. Gronovius and J. Barbeyrac, Amsterdam, 1735.
 De iure prædæ commentarius, [c.1604], with trans. by G.L. Williams and W.H. Zeydel, 2 vols. (Classics of International Law), Oxford, 1950.
 Mare liberum/The Freedom of the Sea, ed. and trans. J. Brown Scott, New York, 1916.
 The Rights of War and Peace in three Books, ed. J. Barbeyrac, trans. anon., London 1738.
 De veritate religionis Christianæ [1623]; in Grotius, *Opera omnia theologica*, 3 vols., Amsterdam, 1679, III, pp. 3–96.
Harrington, James, *The Political Works*, ed. J.G.A. Pocock, Cambridge, UK, 1977.
Hazlitt, William, *An Essay on the Principles of Human Action: to Which are Added Some Remarks on the Systems of Hartley and Helvetius* [1805], in *The Complete Works of William Hazlitt*, ed. P.P. Howe, 21 vols., London, 1930–4, vol. 1, pp. 1–91.
 The Spirit of the Age [1825], in *The Complete Works of William Hazlitt*, ed. P.P. Howe, 21 vols., London, 1930–4, vol. 11, pp. 1–184.
Heineccius, Johann Christian Gottlieb, *De vita, fatis et scriptis Io. Gottlieb Heineccii, IC. commentarius*, in J.G. Heineccius, *Opera omnia*, Geneva, 1744–8, I.
Heineccius, Johann Gottlieb, *Antiquitatum Romanarum syntagma*, Halle, 1719.
 Elementa iuris civilis secundum ordinem Institutionem (1725), Amsterdam, 1733.
 Elemnta juris civilis secundum ordinem Pandectarum [1727], Amsterdam, 1733.
 Elementa juris Germanici tum veteris tum hodierni, 2 vols., Halle, 1735–6.
 Elementa juris naturæ et gentium, Halle, 1737.

Elementa philosophiae rationalis et moralis, Amsterdam, 1728.

A Methodical System of Universal Law: Or, the Laws of Nature and Nations Deduced from Certain Principles, and applied to Proper Cases, trans. George Turnbull, 2 vols., London, 1741.

Hoadly, Benjamin, *The Original and Institution of Civil Government Discuss'd*, London, 1710.

Hobbes, Thomas, *An Answer to a Book published by Dr. Bramhall, late Bishop of Derry, called "The Catching of the Leviathan"* (c. 1688), in Molesworth, ed., *The English Works*, IV.

De cive. The Latin Version/The English Version, ed. H. Warrender, Oxford, 1983.

The Elements of Law Natural and Politic, ed. F. Tönnies, Cambridge, UK, 1982.

The English Works, ed. W. Molesworth, 11 vols., London, 1839–45.

Leviathan, ed. R. Tuck, Cambridge, UK, 1991.

Home, Henry (Lord Kames), *Elements of Criticism*, Edinburgh, 1762.

Essays on the Principles of Morality and Natural Religion, Edinburgh, 1751.

Grundsätze der Kritik, trans. Johann Nikolaus Meinhard and Christian Garve, 3 vols., Leipzig, 1763–6.

Horner, Francis, *The Economic Writings of Francis Horner in the 'Edinburgh Review'*, 1802–6, ed. F.W. Fetter, New York, 1957.

The Horner Papers: Selections from the Letters and Miscellaneous Writings of Francis Horner, M.P., 1795–1817, ed. K. Bourne and W. Banks Taylor, Edinburgh, 1994.

Memoirs and Correspondence of Francis Horner, M.P., ed. Leonard Horner, 2 vols., London, 1843.

Hume, David, *Baron David Hume's Lectures, 1786–1822*, ed. G. Campbell and H. Paton (The Stair Society), 6 vols., Edinburgh, 1952.

Enquiries Concerning Human Understanding and Concerning the Principles of Morals, ed. L.A. Selby-Bigge, Oxford, 1902; 3rd ed., rev. by P.H. Nidditch, Oxford, 1975.

The History of England, From the Invasion of Julius Caesar to the Revolution in 1688, foreword by W.B. Todd, 6 vols., Indianapolis, 1983.

The Letters of David Hume, ed. J.Y.T. Greig, 2 vols., Oxford, 1969.

New Letters of David Hume, ed. R. Klibansky and E.C. Mossner, Oxford, 1969.

Political Essays, ed. K. Haakonssen, Cambridge, UK, 1994.

A Treatise of Human Nature: Being an Attempt to Introduce the Experimental Method of Reasoning into Moral Subjects, ed. L.A. Selby-Bigge; 2nd ed., rev. by P.H. Nidditch, Oxford, 1978.

Hutcheson, Francis, *Collected Works*, 7 vols. Facsim. repr. prepared by B. Fabian. Hildesheim, 1969–71.

An Essay on the Nature and Conduct of the Passions and Affections with Illustrations on the Moral Sense, London, 1728; facsim. repr., in *Collected Works*, vol. 2.

Illustrations on the Moral Sense [London, 1728], ed. B. Peach, Cambridge, MA, 1971.

An Inquiry into the Original of our Ideas of Beauty and Virtue, Dublin, 1725; facsim. repr., in *Collected Works*, vol. 1.

De naturali hominum socialitate oratio inauguralis, Glasgow, 1730.

Philosophiae moralis institutio compendiaria [1742], 2nd ed., Glasgow, 1745; facsim. repr., in *Collected Works*, vol. 3.

A Short Introduction to Moral Philosophy, Glasgow, 1747; facsim. repr., in *Collected Works*, vol. 4.

A System of Moral Philosophy, 2 vols., Glasgow, 1755; facsim. repr., in *Collected Works*, vols. 5–6.

Synopsis metaphysicae, ontologiam et pneumatologiam complectens, 2nd ed., Glasgow, 1744; facsim. repr., in *Collected Works*, 7:203–333.

Two Texts on Human Nature, ed. and trans. T. Mautner, Cambridge, UK, 1993.

Jardine, George, *Outlines of Philosophical Education* [1818], Glasgow, 1825.

Jefferson, Thomas, *The Political Writings of Thomas Jefferson*, ed. E. Dumbauld, Indianapolis, IN, 1955.

The Writings of Thomas Jefferson, ed. A.E. Bergh, 20 vols., Washington, DC, 1907.

Jeffrey, Francis, *Edinburgh Review*, October 1835, Art. II.

Jöcher, Christian Gottlieb, *Allgemeines Gelehrten-Lexikon*, 4 vols., Leipzig, 1750–1.

Kames, Henry Home, Lord. *See* Home, Henry (Lord Kames).

Kant, I. *Essays and Treatises on Moral, Political, and Various Philosophical Subjects*, facsim. repr., of London, 1798 ed., 2 vols., Bristol, UK, 1993.

Gesammelte Schriften, Königlich Preussische Akademie der Wissenschaften, Bd. X, 2. Abt.: 'Briefwechsel', Bd. 1, Berlin and Leipzig, 1922; Bd. XV, 3. Abt., Handschriftlicher Nachlass, Bd. 2.i., Berlin and Leipzig, 1923; Bd. XV, 3. Abt., Handschriftlicher Nachlass, Bd. 2.ii, Berlin and Leipzig, 1928; Bd. XIX, 3 Abt., Handschriftlicher Nachlass, Bd. 6, Berlin and Leipzig, 1934.

Grundlegung zur Metaphysik der Sitten, in *Gesammelte Schriften*, Berlin, 1911, Bd. IV.

Die Metaphysik der Sitten, in *Gesammelte Schriften*, Berlin, 1907, Bd. VI.

Leibniz, G.W., 'Jugement d'un anonyme sur l'original de cet abrégé [*De officio*]: Avec des reflexions du Traducteur [Barbeyrac] . . .', in Pufendorf, *Les devoirs de l'homme, et du citoien*, ed. J. Barbeyrac, Amsterdam, 1718, pp. 429–95.

'Meditation on the common concept of justice', in *The Political Writings of Leibniz*, ed. P. Riley, Cambridge, UK, 1972, pp. 45–64.

'Méditation sur la notion commune de la justice', in *Rechtsphilosophisches aus Leibnizens ungedruckten Schriften*, ed. G. Mollat, Leipzig, 1885, pp. 41–70.

'Monita quædam ad Samuelis Puffendorfii principia, Gerh. Wolth. Molano directa', in Leibniz, *Opera omnia*, ed. L. Dutens, 6 vols., Geneva, 1768, IV.3, pp. 275–83.

'Observationes de principio juris', in Leibniz, *Opera omnia*, IV, pp. 270–5.

'Opinion on the principles of Pufendorf', in *The Political Writings of Leibniz*, Cambridge, UK, 1972, pp. 64–75.

Leslie, Charles, *The Constitution, Laws, and Government of England Vindicated*, London, 1709.

The Finishing Stroke, London, 1711.

Letter from Edinburgh in *Neuer teutscher Merkur*, II (1798), 398–9.

Letters of Sidney, on Inequality of Property. To which is added, A Treatise of the Effects of War on Commercial Prosperity, Edinburgh, 1796.

Locke, John, *The Correspondence of John Locke*, ed. E.S. de Beer, 8 vols., Oxford, 1975–89.

An Essay Concerning Human Understanding [1690], ed. P.H. Nidditch, Oxford, 1975.

Essays on the Law of Nature [1663], ed. W. von Leyden, Oxford, 1954.

'Of ethics in general', in Peter King, Seventh Baron King, *The Life of John Locke with Extracts from his Correspondence, Journals, and Commonplace Books*, new ed., 2 vols., London, 1830, 2:122–39.

A Fourth Letter for Toleration, in *The Works of John Locke*, 9 vols., London, 1824.

A Paraphrase and Notes on the Epistles of St. Paul to the Galatians, 1 and 2 Corinthians, Romans, Ephesians, ed. A.W. Wainwright, 2 vols., Oxford, 1987.

Questions Concerning the Law of Nature, ed. and trans. R. Horwitz, J.S. Clay, and D. Clay, Ithaca, NY, 1990.

The Reasonableness of Christianity, as delivered in the Scriptures, in *The Works of John Locke*, 12th ed., 9 vols., London, 1824, VI.

Some Thoughts Concerning Education, ed. J.W. Yolton and J.S. Yolton, Oxford, 1989.

Two Treatises of Government, ed. P. Laslett, Cambridge, UK, 1960.

Mackintosh, James, *A Discourse on the Law of Nature and Nations* [1799], in *The Miscellaneous Works of the Right Honourable Sir James Mackintosh*, 3 vols., London, 1846.

Dissertation on the Progress of Ethical Philosophy, 2nd ed., Edinburgh, 1837.

Edinburgh Review, July 1808, Art. I; September 1816, Art. 9; December 1818, Art. 8; November 1820, Art. 12; July 1821, pp. 488–509; October 1821, Art. 10; October 1835, Art. 11.

Vindiciae Gallicae: A Defence of the French Revolution and its English Admirers, against the Accusations of the Right Hon. Edmund Burke [1791], *The Miscellaneous Works of the Right Honourable Sir James Mackintosh*, 3 vols., London, 1846, III.

Mackintosh, R.J., ed., *Memoirs of the Life of . . . Sir James Mackintosh*, 2 vols., London, 1836.

Mill, James, *Analysis of the Phenomena of the Human Mind*, New York, 1967.

Edinburgh Review, July, 1809, 407–29; December, 1818, 165–205.

'Education', in *James Mill on Education*, ed. W.H. Burston, Cambridge, UK, 1969.

'Essay on Jurisprudence', in *Essays on Government, Jurisprudence, Liberty of the Press, and Law of Nations*, New York, 1967.

A Fragment on Mackintosh, London, 1835.

The History of British India, 4th ed., with notes and continuation by H.H. Wilson, 9 vols., London, 1840–8.

Literary Journal, vol. 2, October 1803, pp. 325–33, 385–400.

Selected Economic Writings, ed. D. Winch, Edinburgh, 1966.

Utilitarian Logic and Politics: James Mill's 'Essay on Government', Macaulay's Critique and the Ensuing Debate, ed. J. Lively and J.C. Rees, Oxford, 1978.

Millar, John, *An Historical View of the English Government from the Settlement of the Saxons in Britain to the Revolution in 1688. To which are subjoined some Dissertations Connected with the History of the Government from the Revolution to the Present Time* [1787], 3rd ed., ed. John Craig and James Mylne, 4 vols., Edinburgh, 1803.

Letters of Crito e Letters of Sidney, ed. Vincenzo Merolle, Rome, 1984.

The Origin of the Distinction of Ranks, or An Inquiry into the Circumstances which give rise to Influence and Authority, in the Different Members of Society [1771], 4th ed., Edinburgh, 1806.

[Millar, John], *Letters of Crito, on the Causes, Objects, and Consequences of the Present War*, Edinburgh, 1796.

Montesquieu, Charles-Louis de Secondat (Baron), *The Spirit of the Laws*, ed. and trans. A.M. Cohler, B.C. Miller, and H.S. Stone, Cambridge, UK, 1989.

More, Henry, *An Account of Virtue* [1667], trans. E. Southwell, London, 1690.

Neuer teutscher Merkur, publ. C.M. Wieland and C.A. Boettiger, 63 vols., Weimar, 1790–1810.

Ockham, William, *Philosophical Writings: A Selection*, 1957, repr. ed., ed. and trans. P. Boehner, London, 1967.

Ogilvie, William, *Birthright in Land*, with biographical notes by D.C. Mac-Donald, London, 1891.

An Essay on the Right of Property in Land, With Respect to Its Foundation in the Law of Nature, Its Present Establishment by the Municipal Laws of Europe, and the Regulations by Which it Might Be Rendered more Beneficial to the Lower Ranks of Mankind [1781], London, n.d.

Proposals for a Public Library at Aberdeen, Aberdeen, 1764.

Pothier, Robert-Joseph, *Traité des obligations*, Paris-Orléans, 1761–4.

The Preceptor: Containing a General Course of Education. Wherein the First Principles of Polite Learning Are Laid Down in a Way Most Suitable for Trying the Genius, and Advancing the Instruction of Youth, 2 vols., London, 1748.

Price, Richard, *Additional Observations on the Nature and Value of Civil Liberty, and the War with America*, London, 1777.

Observations on the Nature of Civil Liberty, the Principles of Government, and the Justice and Policy of the War with America, 3rd ed., London, 1776.

A Review of the Principal Questions in Morals [1758], ed. D.D. Raphael, Oxford, 1974.

Pufendorf, Samuel, Freiherr von, *Briefe Samuel Pufendorfs an Christian Thomasius (1687–1693)*, ed. E. Gigas (Historische Bibliothek, Bd. II), Munich and Leipzig, 1897.

Les devoirs de l'homme et du citoyen, tels qu'ils lui sont prescrits par la loi naturelle, trans. J. Barbeyrac, Amsterdam, 1706.

Le droit de la nature et des gens, ou système général des principes les plus importants de la morale, de la jurisprudence, et de la politique, trans. J. Barbeyrac, 2 vols., Amsterdam, 1707.

Elementorum jurisprudentiae universalis libri duo [1660], facism. repr., prepared by H. Wehlberg with trans. by W.A. Oldfather, 2 vols. (Classics of International Law), Oxford, 1931.

On the Duty of Man and Citizen According to Natural Law, ed. J. Tully, trans. M. Silverthorne, Cambridge, UK, 1991.

De iure naturae et gentium libri octo [1672], ed. J.N. Hertius, J. Barbeyrac, and G. Mascovius, 2 vols., facsim. repr. of 1759 ed., Frankfurt a.M., 1967.

Of the Law of Nature and Nations, ed. J. Barbeyrac, trans. B. Kennet, 5th ed., London, 1749.

De officio hominis et civis juxta legem naturalem libri duo, ed. A.A. Pagenstecher, Groeningen, 1712.

De officio hominis et civis juxta legem naturalem libri duo, ed. G. Carmichael, 2nd ed., Edinburgh, 1724.

De offico hominis et civis juxta legem naturalem libri duo [1673], facsim. repr. of 1682 ed., with trans. by F.G. Moore, 2 vols. (Classics of International Law), New York, 1927.

The Whole Duty of Man According to the Law of Nature, 4th ed., with the notes of Mr. Barbeyrac . . ., London, 1716.

Reddie, James, *Inquiries Elementary and Historical in the Science of Law,* London, 1840.

Reid, Thomas, 'Cura Prima. Of Common Sense,' ed. David Fate Norton, in L. Marcil-Lacoste, *Claude Buffier and Thomas Reid,* appendix.

Essays on the Active Powers of Man, in *Philosophical Works.* (Abbreviated A.P.)

Essays on the Intellectual Powers of Man, in *Philosophical Works.* (Abbreviated I.P.)

An Inquiry into the Human Mind, on the Principles of Common Sense, in *Philosophical Works.*

'Observations on the dangers of political innovation', *Glasgow Courier,* 18 December 1794, 518–23. Also in Arthur, *Discourses.*

Philosophical Orations of Thomas Reid, ed. W.R. Humphries, Aberdeen, 1937; English trans. by S.D. Sullivan, ed. D.D. Todd, Carbondale, IL, 1989.

Philosophical Works, ed. Sir William Hamilton, facsim. repr. of 8th ed., 1895, introd. Harry M. Bracken, 2 vols. in 1, Hildesheim, 1983.

Practical Ethics: Being Lectures and Papers on Natural Religion, Self-Government, Natural Jurisprudence, and the Law of Nations, ed. K. Haakonssen, Princeton, 1990.

'Unpublished Letters of Thomas Reid to Lord Kames, 1762–1782', ed. I.A. Ross, *Texas Studies in Literature and Language,* 7 (1965), 17–65.

Ricardo, David, *The Works and Correspondence of David Ricardo,* ed. P. Sraffa, 10 vols., Cambridge, UK, 1962–6, vol. 7.

Rutherforth, Thomas, *Institutes of Natural Law* [1754], 2nd ed., Cambridge, UK, 1774.

Selden, John, *De iure naturali et gentium juxta disciplinam hebraeorum libri septem,* London, 1640.

Mare clausum: The Right and Dominion of the Sea in Two Books, trans. J.H., London, 1663.

Sharp, Granville, *A Declaration of the People's Natural Right to a Share in the Legislature,* London, 1774.

A Tract on the Law of Nature, and Principles of Action in Man, London, 1777.

Shute, John (first Viscount Barrington), *Dissertatio philosophica inauguralis de theocratia civili,* Utrecht, 1697.

Dissertatio philosophica de theocratia morali, Utrecht, 1697.

The Rights of Protestant Dissenters, London, 1704.

The Theological Works of the First Viscount Barrington, ed. George Townsend, 3 vols., London, 1828.

Smith, Adam, 'Anderson Notes', in R.L. Meek, 'New light on Adam Smith's Glasgow lectures on jurisprudence', *History of Political Economy*, 8 (1976), 439–77, at pp. 467–77.

The Correspondence of Adam Smith, ed. E.C. Mossner and I.S. Ross, 2nd ed., Oxford, 1987.

An Inquiry into the Nature and Causes of the Wealth of Nations, ed. R.H. Campbell and A.S. Skinner, Oxford, 1976. (Abbreviated *WN*.)

Lectures on Jurisprudence, ed. R.L. Meek, D.D. Raphael, and P.G. Stein, Oxford, 1978.

Theorie der moralischen Empfindungen, trans. Christoph Rautenberg, Braunschweig, 1770.

The Theory of Moral Sentiments, ed. D.D. Raphael and A.L. Macfie, Oxford, 1976.

Smith, Samuel Stanhope, *The Lectures, Corrected and Improved, Which Have been Delivered for a Series of Years, in the College of New Jersey; On the Subjects of Moral and Political Philosophy*, 2 vols., Trenton, NJ, 1812.

Stewart, Dugald, *Biographical Memoirs of Adam Smith . . . William Robertson . . . Thomas Reid . . .* (1793, 1796, 1802; 1811), in *Works*, X.

Collected Works, ed. Sir William Hamilton, 11 vols. [1854–60], facsim. repr. Knud Haakonssen, Bristol, UK, 1994.

Dissertation Exhibiting the Progress of Metaphysical, Ethical and Political Philosophy since the Revival of Letters in Europe (1815–21), in *Works*, I.

Elements of the Philosophy of the Human Mind, 3 vols. (1792, 1816, 1827) in *Works*, II–IV.

Lecturs on Political Economy, 2 vols. (c. 1809–10), in *Works*, VIII–IX.

Outlines of Moral Philosophy (1793), in *Works*, II, VI, and VIII.

The Philosophy of the Active and Moral Powers of Man, 2 vols. (1828), in *Works*, VI–VII.

Suárez, Francisco, *De legibus* [*Tractatus de legibus ac Deo legislatore*]. Ed. crit. bilingüe por L. Pereña et al., 8 vols. (Corpus Hispanorum de Pace, 11–17, 21–22), Madrid, 1971–81.

Selections from Three Works, 2 vols. (Classics of International Law), Oxford, 1944.

Thomas Aquinas, *Summa theologiae* (Latin and English). Blackfriars edition. 61 vols. New York and London, 1964–80.

Turnbull, George, *A Discourse upon the Nature and Origine of Moral and Civil Laws*, London, 1740, in Heineccius, *System of Universal Law*, II, pp. 245–325.

Observations upon Liberal Education, in all its Branches, London, 1742.

The Principles of Moral (and Christian) Philosophy, 2 vols., London, 1740.

'A supplement concerning the duties of subjects and magistrates', in Heineccius, *System of Universal Law*, II, pp. 222–44.

Theses academicae de pulcerrima mundi cum materialis tum rationalis constitutione, Aberdeen, 1726.

Theses philosophicæ de scientiæ naturalis cum philosophia morali conjunctione, Aberdeen, 1723.

Tyrrell, James, *A Brief Disquisition of the Law of Nature* [1692], London, 1701.

Vattel, Emerich de, *The Law of Nations, or Principles of the Law of Nature applied to the Conduct and Affairs of Nations and Sovereigns*, [1758], 2 vols., London, 1759–60.

Veitch, John, 'A Memoir of Dugald Stewart', in Dugald Stewart, *Works*, vol. X.

Verner, David, *Dissertatio philosophica de passionibus sive affectibus . . .*, Aberdeen, 1721.

Voltaire, F.M.A. de, *Voltaire's Correspondence*, ed. T. Besterman, 107 vols., Geneva, 1953–65.

Vox Populi, Vox Dei: Being True Maxims of Government, London, 1709.

Wallace, George, *A System of the Principles of the Law of Scotland*, vol. I (no more published), Edinburgh, 1760.

Wallace, Robert, *Various Prospects of Mankind, Nature, and Providence*, London, 1761.

Watts, Isaac, *The Improvement of the Mind, or, A Supplement to the Art of Logick*, London, 1741.

Willich, A.F.M., *Elements of the Critical Philosophy*, London, 1798.

Wilson, James, 'Lectures on Law', in *Works*, ed. J. Dewitt Andrews, 2 vols., Chicago, 1896.

Witherspoon, John, *An Annotated Edition of 'Lectures on Moral Philosophy'*, ed. J. Scott, Newark, NJ, 1982.

  'The Dominion of Providence over the Passions of Men', in *The Selected Writings of John Witherspoon*, ed. T. Miller, Carbondale, IL, 1990, pp. 126–47.

Wollstonecraft, Mary, *A Vindication of the Rights of Woman*, London, 1792.

Wooddeson, Richard, *Elements of Jurisprudence Treated of in the Preliminary Part of a Course of Lectures on the Laws of England*, London, 1783.

Young, John, *Lectures on Intellectual Philosophy*, edited with a memoir of the author by William Cairns, Glasgow, 1835.

Secondary literature

Allan, David, *Virtue, Learning and the Scottish Enlightenment: Ideas of Scholarship in Early Modern History*, Edinburgh, 1993.

Armytage, W.H.G., 'David Fordyce: A neglected thinker', *Aberdeen University Review*, 36 (1956), 289–91.

Austin, J.L., *How to Do Things with Words*, Oxford, 1971.

Bachmann-Medick, Doris, *Die ästhetische Ordnung des Handelns. Moralphilosophie und Ästhetik in der Popularphilosophie des 18. Jahrhunderts*, Stuttgart, 1989.

Bailyn, B., *The Ideological Origins of the American Revolution*, Cambridge, MA, 1967.

Bain, Alexander, *James Mill: a Biography*, London, 1882.

Banning, L., 'Some second thoughts on virtue and the course of revolutionary thinking', in *Conceptual Change and the Constitution*, ed. T. Ball and J.G.A. Pocock, Lawrence, AR, 1988, pp. 194–212.

Barfoot, M., 'Hume and the culture of science in the early eighteenth century', in *Studies in the Philosophy of the Scottish Enlightenment*, ed. M.A. Stewart, Oxford, 1990, pp. 151–90.

  'James Gregory (1753–1821) and Scottish Scientific Metaphysics, 1750–1800', Ph.D. thesis, University of Edinburgh, 1983.

Barnard, F.M., 'Christian Thomasius: Enlightenment and bureaucracy', *American Political Science Review*, 59 (1965), 430–8.

'The "practical philosophy" of Christian Thomasius', *Journal of the History of Ideas*, 32 (1971), 221–46.

Battaglia, F., *Cristiano Thomasio, filosofo e giurista*, Bologna, 1982.

Baumgold, D., *Hobbes's Political Theory*, Cambridge, UK, 1988.

Bazzoli, M., 'Giambattista Almici e la diffusione di Pufendorf nel settecento Italiano', *Critica storica*, 16 (1979), 3–100.

Behme, Thomas, 'Pufendorf – Schüler von Hobbes?', in *Denkhorizonte und Handlungsspielräume. Historische Studien für Rudolf Vierhaus zum 70. Geburtstag*, Göttingen, 1992, pp. 33–52.

Ben-Israel, H., *English Historians on the French Revolution*, Cambridge, UK, 1968.

Birks, Peter and McLeod, Grant, 'The implied contract theory of quasi-contract: Civilian opinion current in the century before Blackstone', *Oxford Journal of Legal Studies*, 6 (1986), 46–85.

Bishop, J.D., 'The Moral Philosophy of Francis Hutcheson', Ph.D. thesis, University of Edinburgh, 1977.

Blackstone, W.T., *Francis Hutcheson and Contemporary Ethical Theory*, Athens, GA, 1965.

Bloch, R.H., *Visionary Republic: Millennial Themes in American Thought, 1756–1800*, Cambridge, UK, 1985.

Bödeker, H.-E. and Haakonssen, K., eds., *German Political Thought in the Age of Absolutism*, Cambridge, UK, forthcoming.

Bonar, James, ed., *A Catalogue of the Library of Adam Smith*, London, 1894.

Bonomi, P.U., *Under the Cope of Heaven: Religion, Society, and Politics in Colonial America*, New York, 1986.

Bowles, David, 'John Millar, the four-stages theory and women's position in society', *History of Political Economy*, 16 (1984), 619–38.

Brühlmeier, Daniel, *Die Rechts- und Staatslehre von Adam Smith und die Interessentheorie der Verfassung*, Berlin, 1988.

Buckle, S., *Natural Law and the Theory of Property: Grotius to Hume*, Oxford, 1991.

Burns, J.H., 'The light of reason: Philosophical history of the two Mills', in *James and John Stuart Mill: Papers of the Centenary Conference*, ed. J.M. Robson and M. Laine, Toronto, 1976, pp. 3–20.

Burrow, John, *Evolution and Society: A Study in Victorian Social Theory*, Cambridge, UK, 1970.

Cairns, John W., 'Adam Smith's lectures on jurisprudence: Their influence on legal education', in *Adam Smith: International Perspectives*, ed. H. Mizuta and C. Sugiyama, London, 1993, pp. 63–83.

'"Famous as a school for Law, as Edinburgh . . . for medicine": Legal education in Glasgow, 1761–1801', in *The Glasgow Enlightenment*, ed. A. Hook and R.B. Sher, Edinburgh, 1994, pp. 133–59.

'Institutional writings in Scotland reconsidered', *Journal of Legal History*, 4 (1983), 76–117.

'John Millar, Professor of Civil Law at Glasgow (1761–1801)', *Juridical Review* (1961), 218.

'John Millar's lectures on Scots criminal law', *Oxford Journal of Legal Studies*, 8 (1988), 364–400.

'The origins of the Glasgow Law School: The professors of civil law, 1714–61', in *The Life of the Law*, ed. P. Birks (Proceedings of the Tenth British Legal History Conference, Oxford, 1990), London, 1993, pp. 151–94.

'Rhetoric, language, and Roman law: Legal education and improvement in eighteenth-century Scotland', *Law and History Review*, 9 (1991), 31–58.

Camic, Charles, *Experience and Enlightenment: Socialization for Cultural Change in Eighteenth-Century Scotland*, Edinburgh, 1983.

Campbell, T.D., 'Francis Hutcheson: "Father" of the Scottish Enlightenment', in *The Origins and Nature of the Scottish Enlightenment*, ed. R.H. Campbell and A.S. Skinner, Edinburgh, 1982, pp. 176–7.

Carlsen, O., *Hugo Grotius og Sorö Akademi. En Kritisk Studie*, Taastrup, Denmark, 1938.

Carter, J.J. and Pittock, J.H., eds., *Aberdeen and the Enlightenment*, Aberdeen, 1987.

Christian, W., 'James Mackintosh, Burke, and the cause of reform', *Eighteenth-Century Studies*, 7 (1973–4), 193–206.

Christie, J.R.R., 'The origins and development of the Scottish scientific community', *History of Science*, 12 (1974), 122–41.

Clark, Henry C., 'Women and humanity in Scottish Enlightenment social thought: The case of Adam Smith', *Historical Reflections / Réflexions historiques*, 19 (1993), 335–61.

Clive, J., *Scotch Reviewers: The 'Edinburgh Review', 1802–1815*, London, 1957.

Collini, S., Winch, D., and Burrow, J., *That Noble Science of Politics: A Study in Nineteenth Century Intellectual History*, Cambridge, UK, 1983.

Colman, J., *John Locke's Moral Philosophy*, Edinburgh, 1983.

Conrad, Stephen A., *Citizenship and Common Sense: The Problem of Authority in the Social Background and Social Philosophy of the Wise Club of Aberdeen*, New York, 1987.

'Polite foundation: Citizenship and common sense in James Wilson's republican-theory,' *Supreme Court Review*, 1984 (1985), 359–8.

'Metaphor and imagination in James Wilson's theory of 'federal union', *Law and Social Inquiry*, 13 (1988), 170.

Cooper, David C., 'Scottish communitarianism, Lockean individualism, and women's moral development', in *Women's Rights and the Rights of Man*, ed. A.J. Arnaud and E. Kingdom, Aberdeen, 1992, pp. 36–51.

Corsi, P., 'The heritage of Dugald Stewart: Oxford philosophy and the method of political economy', *Nuncius*, fasc. 2 (1987), 89–144.

Crimmins, J.E., 'John Brown and the theological tradition of utilitarian ethics', *History of Political Thought*, 4 (1983), 523–50.

Cropsey, J., *Polity and Economy: An Interpretation of the Principles of Adam Smith*, The Hague, 1957.

Crowe, M., 'An eccentric seventeenth-century witness to the natural law: John Selden (1584–1654)', *Natural Law Forum*, 12 (1977), 184–95.

Darwall, S., 'Norm and normativity in eighteenth-century ethics', ch. 25 in *The*

Cambridge History of Eighteenth-Century Philosophy, ed. K. Haakonssen, Cambridge, UK, forthcoming.

Davidson, J. Morrison, *Concerning Four Precursors of Henry George and the Single Tax*, London, n.d. [c. 1890].

Davie, G.E., *The Scottish Enlightenment*, London, 1981.

Davis, J.C., *Utopia and the Ideal Society: A Study of English Utopian Writing, 1516–1700*, Cambridge, UK, 1981.

Dean, Dennis R., *James Hutton and the History of Geology*, Ithaca, NY, 1992.

Deane, S., *The French Revolution and Enlightenment in England, 1789–1832*, Cambridge, MA, 1988.

Denzer, H., *Moralphilosophie und Naturrecht bei Samuel Pufendorf*, Munich, 1972.

Derathé, R., *Jean-Jacques Rousseau et la science politique de son temps*, Paris, 1988.

Diamond, P.J., 'Witherspoon, William Smith and the Scottish philosophy in Revolutionary America', in *Scotland and America*, ed. Sher and Smitten, pp. 115–32.

Donovan, A.L., *Philosophical Chemistry in the Scottish Enlightenment: The Doctrines and Discoveries of William Cullen and Joseph Black*, Edinburgh, 1975.

Donovan, R.K., 'The popular party of the Church of Scotland and the American Revolution', in *Scotland and America*, ed. Sher and Smitten, pp. 81–99.

Döring, D., 'Samuel Pufendorf (1632-1694) und die leipziger Gelehrtengesellschaften in der Mitte des 17. Jahrhunderts', *Lias*, 15 (1988), 13–48.

Dreitzel, Horst, *Protestantischer Aristotelismus und absoluter Staat. Die 'Politica' des Henning Arnisaeus (ca. 1575–1636)*, Wiesbaden, 1970.

Dufour, A., *Le Mariage dans l'école romande du droit naturel au XVIIIe siècle*, Geneva, 1976.

'Pufendorfs Ausstrahlung im französischen und im anglo-amerikanischen Kulturraum', in *Samuel von Pufendorf, 1632–1982*, ed. K.Å. Modéer, Lund, 1986, pp. 96–119.

Dunn, J., 'The Politics of Locke in England and America in the Eighteenth Century', in *John Locke: Problems and Perspectives*, ed. J.W. Yolton, Cambridge, UK, 1969, pp. 45–80.

Dusen, Robert van, *Christian Garve and English Belles-Lettres*, Berne, 1970.

Dwyer, John, 'Clio and ethics: Practical morality in enlightened Scotland', *The Eighteenth Century*, 30 (1989), 45–72.

'Enlightened spectators and classical moralists: Sympathetic relations in eighteenth-century Scotland', in *Sociability and Society in Eighteenth-Century Scotland*, ed. J. Dwyer and R.B. Sher, Edinburgh, 1993, pp. 96–118.

Virtuous Discourse: Sensibility and Community in Late Eighteenth-Century Scotland, Edinburgh, 1987.

Eckardt, U.M. von, *The Pursuit of Happiness in the Democratic Creed*, New York, 1959.

Eighteenth-Century Scotland: The Newsletter of the Eighteenth-Century Scottish Studies Society, 1987–. Edited by Richard B. Sher.

Eisenach, E.J., 'The dimension of history in Bentham's theory of law', *Bentham Newsletter*, 5 (1981), 2–21.

Emerson, Roger L., 'Lord Bute and the Scottish universities, 1760–1792', in *Lord Bute: Essays in Reinterpretation*, ed. Karl W. Schweizer, Leicester, 1991.

'Natural philosophy and the problem of the Scottish Enlightenment', *Studies on Voltaire and the Eighteenth Century*, 242 (1986), 243–91.

Professors, Patronage and Politics: The Aberdeen Universities in the Eighteenth Century, Aberdeen, 1992.

'Science and moral philosophy in the Scottish Enlightenment', in *Studies in the Philosophy of the Scottish Enlightenment*, ed. M.A. Stewart, Oxford, 1990, pp. 11–36.

'Science and the origins and concerns of the Scottish Enlightenment', *History of Science*, 26 (1988), 333–66.

Fenn, Robert A., 'James Mill's Political Thought', Ph.D. thesis, University of London, 1971.

James Mill's Political Thought, New York, 1987.

Fiering, N., *Jonathan Edwards's Moral Thought and Its British Context*, Chapel Hill, NC, 1981.

Flower E. and Murphey, M.G., *A History of Philosophy in America*, 2 vols., New York, 1977.

Flynn, P., *Francis Jeffrey*, Newark, DE, 1978.

Fontana, B., *Rethinking the Politics of Commercial Society: The "Edinburgh Review", 1802–1832*, Cambridge, UK, 1985.

Forbes, D., *Hume's Philosophical Politics*, Cambridge, UK, 1975.

'Hume's science of politics', in *David Hume: Bicentenary Papers*, ed. G.P. Morice, Edinburgh, 1977, pp. 39–50.

'James Mill and India', *Cambridge Journal*, 5 (1951–2), 19–33.

'Natural law and the Scottish Enlightenment', in *The Origins and Nature of the Scottish Enlightenment*, ed. R.H. Campbell and A.S. Skinner, Edinburgh, 1982, pp. 186–204.

'Sceptical Whiggism, commerce and liberty', in *Essays on Adam Smith*, ed. A.S. Skinner and T. Wilson, Oxford, 1975, pp. 179–201.

'"Scientific" Whiggism: Adam Smith and John Millar', *Cambridge Journal*, 7 (1953–4), 643–70.

Forbes, M., *Beattie and His Friends*, London, 1904.

Francis, Mark and Morrow, John, *A History of English Political Thought in the 19th Century*, London, 1994.

Gagnebin, Bernard, *Burlamaqui et le droit naturel*, Geneva, 1944.

Gallie, Roger, *Thomas Reid and 'the Way of Ideas'*, Dordrecht, 1989.

Gascoigne, John, 'Anglican latitudinarianism, rational dissent and political radicalism in the late eighteenth century', in *Enlightenment and Religion: Rational Dissent in Eighteenth-Century Britain*, ed. K. Haakonssen, Cambridge, UK, forthcoming.

Cambridge in the Age of the Enlightenment: Science, Religion, and Politics from the Restoration to the French Revolution, Cambridge, UK, 1989.

Gauthier, D., 'Artificial virtues and the sensible knave', *Hume Studies*, 18 (1992), 401–27.

The Logic of Leviathan: The Moral and Political Theory of Thomas Hobbes, Oxford, 1969.

Gierke, O. von, *Natural Law and the Theory of Society, 1500–1800*, Cambridge, UK, 1958.

Goldie, Mark, 'Common Sense philosophy and Catholic theology in the Scottish Enlightenment', *Studies on Voltaire and the Eighteenth Century*, 302 (1992), 281–320.

'The Scottish Catholic Enlightenment', *Journal of British Studies*, 30 (1991), 20–62.

Goldsmith, M.M., *Hobbes's Science of Politics*, New York, 1966.

Grave, S.A., *The Scottish Philosophy of Common Sense*, Oxford, 1960.

Green, L.C. and Dickason, O.P., *The Law of Nations and the New World*, Edmonton, 1988.

Grimm, D., 'Europäisches Naturrecht und Amerikanische Revolution: Die Verwandlung politischer Philosophie in politische Techne', *Ius Commune*, 3 (1970), 120–51.

Haakonssen, K., 'The character and obligation of natural law according to Richard Cumberland', in *English Philosophy in the Age of Locke*, ed. M.A. Stewart, Oxford, forthcoming.

'Hugo Grotius and the history of political thought', *Political Theory*, 13 (1985), 239–65.

'Moral philosophy and natural law: From the Cambridge Platonists to the Scottish Enlightenment', *Political Science*, 40 (1988), 97–110.

'Natural jurisprudence in the Scottish Enlightenment: Summary of an interpretation', in *Enlightenment, Rights and Revolution*, ed. D.N. MacCormick and Z. Bankowski, Aberdeen, 1989, pp. 36–49.

'Natural Justice: The Development of a Critical Philosophy of Law from David Hume and Adam Smith to John Millar and John Craig', Ph.D. thesis, University of Edinburgh, 1978.

'Natural law and the German tradition', ch. 9 of *The Cambridge History of Eighteenth-Century Political Thought*, ed. M. Goldie and R. Wokler, Cambridge, UK, forthcoming.

'Natural law and the Scottish Enlightenment', in *Man and Nature*, ed. D.H. Jory and J.C. Stewart-Robertson (Proceedings of the Canadian Society for Eighteenth-Century Studies, IV, Edmonton, 1985), pp. 47–80.

The Science of a Legislator: The Natural Jurisprudence of David Hume and Adam Smith, Cambridge, UK, 1981.

'The Structure of Hume's political theory', in *The Cambridge Companion to Hume*, ed. D.F. Norton, Cambridge, UK, 1993, pp. 182–221.

Haakonssen, K., ed., *Enlightenment and Religion: Rational Dissent in Eighteenth-Century Britain*, Cambridge, UK, forthcoming.

Traditions of Liberalism: Essays on John Locke, Adam Smith and John Stuart Mill, Sydney, 1988.

Haakonssen, Lisbeth M., *Medicine and Morals in the Enlightenment: John Gregory, Thomas Percival, and Benjamin Rush*, Amsterdam, forthcoming. (Wellcome Series in the History of Medicine.)

Haddow, A., *Political Science in American Colleges and Universities, 1636–1900*, New York, 1939.

Hägerström, A., *Recht, Pflicht und bindende Kraft des Vertrages nach römischer und naturrechtlicher Anschauung*, ed. K. Olivecrona (Acta Societatis Litterarum Humaniorum Regiae Upsaliensis, 44:3), Stockholm, 1965.

Halévy, Elie, *The Growth of Philosophic Radicalism*, trans. M. Morris, Boston, 1966.

Hamilton, B., *Political Thought in Sixteenth-Century Spain: A Study of the Political Idea of Vitoria, De Soto, Suárez, and Molina*, Oxford, 1963.

Hammerstein, N., 'Zum Fortwirken von Pufendorf's Naturrechtslehre an den Universitäten des Heiligen Römischen Reiches deutscher Nation während des 18. Jahrhunderts', in *Pufendorf*, ed. Modéer, pp. 31–51.

Hamowy, Ronald, 'Jefferson and the Scottish Enlightenment', *William and Mary Quarterly*, 36 (1979), 503–23.

The Scottish Enlightenment and the Theory of Spontaneous Order (Journal of the History of Philosophy Monographs), Carbondale, IL, 1987.

Hampton, J., *Hobbes and the Social Contract Tradition*, Cambridge, UK, 1986.

Harvey, R.F., *Jean Jacques Burlamaqui: A Liberal Tradition in American Constitutionalism*, Chapel Hill, NC, 1937.

Hatch, N.O., *The Sacred Cause of Liberty: Republican Thought and the Millennium in Revolutionary New England*, New Haven, 1977.

Hayek, F.A. von, *Studies in Philosophy, Politics, and Economics*, London, 1967.

Heimert, A., *Religion and the American Mind: From the Great Awakening to the Revolution*, Cambridge, MA, 1966.

Hinrichs, Hermann Friedrich Wilhelm, *Geschichte der Rechts- und Staatsprinzipien seit der Reformation bis auf die Gegenwart in historisch-philosophischer Entwicklung*, 3 vols., Leipzig, 1848–52.

Hirschman, Albert O., *The Passions and the Interests: Political Arguments for Capitalism before Its Triumph*, Princeton, 1977.

Hochstrasser, Tim, 'Conscience and reason: The natural law theory of Jean Barbeyrac', *Historical Journal*, 36 (1993), 289–308.

Hollander, J.H., 'The founder of a school', in *Adam Smith, 1776–1926*, ed. J.M. Clark et al., New York, 1966, pp. 22–52.

Holzgrefe, J.L., 'The origins of modern international relations theory', *Review of International Studies*, 15 (1989), 11–26.

Hont, I., 'The language of sociability and commerce: Samuel Pufendorf and the theoretical foundations of the "four stages theory"', in *The Languages of Political Theory*, ed. A. Pagden, pp. 253–276.

'The "rich country–poor country" debate in Scottish classical political economy', in *Wealth and Virtue*, ed. I. Hont and M. Ignatieff, pp. 271–315.

Hont, I. and Ignatieff, M., eds., *Wealth and Virtue: The Shaping of Political Economy in the Scottish Enlightenment*, Cambridge, UK, 1983.

Hood, F.C., *The Divine Politics of Thomas Hobbes*, Oxford, 1964.

Horne, T.A., 'Moral and economic improvement: Francis Hutcheson on property', *History of Political Thought*, 7 (1986), 122–3.

Property Rights and Poverty: Political Argument in Britain, 1605–1834, Chapel Hill, NC, 1990.

Howe, D. Walker, 'European sources of political ideas in Jeffersonian America', *Reviews in American History*, 10 (1982), 28–44.

'Why the Scottish Enlightenment was useful to the framers of the American Constitution', *Comparative Studies in Society and History*, 31 (1989), 572–87.

Hruschka, J., *Das deontologische Sechseck bei Gottfried Achenwall im Jahre 1767.*

Zur Geschichte der deontischen Grundbegriffe in der Universaljurisprudenz zwischen Suárez und Kant (Joachim Jungius-Gesellschaft der Wissenschaften/Göttingen), Hamburg, 1986.

'The greatest happiness principle and other early German anticipations of utilitarian theory', *Utilitas*, 3 (1991), 165–77.

Hueber, Anton, *Die philosophische und ethische Begründung des homo economicus bei Adam Smith*, Frankfurt a.M., 1990.

Humphrey, D.C., *From King's College to Columbia, 1746–1800*, New York, 1976.

Ignatieff, Michael, 'John Millar and individualism', in *Wealth and Virtue*, ed. I. Hont and M. Ignatieff, pp. 317–43.

Jägerskiöld, S., 'Samuel von Pufendorf in Schweden, 1668–1688. Einige neue Beiträge', in *Satura Roberto Feenstra Sexagesimum Quintum Annum Aetatis Complenti ab Alumnis Collegis Amicis Oblata*, ed. J.A. Ankum, J.E. Spruit, and F.B.J. Wubbe, Fribourg, 1985, pp. 557–70.

Jensen, H., *Motivation and the Moral Sense in Francis Hutcheson's Ethical Theory*, The Hague, 1971.

Jessop, T.E., *A Bibliography of David Hume and of Scottish Philosophy from Francis Hutcheson to Lord Balfour*, London, 1938.

Johnson, H.C., *Frederick the Great and His Officials*, New Haven, 1975.

Jones, P., 'The polite academy and the Presbyterians, 1720–1770', in *New Perspectives on the Politics and Culture of Early Modern Scotland*, ed. J. Dwyer, R.A. Mason, and A. Murdoch, Edinburgh, 1982, pp. 156–78.

Jones, P., ed., *Philosophy and Science in the Scottish Enlightenment*, Edinburgh, 1988.

Jones, Peter and Skinner, Andrew S., eds., *Adam Smith Reviewed*, Edinburgh, 1992.

Kidd, Colin, *Subverting Scotland's Past: Scottish Whig Historians and the Creation of an Anglo-British Identity, 1689–c. 1830*, Cambridge, UK, 1993.

Kilcullen, John, 'Natural law and will in Ockham', in *Reason, Will and Nature: Voluntarism in Metaphysics and Morals from Ockham to Kant*, ed. K. Haakonssen and U. Thiel (*History of Philosophy Yearbook*, 1), Canberra, 1994, pp. 1–34.

Kirk, L., *Richard Cumberland and Natural Law*, Cambridge, UK, 1987.

Klippel, D., *Politische Freiheit und Freiheitsrechte im deutschen Naturrecht des 18. Jahrhunderts*, Paderborn, 1976.

Kloppenberg, James T., 'The virtues of liberalism: Christianity, republicanism, and ethics in early American political discourse', *Journal of American History*, 74 (1987), 9–33.

Knight, W.S.M., *The Life and Works of Hugo Grotius*, London, 1925.

Kraye, Jill, 'Moral philosophy', in *The Cambridge History of Renaissance Philosophy*, ed. C.B. Schmitt, Q. Skinner, and E. Kessler, Cambridge, UK, 1988.

Krieger, L., *The Politics of Discretion: Pufendorf and the Acceptance of Natural Law*, Chicago, 1965.

Kuczynski, Jürgen, *Zur Geschichte der Wirtschaftsgeschichtsschreibung*, Berlin, 1978.

Kuklick, B., *Churchmen and Philosophers: From Jonathan Edwards to John Dewey*, New Haven, 1985.

Landsberg, Ernst, *see* Stintzing, J.A.R. von.

Landsman, Ned C., 'Presbyterians and provincial society: The evangelical enlightenment in the west of Scotland, 1740–1775', in *Sociability and Society in Eighteenth-Century Scotland*, ed. J. Dwyer and R.B. Sher, Edinburgh, 1993, pp. 194–209.

'Witherspoon and the problem of provincial identity in Scottish evangelical culture', in *Scotland and America*, ed. Sher and Smitten, pp. 29–45.

Lasky, Melvin, *Utopia and Revolution: On the Origins of a Metaphor, or Some Illustrations of the Problem of Political Temperament and Intellectual Climate and How Ideas, Ideals, and Ideologies Have Been Historically Related*, Chicago, 1976.

Lawrence, Christopher, 'Medicine as Culture: Edinburgh and the Scottish Enlightenment', Ph.D. thesis, University of Edinburgh, 1984.

Le Mahieu, D.L., *The Mind of William Paley*, Lincoln, NB, 1976.

Lehmann, W.C., *John Millar of Glasgow, 1735–1801: His Life and Thought and His Contributions to Sociological Analysis*, Cambridge, UK, 1960.

'John Millar, Professor of Civil Law at Glasgow (1761–1801)', *Juridical Review* (1961), 218–33.

'Some observations on the law lectures of Professor Millar at the University of Glasgow (1761–1801),' *Juridical Review*, (1970), 56–77.

Lehrer, K., *Thomas Reid*, London, 1989.

Leidhold, W., *Ethik und Politik bei Francis Hutcheson*, Munich, 1985.

Leyden, W. von, 'John Locke and natural law', *Philosophy*, 31 (1956), 35.

Lieberman, David, *The Province of Legislation Determined: Legal Theory in Eighteenth-Century Britain*, Cambridge, UK, 1989.

Lincoln, Anthony, *Some Political and Social Ideas of English Dissent, 1763–1800* [1938], New York, 1971.

Lindberg, Bo, *Naturrätten i Uppsala, 1655–1720* (Acta Universitatis Upsaliensis, C: 33), Uppsala, 1976.

Lobkowicz, E., *Common Sense und Skeptizismus*, Weinheim, 1986.

Locke, D., *A Fantasy of Reason: The Life and Thought of William Godwin*, London, 1980.

Lovejoy, A.O., *The Great Chain of Being: A Study of the History of an Idea*, Cambridge, MA, 1936, repr. 1974.

Luig, K., 'Zur Verbreitung des Naturrechts in Europa', *Tijdschrift voor rechtsgeschiedenis/Revue d'histoire du droit*, 40 (1972), 539–57.

MacCormick, Neil, 'Law and enlightenment', in *The Origins and Nature of the Scottish Enlightenment*, ed. R.H. Campbell and A.S. Skinner, Edinburgh, 1982, pp. 150–66.

McCoy, Charles S., *History, Humanity, and Federalism in the Theology and Ethics of Johannes Cocceius*, Philadelphia, 1980.

'Johannes Cocceius: Federal theologian', *Scottish Journal of Theology*, 16 (1963), 352–70.

McCracken, C.J., *Malebranche and British Philosophy*, Oxford, 1983.

McDonald, F., *Novus ordo seclorum: The Intellectual Origins of the Constitution*, Lawrence, AR, 1985.

MacIntyre, Alasdair, *Whose Justice? Which Rationality?*, Notre Dame, IN, 1988.

McKenzie, L.A., 'The French Revolution and English parliamentary reform: James Mackintosh and the *Vindiciae Gallicae*', *Eighteenth-Century Studies*, 14 (1981), 264–82.

McLoughlin, W.G., *Revivals, Awakenings, and Reform: An Essay on Religion and Social Change in America, 1607–1977*, Chicago, 1978.

Macmillan, Duncan, *Painting in Scotland: The Golden Age*, Oxford, 1986.

McNeill, J.T., 'Natural law in the teaching of the reformers', *Journal of Religion*, 26 (1946), 168–83.

McNeilly, F.S., *The Anatomy of Leviathan*, London, 1968.

Macpherson, C.B., *The Political Theory of Possessive Individualism: Hobbes to Locke*, Oxford, 1962.

Majeed, Javed, *Ungoverned Imaginings: James Mill's "The History of British India" and Orientalism*, Oxford, 1992.

Malmström, Oscar, *Samuel Pufendorf och hans arbeten i Sveriges historia*, Stockholm, 1899.

Marchi, N. di, 'The case for James Mill', in *Methodological Controversy in Economics: Historical Essays in Honour of T.W. Hutchison*, ed. A.W. Coats, New York, 1983, pp. 155–84.

Marcil-Lacoste, L., *Claude Buffier and Thomas Reid: Two Common-Sense Philosophers*, Kingston, 1982.

'The seriousness of Reid's sceptical admissions', *Monist*, 62 (1978), 311–25.

Martinich, A.P., *The Two Gods of Leviathan*, Cambridge, UK, 1992.

Mautner, T., 'Pufendorf and the correlativity thesis of rights', in *In So Many Words: Philosophical Essays Dedicated to Sven Danielson on the Occasion of His Fiftieth Birthday*, ed. S. Lindström and W. Rabinowics (Philosophical Studies, Philosophical Society and Department of Philosophy, University of Uppsala, no. 42), Uppsala, 1989, pp. 37–59.

'Pufendorf and eighteenth-century Scottish philosophy', in *Samuel von Pufendorf, 1632–1982*, ed. K.Å. Modéer, Lund, 1986, pp. 120–31.

May, H.F., *The Enlightenment in America*, New York, 1976.

Medick, H., *Naturzustand und Naturgeschichte der bürgerlichen Gesellschaft. Die Ursprünge der bürgerlichen Sozialtheorie als Geschichtsphilosophie und Sozialwissenschaft bei Samuel Pufendorf, John Locke und Adam Smith*, Göttingen, 1973.

Medick, H. and Leppert-Fögen, A., 'Frühe Sozialwissenschaft als Ideologie des kleinen Bürgertums: John Millar of Glasgow, 1735–1801', in *Sozialgeschichte Heute. Festschrift für Hans Rosenberg*, ed. H.U. Wehler, Göttingen, 1974, pp. 22–48.

Meek, R.L., 'New light on Adam Smith's Glasgow lectures on jurisprudence', *History of Political Economy*, 8 (1976), 439–77.

'Smith, Turgot and the "four stages" theory', *History of Political Economy*, 3 (1971), 9–27.

Social Science and the Ignoble Savage, Cambridge, UK, 1976.

Meikle, H.W., *Scotland and the French Revolution*, London, 1969.

Meylan, P., *Jean Barbeyrac (1674–1744) et les débuts de l'enseignement du droit dans l'ancienne académie de Lausanne*, Lausanne, 1937.

Micheli, Giuseppe, introduction to *Essays and Treatises on Moral, Political, and Various Philosophical Subjects*, by Emanuel [*sic*] Kant, facsim. repr. of London, 1798, ed., 2 vols., Bristol, UK, 1993, 1:v–liii.

Miller, H., *The Revolutionary College: American Presbyterian Higher Education, 1707–1837*, New York, 1976.

Miller, P., *Errand into the Wilderness*, Cambridge, MA, 1956.

Miller, T.P., 'Witherspoon, Blair, and the rhetoric of civic humanism', in *Scotland and America*, ed. Sher and Smitten, pp. 100–14.

Minowitz, Peter, *Profits, Priests, and Princes: Adam Smith's Emancipation of Economics from Politics and Religion*, Stanford, 1993.

Mizuta, Hiroshi, *Adam Smith's Library*, Cambridge, UK, 1967.

Mizuta, H. and Sugiyama, C., eds., *Adam Smith: International Perspectives*, London, 1993.

Modéer, K.Å., ed., *Samuel von Pufendorf, 1632–1982*, Lund, Sweden, 1986.

Moore, J., 'Locke and the Scottish jurists', paper presented to the conference on 'Locke and the Political Thought of the 1680s' sponsored by the Conference for the Study of Political Thought, Folger Shakespeare Library, Washington, DC, 21–23 March 1980.

'Natural law and the Pyrrhonian controversy', in *Philosophy and Science in the Scottish Enlightenment*, ed. P. Jones, Edinburgh, 1988, pp. 20–38.

'Theological politics: A study of the reception of Locke's *Two Treatises of Government* in England and Scotland in the early eighteenth century', in *John Locke and / und Immanuel Kant*, ed. M.P. Thompson, Tübingen, 1991, pp. 62–82.

'The two systems of Francis Hutcheson: On the origins of the Scottish Enlightenment', in *Studies in the Philosophy of the Scottish Enlightenment*, ed. M.A. Stewart, Oxford, 1990, pp. 37–59.

Moore, J. and Silverthorne, M., 'Gershom Carmichael and the natural jurisprudence tradition in eighteenth-century Scotland', in *Wealth and Virtue: The Shaping of Political Economy in the Scottish Enlightenment*, ed. I. Hont and M. Ignatieff, Cambridge, UK, 1983, pp. 73–87.

'Natural sociability and natural rights in the moral philosophy of Gershom Carmichael', in *Philosophers of the Scottish Enlightenment*, ed. V. Hope, Edinburgh, 1984, pp. 1–12.

Muller, Jerry Z., *Adam Smith in His Time and Ours: Designing the Decent Society*, New York, 1993.

Mullett, Charles F., *Fundamental Law and the American Revolution, 1760–1776*, New York, 1933.

Munz, Peter, *The Place of Hooker in the History of Thought*, London, 1952.

Murdoch, A. and Sher, R.B., 'Literary and learned culture', in *People and Society in Scotland*, ed. T.M. Devine and R. Mitchison, vol. 1 in *A Social History of Modern Scotland, 1760–1830*, 3 vols., Edinburgh, 1988, pp. 127–42.

Nagel, T., 'Hobbes's concept of obligation', *Philosophical Review*, 68 (1959), 68–83.

Noll, M.A., *Princeton and the Republic, 1768–1822*, Princeton, 1989.

Norton, David Fate, *David Hume: Common-Sense Moralist, Sceptical Metaphysician*, Princeton, 1982.

'Francis Hutcheson in America', *Studies on Voltaire and the Eighteenth Century*, 154 (1976), 1547–68.

'Hutcheson's moral realism', *Journal of the History of Philosophy*, 23 (1985), 392–418.

'Hutcheson's moral sense theory reconsidered', *Dialogue*, 13 (1974), 3–23.

'Hutcheson on perception and moral perception', *Archiv für Geschichte der Philosophie*, 59 (1977), 181–97.

'From Moral Sense to Common Sense: An Essay on the Development of Scottish Common Sense Philosophy, 1700-1765', Ph.D. thesis, University of California at San Diego, 1966.

Oakeshott, M., *Hobbes on Civil Association*, Oxford, 1974.

O'Leary, Patrick, *Sir James Mackintosh: The Whig Cicero*, Aberdeen, 1989.

Olivecrona, K., *Law as Fact*, London, 1971.

'Die zwei Schichten im naturrechtlichen Denken', *Archiv für Rechts- und Sozialphilosophie*, 63 (1977), 79–103.

Olson, R., *Scottish Philosophy and British Physics, 1750–1880*, Princeton, 1975.

Onuf, P.S., 'Reflections on the founding: Constitutional historiography in bicentennial perspective', *William and Mary Quarterly*, 46 (1989), 341–75.

Osterhorn, E.-D., *Die Naturrechtslehre Valentin Albertis*, Freiburg i.B.: diss., Albert-Ludwig-Universität, 1962.

Othmer, S.C., *Berlin und die Verbreitung des Naturrechts in Europa. Kultur- und sozialgeschichtliche Studien zu Jean Barbeyracs Pufendorf-Übersetzungen und eine Analyse seiner Leserschaft* (Veröffentlichungen der historischen Kommission zu Berlin beim Friedrich-Meinecke-Institut der Freien Universität Berlin, Bd. 30), Berlin, 1970.

Pack, Spencer J., *Capitalism as a Moral System: Adam Smith's Critique of the Free Market Economy*, Aldershot, UK, 1991.

Pagden, Anthony, 'Dispossessing the barbarian: The language of Spanish Thomism and the debate over the property rights of the American Indians', in *Languages of Political Theory*, ed. Pagden, pp. 79–98.

'The "School of Salamanca" and the affair of the Indies', *History of Universities*, 1 (1981), 71–112.

Pagden, Anthony, ed., *The Languages of Political Theory in Early-Modern Europe*, Cambridge, UK, 1987.

Paladini, F., *Discussioni seicentesche su Samuel Pufendorf. Scritti latini: 1663–1700* (Pubblicazioni del Centro di Studio per la Storia della Storiografia Filosofica, 6) n.p., 1978.

'Le due lettere di Pufendorf al Barone di Boineburg: Quella nota e quella "perduta"', *Nouvelles de la republique des lettres* (Naples), 1 (1984), 119–44.

Samuel Pufendorf, discepolo di Hobbes, Bologna, 1990.

Pangle, T.L., *The Spirit of Modern Republicanism: The Moral Vision of the American Founders and the Philosophy of Locke*, Chicago, 1988.

Passmore, John, 'Enthusiasm, fanaticism and David Hume', in *The 'Science of Man' in the Scottish Enlightenment: Hume, Reid and Their Contemporaries*, ed. P. Jones, Edinburgh, 1989, pp. 85–107.

A Hundred Years of Philosophy, London, 1966.

Ralph Cudworth: An Interpretation, Cambridge, UK, 1951.

Peach, B., introduction to Hutcheson, *Illustrations on the Moral Sense*, ed. Peach, Cambridge, MA, 1971.

Peardon, T.P., *The Transition in English Historical Writing, 1760–1830*, New York, 1933.

Pérez-Ramos, A., *Francis Bacon's Idea of Science and the Maker's Knowledge Tradition*, Oxford, 1988.

Petersen, P., *Geschichte der aristotelischen Philosophie im protestantischen Deutschland*, Leipzig, 1921.

Phillipson, Nicholas, 'Adam Smith as civic moralist', *Wealth and Virtue: The Shaping of Political Economy in the Scottish Enlightenment*, ed. Istvan Hont and Michael Ignatieff, Cambridge, UK, 1983, pp. 179–202.

'Culture and society in the eighteenth century province: The case of Edinburgh and the Scottish Enlightenment', in *The University in Society*, ed. L. Stone, 2 vols., Princeton, 1974, 2:407–48.

Hume, London, 1989.

'Hume as moralist: A social historian's perspective', in *Philosophers of the Enlightenment*, ed. S.C. Brown, Brighton, UK, 1979, pp. 140–61.

'James Beattie and the defence of common sense', in *Festschrift für Werner Gruenther*, ed. B. Fabian, Heidelberg, 1978, pp. 145–54.

'Lawyers, landowners, and the civic leadership of post-union Scotland', *Juridical Review* (1976), pp. 97–120.

'Propriety, property and prudence: David Hume and the defence of the Revolution', in *Political Discourse*, ed. Phillipson and Skinner, pp. 302–20.

'The pursuit of virtue in Scottish university education: Dugald Stewart and Scottish moral philosophy in the Enlightenment', in *Universities, Society, and the Future*, ed. Nicholas Phillipson, Edinburgh, 1983, pp. 82–101.

'The Scottish Enlightenment', in *The Enlightenment in National Context*, ed. R. Porter and M. Teich, Cambridge, UK, 1981, pp. 19–40.

'The Scottish Enlightenment and the science of man', in *Theoretische Geschiedenis*, 8 (1981), 3–19.

The Scottish Whigs and the Reform of the Court of Session, 1785–1830, Edinburgh, 1990.

'Towards a definition of the Scottish Enlightenment', in *City and Society*, ed. P. Fritz and D. Williams, Toronto, 1973, pp. 125–47.

Phillipson, Nicholas and Skinner, Quentin, eds., *Political Discourse in Early Modern Britain*, Cambridge, UK, 1993.

Pocock, J.G.A., 'Clergy and commerce: The conservative Enlightenment in England', in *L'Età dei Lumi: Studi storici sul settecento europeo in onore di Franco Venturi*, ed. R. Ajello et al., 2 vols., Naples, 1985, 2:23–68.

'The concept of language and the *métier d'historien*: Some considerations on practice', in *The Languages of Political Theory in Early-Modern Europe*, ed. A. Pagden, Cambridge, UK, 1987, pp. 19–38.

'Conservative Enlightenment and democratic revolutions: The American and French cases in British perspective', *Government and Opposition*, 24 (1989), 81–105.

'The history of political thought: A methodological enquiry', in *Philosophy, Politics and Society*, 2nd ser., ed. P. Laslett and W.G. Runciman, Oxford, 1969, pp. 183–202.

The Machiavellian Moment: Florentine Political Thought and the Atlantic Republican Tradition, Princeton, 1975.

Politics, Language and Time: Essays on Political Thought and History, London, 1972.

'Post-puritan England and the problem of the Enlightenment," in *Culture and Politics from Puritanism to the Enlightenment,* ed. P. Zagorin, Berkeley, 1980, pp. 91–111.

'Reconstructing the traditions: Quentin Skinner's historians' history of political thought', *Canadian Journal of Political and Social Theory/Revue canadienne de théorie politique et sociale,* 3 (1979), 95–113.

Virtue, Commerce, and History: Essays on Political Thought and History, Chiefly in the Eighteenth Century, Cambridge, UK, 1985.

Presser, Stephen B., *The Original Misunderstanding: The English, the Americans and the Dialectic of Federalist Jurisprudence,* Durham, NC, 1991.

Prest, Wilfrid, 'Law reform in eighteenth-century England', in *The Life of the Law,* ed. P.W. Birks, London, 1993, pp. 113–23.

Rahe, Paul A., *Republics Ancient and Modern: Classical Republicanism and the American Revolution,* Chapel Hill, NC, 1992.

Raphael, D.D., *Adam Smith,* Oxford, 1985.

Hobbes, Morals and Politics, London, 1977.

The Moral Sense, Oxford, 1947.

Raphael, D.D., and Macfie, A.L., introduction to Adam Smith, *The Theory of Moral Sentiments,* ed. D.D. Raphael and A.L. Macfie, Oxford, 1976, pp. 5–10.

Rashid, S., 'Dugald Stewart, "Baconian" methodology, and political economy', *Journal of the History of Ideas,* 46 (1985), 245–57.

Reibstein, E., 'Deutsche Grotius-Kommentatoren bis zu Christian Wolff', *Zeitschrift für ausländisches öffentliches Recht und Völkerrecht,* 15 (1953–4), 76–102.

'J.G. Heineccius als Kritiker des grotianischen Systems', *Zeitschrift für ausländisches öffentliches Recht und Völkerrecht,* 24 (1964), 236–64.

Reid, J.P., *Constitutional History of the American Revolution: The Authority of Rights,* Madison, WI, 1987.

Rendall, Jane, 'The Political Ideas and Activities of Sir James Mackintosh (1765–1832)', Ph.D. thesis, University of London, 1972.

'Scottish Orientalism: From Robertson to James Mill', *Historical Journal,* 25 (1982), 43–69.

'Virtue and commerce: Women in the making of Adam Smith's political economy', in *Women in Western Political Philosophy,* ed. E. Kennedy and S. Mendus, New York, 1987, pp. 44–77.

Reynolds, Rebecca Lynn, 'Samuel Cocceji and the Tradition of Natural Jurisprudence', M.A. thesis, Cambridge University, 1993.

Robbins, Caroline, *The Eighteenth-Century Commonwealthman,* Cambridge, MA, 1959.

'"When it is that colonies may turn independent": An analysis of the environment and politics of Francis Hutcheson (1694–1746)', *William and Mary Quarterly,* 3rd ser., 11 (1954), 214–51.

Robertson, John, *The Scottish Enlightenment and the Militia Issue*, Edinburgh, 1985.

Robertson, J.C., 'A Bacon-facing generation: Scottish philosophy in the early nineteenth century', *Journal of the History of Philosophy*, 14 (1976) 35–45.

Robson, D.W., *Educating Republicans: The College in the Era of the American Revolution, 1750–1800*, Westport, CT, 1985.

Röd, W., *Geometrischer Geist und Naturrecht. Methodengeschichtliche Untersuchungen zur Staatsphilosophie im 17. und 18. Jahrhundert* (Bayerische Akademie der Wissenschaften, Phil.-hist. Klasse, Abhandlungen, N.F. 70), Munich, 1970.

'Weigels Lehre von den entia moralia', *Archiv für Geschichte der Philosophie*, 51 (1969), 58–84.

Rorty, Richard, Schneewind, J.B., and Skinner, Quentin, eds., *Philosophy in History: Essays on the Historiography of Philosophy*, Cambridge, UK, 1984.

Ross, I.S., *Lord Kames and the Scotland of His Day*, Oxford, 1972.

Rossiter, Clinton, *Seedtime of the Republic*, New York, 1953.

Rowe, W.L., *Thomas Reid on Freedom and Morality*, Ithaca, NY, 1989.

Ruddy, F.S., *International Law in the Enlightenment: The Background of Emmerich de Vattel's "Le Droit des Gens"*, New York, 1975.

Rüping, H., 'Gottlieb Gerhard Titius und die Naturrechtslehre in Deutschland um die Wende vom 17. zum 18. Jahrhundert', *Zeitschrift der Savigny-Stiftung für Rechtsgeschichte*, Ger. Abt., 87 (1970), 314–26.

Die Naturrechtslehre des Christian Thomasius und ihre Fortbildung in der Thomasius-Schule, Bonn, 1968.

Ryan, Alan, 'The British, the Americans, and rights', in *A Culture of Rights: The Bill of Rights in Philosophy, Politics and Law – 1791 and 1991*, ed. M.J. Lacey and K. Haakonssen, Cambridge, UK, 1991, pp. 366–439.

Salter, J., 'Adam Smith on feudalism, commerce and slavery', *History of Political Thought*, 13 (1992), 219–41.

Sargentich, T., 'Locke and ethical theory: Two ms. pieces', *Locke Newsletter*, 5 (1974), 24–31.

Sayre-McCord, G., 'The many moral realisms', *Southern Journal of Philosophy*, 24 (1986), suppl. 6–10.

Schlenke, Manfred, *England und das friderizianische Preussen, 1740–1763. Ein Beitrag zum Verhältnis von Politik und öffentlicher Meinung im England des 18. Jahrhunderts*, Munich, 1963.

Schmidt, L.E., 'Sacramental occasions and the Scottish context of Presbyterian revivalism in America', in *Scotland and America*, ed. Sher and Smitten, pp. 65–80.

Schneewind, J.B., 'Autonomy, obligation, and virtue: An overview of Kant's moral philosophy', in *The Cambridge Companion to Kant*, ed. P. Guyer, Cambridge, UK, 1992, pp. 309–41.

'Pufendorf's place in the history of ethics', *Synthèse*, 72 (1987), 123–55.

Sidgwick's Ethics and Victorian Moral Philosophy, Oxford, 1977.

Schneider, H.-P., *Justitia universalis. Quellenstudien zur Geschichte des 'Christlichen Naturrechts' bei Gottfried Wilhelm Leibniz*, Frankfurt a.M., 1967.

'Die wissenschaftliche Beziehungen zwischen Leibniz und den beiden Cocceji (Heinrich und Samuel)', in *Humanismus und Naturrecht in Berlin-Brandenburg-Preussen*, ed. H. Thieme, Berlin, 1979, pp. 90–102.

Schneider, Louis, 'Tension in the thought of John Millar', *Studies in Burke and His Time* (Winter 1971–2), 2083–98.

Schneiders, Werner, 'Naturrecht und Gerechtigkeit bei Leibniz', *Zeitschrift für philosophische Forschung*, 20 (1966), 607–50.

Naturrecht und Liebesethik, Hildesheim, 1971.

Schneiders, Werner, ed., *Christian Thomasius, 1655–1728. Interpretationen zu Werk und Wirkung*, Hamburg, 1989.

Schröder, Jan, *Wissenschaftshteorie und Lehre der 'praktischen Jurisprudenz' auf deutschen Universitäten an der Wende zum 19. Jahrhundert*, Frankfurt a.M., 1979.

Schubart-Fikentscher, G., 'Christian Thomasius. Seine Bedeutung als Hochschullehrer am Beginn der deutschen Aufklärung' (Sitzungsberichte der Sächsischen Akademie der Wissenschaften zu Leipzig, Phil.-hist. Klasse, Bd. 119, Heft 4), Berlin, 1977.

Schulthess, D., *Philosophie et sens commun chez Thomas Reid (1710–1796)*, Berne, 1983.

Scott, J., introduction to J. Witherspoon, *An Annotated Edition of 'Lectures on Moral Philosophy'*, ed. J. Scott, Newark, NJ, 1982, pp. 1–61.

Scott, J.B., ed., *The Spanish Origins of International Law*, Oxford, 1934.

Searle, J.R., *Speech Acts: An Essay in the Philosophy of Language*, Cambridge, UK, 1969.

Seed, J., '"Advocates of an overstrained moderation": The social logic of rational dissent, 1770–1800', in *Enlightenment and Religion*, ed. K. Haakonssen.

Sève, René, *Leibniz et l'école moderne du droit naturel*, Paris, 1989.

Shaver, Robert, 'Hume on the duties of humanity', *Journal of the History of Philosophy*, 30 (1992), 545–56.

Shepherd, C.M., 'The arts curriculum at Aberdeen at the beginning of the eighteenth century', in *Aberdeen and the Enlightenment*, ed. J.J. Carter and J.H. Pittock, Aberdeen, 1987, pp. 146–54.

'Newtonianism in Scottish universities in the seventeenth century', in *The Origins and Nature of the Scottish Enlightenment*, ed. R.H. Campbell and A.S. Skinner, Edinburgh, 1982, pp. 65–85.

Sher, Richard B., *Church and University in the Scottish Enlightenment: The Moderate Literati of Edinburgh*, Princeton, 1985.

'Introduction: Scottish-American studies, past and present', in *Scotland and America in the Age of the Enlightenment*, ed. Sher and Smitten, pp. 1–27.

'Professors of virtue: The social history of the Edinburgh Moral Philosophy Chair in the eighteenth century', in *Studies in the Philosophy of the Scottish Enlightenment*, ed. M.A. Stewart, Oxford, 1990, pp. 87–126.

'Witherspoon's "Dominion of Providence" and the Scottish jeremiad tradition,' in *Scotland and America in the Age of the Enlightenment*, ed. Sher and Smitten, pp. 46–64.

Sher, Richard B. and Murdoch, Alexander, 'Patronage and party in the Church of Scotland, 1750–1800', in *Church, Politics and Society: Scotland, 1408–1929*, ed. Norman MacDougall, Edinburgh, 1983, pp. 197–220.

Sher, Richard B. and Smitten, J.R., eds., *Scotland and America in the Age of the Enlightenment*, Princeton, 1990.

Silverthorne, M.J., 'Civil society and state, law and rights: Some Latin terms and their translation in the natural jurisprudence tradition', in *Acta Conventus Neo-Latini Torontonensis* (Medieval and Renaissance Texts and Studies), Binghamton, NY, 1991, pp. 677–87.

Sinopoli, R.C., 'Liberalism, republicanism and the Constitution', *Polity*, 19 (1987), 331–52.

Skinner, A.S., *A System of Social Science: Papers Relating to Adam Smith*, Oxford, 1979.

Skinner, Q., *The Foundations of Modern Political Thought*, 2 vols., Cambridge, UK, 1978.

Sloan, D., *The Scottish Enlightenment and the American College Ideal*, New York, 1971.

Sommerville, J.P., 'John Selden, the law of nature, and the origins of government', *Historical Journal*, 27 (1984), 437–47.

Sorell, T., *Hobbes*, London, 1986.

Spadafora, David, *The Idea of Progress in Eighteenth-Century Britain*, New Haven, 1990.

Spellman, W.M., *John Locke and the Problem of Depravity*, Oxford, 1988.

St. Clair, W., *The Godwins and the Shelleys: The Biography of a Family*, London, 1988.

Stewart, M.A., 'Berkeley and the Rankenian Club', *Hermathena*, 139 (1985), 25–45.

'George Turnbull and educational reform', in *Aberdeen and the Enlightenment*, ed. J.J. Carter and J.H. Pittock, Aberdeen, 1987, pp. 95–103.

'John Smith and the Molesworth circle', *Eighteenth-Century Ireland*, 2 (1987), 89–102.

'The origins of the Scottish Greek chairs', in *'Owls to Athens': Essays on Classical Subjects Presented to Sir Kenneth Dover*, ed. E.M. Craik, Oxford, 1990, pp. 391–400.

'The Stoic legacy in the early Scottish Enlightenment', in *Atoms, Pneuma, and Tranquillity: Epicurean and Stoic Themes in European Thought*, ed. Margaret J. Osler, Cambridge, UK, 1991, pp. 273–96.

Stewart, M.A., ed., *English Philosophy in the Age of Locke*, Oxford, forthcoming.
Studies in the Philosophy of the Scottish Enlightenment, Oxford, 1990.

Stewart-Robertson, J.C., '"Horse-Bogey Bites Little Boys"; or, Reid's oeconomicks of the family', *Studies in Eighteenth-Century Culture*, 16 (1986), 69–89.

'Sancte Socrates: Scottish reflections on obedience and resistance', in *Man and Nature* (Proceedings of the Canadian Society for Eighteenth-Century Studies), I, ed. R.L. Emerson, G. Girard, and R. Runte, London, Ontario, 1982, pp. 65–79.

'The Well-principled savage, or The child of the Scottish Enlightenment', *Journal of the History of Ideas*, 42 (1981), 503–25.

Stimson, S.C., *The American Revolution in the Law: Anglo-American Jurisprudence before John Marshall*, London, 1990.

'"A Jury of the Country": Common sense philosophy and the jurisprudence of James Wilson', in *Scotland and America in the Age of the Enlightenment*, ed. Sher and Smitten, pp. 193–208.

Stintzing, J.A.R. von, *Geschichte der deutschen Rechtswissenschaft*, edited and completed by Ernst Landsberg, 3 vols. in 4, Munich, 1880–1910.

Stokes, Eric, *The British Utilitarians and India*, Oxford, 1969.

Stolleis, Michael, *Die Moral in der Politik bei Christian Garve*, diss. Ludwig-Maximilians-Universität, Munich, 1967.

Stölzel, Adolf, *Brandenburg-Preussens Rechtsverwaltung und Rechtsverfassung*, 2 vols., Berlin, 1888.

Stout, H.S., *The New England Soul: Preaching and Religious Culture in Colonial New England*, New York, 1986.

Streminger, Gerhard, *Adam Smith*, Reinbek bei Hamburg, 1989.

Tamm, D., 'Pufendorf und Dänemark', in *Pufendorf*, ed. Modéer, pp. 81–9.

Taylor, A.E., 'The ethical doctrine of Hobbes', in *Hobbes Studies*, ed. K.C. Brown, Oxford, 1965, pp. 35–55.

Teichgraeber, R.F., III, *'Free Trade' and Moral Philosophy: Rethinking the Sources of Adam Smith's "Wealth of Nations"*, Durham, NC, 1986.

Thieme, H., ed., *Humanismus und Naturrecht in Berlin-Brandenburg-Preussen* (Veröffentlichungen der Historischen Kommission zu Berlin, Bd. 48), Berlin, 1979.

Thomas, William, *The Philosophic Radicals: Nine Studies in Theory and Practice, 1817–1841*, Oxford, 1979.

Thor, Bruce A., 'The economic theories of John Craig: A forgotten English economist', *Quarterly Journal of Economics*, 52 (1938), 697–707.

Tierney, B., 'Conciliarism, corporatism, and individualism: The doctrine of individual rights in Gerson', *Cristianesimo nella storia*, 9 (1988), 81–111.

'Marsilius on rights', *Journal of the History of Ideas*, 52 (1991), 3–17.

'Villey, Ockham and the origin of individual rights', in *The Weightier Matters of the Law . . . A Tribute to Harold Berman*, Decatur, GA, 1987, pp. 1–31.

Tomasselli, Sylvana, 'Reflections on the history of the science of woman', in *History of Science*, 29 (1991), 185–205.

Townsend, George, ed., 'Life of the first Lord Barrington', in *The Theological Works of the First Viscount Barrington*, 3 vols., London, 1828, vol. 1.

Trapp, Manfred, *Adam Smith – Politische Philosophie und politische Ökonomie*, Göttingen, 1987.

Trendelenburg, Adolf, *Friederich der Grosse und sein Grosskanzler Samuel von Cocceji. Beitrag zur Geschichte der ersten Justizreform und des Naturrechts*, Berlin, 1863.

Trevor-Roper, H., *Catholics, Anglicans and Puritans: Seventeenth-Century Essays*, London, 1987.

Tuck, Richard, '"The Ancient Law of Freedom": John Selden and the civil war', in *Reactions to the English Civil War, 1642–1649*, ed. J. Morrill, London, 1982, pp. 137–61 and 238–41.

'Grotius, Carneades and Hobbes', *Grotiana*, n.s., 4 (1983), 43–62.

Hobbes, Oxford, 1989.

'Hobbes and Descartes', in *Perspectives on Thomas Hobbes,* ed. G.A.J. Rogers and A. Ryan, Oxford, 1988, pp. 11–41.

'The "modern" theory of natural law', in *The Languages of Political Theory in Early-Modern Europe,* ed. Anthony Pagden, Cambridge, UK, 1987, pp. 99–119.

Natural Rights Theories, Cambridge, UK, 1979.

'Optics and sceptics: The philosophical foundations of Hobbes's political thought', in *Conscience and Casuistry in Early Modern Europe,* ed. Edmund Leites, Cambridge, UK, 1988, pp. 235–63.

Philosophy and Government, 1572–1651, Cambridge, UK, 1993.

Tully, J., *An Approach to Political Philosophy: Locke in Contexts,* Cambridge, UK, 1993.

A Discourse on Property: John Locke and His Adversaries, Cambridge, UK, 1980.

Tully, J., ed., *Meaning and Context: Quentin Skinner and His Critics,* Cambridge, UK, 1988.

Villey, M., *La Formation de la pensée juridique moderne,* Paris, 1975.

Warrender, H., *The Political Philosophy of Hobbes: His Theory of Obligation,* Oxford, 1957.

Waszek, N., 'Adam Smith in Germany, 1776–1832', in *Adam Smith: International Perspectives,* ed. H. Mizuta and C. Sugiyama, Houndmills, London, 1993, pp. 163–80.

'Two concepts of morality: A distinction of Adam Smith's ethics and its Stoic origin', *Journal of the History of Ideas,* 45 (1984), 591–606.

Waterman, A.M.C., 'The nexus between theology and political doctrine in Church and dissent', in *Enlightenment and Religion,* ed. K. Haakonssen.

Revolution, Economics, and Religion: Christian Political Economy, 1798–1833, Cambridge, UK, 1991.

Watkins, J.W.N., *Hobbes's System of Ideas,* London, 1965.

Watson, Alan, *Slave Law in the Americas,* Athens, GA, 1989.

Weill, Herman, *Frederick the Great and Samuel von Cocceji: A Study in the Reform of the Prussian Judicial Administration, 1740–1755,* Madison, WI, 1961.

Weinsheimer, J.C., *Eighteenth-Century Hermeneutics: Philosophy of Interpretation in England from Locke to Burke,* New Haven, 1993.

Weinstock, J.A., 'Reid's definition of freedom', in *Thomas Reid: Critical Interpretations,* ed. S.F. Barker and T.L. Beauchamp, Philadelphia, 1976, pp. 95–102.

Welzel, H., 'Ein Kapitel aus der Geschichte der amerikanischen Erklärung der Menschenrechte', in *Zur Geschichte der Erklärung der Menschenrechte,* ed. R. Schnur, Darmstadt, 1964, pp. 238–59.

Werhane, P.H., *Adam Smith and His Legacy for Modern Capitalism,* New York, 1991.

White, M., *The Philosophy of the American Revolution,* New York, 1978.

Philosophy, "The Federalist," and the Constitution, New York, 1987.

Wills, Garry, *Inventing America: Jefferson's Declaration of Independence,* New York, 1979.

Winch, Donald, *Adam Smith's Theory of Politics: An Essay in Historiographical Revision,* Cambridge, UK, 1978.

'The system of the north; Dugald Stewart and his pupils', in *That Noble Science of Politics: A Study in Nineteenth-Century Intellectual History*, by S. Collini, D. Winch, and J. Burrow, Cambridge, UK, 1983, pp. 23–61.

Winkel, H., 'Adam Smith und die deutsche Nationalökonomie, 1776–1820. Zur Rezeption der englischen Klassik', in *Studien zur Entwicklung der ökonomischen Theorie*, vol. 5, ed. H. Scherf, Berlin, 1986, pp. 81–109.

Winkler, K., 'Hutcheson's alleged realism', *Journal of the History of Philosophy*, 23 (1985), 179–94.

Wood, G., *The Creation of the American Republic, 1776–1787*, Chapel Hill, NC, 1969.

The Radicalism of the American Revolution, New York, 1992.

Wood, Paul B., *The Aberdeen Enlightenment: The Arts Curriculum in the Eighteenth Century*, Aberdeen, 1993.

'Science and the pursuit of virtue in the Aberdeen Enlightenment', in *Studies in the Philosophy of the Scottish Enlightenment*, ed. Stewart, pp. 127–49.

'Thomas Reid, Natural Philosopher: A Study of Science and Philosophy in the Scottish Enlightenment', Ph.D. thesis, University of Leeds, 1984.

Wootton, D., 'John Locke: Socinian or natural law theorist?' in *Religion, Secularization and Political Thought: Thomas Hobbes to J.S. Mill*, ed. J.E. Crimmins, London, 1989, pp. 39–67.

Wright, B.F., Jr., *American Interpretations of Natural Law*, Cambridge, MA, 1931.

Wright, John P., 'Metaphysics and physiology: Mind, body, and the animal economy in eighteenth-century Scotland', in *Studies in the Philosophy of the Scottish Enlightenment*, ed. Stewart, pp. 251–301.

Yolton, J.W., *Perceptual Acquaintance: From Descartes to Reid*, Minneapolis, 1984.

Zagorin, Perez, 'Hobbes's early philosophical development', *Journal of the History of Ideas*, 54 (1993), 505–18.

Zurbuchen, Simone, *Naturrecht und natürliche Religion. Zur Geschichte des Toleranzbegriffs von Samuel Pufendorf bis Jean-Jacques Rousseau*, Würzburg, 1991.

Index